Information Retrieval Design

Principles and Options for Information Description, Organization, Display, and Access in Information Retrieval Databases, Digital Libraries, Catalogs, and Indexes

by

James D. Anderson
and
José Pérez-Carballo

Ometeca Institute
ciencia y humanidades • humanities & science • ciência e humanidades
PO Box 12109, St. Petersburg, FL 33733-2109 USA
Distributed by University Publishing Solutions
302 Ryders Lane, East Brunswick, NJ 08816
732-220-1211, fax 732-418-1921, www.upublishing.com

2005

Ometeca Institute

Published in the United States of America
by Ometeca Institute, Inc.
P.O. Box 12109, St. Petersburg, FL 33733-2109

Copyright 2005 by James D. Anderson and José Pérez-Carballo

All rights reserved. No part of this publication may be reproduced, stored in a retrieval system, or transmitted in any form or by any means, electronic, mechanical, photocopying, recording, or otherwise, without the prior permission of the publisher, provisions of "fair use" under the U.S. Copyright law excepted.

The paper used in the cloth library edition meets the minimum requirements of American National Standard for Information Sciences – Permanence of Paper for Printed Library Materials, ANSI/NISO Z39.48 – 1992.
Manufactured in the United States of America.

Cover art by David A. Haywood, the Pennsylvania State University.
Cover design by Jon Hansen, University Publishing Solutions, LLC.

Website

The entire book is available without charges or fees in hypertext format at:
http://www.scils.rutgers.edu/publications/ir-design/

Cataloging in publication, prepared by James D. Anderson
Anderson, James D. (James Doig), 1940-

    Information retrieval design : principles and options for information description, organization, display, and access in information retrieval databases, digital libraries, catalogs, and indexes / by James D. Anderson and José Pérez-Carballo. – St. Petersburg, Fla. : Ometeca Institute ; East Brunswick, N.J. (302 Ryders Lane, East Brunswick, NJ 08816) : Distributed by University Publishing Solutions, LLC, 2005.

    xiv, 617 p. : ill. ; 28 cm.

    Includes glossary (p. 543-565), bibliography (p. 567-590) and index (p. 591-616).

    ISBN 0-9763547-0-5 (trade paper)

    ISBN 0-9763547-1-3 (cloth library edition)

    ISBN 0-9763547-2-1 (ebook)

    I. Pérez-Carballo, José. II. Title. 1. Information retrieval. 2. Indexing. 3. Database design.

Tables of Contents

Brief Table of Contents

Prefatory material : 1

Part I. Chapter 1. Introduction and Background Issues : 7

Part II: Design Decisions : 43

Chapter 2. Subject Scope and Domain : 47

Chapter 3. Documentary Scope : 73

Chapter 4. Documentary Domain : 87

Chapter 5. Display Media : 91

Chapter 6. Documentary Units : 103

Chapter 7. Indexable Matter : 111

Chapter 8. Analysis and Indexing Methods : 117

Chapter 9. Exhaustivity : 177

Chapter 10. Specificity : 185

Chapter 11. Displayed Versus Non-Displayed Indexes : 197

Chapter 12. Syntax : 205

Chapter 13. Vocabulary Management : 297

Chapter 14. Surrogation : 365

Chapter 15. Locators : 373

Chapter 16. Surrogate Displays : 383

Chapter 17. Arrangement of Displayed Indexes : 391

Chapter 18. Size of Displayed Indexes : 441

Chapter 19. Search Interface : 447

Chapter 20. Record Format : 495

Chapter 21. Full-Text Display : 521

Chapter 22. Conclusion: Implementation and Evaluation : 537

Glossary : 543

Bibliography : 567

Index : 591

About the Authors : 617

Tables of Contents

Summary of Contents

Part I. Chapter 1. Introduction and Background Issues : 7

Assumptions and steps required before design begins; terminology; standards and codes of practice, types of databases.

Part II: Design Decisions : 43

Chapter 2. Subject Scope and Domain : 47

Defining the kinds of questions an information retrieval (IR) database will answer, with respect to subject or topical areas and also the operational and cultural domains of potential users; role of subject scope and domain as guide for database producers in the selection of messages and the creation of document descriptions and indexes; role as guide for potential users in the selection and navigation of appropriate IR databases.

Chapter 3. Documentary Scope : 73

Kinds of messages, texts and documents appropriate for fulfilling subject scope and user preferences; definition of searchable documentary features.

Chapter 4. Documentary Domain : 87

Domain (territory) covered in seeking sources for documents and documentary information; methods for discovery, location, and acquisition.

Chapter 5. Display Media : 91

Effective media for the presentation of IR databases.

Chapter 6. Documentary Units : 103

Appropriate size of documentary units to be presented to users; parts of documents versus complete documents and collections of documents.

Chapter 7. Indexable Matter : 111

Portions of documentary units to be analyzed for indexing.

Chapter 8. Analysis and Indexing Methods : 117

Nature of, and appropriate use of, automatic computer-based text analysis and indexing methods versus human intellectual analysis and indexing of messages.

Chapter 9. Exhaustivity : 177

Appropriate level of detail in the indexing of documentary units.

Tables of Contents

Chapter 10. Specificity : 185

Appropriate level of specificity in indexing vocabulary.

Chapter 11. Displayed Versus Non-Displayed Indexes : 197

Support for multiple search modes: displayed indexes for browsing and visual inspection of headings; non-displayed indexes for machine matching of search statements with message, text, and document representations or full text.

Chapter 12. Syntax : 205

Creating intelligible index headings for browsing and visual inspection; syntactic support for user creation of search statements for computer matching.

Chapter 13. Vocabulary Management : 297

Assistance in dealing with alternative and variant terminology, multiple meanings, and conceptual relations among terms.

Chapter 14. Surrogation : 365

Representing messages, texts, and documentary units within the IR database.

Chapter 15. Locators : 373

Links between representations and full documentary units.

Chapter 16. Surrogate Displays : 383

Options for the display of representations in different contexts.

Chapter 17. Arrangement of Displayed Indexes : 391

Options in the display of browsable indexes: alphanumeric versus classed/relational arrangements.

Chapter 18. Size of Displayed Indexes : 441

Estimating the size of indexes when constraints are present (mainly for printed back-of-the-book indexes).

Chapter 19. Search Interface : 447

Presenting IR databases to users; displaying content and search options.

Chapter 20. Record Format : 495

Size and structure of documentary unit records for supporting design features.

Tables of Contents

Chapter 21. Full-Text Display : 521

Options for analysis, encoding, and display of full-text documentary units.

Chapter 22. Conclusion: Implementation and Continuing Evaluation : 537

This book is about design. Once the design is complete, it's time to begin testing, implementation, and ongoing evaluation.

Glossary : 543

The glossary contains most of the definitions for terms included in the main text of the book, arranged in alphabetical order. Most of the definitions will refer back to the sections of the book where the concept defined is discussed in more detail, so the glossary can be used as an index to key concepts.

Bibliography : 567

This is the comprehensive bibliography for the book. Each citation concludes with references to the sections where the item is cited, so the bibliography can be used as an index to discussions of cited works.

Index : 591

The alphabetical subject index was compiled using the NEPHIS system, which is described in chapter 12 on syntax, section 12.2.2.3. Index headings refer to sections or paragraphs, not to page numbers.

About the Authors : 617

Full Table of Contents

Prefatory Material : 1
    0.1. Foreword, by Jessica Milstead : 1
    0.2. Preface, by James D. Anderson : 2
    0.3. Acknowledgments, by James D. Anderson : 4
    0.4. Special Thanks to Scholars and Practitioners of IR for the Use of Their Work : 4
    0.5. Bibliographic Citations : 5
    0.6. Dedication : 5

Part I. Chapter 1. Introduction and Background Issues : 7
    1.1. Purpose : 7
    1.2. Assumptions : 9
    1.3. Terminology : 10
    1.4. Standards and Codes of Practice : 24
    1.5. Types of IR Databases : 30
    1.5.1. Kinds of Objects Represented in Index Terms, Headings, and Entries : 31
    1.5.2. Kinds of Index Terms Used : 32

Tables of Contents

1.5.3. Kinds of Indexable Matter Used : 33
1.5.4. Presentation and Methods for Searching : 33
1.5.5. Arrangement of Index Entries : 34
1.5.6. Methods for Analysis : 35
1.5.7. Methods for Term Selection in Indexing : 35
1.5.8. Methods for Term Combination in Searching : 35
1.5.9. Kinds of Documents Being Indexed : 36
1.5.10. Media of IR Databases : 37
1.5.11. Proximity of Documents Being Indexed : 37
1.5.12. Size of Documentary Units : 38
1.5.13. Periodicity of IR Databases : 38
1.5.14. Authorship of IR Databases : 39
1.5.15. Continuing Examples : 39
1.6. IR Databases Versus Other Types of Databases: A Recap : 39
1.6.1. Two Types of Databases : 40
1.6.2. IR Databases : 40

Part II: Design Decisions : 43

Chapter 2. Subject Scope and Domain : 47

2.1. Specialized Categories : 57
2.2. Presenting the Subject Scope and Domain to Users : 61
2.3. Ranganathan's Facets : 63
2.4. Why Bother? : 66
2.5. Our Examples : 67
2.5.1. A Book Index : 67
2.5.2. An Indexing and Abstracting Service : 69
2.5.3. A Full-Text Encyclopedia/Digital Library : 72

Chapter 3. Documentary Scope : 73

3.1. Authorship : 75
3.2. Titles : 76
3.3. Media : 76
3.4. Forms, Formats, Genres : 77
3.5. Periodicity : 80
3.6. Intended Audience or Level : 81
3.7. Methodological Approaches, Points of View, Biases, Kinds of Treatment : 81
3.8. Language : 81
3.9. Place of Creation, Manufacture, or Publication : 82
3.10. Time of Creation, Manufacture, or Publication : 82
3.11. Specific Documents : 82
3.12. Qualitative Criteria : 82
3.13. Features Versus Topics : 83
3.14. Our Examples : 83
3.14.1. A Book Index : 83
3.14.2. An Indexing and Abstracting Service : 84

Tables of Contents

3.14.3. A Full-Text Encyclopedia/Digital Library : 86

Chapter 4. Documentary Domain : 87
4.1. Primary Versus Secondary Sources : 88
4.2. Monitoring and Covering Documentary Domain : 88
4.3. Our Examples : 89
4.3.1. A Book Index : 89
4.3.2. An Indexing and Abstracting Service : 89
4.3.3. A Full-Text Encyclopedia/Digital Library : 90

Chapter 5. Display Media : 91
5.1. Paper : 91
5.1.1. Card Files : 92
5.1.2. Books : 92
5.1.3. Optical Coincidence (Peek-a-Boo) Retrieval on Cards : 94
5.2. Microforms : 98
5.3. Electronic Media : 98
5.3.1. Online Databases : 99
5.3.2. CD-ROM and Other Machine-Readable Disks : 99
5.3.3. World-Wide Web : 99
5.4. Codes and Symbols : 100
5.5. Our Examples : 100
5.5.1. A Book Index : 100
5.5.2. An Indexing and Abstracting Service : 101
5.5.3. A Full-Text Encyclopedia/Digital Library : 101

Chapter 6. Documentary Units : 103
6.1. Some Examples : 104
6.2. One of the Few "Laws" in Information Retrieval : 106
6.3. Documentary Units Versus Surrogates : 107
6.4. Multiple Documentary Units : 108
6.5. Our Examples : 108
6.5.1. A Book Index : 108
6.5.2. An Indexing and Abstracting Service : 109
6.5.3. A Full-Text Encyclopedia/Digital Library : 109

Chapter 7. Indexable Matter : 111
7.1. Typical Examples of Indexable Matter : 112
7.1.1. Titles : 112
7.1.2. Titles and Abstracts : 112
7.1.3. Preliminary Matter : 113
7.1.4. Initial Paragraphs : 113
7.1.5. Internal Indexes : 113
7.1.6. Reference Citations : 113
7.1.7. Opening Screens of Web Sites : 114
7.1.8. Full Texts : 114
7.1.9. Types of Messages : 114

7.2. Indexable Matter Versus Subject Scope : 114
7.3. Accuracy of Indexing : 115
7.4. Our Examples : 115
7.4.1. A Book Index : 115
7.4.2. An Indexing and Abstracting Service : 115
7.4.3. A Full-Text Encyclopedia/Digital Library : 116

Chapter 8. Analysis and Indexing Methods : 117

8.1. Research Comparing Automatic and Human Indexing : 119
8.2. Human Analysis and Indexing : 123
8.2.1. Cognition Versus Social Construction in Human Analysis and Indexing : 130
8.2.2. Human Indexing Rules : 135
8.2.2.1. Human Indexing Rules for Image Text : 141
8.2.2.2. Human Indexing Rules Based on Probabilistic Analysis : 142
8.3. Automatic Analysis and Indexing : 145
8.3.1. In the Beginning Was the Word : 146
8.3.2. Simple Keyword Indexing : 148
8.3.3. Negative Vocabulary Control: Stop Lists : 149
8.3.4. Counting Words : 149
8.3.5. Comparative Counting and Weighting : 149
8.3.6. Improving the Count: Stemming : 150
8.3.7. Natural Word Distributions : 151
8.3.8. Words Versus Phrases : 156
8.3.9. Managing Vocabulary in Automatic Indexing : 159
8.3.10. Automatic Vocabulary Management : 161
8.3.11. Clustering : 164
8.3.11.1. Latent Semantic Indexing : 166
8.3.12. Citation Indexes : 167
8.3.12.1. Bibliographic Coupling : 167
8.3.12.2. Co-Citation : 168
8.3.13. Relevance Feedback : 168
8.4. Subject Analysis and Indexing in Indexing and Abstracting Services : 169
8.5. Growing Role of Automatic Analysis and Indexing : 171
8.5.1. Censorship or Guidance? : 173
8.6. Our Examples : 175
8.6.1. A Book Index : 175
8.6.2. An Indexing and Abstracting Service : 175
8.6.3. A Full-Text Encyclopedia/Digital Library : 176

Chapter 9. Exhaustivity : 177

9.1. Recall and Precision : 178
9.1.1. A Definition of Recall : 178
9.1.2. A Definition of Precision : 179
9.1.3. The Impact of Exhaustivity on Recall and Precision : 180
9.2. The Calculation of Exhaustivity: Terms Versus Headings : 180
9.3. Our Examples : 181
9.3.1. A Book Index : 181

Tables of Contents

    9.3.2. An Indexing and Abstracting Service : 182
    9.3.3. A Full-Text Encyclopedia/Digital Library : 182

Chapter 10. Specificity : 185

    10.1. Definitions of Specificity : 185
    10.2. Relations between Exhaustivity and Specificity : 190
    10.3. Examples of Specificity : 191
    10.4. Practical Specificity : 191
    10.5. Impact of Specificity on Precision and Recall : 192
    10.6. Impact of Specificity on Vocabulary Size : 193
    10.7. Specificity Versus Syntax : 194
    10.8. Our Examples : 195
    10.8.1. A Book Index : 195
    10.8.2. An Indexing and Abstracting Service : 195
    10.8.3. A Full-Text Encyclopedia/Digital Library : 195

Chapter 11. Displayed and Non-Displayed Indexes : 197

    11.1. Displayed Indexes in Electronic Media : 198
    11.2. Research on Browsing in Information Retrieval : 201
    11.3. Design of Displayed and Non-Displayed Indexes : 202
    11.4. Our Examples : 203
    11.4.1. A Book Index : 203
    11.4.2. An Indexing and Abstracting Service : 203
    11.4.3. A Full-Text Encyclopedia/Digital Library : 204

Chapter 12. Syntax : 205

    12.1. Precoordinate and Postcoordinate Syntax : 206
    12.2. Precoordinate Syntax for Displayed Indexes : 208
    12.2.1. Subject Heading Syntax: *Library of Congress Subject Headings* (LCSH) : 208
    12.2.1.1. *Medical Subject Headings* (MeSH) : 227
    12.2.1.2. Principles for Subject Heading Systems : 228
    12.2.2. String Syntax : 231
    12.2.2.1. Rotated Term Syntax : 231
    12.2.2.2. Faceted Syntax (PRECIS, CIFT) : 234
    12.2.2.2.1. Converting LCSH to Faceted Syntax : 241
    12.2.2.3. Ad Hoc String Syntax (NEPHIS) : 243
    12.2.3. Relational Syntax : 247
    12.2.3.1. Syntagmatic Relationships : 250
    12.2.4. Classification Syntax : 251
    12.2.4.1. Chain Syntax : 257
    12.2.5. Natural Language Syntax : 258
    12.2.5.1. KWIC Syntax : 260
    12.2.5.2. KWOC Syntax : 261
    12.2.5.3. KWAC Syntax : 261
    12.2.6. Permuted Syntax : 262
    12.2.7. Ad Hoc Syntax : 263
    12.2.7.1. Combining Ad Hoc Syntax with Systematic Syntax : 266

Tables of Contents

12.2.8. Syntactic Cross References : 269
12.3. Postcoordinate Syntax for Non-Displayed Indexes : 269
12.3.1. Exact Match (Boolean) Syntax : 273
12.3.2. Best Match (Weighted Term) Syntax : 275
12.4. Our Examples : 280
12.4.1. A Book Index : 280
12.4.2. An Indexing and Abstracting Service : 284
12.4.3. A Full-Text Encyclopedia/Digital Library : 294

Chapter 13. Vocabulary Management : 297

13.1. The Vocabulary Problem : 297
13.2. Research on Vocabulary Issues : 300
13.3. Vocabulary Solutions : 301
13.3.1. Syndetic Structure in Displayed Alphabetical Indexes : 306
13.3.2. Indexing Thesauri : 313
13.3.2.1 Examples of Indexing Thesauri : 318
13.3.3. End-user Thesauri : 332
13.3.3.1. Compiling an End-User Thesaurus : 333
13.3.3.1.1. Sources of Terms : 333
13.3.3.1.2. Selecting Terms : 333
13.3.3.1.3. Categorizing Terms : 337
13.3.3.1.4. Bound Terms Versus Elemental Descriptors : 340
13.3.3.1.5. Term Relationships : 342
13.3.3.1.6. Variant Forms and Equivalent Terms : 352
13.3.3.1.7. Homographs : 353
13.3.3.1.8. Thesaurus Displays : 354
13.3.4. Co-occurrence Term Clustering : 354
13.3.5. Ontologies : 355
13.4. Our Examples : 358
13.4.1. A Book Index : 358
13.4.2. An Indexing and Abstracting Service : 362
13.4.3. A Full-Text Encyclopedia/Digital Library : 364

Chapter 14. Surrogation : 365

14.1. Purpose of Surrogates : 367
14.2. Guidelines and Standards for Surrogates : 367
14.3. Selected Readings on Abstracts and Abstracting : 369
14.4. Surrogates for Machine Searching : 369
14.5. Our Examples : 370
14.5.1. A Book Index : 370
14.5.2. An Indexing and Abstracting Service : 370
14.5.3. A Full-Text Encyclopedia/Digital Library : 371

Chapter 15. Locators : 373

15.1. Our Examples : 380
15.1.1. A Book Index : 380
15.1.2. An Indexing and Abstracting Service : 381

Tables of Contents

    15.1.3. A Full-Text Encyclopedia/Digital Library : 382

Chapter 16. Surrogate Displays : 383
    16.1. Our Examples : 388
    16.1.1. A Book Index : 388
    16.1.2. An Indexing and Abstracting Service : 389
    16.1.3. A Full-Text Encyclopedia/Digital Library : 390

Chapter 17. Arrangement of Displayed Indexes : 391
    17.1. Alphanumeric Displays : 392
    17.2. Alphanumeric Arrangement in Hypertext Displays : 398
    17.3. Relational Classified Displays : 412
    17.3.1 Display of Dewey Decimal Classification in Hypertext : 417
    17.3.2. Constructing and Displaying a Faceted Classification : 421
    17.3.2.1. Display of Faceted Classification in Print Media : 433
    17.4. Our Examples : 438
    17.4.1. A Book Index : 438
    17.4.2. An Indexing and Abstracting Service : 439
    17.4.3. A Full-Text Encyclopedia/Digital Library : 440

Chapter 18. Size of Displayed Indexes : 441
    18.1. Our Examples : 442
    18.1.1. A Book Index : 442
    18.1.2. An Indexing and Abstracting Service : 445
    18.1.3. A Full-Text Encyclopedia/Digital Library : 446

Chapter 19. Search Interface : 447
    19.1. Print on Paper Interfaces : 448
    19.2. Electronic Interfaces : 458
    19.3. Computer Interface Research: Human Computer Interaction : 460
    19.4. Our Examples : 465
    19.4.1. A Book Index : 486
    19.4.2. An Indexing and Abstracting Service : 490
    19.4.3. A Full-Text Encyclopedia/Digital Library : 493

Chapter 20. Record Format : 495
    20.1. The MARC Format for Cataloging Data : 495
    20.2. Record Format for the *MLA International Bibliography* : 500
    20.3. Record Format for ABC-CLIO : 503
    20.4. Record Format for a Class IR Database : 505
    20.5. The Dublin Core Record Format for Internal Metadata : 511
    20.5.1. Dublin Core Qualifiers : 513
    20.5.2. Dublin Core Example : 513
    20.6 Other Metadata Schemas : 514
    20.7. Our Examples : 516
    20.7.1. A Book Index : 516
    20.7.2. An Indexing and Abstracting Service : 517

20.7.3. A Full-Text Encyclopedia/Digital Library : 519

Chapter 21. Full-Text Display : 521

21.1 Linear Versus Hypertext Formats : 521

21.2 Encoding Schemas for Digital Texts : 524

21.3 Browsing Full Texts Online : 530

21.4. Our Examples : 531

21.4.1. A Book : 531

21.4.2. An Indexing and Abstracting Service : 532

21.4.3. A Full-Text Encyclopedia/Digital Library : 534

Chapter 22. Conclusion: Implementation and Continuing Evaluation : 537

Glossary : 543

Bibliography : 567

Index : 591

About the Authors : 617

Figures

Figure numbers begin with a chapter number, followed by a sequential number. After each figure title, locators refer to the chapter and the paragraph number preceding the figure. Thus Figure 2.1 follows paragraph 74 in chapter 2.

Figure 2.1. Opening screen of *Queer Resources Directory* : 2.74

Figure 2.2. Hypothetical preliminary design for an opening screen for the *MLA international bibliography* : 2.74

Figure 2.3. Hypothetical opening webpage screen for the *MLA international bibliography* : 2.77

Figure 2.4. Hypothetical preliminary opening screen design for an indexing and abstracting service for library and information science : 2.94

Figure 2.5. Hypothetical opening screen for *BLISTER — Bibliography of library & information science & technology: evaluation & research* : 2.94.

Figure 5.1. Photographs of the Jonker peek-a-boo IR system, Rutgers University : 5.19

Figure 8.1. Cooper's odds-payoff indexing chart : 8.119

Figure 8.2. Types of clusters, based on Salton (1975a) : 8.216

Tables of Contents

Figure 12.1. Index entries from *America: history & life* : 12.129.

Figure 12.2. Index entries from the *MLA international bibliography* : 12.145

Figure 12.3. Index entries from *Psychological abstracts* : 12.264

Figure 12.4. Index entries from *Readers' guide to periodical literature* : 12.264

Figure 12.5. Comparison of key attributes of displayed and non-displayed documentary unit indexes versus simple vocabulary indexes : 12.279

Figures 19.1-19.9. Opening IR database screen designs by students : 19.73

Figure 19.10-11. Display of browsable facets in IR database designs by students : 19.73

Figure 19.12-13. Display of browsable alphanumeric indexes in IR database designs by students : 19.76

Figure 19.14-15. Interface displays for advanced electronic searches in IR database designs by students : 19.79

Figure 19.16-17. Display of results from advanced electronic searches, with vocabulary assistance, in IR database designs by students : 19.79

Figures 19.18-19.19. Display of full surrogates in IR database designs by students : 19.84

Figure 19.20. Hypothetical opening page for an indexing and abstracting service in library and information science : 19.06

Figure 20.1. Record format for the *MLA international bibliography and database* : 20.17

Figure 20.2. Record format for the *American history and life* database (ABC-Clio) : 20.22

0. Prefatory Material

Contents of Prefatory Material
0.1. Foreword, by Jessica Milstead.
0.2. Preface, by James D. Anderson.
0.3. Acknowledgments, by James D. Anderson.
0.4. Special Thanks to Scholars and Practitioners of IR for the Use of Their Work.
0.5. Bibliographic Citations.
0.6. Dedication.

0.1. Foreword, by Jessica Milstead.

Users of information retrieval databases generally have no idea of the complexity of these databases, or of the effort that goes into development of their structure. This is as it should be; the design of the database should not have to be the users' problem.

Once upon a time, in the days when the most sophisticated information retrieval databases were library card catalogs (which many users of this book probably don't remember), the issue of just how much users should be expected to learn in order to satisfy their needs from the database was actually a lively one. Today all that has changed. Willingly or not, designers of information retrieval databases and the access systems that support them have come to recognize that users just want the information they need. The less effort required of the users, the happier they will be, and the more likely they are actually to use the database – and therefore the more likely they are to support its continuation and growth.

There is another side to the question, of course. The effort has to be undertaken somewhere. The easier a given database is to use, the more effort is required behind the scenes to assure that its use will be transparent. And the number of decisions to be made and issues to be resolved in the design of an information retrieval database is certainly not obvious to anyone who has not actually undertaken such a task. It's not just a matter of dumping in some text and citations and turning a search engine loose – at least not if the information is valuable and you desire quality results.

Twenty years ago I wrote a small book (*Subject Access Systems: Alternatives in Design*, published by Academic Press) that discussed some of the major issues in information retrieval database design, but I didn't even try to cover every aspect. Jim Anderson has now undertaken this daunting task, and in the online environment, which barely existed when I wrote my book. We had online databases, but they were hard to use, requiring the skills of trained searchers to exploit them fully.

Prof. Anderson has distilled his decades of experience in teaching and design of information retrieval databases to produce a work that covers every aspect of design. He spent a number of years as the chair of a National Information Standards Organization committee charged with revising the standard for indexes. His experience with that committee has enriched this, his *magnum opus*.

0. Prefatory Material (Section 0.2)

Sound textbooks for information retrieval database design have been very few, and none have been as comprehensive as this. I particularly enjoyed the practice of defining some examples, and following them as example cases in every chapter. With these example cases it becomes possible to see how the principles discussed in the chapter would be applied in an actual database.

Prof. Anderson's work will serve a variety of users. It synthesizes much that is known, while bringing to bear its author's insights on issues. The case studies make the work particularly useful as a textbook, but it will also serve as a refresher for those already in the field, and as a reference for all audiences.

0.2. Preface, by James D. Anderson.

• purpose of this book; definition of IR databases : 1

This book is for our students, and for others who aspire to design the best possible information retrieval (IR) databases for every type of clientele and every type of message, in whatever medium or format. The overall objective is maximum effective retrieval of useful messages for each particular user.

• scope of this book : 2

The scope of this book is determined by the features of modern IR databases. The term "information retrieval database" or "IR database" is used in the broadest sense. Increasingly IR databases are designed for and implemented in digital media, but the design principles addressed in this book apply just as much to all media, including print on paper, microfilm or fiche, or even card catalogs. They certainly apply to modern digital libraries. The basic definition for the term "IR database" as used in this book is any database in any medium designed or created for the purpose of discovering and retrieving messages, texts and documents. Thus, it includes the whole gamut of IR databases presented to users via online connections, the world-wide web, CD-ROMs, or in print on paper: indexing and abstracting services (regardless of medium), library catalogs (including OPACs: online public access catalogs), bibliographies, and indexes, including back-of-the-book indexes (which can now be presented electronically with electronic books!). This and related definitions are expanded in the first part of the book.

• organization of this book; fundamental issues of IR database design : 3

This book is organized around twenty fundamental design issues in IR database design. See the table of contents for a summary of these issues. These are issues that I have identified during twenty-five years of investigation, teaching, design, evaluation, and creation of IR databases. These issues were further refined between 1991 and 1997 by Committee YY of the National Information Standards Organization (NISO). This committee, which I chaired, focused primarily on indexing and indexes, which are fundamental components for all IR databases. But in fact, the committee addressed all of the fundamental design issues for IR databases.

• NISO Committee YY: new standard for indexes : 4

NISO had charged Committee YY with developing a new standard for indexes that would cover every type of index:

- whether produced by human intellectual analysis or machine algorithm;
- whether presented in print or electronic media;
- whether designed for searching by human visual inspection of index headings or by electronic computer matching of search terms against document records or full text; and

0. Prefatory Material (Section 0.2)

- regardless of the code, medium or format of the messages being indexed (linguistic, musical, pictorial, mathematical; visual, aural, tactile; print, microform, film, video, electronic, digital, etc.; monographic or serial; in any genre or format).

• NISO technical report on design of indexes : 5

The results of the work of this committee, based on input from the NISO member organizations most concerned about the design of IR databases as well as hundreds of individual information professionals, was published in a technical report: *Guidelines for indexes and related information retrieval devices* (Anderson 1997a).

• publications related to this book : 6

This NISO technical report covers the scope of this book in a highly compressed format. Another even briefer presentation of the issues covered in this book, but in a less technical and more discursive style, is contained in my encyclopedia article: "Organization of knowledge," in the *International encyclopedia of information and library science* (Anderson 1997b, revised 2002).

• views of Milstead (Jessica L.) on IR database design : 7

This book rests on the foundations of research and practice in information retrieval, IR database design, indexing and cataloging by persons too numerous to mention. Some of their publications are cited in the bibliography at the end of this book. Here I want to acknowledge one book in particular, which has served as a precursor and exemplar for this book: *Subject access systems: alternatives in design* by Jessica L. Milstead (1984). Like this book, Milstead's emphasis and purpose were to foster intelligent design of IR databases. Although organized differently, Milstead covers many of the same points as we do, and we hardly ever disagree! I highly recommend her book. It has aged very well!

• views of Bates (Marcia J.) on IR database design : 8

I also want to pay special tribute to the work of Marcia Bates. One of her earliest articles, "Rigorous systematic bibliography" (1976) got me started in my analysis of IR database design principles. In that article, she focused on attributes of scope and documentary domain, and also on explicit criteria for selectivity. Since then, she has been a leader in research and commentary on essential aspects of the design and use of IR databases. She summarizes much of her work, and that of others, in "Indexing and access for digital libraries and the internet: human, database, and domain factors" (1998). Here she discusses such essential issues as human factors, indexing and searching terminology and structures, statistical distribution properties of documents in collections and databases, and subject domain-oriented indexing. In this book, her work has been especially influential in the chapters on scope and domain, vocabulary management, and interface design.

• views of Chowdhury (Gobinda G.) on information retrieval : 9

Most books on information retrieval focus on particular approaches to this broad field, such as human indexing, library cataloging and classification, or automatic indexing. A recent book that adopts the same kind of broad view as this book is G. G. Chowdhury's *Introduction to modern information retrieval* (1999). The organization and focus of our two books is different, but readers who desire another viewpoint can benefit from Chowdhury's book.

• Pérez-Carballo (José) as co-author: 10

Dr. José Pérez-Carballo, my former colleague in the School of Communication, Information, and Library Studies at Rutgers University, has joined me as co-author of this book. He has helped with the entire book, but he has taken special responsibility for sections on automatic indexing and interface design.

0. Prefatory Material (Section 0.3)

• **purpose of this book: 11**

I hope that this detailed concentration on the fundamental decision points of IR database design will help members of the information professions to consider all the options, and then to design and create better IR databases. Our society needs the best possible IR databases to cope with the ever growing explosion of information on the internet and the world-wide web, as well as in older print formats, video, film, audio, and electronic formats.

0.3. Acknowledgments, by James D. Anderson.

• **acknowledgment to students : 12**

Many thanks go to my students who have used and critiqued drafts of this book: Debbie Abrams, Jane Achola, Michael Angeles, Shawn Armington, Robert Barbanell, Frances Berman, Michele Lisoski Bond, Elana Broch, Linda Brown, John Burchard, Dorothea E. Clark, Susan Clark, Lisa Coats, Kathleen Creegan, Thomas M. Dolan, Lisa Ellis, Olga Evanusa-Rowland, Loisann Griglak, Ted E. Hamer, Lonnie Johnson, Mary Kearns-Kaplan, Richard K. Kearney, Michael Knies, Scott Kushner, Mariann E. Lucas, Marygrace Luderitz, Ruth Eleanor Lufkin, Mary Marks, Sal Mazzola, Mary McMahon, Daniel Noonan, Megan Palasciano, Antonio M. Pasqualoni, Beth Patterson, José Fernando Peña, Fran Pfeffer, Frances Pinto, Laura Poll, Jill Ratzan, Robert Rittman, Vivian Thiele, Regan L. Tuerff, Susan Turkel, David Utz, Mary O. Walker, Renee Watson, Karen Wenk, Melissa Yonteck, and Zhu Xuening (Sean). Terry Edwards was an especially careful reader, checking not only text for sense and typos, but also the embedded index strings! Jill Ratzan gave parts of the final text a rigorous perusal.

• **13**

I thank them for their valuable editorial assistance. As they worked with earlier drafts of this book, they were very good at pointing out defects.

• **acknowledgment to Milstead (Jessica L.), Wellisch (Hans H.),
members of NISO Committee YY, and executive director of NISO : 14**

Special gratitude goes to my long-term colleagues and primary mentors in the world of indexing, information retrieval, and information science, Dr. Jessica Milstead and Dr. Hans Wellisch, who read intermediate drafts of this book and made many excellent suggestions, most of which I endeavored to implement. I also thank the members of NISO Committee YY, who worked closely with me for many years (1991-1997) on the issues addressed in this book: Barbara Anderson, Knight-Ridder Information, Inc.; Catherine Grissom, U.S. Department of Energy, Office of Scientific and Technical Information; Nancy Mulvany, Bayside Indexing Service; Barbara Preschel, Public Affairs Information Service; Deborah Swain, IBM and Society for Technical Communication; and (again) Hans Wellisch, University of Maryland; and also (again) Jessica Milstead, our liaison from the NISO Standards Development Committee, and Patricia Harris, NISO executive director, both of whom shepherded our work with expertise, care and compassion!

0.4. Special Thanks to Scholars and Practitioners of IR for the Use of Their Work.

• **acknowledgment to scholars and practitioners of special importance : 15**

This book rests squarely on the work of hundreds of colleagues in the world if IR and IR database design. Every author and every published work is listed in the bibliography, but here we want to give special thanks to those colleagues and organizations whose work we have used most extensively, sometimes with extensive quotes. I trust that our use has been within the bounds of scholarly "fair use," but beyond the legalities of use and attribution, we want to express our sincere appreciation for and dependence on their work — indeed, these authors and organizations are co-authors of this work with us:

> ABC-Clio, American Library Association, Marcia J. Bates, *Bliss Bibliographic Classification,* John P. Comaromi, William S. Cooper, Timothy C. Craven, *Dewey Decimal Classification*, Tamas E. Diszkocs, Karen Markey Drabenstott, Dublin Core, *Eurovoc Thesaurus*, Jason, Farradane, *FOLDOC: The Free On-Line Dictionary of Computing*, Bernd Frohmann, Rebecca Green, Stephan Greene, Donna Harman, David Harper, Marti Hearst, Birger Hjørland, Susan Hockey, Robert R. Korfhage, Library of Congress, Gary Marchionini, Jessica L. Milstead, Modern Language Association of America, National Information Standards Organization, Miranda Pao, A. Steven Pollitt, S. R. Ranganathan, Ronald E. Rice, Rutgers University Libraries, Gerard Salton, Ben Schneiderman, Dagobert Soergel, Karen Sparck Jones, Elaine Svenonius, *Unesco Thesaurus*, Brian C. Vickery, Diane Vizine-Goetz, Bella Hass Weinberg, Hans H. Wellisch, Patrick Wilson.

• acknowledgment to students : 16

We also give special thanks to the students of James D. Anderson who shared their design work to help illustrate concepts in chapter 19:

> Matthew Brown, Melissa Hoffman, Eric J. Johnson, Veronica Meyer, Minsoo Park, J. Fernando Peña, Elizabeth Pregill, Robert Rittman, Enola Romano, Lori A. Rowland, Jennifer Schroth.

0.5. Bibliographic Citations.

• style for bibliographic citations : 17

All publications cited in this book are listed in alphabetical order in the bibliography at the end of the book. Citations are presented in accordance with the U.S.A. national standard ANSI/NISO Z39.29-1979. *Bibliographic references* (American National Standards Institute 1979). A revision of this standard was approved in 2003. The only significant change for our purposes was moving the placement of dates for periodical articles from the end of the citation, after volume and issue numbering and pagination, to prior to the volume and issue numbering (National Information Standards Organization 2004?). We did not adopt this small change.

0.6 Dedication.

We dedicate this work to Rafael and Dwayne, the wind beneath our wings.

Part I: Chapter 1. Introduction and Background Issues

Contents of Chapter 1
1.1. Purpose.
1.2. Assumptions.
1.3. Terminology.
1.4. Standards and Codes of Practice.
1.5. Types of IR Databases.
1.5.1. Kinds of Objects Represented in Index Terms, Headings, and Entries.
1.5.2. Kinds of Index Terms Used.
1.5.3. Kinds of Indexable Matter Used.
1.5.4. Presentation and Methods for Searching.
1.5.5. Arrangement of Index Entries.
1.5.6. Methods for Analysis.
1.5.7. Methods for Term Selection in Indexing.
1.5.8. Methods for Term Combination in Searching.
1.5.9. Kinds of Documents Being Indexed.
1.5.10. Media of IR Databases.
1.5.11. Proximity of Documents Being Indexed.
1.5.12. Size of Documentary Units.
1.5.13. Periodicity of IR Databases.
1.5.14. Authorship of IR Databases.
1.5.15. Continuing Examples.
1.6. IR Databases Versus Other Types of Databases: A Recap.
1.6.1. Two Types of Databases.
1.6.2. IR Databases.

1.1. Purpose.

• history of indexing, cataloging, librarianship, IR databases : 1

Ever since humankind learned how to record messages on portable long-lasting media — clay tablets, papyrus, much later paper and more recently various electronic media — we have devised ways to describe and organize these messages so that they could be found, used and enjoyed later on. This ancient practice has evolved over the millennia into the ancient and honorable profession of librarianship and related specializations such as cataloging and indexing. In the twentieth century, this basic human need to analyze and organize messages for later retrieval has become the main preoccupation of information science, under the rubric of "information retrieval."

> Readers interested in the history of indexing and information retrieval databases may want to consult the following book and articles:
>
> Katz, Bill. *Cuneiform to computers: a history of reference sources.* Lanham, MD: Scarecrow Press; 1998. xvi, 417 p. (History of the book series; no. 4). ISBN: 0-8108-3290-9.

Chapter 1. Introduction and Background Issues (Section 1.1)

> Metcalfe, John Wallace. *Information retrieval, British & American, 1876-1976*. Metuchen, N.J.: Scarecrow Press; 1976. v, 243 p. ISBN: 0-8108-0875-7.
>
> Taylor, Arlene G. "Development of the organization of recorded information in western civilization." In: *The organization of information*. Englewood, CO: Libraries Unlimited; 1999: 37-55. xx, 280 p. ISBN 1-56308-498-9.
>
> Wellisch, Hans H. "Early multilingual and multiscript indexes in herbals." *The indexer*. 11: 81-102; 1978 Oct.
>
> Wellisch, Hans H. "How to make an index, 16th century style: Conrad Gessner on indexes and catalogs." *International classification*. 8: 10-15; 1981.
>
> Wellisch, Hans H. "The oldest printed indexes." *The indexer*. 15: 73-82; 1986 Oct.
>
> For more historical references, see:
>
> Wellisch, Hans H. *Indexing and abstracting: an international bibliography*. Santa Barbara, CA: ABC-Clio, c1980. xxi, 308 p. ISBN 0-87436-300-4.
>
> Wellisch, Hans H. *Indexing and abstracting, 1977-1981: an international bibliography*. Santa Barbara, CA: ABC-Clio Information Services, 1984. xix, 276 p. ISBN 0-87436-398-5.

• role of information retrieval in support of civilization : 2

It can certainly be said that civilization is based on the cumulated knowledge that current and former generations have developed, organized, and stored for use by current and future generations. We are long past the time when any educated person could learn and know all of the world's knowledge — if there ever was such a time. Thus, the knowledge base or foundation of civilization must be organized, described, and made accessible through libraries and other systems of information retrieval. It is no exaggeration to say that the preservation and advancement of civilization is absolutely dependent on effective information retrieval.

• origin of "database" as term : 3

The term "database" emerged in the early 1960s among workers involved with military information systems. The term referred to collections of data available to users of computer systems (Oxford English dictionary 1989). The idea implied is that these collections were bases (plural of basis) of data on which decisions might be made — on which decisions could be based. As databases developed since then, they were organized so that data could be accessed in a wide variety of ways.

• libraries compared to databases : 4

Of course libraries have been collecting data, in the form of documents, for millennia and have been describing these documents and organizing them for access. This vital function has been shared with a growing number of indexing and abstracting services and a multitude of separately produced indexes, bibliographies, catalogs, and compendia of data of various types, especially in the 19th and 20th centuries. Recently, digital libraries have been added to this rich mix. All of these systems for information retrieval can now be encompassed by the broad modern term "information retrieval database."

• data versus information, knowledge; varieties of messages : 5

Information retrieval (IR) databases focus on the retrieval of messages more than simple or raw data. Messages are recorded in documents of many varieties in many media and formats. They make use of visual written language and pictorial images, as well as visual texts based on other representation codes (such as musical, choreographic, chemical, and mathematical nota-

Chapter 1. Introduction and Background Issues (Section 1.2)

tion), aural spoken language and musical performances, and even tactile texts for the visually impaired. These messages reflect the knowledge and understandings of the persons, across generations and cultures, that created them. The lines between "data," "information," and "knowledge" are fuzzy. These terms will be discussed in section 1.3 on terminology. Data, information, and knowledge can all be encompassed, represented, or reflected in the messages that humans create. Information retrieval databases are designed to describe and organize such messages so that anyone can find messages they need or desire whenever they want them.

● design of IR databases : 6

Thus this book is about the design of databases that will help retrieve messages. Its purpose is to help the designer consider all the relevant factors and to choose the best available options. In most cases, there are no single correct or right answers, only better and worse choices for given purposes and persons. What this book opposes is simply accepting designs and procedures without considering alternative possibilities and matching them with the needs, desires, preferences, and resources of the persons who will use IR databases, or be served by them.

1.2. Assumptions.

● components of problems in information retrieval : 7

This book assumes that the IR database designer is confronted with an information retrieval problem and that the designer knows quite a bit about this problem. The components of this problem usually consist of:

    a. a large enough set of messages so that it is impossible to easily examine all of them, when certain ones or certain types are desired.

    b. a group of actual or potential users or clientele who need access to these messages for purposes of business, life-enhancement, entertainment, or similar impelling reasons.

● characteristics of messages, of users : 8

The IR database designer needs to know quite a bit about these messages, what they are about, what is significant about them, their format, media, location. Even more important, the IR database designer needs to know even more about the potential users or clientele for the IR database: their interests, needs, and information-seeking experience, skills, habits and preferences.

● user studies and needs assessment not within scope of this book : 9

This book will not discuss and is not meant to guide the conduct of user studies or user needs assessment. For this, the reader might consult *Information tasks: toward a user-centered approach to information systems*, by Bryce L. Allen (1996), and also some of the many publications he cites in his book. The last chapter in this book, chapter 22, discusses literature on methods testing and evaluation of IR databases, including users of these databases. Many of the methodologies discussed there may also be used for initial user needs assessment.

● expert users versus novice users; new users versus frequent users : 10

The discussion of design options throughout this book will assume a wide and varied potential audience for even the most technical or esoteric of IR databases. The reason for this assumption is that we know from decades of information-seeking behavior research that experts rarely consult IR databases for messages falling within their own areas of expertise. For their own literature, they usually have much more direct sources of information, such as colleagues with whom they interact in their research or professional activities and presentations or discussions at conferences and other gatherings. When such experts do consult IR databases, it is usually for information about messages that fall outside their immediate area of expertise, so now they may be playing the role of a new or even a novice user, and perhaps an exploring user. So in all designs, we must welcome new, novice and exploring users of all types. We can add options for frequent and expert users, such as librarians, to enable them to bypass features meant for new and exploring users, but only as special options. Our goal will be to make everyone welcome, and make our IR databases as clear and as easy to use as possible for everyone.

1.3. Terminology.

• terminology of IR database design : 11

It is hard to enter a new field without first learning some of its basic terminology — the special vocabulary used by practitioners and researchers, and the special meanings often given to terms in the context of the field. Here are definitions and discussions of the most important terms related to the design of IR databases. The ways these terms are used also help to lay out some of the assumptions underlying this book. For additional help with terminology, see Hans Wellisch (2000), *Glossary of terminology in abstracting, classification, indexing, and thesaurus construction.*

• 12

Here the major terms are arranged in a logical order, so that whenever possible, definitions that depend on the meaning of other key terms will come later in the list. In some cases, however, you may want to skip ahead in this list of terms. For example, as you read about IR databases, you may want to check the discussions of "message," "text," and "document"!

• 13

All of these terms are also defined in the glossary at the end of the book, where they are arranged in alphabetical order. So later on, if you are looking for a particular definition, it may be easier for you to look there than here.

• definition of database : 14

database. "Database" is a relatively new word for a collection of data that is organized for retrieval. It is sometimes restricted to organized collections of data in electronic media, but in this book, the term "database" is used for any collection of data organized for retrieval, regardless of medium, so that printed indexes, catalogs, encyclopedias, and similar reference works constitute examples of databases as well as electronic retrieval tools on CD-ROM or available online or via the world-wide web. (There is a brief note on the origin of this term in section 1.1 of the Introduction to this book and a recap on IR databases versus other types of databases in section 1.6.)

• types of databases : 15

Databases (along with the systems for access that accompany those in electronic form) can be categorized in many ways: by mission or purpose (such as MIS: management information systems), by subject areas (such as GIS: geographical information systems), by models of organization (such as relational, hypertext, object-oriented, flat-file), or by phenomena represented by data (such as real, concrete entities (things, objects!) and events versus messages about entities and events, including abstract and imaginary entities and events). This book focuses on databases designed for the purpose of facilitating discovery and retrieval of messages of all types, so our databases are called "information retrieval databases" or, for short, "IR databases." Their purpose is information retrieval. The primary data in such databases describe messages rather than concrete entities and events.

Chapter 1. Introduction and Background Issues (Section 1.3)

• relational database model : 16

relational database. One of the most common database models is called "relational," resulting in "relational databases." According to *FOLDOC: The Free On-line Dictionary of Computing* (1997), a relational database is one in which "the data and relations between them are organized in tables." The name reflects a special way for organizing data and for indicating relations among data or categories of data. The name can be misleading, however, because all databases, regardless of data model, record or display relationships to some degree, in one way or another.

• object-oriented database model : 17

object-oriented database. A more recent data model is called "object-oriented," as in "object-oriented databases," related to object-oriented programming (FOLDOC 1997, "object-oriented database"). In these databases, algorithms for processing data are integrated with the data, so that data related to each object of importance have their own associated object-oriented programs.

• flat file database model : 18

flat-file database. In contrast to the rather sophisticated and highly structured relational and object-oriented models, a simple data model calls for nothing more than "a single file containing many records, each of which contains the same set of fields" (FOLDOC 1997, "database"). This simple model, sometimes called a "flat file" design, is quite common for IR databases.

• hypertext database model : 19

hypertext database. With the advent of the world-wide web, hypertext databases have become more and more common. According to FOLDOC (1997, "hypertext"), "hypertext" refers to a "collection of documents (or 'nodes') containing cross-references or 'links' which, with the aid of an interactive browser program, allow the reader to move easily from one document to another." In a hypertext IR database, some of these documents may be summary records or surrogates, which can lead the user to documents containing the full text of messages.

• definition of concrete entity and event database : 20

concrete entity and event database. Databases can also be characterized by the nature of the objects or phenomena that they are designed to describe. Concrete entity and event databases organize data about real concrete entities and events. Examples include airline databases that contain data about airplanes and all their parts, their maintenance, their crews, particular flights, fares, supplies, passengers, including which passengers get special meals, etc.; or bank databases that contain data about all customers, all their accounts, their balances and every banking transaction. The focus of these databases is on concrete entities and concrete events. In contrast, IR databases are designed to describe messages. These messages, of course, may be about concrete entities and events, but just as often, they can be about rather abstract or ephemeral phenomena, such as theories, feelings, emotions, and aesthetics.

• 21

To give one more example of the difference between a concrete entity and event database and an IR database, consider an online or print catalog for a large retail chain like JCPenney or a mail-order house like L.L.Bean. These catalogs are databases that directly describe and organize descriptions of the concrete entities or objects that JCPenney or L.L.Bean would like to sell. On the other hand, an IR database dealing with these products would not directly describe and organize the descriptions of these products, but would describe messages about these products (perhaps the kind of messages one might find in *Consumer Reports* magazine). Thus the focus of concrete entity and event databases is directly on the entities and events that they describe and organize. The focus of IR databases is on messages, their various features and attributes, and what they have to say about concrete, as well as abstract, entities and events.

Chapter 1. Introduction and Background Issues (Section 1.3)

• definition of IR database : 22

IR database. Thus, IR databases have as their primary purpose the organization of data about potential information contained in messages, texts and documents in order to facilitate the retrieval of these information containers. For the most part, IR databases are not directly concerned with concrete entities or events, except as concrete entities and events are represented as topics of messages or features of messages.

• indexing of concrete entities and events compared to indexing of messages : 23

Making a clear distinction between concrete entity and event databases versus IR databases (message databases!) is important because the description and indexing of concrete entities and events are so different from the description and indexing of messages. When one has a carburetor in one's hand, there is little dispute what the object is. There may be questions about what to call it, what type it is, what kind of engine it is designed for, but there is usually a clear consensus on what it is.

• indexing of messages : 24

Messages are entirely different. What a message is, what it is about, what it means, what it is for (or good for) is entirely in the mind of the beholder. Two or more people may see entirely different messages in the very same text. Arguments about what famous texts mean (the Bible for example) have gone on for centuries! This is precisely why the general level of agreement among indexers describing the same text ranges between only 20 and 25 per cent. Searchers, who in effect index information needs or queries, have about the same level of agreement as to appropriate search terms.

• structured data : 25

In the typical concrete entity and event database, the discrete entities and events to be considered are generally known in advance. Their relations are often described and structured in advance (using, for example, a relational database model). Because of the careful structuring of such data, these types of data are sometimes referred to as "structured data."

• unstructured data : 26

In contrast, a typical IR database generally will deal with a defined set of messages, but the number of topics in these messages will be too numerous and varied to predict in advance. These topics may well relate to concrete entities and events, but they may just as frequently deal with abstract or imaginary entities, and abstract or imaginary processes, operations, or conditions. In addition, the possible relations among the topics covered in messages is also enormous and practically impossible to predict in advance. Hence, IR databases are often called "unstructured," or their data can be called "unstructured information." Indeed, in many IR databases, certain fields consist of unprocessed text, such as an abstract, or even the full text of a document. Such full-text fields contain the ultimate in unstructured data! Of course such full-text fields do retain the structure of the original text, but the data represented is not re-structured according to any rules of database structure or data models.

• concrete entities in IR databases; concrete events in IR databases : 27

Despite this general focus on the content and features of messages and texts (and the documents in which they occur), IR databases must also deal with concrete entities and events related to the creation and transmission of messages, texts and documents. They must describe the concrete documents in which messages and texts reside and the persons and organizations that create these messages and texts, and manufacture, publish and disseminate documents.

Chapter 1. Introduction and Background Issues (Section 1.3)

• abstract entities, fictitious entities, imaginary entities in IR databases : 28

Examples of the kinds of abstract, fictitious or imaginary entities that IR databases typically deal with include hypotheses, theories, opinions, beliefs. IR databases also deal with rather abstract or hypothetical processes, such as evolution, growth and development, cognition, consciousness, and with rather abstract attributes such as aesthetics, feelings, emotions. Mythical or fictional figures, characters and events are also fair game for IR databases. In fact, any topic of interest to human beings will be found in IR databases, because all these topics will be found in human messages, and it is human messages that form the focus of most IR databases.

• alternative names for IR databases : 29

IR databases have also been called "bibliographic databases," "document databases," "textual databases," "textbases," and more recently "digital libraries." The modern term "IR database" has come to replace (and to include) a wide spectrum of tools used to organize and provide access to documents: bibliographies, indexes, indexing and abstracting services, information resource guides and handbooks, and reading lists.

• definition of full-text database : 30

full-text database. Full-text databases are IR databases that contain the full text of the documents that they describe and organize for retrieval. Such texts may be based on a variety of representation codes, such as linguistic, pictorial, musical, mathematical, etc. We have long had full-text databases in print media. Examples include handbooks and encyclopedias. In addition, monographs with their own back-of-the-book indexes also qualify as full-text databases, because the text of the monograph is presented together with an index, and this index describes and reorganizes the content and other features of the text for retrieval. But usually, "full-text database" refers to electronic databases.

• definition of digital library : 31

digital library. Digital libraries are full-text IR databases that replicate, in digital media, many of the functions of traditional libraries. They tend to contain a purposefully selected collection of texts plus various means of access to these texts. ODLIS: Online Dictionary of Library and Information Science (Reitz 2000) defines "digital library" simply as: "A library in which a significant proportion of the resources are available in digital (machine-readable) format, as opposed to print or microform. The process of digitization began with indexes and abstracting services, then moved to periodicals and reference books."

• definition of reference database : 32

reference database. Reference databases are IR databases that point to (refer to!), but do not include, the full text of the documents that they describe. Documents are represented by surrogates, such as citations, abstracts, excerpts, notes, and pictures.

• definition of information retrieval system : 33

information retrieval system (or information storage and retrieval system). Information retrieval systems are the systems that make it possible to search IR databases. They provide the interfaces that permit users to compose searches and match them against database indexes or to browse indexes that are displayed for visual inspection. Often the search system is so integrated into the database itself that it is inseparable. This is especially true for print-on-paper databases, such as printed indexes, catalogs, bibliographies, handbooks and encyclopedias. In electronic retrieval, however, the information retrieval system may be completely separate, so that the same IR database can be vended or made available by different vendors or agencies, each of which provides an entirely different information retrieval system, with entirely different interfaces, different search engines, different search commands, and different display options.

Chapter 1. Introduction and Background Issues (Section 1.3)

• definition of index : 34

index. An index is any device that is (or can be) used to indicate or point to something of interest. Indexes are used in many fields in addition to library and information science, such as the consumer price index in economics, where the index points to the rise and fall of prices. In information retrieval, an index is used to indicate the content and features of messages and the locations of these messages and/or the location of particular content or features within these messages. There are many types and varieties of indexes, corresponding to types of IR databases listed in section 1.5. Indexes are produced in many different ways, both by human analysis and computer manipulation.

• definition of message : 35

message. IR databases are used in order to find and retrieve messages. A message is the content of a meaningful communication. In order to be communicated — to be sent and to be received, messages must be encoded into texts, using symbols or representations that can convey meaning to recipients of the message. A message is potential information. If a message is actually received by someone who pays some level of attention to it, that person can be said to have been informed by the message, and the message itself can qualify as information.

• messages versus works : 36

In library cataloging, the term "work" is used in much the same way as "message" is used in this book. In Patrick Wilson's classic treatise, *Two kinds of power: an essay on bibliographical control* (1968, p. 7-14), he makes a considerable effort to make as clear a distinction as possible between a work (a message) and the various texts in which that work (message) may be encoded. He points out, for example, that a particular poem can be translated into other languages, and that a translation of a poem need not itself be a poem. These translations, some in non-poetic forms, are certainly not identical texts, but they each reflect or encode the same work. In another example, he points out that translations of the works of the German philosopher Schopenhauer are still considered texts representing his works (his messages), even though they are in languages different from the one in which he wrote. So the distinction between messages or works and the texts in which they are or can be encoded is fundamental.

• texts versus exemplars : 37

Wilson also makes a distinction between texts and their exemplars, or particular copies or manifestations, pointing out (p. 6-7) that the exemplars of the same text can vary considerably, yet still be said to consist of the same text. We are all aware of this, that the same painting (a text) can be reproduced in copies (reproductions) of different sizes, just as the same language text can be reproduced in different printings with different type faces and sizes and different paginations.

• definition of information : 38

information. This is a slippery concept that is best avoided, except in terms like "information science" (the established name of a discipline) and "information retrieval" (the name of a primary focus in information science). The problem with "information" is that it has come to have too many meanings, and it is therefore often vague and unclear. On the one hand, it is used to refer to the process of informing or becoming informed. But more frequently, it is used to stand for messages, texts, and documents, whether or not these are actually informative for a person confronting them. Does it really make sense to call ancient Greek manuscripts "information" if one can't even read them?

Chapter 1. Introduction and Background Issues (Section 1.3)

• definition of datum, data : 39

datum, data. A "datum" (singular of "data") may be considered to be a single fact or item of evidence. To be informative, a datum needs one or more additional data of different sorts to provide context. Thus it can be said that a message (potential information) needs at least two data. A set of numerical data, such as "70, 90, 28, 64," is meaningless unless some explanation is provided. Do these data refer to temperatures? sport scores? or what? Similarly, a simple datum regarding color, such as "red," carries much more meaning when it is combined with at least one more datum, such as "chair." Data are often presented in tables, along with explanations, e.g., average temperatures by month and place in major cities of the Unites States, or the latest scores of today's football games. Because IR databases focus on messages, they rarely deal with raw data except in the context of messages, where data are placed in context.

• definition of knowledge, wisdom : 40

knowledge. "Knowledge" refers to what someone knows. It resides in the mind and the brain, but it is reflected in messages. "Wisdom" refers to the wise use of knowledge. It is not technically correct to say that knowledge resides in messages. According to the following definitions for "text" and "document," messages are no more than organized sets of symbols. But these symbols refer to what persons know, think, believe, feel, and understand, so it is entirely proper to say that messages, texts, and documents record, reflect, and convey the knowledge of a person, a group, or an entire culture.

• views of Korfhage (Robert R.) on data, information, knowledge, wisdom : 41

Robert Korfhage (1997, p. 8-10) presents a slightly different but useful view of the relations among "data," "information," and "knowledge." He also adds "signal" at the beginning of this continuum and "wisdom" at the conclusion, citing as well Manfred Kochen's treatment of "the chain that begins with signal and ends with wisdom" (Kochen 1974, p. 62). Kochen inserts "understanding" between "knowledge" and "wisdom." But can there be knowledge without understanding? Here are Korfhage's definitions:

• definition of signal : 42

Signal: "At one end [of this hierarchy of increasing complexity], less complex than data, is the signal that must be transmitted from one place to another during information processing. This signal may be a bit stream, an electromagnetic wave form, or some other form" (p. 9).

• definition of data : 43

Data: "Data are impersonal; they are equally available to any users of the system" (p. 8).

• definition of information : 44

Information: "Information, in contrast, is a set of data that have been matched to a particular information need. That is, the concept of information has both personal and time-dependent components that are not present in the concept of data." Information requires "the active intervention of a user" (p. 8).

• definition of knowledge : 45

Knowledge: "Knowledge builds upon information, integrating any new information with that previously known to form a large, coherent view of a portion of reality" (p. 9).

• definition of wisdom : 46

Wisdom: "Finally, wisdom adds to this knowledge a broader view still, encompassing all of known reality, and governing the use of the information that has been obtained and the knowledge that has been developed. It involves the capacity to make balanced judgments in the light of certain value criteria" (p. 9).

Chapter 1. Introduction and Background Issues (Section 1.3)

• definition of text : 47

text. Messages are encoded or recorded in texts. Texts are meaningful collections of symbols assembled to convey a message. The word "text" is related to the word "textile," and just as textiles consist of organized fibers or threads, a text consists of an organized set of symbols. Spoken language (speech) texts consist of meaningful sequences of sounds (phonemes). Writing is the representation of speech, and it uses visual symbols to represent the sounds of speech (phonemes) and sometimes to distinguish among meanings (night vs. knight). Examples of writing symbols include Chinese characters (which represent not only sounds but also meanings), Japanese "kana" syllabaries (in which each symbol represents a syllable — a combination of a consonant and a vowel), and Roman, Cyrillic, Greek and other alphabets (in which each symbol represents one or more phonemes, with separate symbols for vowels and consonants).

• types of texts : 48

In addition to language texts, there are many other kinds of texts that convey messages — musical texts, image texts (such as those embodied in still or moving pictures), three-dimensional texts (such as those created through architecture, sculpture, and industrial design), dance and other performance texts, and mathematical and chemical texts. Music has a well developed symbol system that is used to represent sound, including pitch and length, in visual media such as print on paper. We call these texts "scores." Dance choreography can also be represented symbolically, and scientific disciplines like mathematics and chemistry have well developed sets of symbols and codes for representing mathematical and chemical concepts. The symbol systems of art, as in painting and sculpture, are less formal, but most people would agree that paintings and sculpture convey messages, even if it is not always easy to discern them or to agree on what they are. In painting, the field of iconography is devoted to the study and identification of artistic messages.

• definition of medium, media : 49

medium. Media (the plural of medium) are the physical substances on which or in which a text is conveyed or recorded. Ephemeral media include the airwaves over which sound (including speech) is sent and received. Information retrieval generally deals with longer lasting media, such as stone, clay, metal, paper, film, and the newer media for the recording of electronic digital data: disks, tapes and chips made from various forms of plastic, silicon and metal. An important responsibility of our profession is to make sure that the media on which messages are recorded can actually be preserved for as long as the message has value. This is a big challenge, especially for untested newer magnetic and optical media for digital data. One hopes that these modern media, including silicon (ceramic!) chips, will be as long-lasting as their ancient relatives, the clay tablets of the Middle East and elsewhere.

• definition of format : 50

format. Texts come in many shapes and styles, influenced by the medium on or in which a message is encoded, by the meaning and purpose of the message, and by the intended recipients of the message. Shape and style contribute to something we usually call format. It covers a wide spectrum of attributes, such as literary genre (poetry, narrative, drama, essay, speech, fiction, etc.), type of presentation (chart, diagram, picture, cartoon, list, etc.), and type of publication (such as book versus pamphlet versus broadside or poster on paper media, slide versus motion picture in film media). D. W. Langridge (1992, p. 28) suggests six types of attributes related to "the method of selection, arrangement or display" of message content under the heading of format: 1. order, how material is arranged, e.g., alphabetically, chronologically, or in some classified order according to mutual relations of message content or features; 2. literary forms or gen-

Chapter 1. Introduction and Background Issues (Section 1.3)

res (poetry, drama, essay, narrative fiction, short story); 3. reductions (abstracts, excerpts, quotations, summaries); 4. collections (encyclopedias, compendia, handbooks, readers); 5. keys to other documents (indexes, bibliographies, catalogs); and 6. rules (standards, codes, recipes). The distinction between "format" and "medium" is sometimes cloudy or fuzzy. For example, the meaning of "book" usually includes its medium (paper) as well as its shape (leaves bound together along one edge). When the content of a book is moved to electronic media, is it still a book? Probably the meaning of "book" will continue to shift as the media on or in which book-like messages are conveyed change over time. After all, our word "book" came from the Anglo-Saxon word for beech tree, because ancient runes were once written on beech bark! The connection in German is quite close: "Buche" for "beech tree" and "Buch" for "book."

• definition of document : 51

document. A document is a combination of text and medium. Texts cannot exist without embodiment in some medium, whether ephemeral, like airwaves, or longer lasting, like paper, film, or electronic media for digital data. Usually we use "document" to refer only to texts recorded in the longer-lasting media, and it is these documents that are susceptible to indexing and later retrieval.

• definition of catalog, cataloging : 52

catalog, cataloging. A catalog is an index for a particular collection of messages. A union catalog is an index for several collections. "Cataloging" is the process of creating a catalog, so it is a type of indexing.

• definition of descriptive cataloging, descriptive indexing : 53

descriptive cataloging, descriptive indexing. "Descriptive cataloging" is an old and honorable term that refers to the description and indexing of texts and documents with respect to features other than the content, purpose, or meaning of the text's message. Such features include the authors and other creators of texts (editors, composers, illustrators, translators, artists, etc.); the names or titles of texts (including subtitles, parallel titles, alternate titles, running titles etc.); the publishers or manufacturers and distributors of documents containing texts; the size and medium of documents; and the symbol set and code used to encode the text. Codes and symbols used to encode texts include natural languages and their writing systems (French, German, Chinese), but also codes and symbols for music, dance, chemistry, mathematics, etc., and, at another level, codes for the representation of messages in digital media. Names and index terms are established for the most important features. Descriptive cataloging (along with subject cataloging) is part of the process for making a catalog. "Descriptive indexing" is a rarely used term for the same process outside of the context of catalogs for particular collections of documents.

• definition of subject cataloging, subject indexing : 54

subject cataloging, subject indexing. Whereas descriptive cataloging and descriptive indexing focus on the surface features of texts and documents, subject cataloging and subject indexing focus on analysis, description and indexing of the content, purpose or meaning of messages, in other words, the topics or subjects of messages and texts. The description of certain non-topical features of messages, texts and documents is frequently included in subject cataloging and indexing. Examples include special audiences (books for children), special formats (poetry, fiction, dictionaries, periodicals, statistics), special aspects or approaches (history, case studies), special media (film, video recordings, audio recordings, world-wide web), etc. The goal is to identify and provide access to all important topics and features. The trick, of course, is figuring out what is, or will be, important for future users!

Chapter 1. Introduction and Background Issues (Section 1.3)

• definition of classification : 55

classification. "Classification" literally means to place items in classes, resulting in groupings of items sharing some similarity. By extension, it can refer to the creation and/or naming of these classes. By further extension, it often includes the arrangement of classes in a logical, relational, non-alphabetical or non-alphanumeric order. At the fundamental level, indexing and classification are the same process, because in both operations, messages must be analyzed, and based on this analysis, grouped into categories or classes. Finally, these groupings must be named and arranged to provide access. At the more superficial level, but reflecting its most common usage, classification refers to the logical, relational (non-alphabetical) arrangement of classes, in contrast to alphabetical indexes in which classes are simply arranged in alphabetical or alphanumeric order on the basis of their names.

• definition of documentary unit : 56

documentary unit. A "documentary unit" is the portion of a document that can be directly retrieved by an IR database. Documentary units may be complete documents, such as complete books, or complete periodical articles. Or they may be parts of complete documents — chapters in books, or paragraphs or charts or diagrams or illustrations in periodical articles. This same variety in the size of documentary units applies to all media. An IR database for videotapes, for example, might retrieve only complete videotapes (so that the documentary unit is the complete tape), or it might be able to retrieve individual frames or short sequences of frames, in which cases, either the individual frames, or the short sequences of frames, constitute the documentary units. In all cases, the documentary unit is the unit that is analyzed for indexing (either by machine algorithm or by human inspection). Consequently, the "documentary-unit" is also called the "unit-of-analysis." "Bibliographic unit" has also been used for this concept, indicating the unit described and retrievable via a bibliography. Small documentary units have also been called "information units," but one should hope that all documentary units will be informative! Chapter 6 deals with documentary units.

• definition of indexable matter : 57

indexable matter. "Indexable matter" is the actual portion of a documentary unit on which indexing or classification is based — on which index terms or headings are based or from which terms are extracted. Not all indexes need to be based on the entire text of a message. Sometimes a message can be adequately summarized by a part of its text. Thus, if an index does not need to be very detailed, a good title might be sufficient to represent the message of a periodical article for purposes of indexing or classification. In that case, the title could be the indexable matter for the documentary unit — the periodical article. Abstracts of scholarly articles are a common example of indexable matter. Many indexing and abstracting services base their indexing and classification on the abstracts of the messages that they cover. For important messages, the entire text of the message may need to be consulted, thereby making the entire text the indexable matter. Sometimes, whole categories of messages may be excluded from indexable matter. An index for a scholarly journal, for example, may index only substantive research articles and exclude from indexable matter all advertisements, letters to the editor (unless they comment on articles that are indexed), announcements, calls for papers, etc. (Indexable matter is also called "analysis base," because it constitutes the base (or basis) of analysis — the text on which analysis is based.) Chapter 7 deals with indexable matter.

• definition of term, index term, bound term : 58

term. A "term" is a word or a phrase representing a single concept or multiple concepts that are tightly bound together in the context of a particular IR database. An "index term" is such a

Chapter 1. Introduction and Background Issues (Section 1.3)

word or phrase associated with a documentary unit for the purposes of retrieval. Some concepts need more than one word to express them, for example, "information science" or "venetian blind." Some terms could be divided into two separate terms, but they are used so commonly together in a consistent order, that they are considered a single "bound term" or "compound term." Examples of such bound terms are "information science" (which could be the "science" of "information"), "library schools," "school libraries," "birth control," and "juvenile delinquency." If "information science" were separated into separate terms for "information" and "science," we could get all sorts of "false drops" (unwanted documents) dealing with information problems in science when doing a search for "information" AND "science." We could divide "birth control" into "birth" and "control," but birth control is more about the control of conception than the control of birth, so the bound term "birth control" is more useful. Generally speaking, when two or more terms are almost always used in the same way, in the same order, for a particular concept or set of concepts, they should be kept together as a single bound term. One hardly ever hears anyone refer to "the science of information," the "control of conception or birth," or the "delinquency of juveniles." The National Information Standards Organization guidelines for thesauri has a whole section on compound terms (National Information Standards Organization 1993, section 4).

• definition of complex term : 59

Sometimes "complex term" is used for a single phrase denoting more than two distinct concepts. The Library of Congress introduced the complex term "telephone assistance programs for the poor" in 1990. This single term could be broken up into separate terms for "telephones," "assistance programs" and "poor people," so it could qualify as an example of a complex term.

• definition of descriptor, equivalent term : 60

descriptor. The term "descriptor" is usually reserved for a term that is part of a controlled indexing language. Such indexing languages are often listed in a thesaurus. For each concept included in the indexing language, one descriptor will be chosen to represent the concept, and all other terms that can be used for the same concept are linked to the descriptor by means of cross-references. Thus, if a thesaurus uses the descriptor "lawyer," then it might not use the terms "attorney," "barrister," "solicitor," or "counselor-at-law." Each of these alternative terms can be linked to the preferred descriptor "lawyer" and would be given the status of un-used synonymous or equivalent terms. (Equivalent terms are terms that are not truly synonymous, but are close enough so that they can be considered equivalent in the context of a database. Anyone who knows the English legal system knows that "barrister" and "solicitor" are not exactly the same as U.S. "lawyers," but in many databases, the distinction would not be important enough to make, so that "barrister" and "solicitor" could be considered equivalent to "lawyer.")

• definition of free-text term, keyword : 61

free-text term. Often shortened to "free text," "free-text term" usually refers to the use of uncontrolled words or terms from natural language text for indexing or searching. When one searches the actual text of a document, one is searching the free-text terms that are found in the document. The difference between "free-text terms" and just "terms" is that sometimes terms may be standardized, at least a little, with respect to format, and they may also have links with the most common synonyms or equivalent terms, even if they are not controlled to the extent of formal descriptors. In this paragraph, every term or phrase is a free-text term. Some of the smaller words (such as "to," "the," "of," etc.) may be listed on a "stop list" of unsearchable terms — terms that cannot be searched for by themselves, but they are still free-text terms! "Keyword" is often used to indicate the more important free-text terms.

Chapter 1. Introduction and Background Issues (Section 1.3)

• definition of heading, classification caption : 62

heading. In displayed indexes (indexes that are designed for visual inspection by humans as opposed to non-displayed indexes that are searched by computer algorithm), index terms are combined into headings consisting of multiple terms. It is possible to have index headings with only single terms, but headings of two or more terms are more meaningful, because the lead term is modified or amplified or described by the subsequent term or terms. The subsequent term or terms create a context for the first, or lead, term. Compare, for example, the meaning of the simple heading "United States" versus the more detailed meaning of "United States — history — civil war — bibliography." In the second heading, "United States" has been modified or defined by aspect or approach (history), event or period (civil war), and format (bibliography). An index heading is an essential part of an index entry. When displayed indexes are displayed in classified rather than alphabetical order, the headings are often called "captions."

• definition of syntax for index headings, syntax for search statements : 63

syntax. "Syntax" is a linguistic term meaning (1) "orderly or systematic arrangement," or more precisely, (2) "the arrangement of words as elements in a sentence to show their relationship; sentence structure" (Webster's 1966, p. 1480). It comes from the Greek for putting or arranging together. The first meaning is labeled "obsolete," but it is closer to the meaning intended here in borrowing "syntax" from linguistics and applying it to index headings and search statements. "Syntax" is used in this book to mean rules or patterns for the combination of terms to form meaningful index headings or effective search statements. Index headings consist of terms arranged in a certain order, and they may display a certain structure as well, so the application of the idea of syntax seems appropriate. In modern search statements for electronic IR databases, the order or particular arrangement of terms is often immaterial, but by extension, the idea of syntax is used to refer to the rules or patterns for the combination (as opposed to the arrangement) of terms (for example the use of boolean operators OR, AND, or NOT between terms), and also for the application of techniques for indicating term weights, proximity limits, truncation and wildcards, and for stemming and similar refinements to influence the results of a search. Here the analogy corresponds to the grammatical use of inflections (word endings or changes in form) to indicate the role of words in a sentence with respect to number (singular or plural), case (subject, object, possessive), gender (male or female) or tense (past, present, future).

• 64

In short, indexing or searching "syntax" is used to refer to the rules or patterns for creating index headings or search statements! Chapter 12 deals with syntax.

• definition of postcoordinate syntax, precoordinate syntax : 65

postcoordinate, precoordinate syntax. The terms "postcoordinate syntax" and "precoordinate syntax" are used to indicate when terms are put together to represent documentary units, either before (pre) or after (post) a search begins. All index headings that are constructed for displayed indexes, which users may browse during the searching process, must of necessity be created before the search, so they are called "precoordinate" headings based on precoordinate syntax. Postcoordinate syntax is used almost exclusively for machine matching, where searchers create search statements, putting terms together at the time of the search, then make use of computer algorithms to find matching records or texts.

• precoordinate index headings versus postcoordinate search statements : 66

One big difference between precoordinate index headings and postcoordinate search statements is that the precoordinate headings generally refer to actual existing documents, whereas postcoordinate search statements refer to hoped-for documents.

Chapter 1. Introduction and Background Issues (Section 1.3)

• role of precoordinate index terms in search statements : 67

Even in postcoordinate searches, searchers may take advantage of precoordinate terms or headings that have been attached to documentary units. Such precoordinate terms or headings can prevent false drops — the retrieval of documents based on the presence of two or more terms, when these terms are not actually related in the manner intended. Thus the precoordinated combination of nationality and medium in "French painting" can prevent the retrieval of a document that deals with "French sculpture" and "Dutch painting" when it is "French painting" that is sought. If "French," "Dutch," "painting," and "sculpture" were all separate terms for later combination in postcoordinate searching, then "French" and "painting" would retrieve (in error) the document on "Dutch painting" and "French sculpture."

• definition of index entry, locator : 68

entry. In displayed indexes, an entry represents and points to a documentary unit. An entry consists of a heading (of one or more terms) and a single locator, such as:

```
United States   23
```
or
```
United States. history. civil war. bibliography   44
```

The locator leads to the documentary unit. In this example the numbers 23 and 44 might refer to particular paragraphs or pages or to entries in a list of document citations or to documents on shelves or in a filing cabinet.

• definition of index entry array : 69

When two or more entries have identical headings or subheadings, these duplicate headings are usually merged for display, resulting in "entry arrays" that might look something like this:

```
United States
    Armed Forces
        Afro-Americans. Bibliography   25
                        History   24-30, 339
        California. History. 20th century   54
        China. History. 20th century   332
              Military life. History   442
        Gays   74-80, 445-450
              Government policy   76
              History. 20th century   78-80
              Legal status, laws, etc.   76-78
        History. Civil War, 1861-1865   61
                 Revolution, 1775-1783   55
                 World War, 1939-1945   93-97
        Officers. Death   333, 634
                  Directories   335
                  Education   330-331
        Women. Bibliography   99
               History. Archival resources   98
               Periodicals   97
```

• presentation of entry arrays : 70

Such entry arrays are more compact and often clearer to the user than repeating each term or heading and subheading, as in the following example, which consists of the very same entries, but without merged headings. Punctuation between terms will vary. In the preceding example, dots (or periods or full stops) were used between distinct terms. In the following example, terms are separated by a space-dash-space, as used in *Library of Congress subject headings*.

```
United States — Armed Forces — Afro-Americans — Bibliography 25
United States — Armed Forces — Afro-Americans — History 24-30
United States — Armed Forces — Afro-Americans — History 339
United States — Armed Forces — California — History — 20th century 54
United States — Armed Forces — China — History — 20th century 332
United States — Armed Forces — China — Military life — History 442
United States — Armed Forces — Gays 74-80
United States — Armed Forces — Gays 445-450
United States — Armed Forces — Gays — Government policy 76
United States — Armed Forces — Gays — History — 20th century 78-80
United States — Armed Forces — Gays — Legal status, laws, etc. 76-78
United States — Armed Forces — History — Civil War, 1861-1865 61
United States — Armed Forces — History — Revolution, 1775-1783 55
United States — Armed Forces — History — World War, 1939-1945 93-97
United States — Armed Forces — Officers — Death 333
United States — Armed Forces — Officers — Death 634
United States — Armed Forces — Officers — Directories 335
United States — Armed Forces — Officers — Education 330-331
United States — Armed Forces — Women — Bibliography 99
United States — Armed Forces — Women — History — Archival resources 98
United States — Armed Forces — Women — Periodicals 97
```

• **determination of number of index entries : 71**

When identical portions of headings are merged, one cannot count headings to determine the number of entries in an index. Instead, it is the locators that must be counted. Every entry has a separate locator. It may or may not have a separate heading. Thus, the number of entries (i.e., locators) in an index is not the same as the number of headings, because the same heading can refer to a number of documentary units, and each referral constitutes an entry.

• **sequences of locators : 72**

One area of debate in the indexing community is whether a sequence of locators, such as "76-78," constitutes one locator or three: 76, 77, and 78. The answer should probably depend on the nature of the documentary units to which these locators refer. If they are paragraphs or pages in a continuous text, they could be considered a single locator referring to a three-paragraph or three-page documentary unit. But if the documentary units are independent documents, such as three separate periodical articles, then they are clearly three separate locators.

• **numbers of locators under headings : 73**

One sign of a bad index is too many locators (entries) under individual headings. The National Information Standards Organization (NISO) technical report on indexes (Anderson 1997a, p. 22) recommends that no index heading and no main heading subheading combination should have more than five attached locators, unless these locators themselves convey additional information, as is the case when document citations, with document titles, are used as locators. The rationale for this guideline is that most users do not want to examine too many documentary units in hopes of finding a relevant message. The technical report suggests that users should not have to consult more than five documentary units when they search for a relevant message related to any given index heading. To achieve this goal, indexers can use more specific headings, or they can add more information to headings (by adding additional terms) in order to characterize the documentary unit in more detail and to differentiate among the various messages that might fall together under a more generic heading.

• **criteria for index entries : 74**

According to Timothy Craven (1986, p. 7), a good index entry will provide enough information so that an index user can safely ignore the documentary units to which it refers. This is the principle of eliminability — the need to provide enough information so that the user can eliminate the entry without having to follow up its locators and examine their documentary units. The four other criteria for good index entries suggested by Craven include: predictability, collocation (similar entries falling together in an index), clarity, and succinctness. These criteria will be addressed in chapter 12 on syntax, in section 12.2.

• definition of locator : 75

locator. The "locator" is the part of an index entry that leads the user to the documentary unit to which the index entry refers. It indicates the location of the documentary unit or the location of a representation of the documentary unit (such as a citation, abstract, description, or thumbnail image). The locator can be as brief as a number, representing a page or paragraph in a back-of-the-book index, or it can be long enough to include a full citation that can be used to locate a documentary unit, perhaps in a library or on the internet. Chapter 15 deals with locators. See also ***entry***.

• definition of database record : 76

record. A record (or database record) contains the description of a message, the text in which it is encoded, and the documentary unit that contains the text. All the information or data in a database about a particular message, text and documentary unit goes into its record. Examples of such data include: a citation to the text and its documentary unit, including creator, title, publisher or manufacturer, format and medium; an abstract or some other description of the message content and features of the message, text, and documentary unit, sometimes including a small picture (thumbnail) of an image document or a short segment of sound; and all the content and feature terms, descriptors or headings associated with the documentary unit. The database record is usually structured or formatted according to some regular pattern. For example, many library catalogs use the MARC (Machine-Readable Cataloging) record format, developed initially by the Library of Congress and now a world-wide standard. Many databases create their own record format. In some database models, especially relational databases, the record is not a single unit, but is a node that contains links to all the data related to a particular message, text and documentary unit. For example, the name of a publisher may be recorded in a table of publishers and the name of an author may be in a table of authors. The particular publishers or authors linked to a particular message, text and documentary unit are called into a record display when that display is requested. Chapter 20 deals with record formats.

• definition of relevance : 77

relevance. Judgments of relevance are used in information retrieval as an indication of the usefulness of retrieved documentary units in response to a request or a search. The common measures of retrieval effectiveness, recall and precision, are both based on a determination of relevance (see section 9.1). Sometimes, researchers try to make distinctions between relevance, utility, pertinence, and similar terms, or to distinguish types of relevance, such as topical relevance as opposed to user relevance (the idea being that a document might be on the topic (and therefore topically relevant), but the user can't use it or doesn't want it — perhaps he or she can't read the language or already has the document or the writing is too complex, etc.).

• judges of relevance : 78

An associated controversy is who is qualified to judge the relevance of documents. In earlier (and some current) information science research, so-called expert judges made relevance judgments, but now in most information retrieval circles, these judgments are suspect. There is a growing consensus that to assess the effectiveness of IR databases and information retrieval systems for the actual users or clientele of these systems, the only legitimate judges of relevance, whatever its definition, are the actual users or clientele who have the actual information needs and make the information requests or conduct the searches. If this is the case, then relevance simply means that a user judges a documentary unit to be a useful response to her or his request or query.

1.4. Standards and Codes of Practice.

• **standards versus scientific research : 79**

Since the beginning of librarianship, millennia ago, improvements in practice have come about mainly through the development of new and better standards or codes of practice. Scientific research, as a means to study and understand phenomena and thereby improve practice, is a relatively recent innovation that came into librarianship, for the most part, with the advent and popularity of information science, mostly after World War II. Whereas scientific research is based on empirical testing of hypotheses, standards and codes of practice are based on expert opinion.

• **standards for cataloging, classification : 80**

In the world of indexing, cataloging, and classification, professional bodies have created a wide variety of codes of practice.

Current codes for cataloging and classification include:

- *Anglo-American cataloguing rules* (2002)
- *Library of Congress subject headings* and associated manuals and guides for their application: *Subject cataloging manual: subject headings* and *Free-floating subdivisions*, all issued by the Library of Congress (1996, 1999, 2003);
- many specialized lists of subject headings and thesauri such as *Medical subject headings* (National Library of Medicine 1999), the *ERIC thesaurus* (Educational Resources Information Center), and the *Art and architecture thesaurus* (1994);
- several library classification schemes, including the *Dewey decimal classification* (Dewey 1996), the *Library of Congress classification* (Library of Congress 2004), the *Universal decimal classification* (British Standards Institution 1961), and the *Bliss classification* (1997); and
- codes for the arrangement of alphabetical catalogs and indexes: *A.L.A. filing rules* (American Library Association 1980) and *Library of Congress filing rules* (Library of Congress 1980).

• **standards for indexing : 81**

In the realm of back-of-the-book indexing, the venerable *Chicago manual of style* (1993) has the status of a standard, even though it was never formally adopted by any standard-setting body. But then, neither was *Library of Congress subject headings* nor most classification schemes either. Many codes of practice become de facto standards through wide-spread adoption by practitioners. Formal standards are created by standard-setting bodies such as the National Information Standards Organization (NISO) or the International Organization for Standardization (ISO).

• **standards for alphanumeric arrangement : 82**

The arrangement of alphabetical catalogs and indexes is an interesting example of the impact and use of standards or codes of practice versus research. In the late 1970s, as computers became more and more important in cataloging operations, librarians decided that the older codes for arranging entries in alphabetical catalogs were no longer adequate. There were too many exceptions

Chapter 1. Introduction and Background Issues (Section 1.4)

that required complicated algorithms or human intervention for computer implementation. Examples included the arrangement of abbreviations as if the full term were spelled out, the arrangement of numerals as if the number were written out in the language of the text, and the consideration of heading elements in an order different from their order in certain headings — "Edward II, King of England," for example, was arranged as if it were "Edward, King of England, 2."

• *Library of Congress filing rules* as standard for alphanumeric arrangement : 83

So both the American Library Association (ALA) and the Library of Congress (LC) set up committees of experts to create new codes for the arrangement of alphabetical catalogs. They produced very different and conflicting rules, reflecting deep disagreements on the best way to arrange catalog entries. The Library of Congress continued an old practice of grouping headings on the basis of implicit criteria that are unknown to most users. If headings begin with the same word, the type of heading takes precedence over the content of the heading (the actual words). Names of persons come before names of places. Personal forenames come before family names. Names of places come before names of things (first corporate bodies, then topical subject headings). Names of things and topical subjects come before titles of documents. For example:

```
George III, King of Great Britain, 1738-1820    [forename]
George, Saint, d. 303                           [forename]
George, Alan                                    [family name]
George, William C.                              [family name]
George (Ariz.)                                  [place name]
George (Wyo.)                                   [place name]
George (Motor boat)                             [thing: corporate body]
George, Lake, Battle of, 1755                   [subject heading]
George [motion picture]                         [document title]
George and the dragon                           [document title]
```
(Examples taken from *Library of Congress filing rules*, 1980, p. 24, with two examples and some explanatory modifications added.)

• arrangement of subheadings : 84

Also, according to *Library of Congress filing rules*, subheadings or subdivisions under initial subject headings are not arranged alphabetically, but first grouped by the type of subdivision, such as chronological periods, general forms and topics, place names, limiting adjectives (preceded by a comma), qualifications (enclosed within parentheses), and phrases. This results in many non-alphabetical arrays, such as the following example under "missions," in the 1995 edition of *Library of Congress subject headings*:

```
Missions — African influences
Missions — Theory
Missions — Asia
Missions — United States
Missions, American
Missions, Tamil
Missions (canon law)
Missions and Christian union
Missions to Buddhists
Missions to Mormons
Missions around the world                       [document title]
```
(Actual headings as arranged in the 1995 edition of *Library of Congress subject headings*, with the addition of one document title.)

Chapter 1. Introduction and Background Issues (Section 1.4)

• **A.L.A. filing rules** as standard for alphanumeric arrangement : 85

The ALA rules rejected these non-alphanumeric distinctions, preferring to arrange headings only on the basis of the actual alphabetic letters or numerals of each heading. The ALA experts claimed that users would miss desired headings, because they are unaware of the special non-alphanumeric criteria imposed by the Library of Congress. Take, for example, a library catalog with hundreds of entries under "missions," with a variety of subheadings as well as document titles beginning with the word "missions." When a user comes to "missions" in the catalog, how could he or she be expected to know that "missions, American" comes after "Missions — United States," or that "missions around the world" comes at the very end of the sequence, after "missions to Mormons"?

• **NISO standards for alphanumeric arrangement** : 86

The National Information Standards Organization (NISO) began working on a new standard for the "alphabetical arrangement of letters and the sorting of numerals and other symbols" early in the 1990s (National Information Standards Organization 1996a), but this proposed standard failed to achieve the required consensus among NISO members. The proposed standard was much closer to the ALA rules than the LC, but it differed from both of these de facto standards in significant ways. Most notably, initial articles ("a," "an," and "the" in English) were to be considered for arrangement, whereas most initial articles are ignored in arrangements based on ALA and LC rules. Another departure concerns the arrangement of decimal numbers by numerical value rather than by numerical digits. The problem of fractions was not addressed. NISO later published these recommendations as a technical report (Wellisch 1999).

• **lack of research on alphanumeric arrangement** : 87

In this whole process, there was almost no research as to how users perceived alphabetical or alphanumeric order and which arrangement alternative would be easier for them to use. One exception consisted of several experiments conducted with small groups of students in the United Kingdom (Hartley, Davies, & Burnill 1981). Students were asked to arrange sets of headings as they would expect to find them in a back-of-the-book index. As with the experts, however, these students exhibited no consensus, suggesting a wide variety of possible arrangements. In any case, experiments such as this do not necessarily indicate the impact of different arrangements on searching or browsing effectiveness. These researchers did attempt to assess the speed of access to particular headings in sample alphabetical indexes arranged in different ways, but the differences were of no significance.

• 88

To this day, we do not have any significant body of research on which to base our arguments for particular alphabetical arrangements, and experts are fiercely divided on such issues as whether spaces between words should be considered or ignored (letter-by-letter versus word-by-word arrangement), the appropriate arrangement of subheadings, the arrangements of fractions and decimal numbers, and many similar issues that result in very different arrays of entries in alphabetical or alphanumeric indexes.

• **views of Saracevic (Tefko) on research versus standards** : 89

To be fair, one leading expert in information science (Tefko Saracevic) has declared that there are issues, such as this one, that are simply not amenable to research and must be subject to standards. Indeed, it is not easy to design appropriate, meaningful research to gather empirical evidence on arrangement questions. But what does one do when there is simply no, or insufficient, agreement among experts?

Chapter 1. Introduction and Background Issues (Section 1.4)

• **display of subject headings in online public access catalogs : 90**

In 1992, a Subcommittee on the Display of Subject Headings in Subject Indexes in Online Public Access Catalogs (a subcommittee of the Subject Analysis Committee of the Cataloging and Classification Section of the Association for Library Collections and Technical Services, a part of the American Library Association) brought out a small book entitled *Headings for tomorrow: public access display of subject headings* (American Library Association 1992). In this book, this subcommittee laid out the options and the arguments in favor of various arrangement alternatives, but it made no attempt to reach a consensus on the major controversies or to make recommendations regarding the best kind of arrangement, except in non-controversial areas such as the arrangement of numbers in ascending numerical order (p. 23).

• **lack of consensus among standards on alphanumeric arrangement : 91**

Drusilla Calvert (1996) provides a good summary of the status of standards for alphanumeric arrangement. In an article comparing the latest British and international standards for indexes, she, in effect, throws up her hands in dismay and declares, "Filing, or sorting, is a hornet's nest. All standards seem to disagree with all others" (p. 75). This is indeed the case, resulting in chaos for users, who are mostly unaware that there are major differences in possible alphanumeric arrangements. When they don't find something, they just assume it's not there, not suspecting that it has been placed in a completely unexpected location!

• **92**

We shall return to questions concerning the arrangement of headings and entries to facilitate searching and browsing in chapter 17, Arrangement of displayed indexes.

• **controversies in information retrieval : 93**

This story of alphabetical arrangement can be extended to many other controversies in the world of IR, some very central, such as the role and method of vocabulary control, automatic indexing versus human intellectual analysis, and boolean logic versus ranked weighted retrieval in machine searching.

• **standards for information retrieval : 94**

For IR in the United States, the most important standard-setting bodies are the International Organization for Standardization (ISO) and the National Information Standards Organization (NISO). NISO is a United States body, similar to national bodies in most other developed countries, such as the British Standards Institute in the U.K. These bodies are responsible for a wide range of standards affecting the design and performance of IR databases, on such topics as information interchange formats, international standard numbering for documents in various formats and media, indexes, abstracts, technical reports, thesauri, holding statements, computer character sets, paper permanence, information retrieval protocols (Z39.50), romanization and transliteration of non-Roman writing systems, common command language, interlibrary loan, East Asian character codes, bookbinding, computer software description, library shelving, country codes, CD-ROMs, electronic manuscripts, price indexes, bibliographic references, patron records, circulation transactions, alphanumeric arrangement, preservation, environmental conditions, microforms, library codes, and many more (National Information Standards Organization 1997a, 1997c).

• **NISO Committee YY and new standard for indexes : 95**

In 1991, NISO created a new committee, labeled YY, to revise the 1984 standard for indexes: Z39.4-1984 *Basic criteria for indexes* (National Information Standards Organization 1984). This committee spent five years studying the issues, soliciting and receiving input from NISO member organizations and interested information professionals, and suggesting standards that would encompass all types of indexing (automatic and human) and all types of indexes (print and electronic, displayed indexes for visual inspection and non-displayed indexes for machine searching). Because indexes are so central to IR databases, the committee addressed all aspects of IR database design.

• opposition to standard for indexes : 96

Two NISO members, the American Society of Indexers and the American Society for Information Science, objected to recommendations of Committee YY regarding automatic indexing and non-displayed indexes (indexes that are searched by computer algorithm as opposed to being displayed for searching by human visual inspection). Ironically, these two organizations were also the ones that were most closely involved in the work of the committee. Most members of Committee YY were members of both of these organizations, and both of these organizations sponsored meetings and consultations regarding the development of the standard. An article about the development process for this proposed standard appeared in the *Journal of the American Society for Information Science* (Anderson 1994).

• objections of American Society of Indexers to standard for indexes : 97

The American Society of Indexers (ASI) is primarily an organization of human indexers who earn their living by creating indexes based on their human intellectual analysis of messages and texts. From the very beginning, ASI's official representatives consistently and strenuously objected to any suggestion that finding or searching tools based on simple computer algorithms could be considered indexes. The kinds of tools that ASI objected to included KWIC, KWOC, KWAC (key-word-in-context, key-word-out-of-context, key-word-along-side-context) and permuted indexes, all of which have been widely used and are universally called indexes. The ASI objection also extended to non-displayed indexes that are widely and routinely used in simple full-text searching. ASI argued forcefully that only retrieval tools that actually contributed additional intellectual value (as opposed to simply rearranging or retrieving words as in a concordance) should be called indexes. They appeared to be willing to accept the products of more sophisticated computer algorithms based on term weighting, the identification of term phrases, and clustering as worthy to be called "indexes."

• 98

Committee YY understood and appreciated ASI's concerns, but it felt it could not eliminate any tool or device that pointed to informative messages, in line with its basic definition of an index as any "indicating tool," especially when such tools are universally referred to as "indexes" in the information community. Instead, the committee chose to apply standards for vocabulary management to these simple indexes, something that such indexes almost universally lack.

• endorsement of standard for indexes by American Society for Information Science : 99

The American Society for Information Science (ASIS) gave the first official draft (1993) of the proposed new standard a strong endorsement, saying:

"The people who reviewed NISO Z39.4-199X Guidelines for Indexes and Related Information Retrieval Devices for ASIS feel that it is a very good document. They particularly note that the inclusion of computer indexing is a good enhancement and expansion for the standard" (ballot response from the Standards Committee, American Society for Information Science, 18 February 1994).

• opposition from American Society for Information Science to standard for indexes : 100

But by the time the second official draft went out for a vote in 1995, the membership of the ASIS standards committee had changed, and so did its attitude toward the proposed standard:

"The attempt to extend the standard to electronic information retrieval has resulted in a standard that is overly complex, confusing, and diluted from its primary focus. The standard contains weak,

Chapter 1. Introduction and Background Issues (Section 1.4)

incomplete coverage of online information retrieval concepts and diluted focus on the raison d'etre for the standard, which is the design of indexes such as back-of-the-book indexes. We recommend that the standard be refocussed on traditional index design ...." (ballot response from the Standards Committee, American Society for Information Science, 26 July 1995).

• 101

The new ASIS objections had little to do with the relatively minor changes to the draft standard since the first official draft. Rather they related to the very heart of the draft standard — the attempt to create a standard that would apply to all types of indexes, regardless of medium, type of indexing, or type of searching.

• opposition from American Society for Information Science to terminology for non-displayed indexes : 102

The new ASIS Standards Committee did not like the terminology that NISO's Committee YY had adopted, after wide consultation, for indexes that were not displayed for human inspection, but rather were designed for machine searching. When the Committee YY began its work, there simply wasn't a common vocabulary for such indexes. One visiting member of ASIS declared at a 1992 open meeting of Committee YY that such electronic indexes were not indexes at all, and should not be considered by the committee (Anderson, Record of November 6, 1992 meeting of Committee YY, November 7, 1992). This disagreement, like that of ASI, is fundamentally one of definition. Can the systems that permit computers to search algorithmically legitimately be said to include indexes? Are indexes an essential component of such computer search systems? It is indeed a matter of definition. Definitions can be important when they reflect conflicting models of basic IR processes. And definitions are precursors to standards.

• terminology for non-displayed indexes : 103

Several members of Committee YY represented the IR database industry, and these members, along with a majority of the committee, believed strongly that non-displayed indexes (designed for machine searching) met all the criteria for indexes and were therefore within the purview of the committee. In the end, the committee settled on the term "non-displayed indexes" for these indexes that are not displayed for human inspection. Commonly used "inverted files" are an example of such non-displayed indexes.

• role of search interfaces in non-displayed indexes : 104

A related controversy was whether the search interface for machine searching systems was part of a non-displayed index. The new ASIS Standards Committee said it was not. In contrast, the NISO Committee YY held that the search interface was an essential part of an electronic non-displayed index, because it was the interface that provides the capability for creating search statements that can be matched against the non-displayed index. These search statements, said Committee YY, are closely analogous to index headings in displayed indexes. In fact, according to Committee YY, a non-displayed index can only be considered an index in combination with a search interface. Without a search interface, a non-displayed index is unsearchable.

• lack of consensus on standard for indexes : 105

These views turned out to be irreconcilable. A standard requires a certain level of consensus. There was no consensus, so NISO published the recommendations of its Committee YY as a technical report (Anderson 1997a).

• impossibility of standards for indexes : 106

These stories regarding alphanumeric arrangement and IR indexes serve to illustrate the sometimes contentious atmosphere in which standards of professional practice are developed, especially in the absence of solid, widely accepted research. Standards are based, fundamentally, on expert opinion, and such opinions can be as strongly held and as staunchly defended as the most fundamental religious or cultural beliefs. The key areas of disagreement on the standard for indexes were definitional. Are finding tools created by computer algorithm truly indexes? Do machine searching systems rely on indexes? Are computer search interfaces an essential component of such indexes? Conflicting views and definitions reflect conflicting models of reality, and they may also be perceived to impact or even to threaten future professional roles.

• **chaos and creativity versus stability in IR database design : 107**

The world of indexing and more broadly the world of IR database design and implementation have left behind a period of relative stability (from roughly 1870 to 1970) in which there was a wide consensus on practice. With the advent of computer and information technologies, we have entered a period of chaos and creativity. During the period of stability, almost every library, every indexing and abstracting service, every back-of-the-book index (in short, every IR database!) was pretty much the same with respect to how indexing was done and how indexes were presented to users (with the exception of variations in alphanumeric arrangement!). Now, online public access catalogs in libraries exhibit extreme variety — almost every one is different. The variety of indexing available, especially automatic indexing, for databases in various electronic media, including the world-wide web, digital libraries, and similar resources, increases on a daily basis.

• **impossibility of standards in periods of instability : 108**

In this period of extreme chaos and, one hopes, creativity to deal with and respond to new needs and new opportunities, it may just be impossible to reach the kind of consensus that an official standard requires.

• **responsibility of information professionals in absence of standards : 109**

If that is the case, individual information professionals will have to make their own judgments as to the most appropriate approach to any particular clientele, situation or problem. This book is meant to help them do just that.

1.5. Types of IR Databases.

• **types of indexes : 110**

The NISO technical report (Anderson 1997a) identifies more than 30 types of indexes used for information retrieval. Because indexes are so central to IR databases, influencing as they do the methods for the representation of messages, texts and documents on the one hand and the methods for searching and retrieval on the other, these types of indexes correspond to types of IR databases. They are listed here, with examples. The intent of the NISO technical report, and of this book, is to address design principles that apply to every kind of index and IR database that is intended to describe messages, texts and documents and to provide access to them for subsequent retrieval.

• **attributes of IR databases, of indexes : 111**

Like any complex entity, IR databases and their indexes can be categorized by many different attributes. The major ones are:

- the kinds of objects represented in index terms, headings, and entries;
- the kinds of index terms used;
- the kinds of indexable matter used for indexing;

- the methods for presenting the index to the user and the concomitant method for searching made available to the user;
- the arrangement of entries;
- the methods for analysis of message content;
- the methods for term selection for indexing;
- the methods for term combination in index headings;
- the methods for term combination in searching;
- the kinds of documents being indexed;
- the medium of the IR database;
- the proximity of the documents being indexed to the IR database itself;
- the size of documentary units;
- the periodicity of the IR database;

and finally,
- the authorship of the database.

• 112

WARNING! The types of IR databases and indexes listed below will mention many complexities that haven't been explained yet. After all, most of the book is yet to come. So don't worry. The purpose of this list is to emphasize the wide scope of IR database and index possibilities. It can also be used for reference, later on, simply to review some of the choices available in IR database and index design. So the first time through, just scan it, and don't worry about the details.

• 113

Here is this complex list laid out, one criterion at a time, with some explanation and with some examples of real, existing IR databases.

1.5.1. Kinds of Objects Represented in Index Terms, Headings, and Entries.

• indexes to authors, topics, features : 114

The major categories of objects represented in the terms, headings, and entries of indexes are the persons and organizations responsible for the creation of messages, texts, and documents, and the topics and features of these messages, texts, and documents.

• indexes to authors, illustrators, editors, translators, publishers : 115

a. indexes to persons and organizations responsible for messages, texts, and documents:

    i. author indexes.

    ii. illustrator indexes.

    iii. editor indexes.

    iv. translator indexes.

    v. publisher indexes.

• indexes to composers, choreographers, lexicographers, painters, sculptors : 116

Depending on the nature of messages, authors can be writers, composers (of music), choreographers (of dance), lexicographers (of dictionaries), painters, sculptors, etc.

Chapter 1. Introduction and Background Issues (Section 1.5.2)

• indexes to subjects, places, institutions, documents, laws, quotations, Bible verses : 117

b. indexes to topics addressed in messages and texts.

    i. general subject indexes.

    ii. specialized indexes to types of subjects, such as places, persons, institutions, operations, and documents (e.g., laws, quotations, Bible verses), etc.

• indexes to features : 118

c. indexes to features of messages, texts, and documents.

• indexes to titles : 119

    i. title indexes.

• indexes to genres, science fiction, novels, fiction, short stories, poems : 120

    ii. genre indexes, e.g., an index to science fiction novels or short stories or poems.

• indexes to document numbers, international standard numbers : 121

    iii. document number indexes, e.g., an index to ISBNs (international standard book numbers).

Note: The author of a message and its text is perhaps its most important feature, so category 1.5.1.a could have been subsumed under this more general category — but persons and institutions responsible for documents get their own category because they are so important.

1.5.2. Kinds of Terms Used.

• 122

Index terms usually consist of words, but they can also consist of numbers of various types and also other types of specialized symbols.

• role of words in index terms : 123

a. word indexes.

Word indexes can be further categorized by the types of words, e.g.,

• role of proper nouns, common words in index terms : 124

    i. proper nouns — names of persons, corporate bodies, places.

    ii. common words

• role of numbers in index terms : 125

b. numerical indexes.

• role of symbols in index terms : 126

c. indexes using specialized symbols

• role of mathematical symbols in index terms : 127

    i. mathematical symbols.

• role of chemical symbols in index terms : 128

    ii. chemical symbols.

• role of musical symbols in index terms : 129

    iii. symbols representing music.

1.5.3. Kinds of Indexable Matter Used.

a. indexes based on the full text of documentary units.

● full text as basis for indexing : 130

b. indexes based on summaries of documentary units, e.g.,

● titles as basis for indexing, title indexes : 131

    i. indexes based on titles only.

● abstracts as basis for indexing : 132

    ii. indexes based on titles and abstracts.

c. indexes based on portions of documentary units, e.g.,

● lead paragraphs as basis for indexing : 133

    i. lead paragraph only.

● tables of contents as basis for indexing : 134

    ii. tables of contents only.

● introductory matter as basis for indexing : 135

    iii. introductory matter.

● reference citations as basis for indexing, citation indexes : 136

    iv. reference citations (for citation indexes).

● first lines as basis for indexing : 137

    v. first lines (as in poems).

1.5.4. Presentation and Methods for Searching.

● 138

There are two fundamentally different ways that IR database indexes can be searched: (1) visual scanning and examination of index headings, and (2) mechanical or electronic symbol comparison and matching. (It is also possible to create Braille indexes that are scanned by touch and audible indexes that are listened to, but the first two approaches are the major ones.) The first method is performed by humans. The second method is now performed by computer algorithms. (Prior to the computer, various mechanical means were devised for comparison and matching.) For the first method, the index must be displayed for human visual inspection. For the second method, the user does not necessarily see the index. Some of the best IR designs will combine these two approaches, so that users can take advantage of sophisticated electronic machine matching algorithms but can also see displays of index headings when they wish to browse or make some preliminary judgments about documents or the direction of a search. (Here the focus is on methods of searching. An IR database that provides only for electronic machine matching, with no display of indexes, will still display the results of a search for human examination and consideration!) So we have IR databases that provide:

● displayed indexes : 139

a. displayed indexes for visual searching.

● non-displayed indexes : 140

b. non-displayed indexes for searching by means of computer matching algorithms.

1.5.5. Arrangement of Entries.

• presentation of IR databases; internal computer representation not addressed : 141

Non-displayed indexes may have internal arrangements to facilitate computer comparison and matching, but this book does not address these internal computer issues. The methods and techniques for internal electronic representation and manipulation are constantly changing, and their mastery requires expertise and experience separate from that required for high quality design of IR databases from the point of view of their presentation to and use by human users. The focus of this book is on the presentation of IR databases and their indexes to users. Many different computer methods can be used for the same type of presentation.

• arrangement of displayed indexes : 142

So here, we focus on the arrangement of displayed indexes — those indexes designed for human visual scanning and inspection.

• 143

Such indexes must have an order that facilitates the location of particular entries. Here are the choices:

• alphanumeric arrangement of displayed indexes : 144

a. alphabetic or alphanumeric indexes. At first glance, this is a simple category, and a very popular one for indexes, but as discussed above in section 1.4 on standards, there is no agreement on what constitutes proper alphabetic or alphanumeric order. Consequently, there are many different approaches and versions. These shall be taken up in detail later in section 17.1 on alphanumeric displays.

• relational arrangement of displayed indexes : 145

b. logical, relational or classified indexes. Here, headings are arranged according to various types of relationships among the concepts represented. Criteria for such arrangements can be increasing or decreasing importance, chronology, class inclusion (creating hierarchies from broad topics to narrow ones), or a whole and its parts. These arrangements are often called "classified," but this term tells you nothing about the basis of the arrangement, especially because the classes represented by index headings can also be arranged alphabetically. Relational arrangements will be discussed in some detail later on in section 17.3.

• alphabetical-relational arrangement of displayed indexes : 146

c. combined alphabetical-relational indexes. Some arrangements combine aspects of alphabetical and relational criteria. They are sometimes called "alphabetico-classed." One approach is to arrange broad classes in alphabetical order, with subordinate classes arranged under broad classes on the basis of various relational criteria. The opposite approach is also used. Broad classes are arranged on the basis of relational criteria, but narrower, subordinate classes may be arranged in alphabetical order. The *Library of Congress classification* uses this latter approach quite frequently.

1.5.6. Methods for Analysis.

• 147

As with the arrangement of entries, there are two fundamentally different approaches to the analysis of messages for indexing, with a third approach combining elements of the two basic approaches. Thus we have:

• human intellectual analysis of texts for indexing, human indexing : 148

a. indexes based on human intellectual analysis of messages and texts.

• computer algorithmic analysis of texts for indexing, automatic indexing : 149

b. indexes based on various computer algorithms for the analysis of machine-readable texts. This is often called "automatic indexing."

• combination of automatic indexing and human indexing : 150

c. indexes based on combinations of computer and human analysis.

1.5.7. Methods for Term Selection.

• 151

Index terms can be extracted from texts (if the texts consist of words) or they can be assigned to texts. Extractive indexes are most often associated with automatic computer-based indexing, but human indexers can also limit their selection of terms to those appearing in language texts. Assignment indexing is done most often by human indexers, but computer algorithms also have been developed to assign terms not found in texts. Thus we have:

• extraction of index terms : 152

a. indexes based on extracted terms.

• assignment of index terms : 153

b. indexes based on assigned terms.

• combination of extraction and assignment of index terms : 154

c. indexes based on both the extraction and the assignment of terms.

1.5.8. Methods for Term Combination.

• necessity for combination of index terms : 155

Indexes must provide the capability to search for multiple topics or features at the same time. If indexes provided access to only one topic or feature at a time, they would be pretty worthless. Can you imagine searching a large database for everything related to "United States," with no capability of combining that term with anything else that you want?

• methods for combination of index terms : 156

There are two basic types of methods for the combination of terms, and these are correlated with whether the index is displayed or non-displayed. Thus we have:

• precoordinate combination of index terms : 157

a. precoordinate term combination for indexes that are displayed — terms are combined (or coordinated) before the index is presented to the user for searching.

• postcoordinate combination of index terms : 158

b. postcoordinate term combination for indexes that are non-displayed — terms are combined (or coordinated) after access to the index is presented (via a search interface) to the user, at the time of the search.

• precoordinate and postcoordinate combination of index terms; information science as example of bound term : 159

c. indexes based on both precoordinate and postcoordinate terms. Precoordinate terms are often used in non-displayed indexes to represent complex concepts and to prevent the inaccurate or inappropriate combination of discrete terms. (For examples, see the discussions of pre- and postcoordinate syntax in section 1.3 on terminology.)

1.5.9. Kinds of Documents Being Indexed.

• 160

Here, IR databases are characterized not on the basis of their own features, but on the basis of the types of documents that are included or represented and indexed for the database. These are as various as all the existing types of documents, and new types are being developed or invented all the time. Only some representative examples are listed here:

• IR databases for periodicals : 161

a. periodicals: articles in periodicals or whole periodicals (complete sets); also specialized forms of periodicals or serials, such as newspapers, newsletters, etc.

• IR databases for books, monographs : 162

b. books and monographs, including "back-of-the-book" indexes for single books.

• IR databases for poetry : 163

c. poetry.

• IR databases for fiction : 164

d. fiction; also specialized types of fiction, such as science fiction, romance, historical novels, mysteries, fantasy, short stories.

• IR databases for film media, motion pictures, slides, photographic media : 165

e. film: motion pictures and other types of film or photographic media (such as slides, filmstrips, photographs).

• IR databases for videotapes : 166

f. video; video recordings.

• IR databases for pictures : 167

g. pictures: reproductions, paintings, drawings, photographs, etc.

• IR databases for maps, geographical information systems : 168

h. maps of all types, two-dimensional, three-dimensional; flat maps and charts; globes; geographical information systems.

• IR databases for music, sound recordings : 169

i. music and sound documents, including all sorts of sound recordings — spoken, music, and other types of sounds, such as bird songs, animal sounds, weather sounds, etc. — on various media. Also musical scores.

• IR databases for machine-readable texts : 170

j. machine-readable texts.

• IR databases for computer software : 171

k. computer software.

Chapter 1. Introduction and Background Issues (Section 1.5.10)

l. internet; including world-wide web resources.

• IR databases for internet resources : 172

1.5.10. Media of IR Databases.

• 173

The media of IR databases are as varied as the media of documents in general — after all, IR databases are documents too. The major media used for IR databases are:

• paper as medium for IR databases : 174

a. paper. Before the development of paper, IR databases were recorded on its precursors, such as stone and clay tablets, parchment and other animal skins, papyrus, tree bark and other vegetable matter. Paper media includes card-stock, which was the most popular medium for library catalogs for about a century, until electronic media became viable and popular.

• microforms as media for IR databases : 175

b. microforms. IR databases have appeared in various styles of microfilm and microfiche.

• electronic media for IR databases : 176

c. electronic media. This broad category includes an ever increasing variety of formats, such as compact discs (CDs, CD-ROMs), larger optical disks, magnetic disks and tape, as well as online databases maintained in accessible computer media and of course websites.

• sound media for IR databases : 177

d. sound media. Spoken indexes sometimes accompany sound collections and archives. These are similar to those ever more pervasive voice mail menus that confront you when you call many offices and agencies. Sound indexes can be especially useful for persons with visual impairments.

• braille media for IR databases : 178

e. braille media. Braille is usually recorded on paper, but because it is a specialized combination of symbols for persons with visual impairments, it gets a separate listing.

1.5.11. Proximity of Documents Being Indexed.

• full-text databases : 179

a. full-text databases. Full-text databases contains the full text of the documents to which it points. This includes books published with traditional back-of-the-book indexes, as well as the increasingly popular full-text electronic IR databases, ranging from newspaper and periodical databases to encyclopedias and other reference works of various sorts and digital libraries. If you are surprised to find the printed book with index in this category, just remember that here too, the index is combined with the full text of the document being indexed, so it qualifies!

• reference databases : 180

b. reference databases. Reference databases provide access to documents that are not included in the database. Instead, the IR database provides some sort of locator, such as a bibliographic citation and possibly a call number or notation that can be used to obtain the full document from a library collection, publisher, the internet, or other distributor or document delivery service.

• library catalogs : 181

A library catalog may be seen as a reference database that refers to items in the library's collection. On the other hand, the library as a whole, including its catalog, may be considered a full-text database, because the documents to which the catalog refers are within its collections (unless they are checked out!).

1.5.12. Types and Sizes of Documentary Units.

• 182

Here we categorize IR databases and their indexes with respect to the kind of documentary units (parts of documents, complete documents, collections of documents) that are analyzed for retrieval. These units depend, of course, on the type of document. We give examples mostly from language documents, but analogous examples could be given from visual image documents (photographs, paintings), moving image documents (films, videos), sound documents, etc. In the past these units were often called "bibliographic units," because they were described in bibliographies.

• definition of bibliography : 183

In this book, we have subsumed the term "bibliography" in the broader, newer term "IR database," but "bibliography" and "bibliographies" are fine old words that mean writing (graphy) about books (biblio), thus they have come to mean lists and descriptions of books. There is no reason to limit their meaning to "books," because the "biblio" part of the word comes from the Greek for papyrus leaves! So by extension, bibliographies can deal with messages and texts in any format and medium, just as IR databases can and do.

• IR databases for small documentary units : 184

a. IR databases for small documentary units (parts of complete documents), such as lines, sentences, paragraphs, and pages, or frames in a videotape, segments of pictures or maps). These indexes lead the user inside the full document. Sometimes such small units are referred to as "information units" because they are more likely to lead directly to a precise message that may answer the searcher's query.

• IR databases for complete documents : 185

b. IR databases for complete documents, e.g., periodical articles, chapters in collections, papers in conference proceedings, stories and poems in anthologies, and monographs.

• IR databases for collections of documents : 186

c. IR databases for collections of documents, e.g., anthologies; complete sets of periodicals, serials and series; archives; libraries, etc.

1.5.13. Periodicity of IR Databases.

• monographic databases : 187

a. monographic databases. Like any document, an IR database can be a monograph — a one-time publication, sometimes called a "closed-end" database or index.

• serial databases : 188

b. serial databases. Or an IR database can be designed for updating on a regular or irregular basis. These databases are sometimes called "continuing" or "open-end" databases or indexes.

Chapter 1. Introduction and Background Issues (Section 1.5.14)

1.5.14. Authorship of IR Databases.

• 189

Finally, IR databases can be categorized by authorship, whether an IR database has been created by one or a small number of individuals who can be named and credited with its creation or by a large organization, with the participation of many persons, so that the personal influence of individual authors is not apparent. IR databases relying on automatic indexing are created, in part, by machine algorithms, but human beings "authored" the algorithms that are used.

1.5.15. Continuing Examples.

• examples of IR database design : 190

Throughout this book, design principles related to the topic of each chapter will be applied to three prominent types of IR databases — (1) a book or monograph with its own index (often called a back-of-the-book index); (2) an indexing and abstracting service for a scholarly discipline; and (3) a full-text encyclopedia, which can be seen as a digital library of messages and texts.

• monographs as examples of IR databases : 191

For the example of a single book as an IR database, indexes will be designed for both electronic and print media. The index at the end of this book illustrates the implementation of the design for the print-medium index.

• indexing and abstracting services as examples of IR databases : 192

The example of a scholarly indexing and abstracting service will be an indexing and abstracting service for the literature of library and information science. Every reader of this book likely has some familiarity, or at least interest, in these disciplines.

• full-text encyclopedias and digital libraries as examples of IR databases : 193

The example of a full-text encyclopedia (or digital library) will be an IR database consisting of digital texts on library and information science.

1.6. IR Databases Versus Other Types of Databases: A Recap.

• definition of database : 194

Throughout this book, you will find frequent use of the term "database." As discussed in section 1.3 on terminology, the definition of "database" as used in this book is simple: an organized collection of data designed for retrieval. Although the term "database" (data base, data-base), and its companion term (in earlier days) "databank," grew out of a computer environment, it need not imply any particular medium for the database. In this book, "database" will refer both to print databases and to electronic digital computer-based databases.

• varieties of IR databases : 195

"Database" is a convenient word for the enormous variety of IR tools that librarians, indexers, abstracters, and information specialists of various sorts have developed over the years — indexes, indexing and abstracting services, bibliographies, catalogs, gazetteers, dictionaries, concordances, directories, encyclopedias, handbooks. All of these are organized collections of data designed for retrieval, so all can be legitimately called IR databases.

1.6.1. Two Types of Databases.

• databases for concrete entities and events versus IR databases : 196

As discussed in section 1.3 on terminology, databases can be categorized in many ways — by data models, by purpose, by subject area, and by the kinds of phenomena represented. It is this last categorization that is central to this book. With respect to the primary phenomena represented, databases can be divided into two types: (1) concrete entity and event databases, and (2) IR databases. By far the most common in everyday life are type-1 databases — concrete entity and event databases. These databases are designed to provide information about concrete entities (things, objects) and concrete events (transactions, operations, processes). Bank databases and airline databases were cited as examples in section 1.3. Another example of concrete entity and event databases are university databases, containing as they do information about every student, course, course offering, instructor, classroom, grade, tuition payment — all concrete entities and real events. In contrast, IR databases focus on messages, and these messages frequently relate to phenomena that are abstract, vague, emotional, and imaginary — anything but concrete!

• 197

Concrete entity and event databases are designed around the attributes and relationships among concrete entities and events. For example, students take courses, get grades, and pay tuition. Instructors teach courses and get paid a certain amount every so often. In contrast, most IR databases do not attempt to define possible relations in advance. There are just too many potential relationships among concepts represented in messages and texts, and some of these relationships are only discovered later through subsequent use and analysis.

• exclusion of databases for concrete entities and events from scope of this book:
management information systems, database management systems : 198

This book does not concern itself with the very important category of concrete entity and event databases. If these are the databases you want to read about, get a good book on database management systems (DBMS). Most books using that term are talking about concrete entity and event databases. Management information systems (MIS) also consist largely of concrete entity and event databases, although MIS people are paying more and more attention to IR databases.

1.6.2. IR Databases.

• 199

To close this introductory section of the book, let's return to the basic topic and purpose of the book: the design of IR databases.

• messages as key entities for IR databases : 200

IR databases are databases that focus on messages rather than directly on concrete entities and events. Messages, of course, can and frequently do deal with concrete entities and events, but just as often, they deal with abstract entities, theories, hypotheses, feelings, opinions, ideologies, dreams, emotions, properties, attributes, operations, processes, and even imaginary characters, places, events and times, which are completely foreign to most concrete entity and event databases.

• IR databases as hybrid databases : 201

In fact, IR databases must be hybrid databases. They must deal with certain types of concrete entities and events as well as messages. The primary concrete entities in IR databases are the documents in which texts and messages are embedded and the persons and institutions that create

Chapter 1. Introduction and Background Issues (Section 1.6.2)

messages, texts and documents. IR databases also generally record data about the production and publication of these documents, which are of course concrete events.

• databases for concrete entities and events versus IR databases : 202

But a database that does no more than record the existence of documents is no different, in theory, than a database of car parts, or the products for sale by JCPenney or L.L.Bean. What makes an IR database special is its focus on the content, meaning, purpose and features of messages.

• scope of this book : 203

This book is about the design of IR databases for all types of messages, texts and documents. A special focus will be the enormous variety of indexes that can be used in IR databases, because indexes are essential components of such databases. It is the index that organizes the data for retrieval. Without an index, an IR database loses the element that gives it organization. It is no longer a "collection of data organized for retrieval," and therefore is no longer a database in the usual sense of the term.

• indexes versus IR databases; components of IR databases : 204

The line between an index and an IR database is a very fine and fuzzy one. They are closely related and intertwined. Actually, as we explore the design of IR databases, we will find that an IR database generally consists of three major components, of which the index is one. The other two components are (2) the collection of documents (in full-text databases) and surrogates (representations or descriptions of documents), and (3) the collection of terms that is used for the description and retrieval of documents. In some IR databases, this third component, the collection of index terms, is expanded to include synonymous, equivalent and variant terms and relations among them. Such an elaborated vocabulary component is called a thesaurus.

• software and hardware for IR databases : 205

The focus of this book is on the design of IR databases for the effective presentation of message data to users. The emphasis is on the description and preparation of data for presentation. The book does not concern itself with particular software or hardware for the implementation of electronic databases, nor, analogously, with the technical publishing specifications for print databases.

• design specifications for IR databases : 206

The end product from the study of this book should be the ability to create design specifications for an effective IR database. These design specs can then be used, with experts in database management systems (DBMS), to select an appropriate database model; with experts in interface design to implement presentation specifications in an effective interface; and with experts in software and hardware to select appropriate algorithms and programs and computers. The situation is similar for print IR databases. A book designer will translate specifications for indexing syntax, arrangement, and display into a book design that incorporates the features of the presentation specifications.

• role of IR database designers, information architects : 207

Thus, the IR database designer is not expected to be an expert in every aspect of IR database implementation. But the IR database designer must have a good overview of possibilities. And more than anything else, the IR database designer is the advocate for the user, to insure that the needs and preferences of users will be faithfully represented in the final IR database product. A new term for this role is "information architect." Just as the architect of a building must rely on a whole range of experts to actually construct and maintain the building, so the information architect must rely on a similar range of experts. But the quality of the finished product and users' experience with that product is due, in largest measure, to the architect!

Part II. Design Decisions

• purpose of this book : 1

The primary purpose of this book is to lay out and describe components and attributes of information retrieval (IR) databases and the range and variety of options for each of them, together with the implications of choices. The objective is to encourage designers to weigh options for each component or attribute in relation to the needs and preferences of users, so that the best possible design will result.

• impetus for design : 2

The inspiration or impetus for a new IR database is generally the perception of a group of potential users who have information needs or desires that are not well met, or a collection of documents containing valuable messages that should be made more accessible.

• precursors to design : 3

Before high quality design can begin, the designer must know a great deal about the potential users of the IR database — what kinds of questions they will want to bring to the database and their level of experience with and preferences for IR database searching. Designs for children, for example, will generally be quite different than designs for subject specialists. Also the operational work/action and cultural domains of users' information seeking and use are very important. The domain of an adult seeking novels or movies for entertainment, or messages for spiritual enlightenment, will be very different compared to the literary or film critic's domain or the professional theologian's domain, which in turn will differ from the domain of the sociologist studying religious behavior. Cultural domains may also impact information needs and desires. The situational domains of high-income urban African American lesbians are likely to differ from those of low-income rural subsistence farmers in a barely developing country.

• collections of documents as impetus for design : 4

If the impetus for design is a collection of documents, the designer will want to know quite a bit about the nature of these documents and their content (their messages!), and also about the kinds of users that would find them useful, and the operational or cultural domains of these users.

• user needs assessment : 5

Thus, the assessment of users and their needs, desires, information-searching preferences and the work/action/cultural domains of their information seeking behavior is the first step for any IR design project. This important preliminary step falls outside the scope of this book. For help in designing and implementing a users' needs assessment, a good place to start is with *Information tasks: toward a user-centered approach to information systems*, by Bryce L. Allen (1996). The importance of domain analysis is stressed by Birger Hjørland in his *Information seeking and subject representation: an activity-theoretical approach to information science* (1997).

• attributes and components of IR databases : 6

Twenty key attributes or components have been identified as most important in the design of IR databases. Each will be treated in a separate chapter in an order that seems to make sense with respect to the impact of choices on other options.

• list of attributes and components of IR databases : 7

Here is the list of these twenty attributes and components:

1. ***Subject scope and domain:*** What topics correspond to the kinds of questions that users will want to ask of the IR database? What is the operational or cultural domain to be targeted by the IR database? What is the activity or cultural domain of the intended users?

Part II. Design Decisions

2. ***Documentary scope:*** What kinds of messages, texts, and documents will provide answers or responses to user needs and desires? What features of messages, texts, and documents should be searchable?

3. ***Documentary domain:*** Where and how can these documents be found?

4. ***Display media:*** What media can most effectively display the IR database to users? Which media can provide the most effective searching experiences?

5. ***Documentary units:*** What are the most effective message units to convey answers and responses to users?

6. ***Indexable matter:*** What portions of documentary units should be analyzed for indexing and retrieval?

7. ***Analysis methods:*** How can human intellectual methods and automatic computer-based methods be used most effectively for analyzing the content, meaning, and applications of messages, texts, and documents?

8. ***Exhaustivity of indexing:*** How detailed should indexing be? Will users be more interested in maximum retrieval of useful messages, or in minimum retrieval of uninteresting or useless messages?

9. ***Specificity of indexing terms:*** How closely should indexing vocabulary match the topics and features of messages and the questions of users? How large should the indexing vocabulary be?

10. ***Displayed and non-displayed indexes:*** What kinds of searching opportunities should be provided? Will users want to browse or inspect displayed arrays of topical and feature headings, or will electronic computer matching techniques be sufficient?

11. ***Syntax for index headings and search statements:*** How should terms be combined in headings for effective browsing and visual inspection? How should terms be combined and manipulated for effective searches by means of electronic computer matching techniques?

12. ***Vocabulary management:*** Should users be expected to find the best terminology for their questions on their own? Or should they be assisted with suggestions for synonymous or equivalent terms, clarification for terms with multiple meanings, and suggestions for related terms?

13. ***Surrogation (representation) of documentary units:*** How can messages, texts, and documents be best described for users?

14. ***Locators for documentary units:*** How will message/text/document descriptions be linked to the actual, full documents that they represent?

15. ***Surrogate displays:*** How should message/text/document descriptions be displayed in various situations?

16. ***Arrangement of displayed indexes:*** If the IR database provides for browsing or visual inspection of topical or feature heading arrays, how should these arrays be arranged?

17. ***Size of displayed indexes:*** Are there constraints that will limit the size of a displayed index? How can such an index be designed to fit the available space?

18. ***Search interface:*** How can self-evident and easy-to-use displays be designed to facilitate effective searching of the IR database?

19. ***Record structure:*** How should message/text/documentary units be represented within the IR database? What data should be recorded, and how should it be organized within the database record?

20. ***Full-text display:*** How can full-text documents be effectively displayed for examination?

Part II. Design Decisions

• interaction among design options : 8

As Bates (2002) has reminded us, "each design element or layer in an information system interacts with every other design layer in a synergistic, neutral, or conflicting manner. This cascade of interactions culminates in the interface, where all the prior interactions have either worked to produce effective information retrieval or to produce a hodgepodge of system elements working at cross purposes" (p. 381).

• sequence of design decisions : 9

The interaction and influence of design decisions has been the determining factor in suggesting an effective sequence for considering design options in this book. First comes decisions regarding the subject scope and domain, based directly on user needs assessments. Documentary scope and domain should be determined in manner that meets the goals of the subject scope and domain. IR database display media and policies for indexing (size of documentary units analyzed, appropriate indexable matter, analysis and indexing methods, exhaustivity of indexing, and specificity of terminology) should all reflect the nature of the subject and documentary scope and domain (and the needs, desires, and habits) of users. Similarly, searching and browsing options and the display of documentary surrogates (electronic searching versus displayed index examination, syntax for combining terms in displayed indexes or search statements, vocabulary assistance and management, the design and display of surrogates, and the use of locators) need to be in synch with earlier decisions. The design of browsable indexes, both alphabetical and classified, and the integration of vocabulary assistance are crucial elements of the search interface. Finally, the design of the documentary unit record format must support all previous design choices, and for full-text IR databases, the display and manipulation of retrieved full-text documents should further assist users in finding exactly what they want.

• 10

It is hoped that the ordering of design decisions, and the discussion of each option and its impact on IR effectiveness, will help achieve the goal voiced by Bates (2002): "For effective information retrieval to occur, all layers of a system must be designed to work together ..." (p. 398).

Chapter 2. Subject Scope and Domain

Contents of Chapter 2
2.1. Specialized Categories.
2.2. Presenting the Subject Scope and Domain to Users.
2.3. Ranganathan's Facets.
2.4. Why Bother?
2.5. Our Examples.
2.5.1. A Book Index.
2.5.2. An Indexing and Abstracting Service.
2.5.3. A Full-Text Encyclopedia/Digital Library.

• functions of subject scope and domain analyses : 1

IR databases exist to lead users to messages that relate to questions or problems they have or that will provide desired information, understanding, inspiration, stimulation or entertainment. The subject scope of an IR database describes the kinds of questions or desires that an IR database can respond to. The subject domain sets the subject scope into the context of the work or life situation in which users will be operating and seeking messages. Typical subject domains include the various scholarly disciplines, the professions, industries, business, occupations and trades, but also every other sphere of human life and activity, such as sports and recreation, hobbies, religion, entertainment, travel, child rearing, and home management. Subject domains also include cultural domains, often characterized by such human attributes as economic level, living environment, religious and ethnic heritage, gender, sexual orientation, and age. Subject domain analysis will differentiate between interests and needs in the same subject area for users operating in different domains, such as persons seeking novels for entertainment versus literary scholars; week-end soccer players versus sociologists of sport or students of sports medicine; urban high-income African American gay men seeking health information versus low-income, rural, white migrant worker pregnant women.

• necessary detail in subject scope and domain analyses : 2

It is not sufficient to describe the subject scope and domain of an IR database with only one or a few broad terms for the names of disciplines (like medicine or biology or the social sciences) or broad areas of human endeavor (like art or religion or sports or business). An IR database for medicine, for example, may or may not serve users who are looking for information about particular individuals (such as physicians or researchers or patients) or particular diseases (such as AIDS or the various types of cancer) or parts of the body (such as the wrist or the eye) or institutions (such as a hospital or medical school). An IR database on religion may or may not respond to questions about particular priests, ministers, or rabbis or the doctrines or particular rituals associated with particular religious traditions or religious attitudes toward controversial issues (like abortion or homosexuality). An IR database about sports may or may not provide information about particular players or particular games or equipment or stories, poems, and novels about sports. A business IR database may or may not respond to requests for information on particular companies or business leaders or government regulations or white-collar crime or forecasts of economic conditions.

Chapter 2. Subject Scope and Domain

• **subject scope versus subject domain : 3**

In addition to describing the subject scope, care must be taken to identify the subject domain of IR database users, because two databases with the same or similar subject scope may need very different kinds of messages, texts, and documents depending on the intended domain, and the indexing and description of messages may need to be entirely different as well. To continue with the health and medicine example, a medical database intended for persons working in the domain of medical research and clinical practice will be very different from an IR database covering the very same subject areas but designed for persons in the domain of patients. The context for these two groups is completely different and so, for each group, the useful messages and how they are described will be different in many instances.

• **cultural domains : 4**

In addition to role domains, such as patient versus researcher or medical practitioner, there are cultural domains that may influence the kinds of messages and the kinds of message descriptions that may be appropriate within a given subject scope. Cultural domains are defined or characterized by all the attributes of human culture such as ethnic and religious heritage, gender, age, family situation, sexual orientation, economic and educational levels, living environment (such as urban, suburban, rural), and environmental attributes such as general level of economic development, climate, etc. Thus an Eskimo mother in a remote village in Alaska may "reside" in a very different domain, vis à vis information needs and information seeking, than say an upper-economic-class male to female transgendered Muslim in New York City. IR databases need to be tailored not only to respond to certain subject interests, needs or desires, but also to the domains in which potential users are situated, whether these domains be disciplinary, professional, occupational, hobby-related, or culturally defined.

• **functions of subject scope domain analysis : 5**

Whether an IR database will serve a particular type of need or desire will depend, at least in part, on whether that need or desire was made part of the subject scope, and whether the IR database was tailored to the appropriate subject domain. The description of subject scope specifies the kinds of topics that the IR database will address and therefore should be able to respond to. The description of the subject domain specifies the expected situations or context in which messages on the specified topics will be sought and used.

• **value of subject scope and domain analysis : 6**

A good, well-described subject scope and an appropriate subject domain give value to the user by clearly defining what the IR database is for — what kinds of topics it is designed to address and what kinds of persons it is designed to serve, in terms of their work or life situations. Subject scope and domain statements give value to the database producer by providing criteria for the selection of documents to include in the database — documents with messages that address the topics identified in the subject scope in a manner appropriate for the subject domain. And a well-defined subject scope and subject domain give value to human indexers by guiding their analysis and description of the content, meaning, purpose, and possible applications of messages. Subject scope and domain can even be used to guide sophisticated algorithms for automatic indexing, by suggesting the kinds of terms or attributes that should be more heavily weighted in search procedures.

• **necessity for understanding user needs : 7**

Developing an appropriate subject scope and domain depends on the designer knowing quite a bit about potential users and the kinds of questions, problems and desires they will likely bring to the IR database.

Chapter 2. Subject Scope and Domain

• **goals of subject scope description; number of categories in subject scope analysis : 8**

The goal of a subject scope description is to provide an overview or summary of the kinds of questions that can be asked of an IR database. Generally this can be done by specifying anywhere from ten to thirty categories of topics that the IR database addresses. When IR databases are presented to users electronically, an ideal number of key subject scope categories is between ten and fifteen, because this is the number of topics that can be clearly displayed on an opening electronic screen, where an overall view of the IR database should be presented to potential users.

• **goals of subject domain description : 9**

Similarly, the goal of the subject domain description is to clearly state the domains that the IR database intends to serve. Such a description will help users select the appropriate subject-oriented IR database for the domain in which they find themselves.

• **subject domains of IR databases : 10**

The great majority of IR databases are designed for scholarly/ professional/disciplinary and business domains, or for the general lay public (who are not members of the particular discipline or profession or business connected with the subject scope of the IR databases). Some IR databases have been designed for the domain of students, and some for younger students, or the general domain of children. With the enormous proliferation of specialized IR databases, especially via such channels as the world-wide web, more and more IR databases will be designed for specialized cultural domains.

• **11**

The remainder of this chapter will focus on the design of subject scopes for either disciplinary/professional/business domains or the general lay public, but IR database designers are encouraged to consider much more specialized domains as well, such as culturally defined domains, especially when it comes to appropriate indexing procedures and vocabularies for such domains.

• **role of generic categories in subject scope analysis : 12**

The analysis and definition of a subject scope can often begin with generic categories of topics that pertain to all subject fields. These are categories like:

- entities or things (persons, institutions, artifacts, natural objects and living beings, etc.
- attributes or constituent materials
- actions (operations, processes, and events)
- places
- times

• **contribution of Ranganathan (Shiyali Ramamrita) to facet analysis : 13**

These fundamental categories are like the journalist's "who, what, where, when, why," — fundamental questions or characteristics by which any message can be analyzed and described. These categories are generally called "facets," referring to the faces, dimensions, or aspects of topics. The term comes from the French diminutive for "face," "facette" (Webster's 1966). The analysis of topics with respect to their aspects or facets is called "facet analysis." During the twentieth century, facets such as these have come to be recognized as the fundamental building blocks of most indexing languages and classification systems. The great Indian mathematician, librarian and scholar Shiyali Ramamrita Ranganathan (1892-1972) is universally credited with discovering and explaining the fundamental role of facets in indexing and classification work. A brief summary of Ranganathan's career and impact can be found in *The DDC, the universe of*

Chapter 2. Subject Scope and Domain

knowledge, and the post-modern library, by Francis L. Miksa (1998, p. 65-73). An older work summarizing his influence and its continuation by the Classification Research Group in the United Kingdom is *Faceted classification schemes*, by Brian C. Vickery (1966). In celebration of the centennial of Ranganathan's birth, Mohinder Partap Satija prepared a chronology of the major events and publications connected with his career (Satija 1992). There will be more on Ranganathan below in section 2.3.

• antecedents of facets : 14

The idea of the existence of fundamental types of matter and phenomena long pre-dates Ranganathan — he simply clarified their importance in classification and indexing for information retrieval. Aristotle, for example, suggested basic categories that are very similar to today's fundamental facets: substance, quantity, quality, relations, time, space, position, possession, activities and objects (Iivonen and Kivimäki 1998, p. 91). Post-Ranganathan, others have applied these or similar categories to indexing and classification work. Dahlberg (1978, p. 145; 1981, p. 20), for example, based her "Interconcept" system on entities, including both material objects and immaterial objects or principles; properties (such as quantity, quality, relations); activities (processes, operations, states); and dimensions (time, space, position).

• fundamental facets : 15

Here is a description of some of these fundamental facets in more detail:

• entities in subject scope analysis : 16

• **entities or things, including living beings and inanimate objects, naturally occurring or human-made, concrete or abstract, real or imaginary.**

• concrete entities versus abstract entities in subject scope analysis : 17

• • **concrete entities versus abstract entities.**

Concrete entities are those you can see and touch (at least in theory). Abstract entities are abstractions (constructs abstracted from experience or thought) that can't be seen or touched but whose existence is made known indirectly through various recognized symptoms or indicators. Examples of abstract entities include the American Medical Association, Rutgers University, communism, Islam, and the theory of relativity. Abstract entities, and also imaginary entities such as unicorns, Paul Bunyan, angels and faeries (if they are imaginary), can play the same types of roles in messages as do concrete real entities.

• universities as example of abstract entities : 18

The distinction between concrete and abstract entities can be very fuzzy. Take a university, for example. What exactly is a university? Is it the concrete artifacts like buildings, library collections, together with the persons who make up its student body, faculty, staff, and governing bodies? Or is it something more than its concrete parts, created by their relations and the attitudes and commitments in human minds (and perhaps recorded as messages in documents)?

• institutions versus societies in descriptive cataloging : 19

Old descriptive cataloging rules attempted, in vain, to make distinctions between institutions (which were considered to be more concrete, typically with physical locations) and societies (which were considered to be more abstract, typically without a particular location), but catalogers gave up on this distinction many years ago. Similarly we often categorize institutions and societies together with concrete entities like persons, leaving the category of "abstract entities" for theories, bodies of belief, and similar concepts with lesser physical or concrete manifestations. Indeed, the law recognizes the existence of abstract entities called corporations, which assume many of the responsibilities of real concrete persons. By law, organizations and institutions may

Chapter 2. Subject Scope and Domain

be incorporated (embodied!), and thereby they are formally recognized in law (and in indexing) as entities.

● **abstract entities versus attributes and processes in subject scope analysis : 20**

The crucial question to ask in determining whether an abstract concept represents an entity rather than an attribute (see below!) or a process (see below!) of some other entity, is whether it plays the role of an independent entity, such as having significant attributes of its own, performing operations — or inspiring them, or being the focus or object of operations by other entities. The American Medical Association, for example, publishes books and periodicals and proclaims standards of practice. Christianity and Islam (as systems of beliefs and doctrines, to say nothing of their religious establishments) inspire all kinds of actions, from wars to compassionate care of strangers, and they are the focus of operations such as proclamation and evangelization. Theories, like Einstein's on relativity, serve to explain reality and lead to further hypotheses. While on the one hand opinions and attitudes can be said to be attributes of particular persons or groups, on the other hand theories, ideologies, and religious dogmas can be said to have assumed (taken on) an existence of their own as independent entities. They can be seen as messages that have been codified as standard texts, and as texts, they are entities.

● **messages and texts as entities : 21**

Thus doctrines, dogmas, religious scriptures, ideologies, bodies of belief, theories and similar messages or collections of messages take on the trappings of entities when they have been encoded in texts that are preserved in long-lasting media. In fact, messages can always be considered to be entities. They are the principal objects of our concern in this book, as we struggle to understand them, interpret them, and summarize and describe them to facilitate their discovery and retrieval. It is true that one cannot touch a message, but one can certainly touch its representation in a text when that text is recorded in a tangible physical medium.

● **independent existence of abstract entities : 22**

Abstract entities have, in effect, been institutionalized as independent entities by a culture, much like the formal recognition of corporate bodies by governments. However, if in doubt about whether a phenomenon can be considered an abstract entity, it is usually best to consider it the attribute or a process related to some other entity. Opinions or points of view, for example, can best be related to the persons or groups holding them (in contrast to established bodies of belief). Human institutions like marriage and friendship can't really exist without the persons who engage in them, so they can best be seen as attributes possessed by these persons, or as processes in which these persons are engaged.

● **concepts as abstract entities : 23**

It is possible to consider a concept to be an abstract entity that is recognized and held in the mind. One might, for example, possess concepts for "rain" and "snow" and "running" and "Poland." Some students use the nature of concepts as an excuse to classify just about every phenomenon as an entity. "Friendship is a concept," they say, "and concepts are entities, so friendship is an entity." Even if friendship itself is not an entity (a thing), they argue that the concept of friendship is! But so is the concept of rain and snow and running and Poland. To class all phenomena expressed in messages as concepts, and therefore as abstract entities, would defeat our purpose of classing and organizing concepts according to the types of phenomena they represent. After all, subject scope analysis aims at distinguishing among various types of phenomena, not lumping them all together. We are not so much interested in the "concept" of friendship, but in friendship itself, the attribute of having friends or the process of making or being friends. Making, being and having are never entities in the schema of subject scopes!

Chapter 2. Subject Scope and Domain

• parts of entities in subject scope analysis : 24

• • parts of entities.

When a part of a larger entity or thing is not distinctive enough to stand on its own, it can be categorized as a part of the larger entity. Examples include the parts of plants (flora!) or of human or animal bodies or the parts of a vehicle or other machine. It may be important to identify a carburetor as part of an automobile, rather than a lawn mower, or a liver as part of a human being rather than a rat. The parts of a larger entity can also be considered attributes or properties of that larger entity.

• attributes in subject scope analysis : 25

• attributes.

Often the focus of a topic is not on an entity directly, but on some attribute of the entity. In other cases, a topic relates only to certain types of entities, such as those made out of certain types of materials or possessing certain attributes. Typical attributes of entities consist of their constituent materials and their properties or characteristics.

• constituent materials in subject scope analysis : 26

• • constituent materials.

Constituent materials refer to the materials that something is made out of, like iron or wood or plastic. The ingredients of foods or drugs are other examples. Sometimes these materials or ingredients function as entities in their own right, as when the focus of a topic is on the material itself, as opposed to things made of it, as in a treatise on wood or trisodium phosphate.

• properties in subject scope analysis : 27

• • properties of entities.

Properties of entities are any or all of the characteristics that may be of interest and that pertain or belong to entities. Examples include size, weight, appearance, beauty (or lack thereof), color, emotions, feelings, disease, opinions, relationships, status, and conditions. Sometimes the entities that possess particular properties aren't even mentioned, as in a philosophical treatise on friendship that doesn't concern itself with who the friends are that share, or work at, friendship. In a case like this, the entity is people in general — a phenomenon so general that it may not be worth mentioning!

• actions in subject scope analysis : 28

• actions.

An action is what happens. Whenever a message or a topic focuses on actions, it is usually important to identify the particular kind of action and its relationship to entities, attributes, place and time. Actions may be further categorized or described as operations, processes, or events.

• operations in subject scope analysis : 29

• • operations.

Actions that are performed by one entity, such as a person or group, on or against another entity, may be called operations. In grammar, operations are indicated with transitive verbs — verbs that take direct objects. Examples include cooking, cataloging, translation, management, and murder. Thus one cooks an egg, or a whole meal; one catalogs a book; one manages a company; one translates a poem; one murders an enemy.

Chapter 2. Subject Scope and Domain

• agents versus objects in subject scope analysis : 30

• • agents versus objects.

Sometimes in the subject or topic analysis of particular messages, it is useful to distinguish between objects (or recipients) of operations versus the agents or performers of operations. Thus, in a message about professional librarians versus student interns cataloging maps, the maps are the objects or recipients of the operation of cataloging, while the librarians or the interns are the agents or performers of the operation. These distinctions are called "roles," and some indexing methods will distinguish between these roles. (Chapter 12 on syntax will discuss some of these indexing methods.) Here in broad generic subject scope analysis, however, the focus is on identifying types of phenomena more than roles in complex situations, so for the time being we do not need to worry about who is doing what to whom. Here we concern ourselves only with kinds of actions, kinds of entities, kinds of attributes, kinds of places, and kinds of time. Particular roles may become more important when focusing on more specialized subject scope categories in IR databases of narrower or more specialized scopes. Section 2.1 on specialized subject categories will include some examples of categories based on roles.

• names for actions : 31

Even though we often use verbs to express actions in speech and writing, in describing them for subject scope analysis and later for indexing and classification, we generally use nouns for the names of actions. Often in English, these nouns take the form of gerunds (verbal nouns ending in "ing"), like "cooking" and "cataloging." Words ending in "tion" and "ment" also name actions, like "translation" and "adoption" or "management" and "placement." When there is a "tion" or a "ment" word available, indexers generally prefer it over the gerund. Thus, "translation" is preferred over "translating"; "adoption" is preferred over "adopting"; "management" is preferred over "managing"; and "arrangement" is preferred over "arranging." Words ending in "tion" and "ment" can be problematic, however, because sometimes they refer to the result of the action, rather than the action itself. Thus "translation" can refer to a translated text (an entity!) as well as to the act of translating. "Arrangement" can refer to a particular version (of a piece of music, for example), rather than to the operation of arranging. In contrast, "management" often refers to the people who are doing the managing, not the objects of their management. Later on in the chapters on syntax (chapter 12) and vocabulary management (chapter 13) we will worry about how to deal with these ambiguities.

• 32

English inherited endings such as "tion" and "ment" from the French after the Norman conquest of Britain in 1066. French became the preferred upper-class language, as opposed to English (Anglo-Saxon), with its gerund ending "ing." This preference for French words is unfortunate for clarity in indexing. The English gerund suffix ("ing") consistently refers to actions, whereas the French endings ("ment," "tion") do so inconsistently.

• 33

Some actions have names that are neither gerunds nor words with common endings like "tion" or "ment." Examples include "sex," "birth," "murder," and "war."

• processes in subject scope analysis : 34

• • processes.

Processes are actions that do not take direct objects. Examples include breathing, maturation, evolution, erosion, rusting, flooding and earthquakes. A process is performed or experienced by an entity (a dog breathing, a child maturing, human species evolving, soil eroding; automobiles

Chapter 2. Subject Scope and Domain

rusting; Mississippi River flooding; Japan experiencing earthquakes). In the Mississippi River example, "floods" might be used instead of "flooding," with a slight shift in emphasis from the process or phenomenon of flooding to particular events — particular floods. Major earthquakes are also typically remembered as events. Later on, mainly in chapter 13, we will worry about term standardization.

• processes versus operations in subject scope analysis : 35

Sometimes the same action can be used either as a process or as an operation. If a message is about heavy rains eroding the soil or moisture rusting an automobile, then these processes have been used as operations, with agents that perform or cause the action (rain and moisture) and recipients or objects of the action (soil and automobile). Similarly, "eating" can be seen as a process, without recipient or object in "a dog eating," but as an operation with object in "a dog eating a rabbit."

• events in subject scope analysis : 36

• • **events.**

When an action is a singular event, it can be described as an event. Examples include particular floods or earthquakes, wars, the assassination of President Kennedy, or the 1998 baseball World Series or soccer World Cup games or Le Tour de France.

• places in subject scope analysis : 37

• **places.**

Places, where entities are situated or where actions take place, come in two flavors: particular places, such as Europe, Paris, Antarctica; or types of places, such as deserts, rain forests, planets, outer space. Actually, places are special kinds of entities. When spatial entities like libraries, hospitals, or universities play the role of an environment or locale for actions and other entities, we may consider them places as well.

• time in subject scope analysis : 38

• **time.**

Like place, time is an important dimension or aspect for most entities and actions. Time can be quite specific, like November 22, 1963, or more general, like the 1960s, 20th century, the Jurassic period.

• insurance as example of complex phenomena in subject scope analysis : 39

• **Complex phenomena**

Some phenomena are quite complex, and it is not an easy matter to analyze or deconstruct them in order to identify their fundamental nature or role as entity, attribute, or action. A good example is "insurance." What exactly is "insurance"? In some cases, it is "an insuring or being insured against loss." In this case it is clearly an operation. Company A insures homeowner B against loss by fire. But it can also refer to "a system of protection against loss in which a number of individuals agree to pay certain sums for a guarantee that they will be compensated for any specified loss by fire, accident, death, etc." A "system" is "a set or arrangement of things so related or connected as to form a unity or organic whole" (Webster's new world dictionary 1966, p. 759, 1480). As such, we usually consider systems to be entities, so this meaning of "insurance" could be considered an entity, usually in the form of an insurance company, or an insurance program like Social Security.

Chapter 2. Subject Scope and Domain

• 40

"Insurance" is also "a contract whereby, in return for a fixed payment, the insurer guarantees the insured that a certain sum will be paid for a specified loss" (Webster's 1966, p. 759). But what is a "contract"? One dictionary defines it as "an agreement between two or more people to do something," and also "a document containing the terms of an agreement" (Webster's 1966, p. 320). When actions like agreements and legislation are adopted and are recorded in documents with names like "contracts" and "laws," they take on the role of independent entities, so we can consider them to be entities. Indeed, texts and documents are entities. So in this case, we can consider "insurance" to be an entity. This meaning of insurance is often called an "insurance policy," which is such a signed and sealed contract.

• 41

Being insured, or having insurance can also be considered an attribute of the entity (a person, an institution) that possesses the insurance. Later, in subject analysis, we will attempt to sort out these confusing roles. Here, in subject scope analysis, our only goal is to identify types or categories of phenomena, as opposed to particular phenomena. Just remember, when you face challenging situations such as "insurance," that the purpose of subject analysis is understanding the meaning and intent of a message. Such analysis helps us sort out the various roles of phenomena, so that we can describe them in useful and accurate ways for our users.

• facet analysis by reference librarians : 42

Reference librarians perform this kind of facet or aspect analysis on a daily basis as they seek to unravel and understand the information needs and desires of clients. In subject scope analysis, the IR database designer is doing the analysis in advance, in order to facilitate future information interactions.

• goals of subject scope analysis : 43

The goal in subject scope analysis is to identify a relatively small number of kinds of questions that an IR database can and will respond to. So far, we have considered only quite generic categories, using terms like "entity" and "attribute" — terms that may not be familiar to our potential users. It is useful to translate these technical and generic terms into more meaningful terms for our users. It often helps to include examples with each category name. Here are some examples.

• examples of entities in subject scope analysis : 44

Instead of "entities," "concrete entities," or "abstract entities," (which will appear to be pretty vague to most users), we can use categories such as:

- living beings (like persons, animals, plants, and other organisms); or just "people, animals, plants, and other living beings";
- artifacts, or made objects (like automobiles, buildings, dolls, drugs, equipment, food products); or perhaps even better: "things that people make or construct";
- naturally occurring objects (like rocks, oceans, mountains);
- imaginary objects or characters (like the Wizard of Oz, the Magic Mountain);
- religious or political doctrines or ideologies (like Christianity, Islam, communism, fascism, capitalism);
- documents or publications (like contracts, laws, standards, the *Bible*, the *Koran*, *Gone with the wind*);
- theories and policies (like the theory of relativity, the Monroe Doctrine).

Chapter 2. Subject Scope and Domain

• examples of attributes in subject scope analysis : 45

Instead of "attributes," "constituent materials," "parts" or "properties," consider using categories such as:

- construction materials (like wood, steel, brick, concrete);
- body parts (like eyes, teeth, hearts, livers);
- chemical components (like calcium carbonate, ascorbic acid, zinc oxide);
- ingredients (like wheat, malted barley, salt, yeast, sugar, corn);
- diseases and disabilities (like HIV/AIDS, cancer, blindness, paralysis). Diseases are complex phenomena, like insurance. They can be considered to be attributes, because an entity (a person or an animal) possesses them, or suffers them. But diseases could also be considered as processes. But by simply classifying or labeling them as "diseases," it no longer matters much whether they are fundamentally attributes or processes; they have their own facet!
- conditions or characteristics (like age, ethnicity, gender, educational level, sexual orientation). These examples all relate to persons. Depending on the IR database, examples of characteristics might be very different.

• examples of actions in subject scope analysis : 46

Categories like "actions" and "events" appear to be less problematic and more common as everyday terms. It is usually wise to avoid the use of technical terms like "operations" or "processes," however, because either they have special meanings in certain contexts (like a medical operation), or they do not generally carry the distinctions described here. Instead you might consider creating categories based on the typical performer of actions, as in these examples for a hypothetical medical IR database:

- actions by medical personnel (like diagnosis, therapy, surgery, research);
- actions by patients (like exercise, dieting, sleeping);
- actions by institutions (like advertising, labor relations, managed care).

• examples of events in subject scope analysis : 47

You might not have a category for particular events in a medical IR database, but certainly a historical or political IR database would need categories for:

- historical events (like battles, wars, assassinations, political campaigns, and elections).

• examples of places in subject scope analysis : 48

Some types of IR databases may not consider places to be important at all. In a medical IR database, for example, users might not be interested in where medical actions take place or where entities are situated. Whether this is true or not, of course, should have been determined in the prerequisite assessment of potential user needs and desires. In a historical IR database, you would certainly want categories like:

- particular places, such as Greenwich Village (New York, NY); New Brunswick, NJ; Colorado; Zimbabwe; Africa; Empire State Building (New York, NY);
- kinds of places, such as developing countries, arid regions, densely populated areas, sea coasts.

• examples of time in subject scope analysis : 49

In many IR databases, time is less important as a subject category (time related to message topics) than a message feature category (the time when the message was created), which we shall consider in the next chapter on documentary scope. But certainly any IR database with historical interest will need to offer responses related to time, such as:

Chapter 2. Subject Scope and Domain (Section 2.1)

- particular dates (like December 7, 1941);
- centuries and eras (like 19th century, Renaissance, Victorian period).

• expression of categories in subject scope analysis : 50

In all of these examples, the goal is to use terminology that will be meaningful to potential users.

• avoiding meaningless categories in subject scope and facet analysis : 51

Similarly, it does not help to use categories that do not distinguish among different types of concepts, such as "subjects," "current issues," "themes," or "controversies." The problem with such facet or subject scope categories is that anything can be a subject; anything can be a current issue; anything can be a theme; anything can be a controversy! Such labels do not help to indicate the types or variety of concepts covered by the IR database.

2.1. Specialized Categories.

• 52

So far, this chapter has discussed mostly generic categories that might apply to IR databases with broad, even universal subject scopes. Whenever an IR database focuses on a narrower area, it is helpful and necessary to be much more specific in the analysis of topics. One way to proceed is to first analyze and sort topics into the basic generic categories (entities, attributes, actions, places, times), then to use appropriate sub-categories for the particular database, as in the examples just above.

• specialized categories in subject scope for literature : 53

The Modern Language Association of America has a very well-developed subject scope for its *MLA international bibliography*, which is one of the major print and electronic IR databases for the study of literature, folklore, language, and linguistics. Here are the indexing categories listed on its worksheet for national literatures (Modern Language Association of America 1997). Examples have been added for each category.

• specialized categories in *MLA International Bibliography* : 54

- specific literatures: e.g., English literature, American literature, Chicano literature, Puerto Rican literature.
- performance media: e.g., theater, story-telling, recitation.
- languages (if different from language of national literature): e.g., English, Spanish, Swahili.
- periods: e.g., 20th century, 19th century.
- individuals (real): e.g., Thomas Hardy, Emily Dickinson, Abraham Lincoln, James Baldwin.
- anonymous works: e.g., Beowulf, Mother Goose, The Bible.
- groups/movements: e.g., Avant Garde, Beat Generation, hippies, lesbian poets, African American writers, children.
- genres: e.g., poetry, drama, non-fiction novels.
- works: e.g., *The wind in the willows, Alice in wonderland, Giovanni's room.*

Further Description of Literary Topic:
- features: e.g., dialogue, poetic realism.
- literary techniques: e.g., visual metaphor, imagery, symbolism.
- themes/motifs/figures/characters: e.g., [treatment of] love, hate, war, Manifest Destiny, salvation, Huck Finn, Cinderella.

Chapter 2. Subject Scope and Domain (Section 2.1)

- influences (recipients): e.g., [influence on] Harlem Renaissance, Generation of 1898.
- sources: e.g., [influence of] Harlem Renaissance, Generation of 1898, The Bible.
- processes: e.g., characterization, translation.

Description of Document Author's Processes:

- types of scholarship: e.g., criticism.
- methodological approaches: e.g., sociological approach, psychological approach, Marxist approach.
- theories: e.g., Freudian theory, evolution (as theory).
- devices/tools: e.g., computers, concordances.
- disciplines: e.g., aesthetics, historiography.
- scholars: e.g., critics, folklorists (also particular individuals).
- general/miscellaneous: A place for indexers to add anything that doesn't fit in the established categories!
- special types of documents: e.g., bibliography, film, slides, videotapes, multimedia.
- specialized categories in subject scope for folklore
- specialized categories in subject scope for language

• **specialized categories in subject scope for linguistics : 55**

The MLA index worksheet for folklore is similar, except that "main folklore types" (literature, music and dance, belief systems, rituals, material culture) replaces "specific literatures" and a category for "places" has been added. Also, "genres" has been expanded to include "broad folklore types or genres" (e.g., for folk literature: speech play, narrative, poetry) and "narrow folklore types or genres" (e.g., for folk narrative: legend, myth, tall tale). For language and linguistics, the "language" category is placed first, followed by categories for "places" and "periods." Next comes "major linguistic aspect" for a list of fifteen linguist attributes and operations ranging from dialects (dialectology) and grammar to syntax, translation, and writing systems.

• **non-topical features in subject scope analysis : 56**

A sharp reader will notice that the list of MLA categories is not limited to subject or topical facets. It includes some non-topical features as well, such as "special types of documents" and "methodological approaches."

• **documentary scope versus subject scope : 57**

Chapter 3 on documentary scope discusses the kinds of messages, texts, and documents that an IR database can designate as appropriate for fulfilling its subject scope — documents that will likely include good responses to the kinds of questions and topics described in the subject scope. It is good to make a clear distinction between subjects or topics on the one hand — what a message is about, what it discusses, what it means — as opposed to what it is on the other hand — its medium, its form, shape, format or genre, the point of view or approach that a message creator takes in her/his treatment of topics, its language and level of treatment, and other features of potential interest to users.

• **role of author processes in subject scope versus documentary scope : 58**

The last eight categories in the MLA list are called "description of document author's process." The idea here is to indicate, for the benefit of users, the kind of scholarship that the author brought to the topics indicated in the earlier categories — the methodological approach that the author used, any theories that he or she may have applied, any devices or tools he or she may have employed, any disciplines that the author may have brought to bear on the topics treated,

Chapter 2. Subject Scope and Domain (Section 2.1)

the names of scholars who may have contributed to the study, and any special format or medium in which the message and its text appears.

• topics versus features : 59

In many cases, these author attributes are not the topic of the message. Rather, they are features of the message. For example, the message may be a psychological study of Thomas Hardy, but not about psychological studies.

• role of features as topics : 60

What can be confusing, however, is that each of these feature categories can be subjects or topics as well. It is perfectly possible, and indeed not uncommon, to have messages about various types of scholarship, methodological approaches, theories, the tools or devices that can be used in literary study, the disciplines that can contribute to literary understanding, important literary scholars, and even about types of documents, such as discussion of important bibliographies, films, periodicals, or dissertations.

• distinguishing between topics versus features : 61

What is important in this confusion is to try to be clear about when such a feature is a topic, and when it is a non-topical feature. When users want messages about bibliography (the art of creating bibliographies) or about bibliographies (the lists themselves), they won't want to retrieve hundreds or thousands of actual bibliographies that provide no topical information about bibliography or bibliographies. So even though the same phenomenon is involved, its role can be very different, and for clarity, the different roles need to be specified. This confusion of form and topic is an ancient muddle in indexing, cataloging, and information retrieval.

• subject scope versus documentary scope : 62

This frequent muddle is precisely why, in the design of IR databases, it is important to keep the subject scope separate from the documentary scope, recognizing that many of the same categories may occur in both. Every message, text, and document will have or exemplify some format or genre as a fundamental feature, but genre is also an important topic for literary study. The same is true for all other features of messages, texts, and documents — medium, language, point of view, methodological approach, level of treatment, intended audience, and so on.

• methodological approaches in subject scope versus documentary scope : 63

One of the most important cross-over categories is the methodological approach used by the author of a message. The MLA categories are based on extensive user studies conducted among the members of special interest groups of the Modern Language Association. Most MLA members indicated that one of the topics in which they were most interested was precisely the research methodologies that literary scholars use to study literature. This is why indexers for the MLA bibliography try to indicate every significant example of a methodological approach (Anderson 1979; Anderson 1980).

• role of methodological approaches as topics versus features : 64

But the line between a method used by the creator of a message to analyze, assess, or study a topic (that is, the method as a feature of a message) on the one hand and this same method as a topic of a message can be very fuzzy at times. The question is: is the message *about* the methodological approach used or not. If the main topic of a message is a particular literary work, its characteristics, the techniques of its author, its sources and influences, but at the same time, the author of this message also discusses the methodology that he/she used to elucidate the main topic, or he/she does such a good job of illustrating the application of the method that the message contains an excellent example of the method, such that users who are interested primarily in

Chapter 2. Subject Scope and Domain (Section 2.1)

the method and not in the main topic of the message will still want to see this message, then, in cases such as this, it is quite proper to index the method as a topic.

• **criteria for assignment of index terms : 65**

After all, the most reliable criterion for assigning a particular indexing term to a message is this: if a user who uses this term in a query would want to see this message, then this message should have this term!

• **distinguishing between topics versus features : 66**

The moral of this story is that to the extent possible, a clear distinction should be made between topics and non-topical features, recognizing that many features can play both roles at different times. In the MLA subject scope, all of the categories in the last section (description of document author's process) can be topics. When they are not topics, but features of a message, that should be so indicated to the extent possible. Ways to accomplish this goal will be discussed later on, but one way is to have separate fields in the database records used to describe documentary units — one field or set of fields for topics, another field or set of fields for non-topical features.

• **use of roles in subject scope analysis : 67**

Several of the categories in the MLA indexing worksheet are for roles, rather than for fundamental facets or aspects of literary phenomena. Examples include "themes/motifs/figures," "influences (recipients)," and "sources." Almost anything can be a theme in literature. Phenomena that are treated in a message as a theme are placed in the theme category, rather than in facets relating to their fundamental nature. For example, normally a real person would fall either in the category for "individuals (real)," or perhaps in "scholars," if that was her or his role (another role category!). However, if a real person is treated as a topic or theme in a work of literature, then that person is considered as a theme in the analysis and is placed in the theme category. Similarly, any literary work, or person, or group, or literature, or event can play the role of a source of inspiration for a literary work, or the recipient of influence from a literary work. When an entity or an event is the inspiring source, it is placed in the "sources" category. When it is the recipient of influence (when it is influenced by a literary work or phenomenon), then it is placed in the "influences (recipients)" category.

• **68**

In more generic subject scope analysis for broad-scoped IR databases, there is generally less interest in the particular roles played by various phenomena. The main focus is on the description of the principal types of phenomena addressed by an IR database. However, in more specialized subject scopes such as the MLA subject scope, it is appropriate and important to indicate the kinds of roles that are identified, and that is precisely what these role categories are designed to do. They tell potential users that yes, they may ask questions about various roles in literature — about themes, influences and the role of individuals as scholars.

• **subject scope analysis for artistic works versus critical works : 69**

The MLA bibliography includes only critical literature — that is, works about literary works and folklore. It does not include or index the literary works or examples of folklore themselves. For the critical literature, the themes or topics of artistic works are only one of many attributes to be considered, thus all the various themes and topics of artistic works can be grouped into one facet.

Chapter 2. Subject Scope and Domain (Section 2.2)

• 70

IR databases that cover both artistic works (literature, paintings, photographs, motion pictures, musical works, etc.) and the critical or descriptive literature about such works are especially complex when it comes to subject scope. The subject scope for critical and descriptive works can be similar to that used by the MLA, but lumping all the topics and themes of artistic works into a single facet called (in the case of MLA) "themes/motifs/figures/characters" is not helpful. It does not inform users of the variety of kinds of questions they can ask about the messages of artistic works! Instead, a separate set of subject scope facets is needed to describe the messages of the artistic works. These facets can be very much like the generic facets discussed earlier, such as:

- entities (perhaps with separate facets for special types of entities such as persons, groups, institutions, artifacts, natural objects, etc.)
- attributes.
- actions, operations, processes, events.
- places.
- times.

2.2. Presenting the Subject Scope to Users.

• 71

One of the most important purposes for a clear subject scope description is the ability to inform users of the kinds of topical questions they may ask and the kinds of answers or responses they may expect from an IR database. To achieve this purpose, the subject scope must be presented to users. In print databases, this has generally been attempted in introductions, which few users bother to read. Topical categories have been more effectively presented to users in tables of contents. In a listing of the major categories for the display of document representations, such as abstracts, key topical categories can be presented.

• presentation of subject scope on opening screens : 72

For the current generation of electronic databases, whether accessed via CD-ROM, online, or via the world-wide web, the most effective way to present the subject scope to users is on the opening screen of the IR database. At the very first opportunity, users are informed of the kinds of questions that the IR database is equipped to entertain.

• subject scope on opening screen of *Queer resources directory* : 73

Here is an example of such an opening screen for a world-wide web IR database, the *Queer resources directory* (QRD) (see figure 2.1). Twelve major categories of topical information are listed. Some have brief annotations. This list of topics helps the potential user decide, right away, at the very beginning, whether this might be an appropriate database for a particular search.

• subject scope on opening screen of *MLA international bibliography* : 74

Why don't you try creating a preliminary design for an opening screen for the *MLA international bibliography*, based on the categories listed above in section 2.1? You can use the QRD opening screen as a model. After you give it a try, take a look at a preliminary design for the MLA bibliography in figure 2.2, followed by a prototype opening screen in figure 2.3. Note that the preliminary design can be done in simple typescript, or even pen or pencil. Graphic features can be omitted at this stage, or just hinted at. Your purpose will be to lay out the kind of informa-

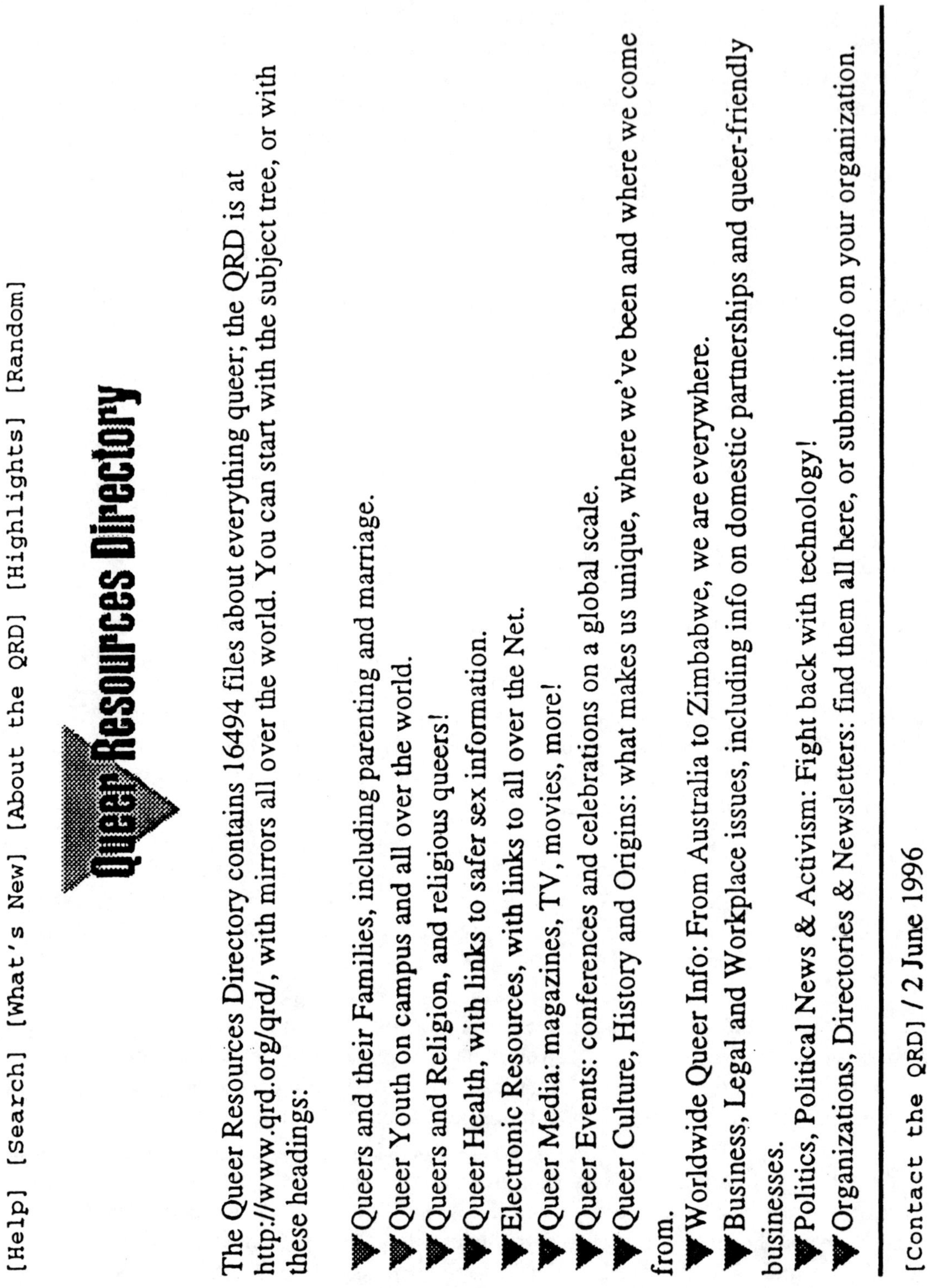

Chapter 2. Subject Scope and Domain (Section 2.2)

[Help] [Search] [What's New] [About the QRD] [Highlights] [Random]

Queer Resources Directory

The Queer Resources Directory contains 16494 files about everything queer; the QRD is at http://www.qrd.org/qrd/, with mirrors all over the world. You can start with the subject tree, or with these headings:

▶ Queers and their Families, including parenting and marriage.
▶ Queer Youth on campus and all over the world.
▶ Queers and Religion, and religious queers!
▶ Queer Health, with links to safer sex information.
▶ Electronic Resources, with links to all over the Net.
▶ Queer Media: magazines, TV, movies, more!
▶ Queer Events: conferences and celebrations on a global scale.
▶ Queer Culture, History and Origins: what makes us unique, where we've been and where we come from.
▶ Worldwide Queer Info: From Australia to Zimbabwe, we are everywhere.
▶ Business, Legal and Workplace issues, including info on domestic partnerships and queer-friendly businesses.
▶ Politics, Political News & Activism: Fight back with technology!
▶ Organizations, Directories & Newsletters: find them all here, or submit info on your organization.

[Contact the QRD] / 2 June 1996

Figure 2.1. Opening screen of *Queer resources directory*.
Reprinted by permission of QRD: Queer Resources Directory, © 1996.

Chapter 2. Subject Scope and Domain (Section 2.3)

tion you would like to provide. A web-page designer can be called upon to actually implement the design and suggest visual features to help convey your message.

```
================================================================
              [Help] [Keyword search] [Browsable subject index]
              [Author, Title, Journal indexes] [Background]
       Welcome to the Modern Language Association of America's
                      MLA INTERNATIONAL BIBLIOGRAPHY

Access to 1,200,000 records for critical scholarship in journal articles,
monographs, dissertations, and proceedings, 1981-2003. Choose Keyword
search, Browsable subject index, Author, Title, Journal indexes, or
select more detailed displays of primary topics below:

 • Literature — or select: specific literatures, performance media, languages,
      periods, individuals, groups/movements, genres, works, literary
      techniques, themes/motifs
 • Folklore — or select: types, performance media, genres, places, periods,
      groups/movements, literary techniques, themes/motifs
 • Language/linguistics — or select: languages, places, periods, linguistic
      aspects, groups/movements
 • Or Select: general aspects — special features, influences (recipients &
      sources), processes, types of scholarship, theories, devices/tools,
      disciplines, scholars, and special types of documents (e.g.,
      bibliographies)
================================================================
```
Figure 2.2. Hypothetical preliminary design for an opening screen for *MLA international bibliography*.

• topics versus features on opening screens : 75

In contrast to our hypothetical opening screens for the *MLA international bibliography*, the opening screen provided to students and faculty at Rutgers University through the Ovid Technologies interface provides indirect access to lots of information about database fields for documentary features, such as author, place of publication, title, date of publication, standard numbers (ISBN, ISSN), journal abbreviation, journal name, document language, publisher, pagination, publication type, etc., but nothing about topical categories. Topical categories are displayed on a search screen only after a preliminary search has been performed, when a searcher asks to limit a search. No guidance is provided to potential users as to subject scope, beyond this general statement at the beginning of the field guide: "critical scholarship on literature, language, linguistics and folklore" (Ovid interface accessed via the Rutgers University Libraries homepage 24 Oct. 2002).

• 76

Do you think this is sufficient?

2.3. Ranganathan's Facets.

• definitions of facets; PMEST acronym for facets : 77

As noted previously, the categories used in describing a subject scope for an IR database are often called facets. This word, related to the word "face" and used for the many "faces" of a cut and polished diamond or other precious gems, has come to refer to the many faces, or aspects, of complex topics in the realm of librarianship and information science. When Ranganathan intro-

Chapter 2. Subject Scope and Domain (Section 2.3)

| Help | Keyword search | Browsable subject index | Author, Title, Journal indexes | Background |

Welcome to the *Modern Language Association of America's*

MLA International Bibliography

An indexing service providing access to 1,200,000 records for critical scholarship in journal articles, monographs, dissertations, and proceedings, 1981-1999. Choose Keyword search, Browsable subject index, Author, Title, Journal indexes, or select more detailed displays of primary topics below:

Literature **or select:** specific literatures, performance media, languages, periods, individuals, groups/movements, genres, works, literary techniques, themes/motifs

Folklore **or select:** types, performance media, genres, places, periods, groups/movements, literary techniques, themes/motifs

Language / linguistics **or select:** specific languages, places, periods, linguistic aspects, groups/movements

Or Select: general aspects: special features, influences (either recipients or sources), processes, types of scholarship, theories, devices/tools, disciplines, scholars, and special types of documents (e.g., bibliography)

Figure 2.3. Hypothetical opening webpage screen for the *MLA international bibliography*.

Chapter 2. Subject Scope and Domain (Section 2.3)

duced the idea of facets, and facet analysis, he admitted that the potential number of topics or subjects and their facets was infinite, but he suggested that all could be encompassed by five fundamental facet categories, which he called:

- Personality (manifested in particular entities, including persons, naturally occurring objects, artifacts, imaginary entities, and abstract entities)
- Material (the constituents of entities, plus their attributes)
- Energy (manifested in operations, processes, and events)
- Space (places, environments)
- Time

• views of Ranganathan (Shiyali Ramamrita) on arrangement of facets; PMEST acronym for facets : 78

Ranganathan also suggested that the preferred order of facets in index headings or classified arrays is the order just presented, which is often referred to as "PMEST," for the initials representing these facets (Miksa 1989, p. 69-71). These facets are essentially the same as the fundamental facets presented in section 2.1.

• facets of Ranganathan (Shiyali Ramamrita) for diesel engines : 79

Nevertheless, in line with his recognition of the infinite number of potential topics, Ranganathan understood the need for much more specific facet analysis for particular subject areas. Here are his facets for a database pertaining to diesel engines (Ranganathan 1965, p. 221-222):

- Brand of engines.
- Country of manufacture.
- Purpose.
- Environment — the element in which an engine will work, under water or in humid climate or in a desert, and so on.
- Cost.
- Compression ratio.
- Cycle of strokes.
- Size.
- Number of cylinders.
- Bore diameter.
- Arrangement of cylinders.
- Piston position.
- Crankshaft speed.
- Displacement.
- Stroke distance.
- Fuel used.
- Fuel & injection system.
- Cooler used.
- Starting method.

Chapter 2. Subject Scope and Domain (Section 2.4)

2.4. Why Bother?

• topical groupings versus facets in subject scope analysis : 80

Many students have difficulty, at least at first, in distinguishing and classifying concepts and phenomena according to the kinds of fundamental characteristics presented in this chapter. Often their reaction is, "why bother?" Or they want to create topical groupings rather than facet groupings, such as a grouping of all topics relating to diseases. They will create a "disease" category that includes not only diseases, but also the body parts affected, symptoms, therapies, drugs, diagnostic techniques, causes or theories about causes, and experts or researchers dealing with diseases.

• deficiency of topical groupings in subject scope analysis : 81

This kind of topical grouping will indicate the possibility of asking the IR database about diseases, but it will mask or hide the possibility of asking about the different types of topics that have been subsumed into the disease topical category, such as body parts, symptoms, therapies, drugs, causes, and experts. The problem is that body parts are not diseases; neither are drugs or symptoms or experts or therapies. At this stage of analysis, each of these phenomena should be moved to their appropriate facet categories. Body parts, drugs, theories, experts and researchers are types of entities. Symptoms are attributes. Therapies and diagnostic techniques are actions. Causes may fall into the entity category (like viruses, bacteria) or they may be actions or attributes (like poor eating habits, smoking, stress).

• tests for membership in facets : 82

A useful test for checking whether a concept belongs to a particular facet is the "is a" test. For each particular disease in the disease facet, you should be able to say that it "is a" disease, such as "AIDS is a disease," "Cancer is a disease," but "chemotherapy is not a disease." "Chemotherapy is a therapy," so it belongs in the therapy facet! This is a basic form of classification, which will prove to be useful in many approaches to message/text/document (information) organization for information retrieval.

• facets in subject scope analysis : 83

Whether the specific categories like drugs or body parts or therapies will be specifically mentioned in the overall subject scope description will depend on the overall scope and the number of categories named. Such categories may be listed in a specialized medical database, but not in a more general database, where therapies might be one of a number of, say, "professional procedures" and "drugs" might be one of many "human-made artifacts."

• topical groupings versus facets in subject scope analysis : 84

Topical groupings can be very effective for information retrieval. Every effective index heading will consist of a grouping of the topics that come together to form the focus of a particular message. Similarly, good search statements for electronic computer searching consist of a topical combination of several (or many) particular aspects pertaining to the topic of interest. These topical groupings are matters of index heading and search statement syntax, to be covered in chapter 12. But for subject scope analysis, there are simply too many topics or potential topics for it to be possible to enumerate topics or topical groupings. Ranganathan has suggested that topics are infinite in number, at least potentially or in theory. This is precisely why, for subject scope analysis, it is best to focus on facets (fundamental types of topics) rather than topics themselves. At this stage, the goal is to identify a small number of fundamental categories. This can be done most effectively by grouping topics according to their fundamental nature rather than by topical relationships.

• purpose of subject scope analysis : 85

Remember, our purpose is to give users (as well as IR database producers and indexers) an overview of the entire content and possible access points of the database, so at this stage, we must not immerse anyone in too much detail.

• number of topics versus facets : 86

While the number of possible topics is very large, the number of fundamental facet categories of phenomena can be summarized in a relatively small number of categories. At this stage, the aim is to characterize the subject scope of an IR database with relatively few terms or categories, from ten to thirty at the most.

2.5. Our Examples.
2.5.1. A Book Index.

• indexes for books : 87

This book that you are reading can be considered an IR database thanks to its indexes — the table of contents and the back-of-the-book index. These indexes provide access to the content of the book, so that users can find discussions of particular topics whenever they want. The design of the back-of-the-book index for this book will serve as our example for book indexes in general.

• subject scope analysis for book indexes : 88

Conventional wisdom suggests that indexers of single books should simply index (indicate!) whatever is important in the book. Such straightforward advice sidesteps the issue of "what is important." There will probably be some degree of agreement on the major themes of a book, but guidance is important for peripheral areas — guidance for the indexer and guidance for the user of the index. For example, in creating the index for this book, should entries be created for the authors and titles of works that are cited in the text? Because this book is mainly about the processes and options for designing IR databases, should entries be created for individual persons, such as Ranganathan, who was mentioned several times in this chapter? Should entries be created for particular IR databases that may be mentioned as examples, such as the *MLA international bibliography* or the *Queer resources directory*? The point here is that even the index to a single book can benefit from an analysis of the probable needs and interests of prospective users, and the results of this analysis can usefully be recorded in a subject scope statement for the guidance of users and the indexer.

• users of book indexes : 89

Why do persons consult an index to an individual book in the first place? There appear to be two major reasons, resulting in two classes of users: (1) Persons who have read or who are in the process of reading the book and wish to find something that they remember having seen, but they don't remember precisely where; and (2) persons who have not read the book, but are looking for answers to some particular question or information related to some interest, such as the maximum number of locators that should be allowed under an undifferentiated heading in a displayed index (to pick a topic at random!). Of course readers in the first category may fall also in the second category for the part of the book they have not yet read.

Chapter 2. Subject Scope and Domain (Section 2.5.1)

• **vocabulary of users of book indexes : 90**

It is not generally feasible to provide different indexes for these two groups of users, tailored to their different needs. Perhaps the biggest difference between them is the use of vocabulary. Readers of the book might be more inclined to use, and expect to find, the vocabulary of the book reflected in the vocabulary of the index. Non-readers can be expected to use the general vocabulary of the field, which may well differ from that of the book. This variability calls for the use of cross-references linking alternative vocabulary, something we will discuss later in chapter 13, vocabulary management.

• **subject scope analysis for this book : 91**

Bearing these factors in mind, here is a possible subject scope for this book:

- **entities or things:**
  - all individuals and groups of persons mentioned, e.g., Ranganathan; indexers; users; designers; librarians; information scientists.
  - authors and titles of documents cited.
  - institutions and organizations, e.g., National Information Standards Organization; American Library Association; Library of Congress.
  - IR databases used as examples.
  - types of IR databases and parts of IR databases.
  - types and parts of messages, texts, and documents.

- **constituent materials:**

This book has little concern for constituent materials of entities, such as the physical materials used to make paper or electronic media. Therefore, this broad category will largely be ignored.

- **attributes or properties:**

All attributes and properties relating to the entities noted above (persons, groups, institutions, IR databases, messages, texts, documents) will be noted. Examples for persons might include searching experience, e.g., level of use, level of experience; for IR databases, this will include properties such as indexing exhaustivity, vocabulary specificity, search recall, search precision, etc.

- **operations, processes, events:**

All operations, processes, and events relating to the design, creation and use of IR databases should be indexed. Examples include scope analysis, message analysis, automatic indexing, vocabulary management, searching, relevance judgment, etc.

- **places:**

Places are of little or no importance and will not be indexed.

- **times:**

Likewise, times and time periods are of little importance and will not be indexed.

Chapter 2. Subject Scope and Domain (Section 2.5.2)

2.5.2. An Indexing and Abstracting Service.

• 92

Now we turn our attention to an appropriate subject scope for a broad-based indexing and abstracting service for library and information science. In the case of an index to a single book, the book comes first and then the indexer designs an index for that book — so the characteristics of the book tend to dominate and determine choices for the design of the index, including the subject scope. This is reversed, at least in theory, in the case of an indexing and abstracting service. First one determines the potential users and the needs and preferences of these users. This leads to the subject scope, which in turn influences the selection of documents to be indexed. So the primary consideration in formulating the subject scope for an IR database for many documents should be the users, not the documents.

• 93

The chief goal will be to represent the major interests and concerns of the students, practitioners, and scholars in the fields of library and information science. Here is a possible subject scope for such an IR database:

- **entities or things:**
  - persons, both individuals and groups. Groups should be indexed on the basis of important characteristics. Users of services, for example, may be characterized by occupation, objectives, level of experience, gender, age, ethnicity, sexual orientation, etc.
  - institutions and organizations, including particular ones by name, and also types. Libraries, for example, should be indexed according to attribute categories such as public, school, academic, special, etc.
  - artifacts. Chief among these will be texts and documents and the tools and other equipment and structures that make them available — catalogs, indexes, databases, shelving, furniture, buildings, etc.
  - natural objects. These will have less importance in the "artificial" (i.e., human created) world of information. Important exceptions may be various pests that attack documents.
  - abstract entities. In addition to the institutions and organizations, with their own subfacet just above, these include the theories and disciplines that contribute to our understanding of information phenomena.
- **constituent materials:**

The materials from which artifacts are created or of which naturally occurring objects consist are generally of little interest for most of library and information science. A notable exception is the sub-field of conservation and preservation, which is concerned with the long-term viability of document media and the impact of the constituent elements in ink, paper, film, and electronic media. Library architecture is of course concerned with building materials and the components of furniture.

- **attributes or properties:**

All attributes or properties relating to relevant entities, materials, operations, processes, events, places and time periods should be noted.

Chapter 2. Subject Scope and Domain (Section 2.5.2)

- **operations, processes, events:**

All operations, processes, and events relating to library and information science should be noted. These include human information behavior, searching, browsing, collection development, document acquisition, cataloging and indexing, reference and information services, management of these operations, conservation and preservation, building and collection maintenance, on-going evaluation, research, and of course IR database design.

- **places:**

Whenever entities or operations, processes and events are associated with a particular place or type of place, it will be noted.

- **times:**

Likewise, whenever entities or operations, processes and events are associated with a particular time or time period, it will be noted.

- presentation of subject scope for indexing and abstracting services : 94

Here is an attempt to translate this rather technical subject scope description into one that can be displayed to users on an opening electronic screen, such as those encountered on the worldwide web or a CD-ROM. Technical terminology is translated into terms that users might find more familiar than "entities" or "attributes." The overall subject scope has been reduced to seven broad category groups. See this attempt in figure 2.4.

```
================================================================================
                [Help] [Advanced search] [Browsable subject index]
                [Author, Title, Journal indexes] [Background]
                                                  _____
BLISTER: Bibliography of Library & Information Science  |                  |
& Technology: Evaluation & Research                     [keyword search]

An indexing and abstracting service providing access to 20,000 scholarly & pro-
fessional journal articles, monographs, multimedia & web resources, disserta-
tions, and proceedings, 1981-2004. Choose Keyword search, Browsable subject in-
dex, Author, Title, Journal indexes, or browse detailed displays of primary
categories below (highlight category headings, then click BROWSE CATEGORIES):

• Participants & Agencies: persons, groups, organizations, institutions,
     companies, libraries, archives.
• Reference & Retrieval Resources: access resources (information retrieval data-
     bases, indexes, catalogs); information resources in all media and formats.
• Tools & Equipment: computers, buildings, furniture, etc.
• Operations, Processes & Events: human information behavior, searching,
     collection development, acquisition, cataloging, indexing, reference &
     information services, conservation & preservation, building &
     collection maintenance, administration & management, design,
     evaluation & research.
• Disciplines & Related Theories: the sciences, applied sciences/technology
     social sciences, history, humanities, arts, law, etc.
• Places: by type; by name.
• Times: by centuries, decades, years.
================================================================================
```

Figure 2.4. Hypothetical preliminary opening screen design for an indexing and abstracting service for library and information science.

Chapter 2. Subject Scope and Domain (Section 2.5.2)

| Help | Keyword search | Browsable subject index | Author, Title, Journal indexes | Background |

BLISTER: Bibliography of Library & Information Science & Technology: Evaluation & Research

An indexing and abstracting service providing access to 200,000 scholarly & professional journal articles, monographs, multimedia & web resources, dissertations, and proceedings, 1981-2004. Choose Keyword search, Browsable subject index, Author, Title, Journal indexes, or browse detailed displays of primary categories listed below (highlight category headings, then click Browse Categories:

Participants & Agencies	Reference & Retrieval Resources	Tools & Equipment	Operations, Processes & Events	Disciplines & Related Theories
persons, groups, organizations, institutions, companies, libraries, archives.	access resources (information retrieval databases, indexes, catalogs); information resources in all media and formats.	computers, buildings, furniture, etc.	human information behavior, searching, collection development, acquisition, cataloging & indexing, reference & information services, conservation & preservation, building and collection maintenance, administration & management, design, evaluation & research.	the sciences, applied sciences / technology, social sciences, history, humanities, arts, law, etc.
				Places
				by type; by name.
				Times
				by centuries, by decades, by years.

Figure 2.5. Hypothetical opening screen for BLISTER — Bibliography of library & information science & technology: evaluation & research.

Figure 2.5 illustrates a hypothetical translation of this opening screen design into a prototype web-page.

2.5.3. A Full-Text Encyclopedia/Digital Library.

The design of an IR database for a full-text collection of important messages will fall somewhere between the design of an index for a single book and a broad-based indexing and abstracting service database. In some cases, the collection of documents to be included in a full-text database already exists. In that case, the content and purpose of these documents will influence the design, including the subject scope, as in the case of a book index. On the other hand, if a new database will be created, for example, a new encyclopedia or digital library for which articles or documents have yet to be selected or will be especially commissioned, then the subject scope should come first, just as in the case of the indexing and abstracting service, so that articles can be chosen or crafted to respond to the identified needs of the projected users.

This design will be for an IR database for a brand new encyclopedia/digital library. Therefore, our subject scope can be identical to that for our indexing and abstracting service.

Chapter 3. Documentary Scope

Contents of Chapter 3
   3.1. Authorship.
   3.2. Titles.
   3.3. Media.
   3.4. Forms, Formats, Genres.
   3.5. Periodicity.
   3.6. Intended Audience or Level.
   3.7. Methodological Approaches, Points of View, Biases, Kinds of Treatment.
   3.8. Language.
   3.9. Place of Creation, Manufacture, or Publication.
   3.10. Time of Creation, Manufacture, or Publication.
   3.11. Specific Documents.
   3.12. Qualitative Criteria.
   3.13. Features Versus Topics.
   3.14. Our Examples.
   3.14.1. A Book Index.
   3.14.2. An Indexing and Abstracting Service.
   3.14.3. A Full-Text Encyclopedia/Digital Library.

• documentary scope versus subject scope : 1

Whereas subject scope defines and describes the kinds of topical questions or concerns that a user can bring to an IR database, the documentary scope defines and describes the kinds of messages, texts, and documents a user can retrieve via the database in terms of non-topical features. Examples of non-topical features include:

- authorship: persons or groups who create or contribute to a message, text, or document;
- the media on which messages and their texts are encoded;
- codes and symbol systems used to encode messages as texts, including the various human languages used for creating language texts;
- the forms, formats, and genres of texts;
- the complexity or technical level of messages, including the kinds of audiences for whom they are intended (children, professionals, general public, etc.);
- points of view, biases, and methodological approaches characterizing the treatment of topics in messages;
- time and place of creation, manufacture or publication.

These features will be discussed in more detail in this chapter.

• importance of documentary scope descriptions for users : 2

Defining documentary scope can be very helpful to users who are looking for particular kinds of messages, texts, or documents. For some users, non-topical features are sometimes more important than topical features, as when a user is seeking poetry by a particular author, or type of author — poetry by African American lesbians, for example. In this case, topics or the meaning of poems are not an issue or concern.

Chapter 3. Documentary Scope

• **importance of documentary scope descriptions for IR database producers : 3**

For an IR database designed to provide access to current messages in one or more fields, a description of the documentary scope will guide the database producer in the search for and the selection of documents to include.

• **documentary scope descriptions for collections of documents : 4**

When an IR database is created to provide access to an already existing collection, it is still helpful to provide a clear description of the kinds of messages, texts, and documents included in that collection, to inform users of the kinds of documents that they may retrieve.

• **documentary scope descriptions for single documents : 5**

The only situation where a formal statement of documentary scope is normally unnecessary is when an IR database consists of a single document and its index or indexes. The most common example of this type of IR database is a book accompanied by a back-of-the-book index. In this situation, the documentary scope of the single document is usually obvious. But this situation is changing. Books can now be published in various electronic media as well as on paper. An index to a single book can now appear in a medium different than the book itself. The book, for example, may be printed on paper, but the index may be distributed on a floppy disk or CD-ROM, or vice versa. So even in the case of a traditional book with back-of-the-book index, it can be useful to specify documentary scope features of the primary document, and of its index.

• **documentary scope descriptions for collections of documents : 6**

When a single print volume is not a single monographic document, but a collection of separate documents, or even an encyclopedia or handbook of many documents, then a documentary scope becomes more important and more useful, because such a collection begins to exhibit some of the variability common in larger document collections. Even if the documents in such a collection all share the same medium, they will have different authors and different types of authors, and they may also exhibit variations in formats or genre; they may include significant charts, diagrams, maps, or illustrations that should be noted; they may vary in level of treatment and methodological approaches; and they may have been created at different times and places.

• **non-topical features combined with topics in searches : 7**

Often users who are primarily interested in topics will also want to search for certain types of documents on the basis of non-topical features as well, so part of the IR database design will consist of decisions as to which non-topical features will be described and made searchable. Most IR databases permit searches on the basis of such features as particular authors (but less often by types of authors); by language; by time or place of publication; and by document type (format, medium and periodicity — monograph versus serial). Searchable features can be combined with topics in order to focus a topical search toward certain types of documents, such as only documents in German in the form of print-on-paper periodical articles.

• **importance of non-topical features for experts: 8**

Experts often do not want everything on the topics that they know about, but rather particular treatments of topics, the applications of particular theories, negative or critical appraisal of topics or procedures, or points of view brought to bear on a topic. Bella Weinberg (1987) has asserted, quite correctly, that many IR databases do not serve experts well because they do not sufficiently indicate non-topical aspects relating to the treatment of topics. Experts already know about the topics. What they want is evidence of something new in relation to analysis or treatment of their topic. Rebecca Green (1997) has related this need for "attribute indexing" to "user (need)-oriented indexing" in contrast to "document-oriented indexing."

Chapter 3. Documentary Scope (Section 3.1)

• role of non-topical features in relevance judgments : 9

Most research in information retrieval has focused on topical representation, but recently there has been growing interest in non-topical aspects of messages, texts, and documents that influence their usefulness to users. One example is Carol L. Barry's dissertation research, summarized in "User-defined relevance criteria: an exploratory study" (1994). Green (1997, p. 73) says Barry "gives perhaps the best available list of attributes that should be considered in indexing documents and requests." Barry cites fundamental work by many leading IR researchers, including Tefko Saracevic and Nicholas Belkin, who have led the shift towards designing IR systems that can respond more directly to user needs and behaviors.

• examples of non-topical features; role of user attributes in relevance judgments : 10

Among the non-topical attributes that Barry explored in her study are: depth and focus of treatment; accuracy or validity of assertions; clarity of presentation; recency; the extent to which a message represents a consensus in a field; the extent to which assertions are supported by external verification; the quality and reputation of the source; ease of document obtainability and cost. Other attributes relate more to the user than to the message, text, or document, such as: background and experience (but this will also relate to the level of treatment in a text); ability to understand; novelty of content or document to the user; and the extent to which the user agrees with, likes, or dislikes the message.

• non-topical features as searchable features : 11

The attributes that are typically important for a documentary scope description are described in the following sections. As you consider these attributes and what role they might play in your IR database, you need to make two decisions: (1) What types of messages, texts, and documents will your IR databases include, with respect to each category or attribute? and (2) will the particular category or attribute be a searchable feature? — will users be able to focus a search on messages, texts, and documents possessing particular varieties of the feature?

3.1. Authorship.

• 12

Messages can be created by many different types of persons and organizations performing a variety of functions. Different authorship (or creation) functions often carry different designations, such as writer, editor, compiler, illustrator, composer, choreographer. The roles designated by these terms are not rigorously defined. The compiler of a bibliography is often the creator or author of that bibliography, deciding what to include, composing the citations and annotations, and designing the arrangement and access methods. Similarly, the compiler of an index creates the index. But a compiler of a collection or anthology of messages and texts by other persons is not considered an author. Sometimes the compiler (the author!) of a bibliography or index is referred to as an editor, but they have not edited the works of others. Such an editor has compiled or created a new work in the form of a bibliography or index. (But of course, there are editors of bibliographies and indexes — persons who check and edit the work of a bibliographer or indexer!)

• types of authors and creators as searchable features : 13

Some IR databases will categorize authors or creators of messages and their texts according to various attributes, so that users may find messages coming from authors of various ethnic backgrounds (e.g., Chicano writers), gender groups (e.g., women poets, transsexual rappers), sexual orientation groups (e.g., gay playwrights), age levels (e.g., drawings by children), nationalities (e.g., Dutch painters), affiliations (e.g., authors connected with Rutgers University), and so on.

• corporate bodies as authors : 14

Sometimes organizations, called "corporate bodies" in cataloging, are considered to be the authors or creators of messages. According to *Anglo-American cataloguing rules* (2002, rule 21.1B2), a corporate body can be considered to be the primary author when a message is "of an administrative nature, dealing with the corporate body itself," when a message is "legal, governmental," or "religious" in nature; when a message records "the collective thought of the body" or the "collective activity" of a conference or a performing group; or when the text consists of cartographic materials.

• types of corporate bodies as searchable features : 15

Corporate bodies, as authors or merely as publishers, can also be categorized by type, to facilitate searching. Examples include governments and government agencies, educational institutions, businesses, non-profit organizations, and so on. Such categories are similar to those indicated by the suffixes one finds in email and world-wide web addresses: ".edu" for educational institutions, ".gov" for government agencies, ".org" for organizations, ".com" for commercial entities, etc.

• messages without human authors; messages from nature : 16

There is another category of messages that have no human authors, even though they may be massaged or organized by human editors or analysts. These types of messages include the massive data sets received via satellites reflecting events and conditions in oceans, on land and in space. Meteorological data are an example. Other examples include recordings of sounds made by animals, such as dolphins or elephants. All of these examples constitute messages of interest to some users, who strive to interpret their meaning and significance.

3.2. Titles.

• 17

Almost all IR databases will provide access to particular messages, texts, or documents by their titles. More sophisticated IR databases will link the main title (or "title proper") with variant titles, such as parallel titles in different languages, subtitles, and conventional titles (such as "Hamlet" versus an earlier title like "The tragicall historie of Hamlet, Prince of Denmarke").

3.3. Media.

• 18

At the most basic level, a message must be encoded as a text of some kind on some medium so that it can be transmitted. Remember from Part I that a document consists of a text recorded on a medium. Texts can be received and perceived aurally (via sound waves directly from a sound source, such as a speaking person, or from a variety of sound recordings), visually (via light waves from a wide variety of visual recording media, including paper and electronic storage media combined with electronic viewing devices), and via touch (a primary example being Braille). Each major means (or channel) of transmission can accommodate a wide variety of media.

• types of visual media : 19

Major types of visual media (media that are designed for human visual inspection) include:

Chapter 3. Documentary Scope (Section 3.4)

- paper, and the precursors of paper, such as animal skins (parchment, vellum), wood and tree bark (the source of the word "book"), papyrus (the source of the words "biblio" and "Bible"), and clay, stone, or metallic tablets;
- film, including both microforms for the recording of mostly language texts (microfilm, microfiche, microcards, etc.) and film for photographic images (such as slides, moving pictures, filmstrips, etc.);
- magnetic plastic tape, used for videos;
- electronic media. This is a rapidly evolving heterogeneous collection of digital and analogue media, made of silicon, plastic, and metallic materials, for the storage of computer-readable data, so that they can later be displayed on electronic monitors for visual inspection.

• types of audio media : 20

Aural messages have used the same types of media as visual messages, especially when one remembers the old paper rolls for player pianos and organs. Soundtracks are recorded on film, along with visual images. Magnetic plastic tape has been used for sound cassettes, as well as for visual video recordings. And audio compact disks are made of the same sorts of materials as are CD-ROMs and similar media for visual texts.

• world-wide web as channel for document transmission : 21

Sometimes, the channel of document transmission assumes major importance. The prime example is the world-wide web. The category of "web documents" is based on this ever more important channel, more than on the basis of the electronic nature of the medium, because the same documents can be transmitted via other channels and media, such as CD-ROMs or floppy disks, for which the channel of transmission is the same as for printed books — physical transport by such means as the post or parcel delivery services or by hand.

3.4. Forms, Formats, Genres.

• 22

Here the focus is on the form or shape of the message and its text. At the most basic level, this is the kind of text in which a message is encoded. One major category is language texts, encoded according to the rules and patterns of the world's human languages. Such language texts may be then transmitted either as speech via aural media and channels, or as writing via visual media and channels.

• varieties of texts : 23

In addition to language texts, however, there are musical texts, mathematical and chemical texts, choreographic texts, and the artistic texts created by painters, sculptors, architects, jewelers, and designers of all kinds.

• codes for composition of texts : 24

While the codes (the rules, conventions, patterns) for text composition are well developed and quite formal for human language and also for mathematics, chemistry and music, they are much more fluid in the visual and plastic arts. Nevertheless, the general rule holds, that for a message to pass effectively from its creator to its intended audience, both the sender and the receiver must share, to some extent, an understanding of the code(s) for the representation of meaning. This need does not, however, stop artists from experimenting and stretching the limits of existing codes and creating new ones.

Chapter 3. Documentary Scope (Section 3.4)

• formats, genres and styles in music : 25

Within each major category of text, a wide variety of shapes, forms, formats, and genres have developed over time. In music, for example, we have symphonies, concertos, and tone poems, to mention only a few traditional forms out of thousands. Mixed up with genres are styles such as jazz, blues, rock, and rap, which inspire new and different genres. Some of these, like rap, musicals, and opera, merge musical with language genres.

• formats and genres for language texts : 26

For language texts, we also have the literary genres: essays, poetry, drama, fiction, short stories, and many sub-types. In addition to these literary types, we have narrative treatises, which can come in the shape or form of short articles in periodicals or anthologies, or as long monographic books. There are also charts, tables, diagrams, lists, and dictionary formats all making use of language texts.

• terminology for formats, genres and media : 27

The terminology for formats and media is not rigorously developed. A photograph, for example, really only indicates the method of creation of a visual image, but that image could be of language text, or of anything else. Naming features such as formats and media can be as problematic as naming topics.

• codes for representation of machine-readable texts : 28

At a more technical level, especially within the realm of electronic digital media, there is the added question of the means and methods for encoding text for machine representation. Here we have an exploding array of competing codes. A useful website for keeping track of the thousands of electronic format codes is http:/whatis.com/. This site includes a section called "Every file format in the world," which "briefly describes every file format (or actually the file name extensions for the formats) that we have been able to learn about" (whatis.com Inc. 1998). Here are some examples, limited to format codes with extensions beginning with 'A':

ABK Corel Draw AutoBackup

ACL Corel Draw 6 keyboard accelerator

ACM Used by Windows in the system directory

ACP Microsoft Office Assistant Preview file

ACT Microsoft Office Assistant Actor file

ACV OS/2 drivers that compress and decompress audio data

AD After Dark screensaver

ADB Appointment database used by HP 100LX organizer

ADD OS/2 adapter drivers used in the boot process

ADM After Dark MultiModule screensaver

ADP Used by FaxWorks to do setup for fax modem interaction

ADR After Dark Randomizer screensaver

AFM Adobe font metrics

AF2 ABC Flowchart file

AF3 ABC Flowchart file

AI Adobe Illustrator drawing

AIF Apple Mac AIFF sound

AIFC Similar to AIF

Chapter 3. Documentary Scope (Section 3.4)

AIFF Similar to AIF

AIS ACDSee Image Sequence file

ALB JASC Image Commander album

ALL Arts & Letters Library

AMS Velvert Studio music module (MOD) file

ANC Canon Computer Pattern Maker file that is a selectable list of pattern colors

ANI Animated Cursor

ANS ANSI text

API Application Program Interface file; used by Adobe Acrobat

APR Lotus Approach 97 file

APS Microsoft Visual C++ file

ARC LH ARC (old version) compressed archive

ARI Aristotle audio file

ARJ Robert Jung ARJ compressed archive

ART Xara Studio drawing

ART Canon Crayola art file

ASA Microsoft Visual InterDev file

ASC ASCII text

ASD WinWord AutoSave

ASF Microsoft Advanced Streaming Format file

ASM Assembler language source file

ASP Active Server Page (an HTML file containing a Microsoft server-processed script)

ASP Procomm Plus setup and connection script

AST Claris Works "assistant" file

ASX Cheyenne Backup script

ASX Microsoft Advanced Streaming Redirector file

ATT AT&T Group 4 bitmap

AU UNIX sound file

AVI Microsoft Video for Windows movie

AWD FaxView document

• codes for representation of word-processing texts : 29

Included in this mass of encoding formats are those used by word-processing programs, each of which seems to have its own separate, often incompatible code for machine representation.

• formats versus media in Dublin Core metadata : 30

Distinctions between media and format are often fuzzy. The recent Dublin Core initiative mushes them together into two of its 15 metadata elements, placing formats like "home page, novel, poem, working paper, preprint, technical report, essay, dictionary" in its "resource type" element, while it uses the "format" element for "data representation" codes, such as "html, ASCII, Postscript file, ... or JPEG images," but also for "physical media such as books, serials or other non-electronic media" (Dublin core metadata element set: reference description 1997;

Metadata, Dublin core and USMARC 1997). Note the careless use of the term "serials," which has nothing to do with format or medium, but everything to do with periodicity. See below! (The Dublin Core is discussed in more detail in section 20.5.)

• physical formats versus presentation formats and media formats : 31

Often a distinction is made between physical (or media) formats and presentation formats, with the physical formats grouped with media. Examples of physical formats include slides, filmstrips, and moving pictures for film media; books, pamphlets, broadsides for print-on-paper media; and tape cassettes, vinyl disks, and compact discs (CDs) for audio media. Presentation formats are all the other formats, including genre, that describe the manner in which the message and its text shapes and presents the message.

• multimedia versus multiformats : 32

The new and popular term "multimedia" is another example of rather fuzzy definitions. The medium of the new "multimedia" is almost always electronic and digital, especially via the transmission channel of the world-wide web. What is "multi" is not the media, but the formats that can be combined into single complex documents. Thus in one electronic digital document one may find still (static) visual images, moving visual images and animation, visual language, spoken language (speech), and music in various combinations.

3.5. Periodicity.

• 33

After the complexities of media and formats, periodicity is fairly simple and straightforward, at least at first glance. All documents can be divided into two camps: those that are issued once (called monographs, for "one" or "single" writing) and those that come out in pieces, over time, called serials. The Anglo-American Cataloguing Rules (2002) has just introduced a broader non-monographic category called "continuing resources," to include both traditional serials and "ongoing integrating resources," such as websites that are periodically updated and loose-leaf services. When serials come out with some regular frequency (usually more often than annually), they are called periodicals. Documents in all formats and all media can be monographic or continuing resources, so it is a mistake to associate these periodicity terms with any particular medium or format.

• revised monographs versus serials : 34

Complications crop up with monographs that are revised or reissued, sometimes with great frequency, so that they take on some of the characteristics of serials. Such documents, like annual tax guides, can now be called "integrating resources." Nevertheless, there is an important distinction between a constantly or frequently changing (improved, revised) monograph (now integrating resource) and a document that is issued periodically or serially. Each issue of a periodical or serial is generally completely different, with different articles or images. There may be continuity in sections or columns, but each issue generally has fresh content. This is not the case in constantly revised monographs. Often the changes are quite small and hard to find. Overall, the document is still pretty much the same as the previous version.

• monographic series : 35

Also between monographs and serials are monographic series, which consist of collections of monographs, issued one after another, so that the set is considered a series. Some IR databases will treat such a series as a serial, and each monograph as a single issue of the serial; others will treat each monograph as a separate document, with links to a record for the series.

Chapter 3. Documentary Scope (Sections 3.6)

• monographs versus books : 36

In popular usage, the term "monograph" is sometimes used for "book," but remember that here, in our more technical atmosphere, any document, of any format in any medium, can appear as a monograph, or as a serial, or as a continuing integrating resource. In no way are monographs restricted to print-on-paper book-like documents!

3.6. Intended Audience or Level.

• 37

Here we can distinguish documents that are designed for children of various ages, for young adults, for adults, for beginners in any subject area, for practitioners, or for research scholars, and similar categories of target audiences that a database may choose to cater to.

3.7. Methodological Approaches, Points of View, Biases, Kinds of Treatment.

• 38

These are features of considerable interest to scholars seeking messages relating to research, but the issues of approach are also applicable to all sorts of users seeking all sorts of messages, texts, and documents. A teen-ager seeking information on gay and lesbian issues might well be interested in knowing whether a particular message reflects an official Roman Catholic or a Southern Baptist point of view, as opposed to a secular or "pro-gay" point of view. Information scientists may want to know whether a work on advanced information retrieval techniques is based on experimental research, field research, a literature survey, or the author's expert opinion.

• methodological approaches in literary study : 39

Users of the Modern Language Association's *MLA International bibliography* database are able to seek examples of anthropological, archetypal, deconstructionist, ethical, feminist, formalist, genetic, hermeneutic, historical, impressionistic, Marxist, philosophical, postmodernist, post-structuralist, psychoanalytic, psychological, reader-response, rhetorical, semiotic, sociological, or structuralist approaches (among others!) to the study of literature (MLA Language Association of America 1999).

• biases as searchable features; as non-topical features : 40

Political, social, and economic issues may be addressed from points of view typical of Democrats, Republicans, Communists, Libertarians, socialists, anarchists, environmentalists, pro-lifers, pro-choicers, and so on. In short, this category includes characterizations of the kind of treatments and biases that authors bring to their topics.

3.8. Language.

• 41

Language played an important role in the discussion of formats (with respect to codes and symbols for text representation), but naming the particular language of a linguistic text is so important, that it is usually listed as a separate category. Of course, language characterization is relevant only for language-based messages, texts, and documents.

3.9. Place of Creation, Manufacture, or Publication.

• 42

Documents are often characterized by where they came from. Most commonly users are interested in the place of publication — where a document was issued or made public. Of course, a message and text could be created in one place, placed into a document (manufactured) in another place, and then made public in a third place.

3.10. Time of Creation, Manufacture, or Publication.

• 43

Here we usually refer to the time or date of publication, but this attribute can also refer to the time of creation or manufacture as well. A poem written first in the 17th century could be first published in 1990.

3.11. Specific Documents.

• 44

Sometimes the documentary scope of an IR database is defined simply in terms of a finite list of documents that are included. An IR database consisting of a single document is the extreme example of this situation. More typical examples are some of the IR databases produced by the H. W. Wilson Company (*Readers' guide to periodical literature, Humanities index, Social sciences index*, etc.) in which a stated list of periodicals is included, and no others. In these cases, the documentary scope is described not so much in terms of the characteristics listed thus far, but in terms of the particular documents covered.

3.12. Qualitative Criteria.

• 45

Given a particular subject scope and a particular documentary scope, an IR database can seek to cover everything that falls within the parameters of these scopes, or it can be selective, covering only those messages, texts, and documents that meet some additional qualitative criteria. When selective criteria are applied, they should be described.

• objective qualitative criteria in documentary scope : 46

Sometimes the criteria are objective, such as votes by certain librarians or subscribers, or recipients of awards, or documents receiving a certain number of reviews, or scholarly publications receiving a certain number of citations by other scholars, or scholarly papers that have undergone double-blind refereeing (where the author is not identified to the referees nor the referees to the author).

• biases and points of view in documentary scope : 47

More commonly, the IR database producer is exercising some judgment of quality or appropriateness. A frank discussion of the biases or points of views or preferences of the database producer will then be most helpful. Marcia Bates (1976, p. 19-25) has contributed a thorough analysis of the "principles of selection."

Chapter 3. Documentary Scope (Section 3.13)

3.13. Features Versus Topics.

• 48

As noted in chapter 2 on subject scope (section 2.1), every non-topical feature of messages, texts, and documents can also be a topic of interest to many users. Scholars are very interested in topical discussions of all those methodological approaches listed in section 3.7; other people are interested in topical treatment of every type of format and medium. Linguists (and many others) are interested in all the languages of the world as primary topics, not just as codes and symbols for encoding messages.

• clear distinction between non-topical features versus topics : 49

It is for this reason (i.e., that every non-topical feature of a message, text, or document can also be a topic of significant interest), that it is essential that IR databases make a clear distinction between when a feature is a topic and when it is a non-topical feature of a message, text, or document. When a user wants a message about a Beethoven symphony, we may assume he or she does not want to be presented with the actual symphony itself, either in the form of a score or a sound recording. A person interested in the French language does not want to be confronted with every text in French! A student who must read about the characteristics of lyric poetry may or may not want to see any actual lyric poems. A Ph.D. student who wants to read about the characteristics of dissertations most likely will not be happy to be presented with every dissertation in an IR database.

• 50

So in the design of your IR database, try to create a clear distinction between messages, texts and documents that are about certain topics versus messages, texts, and documents that manifest or exhibit those very same features. Is a message about dissertations? Or is it a dissertation? It could be both — a dissertation about dissertations!

3.14. Our Examples.
3.14.1. A Book Index.

• 51

As already stated, the documentary scope for an IR database that provides access to a single document is determined entirely by the characteristics of that single document. In such a case, an explicit statement of documentary scope serves little purpose. Nevertheless, this book can be described as a narrative treatise (primary presentation format) with incidental illustrations, mostly of indexes and web pages (secondary formats). It is printed on paper and bound as a book (medium, physical format). It is a monograph (periodicity) in English (language) designed for students and practitioners of library and information science (target audience). It has been published in the United States (place). The time is 2003 (publication date), although the book was created over a period of several years (1995-2003). Because this text was created on a computer, this "book" may also be made available in electronic media. Consequently the design of the IR database for this book will include both a traditional printed back-of-the-book index and electronic indexes, which may be used with a machine-readable version of the book or the printed paper version.

Chapter 3. Documentary Scope (Section 3.14.2)

3.14.2. An Indexing and Abstracting Service.

• 52

Here, the documentary scope is vitally important, because it will describe and guide the search for and the selection and acquisition of documents for the IR database. Also, it will provide potential users with a clear statement of the types of documents that can be retrieved, as well as non-topical searchable features. Here is a possible documentary scope for our indexing and abstracting service:

• media in documentary scope for indexing and abstracting services : 53

• *media.* We shall attempt to cover all media in which documents related to research and practice tend to appear, so this will include print on paper, electronic/digital (e.g., the growing phenomena of electronic journals and other internet resources, as well as CD-ROMs and direct access online files), video and film (e.g., for training materials), and audio media, for training materials and also lectures. The medium of documents will be noted, so that media will be a searchable feature. This will include media formats (physical formats as opposed to presentation formats), such as slides, filmstrips, and moving pictures (for film media); books, pamphlets, broadsides and even punched cards (for print-on-paper media), etc. For electronic digital documents, encoding data that is necessary to display the message will be included.

• formats in documentary scope for indexing and abstracting services : 54

• *formats and genres.* We shall endeavor to cover a wide variety of presentation style formats and genres related to professional research and practice, e.g., research reports, practice reports, committee reports, training materials, standards, codes of practice, conference proceedings, lectures, letters, reviews, news reports, theses, dissertations, databases and other reference tools, and even advertisements. (Advertisements are not often addressed in IR databases, but they are of interest to practitioners, and also to historians!) The formats and genres of messages, texts, and documents will be noted, so that at least the prominent types will be searchable features.

• periodicity in documentary scope for indexing and abstracting services : 55

• *periodicity.* As implied under formats and genres, we shall cover both continuing resources (serials, periodicals, annuals, series, integrating resources) and monographic publications.

• audience and levels of treatment in documentary scope for indexing and abstracting services : 56

• *audience or level of treatment*. Messages and texts will be aimed at students, practitioners, scholars and researchers. We will not attempt to cover materials for the general public, e.g., feature stories in newspapers or general magazines, or material for children or for students in grades K-12 on "how to use libraries or find information." However, reviews of such material, of interest to school librarians, will be included. Intended audience and level of treatment will be noted for searching purposes.

• language in documentary scope for indexing and abstracting services : 57

• *language.* This will be a multilingual IR database, with no restriction on language. However, spin-off databases restricted to major languages, e.g., English, Chinese, Spanish, French, German, Russian, etc., will be available. The great majority of messages will be represented in language texts, but other kinds of texts will not be excluded. Examples might include photographs or portraits of notable librarians, photographs or architectural drawings of notable buildings, etc. Language will be a searchable feature.

• place of publication in documentary scope for indexing and abstracting services : 58

• *place of publication*. There shall be no restrictions as to place of creation or publication. Place of publication will be a searchable feature.

Chapter 3. Documentary Scope (Section 3.14.2)

• **time of publication in documentary scope for indexing and abstracting services : 59**

- *time of publication.* There shall be no restrictions as to time of creation or publication, although efforts will be made to include documents within the year of publication. Year of publication will be a searchable feature.

• **specific documents in documentary scope for indexing and abstracting services : 60**

- *specific documents.* Although the documentary scope obviously cannot be restricted to a list of particular publications, a list of important serials in library and information science will be maintained, and these publications will be comprehensively indexed. The titles of all source documents will be searchable. Similarly, documents may also be searched by names of publishers.

• **qualitative criteria in documentary scope for indexing and abstracting services : 61**

- *qualitative criteria.* This indexing and abstracting service is designed to be a comprehensive IR database that lists all documents within its documentary and subject scope. Qualitative judgments will be encouraged on the part of indexers and users, however, and will be recorded, but they will not be used to eliminate any document from inclusion. Later on, criteria related to quality, or at least popularity or level of use, will be suggested as the basis for determining level and approach to indexing. Users may search for qualitative comments and evidence in a "quality" field of the database record, but unlike other searchable features, there will be no standard method for describing quality.

• **searchable features in documentary scope for indexing and abstracting services : 62**

- *additional searchable features.* All of the features listed so far will be searchable, at least to some extent. The following additional features will also be searchable:

• **authorship in documentary scope for indexing and abstracting services : 63**

- *authors and types of authors.* When authors appear with some frequency in the IR database (a threshold will be established), separate author records will be created for recording whatever biographical data may be available, such as birth and death dates, birthplace, citizenship, ethnicity or nationality, gender, sexual orientation, families (partners, parents, offspring, etc.), professional affiliations, offices held, positions held, etc. These types of data may contribute to an enhanced understanding of possible points of view. Analogous data, as appropriate, will also be collected for corporate bodies.

• **document titles in documentary scope for indexing and abstracting services : 64**

- *titles of documents,* including parallel titles in other languages, subtitles, and conventional titles.

• **methodological approaches and points of view in documentary scope for indexing and abstracting services : 65**

- *methodological approaches, points of view, biases, kinds of treatment.* For important documents (to be determined later based on evidence of popularity or use), an attempt will be made to identify significant methodological approaches, points of view, biases, or kinds of treatment evidenced in messages. Of course, some of these features will be topics for some messages, and in those cases, they will be indexed as topics. But often they are not the topics of messages, but they characterize the authors' treatment of topics. In these cases, they will be noted in a special field for kind of treatment.

• **terminology for non-topical features : 66**

The naming of non-topical features can be as problematic as the naming of topics — a main focus of several sections yet to come. For most of the non-topical features listed here, a thesaurus of terms will be created, to encourage some uniformity in the use of terminology. Included will be terminology for media, formats and genres, continuing resources, integrating resources, periodicals and serials, audiences and levels of treatment, language, places, publishers, authors, and author characteristics.

3.14.3. A Full-Text Encyclopedia/Digital Library.

• 67

Our full-text encyclopedia/digital library will consist of articles especially commissioned for this publication, as well as previously published items of high quality and interest. Here are the features of messages, texts, and documents that will be included:

- *medium*. All articles will be distributed in a digital-based medium capable of displaying linguistic and visual material and of playing sound material.
- *format and genre*. Articles will be in the form of essays, which may be accompanied by bibliographies, pictures, and excerpts from video and sound recordings.
- *periodicity*. All commissioned articles will, by definition, be monographic documents. Reproduced publications can come from both monographic and serial publications, e.g., chapters in books, articles in periodicals. Excerpts will also come from monographic (for the most part) video and sound recordings. The encyclopedia/digital library itself will be a continuing integrating resource, in that individual articles may be updated as needed to cover new material.
- *audience or level*. Articles will be aimed at students and practitioners of library and information science.
- *language*. This will be an English language encyclopedia/ digital library. All articles not originally in English will be translated, and only the English translation will be included.
- *place of publication*. No restrictions as to place of creation or publication of reproduced materials.
- *time of publication*. No restrictions as to time of creation or publication of reproduced materials.
- *qualitative criteria*. Editors will select or commission the best possible treatment of each topic within the subject scope. Qualitative criteria will include accuracy, clarity, timeliness, and citation of important background publications.
- *searchable features*. Within the IR database, users will be able to search for articles on the basis of the following non-topical features: authors, kinds of authors, titles, formats, original place and time of publication (for reproduced articles). Certain articles will be characterized by methodological approach or kind of treatment and point of view.

Chapter 4. Documentary Domain

Contents of Chapter 4
4.1. Primary Versus Secondary Sources.
4.2. Monitoring and Covering Documentary Domain.
4.3. Our Examples.
4.3.1. A Book Index.
4.3.2. An Indexing and Abstracting Service.
4.3.3. A Full-Text Encyclopedia/Digital Library.

• impact of documentary domain on coverage of IR databases : 1

Documentary domain is the territory (domain) from which documents are gathered for an IR database. Two IR databases can have identical subject scopes and identical documentary scopes, yet provide very different coverage because of different documentary domains. An IR database that obtains documents only from the holdings of one library, for example, will have very different coverage compared to an IR database that combs the entire world for documents that fit its subject and documentary scopes.

• views of Bates (Marcia J.) on documentary domain : 2

Marcia Bates promoted the important concept of documentary domain in her 1976 article on "Rigorous systematic bibliography." What she describes as "bibliography" in 1976 had been incorporated into our definition of IR databases by the end of the 20th century. Bates defines documentary domain as "the bibliographical territory searched. Stating domain would in practice mean stating the locations searched in the process of compiling the bibliography" (p. 17).

• views of Wilson (Patrick) on documentary domain : 3

Bates took the idea of documentary domain from Patrick Wilson's book *Two kinds of power: an essay on bibliographical control* (1968). Wilson describes documentary domain as "the set of items from which the contents of the work, the items actually listed, are selected or drawn" (Wilson, p. 59). He continues: "The domain, then, consists of the set of items about which the maker of the instrument is prepared to make a guarantee, the set of items from which he will guarantee to have drawn all that meet the requirements for inclusion" (Wilson, p. 60).

• defining characteristics of IR databases : 4

Before leaving Bates and Wilson, it is interesting to note that Wilson lists only five characteristics of "bibliographic instruments" (IR databases) that need to be specified in order to describe them fully. His five characteristics have now grown to 20 fundamental attributes, which form the basis of chapters 2 through 21 of this book. Here are his five:

- domain;

- selection principles (following Bates called "scope" in this book and divided into subject scope and documentary scope);

- bibliographic units (here called documentary units);

- information fields (the data provided for each message, text and document, which in this book is discussed in chapters 14 on surrogation and 20 on record format);

- organization (which in this book is covered in chapters 11 on displayed and non-displayed indexes, 12 on syntax, and 17 on arrangement of displayed indexes).

Chapter 4. Documentary Domain (Section 4.1)

• principles for selection of documents for IR databases : 5

To Wilson's five characteristics, Bates added a separate specification for scope in her 1976 article, so that "selection principles" (qualitative criteria in this book) could focus more directly on how items are selected for non-comprehensive IR databases. In this book, qualitative criteria are treated more briefly as one of many components of documentary scope. As noted in our discussion of qualitative criteria in section 3.12, the much fuller treatment of selection principles by Bates in her 1976 article is still highly relevant.

4.1. Primary Versus Secondary Sources.

• 6

Closely related to the territory covered to obtain the documents for an IR database is the question of whether IR database producers actually obtain the documents that they list and base their description of these documents on the actual documents themselves. Some IR databases simply copy information about documents from other sources. The actual documents are considered "primary sources" for the description of messages, texts, and documents. All other sources are considered "secondary."

• secondary sources for IR databases : 7

It is quite possible to create a creditable IR database without ever actually seeing the documents that are described and indexed. Instead, the database producer can find and use document descriptions found in other IR databases, such as MARC records in a cataloging utility database, and abstracts, citations, and descriptors in indexing and abstracting services. In this case, the database is based not on primary sources, but on secondary sources, and a large part of the credibility or authority of this new IR database will depend on the credibility and authority of its secondary sources. Therefore, all secondary sources should be identified, both in a general way, and also specifically for each document record in the new database. The identification of any secondary sources used to compile the IR database is thus an important part of the documentary domain description.

• 8

Many IR databases will strive to base their description and indexing of documents on the documents themselves — on primary sources, but occasionally an important document will be hard to obtain. An occasional record based on secondary sources is quite permissible, as long as the database is up front about this, and the source is identified.

4.2. Monitoring and Covering Documentary Domain.

• 9

IR database producers should describe in some detail the documentary domain covered in seeking appropriate documents, and how they go about finding and acquiring the documents that fall within their documentary and subject scopes. Some possible strategies include:

- monitoring the acquisitions of major libraries — these libraries should be identified.
- monitoring other IR databases that cover the same or similar documentary and subject scopes. These source databases too should be listed. They may include very general IR databases, such as *Books in Print* and national bibliographies, and specialized databases.

Chapter 4. Documentary Domain (Section 4.3)

- contact with a network of advisors, e.g., practitioners, teachers, researchers, who collect documents or notify the database producer of documents. This may be a local or an international network.

• role of documentary domain descriptions : 10

The documentary domain description is an important indicator for users who are concerned about the coverage offered by an IR database. Obviously, an IR database on HIV/AIDS (or any other topic) that is limited to materials owned by one particular library, no matter how comprehensive the library may be, cannot expect to be as thorough as an IR database that strives for worldwide documentary domain coverage through links with many major libraries, publishers, research institutes, scholars, researchers, and activists.

4.3. Our Examples.
4.3.1. A Book Index.

• 11

Like documentary scope, documentary domain is not an issue for an IR database for a single publication. Such an IR database, including a traditional back-of-the-book index, will be based directly on the document for which the IR database is designed. This document will constitute a primary source for the database. As you know, the primary source for our exemplar book index is this book you are reading.

4.3.2. An Indexing and Abstracting Service.

• 12

In contrast, the documentary domain is most important for our indexing and abstracting service. All indexing will be based on the actual documents — primary sources, except in those rare cases when the existence of a document is known, but the database producer has not been able to obtain a copy. In this case, a reputable secondary source can be used, and will be fully acknowledged and cited.

• 13

The search and acquisitions domain for this indexing and abstracting service will be the entire world. This world-wide documentary domain will be combed (covered) using all of the techniques suggested in section 4.2 above:

- monitoring the acquisitions of major libraries. Major collections will be identified in libraries around the world and arrangements will be made to receive their acquisitions lists in return for sharing pre-publication records prepared for this database. These libraries will be credited in the documentary domain description.

- monitoring IR databases that cover the same or similar documentary and subject scopes as this database. All major databases around the world that cover library and information science will be identified and regularly monitored. Cooperative agreements will be sought where possible, although some databases may be more comfortable with competition than cooperation. The databases that are regularly monitored will be named in the documentary domain description.

- contact with a network of advisors. The database producer will seek to enlist the help of leading practitioners and scholars around the world, encouraging them to regularly alert the producer of important publications, especially those that may fall through the cracks of more routine surveillance. In addition, all library and information science associations around the world will be invited to set up advisory committees to assist in coverage of documents related to their interests and concerns. All cooperating persons and associations will be listed in the documentary domain description. Contact must be maintained at least on an annual basis.

4.3.3. A Full-Text Encyclopedia/Digital Library.

• 14

Here the documentary domain refers to the sources of the articles that will be reproduced or commissioned for the encyclopedia/digital library. Our goal is to find or commission the best articles possible from around the world. To do this, the database producer will need a network of advisors. Editors of the major journals would be a likely source. Citation indexes can also be used to discover the most cited articles and authors. The techniques used for identifying articles and authors will be included in the documentary domain description.

Chapter 5. Display Media

Contents of Chapter 5
5.1. Paper.
5.1.1. Card Files.
5.1.2. Books.
5.1.3. Optical Coincidence (Peek-a-Boo) Retrieval on Cards.
5.2. Microforms.
5.3. Electronic Media.
5.3.1. Online Databases.
5.3.2. CD-ROM and Other Machine-Readable Disks.
5.3.3. World-Wide Web.
5.4. Codes and Symbols.
5.5. Our Examples.
5.5.1. A Book Index.
5.5.2. An Indexing and Abstracting Service.
5.5.3. A Full-Text Encyclopedia/Digital Library.

• IR databases as messages, texts, and documents : 1

IR Databases are themselves documents as well, sharing many of the characteristics of messages, texts, and documents that were discussed in chapter 3 on documentary scope.

• impact of media on design options for IR databases : 2

In designing an IR database, one of the most crucial decisions will be choosing the most effective medium (or media) for the presentation of the database to users. Like many other design decisions, this one will impact many other options, such as the kinds of searching and browsing that can be offered to users, the kinds of indexing that can be supported, and how the results of searches can be displayed. Many IR databases are presented to users not just in one medium, but in a variety of media, and in a variety of physical or media formats.

• text options for IR databases : 3

As you know from discussions about messages and texts in part I and also in chapter 3 on documentary scope, all messages (including IR database messages) must be encoded in text that can be recorded in a medium, so in this chapter we will also consider options for IR database text types. Human language texts are the most common types of text for IR databases, but many databases, depending on their subject and documentary scopes, may need to also include musical texts, mathematical texts, chemical texts, choreographic texts, and varieties of image texts.

• media options for IR databases : 4

IR databases have been and are displayed in a wide variety of media. The main choices are paper (card files, books), microforms, and electronic media (CD-ROMs, websites, online databases).

5.1. Paper.

• paper as favored medium for IR databases : 5

From the invention of printing with movable type (15th century) through the 1960s, paper was the favored medium for IR databases. During these centuries, IR database producers gained experience in designing effective layouts for all kinds of IR databases on paper, including bibliographies, indexes, catalogs, indexing and abstracting services, thesauri, encyclopedias, handbooks, manuals, dictionaries, and other reference works.

• paper formats for IR databases : 6

Within the print-on-paper category, the two chief media or physical formats have been (1) card files and (2) books.

5.1.1. Card Files.

• card files as favored medium for IR databases : 7

The use of cards as a medium for bibliographies and indexes, but especially for library catalogs, was an innovation developed in the mid-19th century. Card-based files rapidly became the dominant choice for large continuing catalogs and indexes, especially in the United States. The chief advantage was that they could be constantly updated. The chief disadvantage was that they were difficult and expensive to reproduce, so that in most cases, there was only one copy of each catalog or index.

• disadvantages of card files as medium for IR databases : 8

The chief advantage of card files became a major disadvantage in the age of computers. Yes, they could be constantly updated, but only by hand, and the expensive, boring, error-prone, laborious task of inserting new cards, revising old cards, and removing superseded cards was no match for fast and efficient electronic updating of computer files. Furthermore, the card catalogs of large libraries became quite enormous and expensive to maintain, quite apart from updating them. Old card stock deteriorated, especially for those entries representing popular materials or topics, thumbed by countless searchers in pursuit of useful messages. And card catalog cabinets took up lots and lots of very valuable space.

• views of Baker (Nicholson) on card catalogs : 9

As card files pass from the scene, everyone should read the passionate memorial to their glories by Nicholson Baker in his long *New Yorker* article, "Discards: annals of scholarship" (1994).

5.1.2. Books.

• advantages of books as medium for IR databases : 10

The chief advantage of the printed book (including book-form serial issues) as a medium for bibliographies, indexes, catalogs, indexing and abstracting services, handbooks, encyclopedias, dictionaries, directories and a wide range of similar IR databases is the ease of duplication for wide distribution. The chief disadvantage is that as soon as the IR database is published, it is out of date and cannot be updated until a new edition is published (except by hand annotation of individual copies).

• 11

While the card medium is rapidly fading from the current IR database scene, book-form IR databases are still widely published and the printed books remains a viable medium to be considered in the design of a new IR database. For the user, the chief advantages consist of the ability to consult the database without intervening technology, the high visual resolution possible with print on paper, and the relatively large displays possible on two-page spreads, far surpassing in visual scope anything yet possible on electronic display screens. Another advantage is the immediacy and directness of the display medium, which makes it easy for the user to quickly get an overall image of the IR database simply by seeing the size of the volume (or set of volumes, or

Chapter 5. Display Media (Section 5.1.2)

section within a volume) and by scanning a table of contents plus a few sample pages. Another important advantage is the possibility of well-designed index displays for which terms may be selected and precoordinated for effective communication. In such indexes, users can scan and explore possibilities. They do not have to think up in advance appropriate search terms all by themselves. Of course, similar displayed indexes are also possible, and are becoming more popular, in electronic media.

• **advantages of paper as medium for reading : 12**

In the October 1997 issue of *Communications of the ACM* (a principal journal of the Association for Computing Machinery), Richard C. Hsu and William E. Mitchell presented a "viewpoint" article proclaiming, in its title, that "After 400 years, print is still superior." Here is a summary of their points:

- Ergonomics: "it takes a lot of manual dexterity to operate a mouse, buttons, scroll bars, and the like. Books are, by comparison, a low-dexterity device."
- Contrast: the sharp contrast between black print and white (or near white) paper is much sharper than anything available electronically.
- Resolution: "The number of pixels on a printed page is far greater than on any computer monitor, which results in both lower eyestrain and higher 'data density.'"
- Weight: Books are lighter than even the lightest lap-top computer.
- Viewing angle: Laptop screens are hard to read unless you maintain a rather narrow range of viewing angles.
- Durability: A good book will survive spilled coffee, crashes, and similar mis-treatment.
- Cost: Even an expensive book costs a lot less than a computer.
- Life expectancy: Many 16th century printed books are still around.
- Electrical power requirements: Books have none, assuming light is available.
- Editorial quality: The limited capacity of paper encourages succinctness and clarity.
- Search capability: Finally, electronic media have an advantage! At least these authors (Hsu and Mitchell) think so.
- Intangibles: Books don't change, no matter how long you wait to return to them. "Electronic data, particularly on the Web, is nebulous, ephemeral, prone to unexpected editing or complete disappearance."

• **reading versus searching on electronic media : 13**

For the design of IR databases, the key issues appear to be search options on the one hand, and comfortable perusal on the other hand. This contrast is well summarized by James Fallows in his 1996 *Atlantic monthly* article, "Navigating the galaxies." He says, "... the act of reading on the internet seems destined to remain very different from reading a printed page. Reading from even the nicest computer screen is so unpleasant -- and the expectation is so strong that the computer will always be doing something more active than just displaying text -- that computers will remain better suited to jumping from topic to topic than to the sustained intellectual, artistic, or emotional experience that print can provide" (p. 105).

• **paper versus electronic media as media for IR databases : 14**

Thus, IR databases designed to encourage prolonged, leisurely perusal might better be placed on print media, while IR databases designed for quick and effective retrieval of messages (for later perusal) can well be placed on electronic media.

Chapter 5. Display Media (Section 5.1.3)

• cost of electronic media versus paper : 15

Cost is a growing advantage for electronic media as well. Yes, a single monographic book may be cheaper on paper, but large and ever growing IR databases are extremely expensive to print on multiple paper copies, and like the card catalog, they take up lots and lots of expensive space. As the cost of print on paper keeps going up, the cost of electronic storage and retrieval keeps going down.

• electronic media as standard for IR databases : 16

Now and for the foreseeable future, electronic media have become the standard media for IR databases. Almost all IR databases are now produced on electronic media, even when they are still presented on paper media. The only possible exceptions are the indexes of the few back-of-the-book indexers who still use cards or notebooks for their indexing work. Certainly most human indexers have moved to computers to take advantage of many useful programs that help take much of the drudgery out of indexing (such as sorting, formatting, spell-checking, etc.). There are a few libraries as well that still maintain card catalogs, but many of the cards they use are now produced by computer programs, extracting, formatting and printing catalog records from electronic IR databases.

• paper as medium for special types of IR databases : 17

Paper media will be reserved for special types of IR databases, most especially for those that are designed to provide access to particular print-on-paper volumes, and for monographic bibliographies on special topics.

5.1.3. Optical Coincidence (Peek-a-Boo) Retrieval on Cards.

• postcoordinate indexing systems on paper media : 18

Almost invariably, IR databases on paper media will feature displayed indexes, designed for visual inspection and scanning. This was not always the case. For a short period between the end of World War II and the wide availability of electronic media, IR database producers experimented with paper-based postcoordinate indexing systems that could support the same kind of boolean searches that are common today in electronic databases. A prime example is the optical coincidence or "peek-a-boo" system.

• peek-a-boo (optical coincidence) retrieval systems : 19

In the optical coincidence or "peek-a-boo" system, cards approximately a foot square were used to represent index terms or descriptors for topics or features, including names of authors. After a document was indexed, the cards for each term assigned to the document were pulled from an alphabetical file and the document was recorded on these cards by drilling a small hole to represent the document number. On each card was a grid with 100 positions along the vertical and horizontal axes, so that 10,000 unique positions were available to represent 10,000 documents. Each document was given a two part number, corresponding to the vertical and horizontal axes, so that document number 59-23 would get a hole drilled exactly 59 spaces down from the top and 23 spaces to the right of the left margin. A highly calibrated drill press was used to make these holes. See figure 5.1 for an operational example of a "peek-a-boo" optical coincidence system, with equipment manufactured by the Jonker Corporation, circa 1967.

Captions for Figure 5.1. Photographs of the Jonker peek-a-boo IR system, Rutgers University

1. Two documents to be entered into the peek-a-boo system. Each will be assigned a document number, usually in the order that it is processed. In this case, the numbers will be 80-40 and 80-41

Chapter 5. Display Media (Section 5.1.3)

respectively. The documents will be shelved or filed according to these numbers for later retrieval.

On the left is: "The lesbian and gay liberation movement in the Presbyterian Church (U.S.A.), 1974-1996," by James D. Anderson. *Journal of homosexuality.* 34(2): 37-65; 1997. It will get the following descriptors:

```
gay liberation movement
lesbian liberation movement
Presbyterian Church (U.S.A.)
homosexuality
religion
United States
```

The second document, on the right, is: *In every classroom: the report of the President's Select Committee for Lesbian and Gay Concerns.* James D. Anderson, chairperson. Ronald A. Nieberding, editor. New Brunswick, NJ: Office of Student Life Policy and Services, Rutgers, The State University; c1989. 107 p. It will get the following descriptors:

```
gay liberation movement
lesbian liberation movement
Rutgers University
homosexuality
higher education
New Jersey
```

Peek-a-boo cards are pulled from the descriptor card file for each of these descriptors. If there is no card, a new one is created. In the photo are cards for:

```
Rutgers University (on the light box)
homosexuality
gay liberation movement
Presbyterian Church (U.S.A.)
```

2. All the descriptor cards for each document are placed in the tray of the Peek-a-boo drilling machine.

3. The drill is moved to the vertical and horizontal coordinates using the wheels on the right side of the drilling machine. Notice the coordinate numbers in the little windows: 80 in the top window (for the vertical coordinate) and 40 in the lower window on the left side (for the horizontal coordinate). Once the drill is set, a hole is drilled precisely at this point, representing the document.

4. Later, at the retrieval stage, all the cards representing the descriptors in a query are placed on the light box. Here we have cards for "gay liberation movement" (on top) and, underneath it, "religion." The light will shine through when these two cards have a hole at the same place, with the same coordinates, representing the same document. The light should shine through at coordinates 80-40, representing the article on the history of the gay liberation movement in the Presbyterian Church. The calibrated ruler helps the user determine the coordinates where light shines through. Using the coordinate numbers 80-40, the user can go to the document file and retrieve this document.

5. Anderson stands next to the drilling machine.

Chapter 5. Display Media (Section 5.1.3)

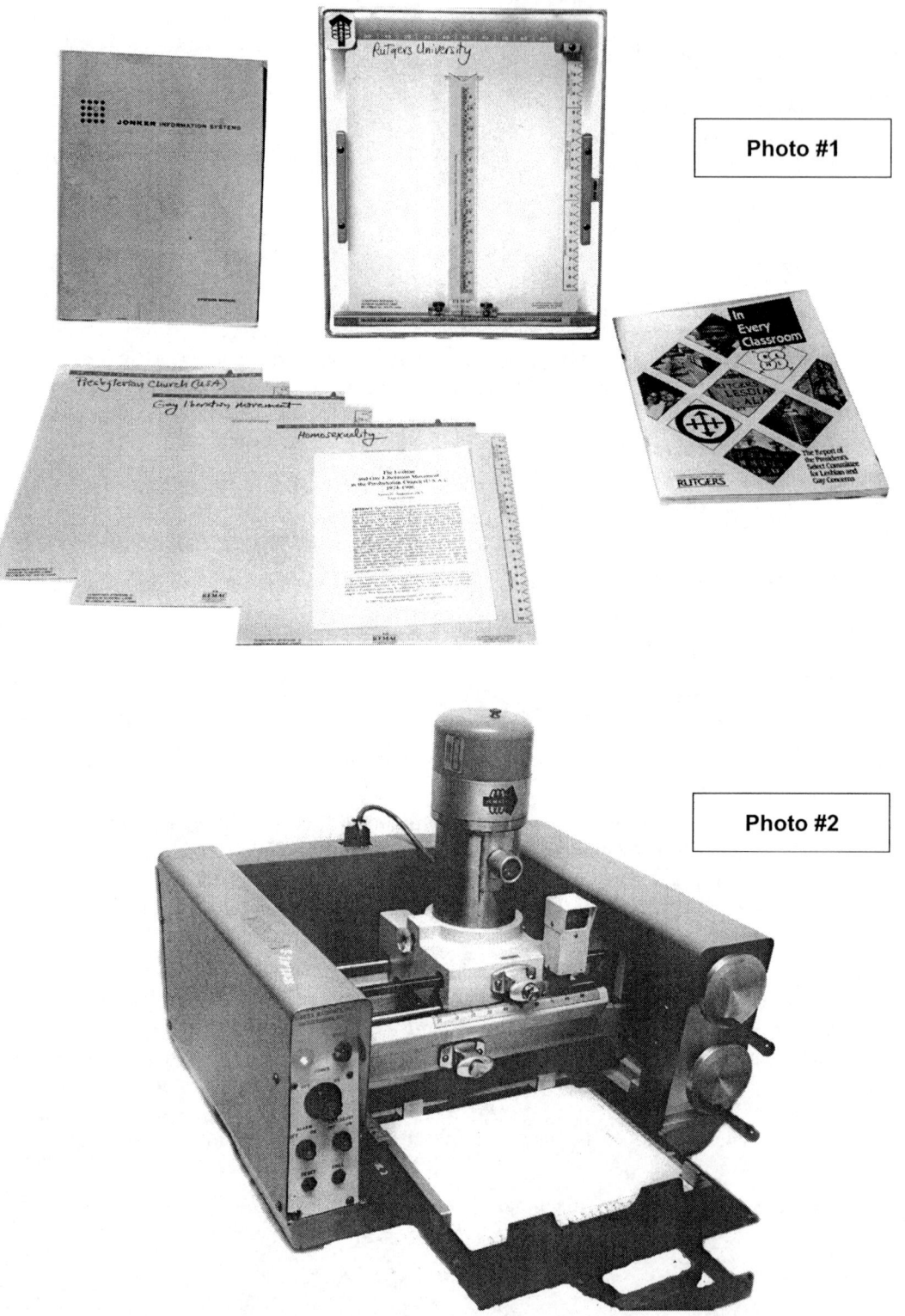

Figure 5.1. Photographs of the Jonker peek-a-boo IR system, Rutgers University.

Photos by Ed Martin. Printed with permission.

Chapter 5. Display Media (Section 5.1.3)

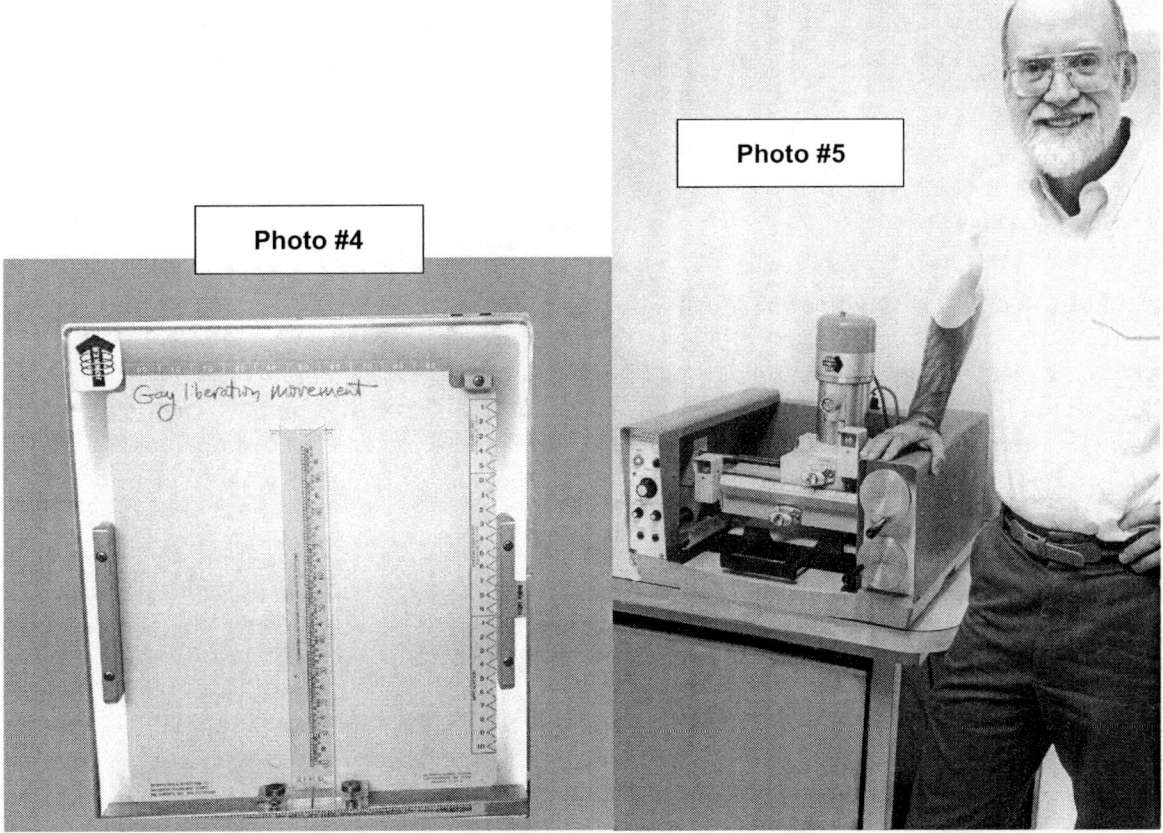

Figure 5.1. Photographs of the Jonker peek-a-boo IR system, Rutgers University (continued). Photos by Ed Martin. Printed with permission.

Chapter 5. Display Media (Section 5.2)

• **boolean searches on peek-a-boo (optical coincidence) retrieval systems : 20**

At retrieval time, a searcher would pull the cards for authors, features or topics of interest and lay them together on a light box -- a small box with a translucent top and a light inside. Wherever the light shone through all the cards, there was a hole standing for a document that shared all the features or topics represented by the individual cards. This was a boolean "AND" search. For a boolean "OR" search, each card would be placed on the light box one at a time, and the document numbers identified.

• **21**

Later in chapter 12 on syntax, we will ponder the question of why boolean searching was the first approach introduced for computer matching of search statements against message, text, or document records or full text in electronic IR databases. The likely reason is that boolean searching was already fairly common and well established. Almost always, the first step in automation in every field is simply to program computers to do, or to support, the practices already in place.

5.2. Microforms.

• **computer-output microfilm as medium for IR databases : 22**

For many decades, microfilm, microfiche, and other microforms have been used as an economical means for reproducing large collections of materials. For a short period of time, mostly in the 1970s, indexes and catalogs were displayed on "computer-output microfilm." This was during the period when large indexes and catalogs were produced in computer-based databases, but direct display of these indexes via electronic media was not yet feasible. Everyone is glad that this period passed rather quickly! Nevertheless, some large indexes are still occasionally produced on one of the microforms, because this is still an economical way to reproduce large bodies of material.

5.3. Electronic Media.

• **unit of manipulation in IR databases : 23**

The great advantage of electronic media for the display and consultation of IR databases is the small size of the unit of manipulation. In print and microform media, the data related to messages, texts, and documents is locked in place, and only elements of the media themselves (e.g., cards, pages, fiche) can be manipulated. The comparatively small unit of manipulation was a chief advantage of the card index or catalog -- each entry was on a separate card, which could be independently manipulated. A single entry could be added, updated, or removed without disturbing the rest of the catalog or index.

• **unit of manipulation in electronic media : 24**

In electronic media, at least for digitized text (where each text symbol is represented by a separate set of computer symbols), each individual computer bit (equivalent to a zero or a one, or an on or off electrical signal) can be manipulated. These very small units are not of much use or interest, so we move up past the byte (usually representing an individual text character, such as a letter of the alphabet or a numeral) to the level of the word. It is the possibility of manipulating each and every word in language text that permits electronic searching of databases by means of combinations of words entered in any order in a search statement.

Chapter 5. Display Media (Section 5.3.1)

• non-displayed searching in electronic media : 25

Thus electronic media support computer matching of search statements against indexes, database records, and full text that have been placed in digital form. Such searching can be called "non-displayed" because the terms and indexes that are matched by the computer are not displayed to the human searcher. Instead, search statements are presented to a search engine and retrieved records are presented to the user. Displayed indexes, which allow users to scan precoordinated entries representing messages, texts, and documents, are also feasible on electronic media, and are becoming increasingly popular, especially for the non-professional searcher. Many databases offer both types of access.

• types of electronic media for IR databases : 26

The major types of electronic media and their delivery systems (channels of transmission) for IR databases are online databases, CD-ROMs and similar machine-readable disks, and the world-wide web.

5.3.1. Online Databases.

• 27

For online databases, access is provided, via communication lines, to a central database. The chief advantage of this approach is that the user always has access to the latest, most up-to-date version of the database. However, the content of the IR database is separated from its presentation to the user. Different vendors may present the same database, using their own interface software. This means that the way the database is presented to users may vary considerably from vendor to vendor. (Chapter 19 deals with search and browsable interfaces for IR databases.)

5.3.2. CD-ROM and Other Machine-Readable Disks.

• 28

Machine-readable disks of various sorts (new types are constantly being developed) permit the publication of electronic IR databases, along with an electronic display interface, for easy, inexpensive, and wide-spread distribution. The end-user of electronic databases on such disks often cannot tell the difference, but these publication media share a chief disadvantage of their printed book counterparts. They are out of date as soon as they are published. Unlike online media, they are never up-to-date!

5.3.3. World-Wide Web.

• 29

The world-wide web (www) is fast becoming one of the most popular transmission channels for electronic messages, texts, and documents, including IR databases. The hypertext format for web documents is very conducive to effective information retrieval, because it supports direct links to related documents, IR database records, or index entries. Many online databases are now available via the www.

5.4. Codes and Symbols.

• nature of codes and symbols for texts : 30

Closely related to the medium on which messages are recorded is the kind of symbols used to represent the message in the form of a text and the rules that give meaning to these symbols. The message that you are reading right now consists of sequences of alphabetic letters, occasional numerals, spaces, and punctuation marks. These symbols have no inherent meaning in and of themselves. By itself, an 'A' or a 'B' has no meaning. Their meaning comes from a social convention that ties certain sounds to these symbols so that they can be used to represent speech. These social conventions, or rules, are called codes, and they include all the rules for presenting the English language in written form. Similar rules exist for other human languages.

• varieties of codes and symbols for texts : 31

Codes and symbols used to represent human speech in various languages are by no means the only types of symbols and codes used to represent messages. Derek W. Langridge, in his wonderful little book on classification (1992), identifies three categories of code and symbol systems for the representation of messages (p. 28): (1) "pictorial, such as drawings, maps and plans"; (2) "mathematical, including formulae and statistics"; and (3) "languages, such as English, French and German." Each of these categories use symbols, and the symbols are given meaning through "codes" that reflect social agreement. But this list is incomplete. There are several other well-developed systems for representing special types of messages. Musical notation is perhaps the most notable, but dance choreography also has a "writing" system, a set of symbols and a code for recording dance steps, and chemistry has a well-developed system for representing the composition of molecules. Symbols and codes are also used in painting, sculpture and similar arts, but here, the symbols and conventions used for communication are less codified and much more idiosyncratic, developed by each artist or by movements or schools of artists.

• codes and symbols for IR databases : 32

The point of all this is that in addition to a medium, a message (including messages in IR databases and their various indexes) must make use of symbols and of codes to give the symbols meaning. Most IR databases use the codes and symbols for written human languages, but there is growing interest in image databases. Designers of IR databases for the retrieval of non-language-based messages (related, for example, to dance, music, mathematics, or the fine arts) may need to use the symbols and codes appropriate to these types of message. In most cases, language-based messages will also be used to represent and describe non-language-based messages, but often there are advantages for direct representation of the original messages.

5.5. Our Examples.
5.5.1. A Book Index.

• multimedia for book indexes : 33

Our book index is to be published on paper, attached to the book to which it is designed to provide access. This index will also be designed for possible electronic publication as well, because publishers are beginning to publish books in both media. Sometimes multimedia publication is simultaneous, but a more cautious approach is to first wait until a print-on-paper book goes out of print, then to make it available on computer disks or via the world-wide web. Note the use of "multimedia" in this paragraph. Publishing the same text in multiple media is true "multimedia," as opposed to the common use of this term, which as pointed out in chapter 3 on documentary scope, usually is meant to indicate the integration of multiple text styles (language-based, musical, speech-based, or image-based texts) in multiple formats or genres in a single document in a single (!) electronic medium.

5.5.2. An Indexing and Abstracting Service.

• 34

Our indexing and abstracting service, like so many of the major comprehensive IR databases, will be published electronically, issued as an online database via multiple vendors, on CD-ROMs, and via the world-wide web. It will also be issued, at least for a time, on paper, issued monthly, with annual and quinquennial cumulations. The phase-out of paper publication of major IR databases has long been predicted, but has arrived more slowly than many thought. However, the cost of paper publication increases as the cost of electronic publication decreases, so in the future, it is likely that electronic media will be the primary choice for publication of large IR databases, especially those designed for updating over time. Print displays of selected portions of a database can be provided on demand to users who wish to peruse a print display. Our design will accommodate this anticipated need.

5.5.3. A Full-Text Encyclopedia/Digital Library.

• 35

Our full-text encyclopedia/digital library will be published on CD-ROM disks and will also be distributed on the world-wide web.

Chapter 6. Documentary Units

Contents of Chapter 6
6.1. Some Examples.
6.2. One of the Few "Laws" in Information Retrieval.
6.3. Documentary Units Versus Surrogates.
6.4. Multiple Documentary Units.
6.5. Our Examples.
6.5.1. A Book Index.
6.5.2. An Indexing and Abstracting Service.
6.5.3. A Full-Text Encyclopedia/Digital Library.

• **information retrieval versus document retrieval : 1**

Occasionally you might hear people debate the merits of "information retrieval" versus "document retrieval." Usually in such discussions, information retrieval is felt to be markedly superior to document retrieval. But such a debate misses the point. By now you know that there can be no recorded or transmitted information without documents. All information, in the form of every kind of message, must be encoded into some form of text, and that text must be recorded on some medium, which, together with the text, constitutes a document. Thus all information retrieval must be the retrieval of documents — documents that, one hopes, contain useful or desirable information.

• **role of documentation in information retrieval : 2**

So it is true to say that there can be no information retrieval without documentation, meaning in this case, the encoding of message texts on or in media to create documents. It is interesting to note that an early name for the field of information science was documentation. The American Society for Information Science and Technology used to be the American Documentation Institute. One of the leading journals of information science in Great Britain is still the *Journal of documentation*.

• **size of documentary units : 3**

Almost always, people who prefer "information retrieval" over "document retrieval" are really arguing about the size of the message, text and document that can be retrieved. The "information retrieval" proponents want small, specific messages targeted closely to their original query, as opposed to large documents like whole books or a whole run of a periodical.

• **4**

So the issue here, and the focus of this chapter, is the optimal size of the documents, or documentary units, that our users should be able to retrieve from our IR databases.

• **complete documents versus parts of documents : 5**

Documents come in all sorts of shapes and sizes. Sometimes it is just fine to organize and retrieve complete documents, but often it is much better to find and retrieve parts of documents. An important choice in the design of an IR database is deciding on the kind or size of messages that can be retrieved. Whatever they are, they will be the documentary units for the database.

• **documentary units as units of analysis : 6**

Documentary units are also called "units of analysis," because they are the units of text that are analyzed for indexing and retrieval.

Chapter 6. Documentary Units (Section 6.1)

6.1. Some Examples.

• **documentary units for indexing and abstracting services : 7**

Traditional abstracting and indexing (A&I) services were designed to retrieve complete periodical articles. (They may also retrieve dissertations, papers in conference proceedings, chapters in collections, and monographs, but periodical articles tend to be the most common document type in most A&I services.) Periodical articles can sometimes be quite long, and a user might be interested only in a particular chart or table or discussion found on a single page of an article. So it might be appropriate for some IR databases to describe and retrieve smaller parts of articles, say pages or individual illustrations, or even individual paragraphs.

• **documentary units for collections of documents and anthologies : 8**

Collections of papers or chapters is also a common form of publication in many fields. Usually an editor invites the authors to focus on aspects of a particular topic. Sometimes, the papers are written in honor of a particular person or institution and published as a festschrift (German for "festival writing"). Library IR databases (library catalogs) may treat these collections as single documents (the whole volume constituting a single documentary unit), but most A&I services will consider each chapter as a separate document, thus as a separate documentary unit for the purposes of indexing and retrieval. Similarly in anthologies of short stories or poems, each short story or poem can be treated as a separate documentary unit.

• **documentary units for video recordings and motion pictures : 9**

Videotapes and motion pictures consist of thousands of individual frames or pictures. In IR databases for moving images, most motion pictures and video recordings have been treated as single whole documents. But more and more, searchers are interested in finding particular frames or pictures, or certain segments or sequences, or certain types of frames or pictures. So there is growing interest in moving the documentary unit down to segments of frames or to the individual frame or picture level.

• **documentary units for music : 10**

In some musical IR databases, there is an effort to identify particular themes, melodies, or sequences of notes, and to identify the particular part of a composition where such sequences occur, so that the documentary unit approaches what is usually called the "measure" in musical notation.

• **documentary units for book indexes : 11**

The traditional-back-of-the-book index has been geared toward finding the pages on which particular topics are discussed. But pointing only to the page means that the user must scan or read the entire page to find the exact point that he or she is seeking, and some pages can be quite dense and long. So it might be better to point to particular paragraphs, rather than whole pages.

• **pages versus paragraphs as documentary units : 12**

Paragraphs in narrative language texts have another advantage that is growing in importance. The page is associated with the physical medium of paper, which is cut up into leaves and bound together to form what we often call a book. The page is an attribute of the paper medium book. It usually has nothing to do with the text in which a message is encoded. This is why you can have the same messages (the same novel, or treatise, or play, or the Bible) in exactly the same version, but in entirely different paginations. The exact same text falls on pages very differently in different publications. So the index created for one set of pages cannot be used for any other set of pages (or can be used only with difficulty).

Chapter 6. Documentary Units (Section 6.1)

• **advantages of paragraphs as documentary units : 13**

In contrast, the paragraph is a conventional unit of narrative prose text. No matter how the text is paginated — how it is laid out on pages, if it is the same text, the division into paragraphs will be the same in all publications of that text. So an index linked to paragraphs can travel with the text to different presentations in the same medium or in different media.

• **paragraphs as documentary units for electronic texts : 14**

This is especially important now that the content (the text) of printed books can be (and with increasing frequency is) published simultaneously or subsequently in electronic formats. A text has no pages in electronic format, unless they are artificially imposed. But paragraphs, as elements of the text, survive in the electronic format, so an index linked to paragraphs will work just as well in the electronic environment as in the paper environment. An index tied to paper pages is nearly worthless in the electronic environment (unless the pages are artificially re-created in the electronic display).

• **NISO recommendation on paragraphs as documentary units; numbering of paragraphs : 15**

The National Information Standards Organization (NISO) technical report on indexes (Anderson 1997a, p. 22) urges publishers and back-of-the-book indexers to begin linking their indexes for language texts to paragraphs rather than printed pages. This will require developing a method for paragraph numbering, so index entries can refer as easily to paragraphs as they now refer to pages. Several approaches have been used. One is to simply number the paragraphs throughout the book. Books that have taken this approach include *Subject analysis and indexing: theoretical foundation and practical advice*, by Robert Fugmann (1993); *Rafael Català: del Círculo cuadrado a la cienciapoesía: hacia una nueva poética latinoamericana*, edited by Luis A. Jiménez (1994); and *El arte autobiográfico en Cuba en el siglo XIX*, by Jiménez (1995). A variation of this approach, used in this book, is to number paragraphs within chapters. Index references must then include both chapter and paragraph numbers.

• **text sections as documentary units : 16**

A slightly different approach is taken by W. J. Hutchins in *Languages of indexing and classification* (1975). His documentary units are sections rather than paragraphs, although many sections consist of a single paragraph. Each section is numbered using a hierarchical notation that begins with the chapter number, then a major section number, and, for subsections, a subsection number. The back-of-the-book index uses these section notations to refer to particular sections.

• **paragraphs as documentary units : 17**

Indexes are often ignored in book reviews, but the paragraph-based index to the book about Rafael Català (Jimenez 1994) got special attention in a review by R. A. Kerr (1995). Kerr wrote, "The edition has an interesting self-contained reference tool that is uncommon in humanities publications. Each paragraph of the text is numbered in consecutive order, and the detailed index at the end of the volume ... [refers] the reader directly to the numbered paragraph in which the reference appears."

• **18**

A more traditional approach is to use the printed pages as they have been for several hundred years, with page numbers only. Index entries linked to paragraphs then include the page number plus a paragraph number that indicates where the paragraph falls on the page, counting full paragraphs from the top of the page. In this approach, an entry to "dogs 34:3, 67:2, 107:4" means that dogs are discussed in the third paragraph on page 34, the second paragraph on page 67, and the fourth paragraph on page 107. But if such a text is moved to a digital medium without pages, these page-plus-paragraph numbers in the index will have to be converted to paragraph numbers only, and corresponding numbers will need to be attached to paragraphs.

• 19

Once the link between an index heading and a paragraph has been made, it may be possible to convert the link into a hyperlink, eliminating the need for the visible numerical reference.

• **documentary units for hypertext : 20**

Hypertext has become a standard document format on the world-wide web and in similar electronic digital environments, such as CD-ROMs. A standard definition of hypertext is "a collection of documents (or 'nodes') containing cross-references or 'links' which, with the aid of an interactive browser program, allow the reader to move easily from one document to another" (FOLDOC 1997, "hypertext"). When a text moves to, or is created in and for digital media, and when its documentary units for the purpose of indexing and retrieval are individual paragraphs, charts, illustrations, sound bites, and similar individual parts and segments, then in effect, the text begins to adopt some of the characteristics of hypertext. Each of these parts becomes a node in a hypertext. Each of the parts or nodes can be accessed directly based on the indexing provided. When cross-references or links are integrated into the individual parts or nodes, then the viewer/reader/listener can move directly from node to node, as in a fully implemented hypertext.

• **documentary units for hypertext on world-wide web : 21**

One sees this transition toward hypertextuality in typical world-wide web sites. The opening screen or page of the site may list a number of nodes (sometimes called web pages, borrowing traditional printed book terminology by analogy). Each of the web pages is therefore a node. At first the viewer can move directly from the opening screen to any of these nodes or pages, but then must return back to the opening screen to get access to the other nodes. But if cross-reference links are also added to each node or page for all closely related nodes or pages, then the complete idea of hypertextuality has been realized.

• 22

In the context of hypertexts, the individual nodes constitute documentary units.

6.2. One of the Few "Laws" in Information Retrieval.

• **documentary units as limiting factor in information retrieval : 23**

One of the few "laws" in information retrieval is that only documentary units can be directly retrieved. Smaller units of texts — segments within documentary units — cannot be directly retrieved via an index or retrieval system, so users must find these smaller units themselves by reading, scanning, viewing, or listening.

documentary units in library catalogs : 24

If a library catalog can retrieve only complete books, then the user who wants a particular chapter, page, paragraph, or statement (an answer to a specific question) will have to search through the book to find it, or begin a new search using the book's own index.

• **advantages of smaller documentary units : 25**

This means that smaller documentary units can often be very advantageous to searchers who are looking for particular answers for fairly narrow, targeted questions.

Chapter 6. Documentary Units (Section 6.3)

6.3. Documentary Units Versus Surrogates.

• **documentary units versus surrogates in reference IR databases : 26**

When considering documentary units, it is important to make a clear distinction between the representation of documentary units within an IR database and the documentary units themselves. This is especially true for reference IR databases, as opposed to full-text IR databases. A reference IR database is one that does not contain the full text of documents, but only provides references to them. In the past, almost all large IR databases were reference databases. Only in the recent past have full-text IR databases become common.

• **abstracts versus documentary units : 27**

Nevertheless, many abstracting and indexing services still do not contain the full text of the periodical articles, conference papers, book chapters, or dissertations to which they refer. Instead, the user retrieves a citation, which can be used to locate the full text in a library or through a document delivery service. Often, an abstract is also provided (hence the name "abstracting and indexing service"). But an abstract is not the documentary unit in such a situation! It is a surrogate or representation of the documentary unit. The documentary unit is the full document that the abstract and the citation point to and represent. (These statements are contradicted only in the fairly rare situation where an author never got beyond the abstract. The full document was never written, or never published. The abstract becomes the full document! In this case, and only in this case, can an abstract be considered the documentary unit.)

• **role of abstracts in information retrieval : 28**

In a reference IR database, which by definition does not include the full text of documents, but does provide citations and possibly abstracts to represent the original documents, all of the index terms and entries, even if they are based only on the abstract and citation, still point to the full original document. The retrieval operation is not completed until the searcher takes the citation and uses it to locate the full original document outside the IR database. Many searchers may choose not to pursue a full document after they see the abstract (indeed, this is precisely why an abstract can be very useful — to eliminate the need to pursue useless documents!). But this doesn't change the fact that, according to the terminology and the framework used in this book, the original document is the documentary unit. It is that original document that is described by such an abstract and linked index terms. The citation plus abstract (if any) is the representation (the surrogate) of the documentary unit, which should not be confused with the documentary unit itself.

• **smaller documentary units in reference IR databases : 29**

If such a reference IR database were using documentary units smaller than complete documents (such as pages or illustrations within complete periodical articles), then it would need to provide separate citations or descriptions (perhaps with abstracts) for each of these smaller documentary units. If the documentary units were paragraphs, an abstract for the paragraph may not be warranted, but to make a paragraph retrievable, a separate citation would need to be provided for each paragraph. Each documentary unit must have a surrogate or representative within the IR database.

• **smaller documentary units in full-text IR databases : 30**

The need for direct access to the documentary units of an IR database is the reason why most IR databases that provide access to smaller documentary units are full-text IR databases. It is much easier to provide direct access to paragraphs, charts, illustrations, motion-picture frames or musical measures when all of these units are directly accessible within the IR database.

• 31

Thus, most reference databases will provide access only to larger documentary units.

6.4. Multiple Documentary Units.

• multiple documentary units in full-text IR databases : 32

A IR database can have more than one documentary unit for each document type. For example, a full-text database might use the paragraph, or a "screen-full" (the amount of text that can be viewed on a computer monitor screen) as the documentary unit for full-text retrieval based on automatic indexing. At the same time, it might use larger text segments, or even complete articles or chapters or books as the documentary unit that is retrievable using descriptors assigned by human indexers.

• documentary units for automatic indexing : 33

The size of the documentary unit for automatic indexing of full-text documents is important not only for the convenience of the user (to be presented with the precise segments of text where a particular topic might be addressed), but also for effective automatic indexing. As Donna Harman (1994) points out (using "record" for our "documentary unit"): "A record which is too short provides little text for the searching algorithms to use, causing poor results. Too large a record, however, may dilute the importance of word matches and cause many false matches. For these reasons it would not be sensible to define a sentence as a record, but a paragraph might be fine. Alternatively it would not be effective to make a very long section a record; it would be better to break it into small subsections" (p. 248-249).

• role of documentary units in IR databases : 34

To summarize: For each document type identified in the documentary scope, the IR database designer must decide on appropriate documentary units, which will be the units that are analyzed, indexed, and labeled to make them retrievable.

6.5. Our Examples.
6.5.1. A Book Index.

• 35

For our book index, we will use the paragraph as the documentary unit. This documentary unit corresponds to the thought processes of most writers, who write in paragraph chunks, so that each paragraph usually focuses on a particular topic, issue or theme. The paragraph is a natural unit in written language text, and for this reason it is a highly appropriate unit for the detailed indexing expected in an index to a single book.

• 36

In addition to each paragraph, each figure, illustration, table, or chart will also be treated as a separate documentary unit.

• documentary units for book indexes in electronic media; books as hypertext : 37

When our book text moves to electronic media, it can be made more hypertextual if all the index headings linked to each documentary unit, along with all the "see also" cross references related to those headings, are displayed with each documentary unit. Then, when a viewer is looking at a particular paragraph or chart or illustration, he or she can click on any of the associ-

Chapter 6. Documentary Units (Section 6.5.2)

ated index headings or cross-references to move directly to paragraphs that are linked to any of these headings.

• books in electronic media as hypertext : 38

A further step toward full hypertextuality can be reached by using some automatic indexing techniques (to be discussed in chapter 8). Every significant word or phrase in a particular paragraph that occurs in an index heading for other paragraphs, or that occurs with a certain frequency in the text of other paragraphs or in illustration captions or section headings can be highlighted, so that choosing these highlighted words or phrases can take the viewer to those linked parts of the text.

6.5.2. An Indexing and Abstracting Service.

• terminology for indexing and abstracting services : 39

First, did you notice that earlier in this chapter the phrase "abstracting and indexing services" was used rather than the more common "indexing and abstracting services"? This switch was intentional, in order to have the phrase correspond to the common abbreviation, "A&I services." Through some quirk of our language, the common full phrase is "indexing and abstracting service," but the common short form is "A&I service."

• documentary units for indexing and abstracting services : 40

The normal documentary unit for our indexing and abstracting service will be the traditional choice: the complete document — the complete periodical article, the complete essay in collections of essays, the complete monograph in the case of books and dissertations. However, our service will also feature augmented indexing for important documents, as measured through signs of use or importance — citation counts, orders through document delivery services, circulation in key libraries, book reviews, etc. (These measures are discussed in section 8.5.)

• documentary units for high-use documents in indexing and abstracting services : 41

These "high use" documents will be featured in a "high use" section of the database and will be indexed on the basis of smaller documentary units. Every chapter in monographs, including dissertations, will be separately analyzed and indexed. In addition, every chart, table, and illustration will be indexed, so that retrieval of these parts of these documents will be facilitated.

• documentary units for full-text searching : 42

Documents that receive augmented indexing will also be incorporated into the database as complete texts (to the extent possible under copyright laws and agreements), so that full-text searching of these documents will be possible. For full-text searches, the documentary unit will be the paragraph or a screen-full of text.

6.5.3. A Full-Text Encyclopedia/Digital Library.

• 43

Our full-text encyclopedia/digital library will have the same kind of multiple documentary units described for high-use documents in our indexing and abstracting service. Users will have direct access to every paragraph of language texts via full-text automatic indexing retrieval. Hypertext indexing will also link related paragraphs or similar segments of texts, including pictures, charts, tables, or diagrams. At another level, searches based on assigned descriptors will lead to complete articles in the encyclopedia. In this way, the encyclopedia will be able to respond to users seeking broader, more comprehensive discussions of topics and issues, and also users seeking particular definitions or information on narrow topics or aspects of topics.

Chapter 7. Indexable Matter

Contents of Chapter 7
    7.1. Typical Examples of Indexable Matter.
    7.1.1. Titles.
    7.1.2. Titles and Abstracts.
    7.1.3. Preliminary Matter.
    7.1.4. Initial Paragraphs.
    7.1.5. Internal Indexes.
    7.1.6. Reference Citations.
    7.1.7. Opening Screens of Web Sites.
    7.1.8. Full Texts.
    7.1.9. Types of Messages.
    7.2. Indexable Matter Versus Subject Scope.
    7.3. Accuracy of Indexing.
    7.4. Our Examples.
    7.4.1. A Book Index.
    7.4.2. An Indexing and Abstracting Service.
    7.4.3. A Full-Text Encyclopedia/Digital Library.

        • **definition of indexable matter : 1**
Indexable matter is the part or portion of documentary units that is actually considered in the indexing process, whether that process is performed by humans through intellectual analysis of the message content and meaning or by machines through manipulation and analysis of textual symbols. Indexable matter is also called the "analysis base" because it provides the base or basis for the analysis of a message and its text.

        • **complete texts versus partial texts as indexable matter : 2**
When language-based documentary units are small, such as a paragraph, table, chart, short sound-bite, or even an entire page of text, then the indexable matter is usually the complete text of the documentary unit. For larger documentary units — complete periodical articles, essays (chapters in books), whole monographs, longer recordings of speech or language performances, or collections of such document-types, the indexable matter is often limited to only a portion of the complete text.

        • **indexable matter for non-language-based texts : 3**
The situation is similar for non-language-based texts and texts that combine language with images, music, and other types of text. If the documentary units for motion pictures or video recordings are single frames or pictures, then the complete documentary unit is generally analyzed. But if the documentary unit is the complete motion picture or video recording, then analysis may be limited to opening (or closing) frames or sequences, often called "credits." Similarly, single slides, paintings, or other images will typically be analyzed as a whole text, but collections of slides, paintings, and other images may be analyzed on the basis of some language-based summary description. Long musical compositions may be described on the basis only of opening measures, but if the documentary unit is the single measure or groups of measures, then of course the complete unit will be analyzed. Topical analysis of musical messages can be based on language-based descriptions, such as the concert notes typically found in concert programs.

Chapter 7. Indexable Matter (Section 7.1)

• **indexable matter and documentary units for mixed-text documents : 4**

In mixed-text documents that receive detailed indexing based on small documentary units, indexable matter may differ for different types of text. In a motion picture or video recording for example, if images are indexed on a frame by frame (for frame sequence) level, then the full image text will likely be considered for indexing. But any accompanying spoken language or musical text may be ignored completely, or indexed at different levels with respect to documentary units and indexable matter. Alternatively, motion pictures or video recordings can be indexed on the basis solely of accompanying language sound tracks as indexable matter, with no direct analysis of the visual images.

• **economic aspects of indexable matter : 5**

Limiting indexable matter is an economic policy decision. It is done to save time and money. Analyzing the entire text of a book takes a lot longer than simply analyzing the title-page, table of contents, and introductory matter. Analysis of an abstract is quicker and cheaper than reading through an entire periodical article. Viewing an entire film or video takes longer than simply checking the openings credits. Furthermore, if the exhaustivity of indexing is low — if only a few terms are to be assigned or extracted — then this type of introductory matter is often quite sufficient to provide an overview of the complete text. (Exhaustivity of indexing is the topic of chapter 9.)

• **impact of size of documentary units and exhaustivity of indexing on indexable matter : 6**

Choosing the indexable matter, in the design of an IR database, will be related to the size of documentary units on the one hand, and the desired exhaustivity of indexing on the other — something we will be discussing later on in chapter 9.

• **variations in indexable matter : 7**

When an IR database covers different types of documents, with different documentary units, there may be different indexable matters for each of them. Sometimes, the size of the indexable matter can vary according to perceived importance of the document.

7.1. Typical Examples of Indexable Matter.
7.1.1. Titles.

• 8

Limiting indexable matter to titles of documents can be risky, because so often the title is designed more to attract attention than to summarize the content, purpose and meaning of a message. Sometimes the title is just too brief to describe the message adequately. Nevertheless, in scholarly circles, especially in the social sciences and the sciences, authors often use long and descriptive titles, so that titles sometimes function quite well. The "Permuterm" indexes that accompany the Institute for Scientific Information's popular *Current contents* publications and its citation indexes are based almost entirely on titles of documents.

7.1.2. Titles and Abstracts.

• 9

Indexing and abstracting services frequently use abstracts, along with titles, as the basis for indexing. IR databases covering non-language-based messages, such as paintings, slides, and music frequently use language-based summaries or descriptions for the indexing of these messages.

Language-based abstracts or summaries are also common for such mixed-text messages as maps, motion pictures, video recordings, and world-wide web sites.

7.1.3. Preliminary Matter.

• 10

Cataloging or indexing the topics and features of books for large databases or library catalogs can often be done quite adequately on the basis of preliminary matter, such as title page, verso of title page, table of contents, and introduction. If library catalogers were to read, or even scan, entire books, only to assign the relatively few headings allowed by most libraries, productivity would fall and their services would become too expensive.

7.1.4. Initial Paragraphs.

• 11

When there is no abstract, articles, especially news stories, can often be adequately indexed based only on the lead paragraph. There is a long tradition in journalism to summarize a story, focusing on the essential points, in the first paragraph of the story.

7.1.5. Internal Indexes.

• 12

Back in the 1970s, Pauline Atherton (1978) (now Pauline Atherton Cochrane) headed up a major "Subject Access Project" to improve access to library materials. Among the many recommendations was the augmentation of typical library descriptions of books with the addition of tables of contents and entries from the indexes of individual books. Back-of-the-book index entries could be chosen on the basis of the number of locators, as a measure of the relative importance of the topics indicated in the particular book. Titles of individual chapters from the table of contents and selected index entries would be accessible through full-text searching of the library catalog records and would provide many additional access points to parts of books. The idea of using an internal index as indexable matter has not been widely implemented, but it is certainly a legitimate example of possible indexable matter. Some library OPACs (online public access catalogs) have begun to automatically index contents notes in catalog records, adding names of authors and titles of chapters, stories or essays to author and title indexes as well as keyword indexes.

7.1.6. Reference Citations.

• 13

Much more common than internal indexes as indexable matter are reference citations found in scholarly publications. These are the basis (the indexable matter!) for all citation indexes, used for many years in the field of law and introduced by the Institute for Scientific Information (1961, 1969, 1976) into the sciences with its *Science citation index* in 1961, the social sciences with its *Social sciences citation index* in 1969, and finally the arts and humanities with its *Arts & humanities citation index* in 1976. All indexing for citation indexes is based solely on the reference citations included in scholarly publications.

7.1.7. Opening Screens of Web Sites.

• role of indexable matter for world-wide web search engines : 14

Indexable matter has become an important issue in the design of opening screens for web sites. Many popular search engines index web sites automatically, and they sometimes limit indexable matter to the title and captions on the opening screen and the first paragraph of visual language text (as opposed to spoken language text). This is why it is wise to include a summary paragraph describing the nature and features of a web site near the beginning of the opening screen.

• language-based texts versus image texts as indexable matter for world-wide-web sites : 15

Also, automatic web-site indexing by search engines is limited to character-based digitized language text. Image and sound texts are ignored. This means that titles, captions, tables of contents or links to web-site nodes or pages must be in character-based language text in order to be indexed. Language text that is embedded in an image will be ignored — that is, when the language text is represented not as digitized language symbols (characters) but as pixels in an image, it will not be indexed by search engines, and the web site will suffer from less exposure.

7.1.8. Full Texts.

• 16

As stated above, if the documentary unit is small, such as a paragraph or page of language-based text, or a single picture or diagram, the full text of the documentary unit will usually serve as the indexable matter.

7.1.9. Types of Messages.

• 17

Sometimes whole categories of messages are eliminated from analysis because they are considered insignificant or of little importance to the principal user groups. An IR database may decide to ignore advertisements, letters to the editor, cartoons, or poems, for example. These types of text are then eliminated completely from indexable matter (and the documentary scope!) for the IR database.

• indexable matter for book indexes : 18

In the case of back-of-the-book indexes, the publisher or the author or the indexer may decide to exclude from indexable matter such categories of text as footnotes, reference citations, illustrations, front matter, and appendices. It will certainly be helpful when any portion of a book has been removed from indexable matter that potential users be informed!

7.2. Indexable Matter Versus Subject Scope.

• 19

Indexable matter is sometimes confused with subject scope. When someone says, "the indexable matter for this IR database, or for this index, consists of persons, institutions, events, relationships, and places," then you know that this is not indexable matter in the sense used here. Rather, these are the topics of interest to potential users. These are the kinds of topics for which indexers will seek evidence in the indexable matter. Indexable matter does not refer to topics of interest, but rather to portions of text that will be analyzed in the hopes of finding discussions of subject scope topics. So answers to the question of indexable matter must always be portions of text, or types of texts.

7.3. Accuracy of Indexing.

• 20

Indexers and IR database producers aim to produce accurate representations of the documents that they want to make fully accessible to their users. To a certain extent, the more complete (or larger) the indexable matter, the more accurate indexing can be. The rationale is that indexing on the basis of the complete text ought to be more accurate than indexing on the basis of only a part or portion of the text. When only a portion of a text is used, some important aspects of the complete text might be lost.

• 21

When only a portion of the text is used for indexing, then the accuracy of indexing will depend on the extent to which that portion accurately reflects the complete text. When only a few terms will be assigned, experience indicates that smaller portions of texts are sufficiently trustworthy for this purpose to make them feasible substitutes.

7.4. Our Examples.
7.4.1. A Book Index.

• 22

Because the documentary unit for our book index is the paragraph, which is quite small as documentary units go, the indexer should consult the entire text of the paragraph, recognizing that it will not always be possible to get the gist of a paragraph from a good topic sentence, if there is one. (Of course every effort will be made to make sure that every paragraph in this book does begin with a clear topic sentence!) And because all figures, diagrams, illustrations, charts, and tables are treated as separate documentary units, their full text will be their indexable matter.

• indexable matter for books in electronic media : 23

An electronic version of this book should also have an index based on electronic full-text indexing. For that index, the indexable matter will, by definition, be the complete text of each paragraph. Some illustrations will be indexed only on the basis of captions however.

7.4.2. An Indexing and Abstracting Service.

• 24

Initial indexing of all documents in our indexing and abstracting service will be based on the abstract or summary that is prepared for each document record. When documents come with their own abstracts, these may be used (with appropriate permission as required), or they may be edited according to database criteria (see the NISO standard for abstracts — National Information Standards Organization 1997b). Where no abstract exists, one will be created. Abstracts in languages other than English will be translated into English. Both the original abstract and the translated abstract will be included in the document record.

Chapter 7. Indexable Matter (Section 7.4.3)

• **indexable matter for high-use documents : 25**

High-use documents will have some smaller documentary units, such as individual diagrams, charts, and illustrations. The indexable matter for these smaller units will be their complete text, when possible, otherwise captions will be used.

• **full texts as indexable matter for high-use documents : 26**

High-use documents will also be included as full text within the electronic database, so that their full text will be searchable via automatic indexing. For such full-text indexing and searching, the indexable matter will be the complete text of each paragraph or analogous segment of text. Full-text access via indexing and searching will be limited to language-based text. The indexable matter for images will be limited to their captions.

7.4.3. A Full-Text Encyclopedia/Digital Library.

• 27

Our full-text encyclopedia/digital library provides three types of access to its content. Access to individual paragraphs via full-text language-based indexing and via hypertext links will be based on the full-text of each language paragraph as indexable matter. For non-language-based elements, such as illustrations and sound-bites, captions or summaries will be used.

• **indexable matter for maps : 28**

Maps are a special case. Even though most maps include language text, this language text is often incorporated into a visual image, represented by pixels rather than by digitized individual language characters. Thus, the place and feature names on maps must often be separately indexed; they are often not accessible via automatic full-text indexing or searching.

• **lead paragraphs as indexable matter • 29**

At the grosser level of indexing, when entire articles constitute the documentary units, then only the lead or introductory paragraphs will be used as indexable matter, because these paragraphs are designed to summarize the entire article. In effect, the introductory paragraph is equivalent to an abstract.

Chapter 8. Analysis and Indexing Methods

Contents of Chapter 8
8.1. Research Comparing Automatic and Human Indexing.
8.2. Human Analysis and Indexing.
8.2.1. Cognition Versus Social Construction in Human Analysis and Indexing
8.2.2. Human Indexing Rules.
8.2.2.1. Human Indexing Rules for Image Text.
8.2.2.2. Human Indexing Rules Based on Probabilistic Analysis.
8.3. Automatic Analysis and Indexing.
8.3.1. In the Beginning Was the Word.
8.3.2. Simple Keyword Indexing.
8.3.3. Negative Vocabulary Control: Stop Lists.
8.3.4. Counting Words.
8.3.5. Comparative Counting and Weighting.
8.3.6. Improving the Count: Stemming.
8.3.7. Natural Word Distributions.
8.3.8. Words Versus Phrases.
8.3.9. Managing Vocabulary in Automatic Indexing.
8.3.10. Automatic Vocabulary Management.
8.3.11. Clustering.
8.3.11.1. Latent Semantic Indexing.
8.3.12. Citation Indexes.
8.3.12.1. Bibliographic Coupling.
8.3.12.2. Co-Citation.
8.3.13. Relevance Feedback.
8.4. Subject Analysis and Indexing in Indexing and Abstracting Services.
8.5. Growing Role of Automatic Analysis and Indexing.
8.5.1. Censorship or Guidance?
8.6. Our Examples.
8.6.1. A book Index.
8.6.2. An Indexing and Abstracting Service.
8.6.3. A Full-Text Encyclopedia/Digital Library.

• 1

In order to retrieve messages, texts, and documents via an IR database, they must be described and indexed (indicated). Description requires some kind of analysis. Two basic approaches are used for the analysis of messages, texts, and documents: by human examination and by machine algorithm. Humans examine documents and texts in order to consider messages that texts represent, plus features of texts and of documents in which texts are recorded. Computers identify and compare components of texts — the symbols that comprise texts — sometimes consulting lexical, thesaural, discourse or other contextual data to expand and characterize sets of textual components; sometimes applying syntactic or pattern indexing algorithms to identify larger units of text; and sometimes calculating attributes for text components and documents based on available data.

Chapter 8. Analysis and Indexing Methods

• **human indexing versus automatic indexing : 2**

These two approaches are often called human indexing and automatic indexing. Our definition of "indexing" simply means pointing or indicating. The focus of this chapter is on these two fundamentally different analysis methods for assessing the content, meaning, purpose, and features of messages, texts, and documents. How the results of these analyses will be translated into indexing terms, descriptors, or headings that can be used for pointing and retrieval involve other aspects of IR database design, such as specificity, syntax, and vocabulary management, which are addressed in subsequent chapters.

• **results of human indexing versus automatic indexing : 3**

Both human and machine approaches are widely used. Research comparing retrieval based on human versus machine analysis and indexing tends to show that the two approaches produce different results, but that users find them, on balance, more or less equally effective. Similar evidence comes from observing the behavior of expert searchers. When they have access to indexing based on both approaches, they generally use both types of indexing, preferring human analysis and indexing for some types of searches and automatic machine analysis and indexing for others. Personal preferences also play a role. Some users prefer one type of analysis and indexing or the other most or all of the time. (Research on these issues is discussed in the next section.)

• **multiple approaches to indexing in IR databases : 4**

Increasingly, IR databases are designed to provide more than one indexing approach in hopes of maximizing the effective retrieval of useful messages, texts, and documents. By offering multiple approaches, it may be possible to take advantage of the strengths and features of different approaches and also to respond to the needs and preferences of users in a variety of situations.

• **automatic indexing of language texts versus image texts and other non-language texts : 5**

This chapter focuses almost exclusively on the analysis and indexing of language texts, as opposed to messages expressed in other types of text, such as pictorial images, music, the fine arts, or mathematical or chemical formulae. Research and experimentation on automatic analysis and indexing of language text has been under way for several decades, and there has been much progress and growing use of automatic analysis and indexing of language texts for retrieval. But the automatic analysis and indexing of image and musical text has barely begun. This is especially true for the topical messages of non-language text, as opposed to non-topical features, such as color, texture, shape, and. for music, pitch, tempo, and pattern. Whereas automatic analysis and indexing of language and mathematical/chemical text is now routine and common, automatic analysis and indexing of image text is usually experimental. IR databases that provide access to most other types of text, especially images, rely for the most part on human analysis and indexing of messages and their texts and documents.

• **recommended resources on indexing processes : 6**

Recent summaries and assessments of the indexing process include the following. A number of other important books and articles on human and automatic indexing will be cited later in the various sections of this chapter.

Hjørland, Birger (1997). *Information seeking and subject representation: an activity-theoretical approach to information science.* Westport, CT: Greenwood Press; 1997. 213 p. (New directions in information management; no. 34). ISBN 0-313-29893-9.

Fidel, Raya; Hahn, Trudi Bellardo; Rasmussen, Edie M.; Smith, Philip J., eds. (1994). *Challenges in indexing electronic text and images.* Medford, NJ: Learned Information for the American Society for Information Science; 1994. ix, 306 p. (ASIS monograph series). ISBN 0-938734-76-8.

Chapter 8. Analysis and Indexing Methods (Section 8.1)

Lunin, Lois F.; Fidel, Raya, eds. (1994). "Perspectives on indexing." *Journal of the American Society for Information Science.* 45(6): 569-636; 1994 September.

Weinberg, Bella Hass, ed. (1988a). *Indexing: the state of our knowledge and the state of our ignorance.* Proceedings of the 20th annual meeting of the American Society of Indexers; 1988 May 13; New York, NY. Medford, NJ: Learned Information; 1989. x, 134 p. ISBN 0-938734-32-6.

Weinberg, Bella Hass (1998). *Can you recommend a good book on indexing?: collected reviews on the organization of information.* Medford, NJ: Information Today; 1998. 161 p. ISBN 1-57387-041-2.

8.1. Research Comparing Automatic and Human Indexing.

• 7

Research comparing the relative strengths and weaknesses of these two basic approaches to analysis and indexing has failed to convince die-hard opponents of the merits of either approach, and in fact, the clarity of research results has been disappointing. Karen Sparck Jones (1981a, 1981c) provides an excellent over-view and assessment of the first twenty years of serious comparative research, including the landmark Cranfield 1 and 2 experiments, conducted under the direction of Cyril Cleverdon in the U.K.

• role of users in IR research : 8

Most of the earlier research was limited to relatively small collections, and the evaluation of search results were usually based on judgments by persons other than real users with real information needs or desires. Since then, there have been increased efforts to put users in the center of information retrieval research, with the recognition that user variables are as important, perhaps more important, than any variation in analysis and indexing methods for determining the effectiveness of IR systems and IR databases. The study of searchers by Saracevic, Kantor, Chamis and Trivison (Part I: 1988; Parts II-III: Saracevic & Kantor 1988b, c) is a good example. Their subjects were functioning intermediary searchers dealing with real queries submitted by real clients, who provided relevance judgments tied to their actual information need perceptions.

• variables in IR research : 9

In all IR research, it has been very difficult to isolate particular variables or differences in order to assess their specific impact on overall performance. The two major components of any information retrieval situation are the user on the one hand and the IR system, including IR databases, on the other hand. Here the focus is on the IR system component (because of the scope of this book). Quite apart from human versus machine analysis and indexing of messages, texts, and documents, other key variables, each of which gets separate attention in this book, tend to co-occur in varying degrees with human or automatic analysis and indexing. Nevertheless, unless these other variables are accounted for, in addition to the type of analysis and indexing (machine versus human), it cannot be clear which variables have the major impact on the results of comparisons. Thus, differences in retrieval results may be due to differences in documentary unit size or extent of indexable matter or exhaustivity of indexing or specificity of indexing terms or index browsability (use of browsable displayed indexes versus non-displayed machine indexes) or searching syntax or displayed heading syntax or vocabulary management or surrogation and surrogate display or interface design, in addition to (or instead of) differences in analysis and indexing methods. These other key variables for IR research include:

Chapter 8. Analysis and Indexing Methods (Section 8.1)

• size of documentary units among variables in IR research : 10

- *size of documentary units.* Human analysis and indexing tend to focus on larger documentary units, such as complete periodical articles, complete chapters in collections, or even complete monographs. With the wide-spread availability of full-text documents within IR databases, automatic analysis and indexing now routinely retrieves individual paragraphs of texts, rather than complete documents. But of course, humans could analyze and index at the paragraph level of documentary unit, so this variable is not directly tied to analysis and indexing method.

• extent of indexable matter among variables in IR research : 11

- *extent of indexable matter.* Tied to the availability of full-text documents are differences in the extent of indexable matter. Automatic analysis and indexing is now routinely based on the complete text, whereas much human indexing may be limited to an abstract or other summary of the complete text. This difference is tied closely also to exhaustivity, because the lower exhaustivity of typical human indexing can be accommodated with briefer indexable matter. But again, humans could analyze complete texts and could index at greater levels of exhaustivity, so these variables are not the same as analysis and indexing method.

• exhaustivity among variables in IR research : 12

- *exhaustivity.* Automatic analysis and indexing tends to be exhaustive, considering most, if not all words in indexable matter as potential indicators of content. In contrast, human analysis and indexing tends to be selective, indexing only topics or aspects that appear to be of most importance for summarizing the content, meaning, or purpose of a message. But, as just noted, humans could analyze and index at higher levels of exhaustivity, so exhaustivity is not directly tied to analysis and indexing method.

• specificity among variables in IR research : 12a

- *specificity.* Automatic analysis and indexing tends to use very specific terminology (and therefore a very large and varied vocabulary), because it uses, or at least begins with, the actual language of the text. Human indexing tends to use more generic terminology (and a much smaller vocabulary over all) in an attempt to summarize topics and to avoid too much scatter of closely related topics. However, humans could use larger vocabularies, so that high specificity is not necessarily an attribute unique to automatic analysis and indexing.

• browsability among variables in IR research : 13

- *browsable displayed indexes.* Browsable displayed indexes with multi-term context-providing headings are certainly possible with automatic analysis and indexing, but they are not as common as with human analysis and indexing, and the types of term combination tend to be more limited for most types of automatic analysis and indexing. Tied to this variable is human browsing and examination versus machine matching. When humans examine displayed indexes, they generally make judgments about possible relevance or usefulness during the examination process. When machine matching is used, users submit search terms to an IR system, which performs some kind of matching and then presents a list of retrieved items to evaluate. These different presentation methods may effect perceptions of performance, but they are not tied to either human or automatic methods of analysis and indexing.

• syntax among variables in IR research : 14

- *searching syntax, display syntax.* Although the increasingly sophisticated methods for selecting, combining, manipulating, and weighting terms for machine matching can also be used with human indexing, most often these techniques are used with automatic analysis and indexing. In contrast, the syntactic possibilities for the combination of terms to create context-providing index headings tend to be richer for human-assigned indexing than for automatic indexing. Such headings are meant to facilitate human browsing, examination and evaluation (as opposed to machine matching). For human-assigned terms, a wide range of syntactic patterns, ranging from traditional

Chapter 8. Analysis and Indexing Methods (Section 8.1)

subject headings to modern contextual string-indexing procedures, are available, whereas the presentation of automatically selected terms is usually limited to KWIC, KWOC, KWAC (keyword in, out of, or along-side context) or permuted formats.

• 15

Thus very different types of syntax are typically used with these different approaches to analysis and indexing, but nevertheless, differences in syntax are not the same as differences in analysis and indexing methods.

• vocabulary management among variables in IR research : 16

• *vocabulary management.* This variable is closely related to specificity. Although there is no necessary connection between type of analysis and indexing on the one hand and vocabulary control or management on the other, nevertheless, the provision of references linking synonymous or equivalent terms, pointing to related terms, and distinguishing among ambiguous homographs tends to accompany human analysis and indexing more commonly than automatic analysis and indexing. However, this type of vocabulary management is increasingly common in automatic experimental systems and more advanced publicly available systems.

• surrogation among variables in IR research : 17

• *surrogation.* Closely related to several of these key variables is the amount, nature, and style of information provided to the user about documentary units. For browsable displayed indexes, this will be connected to the amount and style of information provided in index headings, but also to subsequent documentary unit records that are linked to index headings. For machine matching systems, this variable relates to the size and style of the documentary unit records provided to the user for evaluation, ranging from very brief (such as titles only) to very lengthy (citations, abstracts, outlines, index terms, etc.). Newer methods of using visual displays (such as icons, graphs or network nodes) to characterize retrieved or relevant sets of messages has been more closely tied to automatic analysis and indexing techniques, but there is no inherent reason why they could not also be used with human indexing in the context of electronic IR database displays.

• conflation of variables in IR research : 18

Because variables such as these have typically not been separately analyzed, it has been difficult, if not impossible, to determine whether the results of particular IR systems are due to automatic versus human analysis and indexing, or to different documentary units, different levels of indexable matter and exhaustivity, different types of interface options provided (such as browsable displayed indexes versus electronic searches and machine matching), different levels of vocabulary specificity, different types or levels of vocabulary management, different types of surrogation, or to combinations and interactions among these features.

• views of Cooper (William S.) on variables in IR research : 19

In 1978, William S. Cooper commented on this problem in IR research: "Reflecting the importance of the problem, the indexing process has been investigated extensively and a few insights have been achieved. [However] ... of the ... research that has been addressed to the central issue of finding the normative criteria that ought to govern human and automatic indexing, most has been burdened by the almost insurmountable methodological obstacles involved in making comparative evaluations of retrieval systems as wholes" (p. 107). When IR systems are considered only "as wholes," then it is difficult, if not impossible, to suggest exactly which aspect of the system is contributing to or detracting from desirable results.

• conflation of variables in IR research : 20

Conflation of distinct variables continues to be a problem in IR research. In 1994 in an important anthology assessing the status of human and machine indexing by leaders in the indexing and IR research community (Fidel et al. 1994), Edie Rasmussen characterizes the differences be-

Chapter 8. Analysis and Indexing Methods (Section 8.1)

tween automatic indexing and human indexing as that between the "relative effectiveness of controlled vocabulary versus free text" (Rasmussen 1994, p. 241). With the advent of full-text IR databases, this comparison has progressed to "full-text searching" versus "controlled vocabulary indexing" (p. 245). In each of these examples, two different variables have been conflated. It is possible to present controlled vocabulary terms for searching based on either automatic or human analysis, so the first of these comparisons should appropriately focus on the presence or absence of vocabulary management, separating that attribute from automatic versus human analysis and indexing. Similarly full-text searching has to do with exhaustivity and indexable matter, so in a genuine comparison between human versus machine analysis and indexing, or between free-text terms versus controlled vocabulary, these attributes (level of exhaustivity, extent of indexable matter) should be as similar as possible. All the papers in this anthology are valuable and useful, but they also illustrate the continuing difficulty of isolating the many different aspects of IR database design for assessing the impact of each variable.

• role of users in IR research at TREC : 21

Much research pursued for the annual Text Retrieval Conferences (TREC 1992-2001), sponsored by the U.S. National Institute of Standards and Technology, the U.S. Defense Advanced Research Projects Agency, and the U.S. Advanced Research and Development Activity, have reverted to the older model of IR research, except that the TREC test collections are much larger that earlier ones. For the most part, TREC research has not involved real users with real information needs making real relevance judgments.

• evidence from use of automatic indexing versus human indexing : 22

If research into the merits of automatic versus human analysis and indexing has been inconclusive, the actual experience of IR database producers and users is persuasive. The fact that IR databases that rely solely on automatic analysis and indexing have been economically successful means that the users who are paying for them (either in actual financial outlay or in time spent using them or both) find them sufficiently effective to justify the cost. In some situations, no other options are available.

• user preferences for automatic indexing versus human indexing : 23

Raya Fidel (1991) has verified preferences and usage patterns of professional searchers. When they have a choice between automatic indexing and human indexing as the basis for a search, they often opt for automatic indexing, depending on a whole array of other considerations, which Fidel explores. Again, however, choosing automatic indexing means also choosing, in most cases, a greatly expanded level of exhaustivity, much larger indexable matter, much smaller documentary units, a higher level of specificity, a much larger indexing vocabulary, and little or no vocabulary management. It also provides access to different types of indexing syntax and searching options, which can be much more flexible in certain situations. At the same time, choosing automatic indexing usually limits a user to electronic term-matching searches, as opposed to browsable displays. Thus, when a searcher chooses automatic indexing, it is not clear which features are the most influential. These are not simple choices limited to automatic versus human analysis and indexing.

• effectiveness of automatic indexing : 24

The bottom line is clear, however: automatic analysis and indexing works! And it appears to work just as well as human analysis and indexing, just differently. Automatic analysis and indexing is also considerably faster and cheaper than indexing based on human intellectual analysis. Automatic methods can be applied to enormous collections of messages (such as the world-wide

Chapter 8. Analysis and Indexing Methods (Section 8.2)

web) where the volume of texts and constant change, both within individual texts and in the composition of collections, make human indexing impractical, if not impossible.

• **cost-benefit analysis of human indexing versus automatic indexing : 25**

The challenge for IR database designers is to determine, for particular clientele, particular types of messages, texts and documents, in particular subject areas and for particular purposes, how expensive human analysis and fast, cheap machine analysis can best be deployed to maximize effective retrieval results at the lowest overall cost.

• **26**

This chapter includes brief summaries of techniques used in each approach to indexing, focusing on the initial analysis. The translation or conversion of the results of analysis into formal descriptions or descriptors or headings or other kinds of representations to be searched or presented to users are considered later, mainly in chapter 12 on syntax.

8.2. Human Analysis for Indexing.

• **methods of human analysis for human indexing : 27**

Ironically, much more is known about automatic machine methods of analysis for indexing than about human methods, because machine methods must be rigorously described in detail for the computer to carry them out. Human analysis and indexing has been performed for millennia, at least since the invention of methods for recording messages on long-lasting media, but understanding exactly how it is done is limited to the rather vague guidelines that IR database producers provide to their staffs and the distinctly general explanations that experts suggest in textbooks and training materials, as well as very preliminary results of research into the workings of the human mind and brain.

• **cognitive processes in human indexing : 28**

Brain scientists, neuroscientists, and cognitive psychologists are making progress in understanding how humans think and perform mental tasks. Recent advances were well described for the lay person in a series of articles in *The New York Times* ("Behind the veil of thought: an occasional series about advances in brain research," Hilts 1995), but the steps that might take place in the mind of an indexer are still only suggested hypotheses. A few scholars have begun to address the specific act of indexing as a kind of problem solving (David et al. 1995). Their "research program is an attempt to apply theories and methods from cognitive psychology to the study of indexing behavior" (p. 49).

• **29**

Members of the David et al. research team have reported related research in "Convergent theories: using a multidisciplinary approach to explain indexing results" (Bertrand-Gastaldy et al. 1995), "Psychological approach to indexing: effects of the operator's expertise upon indexing behavior" (Bertrand & Cellier 1995) and "Expertise and strategies for the identification of the main ideas in document indexing" (Bertrand, Cellier & Giroux 1996). Comparing subject-matter experts versus non-experts in the latter study, they found that indexers "not familiar with the content based their judgments on surface-level features of the information. ... Identifying important concepts could be due to perceptual processing based on specific cues, as well as conceptual processing based on prior knowledge of the documentary language and the domain to be indexed" (p. 419, abstract). The "documentary language" is the indexing language or controlled vocabulary used.

Chapter 8. Analysis and Indexing Methods (Section 8.2)

• role of documentary features in human indexing : 30

A 1993 study by Chu and O'Brien, "Subject analysis: the critical first state in indexing," focuses on the use of "document-related factors such as "bibliographic apparatus and presentational layout" (titles, subtitles, abstracts, lead paragraphs, headings, etc.). They also compare analysis difficulty between more factual versus more subjective materials and across disciplines: sciences, social sciences, and the humanities. Their research subjects (participants) were all novice indexers.

• cognitive processes in human indexing : 31

Earlier psychological research on human analysis and indexing is summarized by John Farrow in "A cognitive process model of document indexing" (1991). Farrow notes that "the comprehension of text for indexing differs from normal fluent reading" in the following ways: time constraints; rapid text scanning for perceptual cues "to aid gist comprehension"; task-oriented rather than learning-oriented comprehension; immediate production of some text representation (abstract, index headings or terms, classification category or notation); and the repetition of text processing "by experienced indexers working with a restricted range of text types." He explores the interplay of perceptual (cues from text) and conceptual (prior knowledge) processing and the "allocation of mental resources to text processing" (p. 149).

• analysis steps in human indexing : 32

The general consensus among indexers and theoreticians is that human indexers perceive (read, view, examine, listen to) a text, interpret the message encoded in the text as they understand it (influenced by previous experience and current personal knowledge, including their interpretations of any instructions given to them), and then describe their version of the message, plus any important text or document features, in accordance to rules and patterns for the type of index they are working on. Not much more detail than that is provided by experts in indexing. Here are examples of explanations provided by leading writers on human analysis and indexing:

• views of Mulvany (Nancy) on human indexing : 33

Nancy Mulvany. In *Indexing Books* (1994), Mulvany says:

"I do not believe that indexing can be taught. Rules, and the reasons for following or not following them, can be presented. Various index formats can be discussed. However, the ability to objectively and accurately analyze text and to produce a conceptual map that directs readers to specific portions of the text involves a way of thinking that can only be guided and encouraged, not taught. ... Indexing cannot be reduced to a set of steps that can be followed" (p. vii-viii).

• 34

"... [I]ndexing is an art. We can isolate the methodological components of indexing, but there is another dimension to indexing that does not lend itself to such rigorous examination. Indexing skills can be nurtured and rules can be learned. But the indexer's ability to thoroughly digest the intentions of the author and anticipate the needs of the readers, thereby producing a knowledge structure that is sensible and usable, involves the application of abilities and skills that are inherent in some individuals and not in others" (p. 39).

• 35

"All information presented in the body of the text that is directly relevant to the subject matter, scope, and audience of the book is indexable. An indexer with a clear idea of the scope of the book itself and a general understanding of the subject matter and the audience will be in a position to distinguish between relevant and peripheral information.

Chapter 8. Analysis and Indexing Methods (Section 8.2)

• 36

"Distinguishing between relevant and peripheral information involves judgment. Careful exercise of such judgment is what sets a true index apart from a computer generated list of words" (p. 45).

• cultural factors in human indexing versus automatic indexing : 37

Later, in section 8.3. on automatic indexing, we shall see that modern indexing algorithms go well beyond simply generating lists of words, and that indeed, judgments are made based on a wide range of criteria, including those encoded in knowledge bases reflecting subject area understanding and cultural mores of their creators. Nevertheless, effective human analysis and indexing relies on a very sophisticated use of human intelligence. Machines are very far from simulating the work of a human indexer. Part of what a human indexer does is to interpret the text (understand the message). Human indexers do this in the context of their cultures and their personal experiences, including their prejudices, as well as taking into consideration user needs and desires. Consequently, an index based on human analysis and indexing may not travel well between cultures. A freedom fighter in one culture may be a terrorist in another.

• cultural factors in automatic indexing : 38

But the machine also has a culture: the culture imposed by its programmers. For example, a knowledge base that would associate certain strings of language text with the concept of "terrorism" would use the understanding of that concept in the context of the culture of the programmers. A simpler index, "a computer generated list of words," that would use only a simple manipulation and accounting of the symbols found in the text, would be much closer to an objective index that could be used across cultures.

• views of Chan (Lois Mai) on human indexing : 39

Lois Mai Chan. Cataloging is the application of analysis and indexing procedures to a particular collection of documents. Classification is a form of indexing that results in conceptual groupings of topics, rather than alphabetic arrays of headings. Chan has written widely on cataloging and classification. Here is what she says about subject analysis in her popular introductory textbook, *Cataloging and Classification: An Introduction* (1994):

• 40

"No matter what the subject access system within which a subject cataloger is working, subject analysis of a particular work or document involves basically three steps: (1) determining the overall subject content of the item being cataloged, (2) identifying multiple subjects and/or subject aspects and interrelationships, and (3) representing both in the language of the subject headings list at hand.

• 41

"The most reliable and certain way to determine the subject content is to read or examine the work in detail" (p. 166).

• views of *Chicago manual of style* on human indexing : 42

Chicago manual of style. One of the most widely used guides for back-of-the-book indexing is the venerable *Chicago manual of style*, now in its fourteenth edition (1993). Its chapter on indexing declares that "a good index records every pertinent statement made within the body of the text. The subject matter and purpose of the book determine which statements are pertinent and which are peripheral" (p. 703).

• views of Fugmann (Robert) on human indexing : 43

Robert Fugmann. Writing on "recognizing and selecting the essence of a text," German indexing theorist Fugmann (1993) says:

Chapter 8. Analysis and Indexing Methods (Section 8.2)

"Essence recognition is a most fundamental and cognitive process in science. The kind of subjectivity which is inherent in this process does not detract from its fundamentality. To the contrary, all progress in cognition has been achieved through subjectivity. At some time, a genius saw or hypothetically assumed lawful relations which up to then had been hidden to everybody" (p. 74).

• views of Soergel (Dagobert) on human indexing : 44

Dagobert Soergel. Soergel, whose book *Organizing information: principles of data base and retrieval systems* (1985) won the "Book of the Year" award from the American Society for Information Science, emphasizes the importance of "request-oriented indexing." This means not just indexing according to the message of a text, but according to what users are looking for. He portrays indexers as scouts who are sent out on behalf of users to look for answers to particular questions. Of course, it is economically unfeasible to have an indexer for every information seeker, looking through masses of documents for answers to a single query, so queries must be aggregated or batched, and indexers should look for answers to all of these anticipated requests as they examine documents (p. 50-56). In the design sequence suggested in this book, this is exactly what the subject scope statement is designed to achieve — a description of the kinds of questions that users will want (and therefore should be able) to ask of an IR database. For indexers the subject scope statement can serve as a kind of questionnaire that needs to be answered for each document that is indexed. For each topic specified in the subject scope, the users are, in effect, asking the indexer, "does this document have anything of value on this topic?"

• views of Lancaster (F. W.) on human indexing : 45

F. W. Lancaster. Widely recognized as an authority on indexing, abstracting, and vocabulary management, Lancaster echoes Soergel's ideas when he writes:

"Effective subject indexing involves deciding not only what a document is about but also why it is likely to be of interest to a particular group of users .... The same publication could be indexed rather differently in different information centers and should be indexed differently if the groups of users are interested in the item for different reasons" (1991, p. 8).

• views of Fairthorne (Robert) on human indexing : 46

Robert Fairthorne. Writing earlier, the British information scientist Fairthorne (1971) also deals with the thorny issues of aboutness and purpose:

"What discourse speaks of, — that is, what it mentions by name or description —, are amongst its extensional properties. What discourse speaks on, — that is, what it is about —, is amongst its intensional properties. Thus, its topic, cannot be determined solely from what it mentions. For this, one must take into account extra-textual considerations, such as who is using it for what purpose, what purpose the author intended it to be used for, and for whom or for what the librarian, or other manager of messages, acquired it. ... [T]opics are not the properties of text marks as such, but of discourse. ... [T]o create or assign topics to a text we must consider it in the wider context of what kind of person uses it for what, what other texts are used, and in what ways do these texts depend on each other" (p. 361, 362).

• views of O'Connor (Brian) on human indexing : 47

Brian O'Connor. In his philosophical *Explorations in indexing and abstracting: pointing, virtue, and power*, O'Connor (1996) defines "subject" as "a relationship between each individual and the squiggles that constitute the document. If the subject were a single, self-evident entity, then subject representation would be only a slight challenge. ... The circumstances of the patron and the nature of the squiggles combine to generate a unique, user-dependent meaning for each engagement with each document" (p. 51). O'Connor's "squiggles" and Fairthorne's "text marks" are the symbols used to create a text that represents the message of the creator of the text. Later, O'Connor addresses the concept of "aboutness," which is usually central to the human indexer's analysis and subsequent description of a message: "Aboutness is the behavioral reaction of a person to a document. Each patron may have a different experience with the same document" (p. 147). It is clear that indexers, as well as users (patrons), each have different experiences with messages and texts.

• views of Wellisch (Hans) on human indexing : 48

Hans Wellisch. Veteran indexer and scholar of indexing, Wellisch writes in the first edition of his encyclopedic *Indexing from A to Z* (1991) that:

"[T]he mental activities resulting in the formulation of index entries cannot be observed and can therefore not be objectively described, measured, or reduced to fixed rules similar to those that govern the purely technical aspects of indexing such as filing or capitalization of words" (p. 175). A little later he explains that "The problem is that the topics or subjects dealt with in a document (or the 'aboutness' of that document) and their relevance for its intended or prospective users is in many if not most cases vague and difficult or even impossible to pin down exactly, because it is almost always a matter of subjective opinion" (p. 178).

• 49

Wellisch expands on these ideas in the second edition of this book (1996):

"Beginning indexers often ask whether there is a theory of indexing. If by this is meant a coherent system of propositions explaining the mental activities involved in transforming a text into its index, the only honest answer is that we do not have such a thing. To be sure, whole books and numerous articles have been written, purporting to reveal an indexing theory, but these are either mere discussions of technical rules and their interpretation, or they are more or less conjectural speculations on what goes on in the mind of a person who is indexing a text.

• 50

"All we know is that indexing is a highly complex intellectual process involving the use of language in a specific and somewhat artificial way, and that it is also to a considerable extent a matter of intuition, the workings of which cannot be reduced to fixed rules. ... In this respect, indexing is similar to other mental operations such as the recognition of faces and voices: we know that we can do it, but cannot describe in so many words how we do it, nor can we reduce it to a set of rules" (p. 218-219).

• views of Wilson (Patrick) on human indexing : 51

Patrick Wilson. One of the most detailed analyses of the challenges of human indexing appears in the chapter "Subjects and the sense of position" in Patrick Wilson's classic treatise *Two kinds of power: an essay on bibliographic control* (1968). Remember that in 1968 "man" and "his" were thought to refer, when appropriate, to all of humankind. He writes:

• 52

"It is difficult enough in any field of human behavior to discover a man's purposes by examining the results of his activity; and the difficulties must be much greater than ordinary in the case of those most complex products of human effort, writings" (p. 81).

• 53

He continues:

"The notion of the subject of a writing is indeterminate, in the following respect: there may be cases in which it is impossible in principle to decide which of two different and equally precise descriptions is a description of the subject of a writing, or if the writing has two subjects rather than one" (p. 89).

Chapter 8. Analysis and Indexing Methods (Section 8.2)

• 54

He concludes:

"Any actual physical object is, as the old philosophers would have said, 'determinate in every respect'; whether we can decide on its actual shape and size and weight and color, it must have some definite shape and size and so on, at any moment. There are no doubt limits to the precision of measurement and description possible to us, but there must be some descriptions which are the exactly correct descriptions of its various characteristics, even if we cannot, because of physical limitations, tell which ones those are. Things are what they are; our descriptions may be vague and imprecise and indefinite, but there can be no vagueness or indefiniteness about the things themselves. Now we have an inclination to say that what is true of things must be true of writings 'about' things; a writing must have a definite subject, and there must be some description of the subject that is absolutely precise and accurate, all other descriptions being imprecise or inaccurate. It is this inclination which must, I think, be resisted; of course we can always formulate descriptions which are obviously and definitely *not* descriptions of what a writing is about, but we cannot expect to find one absolutely precise description of one thing which is *the* description of *the* subject, all others being mere approximations to that one description, or being descriptions of what is not the subject. The uniqueness implied in our constant talk of *the* subject is non-existent" (p. 89-90)

• concrete entity and event databases versus IR databases : 55

This basic difference between "things" and "messages" (and their texts) — which Wilson calls "writings" — creates the fundamental difference between concrete entity and event databases on the one hand (databases of data about things and events!) and IR databases (databases of data about messages, texts, and documents) on the other (a distinction discussed at some length in section 1.3 on terminology and section 1.6.2 on IR databases). Concrete entity and event databases focus on things and events — on the description of things and events and the retrieval of information about things and events; IR databases focus on messages — on the description of messages, the texts in which they are encoded, and the documents in which texts are recorded. The purpose of IR databases is the retrieval of information about messages, texts, and documents, or the retrieval of the texts of messages. Wilson explains why the goal of concrete entity and event databases is possible and why the goal of IR databases is fraught with difficulty and challenge!

• views of Taylor (Arlene) on human indexing : 56

Arlene Taylor. Taylor (1999) has analyzed Patrick Wilson's commentary on concept analysis and has named the approaches that he has identified (p. 138-139):

"***Purposive method***. One tries to determine what the author's aim or purpose is. If the creator of the information package gives a statement of purpose, then we can presume to know what the work is 'about.' ...

"***Figure-ground method***. Using this method, one tries to determine a central figure that stands out from the background of the rest of the information package. However, what stands out depends on the observer of the package as well as on its creator. What catches one's interest is not necessarily the same from person to person, and may not even be the same for the same person a few weeks later.

"***Objective method***. One tries to be objective by counting references to various items to determine which one vastly outnumbers the others. Unfortunately, an item constantly referred to might be a background item (e.g., Germany in a work about World War II). ...

"***Appealing to unity or to rules of selection and rejection***. When using this method one tries to determine what holds the work together, what cohesiveness there is, and what has been said (se-

Chapter 8. Analysis and Indexing Methods (Section 8.2)

lection) and not said (rejection). Again, the observer of the information package has to be objective and also has to know quite a lot about the subject in order to know what was rejected."

• views of Hjørland (Birger) on human indexing : 57

Birger Hjørland. We close this section with quotes from one of the most recent analyses of the nature and purpose of human indexing, and more broadly, the whole field of information science: *Information seeking and subject representation: an activity-theoretic approach to information science* (1997) by Birger Hjørland, a professor in the Royal School of Librarianship in Copenhagen. Hjørland urges the study and practice of indexing (or more broadly, the facilitation of information seeking through subject representation) guided by an "activity theory" that focuses on the working domains of users as the context and impetus for their information seeking. This might encompass, as well, various social or cultural domains for users seeking informative or uplifting or entertaining messages relating to such life concerns as occupational or career options, spiritual life, family issues, or entertainment. Hjørland writes:

• activity theory: treatment of knowledge organization : 58

... [K]nowledge is organized in learned institutions, in professionals [i.e. professions?], in journals, in libraries, and so on. Knowledge is produced as a part of human activities and tied to the division of labor in society. From the point of view of activity theory, this is the primary organization of knowledge. The organization of knowledge in IS [information science] is secondary or derived, and so is, in certain ways, the cognitive organization of knowledge in individual minds. The organization of knowledge is determined by evolution of different kinds of functional forms and principles which vary according to specific needs, contents, and conditions" (p. 45.)

• paradigms of information science : 59

Hjørland advocates the use of activity theory and domain analysis as the best framework, model, or paradigm for pursuing IR. He contrasts domain analysis and activity theory with other current models/paradigms of IR, which he labels the "information object paradigm" (in which messages, texts, and documents are central), the "behavioral paradigm" (in which human behavior, especially vis a vis information, is central), the "cognitive paradigm" (in which the functioning of the individual human mind is central), and the "communication paradigm" (in which IR is seen as an aspect of human communication). He concludes:

• role of domain analysis in information understanding : 60

"The domain analytic paradigm is a theoretical approach to information science (IS) which states that the best way to understand information in IS is to study the knowledge domains as discourse communities, which are parts of the society's division of labor. Knowledge organization and structure, cooperation patterns, language and communication forms, information systems, and relevance criteria are reflections of the objects of the work of these communities and of their role in society. The individual person's psychology, knowledge, information needs, and subjective relevance criteria should be seen in this perspective" (p. 106).

• views of Hjørland (Birger) on nature of subjects : 61

In this context, Hjørland asserts:

"What constitutes a subject according to activity theory is not independent of purpose, viewpoint, or theoretical influences. What constitutes a subject for one discipline or theory need not constitute a subject for another (p. 84). ... Another consequence of this view is that different theoretical backgrounds, paradigms, world views or metaviews — which can be either disciplinary, interdisciplinary, or cross-disciplinary views — are central to subject analysis" (p. 85).

• 62

This concern for operational, social or cultural context is very much in line with the need for subject interest and domain analysis of potential users in the initial formulation of the subject scope and domain focus of IR databases.

• variability in human indexing : 63

One conclusion that must be drawn from this survey of expert commentary on human intellectual analysis of messages is this: the one thing we definitely do know about human indexers is that they rarely agree on what is important in a message, or what to call it. Research on human analysis and indexing shows that human indexers share the enormous variability that characterizes all human use of language. Tefko Saracevic (1991), synthesizing "major findings from several decades of research on the magnitude of individual differences in information retrieval (IR) tasks," summarizes this variability in this way: "the degree of agreement (expressed by a variety of measures) in human decisions related to organizing, representing, searching and retrieving of information is relatively low and the range of performance relatively high. The agreement hardly reaches about one fourth of cases involved (and often it is lower), and the range of performance routinely varies tenfold or more. However, the notion of 'low' or 'high' here may be inappropriate. The observed ranges may be all that is expected for these tasks, i.e., they may be 'normal'" (p. 85). "Range of performance" refers to such measures as time taken to perform given tasks, error rates, number of documents retrieved in order to achieve a pre-determined level of recall, or recall and precision ratios (which measure the percentage of relevant documents retrieved and the ratio of relevant to irrelevant documents retrieved, respectively; these ratios will be discussed in chapter 9).

• consistency in human indexing : 64

There is a large literature on indexer (and searcher) inconsistency. Overviews and summaries have been provided by Lawrence E. Leonard in *Inter-indexer consistency studies, 1954-1975: a review of the literature and summary of the study results* (1977) and Karen Markey (now Drabenstott) in "Interindexer consistency tests: a literature review and report of a test of consistency in indexing visual materials" (1984).

• 65

Mirja Iivonen (1994a, b) has analyzed the nature of indexer inconsistencies and distinguished differences in conceptual analysis from differences in naming. She found the latter differences — what to call topics — to be more prevalent than disagreements on key concepts.

• inconsistency in searching : 66

Saracevic and Kantor et al. (1988a, b, c) have investigated variation among searchers, verifying that searchers behave much the same way as indexers. After all, searchers describe (that is, they analyze and index) information needs or desires and hope that their indexing will match that of indexers of potential answers or responses. Lourdes Collantes (1995) focused on variation in naming among potential cataloging users.

8.2.1. Cognition Versus Social Construction in Human Analysis and Indexing.

• views of Frohmann (Bernd) on human indexing : 67

The prevailing view among indexers and indexing experts is that human analysis and indexing of messages and texts is largely a cognitive process of the human mind. Bernd Frohmann has vigorously protested what he considers to be excessive preoccupation with the mental (cognitive) aspects of indexing. Yet almost everyone who has studied the indexing process has described it as a cognitive process governed or influenced by the workings of the individual minds of index-

Chapter 8. Analysis and Indexing Methods (Section 8.2.1)

ers. Emphasis has been on the essential characteristics of human mental operations. Proponents of this approach call it the cognitive view or approach to information retrieval. Frohmann considers this to be useless "mentalism."

• 68

In his 1990 article, "Rules of indexing: a critique of mentalism in information retrieval theory," Frohmann quotes a number of scholars on the nature of human indexing, which he describes as "the implicit or explicit representation of a document by an indexing phrase." He summarizes current understanding of the indexing process as one that "continues to be lamented as an intellectual operation both fundamental to indexing yet so far resistant to analysis" (p. 82). Here are some examples of the passages that Frohmann quotes, not unlike those already quoted in the previous section:

• views of Foskett (A. C.) on human indexing : 69

A. C. Foskett.

"Scanning a text to decide what it is about is the key operation in indexing, yet it is the least discussed and the least reducible to rule" (Frohmann cites Foskett 1982; similar statements occur in that book, but this particular statement could not be found).

• views of Farradane (Jason) on human indexing : 70

Jason Farradane.

"The indexer's 'output' is a stylized form of 'information' whose relationship to the original document needs more study than it usually receives" (Farradane 1979, p. 13).

• 71

"... the more we study the two cognitive ends of the picture, that is, the cognitive processes which produce information, and the cognitive processes which occur on the receipt of information, the more we may be able to improve and control the processes of information storage and retrieval to attain desired results. ... [I]n a large part of its scope information science is a cognitive science, that is, it deals with thought processes" (Farradane 1980a, p. 75).

• views of Beghtol (Clare) on human indexing : 72

Clare Beghtol. Basing her analysis on the work of Teun Adrianus van Dijk, Beghtol writes:

"The ability to restate the semantic aboutness of a discourse ... originates in an automatic reductive cognitive process of summarisation that allows a reader to construct during reading a notion of the text topic and to store it in hierarchically-arranged memory structures for later recollection. ... During the act of reading a text the reader notices the presentation of each sentence, automatically transforms its surface verbal structures into its deep conceptual propositions and establishes an understanding of the local relationships between the words and sentences of the text. ... At the same time, the reader engages in a global, textual or macro-level analysis of the text in order to arrive at an overall understanding of the aboutness and meaning of the complete text as a whole. ... These cognitive actions of compressing a text in order to generate a semantically accurate statement of discourse aboutness are, according to Van Dijk, governed by macro-rules .... One may say that the subject of a document is the highest specific macroproposition that is produced and can be expressed by a reader during cognitive reduction of a text by microanalysis. ... Van Dijk has formally described and analysed a cognitive process that can be assumed to operate during the aboutness analysis of a text for the purpose of classifying it by means of a particular classification system" (Beghtol 1986, p. 90, 92).

Chapter 8. Analysis and Indexing Methods (Section 8.2.1)

• views of Anderson (James D.) on human indexing : 73

James D. Anderson. Anderson is greatly honored to be classified, along with his contemporary Clare Beghtol, with leaders of an earlier generation of information scientists such as Foskett, Farradane, and Artandi. Frohmann writes:

"James D. Anderson (1985) is in the vanguard of library science's appropriation of mentalism by boldly representing the mind as a library, complete with a technical services department performing indexing operations of which, at least until we have read Anderson, we are completely unaware" (p. 84-85).

• 74

Here's Frohmann's Anderson quote:

"Indexing systems turn information storage and communication systems into information retrieval systems analogous, in widely varying degrees, to the human information retrieval system of the mind (Anderson 1985, p. 287-288). ... [T]he mind of a human indexer ... receives the symbols via normal perception processes, matches them against those stored in the mind, determines what concepts are represented and which are important, then chooses symbols to represent these concepts in the index (p. 295). ... Just as a well selected library is very discriminating in choosing what to add to its permanent collection, the mind selects only a small portion of its perceptions for processing into long-term memory. ... It is this selected and stored information which is indexed by the mind as part of its information retrieval system (p. 292, 293). ... Just as a well-run library [...] will discard documents no longer needed, the human mind will forget information which, although indexed initially into long-term memory, was of less importance when received and therefore indexed less thoroughly (p. 293). ... The human mind is like a library collection or a full-text database in that its documents are included in its indexing system in full, not represented by abbreviated surrogates. ... [T]he mind does not store the original texts ... which it processes .... Instead, from the mass of information perceived, it selects the information (concepts and their relations) of interest and creates new 'documents' which are integrated into semantic memory. It is the full text of these new documents which the mind stores and indexes (p. 314)."

• views of Artandi (Susan) on human indexing : 75

Susan Artandi. Artandi, Anderson's former colleague and an information science pioneer at Rutgers University, asks: "Do we know enough about how we behave when we say we are thinking that we can describe the process explicitly for the machine?" — [referring to] "the understanding of the human processes that the machine is to duplicate" (1975, p. 235).

• human indexing as model for automatic indexing : 76

Is Artandi suggesting that automatic analysis and indexing should seek to mimic human analysis and indexing? Human indexing is so variable and inconsistent that it seems unwise to make it the model or measure of effective machine indexing. The best test of effectiveness is the satisfaction of users, and automatic indexing should use whatever techniques are at its disposal to achieve this, regardless of how they may relate to human indexing methods. We may aim to "duplicate" in the sense of "replace," or even better "complement," but improvement of IR performance does not lie in the direction of simply replicating the variability of human indexing. In any case, the experience of fifty years of research in artificial intelligence would suggest that the answer to Artanti's question is a resounding "No!"

• positive attributes of human indexing : 77

Nevertheless, there are some very positive attributes of human analysis and indexing that have been highlighted in many of the preceding quotes. Perhaps the most important, and the most difficult for machines to approach, at least in the foreseeable future, is attention to features or characteristics of texts related to potential users and uses that are not explicit in the texts themselves. It is in this matching of often vague and qualitative message, text and document attributes to often even vaguer user needs and desires where expert human analysis and indexing appears to offer the greatest value, over and above the best possible machine analysis and indexing, which almost by definition, must focus solely on the actual text that is being analyzed.

• application of views of Wittgenstein (Ludwig) to human indexing : 78

Frohmann (1990) appeals to the philosopher Ludwig Wittgenstein to contest the "mentalism" represented in current work on human indexing. Frohmann contends that indexing "rules" are not (or should not be?) based on cognitive processes resident in the mind, but on socially constructed rules apprehended by indexers. So he argues that the focus must shift "indexing theory away from rule *discovery* and toward rule *construction*." He continues:

• 79

"By Wittgenstein's lights, indexing rules governing the derivation of indexing phrases from texts are properly seen as instruments of particular social practices. Theory in indexing is therefore confronted with the challenge, not of discovering rules followed unconsciously, but of constructing, consistent with stated purposes, explicit, well-formulated, and strict rules which may be used to yield indexing phrases from texts. The problem of indexer inconsistency, for example, is not solved by first discovering and then bringing order to the motley of tacitly known rules unconsciously followed by indexers, but by replacing prevailing vague rules, for example, those providing no more guidance than 'express the subject of this text in a concise statement,' which indexers perforce interpret variously, with rules sufficiently precise to serve as justifications, as standards of correctness, and as instruments of indexer training." (p. 94).

• application of views of Wittgenstein (Ludwig) to social construction of indexing rules : 80

However, it is not at all clear how Wittgenstein's views might be applied to create more precise rules for human analysis and indexing. Frohmann does not suggest how this should be done, only that it ought to be done. If indexing rules are vague and difficult to formalize when they reflect an individual's cognitive processes, how can it be argued that they will become more precise when they reflect the "stated purposes" of a user, a group, a culture, or society in general? Would the vague rule "express the subject of this text in a concise statement" become somehow less vague if it were to read something like "determine and express the subject of this text according to the purposes of the intended user"? Indeed, it could perhaps be argued, according to Wittgenstein, that cognitive processes are themselves a reflection and a construction of the individual's culture. Persons, including indexers, understand a text based on what they are, who they are, when they are, where they are.

• queer theory compared to indexing theory : 81

This controversy regarding the proper basis for indexing research and theory has regrettably attracted little attention in the primary literature of message and text analysis or indexing and cataloging, whether by humans or machines. It is much closer to similar and sometimes fierce debates in some of the newer post-modern disciplines. A prominent example is queer theory, "an ensemble of strategies of reading and interpreting texts (whether literary or social) that has emerged in the last decade and has been profoundly influenced by poststructural theory. ... Queer theory has evolved as an eclectic and diffuse ensemble of practices influenced by the contestatory realms of psychoanalysis, Marxism, cultural materialism, semiotics, social constructionism, structuralism, and feminism" (Bredbeck 2000).

• queer theory : 82

A dominating feature of queer theory is an on-going argument with essentialists, who see sexual orientation as something innate and rather constant across humankind (and indeed, beyond our species) on one side versus social constructionists, who see sexual orientation as very much a social creation of every culture on the other side. The essentialist position in queer theory is comparable to that of the cognitive approach in human indexing (mentalism to Frohmann), which seeks to understand the essential nature of the mental processes of the human mind as applied to message and text analysis and indexing. Frohmann is clearly on the side of the social constructionists. It is likely that both camps possess some truth — perceptions that will lead to more complete and accurate understanding of complex phenomena. It may indeed be the case that there is something "essentially" innate and constant about being homosexual, heterosexual, or bisexual, but what that means and how it is played out is certainly a consequence of one's cultural context. Similarly it is hard to imagine that fundamental (essential) human cognitive processes do not play a large role in human analysis and indexing, but the application of these processes are just as surely influenced, even determined by, social forces and contexts. For a good summary of this debate in queer theory, with references to relevant publications, see "Constructionism vs. essentialism" in *Completely queer: the gay and lesbian encyclopedia* (Hogan & Hudson 1998).

• **essentialism versus social constructionism in gender studies : 83**

Another arena where the battle between the essentialists and the social constructionists rages is gender studies. Carol Tavris (1998) does a good job of describing these two approaches in "The paradox of gender," a review of *The two sexes: growing up apart, coming together*, by Eleanor E. Maccoby. Tavris calls the two points of view "two antithetical trends in the current study of gender" (p. 127):

• **84**

"One, the oldest empirical tradition, takes an essentialist approach. Essentialists regard a gender-related attitude, trait or behavior as being something embedded in the person — internal, persistent, consistent across situations and time — and thus they tend to regard the sexes as 'opposites': men are aggressive, women pacifistic; men are rational, women emotional. ... For some feminist psychologists, men and women have inherently different ways of knowing, ways of speaking, ways of moral reasoning and the like. For neuroscientists, men's and women's brains operate differently. For sociobiologists, male promiscuity and female monogamy are opposite, hard-wired reproductive strategies. (When sociobiologists learned that the males of many species are nurturant and monogamous and the females of most species are promiscuous, they reconnoitered and decided that these reproductive strategies too are adaptive)."

• **role of gender in human indexing : 85**

As an aside, if we were to accept this essentialist approach to gender studies, then we must make sure that gender is considered as an essential factor in our cognitive study of human indexing! Tavris continues:

• **social construction of gender : 86**

"In contrast, researchers who take a social constructionist approach vigorously dispute all forms of essentialism. Social constructionists hold that there is no "essence" of masculinity and femininity, for these concepts and labels are endlessly changing, constructed from the eye of the observer and from the historical and economic conditions of our lives. 'Opposition,' for example, is a social construction, not an empirical reality; it is a stereotype that blinds us to the greater evidence of gender similarity. ... Constructionists regard gender as a performance, not an attribute. People don't *have* a gender, they *do* a gender, which is why their behavior changes so much depending on the situation."

Chapter 8. Analysis and Indexing Methods (Section 8.2.2)

• **culture versus cognition in human indexing : 87**

Returning to the arena of indexing, Frohmann is surely correct that much of indexing rests on rules or customs informed by culture, and his efforts to persuade our field to create more effective rules to guide our efforts at indexing are very important and to be encouraged. The cultural bias of classification schemes (a form of indexing language) has long been recognized, along with the prejudicial nature of many established subject headings in alphabetical indexing (such as the Library of Congress headings "Pilgrim Fathers" and "Hotel maids," changed to "Pilgrims (Plymouth Colony)" and "Hotel cleaning personnel" in 1976 and 1989 respectively). (Indexing languages will be considered later in chapter 12 on syntax and chapter 13 on vocabulary management.) With respect to the human analysis process, however, it also seems clear that much of that process is also governed by the cognitive procedures of our minds. As in the contending sides in queer theory, gender studies, and many other of the human and social sciences, both sides, both approaches, contribute important aspects toward more complete and accurate understanding.

• **views of Frohmann (Bernd) on social context of human indexing : 88**

Here is one final quote (for the time being) from Frohmann (1990), emphasizing the social context of the rules that he advocates:

"... [M]entalism's focus on processes occurring in minds conceals the crucial social context of rules. Since we do not understand the rule we are constructing without understanding its social context, or the way it is embedded in the social world, its point, its purpose, the intentions and interests it serves, in short, the social role of its practice, indexing theory cannot avoid investigation into the historical, economic, political, and social context of the rules in its domain. Mentalism, on the other hand, either erases the social dimension altogether by conceiving rules as operating in disembodied, ahistorical, classless, genderless, and universal minds, or else acknowledges it only by expanding the set of rules of mental processing" (p. 96).

• **89**

We will return to these issues at the end of the next section on rules for human indexing.

8.2.2. Human Indexing Rules.

• **human indexing as two step process : 90**

Just about everyone agrees that there is a two step process in human indexing: (1) the analysis of a text, resulting in the creation of some kind of notion, phrase or statement representing the meaning and/or features of a message and possibly also of its text and document; and (2) the translation of this notion, phrase or statement into the indexing language or format prescribed by the IR database producer or the design of the index.

• **rules for analysis in human indexing : 91**

Most of the rules regarding indexing, cataloging, and classification relate to the second step — the translation of the result of message/text/document analysis into terms and forms mandated by an indexing language or presentation format. These rules and procedures relate to term specificity, vocabulary management, syntax for index strings and headings, surrogates and surrogate displays, and search interfaces, all of which are treated in separate chapters later in this book. Here the focus is on attempts to formulate rules, guidelines, or procedures for the first step, the analysis of messages, texts and documents and the creation or production of the preliminary notion or statement of meaning, topic, importance or application. These attempts may be seen as at least initial efforts to respond, at least in part, to Frohmann's plea for the construction of effective rules that will contribute to better indexing.

Chapter 8. Analysis and Indexing Methods (Section 8.2.2)

• **standards for analysis in human indexing: British and international : 92**

Both the British Standards Institute (BSI) and the International Organization for Standardization (ISO) have issued standards (BS 6529: 1984, ISO 5963-1985) with recommendations on "methods for examining documents, determining their subjects, and selecting index terms" (International Organization for Standardization 1985). These methods include the following list of questions an indexer should ask of a text (International Organization for Standardization, p. 2). The British standard contains the same list, in slightly different wording (British Standards Institute 1984, p. 3):

a) Does the document deal with the object affected by the activity?

b) Does the subject contain an active concept (for example an action, an operation, a process, etc.)?

c) Is the object affected by the activity identified?

d) Does the document deal with the agent of this action?

e) Does it refer to particular means for accomplishing the action (for example special instruments, techniques or methods)?

f) Were these factors considered in the context of a particular location or environment?

g) Are any dependent or independent variables identified?

h) Was the subject considered from a special viewpoint not normally associated with that field of study (for example a sociological study of religion)?

These are offered as examples of general factors that are likely to apply in any subject field. Other questions may need to be formulated within a special discipline.

• **guidelines for analysis in cataloging and classification at Rutgers University : 93**

This ISO list is similar to guidelines for initial analysis of messages and texts used in cataloging and classification classes in the School of Communication, Information, and Library Studies of Rutgers University. These guidelines are based on the work of the Classification Research Group (U.K.) as reported by Brian C. Vickery (1966, p. 46-47) and also subsequent work by Derek Austin (1984) on PRECIS (Preserved Context Indexing System). Here they are:

Analyze prominent topics and features using the following outline of facets. Not all facets will be represented in all documents.

Describe topics and features using "descriptors" representing single concepts (including "bound terms" such as "information science" or "birth control"). Place descriptors in the most appropriate category.

In general, aim for an exhaustivity level of no more than 10-20 descriptors.

a. discipline/s or work/action domain/s (related to the "approach" facet below, but placed here for the purpose of classing according to library classification systems, all of which put primary emphasis on discipline, work/action domain or professional field having a claim on or special interest in the message of the document).

b. entity/ies (persons or things, concrete/real or abstract/imaginary mental constructs — if action is present, may be object or recipient of action, or performer of action, if action has no object).

c. attribute/s and part/s, including raw material/s pertaining to entity/ies, if present.

d. action/s, activity/ies, operation/s, process/es, event/s, condition/s.

e. agent/s (thing/s or person/s performing actions if entity is recipient of action; may also be means or method of performing action).

f. place/s (as topic!).

Chapter 8. Analysis and Indexing Methods (Section 8.2.2)

g. time or time period/s (as topic!).

h. author's treatment or approach to topic (compare to discipline); point of view, bias.

i. unusual/special organization & format of text.

j. unusual/special medium of text.

k. unusual/special audience intended, including cultural domains (ethnic, religious, gender, sexual orientation, family status, economic-level, urban/rural, occupational, etc.)

• subjective nature of guidelines for indexing : 94

These guidelines are meant to suggest a general approach to analysis, but they certainly don't constitute anything like a rigorous procedure that would produce predictable results. The very first sentence of the guidelines asks the student to analyze "prominent" topics and features, reminding us of efforts by Patrick Wilson, Arlene Taylor and many others (described in previous section) to suggest ways in which "prominent" or "important" might be determined.

• views of Hjørland (Birger) on guidelines for indexing : 95

Commenting on the ISO guidelines, Birger Hjørland (1977) notes, in line with his concern for domain analysis quoted previously, that:

> "Even though the ISO standard can in many ways be reasonable and useful, it can be noted that the prescribed guidelines for subject analysis are fairly document-centered .... The standard does not offer any specific insights into how disciplines or user groups differ or explain the fact that they require particular domain-specific analyses. The document could, for instance, have mentioned that where social science and humanities disciplines are concerned, the indexers need to pay special attention to worldviews and theoretical orientation; that is, it could have emphasized the importance of the subject-object relation in these disciplines. The fact that this was not done shows the danger in publishing international standards in this area: paying attention to inconsequential external features in the analysis gives a false impression of general, objective criteria that in reality cannot be described in a standard, since subject analysis is a theoretical and intellectual process that is dependent on the concrete situation within the knowledge domain in question" (p. 44-45).

• relation of subject scope and documentary scope to rules for human indexing : 96

These lists of questions to ask of, or aspects to look for, in the analysis of a message and its text and document are similar to procedures recommended for assessment of user needs, interests, and operational work/activity and/or cultural domains leading to the formulation of subject scope and domain, as well as documentary scope, for an IR database, as described in chapters 2 (subject scope and domain) and 3 (documentary scope). These assessments are the initial steps in overall IR database design, long preceding any analysis or indexing of individual messages, texts and documents. Indeed, guidelines for indexers should be based directly on assessments of subject scope and domain as well as key documentary types and features, so that indexers will be encouraged to look for evidence that will more likely respond to the requests, interests and needs of users. If the subject scope and domain, plus the identification of key searchable features related to documentary scope, are an accurate reflection of user interests and situations, and if they serve to guide the attention of indexers, then indexers may more nearly fulfill the role envisioned by Dagobert Soergel in request-oriented indexing — as information scouts acting on behalf of searchers, seeking the answers to their questions or appropriate responses to their desires (Soergel 1985, p. 50-56). Similarly, this attention to particular work/activity and cultural domains is also in line with the concerns of Birger Hjørland for effective domain analysis as the context for message analysis and indexing.

Chapter 8. Analysis and Indexing Methods (Section 8.2.2)

• specialized rules for human indexing : 97

But as Hjørland has pointed out, guidelines like the ISO/BSI and the Rutgers lists consist of broad generic categories that can be applied to most if not all messages, texts and documents, with little or no attention to the special needs or interests associated with particular domains of human activity. Specialized domains deserve more specific lists of aspects to guide indexers. Two examples of such specialized lists are (1) the categories currently used by the Modern Language Association of America for its international literary studies database and (2) the facets suggested by Shiyali Ramamrita Ranganathan many years ago for the analysis of messages on diesel engines. They were listed in chapter 2. Here they are again:

• rules for indexing for *MLA international bibliography* : 98

(1) MLA Categories for Analysis of National Literatures (Modern Language Association of America 1997). Examples have been added for each category:

- specific literatures: e.g., English literature, American literature, Chicano literature, Puerto Rican literature.
- performance media: e.g., theater, story-telling, recitation.
- languages (if different from language of national literature): e.g., English, Spanish, Swahili.
- periods: e.g., 20th century, 19th century.
- individuals (real): e.g., Thomas Hardy, Emily Dickinson, Abraham Lincoln, James Baldwin.
- anonymous works: e.g., Beowulf, Mother Goose, The Bible.
- groups/movements: e.g., Avant Garde, Beat Generation, hippies, lesbian poets, African American writers, children.
- genres: e.g., poetry, drama, non-fiction novels.
- works: e.g., The wind in the willows, Alice in wonderland, Giovanni's room.

Further Description of Literary Topic:

- features: e.g., dialogue, poetic realism.
- literary techniques: e.g., visual metaphor, imagery, symbolism.
- themes/motifs/figures/characters: e.g., [treatment of] love, hate, war, Manifest Destiny, salvation, Huck Finn, Cinderella.
- influences (recipients): e.g., [influence on] Harlem Renaissance, Generation of 1898.
- sources: e.g., [influence of] Harlem Renaissance, Generation of 1898, The Bible.
- processes: e.g., characterization, translation.

Description of Document Author's Processes

- types of scholarship: e.g., criticism.
- methodological approaches: e.g., sociological approach, psychological approach, Marxist approach.
- theories: e.g., Freudian theory, evolution (as theory).
- devices/tools: e.g., computers, concordances.
- disciplines: e.g., aesthetics, historiography.
- scholars: e.g., critics, folklorists (also particular individuals).
- general/miscellaneous: A place for indexers to add anything that doesn't fit in the established categories!
- special types of documents: e.g., bibliography, film, slides, videotapes, multimedia.

Chapter 8. Analysis and Indexing Methods (Section 8.2.2)

The MLA list is based directly on a detailed analysis of the working habits and interests of literary scholars (Anderson 1979).

• rules for indexing about diesel engines by Ranganathan : 99

(2) Ranganathan's Facets for Diesel Engines (Ranganathan 1965, p. 221-222):

- Brand of engines.
- Country of manufacture.
- Purpose.
- Environment — the element in which an engine will work, under water or in humid climate or in a desert, and so on.
- Cost.
- Compression ratio.
- Cycle of strokes.
- Size.
- Number of cylinders.
- Bore diameter.
- Arrangement of cylinders.
- Piston position.
- Crankshaft speed.
- Displacement.
- Stroke distance.
- Fuel used.
- Fuel & injection system.
- Cooler used.
- Starting method.

• role of specialized categories in human indexing : 100

Such specialized lists of categories are designed to increase the chances that indexers will not miss important aspects of topics or features, but they do not insure uniformity in the identification of important aspects. This variability appears to be due to those subjective, cognitive, "mentalist" processes going on in our minds, and the fact that the mind of every individual is different.

• limitations of rules for human indexing : 101

Most guidelines for indexers, including those illustrated here, and the implied rules for analysis that they suggest, focus mostly on the content and features of messages, texts and documents, and less on potential uses by interested persons (this document would be good for ...), and even less on the relevant characteristics of potential users, their information needs and information seeking behavior. In addition, they side-step entirely issues of quality, authority, accuracy, and appropriateness, other than some general categorization for intended audience by age level and possibly by occupation or level of expertise.

• qualitative judgments in request-oriented human indexing : 102

Dagobert Soergel (1985) is a strong proponent of the need for qualitative judgments in request or user-oriented indexing — the indexing of messages for particular users, rather than just indexing the content and features of messages, texts, and documents. Thus, he suggests the use of index terms like "read immediately" and "danger to our business" which indicate the impor-

Chapter 8. Analysis and Indexing Methods (Section 8.2.2)

tance of messages for particular users or purposes and at specific times (it is urgent now!) (p. 229).

• **views of Frohmann (Bernd) on rules for human indexing : 103**

Frohmann (1990) is seeking much more thorough and rigorous rules than those presented here — rules based on a careful analysis of social purpose. Here are questions that Frohmann asks us to consider in formulating such rules (p. 97-98):

• **purposes of information retrieval for diverse users : 104**

"What are the purposes of text retrieval in various social contexts and of various kinds of users? The problems involved in constructing rules for indexing languages incorporating the categories of the dominant social institutions of industry, research and development, commerce and finance, universities and the like, are not identical to those involved in designing text retrieval services for marginal groups outside the dominant institutions, such as the economically disadvantaged or the victims of racial, class or gender discrimination. Not only are text retrieval practices of the socially, economically and politically marginalised more difficult to discern, but also the construction of indexing rules aimed at meeting their needs may quite explicitly become part of the exercise of building new and alternative social practices."

• **domain analysis as basis for rules for human indexing : 105**

These questions are right in line with Hjørland 's call for careful domain analysis of potential users, based on the role of information in their work tasks.

• **wants versus needs in information retrieval : 106**

Frohmann continues:

"Some questions demand critical inquiry. Does text retrieval fulfil a need, or does it satisfy a want? Indexing rules will look quite different depending upon how this question is answered. Wants are explicitly recognised and admitted; they reflect the agents' goals, purposes, and intentions. Not all needs are known, and some fly in the face of wants. For example, not everyone knows what they need to prevent AIDS, and not everyone wants what they need. Identification of needs depends upon a conception of human nature and the social world; wants can be identified by questionnaire. If want satisfaction alone is considered the end of text retrieval, then most indexing rules will serve the retrieval practices of the prevailing form of social organisation. Among the important indexing rules for want satisfaction in consumer capitalism, for example, are those which efficiently represent goods for consumption. On the other hand, if text retrieval is taken to fulfil needs, then rules for its practice may not only be inconsistent with the aims of the dominant social order, but may also be antagonistic to them.

• **political aspects of information retrieval : 107**

"Other questions demand political analyses. What and whose aims, goals, strategies, and intentions are fulfilled by text retrieval in the social world in which indexes, abstracts, online databases, catalogues, thesauri, bibliographies and the whole range of retrieval apparatus make their appearance? Is the retrieval of truth a desirable (or even feasible) retrieval practice, as Patrick Wilson (1978) has suggested? If so, this purpose imposes a serious constraint on the kind of indexing rules governing the derivation of indexing phrases. Is the spread of disinformation in the service of ruling elites the purpose of text retrieval? If so, this purpose imposes a rather different constraint on indexing rules. Is text retrieval an economic transaction yielding a profit for the database owner, and therefore a social practice whose participation is constrained by ability to pay, or is it a fundamental right that ought to be guaranteed by government? Again, differing conceptions of the social role of text retrieval will determine the kinds of indexing rules we construct.

Chapter 8. Analysis and Indexing Methods (Section 8.2.2.1)

• identification of non-topical features in human indexing; bibliographic coupling and co-citation as basis for indexing : 108

"Some questions have already been raised in the literature. Is there a large category of document uses for which the *subject* of a text as identified by inter- and intratextual criteria of significance, is quite irrelevant? Are certain other features, such as those identified by Swift [et al. 1977a, 1977b, 1978] and Weinberg (1988b) [point of view, methodological approach, etc.], more significant than a text's 'aboutness'? Does investigation of the uses of documents show that a text should be considered in light of 'the projects in which it can be used, the decisions it can facilitate, the arguments it can support, the predictions it can warrant'? (Wilson 1978, p. 22). If so, we need to find ways of constructing rules yielding index phrases representing projects, decisions, arguments, and predictions. Are the practices of document production relevant for text retrieval? If so, then retrieval practices based on document clusters mapped by bibliographic coupling and co-citation patterns can eliminate the need for rules for the derivation of indexing phrases altogether" (p. 97-99).

(Bibliographic coupling and co-citation analysis as methods of automatic indexing are discussed later in section 8.3.12.)

• 109

Frohmann has raised important questions, most of which our field has largely ignored.

8.2.2.1. Human Indexing Rules for Image Text.

• views of Jorgensen (Corinne) on indexing of image texts : 110

Most rules for indexing focus on language text. Several researchers are working specifically with image texts, attempting to identify useful approaches to their analysis and description. One example is Corinne Jorgensen's dissertation, *Image attributes: an investigation* (1995). Based on patterns exhibited by persons assigned tasks of description, categorization, and searching, she suggests that "indexing of literal object is of prime significance, as is indexing of the human form and other human characteristics and associated attributes. The concept of location ... needs to be addressed. Color ... appears to cue attention to certain attributes .... 'Content/story' and other abstract and affective attributes are also typically described, suggesting that image indexing may benefit by application of concepts associated with indexing of fiction. ... Similarity among images cannot be represented solely by perceptual attributes but must take into account interpretive attributes as well" (dissertation abstract). This work was summarized in Jorgensen (1998).

• views of Pérez-López (Kathleen Golitko) on automatic indexing of image texts : 111

Kathleen Golitko Pérez-López (1995) has focused on scientific images, including "remotely sensed terrain images and radiological images of human tissue [that] do not generally consist of uniform regions separated by distinct, straight line edges, as is often the case for images of manufactured objects" (dissertation abstract). She suggests computer methods for automatic analysis of such images, related more to the next section on automatic indexing.

• recommended resources on human indexing of image texts : 112

The indexing of images has also been addressed by:

Heidorn, P. Bryan; Sandore, Beth, eds. (1997). *Digital image access & retrieval*: papers presented at the Clinic on Library Applications of Data Processing; 1996 March 24-26. Urbana-Champaign, IL: Graduate School of Library and Information Science; 1997. 191 p. ISBN 0-87845-100-5. This collection also has several papers that address the automatic analysis of images.

Chapter 8. Analysis and Indexing Methods (Section 8.2.2.2)

Keister, Lucinda H. (1994). "User types and queries: impact on image access systems." In: Fidel, Raya; Hahn, Trudi Bellardo; Rasmussen, Edie M.; Smith, Philip J., eds. (1994). *Challenges in indexing electronic text and images*. Medford, NJ: Learned Information for the American Society for Information Science; 1994: 7-22. ix, 306 p. (ASIS monograph series). ISBN 0-938734-76-8.

Lunin, Lois F. (1994). Analyzing art objects for an image database. In: Fidel, Raya; Hahn, Trudi Bellardo; Rasmussen, Edie M.; Smith, Philip J., eds. (1994). *Challenges in indexing electronic text and images*. Medford, NJ: Learned Information for the American Society for Information Science; 1994: 57-74. ix, 306 p. (ASIS monograph series). ISBN 0-938734-76-8.

Shatford Layne, Sara (1994). "Some issues in the indexing of images." *Journal of the American Society for Information Science*. 45(6): 583-588; 1994 September.

Svenonius, Elaine (1994). "Access to nonbook materials: the limits of subject indexing for visual and aural languages." *Journal of the American Society for Information Science*. 45(6): 600-606; 1994 September.

• **terminology for image texts and sound texts : 113**

(Note that Svenonius refers to "visual and aural languages." In this book, we use the term "language" and "language texts" in the narrower sense that limits the meaning of "language" to human verbal or word-based speech and the texts that represent human spoken languages in their aural and written forms. For other types of messages and symbol systems, we use terms like "images" and "image text" or "music" and "musical text." Written language is also visual, so we try not to use "visual" when we mean non-language images. Similarly, spoken language is also "aural" or "audio," consisting of sound!)

8.2.2.2. Human Indexing Rules Based on Probabilistic Analysis.

• **views of Frohmann (Bernd) on rules for human indexing of Cooper (William S.) : 114**

William S. Cooper (1978) is cited by Frohmann (1990) as one who merits special praise for his search for indexing rules: "Whether or not one agrees with Cooper's proposed indexing rules ..., their theoretical base is nonetheless exemplary, because his explicit recognition of rules as instruments of training and as standards of evaluation locates them within a conception of rule-following as a practice, a custom, or a technique" (p. 94).

• **views of Cooper (William S.) on human indexing : 115**

Cooper writes in "Indexing documents by gedanken experimentation" (1978):

"It is widely acknowledged among information scientists that the problem of indexing ("cataloging," "classification," etc.) is one of the fundamental problem areas, if indeed not *the* central theoretical problem, of document and reference retrieval. If correct normative rules of indexing could be formulated, the accessibility of man's [sic, but remember this was written in 1978!] entire store of recorded knowledge would be enhanced. However ... there is as yet no consensus among experts about the answers to even some of the most basic questions of what indexers ought to be told to do or of how an indexer's performance should be evaluated" (p. 107).

• **decision theory, utility theory, and gedanken experimentation in rules for human indexing : 116**

Using decision theory and utility theory, Cooper suggests a rule for indexing, which he reduces to this: "The assignment of a term to a document is justified if the average utility associated with that assignment is positive, and unjustified if it is negative" (p. 110). He then introduces a method of "gedanken experimentation" (thought experimentation, from the German for "thought") by which an indexer may estimate average positive and negative utilities.

Chapter 8. Analysis and Indexing Methods (Section 8.2.2.2)

• 117

In the context of language texts, Cooper insists that "the gedanken indexer must read or at least scan the document to be indexed in order to do his job well, gain some idea of what it is about, and keep his user population clearly in mind" (p. 112). For a broad-based assessment of utility, the indexer must "take into account many aspects of utility often neglected in traditional subject cataloging, such as whether the document is written in a language and on a level which the users will be able to understand, whether it is up-to-date enough for his user population, even (if he can) whether the document is of 'high quality'" (p. 112).

• 118

After simplifying the recommended procedure as much as he can, Cooper asks the gedanken indexer to make two utility predictions: (1) the odds against satisfaction, to indicate the chances that a searcher using a particular term would not find a particular document associated with that term useful; and (2) and the average predicted payoff — the amount a satisfied user would be willing to pay for the document. To make the process as easy as possible, Cooper provides an "odds-payoff indexing chart" (reproduced below). In the chart, he suggests that the odds against satisfaction might range from more than 1000:1 down to less than 1:1, indicating at the low end of the scale that as many as half the potential users who use a particular term would find a particular document associated with that term useful. In the same chart, the payoff is measured in money that a user might be willing to pay for a document, ranging from ten cents to $100 or more (in 1978 dollars!). These opposing measures are paired, with the predicted odds against satisfaction on the left and the predicted payoff on the right. Cooper points out that the particular relationships displayed in the chart reflect a particular hypothetical user group, and would need to be adjusted for the particular group of users under consideration.

• odds-payoff indexing chart : 119

```
                    Odds        |  |     Payoff
                                |  |
                   {            |  |            } Higher
        High       {            |  |            } than
                   {            |  |            } Average
                      1000:1   _|  |            }
        Above      {             |  |_ $100.00  }
        Average    {             |  |
                   {             |  |           }
                   { 100:1      _|  |           }
        Average    {             |  |_ $10.00   } Average
                   {             |  |           }
                   {             |  |           }
                   { 10:1       _|  |           }
        Below      {             |  |_ $1.00    }
        Average    {             |  |           }
                                 |  |           } Lower
                   {             |  |           } than
        Low        {             |  |           } Average
                   {  1:1       _|  |           }
                   {             |  |_ $.10     }
                                 |__|
```

Figure 8.1. Cooper's odds-payoff indexing chart
"Possible format for a graphic aid to gedanken indexers.
The data are fictitious" (Cooper 1978, p. 117)

Chapter 8. Analysis and Indexing Methods (Section 8.2.2.2)

• 120

For each potential indexing term, the gedanken indexer will place a mark on the left side of the chart to represent the predicted odds against satisfaction for a user using a particular index term. For example, an indexer may want to decide whether to index Cooper's "Indexing documents by gedanken experimentation" with the term "experimentation." The indexer might predict that among a certain group of users, the odds that they would not find this discussion a useful discussion of "experimentation" might be 10 to 1 (10:1) — 10 users would not find this a useful message for every user who would find it useful. At the same time, the indexer might predict that those who do find this discussion useful might, on the average, be willing to pay $10.00 for it. When we plot these two values on the Cooper chart, the slant is upward to the right, indicating that the potential value for the minority who find this discussion useful outweighs the potential negative impact experienced by the majority. Therefore the term should be assigned.

• 121

Another potential term, say "decision theory," might generate an odds against satisfaction prediction of 100:1, with a predicted average payoff value of only $1.00. Now the line linking these two values slants downward to the right, indicating that the predicted overall negative utility outweighs the predicted positive utility, so the term should not be assigned.

• 122

In actual practice, this decision and utility theoretic approach is often simplified even further and shortened to: if a person using this term is likely to want this document, then use the term.

• 123

Cooper's rules for estimating the utility of documents for persons using particular search or index terms for topics and features can be combined with the lists of aspects to look for, with which this section on rules for human indexing began. When an indexer sees evidence of material related to a topic or feature of known interest, then he or she should note it and assign an appropriate candidate term. The candidate term can then be analyzed by Cooper's decision/utility theoretic procedure as a way of gauging whether the treatment of the topic or the manifestation of the feature is really good enough or significant enough or clear enough or up-to-date enough (etc.!) to be tagged for retrieval.

• numerical values for decision making in human indexing : 124

Cooper's suggestions never caught on in the human indexing community. Adding numerical values to the procedures that expert indexers already follow (assessing needs and interests of potential users and comparing them to the characteristics of messages) did not seem to provide much added value. The fundamentals of just how user needs and desires might be assessed and message, text, or document characteristics be evaluated were not addressed. Cooper's ideas about collecting data about actual term utility values for the purpose of training indexers and evaluating indexing performance had value, but they had no obvious advantage over other approaches to testing and evaluation of indexing effectiveness (e.g., precision, recall, satisfaction, or utility based on user judgments). The addition of numerical values doesn't change the basic fact that the judgments of human indexers are still very subjective, and their precise basis is still very difficult to specify. Despite praise by Frohmann, it does not appear that Cooper has laid down the rigorous rules that Frohmann was seeking.

Chapter 8. Analysis and Indexing Methods (Section 8.3)

8.3. Automatic Indexing.

• **automatic indexing versus human searching : 125**

We now turn from human analysis and indexing to machine indexing, or the analysis of text by means of computer algorithms. Here the focus is on automatic methods used behind the scenes with little or no input from individual searchers, with the exception of relevance feedback. Searching options and techniques, such as methods for creating effective search statements, adding weights to terms, specifying proximity requirements, using truncation, wild cards, or combining terms with boolean or role operators, are considered later in chapter 12 on indexing and searching syntax.

• **automatic indexing of language texts versus image texts and sound texts : 126**

Operational automatic indexing has thus far been restricted, for the most part, to language text. Research into ways to apply automatic techniques to image, sound, and other types of text is still in its infancy, compared to the half century of work on automatic indexing of language text. As suggested in the previous section, some researchers are working on methods for applying pattern recognition techniques to image data, such as the massive amounts of data resulting from satellite surveillance of space and the earth. Their hope is to identify meaningful patterns and thereby indicate (index!) important phenomena hidden in these masses of data that might contain important messages.

• **indexing of image texts by Altavista web search engine : 127**

The search engine Altavista (http://www.altavista.com), began to offer a search option in late 1998 that attempts to locate images that are "visually similar" to a retrieved image. "Visually similar" is not the same as "conceptually similar," so that the results often appear to be based on color, shapes, contrast, and density patterns, rather than particular objects or activities portrayed.

• **theoretical models for automatic indexing: vector-space model, probabilistic model : 128**

Throughout the history of automatic indexing, two major theoretical models have emerged: the vector-space model and the probabilistic model. Sparck Jones, Walker, and Robertson (2000) have provided a thorough review of the development, versions, results, and current status of the probabilistic model. In comparing this model to others, they conclude that "by far the best-developed non-probabilistic view of IR is the vector-space model (VSM), most famously embodied in the SMART system (Salton 1975; Salton & McGill 1983a). In some respects the basic logic of the VSM is common to many other approaches, including our own [i.e., the probabilistic model] .... In practice the difference [between these two models] has become somewhat blurred. Each approach has borrowed ideas from the other, and to some extent the original motivations have become disguised by the process. ... This mutual learning is reflected in the results of successive round[s] of TREC [Text REtrieval Conferences]. ... It may be argued that the performance differences that do appear have more to do with choices of the device set used, and detailed matters of implementation, than with the foundational differences of approach" (part 2, p. 829-830).

• **language model for automatic indexing : 129**

Recently, a "language model" for IR has been proposed, as a modification or simplification of the probabilistic model. The differences are subtle. Instead of attempting to predict the probability of document relevance for an IR query statement, the language model is used to predict probable query search terms. Retrieval is effected when predicted (highly probably) search terms match the actual search terms of users. Like all basic models, probabilities are based, for the most part, on term frequencies within documents and the distribution of terms across collections or IR databases (Ponte & Croft 1998).

• recommended resources on automatic indexing : 130

The focus of our discussion will be on the automatic indexing of language texts. The various tactics and strategies are emphasized, rather than the underlying theoretical models. Useful background and further detail can be found in the following resources:

Croft, Bruce (1989). "Automatic indexing." In: Weinberg, Bella Hass, ed. *Indexing: the state of our knowledge and the state of our ignorance.* Proceedings of the 20th annual meeting of the American Society of Indexers; 1988 May 13; New York, NY. Medford, NJ: Learned Information; 1989: 86-100. x, 134 p. ISBN 0-938734-32-6.

Harman, Donna (1994). "Automatic indexing." In: Fidel, Raya; Hahn, Trudi Bellardo; Rasmussen, Edie M.; Smith, Philip J., eds. *Challenges in indexing electronic text and images.* Medford, NJ: Learned Information for the American Society for Information Science; 1994: 247-264. ix, 306 p. (ASIS monograph series). ISBN 0-938734-76-8.

Korfhage, Robert R. (1997). *Information storage and retrieval.* New York: Wiley Computer Publishing; c1997. xiii, 349 p. ISBN 0-471-14338-3.

Kowalski, Gerald (1997). *Information retrieval systems: theory and implementation.* Boston: Kluwer Academic Publishers, c1997. xiii, 282 p. (The Kluwer international series on information retrieval; 1). ISBN: 0-7923-9926-9.

Salton, Gerard (1989). *Automatic text processing: the transformation, analysis, and retrieval of information by computer.* Reading, MA: Addison-Wesley; 1989. xiii, 530 p. (Addison-Wesley series in computer science).

Sparck Jones, Karen; Willett, Peter, eds. (1997). *Readings in information retrieval.* San Francisco: Morgan Kaufman Publishers; 1997. 576 p. ISBN 1-55860-454-5.

8.3.1. In the Beginning Was the Word.

• definitions of words in automatic indexing : 131

Automatic indexing of language text has traditionally begun with individual words. The first step is to decide what constitutes a word. The usual definition is one or more characters separated by spaces or punctuation. The hard part in this definition (and the part in which systems vary, leading to very different results) is how to deal with punctuation. When are marks of punctuation part of a word, as in 501(c)(3) or A.L.A.? Some researchers are experimenting with procedures that bypass words all together, by simply matching sequences of characters — for example, all sequences of three, four, or five characters, without regard to spaces or punctuation (Mayfield & McNamee 1998; Huffman 1995; Cavnar 1994).

• definitions of words in Chinese language : 132

Defining words on the basis of spaces and punctuation works for most alphabetic or syllabic writing systems, but in Chinese, for example, where each character represents a morpheme or syllable rather than a "word" as generally understood, the determination of word boundaries is much more difficult and is similar to attempts to identify multi-word phrases in English. Several participants in the Text REtrieval Conferences (TREC), especially TREC 5 and TREC 6, have worked on this problem in relation to the indexing and retrieval of Chinese text (TREC 1992-2001).

Chapter 8. Analysis and Indexing Methods (Section 8.3.1)

• treatment of punctuation in automatic indexing : 133

The most troublesome punctuation marks are the hyphen, the slash, and occasionally the apostrophe, the comma, and the period or full stop. Parentheses and underscores can also be significant. Our discussion will focus on the English language, so we will ignore the problem of diacritical marks or accents, but these are also problematic, because in some languages, they can distinguish between very different words, such as "ano" (anus) and "año" (year) in Spanish.

• treatment of hyphens in automatic indexing : 134

Hyphens are tricky because they can be used to connect two separate words, as in "full-text." In this book, for example, we use "full text" when text is used as a noun, but we link these two words with a hyphen when they are used together as an adjective, as in "full-text database." Hyphens are also used to create compound words, such as "data-base." In English, new compound words often lose their hyphens over time, so that "data base" became "data-base," which evolved into today's "database." Some automatic indexing algorithms treat the hyphen as a space, so that the characters before and after the hyphen become separate words ("on-line" becomes "on" and "line"!). Some systems ignore the hyphen, treating it as nothing, so that "MS-DOS" becomes "MSDOS" and "full-text" becomes "fulltext." One solution is to use all possible combinations, so that "on-line" would become "on" and "line," "online," and "on-line."

• treatment of slashes in automatic indexing : 135

The same approach can be used with the slash, which is sometimes used as an integral part of a word or acronym, as in "OS/2," but perhaps more often is used to combine two different, often contrasting or complementary words, as "high/low" or "lesbian/gay." If all possible combinations are used, then we would have "lesbian," "gay," "lesbiangay," and "lesbian/gay." Slashes are used in universal resource locators (URLs) for world-wide web documents, so they should not be ignored. Slashes are also important in UNIX directory syntax, and back slanting slashes (\) are used in MS-DOS directory and file names.

• treatment of underscores and full stops (periods) in automatic indexing : 136

Like slashes, underscores and full stops have become common elements within email addresses and URLs. Full stops are also common in initialisms. If character sequences containing full stops (without following spaces) are treated in all possible ways, then "A.L.A." would also be treated as "ALA" and "A," "L," and "A."

• treatment of parentheses in automatic indexing : 137

Parenthesis can also appear within various types of words, but even more commonly in section headings, such as "501(c)(3)," the provision in the U.S. Internal Revenue Code that provides for tax-deductible contributions to many non-profit organizations. As a result, many organizations are called "501(c)(3)" organizations, and that sequence of characters can be an important searchable word. A possible solution is to treat parentheses as parts of words if there is no space to the left of a left parenthesis or to the right of a right parenthesis.

• treatment of apostrophes in automatic indexing : 138

If the apostrophe is ignored, "can't" would become "cant" and "I'll" would become "Ill." Here too, perhaps the best solution is to include all possibilities. In syntactic analysis, the difference between "its" and "it's" may be important.

• treatment of numbers in automatic indexing : 139

"501(c)(3)" also illustrates the importance of including numbers as words. And if numbers are included as words, then internal commas and full stops become important. It might be O.K. to treat "1,998" as the same as "1998" (possibly confusing an integer number with a date), but there is a big difference between ".103" and "103."

Chapter 8. Analysis and Indexing Methods (Section 8.3.2)

• 140

However, including numbers as indexable words may have an important negative impact as well. Harman (1994, p. 250) points out that there are an unlimited number of unique numbers, so that including them can cause the number of unique words to "explode," slowing down the whole indexing process. The role of numbers will vary among different types of texts.

• 141

One possible solution would be to index only numbers that are combined with alphabetic letters, such as our "501(c)(3)" example. But that would make it impossible to search for tax forms like "1040" or "1099" or a movie like "2001"! Despite possible problems, the best solution appears to be to include all numbers and number-letter combinations within the definition of words to be indexed. In many automatic indexing systems, words that occur only once are eliminated from the index, and because many numbers occur only once, they will be eliminated in any case. But common numbers, such as "1999," "2000" and "2001" would be retained.

• treatment of single characters in automatic indexing : 142

A similar issue is whether to include single character words. The most common single character words in English are "I" and "a," and in many indexing procedures, these words end up on a stop list. Not to include single-character words will make it hard to find "vitamin C"! If single characters are included, but "a" is on the stop list (see section 8.3.3), how can "vitamin A" be found? Some of these problems can be eliminated through a careful sequencing of analysis steps. For example, if phrases are identified first (section 8.3.8), then "vitamin A" would be considered as a phrase rather than two separate words. However, if stemming is performed first (section 8.3.6), some words may be reduced to forms that are on a stop list.

• definition of words in automatic indexing : 143

All these examples are evidence that defining a word for automatic indexing (and electronic searching) is not a simple and straightforward task. These problems have been discussed by Terrance A. Brooks (1998), who gives many more examples and cites relevant literature.

• treatment of upper- and lower-case letters in automatic indexing : 144

Upper and lower-case letters can also be problematic. Upper and lower-case letters are usually merged for calculating term frequency, but retaining upper-case letters can be useful for identifying proper nouns such as names of persons, organizations, and countries. But certainly, searchers should not have to worry about whether particular terms may have upper or lower-case letters.

8.3.2. Simple Keyword Indexing.

• 145

The simplest automatic indexing is based on providing access to every occurrence of every word. In displayed indexes (browsable by humans), this kind of indexing can be presented to users in formats known as permuted, keyword-in-context (KWIC), keyword-out-of-context (KWOC), keyword-along-side-of-context (KWAC), which will be discussed in chapter 12 on syntax. For machine matching, this is straightforward free-text, full-text indexing and retrieval, the kind common in many word processing programs. It will find every occurrence of every character or combination of characters, even the most insignificant of words (from the topical stand point), such as "an" or "the."

8.3.3. Negative Vocabulary Control: Stop Lists.

• **stop lists for reducing size of indexes : 146**

The first attempt to improve simple keyword indexing is often a stop list of insignificant words, designed to eliminate indexing and retrieval of words like "an" and "the." Eliminating stop words can reduce the size of the index significantly, and speed up processing. Francis, Kučera and Mackie (1982) suggest that the ten most frequently used words in English can account for twenty to thirty percent of the words in a text.

• **choice of words for stop lists : 147**

The obvious words for a stop list are prepositions, articles, and conjunctions. Beyond that, expanding the stop list can be problematic, because one person's meaningless word is another person's essential word. "Aspect," for example, might be a good candidate for a stop list, but then "aspect" is an important attribute of verbs in the Russian language, so it could be an important keyword in the context of Russian grammar or linguistics. Some electronic databases have dropped "a" as a stop word because of topics like "vitamin A."

• **number of words in stop lists : 148**

Some automatic indexing systems use stop lists of several hundred words, but to be on the safe side, some IR databases have reduced their stop words to as few as eight: "and," "an," "by," "from," "of," "or," "the," and "with." According to Harman (1994), MEDLARS (MEDical Literature Analysis & Retrieval System) of the U.S. National Library of Medicine has even fewer stop words (p. 252).

• **negative vocabulary control : 149**

Using a stop list can be considered negative vocabulary control. The usual approach to vocabulary control is to list the terms that may be used (preferred terms). In this case, exactly the opposite approach is used: the terms that may not be used are listed.

8.3.4. Counting Words.

• **use of frequency of words for ranking texts : 150**

It quickly became apparent in the early days of automatic indexing that the simple occurrence of a word did little to indicate the theme, meaning or purpose of a language text. So algorithms began counting words in texts, their designers hoping that the term frequency would better indicate what is important in a message. Of course, the most meaningless words — the function words like conjunctions, articles, and prepositions — are also the most frequently occurring words, and these, as already suggested, are not very helpful. But if these words have been eliminated by placing them on a stop list, then counting words can provide a criteria for ranking likely candidate texts in response to a keyword search.

8.3.5. Comparative Counting and Weighting.

• **inverse document frequency of words : 151**

Next came the realization that sometimes term frequency (TF) within documents does not help much in distinguishing one text from another within a single collection or IR database. Take librarianship, for example. The word "library" will probably occur in most if not all texts in a collection or IR database on librarianship, so the mere fact that it occurs in a text doesn't tell us very much. But comparing frequency counts in single texts with the overall occurrence for the same words in an entire collection or IR database might help to pinpoint the more important terms. We can identify words that are unusually frequent in a particular text — words that occur frequently in some texts but do not occur frequently across the entire collection. This relative frequency could be more useful in finding useful documents than simple word frequency within documents. "Inverse document frequency (IDF)" is the measure used to indicate the frequency of terms across documents in the collection. The fewer the documents that have a term, the higher the IDF score, hence the name "inverse" document frequency. The IDF score can be combined with term frequency (TF) within particular documents to help identify useful documents.

• **calculation of document weights : 152**

Term statistics such as IDF and TF have been combined into more or less complex mathematical formulas in order to compute a weight for each of the terms that appear in a document. This weight is then used to compute a score for the whole document in relation to a particular query or search statement. The essential point of these formulas is to assign weights to terms in a document according to how good these terms are for distinguishing among documents. For example, as noted, terms that appear in almost all documents in the IR database are not as good as terms that appear frequently within some documents but not in the whole collection.

• **153**

Some of these formulas do not have a very strong theoretical basis, but are created through trial and error. Others have a much more solid foundation based on probability theory, for instance. Quite a bit of effort has gone into refining these formulas because very significant performance increases can be obtained.

• **154**

Weighting schemes have been a major component of papers presented at TREC (annual Text REtrieval Conferences), organized by the U.S. National Institutes for Standards and Technology (TREC 1992-2001). Gerard Salton was long an advocate for term weighting approaches and was himself a pioneer in developing techniques for weighting. He and Christopher Buckley summarize the results of the previous twenty years in their paper "Term-weighting approaches in automatic text retrieval" (Salton & Buckley 1988), which was reprinted by Karen Spark Jones and Peter Willett (1997) in *Readings in information retrieval.*

8.3.6. Improving the Count: Stemming.

• **impact of stemming on frequency of words : 155**

There are sets of related words that are derived from a common root and appear in a variety of forms, depending on particular functions in a sentence or variations in meaning. Thus we have "index," "indexes," "indexer," "indexing," "indexable." We also have variants, such as "indices" as another form for the word "indexes." Stemming was developed to automatically remove certain common suffixes, or word endings, (and sometimes prefixes, like "re" or "re-" as in "re-indexing") in order to increase the count for important words, and also in order to find word occurrences when the word form in the text does not match the word form in the search statement.

• **identification of word roots in stemming : 156**

The purpose of stemming is to conflate or merge many different words into a single form. The hope is that stemming will increase recall of relevant documents, without too great a cost in decreased precision. But automatic stemming tends to produce errors. The study of word forms or internal structure is called "morphology" in linguistics. Morphological analysis of language is not an easy task, and the more simple or routine stemming procedures do not attempt morphological analysis. Robert Krovetz (1993) has pointed to the kinds of errors that can result from ignoring morphology and the relationship between form and meaning. His examples include the erroneous merging of "organization" and "organ," "doing" and "doe," "policy" and "police," "past" and "paste," and "arm" and "army" (p. 193).

• stemming of plural "s" suffixes : 157

The simplest stemming is limited to removing the "s" used to make words plural. Of course, all "s"s could simply be removed, regardless of their function, but a more careful "s" stemming algorithm attempts to distinguish among different types of concluding "s"s, as in "business," "businesses," "tomatoes," "mathematics," etc.

• stemming of multiple suffixes : 158

A much more complicated stemmer (named for its creator Lovins) goes after more than 260 possible suffixes, while a popular middle-of-the-road stemmer (called Porter after its creator) settles on 60 or so suffixes. Harman (1994, p. 253) illustrates their differences with the search statement "panels subjected to aerodynamic heating." The Porter stemmer would not only reduce to the same root "aerodynamic" and "aerodynamics" (as would a simple "s" stemmer), but also "aerodynamically." It would also combine "heating" and "heated," as well as "subjected," "subject," "subjective," and "subjects." The more comprehensive Lovins stemmer would also deal with "aerodynamicist," as well as "heat," "heats," and "heater."

• impact of stemming : 159

As noted by Krovetz (1993), stemming may produce unwanted results. After all, an "indexer" is not the same thing as an "index"; "indexing" is a process as opposed to the entity "index"; and "indexable" is an attribute. According to Harman (1994, p. 253), "research has shown that *on the average* results were not improved by using a stemmer." Her 1991 paper, "How effective is suffixing," focuses on this question (Harman 1991). Other researchers, however, show improved results in a variety of studies (Hull 1996; Paice 1996), especially when more attention is paid to morphological analysis (Krovetz 1993). Many factors can affect performance, such as "the length of queries, the length of documents, the distribution of the different variants of the word forms ..., and the way queries are presented." Results can be better, for example, if phrases are identified in queries, because phrases help to eliminate some errors (Krovetz 1999). But no matter what the results, searches have grown to expect at least simple "s" stemming so that they don't have to worry about singular and plural forms.

8.3.7. Natural Word Distributions.

• Zipf's law on distributions of words in texts : 160

The purpose of counting word frequency in texts, and also of comparing term frequency within documents to term frequency across documents in collections or IR databases, has been to identify important words for indexing. Another approach to selecting the more important words is based on the distribution of words in texts. George Kingsley Zipf studied word distributions, so we now call the typical word distribution pattern a Zipfian distribution based on "Zipf's law," which consists of mathematical formulas that describe the distribution of high and low frequency words. Here, it is sufficient to say that relatively few words, including the most common function words like articles, prepositions, and conjunctions, occur many times in any normal language text, while the great majority of words occur few times or only once.

Chapter 8. Analysis and Indexing Methods (Section 8.3.7)

• identification of keywords based on transition points in Zipfian distributions : 161

Miranda Pao (1978) presents a procedure for selecting important indexing words based on this Zipfian distribution of words in texts and the identification of a transition point between the highest frequency words and lower frequency words. Words occurring with the highest frequency tend to fall into separate ranks when arranged by frequency, whereas the lower frequency words fall in groups of words, each of which occur with the same frequency. In 1999, Qinglan Sun, Debora Shaw, and Charles H. Davis suggested a new method for identifying this transition point.

• automatic indexing compared to human indexing : 162

Pao compares the terms selected by this automatic procedure with terms selected by her students. Her example is based on Andrew Donald Booth's article "On the geometry of libraries" (1969). Here is Booth's abstract for this article:

"It is shown that to minimize access time to a library collection the items should be arranged so that the access point is distant from individual books in inverse order of their frequency of use.

"This is shown to lead to several interesting geometrical arrangements for library stacks. The library as a push-down store would mean that after any book has been withdrawn it is replaced at the head of the shelf, all other books being pushed down to accommodate it.

"The frequency-ordered arrangement leads to increases in access efficiency by as much as ten times.

"Finally an analogy is drawn between such a push-down arrangement and human memory as a push-down store in the brain."

• Zipfian distribution of words in article by Booth (A. D.) : 163

Here is the word distribution for the more frequently occurring words in the Booth article, as calculated by Pao (1978, p. 122):

```
       word          rank      frequency

 1.   the            1         218
 2.   of             2         120
 3.   is             3         105
 4.   in             4          70
 5.   to             5          65
 6.   that           6          64
 7.   and            7          55
 8.   a              8          53
 9.   be             9          46
10.   this          10          39
11.   for           11          35
12.   it            12          33
13.   book          12          33
14.   access        13          26
15.   frequency     14          23
16.   library       15          22     <— transition point
17.   which         15          22
18.   collection    16          19
19.   by            16          19
20.   are           16          19
21.   has           17          17
22.   distance      18          16
23.   most          18          16
24.   so            18          16
```

Chapter 8. Analysis and Indexing Methods (Section 8.3.7)

```
25. shown       19    15
26. shelf       20    14
27. stack       20    14
28. from        20    14
29. analysis    21    13
30. use         21    13
31. can         21    13
32. as          21    13
```
— etc. for a total of 559 different words, 256 of which (46% of the total number) occur only once.

• **transition point in Zipfian distribution of words : 164**

In this frequency distribution, there is a transition point at around rank 15. For all ranks from 1 through 14, with the exception of rank 12, there is only one word at each frequency, and therefore only one word in each rank. From rank 15 on, with the exception of ranks 17 and 19, multiple words share the same frequency, and therefore fall in the same rank. The number of words in each rank increases as the frequency of occurrence decreases. The largest number of words (256, 46% of the total of 559 different words in this text) fall in the last rank, for all words that occur only once.

• **identification of keywords based on transition points in Zipfian distributions : 165**

Experts in information retrieval have found that the most effective words for identifying useful texts tend to be those that occur with some frequency, but not the highest frequency. Miranda Pao (1978), pursuing theories advanced by William Goffman, suggested that useful words might be those that occur in a frequency distribution around the Zipfian transition point, where ranks change from having only one word per rank to having multiple words per rank. In her technique, she identifies the transition rank, which in this example is rank 15. She then doubles this number and takes that number of words, beginning with rank 1, but ignoring all words on a stop list. In this example, she took the first 32 words, beginning with "the" and ending with "as," but ignoring stop list words. The resulting words are:

```
book
access
frequency
library
collection
distance
shelf
stack
analysis
use
```

• **effectiveness of keywords : 166**

How effective are these keywords in describing the content, meaning and purpose of this text? The only real test for this question is to assess actual retrieval performance in response to real searches by users with real needs who can make real relevance judgments regarding the usefulness of this particular document.

• **keywords based on Zipfian distributions compared to human indexing : 167**

Nevertheless, it is interesting to compare the results of this automatic indexing technique with the result of human indexing of the same document. Here are the terms selected by Pao's students (p. 123):

Chapter 8. Analysis and Indexing Methods (Section 8.3.7)

term	frequency
frequency of use	9
Zipf's law	9
library geometry	7
library layout	6
push-down principle	4
frequency	3
shelf arrangement	3
rank	2
layout	2
library architecture	2
access	2

• incompatibility of human indexing compared to automatic indexing : 168

The first thing to notice is that unlike the automatically generated keywords, most of these terms consist of more than one word, and it is true, that much of the time, a word phrase is more meaningful than a single word. Later on, automatic methods for locating or generating word phrases will be discussed, but here we are comparing automatically selected single words with human-generated phrases, which is like comparing apples and oranges, so to even out the comparison, we will convert the students' list of terms to single words, as follows.

library	15
frequency	12
use	9
Zipf's	9
law	9
layout	8
geometry	7
push-down	4
principle	4
shelf	3
arrangement	3
rank	2
architecture	2
access	2

• automatic indexing compared to human indexing : 169

Now we can compare the two lists. The following words are on both lists:

    library
    frequency
    use
    shelf
    access

• 170

The following words are only in the computer-generated list:

    book
    collection
    distance
    stack
    analysis

Chapter 8. Analysis and Indexing Methods (Section 8.3.7)

• 171

The following words are only in the student's list:

```
Zipf's
law
layout
geometry
push-down
principle
arrangement
rank
architecture
```

• 172

When students at Rutgers University indexed this document in the Spring of 1995, they chose the following terms, with the following frequencies. They were told to select only single terms, but there are still some multi-word terms, because it is very hard for human indexers to avoid them. It is often hard to convey meaning with only a single word! The terms with asterisks are also on the computer generated list:

```
  term                 frequency
* access               27
* frequency            25
* library/libraries    23
  Zipf                 22
  geometry             15
  Zipf's law           13
* book(s)              13
* stack(s)             12
* shelf                12
  push-down            12
  spiral               10
  frequency of use     10
* collection           10
  radial               8
  linear               8
  layout               8
  arrangement          7
  language             6
  frequency ordered    6
  frequency order      6
  efficiency           6
  circular             6
  access time          6
```

• 173

The remaining terms chosen by Rutgers students had frequencies of five or less. (The distribution of terms chosen by indexers, or students, have the same type of distribution as words in a text! A few terms occur frequently, but many different terms occur with less and less frequency.)

• 174

Of the thirteen terms chosen most frequently (ten or more times) by Rutgers students, seven, or more than half, were also selected by the computer algorithm. Only two words selected by the computer were not among the twenty-three terms chosen by Rutgers students with frequency greater than 5: "distance" and "analysis." "Use" was selected by the computer algorithm as a single word term, whereas students combined it with "frequency" in the phrase "frequency of use."

In contrast, the most important indexing and abstracting services, using human indexing, were much less generous in their indexing of this article. *Library literature* (1967-1969) gave this document only one term: "Shelf-arrangement." *Information science abstracts* (1971) gave it the rather surprising heading: "Information centers and libraries — operation — conventional." Most people reading this interesting article would call it anything but "conventional"! *Library and information science abstracts* (March-April 1969) gave this document the terms: "Shelf arrangement. Frequency of use."

• 176

Machine techniques have many problems, but at least one merit is guaranteed results with a consistent quality. With human indexing, results can vary widely, and sometimes they can be quite perplexing.

• 177

Even without verification by actual retrieval tests with real users and real queries, this automatic indexing technique did rather well, compared to amateur (student) and professional indexing (by indexing and abstracting services). Nevertheless, this algorithm based on word frequency ranks within single documents is rarely used, because it does not take into account the relative frequency of terms in other texts in a collection or IR database. We have included it here because it allows easy comparison between human and machine analysis and indexing.

8.3.8. Words Versus Phrases.

• importance of phrases in automatic indexing : 178

Sometimes single words just aren't sufficient to name or describe a topic. "Information science," for example, is not the same as "information" and "science." Nor is "birth control" simply "birth" and "control" (it is actually control, or prevention, of conception, not of birth!). One of the most oft-cited examples is "venetian blinds," which if not treated as a phrase, could be retrieved by a query about blind Venetians.

• proper nouns in indexing : 179

The names of persons and organizations also suffer when reduced to individual words. What is the significance of single words like "Smith" or "National"? The single term "Smith" is not very helpful in identifying a particular individual, nor is "National" (when, for example, the National Information Standards Organization" is reduced to single words). So automatic indexing researchers have worked on methods and algorithms for identifying phrases in text, including proper nouns, in an attempt to keep such phrases together. There are also procedures for identifying proper names per se: names of persons, organizations, countries, brand names — all of which are very important terms in certain kinds of searches.

• cost versus benefits in identification of phrases in automatic indexing : 180

Analyzing or parsing the grammatical structure of text can help distinguish between "junior college" versus "a junior in college." Sophisticated procedures can also combine variations such as "college junior" and "junior in college" into a single form. But such careful analysis procedures tend to be expensive and time-consuming, and the pay-off in terms of results versus investment is still an open question in a variety of contexts. Research in this area is very much a work in progress. Some recent preliminary results are described in reports on TREC experiments (Callan, Croft & Broglio 1995; Strzalkowski, Lin, & Pérez-Carballo 1997). Pérez-Carballo and

Chapter 8. Analysis and Indexing Methods (Section 8.3.8)

Strzalkowski (2000), Sparck Jones (1999), Strzalkowski, Pérez-Carballo and Marinescu (1996); and Strzalkowski, Lin, Wang and Pérez-Carballo (1999) provide overviews of several natural language processing techniques in information retrieval, including phrase identification.

• identification of phrases in automatic indexing and in searching : 181

The identification of some phrases can be accomplished in electronic searches by simply specifying that certain words must be contiguous or in close proximity. But for displayed indexes, where the indexing must be done in advance and displayed in meaningful headings, some sort of automatic phrase identification is helpful. Automatic phrase identification is also potentially useful for searching systems that accept natural language queries in the form of sentences or paragraphs, where the user is not expected to indicate phrases. Phrase identification techniques can be applied against both the query and the indexable matter of messages (abstracts or full texts).

• 182

One approach that has been tried in some automatic indexing situations could be called a "brute force" or "try everything" method. Over time a list of word phrases important to the subject area is compiled. Then all word pairs and word triplets (possibly quadruplets as well, and so on) are matched against this list. Any such combination that matches is kept as a word phrase in the indexing system. Take, for example, the first sentence of this paragraph. The following word pairs would be matched:

```
one approach
approach that
that has
has been
been tried
tried in
in some
some automatic
automatic indexing
indexing situations
situations could
could be
be called
called a
a "brute
"brute force"
force or
or "try
"try everything"
everything" method
```

• 183

In this case, only "automatic indexing" (and perhaps "brute force") would probably be matched, and therefore kept as a single term of two words. In an earlier sentence, "National Information Standards Organization" might have been found and identified as a meaning phrase if all four-word sequences were matched against a list of important phrases, including organizational names. A similar approach does not rely on a pre-existing list of phrases, but matches potential phrases against large collections of texts. Word combinations that frequently occur together are accepted as potential phrases.

Chapter 8. Analysis and Indexing Methods (Section 8.3.8)

• 184

More sophisticated approaches involve parsing of texts to identify parts of speech and syntactic structures. It is this type of analysis that seeks to distinguish between "college junior" and "junior college," and also to match "college junior" with "junior in college" (Strzalkowski et al. 1999).

• identification of phrases in automatic indexing : 185

An example of using a variety of techniques to identify phrases and to select the more useful ones in texts is the Keyphind (key phrase find) system created by Gutwin, Paynter, Witten, Nevill-Manning, and Frank (1998; Gutwin et al. 1999). Theirs is a hybrid approach, relying on both syntactic analysis of text patterns and statistical analysis of frequency counts. Important attributes for identifying key phrases include location of its first occurrence in a text; frequency within text; and frequency in a collection of documents. Using these techniques, the twelve potentially most important phrases for each document are selected. Some stemming is performed to merge singulars and plurals and alternative spellings.

• role of phrases in browsing : 186

Phrases are especially useful for browsable displayed indexes. Gutwin et al. (1998) demonstrate this with examples from a portion of the New Zealand Digital Library (Witten, Nevill-Manning, McNab & Cunningham 1998, www.nzdl.org).

• 187

In one example, a user types in a query term "text," and in response, the phrase browser (Keyphind) lists key phrases containing the word "text," ranked by the number of documents containing the key phrase, in an initial window:

```
Phrase                  # Docs

text editor             12
text compression        11
text retrieval          10
full text               8
program text            8
text database           7
text generation         7
structured text         6
input text              5
plain text              5
text element            5
text entry              5
text line               5
text processing         5
text widget             5
text window             5
free text               4
text editing            4
text file               4
text search             4
block of text           3
handwritten text        3
natural language text   3
parallel text           3
```

Certainly these phrases are more indicative of possible topics discussed in documents than just the word "text." By browsing these phrases that actually occur in documents, a user can survey

Chapter 8. Analysis and Indexing Methods (Section 8.3.9)

what is available and pick the phrase closest to her/his desire or need, guided also by the information about the number of documents that are available containing the phrase.

• 188

If the user now selects the phrase "text retrieval," brief surrogates for the ten documents containing this phrase are displayed at the bottom of the browser. However, in a second window beside the initial phrase window, other phrases that co-occur with "text retrieval" are displayed according to frequency. These phrases can be used to further refine the search, or they may suggest other paths of inquiry to the user. Here are the key phrases that co-occurred with "text retrieval":

```
Occurring with "text retrieval"      # Docs

information retrieval                 4
full text                             2
natural language processing           2
retrieval system                      2
document retrieval                    2
signature file                        2
engineering sector                    1
signature length                      1
office information system             1
search string                         1
signature size                        1
machine learning                      1
scheme-independent retrieval          1
term clustering                       1
feature selection                     1
navigation tool                       1
office system                         1
relational database system            1
feature set                           1
recognition error                     1
recent development                    1
information retrieval system          1
natural language indexing             1
feature extraction                    1
```

• 189

Now, if the user selects the co-occurring phrase "natural language processing," surrogates for the two documents containing both "text retrieval" and "natural language processing" will be displayed in the lower window. By selecting one of these surrogates, the full text can be retrieved.

8.3.9. Managing Vocabulary in Automatic Indexing.

• 190

The main theme of chapter 13 is vocabulary management for IR databases, but here we will consider briefly the application of some vocabulary management techniques to automatic indexing.

• positive vocabulary management in automatic indexing : 191

In section 8.3.3, negative vocabulary control was based on the creation of a list of excluded words, the stop list. Positive vocabulary control or management can be applied to the remaining words, in an effort to combine, link, and standardize variant forms and also synonyms and

Chapter 8. Analysis and Indexing Methods (Section 8.3.9)

equivalent terms, such as "lawyer," "attorney," "barrister," "solicitor," and "counselor at law." Other examples of variant terms are "vocabulary control" and "vocabulary management." They are sometimes used interchangeably, but sometimes, "vocabulary control" implies limitations on the possible use of terms, while "vocabulary management" is more permissive and facilitative.

• **vocabulary management of equivalent and synonymous terms : 192**

There are in fact very few true synonyms — two words that mean exactly the same thing — and in this lawyer example, it is true that each of these words have different connotations. For example, in some states, anyone can be an attorney for another person as long as the person being represented signs a "power of attorney" document, but anyone using the title "lawyer" must have passed the state bar exam. However, in most situations, for information seeking purposes, these terms can be considered to be equivalent. The terms "barrister" and "solicitor" are British terms, indicating different lawyer-like functions, but for U.S. databases, these terms might also be merged with lawyer and attorney for many types of searches.

• **vocabulary management of minor terms : 193**

In addition to such essentially equivalent terms, an IR database producer may choose to merge minor terms (terms peripheral to the main subject scope of the database) into broader categories and treat these terms as equivalent. For example, an IR database on literature may not need to identify every brand and model of automobile, so it may treat "Buick," "Ford," "Chevrolet," "Dodge," "convertible," "sedan," "station wagon," "jalopy," and "car" as all equivalent to "automobile."

• **vocabulary management in automatic indexing : 194**

Vocabulary management in conjunction with automatic indexing can be accomplished by having a large thesaurus in which all preferred terms and their variant, synonymous, equivalent, and minor (i.e. insignificant) narrower terms are recorded. During the automatic indexing process, all words and phrases not on the stop list are matched against this thesaurus. (The creation of such a thesaurus will be discussed in chapter 13 on vocabulary management.) All terms that match non-preferred terms (variant, misspelled, equivalent, synonymous, minor narrower terms) would be automatically converted to or linked to the corresponding preferred terms.

• **vocabulary management for displayed indexes : 195**

This kind of vocabulary management is very useful for displayed indexes, where it is very inconvenient for users to have separate entries under, say, "lawyer," "attorney," "counselor at law," "barrister," and "solicitor." Preferred terms can also be linked to other preferred terms (narrower terms, broader terms, other related terms) by means of suggestive references to facilitate searching. (These kinds of links or references will also be discussed in more detail later on in chapter 13 on vocabulary management).

• **vocabulary management for electronic searching : 196**

For electronic term-matching searches, terms don't need to be actually converted to preferred terms. Instead, all linked terms can be added to the search, either automatically or at the option of the searcher.

• **addition of terms to thesauri in automatic indexing : 197**

For comprehensive on-going vocabulary management, all words and phrases that do not match terms already in the thesaurus can be routed to the thesaurus editor, who would add the new terms to the thesaurus as one of the following types. These words can come from search statements, if that is feasible, otherwise from the texts of documents as they are added to the IR database. When vocabulary management is a priority, the terms used by searchers are usually considered to be the most important source of new terms, followed by terms used in documents:

Chapter 8. Analysis and Indexing Methods (Section 8.3.10)

- stop list terms — terms that have little or no significance for potential searches, and therefore can be ignored in indexing and searching. These terms are stored in the thesaurus so that every time the same term is matched against the thesaurus, it will not be referred again to the thesaurus editor.

- alternative equivalent or variant terms — new terms that have essentially the same meaning as preferred terms already in the thesaurus. These new terms would be added to the record for their preferred term equivalents, and occurrences of the variant or alternative equivalent terms would be automatically converted to the preferred term, or linked to them for possible addition to searches.

- new preferred terms — new terms that represent new concepts in the thesaurus. New preferred term records would be established for each of them, with links to broader, narrower, and related terms, as appropriate.

- new candidate terms — a fourth category could be "candidate" terms, for terms on which the thesaurus editor is undecided.

- bypassing vocabulary management in electronic searching : 198

Sometimes a searcher will not want the more generic terms that vocabulary management might suggest. In the "lawyer" example, a searcher might want only documents that touch on barristers, and no other related terms (solicitor, lawyer or attorney). A searcher should always have the option of by-passing any vocabulary management when it is judged to be unhelpful.

8.3.10. Automatic Vocabulary Management.

- 199

The negative and positive vocabulary control discussed so far as possible adjuncts to automatic indexing is based on stop lists or thesauri generated by humans, relying on human judgments. It is also possible to perform some interesting and potentially useful vocabulary management through automatic means, based on co-occurrence of words or terms. In this approach, related terms are identified not through human intellectual analysis, but through patterns of usage that can be identified by computer analysis. The underlying idea is that if two or more terms occur together more frequently than terms at random, they may have a meaningful, useful relationship that might be worth exploiting in information retrieval searching.

- Associative Interactive Dictionary as example of automatic vocabulary management : 200

An early example of this approach is the Associative Interactive Dictionary, developed by Tamas E. Doszkocs (1978) at the National Library of Medicine. In this system, the user does a preliminary search, then asks the Associative Interactive Dictionary to list the terms, in rank order, that are most closely related to the terms in the initial search. The user may choose an analysis based on text words (in this example, words in titles and abstracts), Medical Subject Headings (MeSH), or chemical registry numbers. After the results of the analysis are presented, the user can select any of these related terms to augment the search. Doszkocs gives an example of a Boolean search for the text words "prenatal AND toxicity" in the Toxline database. "Prenatal" has 852 postings (meaning that this term is linked to 852 documents — that it is "posted" to the record for each of these documents). "Toxicity" has 32,880 postings (after all, this is a toxicity database!). Together, they retrieve 117 documents that have both "prenatal" and "toxicity" in their titles or abstracts.

- identification of related terms by co-occurrence : 201

Here are the terms most closely related to "prenatal" and "toxicity" as determined by the co-occurrence ranking algorithm of the Associative Interactive Dictionary:

Chapter 8. Analysis and Indexing Methods (Section 8.3.10)

term	rank score	extra postings
1. prenatal	0.9971	647
2. postnatal	0.9872	681
3. gestational	0.9808	781
4. fetus	0.9793	2375
5. gestations	0.9788	1826
6. teratogenicity	0.9770	951
7. embryocidal	0.9770	42
8. perinatal	0.9758	328
9. placental	0.9754	1403
10. mothers	0.9748	1090
11. clefts	0.9739	580
12. retardation	0.9738	864
13. fetuses	0.9736	1257
14. stillbirths	0.9723	45
15. resorptions	0.9708	1020
16. rubratoxins	0.9707	74
17. developmental	0.9706	816
18. palates	0.9704	611
19. organogenesis	0.9703	188
20. fetal	0.9701	5049
21. pregnant	0.9669	3492
22. supernumerary	0.9663	31
23. embryotoxic	0.9650	429
24. photodieldrin	0.9644	59
25. teratogenic	0.9642	2516
26. teratogens	0.9626	762
27. malformations	0.9611	1511
28. CD-1	0.9598	126
29. born	0.9588	587
30. teratology	0.9574	315
31. neurobehavioral	0.9567	15
32. chac	0.9563	19
33. embryotoxicity	0.9558	184
34. utero	0.9552	355
35. alternate	0.9552	517
36. pregnancy	0.9551	8635
37. nitrosomethylurethane	0.9548	36
38. anomalies	0.9541	874
39. paraoxon	0.9505	440
40. neonates	0.9481	297
41. maternal	0.9481	3118
42. transfers	0.9478	3702
43. abnormalities	0.9469	4155
44. conceptions	0.9464	322
45. trimesters	0.9437	564
46. skull	0.9435	159
47. hydrogenation	0.9433	161
48. dutch	0.9431	163
49. embryos	0.9420	3747

• ranking of related terms by frequency of co-occurrence : 202

The rank score was calculated on the basis of how frequently a term co-occurs with the two preliminary terms ("prenatal" and "toxicity") in the title or abstract of retrieved documents, as compared to its average frequency in document titles and abstracts in the entire database. The

Chapter 8. Analysis and Indexing Methods (Section 8.3.10)

higher the term rank score, the higher the co-occurrence frequency with "prenatal" and "toxicity" compared to the average frequency of that term.

• 203

The highest ranking term is, not surprisingly, "prenatal," because "prenatal" obviously occurs in every title and abstract that contains the two preliminary terms. So we can ignore "prenatal." Our first related term of interest is "postnatal," followed by "gestational," "fetus," "gestations," etc. Some of these terms are clearly related to "prenatal." "Embryocidal" and "stillbirths," which fall later in the list, are possibly related to "toxicity." For each term, the number of extra postings is given (the number of additional documents that would be retrieved if the new term were added to the search with the Boolean operator "OR"). This number gives the searcher an idea of how many documents in the database have these terms.

• 204

As the rank score of association becomes lower, the relationship between the new term and the original terms become less close and more coincidental. An example of this incidental co-occurrence is the term "dutch" which falls in the 48th rank. Some of the papers indexed may have involved Dutch patients or Dutch practitioners or Dutch researchers or perhaps took place in Dutch institutions.

• 205

Careful readers of the ranked list of terms with their extra postings may wonder why the extra postings for the very first term, "prenatal" is not 735 instead of 647, because the total number of postings for "prenatal" is 852 and the combined postings for "prenatal" AND "toxicity" is 117. If "prenatal" were added back into the search with a Boolean OR, then the total postings should return back to the original 852, so that the extra postings would be 852-117, or 735. The difference appears to be related to operational procedures in which representative subsets of postings are used in the computations. Consequently, in this example, the extra postings are a relative, as opposed to an absolute, guide.

• 206

Careful readers may also wonder why "toxicity" didn't make the list of frequently co-occurring terms (as "prenatal" did). A likely reason is that because this is a toxicity database, "toxicity" occurs so frequently throughout the database that its frequency among the retrieved items was not markedly different from its frequency in the rest of the database.

• 207

This technique of displaying automatically generated lists of related terms was not widely implemented because it demands a large amount of computing power, involving the calculation of co-occurrence scores for the large numbers of terms linked to every document. Now that computing power has become more readily available, this kind of display of possibly related terms for consideration is becoming more common. Some web search engines offer this type of feature, and it is sometimes used in conjunction with relevance feed-back (see section 8.3.13 below).

• **impact of automatic vocabulary management : 208**

Lists of related terms generated through co-occurrence analysis can be helpful for searchers trying to think of terms to use to expand a search. Such lists might also help users find terms that better describe a precise need — better than the original terms entered into a search statement. Of course, the actual efficacy of such systems needs to be tested in careful investigations involving real searchers with real queries using real databases.

8.3.11. Clustering.

• **definitions of classing and clustering : 209**

All indexing is based on classing or clustering items based on similarities among characteristics. "Classing" simply means to create or define classes of items and/or to assign items to classes. "Clustering" means to create or identify groupings or clusters of items. When an indexer assigns the term "dogs" to a document, or when a computer finds the term "dogs" in a document, a class is created and this document is associated with all other documents that have been indexed with the term "dogs." The common meaning of "classification," which often has less to do with creating classes than with the arrangement of classes in a logical and meaningful order, is an important issue for the creation of browsable displayed indexes — a topic outside the scope of this chapter, which we will be discussing in chapter 17 on the arrangement of displayed indexes. The term "clustering" is used more often when the classing, or gathering together, is done through automatic, or algorithmic, means. The term "classing" usually implies human judgment.

• **criteria for clusters : 210**

The Associative Interactive Dictionary (discussed in the previous section) is based on clustering — the formation of clusters based on the co-occurrence of terms in documents or the co-occurrence of index terms assigned to them. Similar clusters can be generated on the basis of any document characteristic — other examples include authors' names, journals in which articles are published, and reference citations.

• **clusters in searching : 211**

In machine-matching searches, classes or clusters of documents are created based on the terms in a search statement.

• **document similarity as basis for clustering : 212**

Another example of clustering is the popular feature in modern IR systems that allows a user to request other documents like one he or she already knows about. In this case, the search program creates a cluster of documents that are similar with the original document and with each other. This similarity can be computed in any number of ways based on a range of characteristics, such as authors, affiliations, index terms, abstract terms, other text terms and reference citations. A number of documents can be identified and can be ranked by their degree of similarity.

• **types of clusters: string clusters : 213**

Gerard Salton named a variety of cluster types in his book *Dynamic information and library processing* (1975a, p. 327), illustrated in figure 8.2. In a string cluster, each member of the cluster — each document, for example — is linked to only one or two others. Items A and B may share one or more terms or one or more reference citations, but A shares none of them with item C. Item B also shares one or more terms with item C, but none with item D, and so on.

• **star clusters : 214**

In the star cluster, the central item is linked to all other items, but they are linked only to the central item, not to each other.

• **clique clusters : 215**

The clique cluster is the most highly interconnected one, in which each item is equally connected to every other member of the group.

• **clump clusters : 216**

Finally, among these examples, the clump cluster is simply one in which the members have a variety of connections.

Chapter 8. Analysis and Indexing Methods (Section 8.3.11)

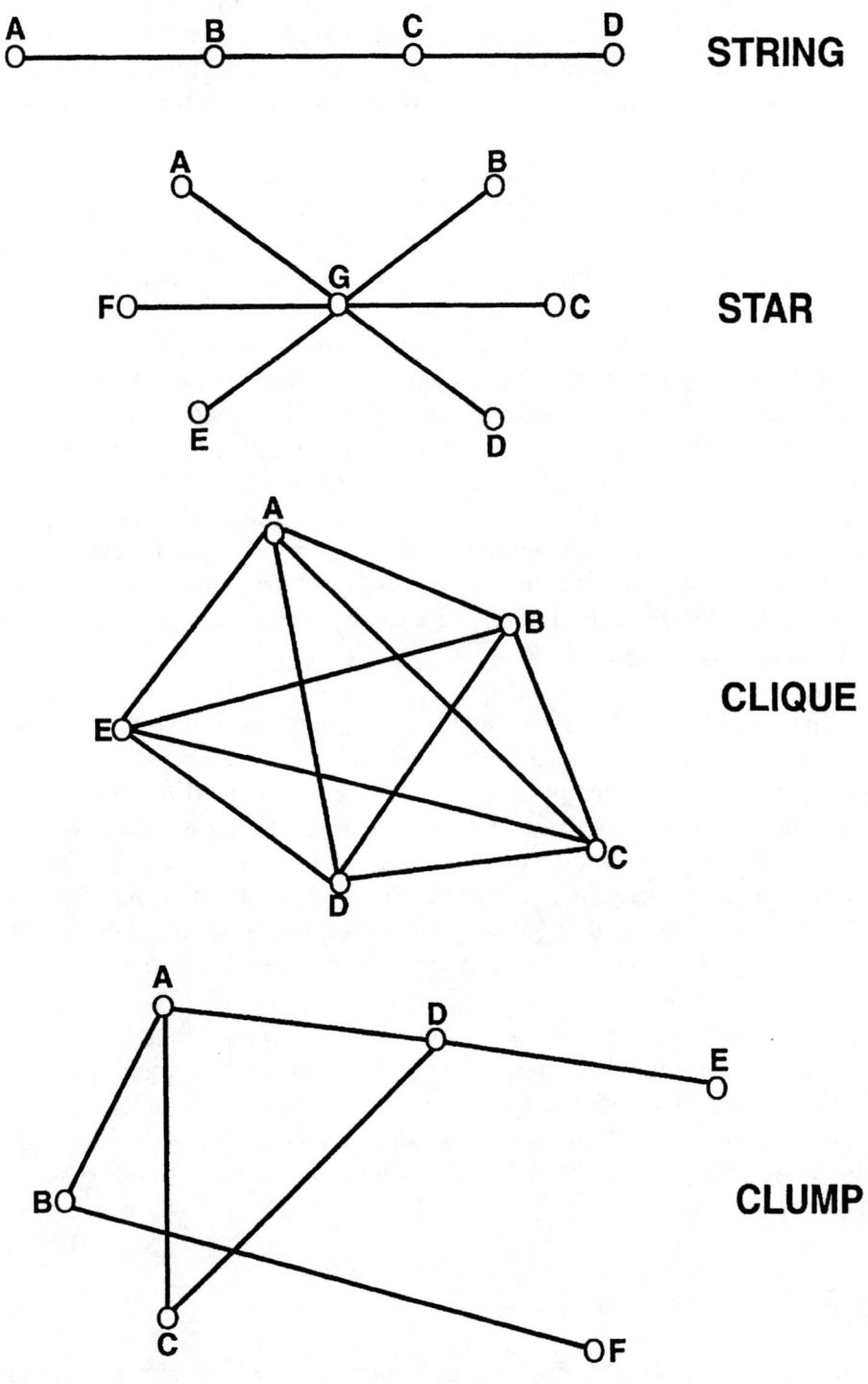

Figure 8.2. Types of clusters, based on Salton (1975a).

Chapter 8. Analysis and Indexing Methods (Section 8.3.11.1)

• **thresholds in automatic clustering : 217**

Thresholds are important in automatic clustering. We saw in the case of the Associative Interactive Dictionary that terms were ranked by the level of association — in that case, by the relative frequency of co-occurrence. Different clusters can be formed by raising or lowering the required level of association — the number of authors, or index terms, or reference citations, etc. that items must share in common. Clustering algorithms can thus specify that items must have a certain number of items in common — two, or three, or four, or more.

• **automatic clustering techniques: static clustering, dynamic clustering, scatter-gather clustering : 218**

Automatic clustering techniques are attempts to compute degrees of association among either terms (term-clustering, as in the Associative Interactive Dictionary, discussed previously) or documents (document clustering). Document clustering may be used to organize document files (static clustering) or on the fly in order to present sets of retrieved documents to the user (dynamic clustering). Clustering has been used in attempts to improve the efficiency and efficacy of IR systems. Work on clustering has been reported since the early days of IR research (Stiles 1961) to the present (Hearst 1999). Early work suggested that clustering techniques could improve retrieval performance. More recent work on clustering has failed to show significant improvements in retrieval effectiveness. Nevertheless, modern applications of clustering seem to be useful to support user interaction with IR systems. For example, Hearst (1999) describes "scatter-gather" techniques based on dynamic document clustering to facilitate the evaluation of retrieved documents. Documents are first "scattered" into clusters based on document similarities. The documents "gathered" into selected initial clusters can again be scattered and gathered into new clusters to further refine groupings.

• **static clustering : 219**

The idea of storing documents in clusters such that "similar" documents are "near" each other has been proposed and explored since Salton and colleagues' early work in the sixties. This idea is supported by the cluster hypothesis: similar documents tend to be relevant to the same queries. In Salton & McGill (1983a, b) the document clustering techniques used in the 1983 implementation of SMART are described. Clustering results in a file organization that may reduce file accesses and improve the efficiency (speed) of the system but not necessarily its retrieval efficacy. Clustering research through the mid-1980s was described and assessed by Willett (1988) in "Recent trends in hierarchic document clustering: a critical review."

• **220**

The intimate details of how the files are organized inside the computer is better left to programmers. Such details may change depending on changes in the hardware and lower level operating system details without any noticeable affect on any of the higher level operations. A change in file organization might result in changes in performance speed but not in the retrieval performance of the system. At the conceptual level that interests us here it doesn't matter how the document files are organized.

8.3.11.1. Latent Semantic Indexing.

• **221**

Latent semantic indexing (LSI) is one of the most sophisticated modern attempts at high quality automatic indexing. It is based on co-occurrence clustering of terms and the identification of documents associated with these term clusters. By relying on co-occurrence data, LSI is also able to deal with the problem of the variety of terms that can be used to express similar ideas.

Chapter 8. Analysis and Indexing Methods (Section 8.3.12)

LSI is described by its creators in Deerwester, Dumais, Furnas, Landauer, and Harshman (1990). Michael Gordon and Susan Dumais (1998) describe its application in the search for relationships in widely separated literatures.

• vocabulary management in latent semantic indexing : 222

As an example of LSI's capability of dealing with divergent terminology, let's imagine documents on the repair and maintenance of automobiles. Different documents may use a number of different terms like "automobile," "car," "motor vehicle," "sedan," plus the names of particular brands and models — "Buick," "Plymouth," "Cherokee." The LSI program is likely to associate these terms together because of their high level of co-occurrence with terms like "oil," "gasoline," "fuel," "carburetor," "tires," "air-conditioning," etc. The LSI program creates clusters of highly related (through co-occurrence) terms, so that when a sufficient number of these terms occurs in a document, the document can be linked to that cluster. In this way, a search for the care and maintenance of carburetors in gasoline-powered automobiles can be made without regard to the particular words used for automobile. All words that mean more or less the same thing as automobile will be linked to the same cluster, as long as a sufficient number of other co-occurring terms match terms in the cluster. LSI is an example of current attempts to use computing algorithms to get underneath the actual words used, in order to identify the underlying ideas expressed.

8.3.12. Citation Indexes.

• citation links to older documents : 223

Reference citations have always been a useful basis for indicating (indexing!) possibly useful relationships. Almost every writer of a term paper, to say nothing of more serious researchers, has pursued reference citations in good documents as a way to find other documents of interest. In effect, a string cluster is created, with each link through a reference citation leading to an older article that was cited in the later paper. This kind of citation indexing can only lead backwards in time, because it is impossible to cite a document that has not yet been created!

• citation indexes to newer documents : 224

Creating indexes that could trace reference citations forward in time was extremely laborious before the advent of the computer. Such citation indexing was limited largely to the legal literature until the Institute for Scientific Information (1961, 1969, 1976) introduced the *Science citation index* in 1961, followed by the *Social science citation index* in 1969 and the *Arts and humanities citation index* in 1976. These indexes have now become standard tools, available in both print and electronic forms. They permit the user to begin with a given document and to trace its citation in subsequent documents forward in time. To the extent that a reference citation indicates a link between messages related with respect to topic, purpose, meaning or significance, these links can be quite useful for IR searching.

8.3.12.1. Bibliographic Coupling.

• definition of bibliographic coupling : 225

Bibliographic coupling is a special form of clustering based on reference citations. The underlying idea is that two or more documents are related ("bibliographically coupled") if they share the same reference citations. The more reference citations they share (the higher the threshold), the more closely related they may be. The technique for identifying related documents through bibliographic coupling was described by Maxwell Kessler (1963).

- bibliographic coupling compared to co-citation : 226

Clusters based on bibliographic coupling are static, because the reference citations in a given document never change after the document is finished and published. Henry Small (1973) invented, or discovered, co-citation clustering as an alternative method for creating dynamic clusters of related documents that tend to focus on new (as opposed to older) documents and are thought to point to active research fronts.

8.3.12.2. Co-Citation.

- definition of co-citation; identification of research fronts by co-citation : 227

In co-citation clustering, clusters are not based on reference citations shared by documents (as in bibliographic coupling) but on two or more documents being cited together in a subsequent document. If new papers, hot off the press, frequently cite both documents A and B, then, the reasoning goes, documents A and B must be related, and the more often they are co-cited (cited together in later papers), then the closer the relationship is. Because new documents keep coming out, with different sets of reference citations, the co-citation clusters keep changing over time, showing new patterns of emerging relationships among documents, authors, and the topics they address. This constant change, incorporating new citation patterns, is the basis of the claim (or hope) of its proponents that these co-citation clusters can identify hot topics and emerging research fronts.

8.3.13. Relevance Feedback.

- feedback in automatic indexing and in searching : 228

All automatic indexing techniques are the creations of human designers, but in most cases, once these techniques are set in motion, they go their own way with no opportunity for human intervention or feedback. When automatic indexing techniques are combined with machine-matching electronic searches, human searchers have the opportunity to influence the matching procedures or criteria by specifying a range of parameters. In addition to choosing or changing search terms, they may, depending on what a particular search system permits, be able to indicate relative importance or weights for terms, truncate terms, require certain proximity of terms in text, specify whether case (upper or lower case letters) is to be considered, and similar modifications, which will be considered in chapter 12 on syntax. But even with these searcher-specified modifications, once the automatic matching process is invoked, it proceeds according to algorithm without modification.

- purpose of relevance feedback : 229

The idea behind relevance feedback is to permit evaluation of preliminary results in order to influence (hopefully to improve!) subsequent performance. This process is analogous to the common practice of searchers browsing displayed indexes. As they examine potential entries, they are constantly making judgments of relevance, and making adjustments in their approach in accordance with these judgments.

- 230

Relevance feedback represents an effort to build this natural feedback process into searching and automatic matching procedures. Of course, even without the techniques described here, a searcher can review the results of a search, make modifications in the original search statement based on these results, eliminating some terms, adding some terms, and perhaps changing weights or other parameters. The more formal relevance feedback techniques are designed to make the process easier and a little more automatic. Current applications have been described by Gerard Salton and Chris Buckley (1990) and Amanda Spink (1995).

• procedures in relevance feedback : 231

The usual approach to relevance feedback is for a preliminary search to proceed using terms (and modifications such as term weights, truncation, proximity limits, etc.) provided by the user. The results of this initial search are presented to the user, along with an evaluative questionnaire in which the user can indicate preliminary relevance judgments concerning the value of the retrieved documents. These judgments are then used by the system to modify the initial search, and a second search is performed. This interaction can continue as long as the user wishes.

• 232

Two types of modifications are generally made. Terms are added or deleted, and weights for terms are increased or decreased. Terms that are closely associated with documents that received low or negative relevance ratings may be given lower weights or may be removed from the search altogether. Terms that are associated with documents that received high relevance ratings can be given higher weights. Also, terms not in the original search but which are closely associated with highly rated documents can be added to the search.

• relevance feedback in selective dissemination of information and filtering : 233

This same approach to ongoing semi-automatic modification of search statements can be used to update search filters for continuously identifying new documents of possible interest as they are added to databases. The resulting profile of user interests serves as the basis for "selective dissemination of information" (SDI) to clients over time. The newer applications of this ongoing indexing and searching of new material is often called "information filtering" (Belkin & Croft 1992).

• role of human searching behavior in automatic indexing : 234

Current research is attempting to find ways to improve automatic indexing by tracking patterns of human searching behavior and decision making, then using the results to influence subsequent matching procedures. Whereas current efforts at relevance feedback tend to focus on individual searchers and individual searches, the hope is that longer term group patterns can be used to tailor systems to more closely match the needs of groups of users.

• pseudo relevance feedback : 235

Some researchers are experimenting with systems that don't require user input or evaluation at all. The initial search is simply modified on the basis of the most highly-ranked documents in the initial retrieval set. This technique is called "pseudo relevance feedback."

8.4. Subject Analysis and Indexing in Indexing and Abstracting Services.

• 236

Modern indexing and abstracting services (also known as A&I services), such as BHA: Bibliography of the history of art/Bibliographie d'histoire de l'Art (J. Paul Getty Trust), BIOSIS/Biological abstracts, Chemical abstracts, EMBASE (Elsevier Science), Engineering index/Compendex, MLA international bibliography (Modern Language Association of America), MEDLINE (National Library of Medicine), Psychological abstracts/PsychINFO (American Psychological Association), PAIS (Public Affairs Information Service), and the several indexing services of the H. W. Wilson Company, all use some sort of human subject analysis and indexing to create their IR databases. Jessica Milstead (1992) surveyed and discussed their practices in

Chapter 8. Analysis and Indexing Methods (Section 8.4)

"Methodologies for subject analysis in bibliographic databases." A major focus of F. W. Lancaster's (1991, 2d ed. 1998) book on *Indexing and abstracting in theory and practice* is on the practices of major indexing and abstracting services.

• 237

Actual analysis methods, the topic of this chapter, is only one part of indexing practice. In discussions and descriptions of production methods, procedures, and rules, the basic methods of analysis often play second fiddle to aspects that are treated elsewhere in this book, such as syntactic rules or patterns used for creating headings, exhaustivity policies for appropriate detail in analysis and indexing, specificity policies for terms or descriptors, vocabulary management and use of thesauri, and the nature of displayed indexes and interfaces. However, some A&I services have attempted to describe and regularize some of the analysis procedures that indexers use or are expected to employ, and some work has begun in moving analysis rules, patterns, and procedures into expert systems that can be used to assist in both the analysis and the indexing stages.

• MedIndEx as example of expert system for subject analysis and indexing : 238

A prominent example of attempts to regularize and encode analysis procedure is the Medical Indexing Expert (MedIndEx) project of the National Library of Medicine. MedIndEx is a prototype for knowledge-based indexing which makes use of "encoded domain knowledge, including domain-specific relationships between concepts, as well as computer-executable rules that, using this knowledge, participate both actively and specifically ... in the steps of a complex intellectual task" (Humphrey 1984, p. 166). Humphrey gives an example of an indexer having indicated a medical therapy, "estrogen replacement therapy." MedIndEx prompts the indexer to indicate the "problem" by naming the particular disease to which the therapy is being applied, if known. A list of possibilities is automatically provided from Medical Subject Headings (MeSH), the thesaurus of medical terminology maintained by the National Library of Medicine. When the indexer chooses "osteoporosis, postmenopausal," MedIndEx asks for body location, by suggesting "one of the following organ-disease terms, if appropriate: spinal diseases; orbital diseases; maxillary diseases; mandibular diseases; jaw diseases" (Humphrey 1984, p. 167.

• use of checktags in subject analysis and indexing : 239

A less ambitious example, also from the National Library of Medicine, but also in use elsewhere, is the use of checktags. Checktags are lists of important facets or aspects of subject analysis (like the subject scope facets discussed in chapter 2). Their purpose is to remind indexers to consider all important aspects of a topic. Thus, in indexing for MEDLINE at the National Library of Medicine, the "Automated Indexing and Management System (AIMS)" has used checktags to remind indexers to indicate gender and species of patients or subjects of experiment when relevant. In some cases, the system would automatically insert the term for a concept. For example, if an indexer indicated the concept "pregnancy," AIMS would insert the term "female," but a checktag would ask for information as to "human" or "animal" (Humphrey 1994, p. 165).

• computer-aided subject analysis and indexing for indexing and abstracting services : 240

Increasingly, indexing and abstracting services have experimented with and implemented various methods to take fuller advantage of capabilities offered by advancing research in automatic indexing. Gail Hodge and Jessica Milstead (1998) focused on this evolving aspect of large-scale indexing operations in a survey of major A&I services. Their results are reported in *Computer support to indexing*, a special report for the National Federation of Abstracting and Information Services. They conclude that:

"The final resolution to the debate over natural language processing [i.e., advanced automatic indexing] versus human indexing remains to be determined. However, it is certain that the degree to

Chapter 8. Analysis and Indexing Methods (Section 8.5)

which natural language processing and its incorporation into Internet-based search technologies can be perfected will have a profound effect on the future of indexing. Both natural language processing and increased demand for human indexing and knowledge organization (whether by the building of organized virtual-digital libraries or by the development of knowledge representation systems based on thesauri) will require increased computer support" (p. 80).

8.5. Growing Role of Automatic Analysis and Indexing.

• allocation of automatic indexing versus human indexing : 241

It is clear from research and the experience of users that automatic machine-based indexing and human intellectual analysis-based indexing both make important, but very different, contributions to successful information retrieval. At the same time, expert human indexing keeps getting more expensive, while automatic indexing becomes, comparatively, less and less expensive. Therefore, it seems likely that future IR databases will seek to maximize benefits by allocating human analysis and indexing to situations where the benefits of human expertise are most apparent and immediate.

• allocation of human indexing to important documents : 242

In order to improve the effectiveness and efficiency of the information retrieval enterprise, librarians and other information professionals need to stop treating every document as if all documents, all texts, and all messages were equally important. We know this is not the case. We need to be more judgmental and discriminating, in the best sense of these terms. We all learn about the so-called "80-20 rule" that suggests that in any large collection of documents, 20% will get 80% of the use, or, to put it differently, 20% of the documents will answer 80% of the questions, or respond to 80% of the needs or desires of users. To allocate human analysis expertise in a rational, cost-effective manner, we need to develop methods for predicting the more important documents and devoting human analysis to them. All documents can receive inexpensive, relatively effective automatic, machine-based analysis and indexing. For important documents, automatic indexing can be augmented by human indexing, to make these documents even more accessible to a broader clientele.

• 243

In highly selective libraries and databases, it will probably continue to make sense to apply human analysis to all selected documents, but in IR databases that seek to be comprehensive within their domains, then it makes sense to apply some discriminating criteria within the database collection in an attempt to identify the more important documents. (See chapter 4 on documentary domain and also section 3.12 on qualitative criteria for selection of documents within the documentary scope of an IR database.) As IR databases grow ever larger, such discriminating criteria can be beneficial for users who often want not everything on a topic, but only the best and most appropriate items.

• use of human indexing for identification of useful documents : 244

Investing human analysis and indexing in more important documents can make those documents more accessible to users by identifying themes, relationships, methodological approaches, points of view, prejudices, biases, slants, purposes, values, and qualitative aspects that cannot be easily identified through automatic techniques. The role of the human indexer can take on that of the "readers' adviser" in traditional reference services, moving beyond simple topical description. Such human indexing should be guided by the subject scope and domain, mission and objectives of the IR database (chapter 2), which if well formulated, will reflect the needs and desires of potential users.

Chapter 8. Analysis and Indexing Methods (Section 8.5)

• views of Bates (Marcia J.) on role of human indexing : 245

Human indexing also has a potentially important contribution to make in combating the inevitable scatter of relevant messages in large collections or IR databases. Marcia Bates (1998, p. 1193-1198) summarizes the naturally occurring statistical distributions that characterize information phenomena and IR databases. The Zipfian distribution of words in texts has already been discussed with respect to a possible automatic indexing technique (section 8.3.7). Similar Zipfian distributions (so named because George Kingsley Zipf first described them in mathematical terms) characterize many other information phenomena as well. One of the most important, called Bradford's Law in honor of Samuel Bradford, describes the greater and greater dispersion of relevant documents beyond a core group of the most relevant documents. Bates asserts that "even in the best-designed database, users will usually retrieve a number of irrelevant records, and the more thorough they are in trying to scoop up every last relevant record by extending their search formulation with additional term variants, the greater the proportion of irrelevant records they will encounter. However, as the 'core' terms will probably retrieve a relatively small percentage of the relevant records (certainly under half, in most cases), they must nonetheless tolerate sifting through lots of irrelevant records in order to find the relevant ones. *It is the purpose of human indexing and classification to **improve** this situation, to pull more records into that core than would otherwise appear there,* [emphasis added] but it should be understood that even the best human indexing is not likely to defeat the underlying Zipfian patterns" (p. 1198). This points to the need to design tools (and systems) that help users do the sifting more efficiently!

• 246

Certainly, it is unlikely that the deployment of human indexing expertise to combat the Zipfian or Bradfordian scatter of relevant documents can be undertaken willy-nilly across the board. Instead, human expertise can better be devoted to documents that possess some predictable attributes associated with potential importance.

• criteria for allocation of human indexing : 247

Here are some examples of ways in which "more important" documents might be identified. Whatever criteria are used should be made explicit, in line with Marcia Bates' plea in her landmark 1976 paper "Rigorous systematic bibliography."

- **use**. In libraries, especially special libraries, circulation or other use data can be used to identify high-use documents. Downloading digital documents is a similar indicator.

- **citation**. Citations to scholarly literature can be monitored through citation indexes. Most active scholars and researchers learn about important documents in their areas of interest not through indexing and abstracting services or other IR databases, but via the informal networks that characterize the "invisible colleges" of scholars — interaction at conferences, telephone calls, email discussion groups, world-wide web sites, personal email, and mention by colleagues. Thus initial use and citation is generated in many cases by means independent of indexing and abstracting services and other IR databases. The augmented indexing given to documents identified by use and citation data helps to make these same important documents available to users who are not tied into the scholarly networks — students, scholars in other fields, and other interested persons. Indeed, persons who want to find only the most important documents could limit their searches to such documents.

- **publisher prediction**. Documents published as trade or scholarly monographs represent a tiny percentage of the universe of documents, both print and electronic, in our information environment. When a publisher decides to invest the large amount of money necessary to publish and market a book in print form, in almost all cases, such a document deserves an index based on human intellectual analysis. Fiction, drama, poetry, and other belles-lettres are possible exceptions, but a growing number of scholars and other users advocate indexing for these works as well.

- **reviews and awards**. Documents that are reviewed or receive awards should receive augmented indexing. Such documents represent a tiny percentage of all documents, and their selection is based on judgments by reviewers, editors, or practitioners that a document is significant for some reason.

- **searcher nomination**. As modern IR databases and search interfaces become more interactive, they can include features to encourage users to provide feedback to indexers and publishers of databases on a variety of issues, such as indexing terminology and the selection of terms for the description of particular messages. Another area of user input could be the nomination of "important" documents to receive augmented indexing. Searchers who find particular documents useful could say so in a response form, and these responses could be incorporated into the record for the document so that searchers interested in the comments of other users could see them. At the same time, user nomination could also be used to select documents to receive human indexing.

Searcher nomination or recommendation is spreading on the world-wide web, where users often comment on other websites and add links to them in their own websites, thus making the recommended sites easier to find by others. There are also a growing number of "recommender systems" on the web, which use the experience of previous users to recommend documents or sites to new users. The invitation of Amazon.com (and similar sites) to users to add their recommendations or reviews are examples of searcher nominations.

- **advisory board**. IR databases that have a board or network of advisors to assist with documentary domain coverage (see chapter 4) can also make use of these expert users to nominate documents or classes of documents that deserve treatment as important documents.

- **indexer nomination**. Expert indexers, especially those with experience in a subject domain, can also identify potentially important documents.

- **exemplary documents**. David Blair and Steven Kimbrough (2000) have advocated the identification of exemplary documents to facilitate focused information retrieval, especially for newcomers to a field. Such documents, which would "describe or exhibit the intellectual structure of a particular field of interest," are a prime example of important documents that would merit the attention of human indexers. Indeed, a primary role of human indexers might be to identify such documents. These documents could then be used, in accordance with Blair and Kimbrough's proposal, as gateways to related literature connected through vocabulary usage, reference citations, authorship, assigned descriptors, etc., to a broader range of documents.

8.5.1. Censorship or Guidance?

- measures of use versus censorship : 248

Some students and colleagues argue that limiting expensive, expert human analysis and indexing to important documents constitutes a kind of censorship. One response is that such limits would be censorship only if criteria related to political, social, religious, ideological, personal, or other prejudices were used to limit access.

- expert judgment versus use in evaluation of importance : 249

But human judgments are always mixed with cultural world views, prejudices, biases and values, both conscious and unconscious, so it could be argued that choosing documents based on actual use rather than on the judgments of a relatively small number of humans could be considered a safeguard against censorship. When measures of importance are based on actual use and recommendations by users, gathered on a relatively large and representative scale, then the user community can be said to be choosing what is important to it.

• selection of useful documents by advisory groups and indexing staff : 250

In addition, selection of useful documents based on nomination or recommendation by advisory groups and indexing staff might further insure an openness to consider documents that might not otherwise be given additional analysis. What should be avoided is a closed circle of popularity, such as that created when an IR database limits its documentary scope to journals selected by votes of librarians, who may tend to purchase journals that are indexed, and then to vote for the journals that they own.

• expert judgment versus user preferences in IR database design : 251

Some critics argue that popularity criteria are similar in kind to those used by all sorts of marketers of entertainment, news, and other consumer products, resulting in excessive blandness. This is only partly true. In marketing, consumer surveys are conducted to ascertain consumer tastes and views, but then advertisers go out of their way to seek to influence and change these tastes and opinions. In a way, librarians and information experts who seek to influence the use of documents are comparable to advertisers. In librarianship, there is a long, and sometimes controversial tradition, of providing to our users what they ought to be using, rather than what they ask for. A growing consensus seems to be swinging in the other direction. That the user is the best judge of what is useful, beneficial, and to be desired. This controversy is often associated with collection development in libraries, but the principles are the same when applied to indexing and the creation of IR databases.

• expert judgment in indexing : 252

As in many controversies, both sides have some of the merit. The opinions and desires and information-seeking behavior of our users must be respected. But in addition, in some cases, expert librarians and other information specialists are indeed equipped to make judgments of importance, and they should be encouraged to do just that on behalf of users. Librarians have always done so and must continue to do so in selecting books and other documents for library collections and in defining the coverage of databases with respect to subject and documentary scope and domain. However, in the realm of human indexing and cataloging, indexers and catalogers have traditionally been loathe to express qualitative judgments or opinions. This avoidance is unfortunate and should stop. It is one area where human indexing can be clearly superior to machine indexing. We need to add to the value of our contributions to information retrieval by expressing qualitative judgments and by high-lighting what we believe is best and most appropriate for various categories of users. There is no reason why our indexing should not reflect this. In short, expert opinion can be yet one more criterion for identifying important documents that should receive the attention of human indexers.

• role of human indexers in assessments of authority : 253

Indeed, a few indexing theorists, such as Patrick Wilson (1978) and Bernd Frohmann (1990) have advocated much more attention to the identification of "truth" or accuracy in messages. Such assessments require careful analysis and would mean allocating more time and attention on fewer documents, but such assessments might be very valuable in some contexts.

• identification of contributions by human indexers : 254

If we ask human indexers to play a larger role in assessing messages, then we may want to let our users know who they are, much like book or movie reviewers who gain followers among those who respect their judgments (or whose names warn others to ignore their views). Expert judgments, in addition to prejudices, biases, and values, can be made more explicit by identifying

Chapter 8. Analysis and Indexing Methods (Section 8.6)

and giving credit to the evaluators. Indeed IR databases featuring the views of such expert indexers will take on the trappings of "expert" websites!

• discovery of controversial documents : 255

By relying on mass judgments of importance, coupled with experts imposing their assessment of accuracy and value on messages, will we run the risk of finding only the bland and conventional at the cost of the truly original, unconventional, controversial? For this task of discovery, perhaps we must place reliance and hope on intrepid explorers using the kind of full-text browsing techniques that were described previously in the section on phrase indexing (8.3.8).

• inequality of documents : 256

What we cannot afford to continue to do is to treat all documents that enter our collections and our IR databases as if they were all equally important and equally deserving of our expert analysis and indexing. They simply are not, and to continue to do so is to waste precious resources.

• application of expert judgment to world-wide web and internet : 257

The exploding internet and world-wide web is a prime example where selectivity in deploying human expertise is absolutely essential!

• machines versus humans in indexing : 258

To bring this discussion of humans versus machines in analysis and indexing to a close, here is Hans Wellisch's (1998) concluding quote in an essay on "Indexing after the millennium ...: the indexer as helmsman," reflecting predictions from Norbert Wiener's (1950) book *The human use of human beings*: "[C]ontrol exercised by machines, far from enslaving human beings, will liberate men and women for tasks only they can perform. Let us hope that the coming century will see an increasing use of human indexers for the forging of keys to the hidden treasures of information in all its forms."

8.6. Our Examples.
8.6.1. A Book Index.

• 259

Our book index will be created by a human indexer, based on intellectual analysis of the text of the book and its message. This same index can be made available with electronic versions of the book. However, users of the electronic version of the book will also be able to search the full text of the book using a full-text automatic indexing and retrieval system, providing them with the advantages of both types of indexing.

8.6.2. An Indexing and Abstracting Service.

• 260

Our indexing and abstracting service will use both types of indexing as well. All documents will be analyzed and represented initially by automatic indexing of abstracts, titles, statements of authorship, publication information, and reference citations. Selected documents, identified through citation data, reviews, awards, use in a network of cooperating libraries, and nomination by users, advisors and indexing staff will receive augmented human indexing. The full-text of these selected (important) documents, to the extent possible, will be added to the database, so that full-text automatic indexing will also be made available for them. Users will have the option of limiting electronic searches to selected (important) documents, or searching the entire database.

8.6.3. A Full-Text Encyclopedia/Digital Library.

• 261

All articles in our encyclopedia will receive both human and automatic indexing, because selection for inclusion in the encyclopedia indicates a positive judgment of importance, justifying the expenditure of expensive intellectual analysis in addition to algorithmic, computer-based analysis.

Chapter 9. Exhaustivity

Contents of Chapter 9
9.1. Recall and Precision.
9.1.1. A Definition of Recall.
9.1.2. A Definition of Precision.
9.1.3. The Impact of Exhaustivity on Recall and Precision.
9.2. The Calculation of Exhaustivity: Terms Versus Headings
9.3. Our Examples.
9.3.1. A Book Index.
9.3.2. An Indexing and Abstracting Service.
9.3.3. A Full-Text Encyclopedia/Digital Library.

• definition of exhaustivity of indexing 1

Exhaustivity of indexing refers to the detail with which the topics and features of messages, texts, and documents are described. How many different descriptors or terms are used to describe the content or features of a typical documentary unit? This number of terms or descriptors is a measure of exhaustivity.

• 2

A simple example from descriptive cataloging, where the document and its text are described rather than the topic or features of the message, is the question of how many authors should be mentioned. Many research reports can have ten, twenty or more authors listed. In library descriptive cataloging, there is a long tradition called "the rule of three," which says that up to three authors (illustrators, translators, editors, etc.) may be mentioned, but if there are more than three, then only the first is mentioned, followed by an "et al." (et alia, Latin for "and others") (Anglo-American cataloguing rules 2002, rule 1.1F5).

• exhaustive indexing of authors : 3

Some science and technology IR databases that cater to the "publish or perish" syndrome in academia list every single author, knowing that they, if no one else, will want to see every one of their publications listed under their names. But this exhaustive indexing of authors also serves users who may want all the publications by a particular individual, even if they were one of 50 or more collaborators.

• range of exhaustivity : 4

The same issue is at play when we index the content, meaning, purpose, and features of a message and its text. How detailed shall our description be? Shall we give a message the single best term that matches its overall content, or shall we index every topic and every feature, even the minor ones, with, say, 100 or more terms?

• relationship of exhaustivity to size of documentary units : 5

As with all design issues, exhaustivity is closely related with other factors, especially with the size of the documentary unit (chapter 6). Low exhaustivity with small documentary units may be just as exhaustive, and more useful, than high exhaustivity with large documentary units. For example, the overall number of terms may be the same if we index every paragraph of periodical articles (small documentary units) with the single best term (low exhaustivity), compared to indexing the entire article as a single unit, but giving it 25 to 100 terms.

Chapter 9. Exhaustivity (Section 9.1)

• advantages of high versus low exhaustivity : 6

There are advantages to both high and low exhaustivity, so choosing the best approach is not easy or straightforward. The best exhaustivity level depends on the needs and desires of the user, but different users will have different needs and desires (and the same users will have different needs and desires at different times). For example, one student (writing a short term paper) may want only a few of the most relevant documents on a topic, while another student (one writing a dissertation on the topic) wants absolutely everything. A patent attorney also wants comprehensive retrieval, based on exhaustive indexing, while researchers or engineers checking on something outside their main field may want only a single reference.

• examples of low exhaustivity : 7

Imagine a message about the care and feeding of dogs and cats as pets. One section deals with the dreaded topic of fleas, and one paragraph discusses one particular species of fleas. Low exhaustivity indexing requires a high threshold of importance before a topic gets an index term. Would fleas, or this special species of fleas, get an index term on the basis of high importance? Is this text primarily on fleas? No. Would the student needing six references on fleas for a six page paper (the purported ratio of references to pages among Rutgers undergraduates) want this text? Most likely not.

• examples of high exhaustivity : 8

Would the biologist writing a dissertation on the impact of this species of fleas on domestic animals want this document? Perhaps so (perhaps as an indication of the treatment of the problem in documents aimed at pet owners), so exhaustive indexing might give this species its own index term.

9.1. Recall and Precision.

• impact of exhaustivity on recall and precision : 9

We will use this flea example to illustrate the possible impact of the exhaustivity of indexing on the precision and recall of retrieval in a search. This is the first time we have mentioned these two traditional measures of retrieval effectiveness, so first we will define their meaning.

9.1.1. A Definition of Recall.

• 10

Recall refers to the extent to which a retrieval system, including the indexing provided, is able to retrieve everything useful within its reach in response to a search. Its formal definition is the ratio of the number of relevant documents retrieved over all the relevant documents in an IR database or collection:

$$\text{recall} = \frac{\text{number of relevant documents retrieved}}{\text{number of relevant documents in database or collection}}$$

• impossibility of recall calculation : 11

Recall is easy to think about but just about impossible to calculate or measure in the real world. How in the world do we determine the number of relevant documents in an IR database or collection? If we knew how to do that, we would retrieve all of them, always achieving 100% recall, and be done with it. But we don't know how to identify (index) all possibly relevant documents. The only way to achieve 100% recall is to retrieve the entire IR database or collection, in which case our troubles have just begun, because our relevant items may constitute a

Chapter 9. Exhaustivity (Section 9.1.2)

very small percentage of the IR database or collection, perhaps less than .000001% of all the documents.

• recall versus relative recall : 12

Whenever researchers talk about recall, you should try to find out how they determined it. Often they are using something that is often called "relative recall," which is based on the relevant documents retrieved through multiple searches, sometimes using multiple retrieval techniques or systems. All the relevant documents from all the searches are lumped together to approximate the total number of relevant documents in the database or collection, so that the recall ratios for each individual search or system consist of the relevant documents retrieved by that search or system over all the relevant documents retrieved by all the searches or systems. But we have no evidence that even this combined set of relevant documents is even close to all the relevant documents in the entire database or collection.

• definitions of relevance : 13

Another problem is the meaning of "relevance." There is an enormous literature just on this topic, including the dissertation of our Rutgers colleague Tefko Saracevic (*On the concept of relevance in information science*, 1970). He has summarized his research and that of many others in "Relevance: a review of the literature and a framework for thinking on the notion in information science" (1976). One might summarize this massive literature in just one or two sentences by suggesting that relevance is whatever the user says it is, so that what is relevant is what a particular user finds useful at a particular time. If you agree with this definition, then you will look askance at all recall figures based on judgments by the researcher or other persons, even experts, who are not the end user.

9.1.2. A Definition of Precision.

• 14

While true recall is difficult, if not impossible, to determine, precision is easy to calculate — at least it would be easy if making relevance judgments were easy. It is based only on retrieved documents. It's the ratio between the number of relevant documents retrieved over all the documents retrieved — both the relevant and the junk:

$$\text{precision} = \frac{\text{number of relevant documents retrieved}}{\text{number of all documents retrieved}}$$

• inverse relationship of recall and precision : 15

Recall and precision often have an opposing, or inverse, relationship. We can generally improve recall by pulling in more and more documents, but as we pull in more and more documents, we get more and more junk, so as we improve recall, we make precision worse. The extreme example is pulling in the entire IR database or collection in order to insure 100% recall. At the same time, we pull in so much junk that our precision may be near zero, e.g.,

$$\frac{100 \text{ relevant documents retrieved}}{1{,}000{,}000 \text{ total number of all documents retrieved}} = .0001$$

Chapter 9. Exhaustivity (Section 9.1.3)

9.1.3. The Impact of Exhaustivity on Recall and Precision.

• 16

The higher the number of index terms associated with a document, the more often it is likely to be retrieved in response to a search. With high-exhaustivity indexing, a document will be retrieved both for its central theme, meaning, and purpose, such as the care and feeding of dogs and cats as pets, and also for minor topics, such as the species of fleas that infect dogs and cats and the ingredients that go into pet food. Such a document might be retrieved, for example, in a search on the presence of vitamin A in processed foods.

• 17

The higher the exhaustivity of indexing, the better the chances are that a searcher will find everything on a particular topic, both those documents in which the topic is the central theme, and those documents for which it is a minor, even insignificant topic. This kind of retrieval is fine for users who want comprehensive retrieval — who want everything. But such persons are probably a small minority of searchers. Most users most often want a few good items on a topic, especially the best items.

• role of high-threshold indexing in high-precision IR : 18

In order to accommodate users who want only a few good items, we raise the threshold of importance before associating a term with a document, hoping in this way to insure that a document will only be retrieved when its central theme is related to a user's need and desire. A high threshold of importance will reduce the number of terms assigned, reducing the exhaustivity of indexing. Each document will be retrieved less often, reducing the potential recall of searches, but the potential precision of searches will be improved.

• role of automatic indexing in high-recall IR : 19

Increasingly, database producers try to accommodate multiple user needs by providing different types of indexing with different levels of exhaustivity to cater to differing needs and desires of users. For example, automatic indexing can be used for language texts, based on all the terms in an abstract, or even the full text of the document. Such automatic indexing tends to result in the highest exhaustivity, because every term is considered. This type of indexing, especially when combined with forms of vocabulary management to take care of linguistic variety, can be very helpful for comprehensive high-recall retrieval.

• role of human indexing versus automatic indexing in high-precision IR : 20

For high-precision retrieval, a few terms can be assigned by human indexers, or tagged by sophisticated computer analysis, as representing the central themes or topics of a document. This low exhaustivity indexing can be used by those users wanting only a few good items.

9.2. The Calculation of Exhaustivity: Terms Versus Headings

• terms versus headings for calculation of exhaustivity : 21

Throughout our discussion of exhaustivity, we have defined it on the basis of index terms or descriptors — the number of index terms or descriptors associated with a documentary unit. Because index terms or descriptors each represent single concepts (more or less), they are a much more stable criterion for calculating exhaustivity than are index headings, which can encompass any number of terms, depending on the syntax of the indexing system. (We will be discussing

Chapter 9. Exhaustivity (Section 9.3)

syntax later on in chapter 12.) For example, the following Library of Congress subject headings each comprise multiple terms representing multiple concepts (El-Hoshy 1992, p. 126):

```
Railroads — France — Cars — History — 19th century — Pictorial works
(one subject heading, but six separate terms)

Tuberculosis — Patients — Hospital care — Maryland — Baltimore — History — 20th century — Bibliography (one subject heading, but eight or
nine separate terms; Hospital care could be divided into separate terms
for the environment "Hospitals" and the operation "Care.")
```

• calculation of exhaustivity in displayed indexes versus non-displayed indexes : 22

Furthermore, headings are not needed in non-displayed indexes that are designed for electronic searching, rather than human visual browsing or inspection. But if we counted headings in displayed indexes while counting individual terms or descriptors in non-displayed indexes, that would be like comparing automobiles and steering wheels. To be consistent, and in order to make useful comparisons, we calculate the exhaustivity of indexing on the basis of individual index terms or descriptors, not on the basis of index headings.

• 23

When multiple headings are used for the same documentary unit, often the same term will occur in more than one of these headings. When counting terms for assessing the level of exhaustivity, however, each distinct term should be counted only once, even if it occurs in more than one heading. To count the same term more than once would inflate the exhaustivity of indexing headings compared to single terms used for electronic searching.

9.3. Our Examples.

• relationship of documentary units to exhaustivity : 24

Exhaustivity is always determined, and measured, with respect to the documentary unit of the IR database or indexing system. As was pointed out, changes in documentary units can have a large influence on exhaustivity. For example, for several centuries, the traditional documentary unit for back-of-the-book indexes has been the page, so for these indexes exhaustivity would be expressed as the average number of single concept terms associated with each page. In our book index, we have shifted the documentary unit to the paragraph, so that the same index may be used in print-on-paper media and in electronic media, where pages don't normally exist.

• 25

But because a typical printed page can encompass several paragraphs, the exhaustivity counts will be very different. So it's very important to consider the documentary unit when discussing or comparing exhaustivity of indexing.

9.3.1. A Book Index.

• exhaustivity of human indexing for book indexes : 26

Our book index, with paragraph documentary units, will have an exhaustivity that ranges from 1 to 10 terms assigned by a human indexer to each paragraph. Examples of this exhaustivity can be seen throughout this book, because index entries are printed in the margins next to most paragraphs (in addition to being placed in the comprehensive back-of-the-book index).

• exhaustivity of automatic indexing for book indexes : 27

At the same time, in the electronic version of our book, users will have access to automatic indexing based on the full text of the book, so that the exhaustivity for each paragraph will approach the maximum, based on every word in each paragraph, minus a stop list.

• alternative levels of exhaustivity for book indexes : 28

In this way, users of the electronic version of the book will have a choice between high-threshold-of-importance indexing, which should lead to higher precision when users want to find where a topic receives major attention, and low-threshold-high-exhaustivity indexing when the user wants to find every mention of a word or topic.

9.3.2. An Indexing and Abstracting Service.

• 29

Our indexing and abstracting service has three levels of indexing, each with a different exhaustivity level:

• exhaustivity for routine documents : 30

• New and routine documents. All documents entering the database will be accessible through automatic indexing based on statements of authorship, titles, abstracts, and citations. Exhaustivity will be maximum, based on every word except stop words, but it will be limited to this restricted indexable matter, as opposed to full-text indexing.

• exhaustivity of human indexing for important documents : 31

• Important documents, as identified through evidence of usage or recommendations (see section 8.5), will have augmented indexing by human analysts. In addition to documentary units consisting of complete documents (periodical articles, conference papers, book chapters, video recordings, dissertations, monographs, research reports, etc.), this second level of indexing will also focus on individual charts, tables, illustrations, diagrams, and individual chapters in monographs and dissertations. For each of these smaller documentary units, from 1 to 10 terms will be assigned.

• exhaustivity of automatic indexing for important documents : 32

• The full text of important documents will also be incorporated into the database, so that automatic indexing for these documents will have greatly expanded indexable matter, with the result that the overall exhaustivity of the automatic indexing will be much higher.

9.3.3. A Full-Text Encyclopedia/Digital Library.

• 33

Our full-text encyclopedia/digital library also has three levels of indexing exhaustivity with different documentary units:

• Complete individual articles will be assigned from 1 to 10 terms by human analysts. Searches on these terms should result in high potential precision.

• Automatic full-text indexing will provide access based on maximum exhaustivity, for users interested in every mention of a word or topic.

• Once a user has retrieved an article, hypertext links may be used to retrieve related articles. The number of links per paragraph (or analogous non-language units, such as pictures, maps, diagrams, etc.) will vary from none to 10 or more. At first, links will consist of highlighted terms whenever the topic represented by a term has its own article in the database (a practice used in print databases for a long, long time). In addition, over time, associative links will be established

Chapter 9. Exhaustivity (Section 9.3.3)

:tual use patterns observed in test sites. As users move from article to article within the
1ese movements will be recorded. The articles that are most frequently linked through
equent use will receive an automatic link, consisting of a note appended to the article:
ing associated articles may also be of interest." This associative indexing is based on
nderlying idea of co-occurrence as the clustering that was discussed in section 8.3.11.
, it is co-occurrence of consultation by users. This is the same technique that is used by
ich as Amazon.com, who tell customers that other customers who bought "this book"
t "these other books."

Chapter 10. Specificity

Contents of Chapter 10
10.1. Definitions of Specificity
10.2. Relations between Exhaustivity and Specificity.
10.3. Examples of Specificity
10.4. Practical Specificity
10.5. Impact of Specificity on Precision and Recall.
10.6. Impact of Specificity on Vocabulary Size.
10.7. Specificity Versus Syntax.
10.8. Our Examples.
10.8.1. A Book Index.
10.8.2. An Indexing and Abstracting Service.
10.8.3. A Full-Text Encyclopedia/Digital Library.

10.1. Definitions of Specificity.

• specificity as closeness of relationship between index term and topic : 1

"Specificity" has been a rather slippery term with respect to its meaning and applications in library and information science. In this book, specificity refers to the degree of correspondence between an index term or descriptor and the topic or feature to which it refers. The criterion is how closely do the meanings of index terms fit the topics that are discussed in messages or the features that messages, texts, or documents exhibit or possess. Thus, our definition is a relational one — referring to the relationship between the meaning of a term and a topic or a feature. We can refer to this definition as the "semantic term-document relational definition." In this phrase, "document" is short-hand for "message, text, or document"!

• 2

This semantic term-document relational definition is based most directly on the work of the NISO committee that created the 1997 *Guidelines for indexes and related information retrieval devices* (Anderson 1997a), which was approved by the great majority of members of NISO. However, this definition has a long ancestry, going back at least to Charles Ammi Cutter and his *Rules for a printed dictionary catalogue* (1876).

• specificity versus scope of index terms : 3

According to this semantic term-document relational definition, specificity has nothing directly to do with the scope of terms themselves — the narrowness or the breadth (broadness) of the meaning of terms. A narrow term is not necessarily more specific than a broad term. In fact, it may be too narrow or too broad for the topic or feature it is intended to indicate, and therefore non-specific in either case. Specificity has to do with the use of appropriately narrow terms for narrow topics and appropriately broad terms for broad topics.

• views of Cutter (Charles Ammi) on specificity : 4

This semantic term-document relational definition corresponds well to the traditional definition used in library cataloging. In his 1876 rules, which laid the foundation for modern subject heading practice, Charles Ammi Cutter (1876, p. 37) wrote: "Enter a work under its subject-heading, not under the heading of a class which includes that subject. Ex. Put Lady Cust's book on 'The Cat' under CAT, not under ZOOLOGY or MAMMALS or DOMESTIC ANIMALS."

Chapter 10. Specificity (Section 10.1)

• views of Library of Congress on specificity : 5

The Library of Congress has continued this principle (with occasional lapses) in the application of its Library of Congress Subject Headings, probably the most widely applied indexing language ever created. In its *Subject cataloging manual: subject headings* (1996, H 180, p. 2), it explains "specificity" as follows:

> Specificity. Assign headings that are as specific as the topics they cover. Specificity is not a property of a given subject heading; instead, it is a relative concept that reflects the relationship between a subject heading and the work to which it is applied. For example, a seemingly broad heading like "Psychology" is specific when it is assigned to an introductory textbook on psychology. ...

• alternative definitions of specificity : 6

Despite the honorable pedigree for this semantic term-document relational definition of specificity, other definitions have been used, especially in information science research.

• views of Svenonius (Elaine) on specificity : 7

Perhaps the most extensive study of specificity and its impact on indexing and retrieval effectiveness was Elaine Svenonius' dissertation research (1971, 1976). She developed seven potential definitions of specificity (p. 23-50), all of them differing from the semantic term-document relational definition used in this book. Most of her definitions have to do with the semantic relationships among terms — their hierarchical relationships and their relative breadth or narrowness of meaning. These are relationships solely among terms, without regard for the nature of topics or features in documents to which they may refer. According to this definition, "cat" would always be more specific than "mammal," because in a broad-to-narrow hierarchy of terms, "cat" is always subordinate and narrower in scope than "mammal." This definition may be called the "semantic inter-term relational definition."

• operational specificity; number of postings as specificity : 8

Svenonius' seventh definition, and the one on which her research is based, is called "operational specificity." It has also been the definition used in most subsequent information science research on specificity. "Operational specificity" is determined or measured by the number of postings — the number of documentary units associated with a term. ("Postings" refers to the assignment or "posting" of a term to a record for a documentary unit. It is used for term-document associations regardless of whether a term was assigned by a human or by machine algorithm.) The fewer the postings, the higher the level of operational specificity. Terms linked to few documentary units are considered to be highly specific. Terms linked with many documentary units are considered to lack specificity.

• operational specificity : 9

Operational specificity is the only one of Svenonius' seven definitions that refers to a relationship between a term and a document or documentary unit. However, the relationship in operational specificity is statistical rather than semantic. It is based on numbers of occurrences, not on the meaning of a term and the significance of a topic or the nature of a feature.

• 10

The primary advantage of Svenonius' operational definition is just that — it is operational. It is easy to determine without ambiguity. In any IR database, it is possible to determine the number of postings per term, and experienced searchers find this information quite valuable as they create search statements. In general, terms with too many postings are not very useful!

Chapter 10. Specificity (Section 10.1)

• **semantic specificity versus operational specificity : 11**

At first glance, this operational definition appears to be quite at odds with the semantic term-document relational definition. To use one of Svenonius' own examples (p. 42), in a particular IR database, there may be ten documentary units indexed by "dogs" (that is, ten postings), and only five documentary units indexed by "mammals." Hence, according to the operational definition, the term "mammals" is more specific than the term "dogs."

• 12

But this situation is quite permissible and possible according to the semantic term-document relational definition as well, because it too divorces the meaning of specificity from the breadth or narrowness of meaning of particular terms. According to the semantic term-document relational definition, you cannot automatically assume that "dogs" is more specific than "mammals." Specificity depends solely on the relationship between the term and the topic or feature to which it refers. The only way you could determine the specificity of these terms is to compare each one to the documentary unit to which it refers — a rather tedious, subjective, and not very "operational" procedure!

• 13

The practical significance of Svenonius' operational specificity (number of postings) and the semantic term-document relational definition (closeness in meaning) are similar. In both cases, the point is more precise retrieval. When terms like "dogs" and "mammals" are applied specifically (according to the semantic term-document relational definition), then "mammals" will retrieve only messages that discuss mammals *per se*, as opposed to particular mammals like dogs. When "mammals" is used in this way, there will be fewer postings, and searchers who are interested in "mammals" will not be bothered with irrelevant documents on all the particular mammals. On the other hand, if "mammals" is indiscriminately applied to every particular mammal, then the number of postings will be very much larger. Thus indeed, there is a likely correspondence between the specific semantic relations between terms and topics (or features) on the one hand and the number of postings on the other. Svenonius' operational definition does not therefore conflict, in purpose or intent, with the traditional semantic term-document relational definition. If terms are assigned to topics or features as specifically as possible, then it is likely that they will be assigned to fewer documents, and therefore, that such terms will be more operationally specific than terms assigned less specifically.

• 14

The conflict between these two definitions comes to the fore in relation to core topics of a database, such as, for example, "libraries" in a library science database. Even if the term libraries is assigned only to documents where libraries in general (not specific types of libraries or aspects of librarianship) are indeed the topic discussed, the term "libraries" is still likely to be posted to a large number of documents. It can still be considered a highly specific term, with respect to each assignment according to the semantic term-document relational definition, but because it is assigned frequently, it would be considered a less specific term according to operational specificity.

• 15

Semantic term-document relational specificity is based on each term-document relationship. Operational specificity is based on the overall usage of a term in an IR database or collection.

• **alternative definitions of specificity: views of Balnaves (John) : 16**

In 1976, John Balnaves wrote a paper entitled, simply, "Specificity" in honor of the prominent Australian librarian John Wallace Metcalfe. Exploring notions of and impact of specificity,

Chapter 10. Specificity (Section 10.1)

Balnaves begins by quoting F. W. Lancaster: "exhaustivity of indexing controls the recall capabilities of an index, while specificity of the index language controls its precision capabilities" (Lancaster 1968, p. 20). Balnaves concludes his essay with five senses or definitions of specificity, all but one of which are close to the semantic term-document relational definition used in this book. The definition that he suggests is "the most promising, from the point of view of a general theory of indexing" is the second: "The extent to which a characteristic which distinguishes a document class is precisely labeled by a descriptor." Here, a document is placed into a class of documents according to a distinguishing characteristic (a topic or a feature), and then that characteristic is "precisely" labeled. This corresponds quite well to our semantic term-document relational definition of specificity. It refers to a semantic, or meaning-related, relationship between a term and a topic or feature to which the term refers.

• 17

Balnaves concludes his essay by recalling the point and purpose of specificity: "Specificity has to do with the accuracy of document representation ...." (p. 55).

• views of Wilson (Patrick) on specificity; specificity in Library of Congress subject headings : 18

Other prominent writers who have focused on the issue of specificity include Karen Sparck Jones, Patrick Wilson, and Bella Hass Weinberg. In a 1979 article entitled "The end of specificity," Patrick Wilson attacks the Library of Congress for not following its own oft-stated principle of specific entry. This is a continuing controversy. A similar theme pervades Mary Dabney Wilson's 1998 article "Specificity, syndetic structure, and subject access to works about individual corporate bodies." The controversy hinges on the relationship between the use of specific terms or headings on the one hand, and links among hierarchically related terms on the other. (These links between broader and narrower terms are an aspect of vocabulary management, discussed in chapter 13.) In subject heading systems like Library of Congress subject headings, part of the system includes such linking references, designed to lead users from broader terms to narrower terms (as well as other related terms). Mary Dabney Wilson gives the example:

```
Presidents — United States
    see also narrower term
        Lincoln, Abraham, 1809-1865
```

• specificity versus broader-narrower cross references, up-posting, and generic posting : 19

When such links are present, there is no need to violate the principle of specificity and use the heading "Presidents — United States" for a biography of Lincoln. Users who search on the terms "Presidents — United States" will be presented with a list of all the particular presidents for whom there are biographies.

• 20

But many libraries have dropped cross-reference links from their catalogs. So the Library of Congress began to assign non-specific terms, like "Presidents — United States" to biographies of individual presidents, in order to help users who were looking for presidential biographies, but had no particular president in mind. This practice of using broader more generic terms in addition to specific terms is called "generic posting" or "up posting." Some experts make a distinction between these two terms: "generic posting" is sometimes limited to the use of a broader, more generic term in place of a specific term (e.g., using "furniture" in place of "sofas") while "up-posting" is used for using both a specific term and a broader, more generic term (using both "sofas" and "furniture").

Chapter 10. Specificity (Section 10.1)

• **facets and hierarchical relationships : 21**

But there is an alternative view in this controversy, based on facet analysis. When you consider the terms "United States," "Presidents," and "Lincoln, Abraham," each falls in a different facet: "places," "occupations," and "individual persons" respectively. There is a strong theoretical position that broader-narrower relations exist only with facets (Kwasnik 1999). Thus it makes no sense to say that "Presidents" is either narrower or broader than "Lincoln, Abraham." Each of these terms can be considered highly specific in this case. Lincoln's occupation was "president," so this is a specific term; and so is United States. After all, he was president of the United States!

• **views of Sparck Jones (Karen) on specificity : 22**

Writing at almost the same time as Svenonius, Karen Sparck Jones lays out "A statistical interpretation of term specificity and its application in retrieval" (1972). She begins with something like the traditional semantic relational definition, except that it is not completely clear whether she is referring to relationships among terms per se, or relationships between terms and the topics or features of documents: "specificity of an individual term is the level of detail at which a given concept is represented. ... Specificity ... is a semantic property of index terms: a term is more or less specific as its meaning is more or less detailed and precise" (p. 11). Is "mammal" more or less detailed and precise than, say, "dog"?

• **23**

But then, Sparck Jones quickly moves on to considering the discriminating value of a term: "It is not enough ... to think of index term specificity solely ... as having to do with accuracy of concept representation. We should think of specificity as a function of term use. It should be interpreted as a statistical rather than semantic property of index terms. ... We can thus redefine ... specificity ...: the specificity of a term is the number of documents to which it pertains" (p. 13). Thus, Sparck Jones' statistical definition is the same as Svenonius' operational definition. In both cases, the concern is the capability of a term to pin-point relatively few highly relevant documents, and the assumption is that a term associated with fewer documentary units will do this better than a term associated with many documentary units. As with operational specificity, if index terms are truly specific, in the semantic term-document relational sense, then it is likely that they will also be more specific (or more discriminating) in the sense of Sparck Jones' statistical definition. Conversely, when a given term is used both specifically and generically (assigning, for example, "mammals" not only to messages that focus on mammals per se, but also to all messages about particular mammals), then its number of associated documentary units (number of postings) will greatly increase and its discriminating power will greatly decrease.

• **views of Weinberg (Bella Hass) on specificity: hierarchical specificity : 24**

In 1984 and 1985, Bella Hass Weinberg published two studies of specificity, seeking to explore the relationship between specificity and the number of postings — the very criterion that forms the basis of Svenonius' operational specificity and Sparck Jones' statistical definition. However, Weinberg's definition of specificity was based solely on hierarchical (broader-narrow) relations among terms in thesauri (1984, p. 145). This term-term relationship is entirely different from the term-document relationship that forms the basis of the semantic term-document relational definition.

• **25**

Therefore, the fact that Weinberg did not find a close association between number of postings and the breadth or narrowness of terms neither invalidates nor affirms the traditional term-document semantic relational definition of specificity or Svenonius' and Sparck Jones' operational/statistical definition. Instead, Weinberg was exploring quite a different phenomenon and relationship (term breadth and term postings — not term-document specificity and term postings). According to both the semantic term-document relational definition and the operational/statistical definition, broad terms can indeed be more specific than narrower terms. Broad terms can have fewer postings (the operational/statistical definition) and broad terms can sometimes correspond more closely to a topic or feature than a hierarchically subordinate narrower term (the semantic term-document relational definition).

• 26

The fact that different experts use "specificity" in very different ways means that the reader must take special care to find out exactly what they mean!

10.2. Relations between Exhaustivity and Specificity.

• 27

As chapter 9 on exhaustivity indicated, the expected relationship between exhaustivity on the one hand and recall and precision on the other is that high exhaustivity will likely increase recall and may reduce precision, while low exhaustivity will likely increase precision as it reduces recall. In contrast, the expected relationship between specificity on the one hand and recall and precision on the other is exactly the reverse. Highly specific terms should help precision while they may hurt recall, whereas generic terms should help recall, while precision will likely suffer. Thus, all other things being equal (which they never are), specificity and exhaustivity should have opposite impacts on retrieval.

• 28

Indeed, there is a clear relationship between exhaustivity and specificity, especially when the operational or statistical definition of specificity is considered. Exhaustivity is the number of terms or descriptors assigned to or extracted from a documentary unit. When exhaustivity is high, then it is likely that a given term will be assigned more frequently, so that its number of postings will increase and its discriminating power will decrease, because as it is used more frequently it will retrieve a larger number of documents. Also, with high exhaustivity indexing, terms will be assigned for even minor topics, so even though the term may be quite specific for the topic (in the sense of semantic term-document relational specificity), the document, once retrieved, may be judged irrelevant by a searcher who only wants messages that focus on the topic as the main theme. In these cases, high exhaustivity has over-powered high specificity.

• 29

Thus, in a message that is mostly about dogs, there may be a rather minor discussion of some of the mammalian features of dogs. Therefore, with high exhaustivity indexing, the term "mammals" may appropriately be assigned or extracted. In such a case, "mammals" may be considered to be a specific term in the sense of semantic term-document relational specificity, but the number of postings for "mammals" will increase with this level of exhaustivity, so the term "mammals" will retrieve many more documents, some of which a user may well consider irrelevant, depending on the level of treatment he or she desires. With high-exhaustivity indexing, even minor topics are indicated, so even with highly specific indexing, such terms are less discriminating and will retrieve minor discussions of topics as well as major discussions.

Chapter 10. Specificity (Section 10.3)

10.3. Examples of Specificity.

• 30

Returning to our fleas on dogs example (which we used in chapter 9 on exhaustivity), if we have a significant discussion of "ctenocephalides felis" or the "cat flea," which is one of the species of flea most common on dogs and cats in the United States, do we indicate (do we index!) this discussion with a term like "animals," "pests," "fleas," "cat fleas," or "ctenocephalides felis"? If the discussion is specific to Labrador retriever dogs, do we indicate (index!) this with terms like "animals," "mammals," "pets," "canines," "dogs," or "Labrador retrievers"? None of these terms would be wrong — they just differ in level of specificity! For the dogs, only "Labrador retrievers" is specific; each of the other possible terms (dogs, canines, pets, mammals, animals) is less and less specific and more and more generic. Among these terms, "animals" or possibly "pets" are the furthest removed, conceptually or hierarchically, and therefore compete for "most generic" and "least specific." For fleas, the only specific term would be "cat fleas" or "ctenocephalides felis." Whether we use the popular name or the scientific name or both is a separate question in the realm of vocabulary management (treatment of synonymous or equivalent terms), to be considered in chapter 13.

• hierarchical relationships versus roles : 31

A careful reader might appropriately object to the presence of "pets" in the list of broader terms related to dogs, or the presence of "pests" in the list of broader terms related to fleas. After all, not all dogs are pets, and not all fleas are pests (some perform in little circuses!). These terms, "pets" and "pests" describe possible roles that are commonly played by dogs and fleas. Therefore, in a message about dogs as pets, the term "pets" could be considered quite specific; and in a discussion of fleas as pests, "pests" could likewise be considered specific. Similarly, if a message pertains to fleas in circuses, then "circus performers" could be considered a specific index term. Indeed, as noted previously, it is technically correct to speak of hierarchically broader or narrower relationships only within the same facet. Dogs, fleas, mammals, and insects all fall into the animal species and families facet, but pets and pests do not. They can be considered to be members of the "animal roles or functions" facet, so they should not be considered broader or narrower than particular animal species or family of species.

10.4. Practical Specificity.

• 32

Most indexing theorists recommend what could be called "practical specificity." This means using the narrowest term that fits, without getting so specific that no-one (or very few users) will find or use a term. For our flea discussion, we would probably want to use "fleas" for most IR databases. We would probably only use "ctenocephalides felis" when the index or database has lots of materials on different types or species of fleas and is aimed at zoologists or veterinarians specializing in fleas. On the other hand, we should probably use "Labrador retrievers," because the names of dog breeds are fairly well known (as opposed to the Latin names for flea species!). However, if dogs are a very peripheral topic in our IR database, we might opt for much more generic indexing, using "dogs" or even "animals."

• vocabulary of users versus specificity : 33

Thus, an important consideration in deciding on the appropriate level of specificity is the probable vocabulary of the IR database user — the persons for whom the database is designed.

Chapter 10. Specificity (Section 10.5)

Anyone dealing with dogs knows and uses the word "flea," but the use of "cat flea" is rare, and the use of "ctenocephalides felis" is even more so!

• narrow-scoped searches versus broad-scoped searches : 34

If you use the names of breeds to index dogs, what happens to users who want everything on dogs? If you index motor vehicles under narrower terms like "pick-up trucks," "off the road vehicles," "buses," "vans," "automobiles," "sedans," "limousines," etc., what happens to the users who want everything on motor vehicles? This brings us back to the conflict between generic or up-posting versus term references linking broader to narrower terms, mentioned previously in the context of Library of Congress subject headings. The term-linking solution would link all dog breeds to the broader term "dogs" and all types of motor vehicles to the broader term "motor vehicles." Then anyone who asked for "dogs" would be shown a list of dog breeds, each of which could be selected. And anyone who asked for motor vehicles would be shown a list of particular types of motor vehicles. On the other hand, users who wanted to retrieve more general works on dogs or motor vehicles would not be swamped with masses of documents about particular types of dogs or vehicles. These are simple examples of hierarchical relationships that can, and should be, handled through vocabulary management, something we will discuss in more detail later in chapter 13.

10.5. Impact of Specificity on Precision and Recall.

• impact of specificity on precision : 35

What we try to avoid, through the use of specific terms, is retrieving unwanted material. Specificity contributes to the precision or preciseness of a search. If the user is interested in dachshunds, but is forced to search for "dogs," many "dog" documents will be retrieved that have absolutely nothing to do with dachshunds.

• impact of specificity on recall : 36

But as we try to improve precision through high specificity, we may lose some documents that might be relevant. Documents whose messages discuss a number of breeds may be indexed only with the term "dogs." A policy or practice of low exhaustivity (relatively few terms per documentary unit) generally prevents the use of terms for each of the breeds when more than, say, three particular breeds are discussed, so that such a document will not be retrieved by the term "dachshunds," even though this breed is discussed. Thus, specific indexing may help precision, but it may hurt recall, especially when comprehensive retrieval is desired but indexing is characterized by low exhaustivity (high threshold of importance).

• 37

The solution to this problem may be an additional search, using key words to search document records or full text to find any mention of "dachshunds." This would be an appropriate strategy for users wanting a comprehensive search, rather than a few good items on their topic. A less attractive solution would be to search also for "dogs," and then to wade through all the retrieved "dog" documents looking for discussions on dachshunds.

Chapter 10. Specificity (Section 10.6)

10.6. Impact of Specificity on Vocabulary Size.

• 38

The higher the level of specificity in the assignment of indexing terms, the larger the size of the indexing vocabulary. If an indexing vocabulary were to be limited, say, to only ten terms, then all fleas and all dogs would likely be indexed only with the term "animals." On the other hand, if every breed of every species is indexed with its own name, then of course, the indexing vocabulary will be very much larger.

• impact of vocabulary control on specificity : 39

Larger vocabularies are more difficult and expensive to maintain as carefully regulated or controlled vocabularies, especially when one attempts to indicate all the various relationships among terms and accommodate shifts in meaning and usage over time. IR databases that use controlled vocabularies for indexing tend, therefore, to use fewer, broader-scoped terms, especially for areas peripheral to the main focus of the database. Such broader-scoped terms will be specific only for broad-scoped topics or broad categories of features. For many narrower-scoped topics or less usual features they will function as generic, rather than specific terms.

• collocation of minor concepts by generic terms : 40

Some users find the use of generic terms helpful because they tend to gather topics that otherwise would be scattered under their own names. However, this can be a problem when a user is seeking one of these gathered topics and must wade through all the others. Gathering related topics versus discrimination among related topics is the trade-off between smaller, more generic vocabularies versus larger vocabularies that permit more specific indexing.

• impact of free uncontrolled vocabulary on specificity : 41

In contrast to controlled vocabularies, free uncontrolled vocabularies tend to be highly specific, using the actual terms found in texts and/or in search statements. Searching with such free and uncontrolled terms, however, may mean that topics or features characterized by synonymous or equivalent or more generic terms may be missed, unless the searcher managed to include all relevant synonymous or equivalent or broader terms in the search description.

• controlled vocabularies versus un-controlled vocabularies for indexing : 42

The pros and cons of controlled vocabularies is a main theme of chapter 13. One increasingly popular approach in IR databases is to use both types of vocabulary — both controlled terms and free, uncontrolled terms. If a smaller, carefully controlled vocabulary is applied to messages, texts and documents with care and expertise (by expert indexers), then its terms can be used to facilitate browsing (a major theme in chapter 11 on displayed indexes). Controlled vocabulary may also be preferred in situations when terms appropriately specific for a search are available. Depending on the circumstances, a controlled vocabulary search may result in higher recall or higher precision, or both.

• 43

For example, an IR database might use the controlled vocabulary descriptor "banks (financial institutions)" for all types of financial institutions that receive deposits and make loans. Depending on the exhaustivity of indexing, using this term should retrieve only documents having some level of treatment of banks, credit unions, mortgage companies, and similar institutions, while eliminating documents that might use "banks" in other senses, such as river banks. If indexing is good, then this should be a high-precision search for "banks." It would be a low-precision search for "saving banks," however, because lots of non-savings-bank messages would like be included.

On the other hand, recall might be good, especially for messages that use unusual terminology, or for non-language texts, such as pictures.

• **interactions of specificity with exhaustivity and vocabulary management : 44**

What we have here are the interacting influences of several design features: size of vocabulary and specificity of terms; controlled vocabulary versus free, uncontrolled terms (to be treated in chapter 13); and exhaustivity of indexing. In every instance these three factors will be at play, so it is difficult, if not impossible, to predict the impact of any one feature, such as specificity of indexing terms, without also considering the impact of the other closely associated features.

• 45

For example, to recapitulate, specific indexing generally contributes to more precise retrieval (higher precision), with the possible loss of some recall when the particular specific term used in the search has not been assigned to a document because the concept has been indicated (indexed) with a broader or synonymous or equivalent term. On the other hand, higher exhaustivity — the number of terms used, on average, per documentary unit — tends to increase recall, at the cost of retrieving more messages that may be judged to be irrelevant (lower precision), depending on how focused the user wants a message to be on a particular topic. At the same time, a smaller, controlled vocabulary may help recall by gathering in messages on the precise, or a broader, topic when the usual words for that topic have not been used. But, if the controlled term is not very specific, then the higher recall may result in lots of irrelevant messages (lower precision). Vocabulary control can also help to increase recall (without much damage to precision) when synonymous and equivalent terms are linked.

• 46

Because of these interactions, it is not easy to predict in any given situation what impact specificity, or exhaustivity, or vocabulary management will have. Making these judgments in an effective way is a mark of an expert searcher. Such searchers prefer IR databases that provide as many options as possible regarding these attributes. For novice searchers, the design challenge is to provide a default level of exhaustivity, specificity, and vocabulary management that will lead to effective results without confusing or frustrating the searcher.

10.7. Specificity Versus Syntax.

• 47

Specificity in the sense treated in this chapter refers only to individual index terms or descriptors, not to strings of terms or multi-term headings or to search statements consisting of multiple terms. The specificity discussed in this chapter might more appropriately be called "term specificity," because of course, the word "specificity" can indeed be applied to headings and search statements. Headings and search statements can also be more or less specific!

• 48

The specificity of individual terms will contribute to the specificity of multi-term headings and to multi-term search statements. However, the specificity of index headings can also be increased by combining two or more terms; the potential specificity of search statements can likewise be increased by combining two or more terms. Thus "dogs — New Jersey" could be a more specific heading than "dogs" by itself, or "New Jersey" by itself. And a search for "dogs" and "fleas" could be a more specific search than "dogs" by itself or "fleas" by itself, even though the term specificity of "dogs," "New Jersey," or "fleas" has not changed.

Chapter 10. Specificity (Section 10.8)

• 49

The means and methods for this combination of terms are governed by rules and patterns of syntax, not by term specificity. Syntax is the topic of chapter 12.

10.8. Our Examples.
10.8.1. A Book Index.

• specificity of index terms assigned by human indexing in book indexes : 50

For our book index, we will prescribe maximum practical specificity for the terms assigned by our human analyst/indexer. This means that any significant topic discussed in a paragraph of the book will be named as tightly, or as specifically, as possible. It is unlikely that we will have to worry about excessively specific terms, as long as we are naming the main topics of each paragraph.

• specificity of index terms assigned by automatic indexing in book indexes : 51

In the automatically generated full-text index to our book in electronic media, index terms will be based on the actual terms used in the text, so that ultimately, the specificity will be determined by the authors' choice of terms. Generally speaking, automatic full-text indexing is characterized by maximum specificity, assuming that an index cannot be more specific than the text it is indexing. Of course, there are exceptions to every such statement. We can imagine a text that discusses a topic, say a certain variety of sexual act, without ever actually naming it!

10.8.2. An Indexing and Abstracting Service.

• 52

The specificity policy for our indexing and abstracting service will be the same as for our book index — maximum practical specificity for the terms assigned by human analyst/indexers, while relying on the automatic indexing of citations, abstracts, and, for selected documents, full texts for maximum specificity. But unlike our book index, expert indexers may appropriately choose to use non-specific terms when topics discussed are not central to the subject scope of our database. In other words, a topic that is central to a documentary unit covered by the index, but that is peripheral to the subject scope of the database, will appropriately get a term that is more generic than the topic. For example, we may have a document about indexing systems for medicine. One documentary unit might focus on highly technical details about advanced medical diagnostic procedures or the ingredients of a particular drug. Because this is not a medical database, we need not index these details specifically.

10.8.3. A Full-Text Encyclopedia/Digital Library.

• 53

The documents in our full-text encyclopedia/digital library have already been selected for their relevance to the overall subject scope and domain. Therefore, we can implement a policy of uniform specificity for human indexing, in the same way as laid out for our book index. We do not expect to have the exceptions to specificity that may occur with some frequency in our indexing and abstracting database.

Chapter 10. Specificity (Section 10.8.3)

• 54

Our full-text automatic index will, as usual, rely on the specificity of the terms in the text. Similarly, the hypertext links from within linguistic text segments will rely on the terms used there.

Chapter 11. Displayed Versus Non-Displayed Indexes

Contents of Chapter 11
11.1. Displayed Indexes in Electronic Media.
11.2. Research on Browsing in Information Retrieval.
11.3. Design of Displayed and Non-Displayed Indexes.
11.4. Our Examples.
11.4.1. A Book Index.
11.4.2. An Indexing and Abstracting Service.
11.4.3. A Full-Text Encyclopedia/Digital Library.

• **index headings versus search statements : 1**

In the next chapter our topic is syntax. Syntax deals with rules or patterns for the combination of terms in order to create more precise — more specific — index headings or search statements to describe topics and features of interest.

• **displayed indexes versus non-displayed indexes : 2**

Index headings are used in displayed indexes — indexes that are displayed for human visual inspection. Search statements are used with non-displayed indexes — indexes designed for machine algorithms that match terms in search statements against terms in message, text, and/or document descriptions (citations, abstracts, surrogates) or full text.

• **3**

Before we can discuss syntax in detail, we must focus on these two fundamentally different kinds of indexes: Indexes that are displayed so that they can be scanned, browsed or read by the human eye (displayed indexes), and indexes that are meant for computer term-matching algorithms rather than human inspection.

• **4**

We have mentioned these two types of indexes before, but here we focus directly on this fundamental distinction.

• **5**

Note that in this chapter we focus on the question of whether or not to provide displayed, browsable indexes. The options for arranging such indexes are treated in chapter 17 on the arrangement of displayed indexes (both alphanumeric and classified relational displays), and the design of effective interfaces for displays in both print and electronic environments is the chief topic of chapter 19 on the search interface.

• **history of displayed indexes : 6**

Humankind has used displayed indexes for millennia, ever since our ancestors learned how to encode messages onto long-lasting media and began creating collections of the resulting documents. As soon as these documents became too numerous to keep track of in informal ways, lists were devised to manage and find them. These lists were indexes, and they were displayed usually in the same medium as the documents that they indicated — clay tablets, bone, leaves, bark, animal skins (parchment, vellum), paper.

• **history of non-displayed indexes : 7**

Only in the past half century have we begun creating indexes that are used for machine matching rather than for visual inspection by the human eye. The earliest such indexes predated the computer, but relied on early examples of the same kind of matching techniques that became

Chapter 11. Displayed Versus Non-Displayed Indexes (Section 11.1)

nearly universal with the advent of computer retrieval systems. An example of a pre-computer non-displayed index are the cards used in the optical coincidence, or peek-a-boo, retrieval system that was described back in chapter 5 on display media (section 5.1.3).

• **inverted files as non-displayed indexes : 8**

But now, non-displayed indexes are almost always used by computer programs. Such indexes may not even exist until a search is performed. They may be created "ad hoc" or "on the fly" for each search, or inverted files of terms may be created in advance of searches in order to speed up the machine matching process. Inverted files are created by taking all, or selected, terms from message, text, or document descriptions or from full text, and sorting them in ways that speed up the machine matching process.

• **syntax for displayed indexes versus non-displayed indexes : 9**

Obviously, the syntax for index headings that are displayed for human visual inspection will be very different from the syntax for search statements used for computer matching of terms in an index designed for computer use.

11.1. Displayed Indexes in Electronic Media.

• 10

Almost invariably today, an index on paper media will be a displayed index. Non-displayed indexes are almost always relegated to electronic media. However, displayed indexes are becoming more and more popular in electronic databases, especially when they are designed for non-professional "end user" searching.

• **browsing and navigation : 11**

While it is now very uncommon, and not very practical given current technological options, to present non-displayed indexes and search options in paper or paper-like media (such as the cards used in the optical coincidence system), it is easy to provide for both displayed and non-displayed indexes in electronic media. Consequently, IR database designers must consider the pros and cons of both types of indexes. There is a growing tendency to offer users both types of indexes, in order to increase the options for searching — the option of searching by means of "behind-the-scenes" computer matching, or the option of searching by means of visual inspection or browsing of displayed index arrays.

• **characteristics of non-displayed indexes : 12**

A user does not normally see the non-displayed index during an actual search — hence the term "non-displayed index." When searching a non-displayed index, users are presented with a search screen in which they must describe the topics or features that interest them. Users may or not be offered assistance in describing their interests. They may be able to consult a list of terms used in the database, or perhaps a full-fledged thesaurus. Relationships among terms may also be displayed to help users broaden, refine, or redirect their search. (These vocabulary management options will be discussed in chapter 13.)

• **vocabulary lists versus non-displayed indexes : 13**

Even when a full-fledged thesaurus is not provided, it is not uncommon for an IR system using non-displayed indexes to provide the user with opportunities to see lists of terms from database records or texts. Such lists can help users pick useful search terms. However, these lists of terms are not properly called message, text, or document indexes, because they list only single terms — sometimes only single words — rather than complete index headings consisting of multiple terms. Index headings (multiple terms combined according to syntactic rules) are designed

Chapter 11. Displayed Versus Non-Displayed Indexes (Section 11.1)

to represent the content (or the features) of a message, text or document (a documentary unit). It is rare that a single term can adequately represent the content or features of a documentary unit, so most index headings will (or should!) consist of two or more terms. Similarly, in computer matching search systems, an effective search statement rarely consists of only a single word or term. Such a very short search statement would simply match entirely too many records or texts to be useful for retrieval. Thus, search statements, like index headings, will often need multiple terms to adequately represent desirable documentary units. In contrast to index headings or search statements, lists of terms are designed only to present available search terms. They do not represent documentary units in the way that index headings or search statements do, so it is inappropriate to call them "displayed indexes," at least in the context of the terminology used in this book! Technically, these lists of terms — usually in alphanumeric order — are indexes to (indicators of) possible search term vocabulary, rather than indexes to (indicators of) potentially useful documentary units. We will return to this distinction between indexes to documentary units versus indexes to terms in the next chapter on syntax (section 12.3).

• advantages of non-displayed indexes : 14

Computer matching of search terms against non-displayed indexes has many advantages. Searchers may use any terms they want to, and there is no need to worry about the order of terms. There are often no constraints in what users can search for or how they describe it. Syntactic options for search statements (see chapter 12) provide ways to narrow and broaden searches (truncation, wild cards, proximity requirement, Boolean operators, weights, etc.). If users know what they want, and how to describe it, a quick computer match against a non-displayed index can be the fastest way to find a useful documentary unit. However, there is no guarantee that such a search statement will match any database records or texts, or that a reasonable number of items will be retrieved. Often searchers are faced with either zero hits (no retrieved items) or entirely too many items to cope with.

• 15

So, to repeat, searching non-displayed indexes is often fast and efficient when a searcher knows exactly what they want, and how to describe it.

• disadvantages of non-displayed indexes : 16

But computer matching of search terms against non-displayed indexes can be difficult and frustrating in many situations, especially when users are not quite sure what they are looking for. It is often hard to get an overall idea of IR database content when there are no displayed indexes, because the content of the database is often not displayed in any global way that presents an overview of possibilities. The syntax for creating a sophisticated search statement can be quite daunting, and sometimes the results of a search consists of hundreds, even thousands, of undifferentiated records. In these cases, the user may prefer a visible displayed index that can be scanned and browsed.

• characteristics of displayed indexes : 17

In contrast to non-displayed indexes, displayed indexes attempt to show users what is in the database. Index headings are created to describe in advance the topics and features of possible interest in the documentary units of the database. Users may then choose from among the index headings, selecting those that most closely match their interests. Users are not required to come up with any search statement on their own. In effect, the system has created potential search statements in advance, and now displays them to users, for the users to pick from. It is often much easier to recognize potentially relevant headings than to think up in advance, on one's own, the best possible terms to represent potentially relevant documentary units.

Chapter 11. Displayed Versus Non-Displayed Indexes (Section 11.1)

• advantages of displayed indexes : 18

Also in contrast to non-displayed indexes, when working from a displayed index, users are guaranteed retrievals, if they pick an existing index heading. If the indexing system is well designed and well implemented, then the retrieved items should reflect the index heading fairly closely and should not be too numerous. The NISO *Guidelines for indexes and other information retrieval devices* (Anderson 1997a), for example, suggests that no more than five items should share the same index heading.

• disadvantages of displayed indexes : 19

The main disadvantage of a displayed index is the requirement that users must figure out how the index is arranged and what the terms are that are used to describe the concepts in which they are interested. Some classified relational arrangements can be quite complex (these will be discussed in chapter 17), involving hierarchical, spatial, chronological, operational and other relationships among entities and associated phenomena. Even alphabetical arrangements can be challenging, as described in chapter 1 in the discussion of standards for alphanumeric arrangement (section 1.4). Good displayed indexes will provide lots of help for vocabulary problems, with cross references leading users from unused terms to used terms and suggestions for consulting narrower, broader or other related terms. Unfortunately, however, some displayed indexes are completely lacking in this kind of vocabulary and navigation assistance.

• challenges for displayed indexes : 20

Among the many challenges in the design of effective displayed indexes are:

• matching the vocabulary of users so that they can find index headings of interest. This means including a vocabulary management component so that users who look for "attorneys" will find them even if the index calls them "lawyers." It also means providing guidance for users who begin their exploration with broad terms, like "animals," "pets," or even "dogs," when what they really want is information on the care and feeding of dachshunds! In other cases, users may benefit from similar guidance to broader or related terms. (These are major themes of chapter 13 on vocabulary management.)

• creating a display that is effective in showing users what is available. For some users this may be an alphabetical display of key terms representing the topics and features of the documentary units in the IR database; for others it may mean a classified or grouped display of broad categories of topics, which users can browse, via descending hierarchies of terms, as they see options and use them to refine their search. Creative displays may also use graphical methods for providing visual overviews of the entire content of the IR database. These challenges are the main theme of chapter 19 on user interfaces.

• mental images of IR databases : 21

One advantage of displayed indexes is that they can be effective in conveying a mental image of the scope, content and organization of the IR database to users. This is often a serious problem for electronic IR databases. When users, especially new users, are confronted with essentially empty search screens in which they must describe their search, it is often hard for them to get a grasp of what is actually available to them — to visualize the entire IR database and what is in it.

• 22

Contrast this situation with traditional print-medium databases. When a user approaches the printed version of *Chemical abstracts*, for example, they are first impressed by its immense size, seeing row on row of massive volumes. If they pick the first volume of the latest year available, they will see a table of contents that lays out the various parts — grouped or classified arrays of abstracts and a variety of alphanumeric indexes that can be searched.

Chapter 11. Displayed Versus Non-Displayed Indexes (Section 11.2)

• 23

When they choose a particular index, they immediately see the actual index, so they can get a picture of the kind of document descriptions provided in the index headings, how the index is arranged, and how it might be searched.

• 24

One of the purposes of displayed indexes in electronic IR databases is to portray the scope of the IR database and to permit and encourage the kind of exploration that new users typically engage in when they approach for the first time a print-medium IR database like *Chemical abstracts*.

• role of browsing in IR : 25

The main reason for providing displayed indexes, whether they are arranged in an alphabetical order, or in a grouped, hierarchical, classified order, is to facilitate browsing. When only non-displayed indexes are available, browsing is generally limited to lists of possible search terms and to the results of a search. With displayed indexes, users may browse the entire database, or they may select portions of the database to browse.

11.2. Research on Browsing in Information Retrieval.

• 26

Research on the role and importance of browsing in information retrieval reinforces the need for providing users with the opportunity to browse IR databases. With the advent of online public access catalogs (OPACs) and CD-ROM and online IR databases, followed by the explosion of the world-wide web, end-user searching without the help of professional search intermediaries has grown by leaps and bounds. OPACS are now the most common form for library catalogs, and like nearly all library catalogs, they are intended primarily for end-user searching. The burgeoning number of digital libraries — large collections of texts in digital form representing a wide range of formats and media — require effective and user-friendly search procedures as well. Many end-users are more comfortable when they can see what they are looking for. Hence, there is growing interest in browsing as an important component of information searching. And the bottom line is, displayed indexes support browsing.

• literature reviews on browsing : 27

Chang and Rice (1993) have provided a comprehensive review of the research literature on browsing as it applies, not only to information retrieval, but also to consumer behavior, mass media, organizational communication, and environmental design. Their review is related to Chang's dissertation, "Toward a multi-dimensional framework for understanding browsing" (1993). Rice was Chang's dissertation advisor at Rutgers University.

• 28

Later, Rice, McCreadie, and Chang (2001) expanded on this research in *Accessing and browsing information and communication*. Christine Borgman, a leading IR researcher at UCLA provided a pithy quote for the book's jacket: "In the networked world, browsing has supplanted direct searching as the primary means to locate information."

• 29

In addition, Kurth and Peters (1995) have provided an "extensive annotated bibliography" on "browsing in information systems."

Chapter 11. Displayed Versus Non-Displayed Indexes (Section 11.3)

• definitions of browsing; views of Chang (Shan-Ju) and Rice (Ronald E.) on browsing : 30

Here are selected statements from Chang and Rice (1993):

- "Browsing is common but not well understood. We all browse in various contexts to make sense of the world around us, such as when we read newspapers, scan television channels, go window shopping, or seek information in libraries" (p. 232).
- "Browsing has been loosely described as a kind of searching, in which the initial search criteria or goals are only partly defined or known in advance" (p. 235).
- "Browsing has become an important heuristic search strategy to be used in situations such as when the user does not look for anything specific or is unable to specify initial search requirements or is unfamiliar with the terminology of a domain of interest, or when he or she wishes to discover the general information content of the database" (p. 238).
- "Browsing has been associated with visual recognition and spatial reasoning as opposed to linguistic specification and logical reasoning" (p. 239).
- "... it takes less cognitive load to browse than it does to plan and conduct an analytical search" (p. 241).
- "... browsing is the most important form of searching for casual use" (p. 241.)

• views of Marchionini (Gary) on browsing : 31

Marchionini has devoted two major chapters to browsing in his book *Information seeking in electronic environments* (1995). He introduces the first of these chapters (6. Browsing strategies) as follows (p. 100):

"In contrast with the formal, analytical strategies developed by professional intermediaries, information seekers also use a variety of informal, heuristic strategies. These informal, interactive strategies are clustered together under the term "browsing strategies." In general, browsing is an approach to information seeking that is informal and opportunistic and depends heavily on the information environment. Four browsing strategies are distinguished in this chapter: scanning, observing, navigating, and monitoring. The term "browsing" reflects the general behavior that people exhibit as they seek information by using one of these strategies.

"Browsing is a natural and effective approach to many types of information-seeking problems. It is natural because it coordinates human physical, emotive, and cognitive resources in the same way that humans monitor the physical world and search for physical objects. It can be effective because the environment and particularly human-created environments are generally organized and highly redundant — especially information environments that are designed according to organization principles. Browsing is particularly effective for information problems that are ill defined or interdisciplinary and when the goal of information seeking is to gather overview information about a topic or to keep abreast of developments in a field."

11.3. Design of Displayed and Non-Displayed Indexes.

• 32

Indexes are a major component of any IR database. Their design consists of several aspects that are treated in separate design chapters in this book. Displayed indexes will depend on the syntax chosen for index headings (chapter 12), methods of vocabulary management (chapter 13), arrangement options (chapter 17) and the interface for the display of indexes (chapter 19). These same design issues impact non-displayed indexes as well, with the exception of the arrangement of indexes. Because users don't see non-displayed indexes, their arrangement does not play a role in the interaction between human searchers and the index. Electronic non-displayed indexes often do have arrangements, but they are created to facilitate behind-the-scenes computer matching and are outside the scope of this book.

11.4. Our Examples.
11.4.1. A Book Index.

• 33

Our book can be published in two media: paper and electronic. The paper book will have a traditional displayed index, locked onto paper pages at the end of the book.

• 34

Our electronic book will get two indexes, one displayed and one non-displayed. The displayed index will look very much like the displayed index in the print book. Users will be able to browse up and down the index using arrow keys or a mouse. They can zoom to another section of the index (like turning a page) by typing one or more letters. The display will "zoom" to the headings beginning with the letters typed, or the closest headings to them if there is no exact match. In addition, users can do keyword searches of the displayed index, which will find every heading containing the words, or letters, typed in, no matter where they occur in the heading.

• 35

If users of the electronic book prefer, they can opt for the non-displayed index by submitting freely constructed search statements, using syntax appropriate for computer matching (to be described in chapter 12). Such computer matching searches can be restricted to terms assigned by human indexers, or they can include the full text of the book as well.

11.4.2. An Indexing and Abstracting Service.

• 36

Our indexing and abstracting service will also have both displayed and non-displayed indexes, but the non-displayed indexes will be available only in the electronic version. The print version will have two distinct displayed indexes, one for the indexing based on terms assigned by human indexers to high-use documents, and one for keyword indexing based on the words in titles, abstracts, and statements of authorship.

• 37

Users of the electronic version of our indexing and abstracting service may use a displayed index based on human indexing of high-use documents, or a non-displayed index for computer-based matching of search statement terms. If a searcher desires a more focused search, the non-displayed index for computer matching may be restricted to:

- terms assigned by our human indexers to high-use documents;
- titles, abstracts, and statements of authorship of high use documents;
- the full text of high use documents;
- titles, abstracts, and statements of authorship of all documents;
- any combination of these sets of documents and types of indexing.

Chapter 11. Displayed Versus Non-Displayed Indexes (Section 11.4.3)

11.4.3. A Full-Text Encyclopedia/Digital Library.

• 38

Our full-text encyclopedia/Digital Library also gets both displayed and non-displayed indexes, and in addition, hypertext links within individual articles, linking them to related articles. The displayed index features headings based on human analysis, while the non-displayed index provides access via computer term-matching algorithms to the complete text of the articles, in addition to the terms assigned by the human indexers.

Chapter 12. Syntax

Contents of Chapter 12
12.1. Precoordinate and Postcoordinate Syntax.
12.2. Precoordinate Syntax for Displayed Indexes.
12.2.1. Subject Heading Syntax: *Library of Congress subject headings* (LCSH).
12.2.1.1. Medical Subject Headings (MeSH).
12.2.1.2. Principles for Subject Heading Systems.
12.2.2. String Syntax.
12.2.2.1. Rotated Term Syntax.
12.2.2.2. Faceted Syntax (PRECIS, CIFT).
12.2.2.2.1. Converting LCSH to Faceted Syntax.
12.2.2.3. Ad Hoc String Syntax (NEPHIS)
12.2.3. Relational Syntax.
12.2.3.1. Syntagmatic Relationships.
12.2.4. Classification Syntax.
12.2.4.1. Chain Syntax.
12.2.5. Natural Language Syntax.
12.2.5.1. KWIC Syntax.
12.2.5.2. KWOC Syntax.
12.2.5.3. KWAC Syntax.
12.2.6. Permuted Syntax.
12.2.7. Ad Hoc Syntax.
12.2.7.1. Combining Ad Hoc Syntax with Systematic Syntax.
12.2.8. Syntactic Cross References.
12.3. Postcoordinate Syntax for Non-Displayed Indexes.
12.3.1. Exact Match (Boolean) Syntax.
12.3.2. Best Match (Weighted Term) Syntax.
12.4. Our Examples.
12.4.1. A Book Index.
12.4.2. An Indexing and Abstracting Service.
12.4.3. A Full-Text Encyclopedia/Digital Library.

• **definition of syntax; syntax in index headings compared to search statements : 1**

Syntax (from the Greek "syn" for "together" and "tassein" for "to arrange") refers to patterns or rules for putting words together to create texts for messages in a language. Indexing syntax refers to patterns or rules for putting terms together in index headings to indicate the topics and features of messages, texts, or documents in displayed indexes. For non-displayed indexes designed for electronic searching by means of computer-matching algorithms, syntax refers to patterns or rules for putting terms together in search statements to indicate the topics or features of desired messages, texts, or documents.

• **role of syntax in indexing : 2**

It is almost impossible to communicate in one-word utterances. "Help!" is an obvious exception, and so is "Thanks!" and "Sorry!" But most of the time, we need to put words together to convey the meaning we want to communicate. The same is true in indexing, whose fundamental purpose is "indicating" (from the same Latin word "indicare" whence comes "indexing") the meaning, purpose, content, and features of messages, texts and documents (i.e., documentary units). If indexing were limited to single words or terms, it would be a pretty weak method for indicating anything of significance.

• **impact of syntax on precision : 3**

Syntax is especially helpful for increasing the precision of searches. As more terms are put together, more fully describing desirable documentary units, the documentary units that are retrieved may be more precisely what is desired. At the same time, some other documentary units that are similar (but whose associated terms may not match all of the terms in a heading or a search statement) may be left behind. So as usual, as we take steps to increase precision, we may be hurting potential recall. (Experienced searchers will recognize that there are syntactic options for including terms without insisting that they be present in every documentary unit or in their database records. More on this later!)

• **example of impact of syntax on precision : 4**

An example: In many databases and collections, there may be thousands, if not millions, of documents relating in some way to the United States. If we can search only on "United States" (two words but a single term!) we can retrieve all of them, but it would be the rare situation where anyone wants all of them, everything from documents on agriculture in the U.S. through zoos. For any kind of precision, it is absolutely essential that terms be combined, and indexing syntax provides the means for combining them.

• **syntax as essential attribute of indexes : 5**

Syntax is so important in indexing that it constitutes one of the two essential attributes of an index according to the NISO *Guidelines for indexes and related information retrieval devices* (Anderson 1997a). (The other essential attribute is some form of vocabulary management or control, the theme of chapter 13.)

• **syntax in index headings compared to search statements : 6**

To summarize, terms are combined by means of syntax to form index headings in displayed indexes. For non-displayed indexes designed electronic searching, syntax is used to combine terms in search statements.

12.1. Precoordinate and Postcoordinate Syntax.

• **purpose of index headings and search statements : 7**

Index headings (in displayed indexes) and search statements (for computer matching of terms in non-displayed indexes) play similar roles in the information retrieval process. The index heading or the search statement is meant to present a succinct summary of the content, purpose, meaning, and/or features of documentary units.

• **precoordinate index headings : 8**

But index headings and search statements do this in very different ways. Index headings are created in advance (before a search) by indexers (or by indexing algorithms) to describe documentary units in an IR database. Index terms are precoordinated into headings, which users then examine as they search for useful documentary units. One advantage of these precoordinate headings is that users can look at them and judge their potential usefulness, without having to think of appropriate terms to describe their desires. It is often easier for users, especially if they are looking for unfamiliar material, to recognize something of interest than to compose a statement that describes exactly, or even approximately, what will interest them.

Chapter 12. Syntax (Section 12.1)

• **postcoordinate search statements : 9**

Search statements, in contrast, are created by the user (or by a search intermediary on behalf of the user). Instead of being precoordinated in advance during the production or updating of the IR database, terms are postcoordinated, that is, they are put together after the creation of the IR database.

• **differences between displayed indexes and non-displayed indexes : 10**

Because of the major differences between displayed indexes with precoordinate index headings, and non-displayed indexes designed for computer matching of postcoordinate search statements, appropriate syntax is very different for each type of index. First we will examine syntax for displayed indexes; then for non-displayed indexes.

• **views of Svenonius (Elaine) on precoordination versus postcoordination : 11**

Svenonius (1995) provides a good overview and a brief history of the arguments pro and con concerning precoordinate versus postcoordinate syntax. On the pro-postcoordination side, she begins with the ideas of Mortimer Taube. In the 1950s Taube developed the "uniterm" method of indexing — an example of extreme post-coordination with a minimum of pre-combined terms. He also offered me — James D. Anderson — my very first job right out of library school in 1964. Who knows where I would have ended up had I accepted his offer! In her discussion, Svenonius applies twenty criteria for the evaluation of indexing languages, sixteen suggested by Taube (1953) and four of her own (precision, recall, browsability, and contextuality). The names and numbering of the criteria are from Svenonius rather than Taube. Here they are:

• **criteria for indexing languages : 12**

- Logical syntax
- Simplicity
- Speed in cataloging or indexing
- Size
- Rate of growth
- Rate of obsolescence
- Suitability for cumulative dissemination
- Cost
- Universality (the capability of indicating new concepts, often called "hospitality")
- Neutrality (the capability of being merged or combined with other indexing languages)
- Specificity (see chapter 10)
- Browsability (see chapter 11)
- Precision (see chapter 9)
- Recall (also covered in chapter 9)
- Number of access points.
- Speed in searching
- Suggestibility (the capability of suggesting aspects of topics)
- Contextuality (the capability of placing terms in context)
- Familiarity
- Adaptability to a machine environment

Chapter 12. Syntax (Section 12.2)

12.2. Precoordinate Syntax for Displayed Indexes.

• 13

The following sections survey the characteristics of the major varieties of precoordinate syntax as they are used to create index headings for displayed indexes. these varieties include:

- subject heading syntax.
- string syntax (rotated, faceted, ad hoc).
- relational syntax.
- classification syntax (for enumerative, synthetic, faceted classifications); chain syntax.
- natural language syntax (KWIC, KWOC, KWAC).
- permuted syntax
- ad hoc (made to order) syntax.

• views of Craven (Timothy) on purpose of precoordinate syntax : 14

The purpose of precoordinate syntax is to combine terms in such a way that the resulting index headings will be as helpful as possible to persons searching for useful documentary units. According to Craven (1986, p. 7), such headings should possess five important attributes or capabilities (which can be compared to the twenty criteria suggested by Svenonius!):

• criteria for precoordinate indexing languages : 15

- Eliminability: index headings should be sufficiently full so that the documentary units represented can be safely ignored (eliminated!) as inappropriate.

- Predictability: the terminology, format and syntax of index headings should be as uniform and regular as possible, so that users will be able to learn how to predict what desirable index headings will look like and where they can be found.

- Collocation: terms should be combined into index headings in such a way that closely related headings will be close to each other in displayed indexes — they will be closely "co-located."

- Clarity: the resulting index headings should be as clear as possible!

- Succinctness: and they should be as succinct as possible!

12.2.1. Subject Heading Syntax: *Library of Congress subject headings.*

• development of subject headings in 19th century : 16

Subject headings are the most widely-used type of pre-coordinate headings in indexes and catalogs. They were developed in the 19th century in order to provide predictable, uniform and direct alphabetical access to topics in library catalogs, indexes, and bibliographies. Prior to subject headings, subject access to documents — mainly books — had been provided through classification schemes and "catch-word titles." Classification schemes were generally used to arrange books on shelves, but also sometimes to arrange entries in catalogs, which were usually printed as books. Catch-word titles were titles of books and other documents rearranged under their most important word or words (usually only the single most important word). A modern version of catch-word titles is the computer-produced KWIC, KWOC, and KWAC indexes, which will be discussed later on in section 12.2.5 on natural language syntax.

Chapter 12. Syntax (Section 12.2.1)

• **subject headings in the United States** : 17

In the United States, the two most widely used subject heading systems are *Sears list of subject headings* (Sears 1997), for smaller libraries, and the *Library of Congress subject headings* (Library of Congress 2003), for larger libraries. Specialized lists of subject headings have been developed for many subject areas, such as *MeSH: Medical subject headings* (National Library of Medicine 1999).

• *Library of Congress subject headings* : 18

As the largest and oldest system of subject headings in continuous use, we will use *Library of Congress subject headings* (LCSH) as our primary example for illustrating subject heading syntax. This indexing language of over "245,000 authorized headings" (Library of Congress 2003, 1999 ed. p. vii) just celebrated its 100th birthday in 1998. It is by far the most widely used indexing language in the world.

• **types of subject headings in** *Library of Congress subject headings* : 19

The Library of Congress has created subject headings for:

- individual persons and corporate bodies, established according to rules for descriptive cataloging;
- places, regions, types of environments, and political jurisdictions, also established according to rules for descriptive cataloging;
- messages (called "works" in cataloging, also established according to rules for descriptive cataloging;
- groups and classes of persons (ethnic groups, occupational groups, gender groups, sexual orientation groups, disability groups, age groups, etc.);
- institutions and types of institutions;
- naturally occurring objects, both named (Rocky Mountains) and generic (mountains);
- artifacts, including buildings, both named (Empire State Building) and generic (castles);
- conditions, emotions, attributes, properties, and parts of entities that belong to all the preceding categories;
- events;
- activities, operations, and processes;
- time periods or eras (both geologic and historic);
- formats, genres, and media of documents.

• **syntax of** *Library of Congress subject headings* : 20

Subject headings can consist of single words or phrases. They can be used alone or in combinations of main headings and subheadings, called "subdivisions" by the Library of Congress. The combination of terms is governed by complex and inconsistent rules that have developed over the more than 100-year life of the system and are now embodied in the four-volume looseleaf *Subject cataloging manual: subject headings* (Library of Congress 1996).

• **history of syntax in** *Library of Congress subject headings* : 21

The Library of Congress has been quite frank about the inconsistencies of the system:

"Because the list [of headings] has expanded over time, it reflects the varied philosophies of the hundreds of catalogers who have contributed headings. As described by David Judson Haykin in the introduction to the fourth edition (1943): 'The failures in logic and consistency are, of course, due to the fact that headings were adopted in turn as needed, and that many minds participated in the choice and establishment of headings.' This was expanded by Richard S. Angell in the introduction to the sixth edition (1957): 'The list is the product of evolutionary forces, among them the growth of the Library's collections, semantic change, and varying theories of subject heading practice over the years. As a consequence the list is, at any point in time, an accurate reflection of practice but not a complete embodiment of theory'" (Library of Congress 2003, 1992 ed. p. viii). Unfortunately, these comments were eliminated from subsequent introductions to the annual editions of LCSH.

• main headings in *Library of Congress subject headings* : 22

Even the patterns for formulating main headings have changed over time. In earlier years, inverted headings were quite common, resulting in headings like "Lullabies, Urdu," "Songs, French," "Art, American," and Drawing, Australian," or "Love, Maternal," "Bridges, Concrete," and "Insurance, Fire." But later, natural word order came to be preferred, so newer headings are "Nuclear physics," "Local taxation," and "Pumping machinery" (most examples from Library of Congress 1986-1999, 1998 ed. p. viii).

• combination of entities and actions in *Library of Congress subject headings* : 23

Another area of inconsistency is the combination of entities and actions. The most common order for combining entities and actions in indexing and classification is: entity + action, as in:

```
Animal food — Contamination
Baby foods — Contamination
Fibers — Reclamation
Fire arms — Design and construction
        — Identification
        — Maintenance and repair
        — Taxation
        — testing
Plants — reproduction
```

But LCSH also uses:

```
Fertilization of plants
```

and

```
Fire investigation
Fire engine driving
Fire prevention
Food contamination
(examples from Dykstra 1992, p. 40).
```

• 24

The heading "Fertilization of plants" places the action first; "Fire investigation," "Fire engine driving," "Fire prevention" and "Food contamination" converts the entity to an adjectival form modifying the action. For consistency, these variant headings could be converted to:

```
Plants — Fertilization
Fires — Investigation
Fire engines — Driving
Fires — Prevention
Foods — Contamination (which would then match the pattern
     in "Animal food — Contamination" and "Baby Foods — Contamina-
     tion."(Yes, it's "Animal food" but "Baby
     foods"!)
```

• subdivision practice in *Library of Congress subject headings* : 25

LCSH adds subdivisions to main headings in order to add context and thereby characterize a documentary unit with greater specificity. El-Hoshy (1992) has summarized current practice.

Chapter 12. Syntax (Section 12.2.1)

Many of the following examples are taken from her paper. LCSH uses four categories of subdivisions to indicate aspects of main heading topics:

- form subdivisions
- geographical subdivisions
- chronological subdivisions
- topical subdivisions

• form subdivisions in *Library of Congress subject headings* : 26

Form subdivisions are used to indicate the form or format of documents, such as "— Pictorial works," "— Indexes," "— Catalogs," and "— Handbooks, manuals, etc." Form subdivisions also include indications of intended audiences, as in: "— Amateurs' manuals," "— Popular works," "— Juvenile literature," and "— Textbooks for foreign speakers."

• 27

Sometimes, however, these same form subdivisions are used to indicate topics rather than forms, and the distinction is often unclear, as between "Art — Exhibitions" for an art exhibition catalog (a form) versus a book on how to mount an art exhibition (a topic).

• 28

Some form subdivisions indicate the approach the author has taken to a topic, as in "— History." This subdivision is generally applied to documentary units that are histories of a topic or place, rather than documentary units that discuss, or are about the nature of history as a topic (the doing of history, historiography) or methods of creating or writing histories. Thus "— History" is often used to describe the form of the documentary unit rather than its topic.

• 29

Whether "— History" is actually considered to be a form subdivision or a topical subdivision by the Library of Congress is a source of confusion. Lynn El-Hoshy, who is described as a "Subject Cataloging Policy Specialist in the Office for Subject Cataloging Policy at the Library of Congress" (Conway 1992, p. 144) cites "— History" as an example of a form subdivision (El-Hoshy, p. 118), but "— History" is not marked as a form subdivision in the *Subject cataloging manual: subject headings* (Library of Congress 1996).

• geographic subdivisions in *Library of Congress subject headings* : 30

Many main headings in LCSH carry the note "(may subd geog)." This means that the heading may be modified by the names of cities, towns, states or provinces, countries, regions or geographic features such as rivers or mountains.

• 31

Whenever a heading is subdivided by a small or local place, the larger place — the country or, for United States, Canada, and the United Kingdom, the state, province, or constituent country, is inserted first, in order to gather together all local places within countries or states or provinces, as in:

```
Clocks and watches — England — London
Children — Mortality — Brazil — Rio de Janeiro
```

• 32

Many subdivisions may also be subdivided by place, and when both the main heading and the subdivision has the (may subd geog) note, then the place must go as far toward the end of the complete heading as possible, creating a rather chaotic pattern as in:

Chapter 12. Syntax (Section 12.2.1)

```
Construction industry — Italy
Construction industry — Italy — Finance
Construction industry — Finance — Law and legislation — Italy
Construction industry — Government policy — Italy
Construction industry — Italy — Mathematical models
 (examples taken from Library of Congress 1986-1999, 1998
     ed. p. xii).
```

• 33

Which subdivisions may be followed by a geographic subdivision is difficult (perhaps impossible) to predict. Why can a geographical subdivision follow "— Law and legislation," but not "— Finance"?

• chronological subdivisions in *Library of Congress subject headings* : 34

Subdivision by time is used sparingly in LCSH. For many historical topics, including major places with subdivisions like "— History," "— Politics and government," "— Economic conditions," "— Social conditions" and "— Description and travel," time periods appropriate for these places or topics are "built in" — actually listed under the main heading for the place plus subdivision in published lists. When this is not done, the usual way for indicating time is by using the subdivision "— History" plus century, as in "— History — 18th century," "— History — 19th century," etc. However, there is a list of subdivisions that cannot be modified by "history"! For a few of these subdivisions, rules permit the direct addition of particular time periods, but only if the main heading is a place (e.g., "— economic conditions," "— social conditions," "— social life and customs") (Library of Congress 1996, v. 3, H 1578 p. 2, v. 4, H 2055 p. 2, H 2057 p. 1). By 1999, LCSH had added provisions for direct subdivision by century for several of the important subdivisions that cannot be followed by "—history," such as "— economic conditions" and "— social conditions" (Library of Congress 2003, 1999 ed.).

• 35

But why can't "— Social conditions" or "— Economic conditions" be followed by "— History"? These are just two of the many subdivisions after which further subdivision by "— History" is forbidden, for no apparent reason! Others include: "— Ethnic relations," "— Foreign relations," "— Intellectual life," "— Military policy," "— Politics and government," and "— Race relations" (Library of Congress 1996, v. 3, H 1647 p. 5). This is an example of the seemingly arbitrary rules that drive catalogers crazy!

• topical subdivisions in *Library of Congress subject headings* : 36

Topical subdivision involves adding one topical heading to another. The most common order of elements is: entity (or thing) + action, as in:

```
Construction industry — Management
Construction industry — Management — Employee
    Participation
```

or whole entity (or thing) + part of entity, as in:

```
Automobiles — Axles
            — Bodies
            — Clutches.
```

A combination of these two patterns occurs in:

```
Automobiles — Bodies — Alignment
```

Chapter 12. Syntax (Section 12.2.1)

Another common pattern is entity (thing) + attribute, as in:

```
Automobiles — Speed
Automobiles — Stability.
```

• **subdivision by place versus topic** in *Library of Congress subject headings* : 37

Because both non-place topics and places can be main headings in LCSH, there is often confusion about which should come first, place or non-place topic. Thus, LCSH uses "United States — Archival resources," but also "Archives — United States."

• **syndetic structure** in *Library of Congress subject headings*; **definition of syndetic structure** : 38

A key element in LCSH is the "syndetic" structure, which consists of cross-reference links between headings. "Syndetic" comes from the Greek words "syn" for "together" and "dein" for "to bind or tie." Thus, the syndetic structure ties or binds the individual headings into a complete and connected subject access system. Syndetic structure results from vocabulary management, a key element of the subject heading system. As such, it will be discussed in the context of vocabulary management in chapter 13. Nevertheless, we present a summary here.

• 39

LCSH uses five types of cross references:

• **equivalent term cross references** in *Library of Congress subject headings* : 40

Equivalent term cross references lead users from unused terms to the terms that are used for the same concept. Sometimes these cross references lead from narrower terms that are not used to broader terms that are used. Traditionally, libraries used "see" in these cross references, but recently the Library of Congress changed "see" to "use." Examples include:

```
Cars (Automobiles)
    USE
        Automobiles
Food, Raw
    USE
        Raw foods
Uncooked food
    USE
        Raw foods
Catalogs, Online
    USE
        Online catalogs
```

An example of an equivalent term cross reference leading from a narrower unused term to a broader term that subsumes it is:

```
Iron-clad vessels
    USE
        Armored vessels
Ironclads
    USE
        Armored vessels
```

• **narrower term cross references** in *Library of Congress subject headings* : 41

Narrower term cross references suggest narrower, possibly more specific, headings that a user may be interested in, as in:

```
Vehicles
     SEE ALSO NARROWER TERM
          Motor vehicles
Motor vehicles
     SEE ALSO NARROWER TERM
          Trucks
Trucks
     SEE ALSO NARROWER TERM
          Dump trucks
```

• 42

There is some evidence that some users interpret these see-also cross references more as commands than suggestions, so some catalogers have experimented with fuller, more explicit "directives," as in:

```
Vehicles
     IF YOU ARE INTERESTED IN PARTICULAR TYPES OF VEHICLES,
     YOU MAY ALSO WANT TO CHECK THE HEADING:
          Motor vehicles
```

• **broader term cross references in** *Library of Congress subject headings* : 43

Some libraries will also include cross references to broader terms, in case a user might wish to broaden a search. Broader term cross references are also very useful if there is very little (or nothing!) under the narrower term first consulted:

```
Dump trucks
     SEE ALSO BROADER TERM
          Trucks
```

• **related term cross references in** *Library of Congress subject headings* : 44

LCSH uses related term cross references to link terms that are related in ways other than hierarchically (genus-species or whole-part relations), as in:

```
Ornithology
     SEE ALSO RELATED TERM
          Birds
Birds
     SEE ALSO RELATED TERM
          Ornithology
```

The term "Birds" is neither narrower nor broader than the term "Ornithology," which is used for "the study of birds."

• **general cross references in** *Library of Congress subject headings* : 45

LCSH was designed for card catalogs, so general cross references (as opposed to specific cross references) were created to save space. Some of these general cross references are still in use, such as:

```
Woodworking industries
     SEE ALSO names of specific industries, e.g., Furniture
industry and trade
```

The trouble with this kind of non-specific cross reference is that the names of appropriate headings are not actually listed in the reference. There is no reason in modern online public access catalogs (OPACs) not to list all appropriate headings, but this was not done in older card catalogs in order to save space on the 3x5-inch cards.

Over time, some of these older general cross references have been converted to specific cross references. Now, under the broad heading "Indians of North America," particular tribes are listed. Tribes residing in particular states of the United States are listed under the broad heading followed by the name of the states, as in:

```
Indians of North America — Alabama
    NT Creek Indians
        [etc.]
```

This is the form of abbreviated reference used in the published lists for librarians. In OPACS designed for the general public, this reference should be translated for users to read:

```
Indians of North America — Alabama
    SEE ALSO narrower terms:
        Creek Indians
        [etc.]
```

• 47

As of 1991 (14th ed.), the smaller Sears list of subject headings still used the general see-also reference under this heading:

```
Indians of North America
    SEE ALSO ... names of peoples and linguistic families,
        e.g., Navajo Indians, etc.
```

Users who want to follow this suggestion must first go to other reference sources to find the names of particular tribes before continuing their search. For years students assigned term papers on particular Indian tribes had to detour to the *World book encyclopedia* to find the names of candidates tribes.

• 48

Other types of general see-also cross references are less problematic because users are given clues for finding the related headings, as in:

```
Chemistry
    SEE ALSO headings beginning with the word "Chemical"
Economic history
    SEE ALSO subdivision "Economic conditions" under names
        of countries, cities, etc.
```

In this last example, users can conduct a keyword search in most OPACs to locate headings containing the term "economic conditions." (Most examples of cross references were taken from Library of Congress 1986-1999, 1999 ed. p. ix-xi).

• absence of cross references in library catalogs : 49

It is truly unfortunate that many libraries, when they first converted their card catalogs to OPACs, eliminated all cross references from their subject heading systems. Many user studies have indicated that it is already difficult to conduct subject searches in library catalogs. By removing all cross references, the number of headings that users can try, at least initially, is sharply cut, and all assistance in moving from one heading to other possibly more appropriate headings is missing. In these catalogs, only half the subject heading system is present. The syndetic structure is a crucial part of the original design. Some libraries are now working to restore missing cross references to their catalogs.

Chapter 12. Syntax (Section 12.2.1)

• **syndetic structure as vocabulary management : 50**

Syndetic structure, or the system of cross references in an indexing language such as LCSH, is a form of vocabulary management, which is the focus of chapter 13. Vocabulary management is a desirable adjunct for all types of subject access syntax. However, as we survey other types of syntax in this chapter, we shall postpone additional consideration of vocabulary management to chapter 13.

• **modernization of *Library of Congress subject headings* : 51**

Over recent decades, there have been many calls for the Library of Congress to abandon or modernize its subject heading system. At one point, there was a push for the Library of Congress to substitute a modern string indexing system (PRECIS, which will be described later in this chapter), but the Library of Congress declined to do so after a brief study. The Library appears to be committed to continuing LCSH indefinitely, with gradual improvements implemented as they become feasible. (Conversion of LCSH to a fully faceted syntax system is discussed later in section 12.2.2.2.1.)

• **conference on future of subdivisions in *Library of Congress subject headings*:**
  recommendations for improvement : 52

In 1991, the Library of Congress convened a high level conference of experts to consider "The future of subdivisions in the Library of Congress Subject Heading system" (Conway 1992). The conference considered proposals to limit the use of "free-floating subdivisions" (subdivisions that may be freely applied by catalogers according to the rules in the 4-volume *Subject cataloging manual: subject headings*); to expand the use of free-floating subdivisions; alternatives to subject strings; and ways to streamline subdivision selection. In the end, conference participants came up with the following recommendations, some of which have been partially implemented, but most of which are still being studied (Conway 1992, p. 6-10):

• **arrangement of subdivisions in *Library of Congress subject headings* : 53**

"1. Under topical headings (as opposed to name or place headings), place, chronological, and form subdivisions shall be applied as needed and on an individual basis, based upon the judgment of the cataloger as to their appropriateness to the item being cataloged. If the cataloger chooses to apply subdivisions, the subdivisions should always appear in the following order: topical, geographic, chronological, form. ..."

• 54

This recommendation has not been implemented because the meaning of a complete heading is often affected by the order of subdivisions, e.g., "Spanish literature — 18th century — History and criticism" is not the same as "Spanish literature — History and criticism — 18th century"!

• **national authority file for *Library of Congress subject headings* : 55**

"2. The developing "national authority file" should contain authority records for topical headings and for topical heading-topical subdivision(s) combinations. Further non-topical elements in any given string will not normally be established, unless such a record is desirable for cross-reference purposes. ... The conference encourages the Library of Congress to continue and expand its programs by which other libraries contribute to a national subject authority file."

The idea here is to have a national authority file against which libraries could check LCSH heading and subdivision combinations for "correctness."

• 56

Authority records had not previously been created for heading-subdivision combinations with free-floating subdivisions. This recommendation calls for creating authority records for combinations such as:

Chapter 12. Syntax (Section 12.2.1)

```
Economics — Authorship — Marketing
Football — Coaches
Murder — Biblical teaching
Swine — Behavior
Turkey industry — Employees — Effect of technological innovations on
```

● chronological subdivisions in *Library of Congress subject headings* : 57

"3. Chronological subdivisions under topical headings should relate to the coverage of the content of the publication and not to its date of issue. The Library of Congress should investigate using numerals as dates or date ranges in chronological subdivisions. The Library of Congress should consider the pros and cons of the use of free-form chronological subdivisions. ..."

This would mean that catalogers could use any date span related to a documentary unit. Compare the following two examples, the first illustrating current practice, the second illustrating proposed practice:

```
Clocks and watches — England — History — 17th century — Catalogs
Clocks and watches — England — 1647-1782 — Catalogs
```

● categorization and display of subdivisions in *Library of Congress subject headings* : 58

"4. The question of whether subdivisions should be coded specifically to improve online displays for end users should be considered by organizations such as the Network Development/MARC Standards Office of the Library of Congress, MARBI [Machine-Readable Form of Bibliographic Information] and SAC [Subject Access Committee] of the American Library Association, and the [cataloging] utilities [such as OCLC (Online Computer Library Center) and RLIN (Research Libraries Information Network)], among others. In particular, the Library of Congress should investigate implementing a separate subfield code for form subdivision.

"The consolidation of subdivisions into broad, conceptually-based categories could significantly reduce the length of the index display under a specified search term. A compressed display based upon unique subfield coding for subdivisions representing economic aspects (e.g., — Accounting, — Costs, — Custom rates, — Economic aspects, — Finance, — Forecasting, — Taxation, etc.), technical aspects (e.g., — Documentation, — Energy conservation, — Energy consumption, — Quality control, — Safety measures, — Technology transfer, etc.), and form of material (e.g., — Bibliography, — Handbooks, manuals, etc., — Maps, — Statistics, — Terminology, etc.) could look like this:

```
"Agriculture — [economic aspects]
Agriculture — [technical aspects]
Agriculture — [place]
Agriculture — [bibliographies, dictionaries, etc.]"
(Brackets are used in the original example.)
```

The idea here is to improve the display of headings in online public access catalogs (OPACs). Users would first see the above abbreviated display. If they select one of these generic categories, they would then see the specific subdivisions that are gathered under that generic category. This would relieve them of the need to wade through all subdivisions in order to find the ones of interest. The Library of Congress already had a special subfield code for topical, place, and chronological subdivisions. They have now added a code for form subdivisions. See our discussion of the display of LCSH below.

● geographic subdivisions in *Library of Congress subject headings* : 59

"5. The current policy of indirect geographic subdivision should be continued [— that is, including larger place names before smaller place names when topics are subdivided by small places.]

Chapter 12. Syntax (Section 12.2.1)

The Library of Congress should investigate including the indirect form of geographic headings in authority records for geographic names [as in the following example:]

```
151  Boston (Mass.)
7xx  Massachusetts $z Boston
Note: 151 is the field tag for the established form of a place name in
the MARC authority record format. 7xx is a suggested but unspecified
field tag number for the suggested inclusion of the form for subdivi-
sion by "Boston," preceded by the larger place "Massachusetts." $z is
the subfield code for further subdivision by place. The actual charac-
ter preceding the "z" is a special delimiter that looks like a dagger
but is missing from most character sets, so the $ is commonly used in-
stead.
```

• subdivisions in *Library of Congress subject headings* : 60

"6. The conference strongly recommends that the Library of Congress simplify subdivisions in the *Library of Congress subject headings* system. Target areas for simplification include:

- reduction of overly fine distinctions, e.g.:
    ```
    — Administration, [versus] — Management, and — Personnel management
    — Amateurs' manuals [versus] — Handbooks, manuals, etc.
    — Description [versus] — Description and travel
    — Resignation [versus] — Resignation from office
    ```

- consolidation of pattern lists, e.g.:
    ```
    Animals (general) [versus] Domestic animals
    Names of persons [versus] Individual literary authors
    ```

- and increased consistency in syntax, e.g.:
    ```
    Hospitals — Finance [versus] Library finance.
    ```

• display of *Library of Congress subject headings* : 61

When the LCSH system was begun in 1898, it was designed for card catalogs. The full heading had to be written, typed, or printed on the top of each card so that it could be placed in its proper alphabetical position. Most current library OPACS continue to display subject headings in this old card-based way, even though there is no longer any need for such excessive duplication of terms. The display of similar kinds of headings in print-on-paper indexes (such as back-of-the-book indexes) long ago eliminated such useless repetition, as illustrated in the following examples.

• 62

First, here is the traditional card-oriented display, (taken from an older Rutgers University OPAC in 1997). The numbers on the far right indicate the number of items under that heading (the number of postings). Note that when the heading is too long, it is simply lopped off!:

```
Homosexuality and literature — England — History — 16th centur>       4
Homosexuality and literature — England — History — 17th centur>       3
Homosexuality and literature — England — History — 19th centur>       1
Homosexuality and literature — England — History — 20th centur>       3
Homosexuality and literature — England — Oxford — History — 19>       1
Homosexuality and literature — Europe.                                1
Homosexuality and literature — France.                                1
Homosexuality and literature — France — History — 19th century>       1
Homosexuality and literature — France — History — 20th century>       3
Homosexuality and literature — Great Britain.                         2
Homosexuality and literature — Great Britain — Colonies — Hist>       1
Homosexuality and literature — Great Britain — History.               2
```

Chapter 12. Syntax (Section 12.2.1)

```
Homosexuality and literature — Great Britain — History — 19th >     5
Homosexuality and literature — Great Britain — History — 20th >     3
```

• 63

Here are the same headings formatted as they might appear in a print-on-paper display:

```
Homosexuality and literature
    England
        History
            16th century (4)
            17th century (3)
            19th century (1)
            20th century (3)
        Oxford
            History
                19th century (1)
    Europe (1)
    France (1)
        History
            19th century (1)
            20th century (3)
    Great Britain (2)
        Colonies
            History (1)
        History (2)
            19th century (5)
            20th century (3)
```

• 64

The current Rutgers University OPAC (1999) has removed all punctuation from subject headings, so at least more of the headings can be displayed. Here are the same headings, with a few additional postings reflecting growth in the collection. The entire string of terms continues to be displayed:

```
Homosexuality and literature England History 16th century [7]
Homosexuality and literature England History 17th century [4]
Homosexuality and literature England History 18th century [2]
Homosexuality and literature England History 19th century [2]
Homosexuality and literature England History 20th century [5]
Homosexuality and literature England Oxford History 19th century [1]
Homosexuality and literature Europe [2]
Homosexuality and literature France [4]
Homosexuality and literature France History 18th century [1]
Homosexuality and literature France History 19th century [2]
Homosexuality and literature France History 20th century [3]
Homosexuality and literature Great Britain [5]
Homosexuality and literature Great Britain Colonies History [1]
Homosexuality and literature Great Britain History [5]
Homosexuality and literature Great Britain History 17th century [2]
Homosexuality and literature Great Britain History 18th century [5]
Homosexuality and literature Great Britain History 19th century [14]
Homosexuality and literature Great Britain History 20th century [5]
```

• views of Drabenstott and Vizine-Goetz on display of *Library of Congress subject headings* : decision trees : 65

Many researchers have been exploring alternative displays in electronic OPACs. Chief among them is Karen Markey Drabenstott, who has made subject headings one of the chief targets of her research agenda. In *Using subject headings for online retrieval: theory, practice, and potential* (1994), Drabenstott and her co-author Diane Vizine-Goetz suggest alternatives to the

Chapter 12. Syntax (Section 12.2.1)

traditional static and repetitious displays. Their chief recommendation is to use a set of search decision trees by which a more intelligent OPAC would determine the most effective display based on the kind of search statement a user entered. Here are some examples.

• exact-match searches using *Library of Congress subject headings* : 66

If a search statement matches a LCSH heading or one of its equivalent term cross references exactly, then that heading should be displayed in what Drabenstott and Vizine-Goetz call the "exact" approach. If the search statement matches a heading that has qualifiers, the user should be asked to choose which heading they want, as in this example (p. 306):

```
1. Korea
2. Korea (North)
3. Korea (South)
```

• 67

The user chooses 2. Korea (North). The exact approach then displays only that heading, followed by a summary of possible subdivisions. The use of a summary (or condensed) list of subdivisions was one of the recommendations of the 1991 Subject Subdivisions Conference (Conway 1992, recommendation 4, p. 9-10). The Drabenstott Vizine-Goetz list is different, but the idea of summarizing subdivisions, rather than showing them all at once, is the same. Here is the Drabenstott Vizine-Goetz list (p. 308):

```
Broad topic:        Korea (North)
Broad category:     Armed forces
                    Business and economics
                    Culture and civilization
                    General
                    Foreign relations
                    History
                    Politics and government
                    Society, ethics, and religion
```

Also in this display, searchers are given the opportunity to select:

- "General works" for documentary units having the un-subdivided heading "Korea (North)";
- "Notes" for detailed information about this heading, such as scope notes, *Library of Congress classification* notation for the general topic; or
- "Related topics" for displays of narrower, broader, and other related headings (p. 249).

• 68

If the searcher selects the broad category "Politics and government" from the display under the broad topic "Korea (North)," then the more detailed subdivisions belonging to that broader category are displayed (p. 309):

```
Broad topic:        Korea (North)
Broad category:     Politics and government
Topic:              Constitutional history
                    Constitutional law
                    Officials and employees
                    Politics and government
```

• 69

Sometimes, the "exact" approach turns out not to be helpful. Drabenstott and Vizine-Goetz give the example of a search on the term "translation." This term matches "translation (genet-

Chapter 12. Syntax (Section 12.2.1)

ics)," which is likely not what the searcher had in mind. When the searcher is not satisfied and chooses to terminate this search, the system can ask (p. 310):

> Additional topics in the dictionary may express your query *Translation*. Continue searching for *Translation*?

We could reword this notice to something like: "There are additional topics in the catalog that may relate to your query *Translation*. Continue searching for *Translation*?"

• **alphabetical browsing using** *Library of Congress subject headings* : 70

If the searcher replies yes, the OPAC moves to the "alphabetical approach," which displays the alphabetical sequence of headings surrounding the word "translation" (p. 310):

```
Translating services
Translatio imperii
translation [not an authorized heading!]
Translation (Genetics)
Translation bureaus
Translation glide (Crystallography)
Translation planes
Translation to heaven
Translations
Translators
Translators (Computer programs)
Transluminal angioplasty
Transmission of texts
```

• 71

Initial search statements that do not match authorized subject headings are submitted first to this "alphabetical" approach, giving the searcher the opportunity to select an authorized heading, which will take them to the "exact" approach, as in the "Korea (North)" example just above.

• 72

Here are two examples of initial search statements that would begin with the alphabetical approach — first a one-word search statement, then a multi-word search statement (p. 314, 318):

```
Subject:      regulation

Broad topics:     Regular functions
                  Regular rings, Von Neumann
                  regulation [not an authorized heading]
                  Regulation, Biological
                  Regulation of blood circulation
                  Regulation of body fluids
                  Regulation of body weight
                  Regulation of cancer cell growth
                  Regulation of cell growth
                  Regulation of enzyme activity
                  Regulation of fruit development
                  Regulation of growth
                  Regulation of heart growth
```

• 73

So far, all of these "regulation" topics relate to biology or medicine. However, if the searcher browses further down the list, using a scroll bar or arrow key, they would come to "Regulation of prices," "Regulation of trade," "Regulatory agencies." Note that in the "alphabetical approach," users are shown only main headings. Subdivisions are not shown until the display shifts to the "exact approach," after a searcher selects one of the main headings. This staged display helps the user find an appropriate main heading without getting bogged down in lengthy lists of irrelevant subdivisions.

• 74

Now a multi-word search example:
```
Subject:     civil rights movement

Broad topics:    Civil rights and socialism
                 Civil rights and demonstrations
                 civil rights movement [not an authorized heading]
                 Civil rights movements
                 Civil rights workers
                 Civil service
                 Civil service, Colonial
                 Civil service, International
                 Civil service ethics
                 Civil service examinations
                 Civil service furloughs
                 Civil service jobs
                 Civil service pensions
```

• keyword searches using *Library of Congress subject headings* : 75

A third approach to searching is the "keyword" approach. It should be invoked by the intelligent OPAC in several instances. In this first example, a searcher has used the "exact" approach to "jazz music" but wants more options. The next step would be to apply the "keyword-in-main-heading approach," which would retrieve (p. 311):

```
Double-bass and piano music (Jazz)
Guitar music (Jazz)
Monologues with music (Jazz ensemble with chamber orchestra)
Piano music (Jazz)
Saxophone music (Jazz)
```

In this case, "music" and "jazz" are treated as independent keywords.

• 76

The "keyword-in-subdivided-heading" approach may be useful when the search statement includes geographic names, because place names often appear in subdivisions, as well as main headings, as in (p. 312):

```
Food supply — Africa
Industrial management — Japan
Small business — Ontario — London
```

• 77

When a one-word search statement does not match an authorized heading (leading to the "exact" approach) or the initial term of one or more authorized heading (leading to the "alphabetical" approach), then the search statement should be submitted to the "title keyword" approach. An example is a search for "McCarthyism." If there are any items in an OPAC with "McCarthyism" in their titles, then the authorized subject headings for these items can be displayed for leads to additional material. Examples of authorized headings often associated with the title keyword "McCarthyism" are (p. 314):

Chapter 12. Syntax (Section 12.2.1)

```
McCarthy, Joseph, 1908-1957
Subversive activities — United States
Internal security — United States.
```

• 78

When multi-word search statements do not match at least the initial terms of an authorized heading, then the OPAC can submit the individual words to the "keyword-in-record" approach to make sure that the individual words at least occur in some records in the OPAC. If they don't, the searcher must be asked to check spelling. (Of course, an OPAC may also employ a spell checker to help with obvious errors.) When the OPAC determines that there are records with the keywords submitted, it should begin displays using the "keyword in main heading" approach. This will help insure the display of potentially more relevant records (p. 318-321).

• 79

If there are no matches in main headings, the OPAC can continue on to the "keyword-in-subdivided-heading" approach, then to the "title keyword" approach, and then to the "keyword-in-record" approach. Finally, if necessary, such search techniques as automatic stemming may be applied to terms in the search statement (p. 322-323).

• 80

Here are some examples of multi-word statements that matched neither authorized headings nor the initial terms of authorized headings, and were therefore submitted to keyword approaches (p. 322):

• Jewish humor: matched the authorized heading "Jewish wit and humor" via the "keyword-in-main-heading" approach.

• English grammar: matched the authorized heading "English language — Grammar," and also many headings with the subdivisions "Grammar, Comparative — English" via the "keyword-in-subdivided-heading" approach.

• scopes trial: matched the title "The roots of bias: an empiricist press and coverage of the Scopes trial" via the "title keyword" approach;

• scopes trial: matched records for "The great monkey trial," "The Scopes case," and "Bryan and Darrow at Dayton" via the "keyword-in-record" approach

• search decision trees for *Library of Congress subject headings* : 81

Drabenstott and Vizine-Goetz' main point is that these search tree decisions should be made by the OPAC, based on the nature of the search statement — whether or not it matches exact authorized headings, initial terms in headings, keywords in main headings or subdivision, keywords in titles or records. The user should not be expected to understand or know how to invoke all these options.

• views of American Library Association on display of *Library of Congress subject headings* : 82

The Subcommittee on the Display of Subject Headings in Subject Indexes in Online Public Access Catalogs, of the Subject Analysis Committee, of the Cataloging and Classification Section, of the Association for Library Collections and Technical Services (ALCTS), a division of the American Library Association, has also dealt with the problem of displaying subject headings in OPACS (Association for Library Collections and Technical Services 1992). However, the emphasis in their report is the ongoing debate between strictly alphabetical displays versus so-called structured displays, such as those advocated by Library of Congress Filing Rules (Library of Congress 1980). See sections 1.4 on standards and 17.1 on alphanumeric displays for discussions of this controversy. The so-called structured approach works well with the kind of guidance advocated by Drabenstott and Vizine-Goetz. Otherwise, users can become hopelessly confused by displays that purport to be alphabetical (or alphanumeric), but are actually governed by all sorts of non-alphanumeric considerations unknown to the user.

• 83

The ALCTS report offers no recommendations. Its purpose is to lay out the arguments for the strictly alphabetical or alphanumeric display versus a structured display. In line with the NISO *Guidelines for indexes and related information retrieval devices* (Anderson 1997a), we recommend the strictly alphanumeric arrangement of headings in displayed indexes unless an OPAC or IR database can offer the more sophisticated guided displays suggested by Drabenstott and Vizine-Goetz.

• **comprehensibility of** *Library of Congress subject headings* : 84

Do users actually understand what catalogers intend to convey in LCSH headings and subdivisions? Drabenstott, a participant in the 1991 Library of Congress Subject Subdivisions Conference (Conway 1992), wanted to find out. During the years following the conference, with Simcox and Fenton (1999), she pursued research related to the conference recommendation that a standard order be adopted for the four categories of LCSH subdivisions (topical, geographic, chronological, and form). Using large samples of 144 adults and 144 children recruited from three Michigan public libraries, they sought to discover whether the new format might be more understandable than the old. Their results indicated that these alternative orders didn't make much difference — in fact their users understood the old order slightly better, but not significantly better. Regardless of order, however, only 36% of the users in their sample actually understood what the headings they were shown were supposed to mean, when compared to the opinions of an expert cataloger employed to determine the correct meanings of the headings used in the research.

• 85

The headings used in the research were fairly complex. Here are some of them in their original format with respect to the order of subdivisions:

```
Spanish drama — 18th century — History and criticism
Jews — Germany — Berlin — Intellectual life — Congresses
Art, Modern — 20th century — Germany — Berlin — Exhibitions
Combined sewers — Illinois — Chicago Metropolitan Area — Overflows
Art, Modern — 20th century — Public opinion
```

Here are the same headings with the proposed revised order of subdivisions (1. topical, 2. geographical, 3. chronological, 4. form):

```
Spanish drama — History and criticism — 18th century
Jews — Intellectual life — Germany — Berlin — Congresses
Art, Modern — Germany — Berlin — 20th century — Exhibitions
Combined sewers — Overflows — Illinois — Chicago Metropolitan Area
Art, Modern — Public opinion — 20th century
```

• 86

Sometimes there are subtle changes in meaning between a heading in the original LCSH order and the proposed new order. The expert employed in the research to determine the meaning of headings interpreted the current heading "Art, Modern — 20th century — Public opinion" to mean "public opinion of twentieth century modern art." In contrast, the expert stated that the proposed heading "Art, Modern — Public opinion — 20th century" means "20th century public opinion of modern art." When users responded to the heading "Art, Modern — Public opinion —

20th century" with explanations such as "public opinion of 20th century modern art" or "what the public thinks about 20th century modern art," they were marked wrong.

• 87

These are sometimes subtle distinctions. In this particular case, the public opinion had to be 20th century public opinion. Of course during the 21st century, there will also be 21st century public opinion! However, the span of "Art, Modern" in LCSH ranges from the 17th century to the present, so whether this heading refers to 20th century public opinion of all of modern art, or public opinion just of 20th century modern art could be significant.

• 88

More substantial changes in meaning are affected by the rearrangement of terms in other headings. According to the Drabenstott (et al.) expert, "Spanish drama — 18th century — History and criticism" means "18th century history and criticism of Spanish drama" and "Spanish drama — History and criticism — 18th century" means "history and criticism of 18th century Spanish drama." One of the authors of this book, James D. Anderson, a long-time "expert" teacher of subject cataloging, believes these interpretations are exactly backwards! "Spanish drama — 18th century" clearly means "18th century Spanish drama." Adding "history and criticism" to this heading should mean "the history and criticism of 18th century Spanish drama." Similarly, "Spanish drama — History and criticism" clearly means "history and criticism of Spanish drama." Adding the chronological subdivisions "18th century" should make this heading mean "18th century history and criticism of Spanish drama." But regardless of who is correct, it is clear that the meanings do change, and the disagreement of experts just reinforces yet again the fact that that the meanings of headings are not necessarily obvious.

• 89

Drabenstott and colleagues pursued some of these difficulties in interpretation by expert catalogers in a follow-up article (Drabenstott, Dede & Leavitt 1999). Here they explain that their expert actually gave different meanings to the heading "Spanish drama — 18th century — History and criticism" in different contexts: the heading in isolation; the heading with the bibliographic record; and the heading in an alphabetical list.

• confusion between form versus topical subdivisions in *Library of Congress subject headings* : 90

Part of the problem with this heading (Spanish drama — 18th century — History and criticism) is that it is unclear whether "history and criticism" should be considered a topical subdivision or a form subdivision. In the 11th edition of *Free-floating subdivisions: an alphabetical index* (Library of Congress 1999), Library of Congress experts address, but do not resolve this confusion: "It should be noted that most subdivisions identified as form subdivisions ... may also be assigned as topical subdivisions to works that are about these bibliographical forms. ... The Library has made the decision to consistently treat certain problematic subdivisions such as '— History,' '— History and criticism,' and '— Law and legislation' as topical ...."

• 91

The confusion over the meaning of subdivisions like "history" and "history and criticism" is compounded by the varying roles of "history" and "criticism." As with the case of "exhibitions" mentioned above, these subdivisions are used both for documentary units that discuss the "doing" of history and/or criticism — that is, the topic is doing or creating history or criticism, but much more frequently they are used as a form subdivision for documentary units that are (that take the form of) histories or critical appraisals, that are the result of historical work or critical work. Thus the same subdivisions are used both as topical subdivisions and form subdivisions.

Chapter 12. Syntax (Section 12.2.1)

• 92

The recommended standard order for subdivisions (Conway 1992) could help to resolve this confusion. When "history and criticism" refers to a topic (the doing of history and criticism), it would come directly after the main heading, but when it is used to indicate the form of the documentary unit, it would come last. Thus, "Spanish drama — History and criticism — 18th century" would indicate a documentary unit that discusses the art or methods or attributes of creating histories and criticism of Spanish drama in the 18th century; while "Spanish drama — 18th century — History and criticism" would indicate documentary units that are histories and criticisms of 18th century Spanish drama, regardless of when they are created. This last heading could be given to a brand new late 20th century (or early 21st century) history and criticism of 18th century Spanish drama!

• 93

Similarly, "Art, Modern — Germany — Berlin — 20th century — Exhibitions" would indicate a documentary unit that is an exhibition catalog or a description of an actual exhibition, whereas "Art, Modern — Exhibitions — Germany — Berlin — 20th century" would be about the topic of mounting exhibitions of modern art in 20th century Berlin.

• 94

Do these different interpretations really matter? It would be good if further research could explore whether these kinds of distinctions, often quite subtle, actually make any difference in the ability of users to find useful documents. The question as to whether our index headings are comprehensible is a very important question, and the research pursued by Drabenstott et al. (1999) is an important first step.

• 95

A major difference among the more modern syntax patterns that follow in this chapter is the degree to which the order of terms is meant to enhance the meaning of an index heading. If the order of terms doesn't really matter in terms of user comprehension or user results, then the efforts to create meaningful orders of terms in headings may be a waste of time.

• professional and research literature on *Library of Congress subject headings* : 96

There is an enormous literature on LCSH. Here are just a very few of the most important recent works:

Berman, Sanford (1993). *Prejudices and antipathies: a tract on the LC subject heads concerning people*. With a foreword by Eric Moon. 1993 ed. Jefferson, NC: McFarland & Co.; 1993. xvii, 211 p. ISBN 0899508286.

Chan, Lois Mai (1995). *Library of Congress subject headings: principles and applications*. 3rd ed. Englewood, CO: Libraries Unlimited; c1995. xiv, 541 p. ISBN 1563081954.

Cochrane, Pauline A. (1986). *Improving LCSH for use in online catalogs: exercises for self-help with a selection of background readings*. Littleton, CO: Libraries Unlimited; 1986. xiii, 348 p. ISBN 0872874842.

Drabenstott, Karen Markey; Vizine-Goetz, Diane (1994). *Using subject headings for online retrieval: theory, practice, and potential*. San Diego: Academic Press; c1994. xvii, 365 p. Published under the auspices of OCLC Online Computer Library Center, Inc. ISBN 0-12-221570-2.

Stone, Alva T., ed. (2000). The LCSH century: one hundred years with the *Library of Congress subject headings* system. *Cataloging and classification quarterly*. 29(1-2): 1-234; 2000. Includes "A brief history," by Alva T. Stone; "LCSH: semantics, syntax and specificity," by Elaine Svenonius; "Entering the millennium: a new century for LCSH," by Lois Mai Chan and Theodora Hodges.

Chapter 12. Syntax (Section 12.2.1.1)

• *Sear's list of subject headings* : 97

There are many other subject heading systems, but the only other general system widely used in the United States is *Sears list of subject headings* (Sears 1997). It is a much smaller list designed for school and smaller public libraries, but it is modeled on LCSH, so that it shares many of its problems and inconsistencies. However, headings tend to be shorter and less complex.

12.2.1.1. *Medical Subject Headings* (MeSH).

• 98

Many subject heading systems focus on particular subject areas or domains. One of the most important, and the only one we will cite as an example of a specialized list, is Medical subject headings (1999). This a much newer system than LCSH, and of course the subject scope is much narrower. Its syntactic rules are much simpler. All of its main headings are classified into hierarchies or facets, called "tree structures."

• 99

Up to 1999, Medical subject headings (MeSH) used a standard order for subheadings attached to main headings:

```
Main heading — topical subheading — geographic subheading
    — form (genre or physical format) subheading — language
    subheading.
```

Beginning in 1999, however, the MeSH syntax was further simplified by eliminating geographic, form, and language subheadings from subject headings. Instead, geographic and form headings will be placed in separate fields in the MARC (Machine readable cataloging) format. Language and physical format information will be recorded in descriptive cataloging fields rather than with subject headings (National Library of Medicine 1999, p. I-74).

• 100

In addition, age groups will no longer be indicated as subheadings, but as independent main headings. Here are some examples of pre- and post-1999 MeSH headings displayed in MARC record format (National Library of Medicine 1999, p. I-75, I-76). The MARC format will be discussed later in chapter 20 on record formats. "650" is the MARC field tag for topical subject terms. Next come two numerical indicators: the first of these (1 or 2) indicates a (1) primary or a (2) secondary topic; the second indicator (a 2 in these examples) indicates that these are MeSH terms. The subfield code $a indicates a main heading; $z indicates a place subheading; $x indicates a topical subheading; and $v indicates a form subheading. "651" is the MARC field tag for a place as main heading. No first indicator is used. The subfield code "$9 a" is used to indicate that an age-group term is being used as a separate heading. "655" is the MARC field tag for form or genre terms. The second indicator "7" indicates that the source of the term is indicated later in the subfield $2.

Pre-1999 practice:

```
650 12 $a Acquired Immunodeficiency Syndrome $x epidemiology $z United
       States
650 22 $a Acquired Immunodeficiency Syndrome $x in adolescence
650 22 $a Acquired Immunodeficiency Syndrome $x prevention & control $z
       United States
650 22 $a Adolescent Health Services $x organization & administration
       $z United States
```

New practice:

```
650 12 $a Acquired Immunodeficiency Syndrome $x epidemiology
650 22 $a Acquired Immunodeficiency Syndrome $9 a
650 22 $a Acquired Immunodeficiency Syndrome $x prevention & control
650 22 $a Adolescent Health Services $x organization & administration
650 22 $a Adolescence
651 _2 $a United States $x epidemiology
```

Pre-1999 practice:

```
650 12 $a Child Development
650 22 $a Communication $x in infancy & childhood
650 22 $a Learning $x in infancy & childhood
650 22 $a Thinking $x in infancy & childhood
```

New practice:

```
650 12 $a Child Development
650 22 $a Communication $9 a
650 22 $a Learning $9 a
650 22 $a Thinking $9 a
650 22 $a Infant
650 22 $a Child
```

Pre-1999 practice:

```
650 12 $a Medicine $v dictionaries
650 12 $a Medicine $v bibliography
```

New practice:

```
650 12 $a Medicine
655 _7 $a Dictionary $2 mesh
650 12 $a Medicine
655 _7 $a Bibliography $2 mesh
```

• browsing versus searching using *Medical subject headings* : 101

These changes in syntax clearly move MeSH from more precoordination toward more postcoordination. This is fine for postcoordinate electronic searching, but it is disastrous for browsing displayed indexes. Single descriptors in isolation, such as "Learning," "Infant," "Child" simply cannot provide enough context for effective browsing. The precoordinate heading "Learning — in infancy & childhood" provides valuable context for "Learning." It is sad that the National Library of Medicine moved in this direction just when browsing was becoming more important in information retrieval!

12.2.1.2. Principles for Subject Heading Systems.

• 102

The Working Group on Principles Underlying Subject Heading Languages, sponsored by the Section on Classification and Indexing of the International Federation of Library Associations and Institutions (IFLA) has been working on defining principles for subject heading systems. These principles are summarized here, based on Julianne Beall's discussion (1995) at a 1993 IFLA Satellite Meeting in Lisbon and a subsequent review by Pauline Atherton Cochrane (1996).

Chapter 12. Syntax (Section 12.2.1.2)

The principles are divided into two sections, one for construction of subject heading systems, and one for their application in cataloging or indexing.

• principles regarding construction of subject heading systems : 103

Construction Principles

• principles regarding uniform headings in subject heading systems : 104

1. **Uniform Heading Principle (Terminology Control and Predictability of Representation):** "To facilitate synonym control and to collocate subjects in the display of bibliographic records, each concept or named entity that is indexed by a subject heading language should be represented by one authorized heading" (Bell, p. 292).

• principles regarding synonymy in subject heading systems : 105

2. **Synonymy Principle:** "To collocate all material on a given subject and to increase the recall power of a subject heading language, synonymy should be controlled in the subject heading language" (Beall, p. 292).

• principles regarding homonymy in subject heading systems : 106

3. **Homonymy Principle:** "To prevent the retrieval of irrelevant materials and to increase the precision power of a subject heading language, homonymy should be controlled in the subject heading language" (Beall, p. 292).

• principles regarding semantics in subject heading systems : 107

4. **Semantic Principle:** "To express the semantic (paradigmatic) structure of a subject heading language, subject headings should be linked by equivalence, hierarchical and coordinate relationships" (Beall, p. 294). (Less agreement on this principle — Cochrane, p. 186).

• principles regarding syntax in subject heading systems : 108

5. **Syntax Principle:** "To express complex and compound subjects, the syntax of a subject heading language should link the compound parts of a subject heading by syntagmatic relationships rather than semantic (paradigmatic) ones" (Beall, p. 295). (This principle had the least agreement — Cochrane, p. 186).

Syntagmatic relationships are those that actually exist in documentary units, such as a relationship between "dogs" and "breeding" or between "cats" and "care" or "feeding" in the "United States" or "Brazil." These are the kinds of relationships that a subject heading language should express through the use of syntax. The semantic (paradigmatic) relationships that should be avoided in compound or complex subject headings (main headings plus one or more subdivisions) are those that always exist, such as the taxonomic relationships among "dogs" and "canines" and "mammals" and "vertebrates" and "animals." Principle 4 states that these semantic (paradigmatic) relationships should be handled by means of linking references to narrower, broader, and other related headings.

• principles regarding consistency in subject heading systems : 109

6. **Consistency Principle:** "To achieve and maintain consistency, each new subject heading admitted into a subject heading language should be similar in form and structure to comparable headings already in the language" (Beall, p. 293).

• principles regarding naming in subject heading systems : 110

7. **Naming Principle:** "To facilitate integrated retrieval, names of persons, places, families, corporate bodies and works when used in a subject heading language of a given catalogue, bibliography or index should be established according to the rules used for author and title entries in that catalog, bibliography or index" (Beall, p. 293-294).

Chapter 12. Syntax (Section 12.2.1.2)

• principles regarding literary warrant in subject heading systems : 111

8. **Literary Warrant Principle (A Posteriori Principle):** "To reflect the subject content of documents, the vocabulary of a subject heading language is [i.e. should be] developed dynamically, based on literary warrant, and integrated systematically with existing vocabulary" (Beall, p. 297).

Literary warrant simply means that the vocabulary of indexed or cataloged documents should be accepted as terminology for a subject heading system, because it is warranted (authorized) through actual usage in documents. Literary warrant is complemented by the "user warrant" of the next principle.

• principles regarding user needs in subject heading systems : 112

9. **User Principle:** "To meet users' needs, the vocabulary of subject headings in a subject heading language should be chosen to reflect the current usage of the target audience for the subject heading language, whatever that might be, for example the general public or users of a specific type of library" (Beall, p. 296).

This principle is sometimes called "user warrant," to correspond to literary warrant, just above. Thus the vocabulary of a subject heading system should reflect both the vocabulary of its documents and its users.

• principles regarding application of subject heading systems : 113

Application Principles

• principles regarding subject indexing policy for subject heading systems : 114

10. **Subject Indexing Policy Principle:** "To meet user needs and give consistent treatment to documents, indexing policies giving guidance for subject analysis and representation should be developed" (Cochrane, p. 187 — not included in Beall).

• principles regarding specific and coextensive subject headings in subject heading systems : 115

11. **Specific Heading Principle (Specificity Principle):** "To increase the precision power of a subject heading language, a subject heading [or a set of subject headings] should be coextensive with the subject content to which it applies" (Beall, p. 297, Cochrane, p. 187).

Cochrane adds the phrase "or a set of subject headings." The principle as stated by Beall implies string syntax, to be discussed in the next section, which attempts to create more comprehensive strings of terms that are co-extensive with the content of documentary units. This "co-extensive" principle is beyond the reach of single subject headings in most situations. Also, this principle confuses (conflates) the specificity of individual terms or headings and the specificity (or coextensivity) of a string of terms (main headings and subdivisions or subheadings).

• future of subject headings : 116

Subject headings were first developed in the 19th century. They tend to be labor intensive, because human indexers or catalogers not only select main headings and subdivisions or subheadings, but each complete heading is constructed, one at a time, by the indexer or cataloger. We now move on to modern "string" syntax systems for displayed indexes. Their distinguishing feature is that headings, or strings of terms, are created by computer algorithms, not one by one by indexers or catalogers.

• 117

Subject headings continue to be important because so much subject analysis over the past 100 years has been recorded using subject headings. It is doubtful that any new IR system would or should adopt the 19th century technology of subject headings unless it needs to conform to other systems that already use subject headings.

12.2.2. String Syntax.

• definition of string syntax : 118

String syntax is the modern version of subject headings, inspired by the desire to take advantage of computer technology for the creation of headings. Because instructions for the combination of terms into headings are programmed for the computer, string syntax tends to be much more regular than the idiosyncratic variety exhibited by subject heading syntax.

• 119

The name "string syntax" or "string indexing" comes from the custom of displaying headings as "strings" of terms — terms strung together in various configurations. The variety of string syntax approaches is mostly related to how terms are arranged in these strings.

• principles regarding specific and coextensive index headings in string syntax : 120

Most string indexing systems attempt to include as many terms as necessary to provide a comprehensive description of the content of a documentary unit. Thus string indexing aims to fulfill the IFLA "specific heading principle" (section 12.2.1.2) in a single string (or set) of terms. Such a string should be co-extensive with the topical content of a documentary unit.

• 121

In the following sections, we illustrate the major types of string syntax.

12.2.2.1. Rotated Term Syntax.

• definition of rotated term syntax : 122

The simplest of all string syntax patterns is simply to place all terms or descriptors assigned to a documentary unit in alphabetical (or alphanumeric) order within the string, and then to rotate each term to the lead position, one at a time, for access purposes.

• examples of rotated term syntax : 123

Here is a set of such headings taken from *America: history and life* (ABC-Clio 1999a, 1980 ed.). In an alphabetical displayed index, these headings would be placed in their alphabetical positions:

```
American Mercury (periodical). editors and editing. Ku Klux Klan.
     Mencken, H. L. Methodist Episcopal church (South).
     temperance movements. 1910-33. [locator]
editors and editing. American Mercury (periodical). Ku Klux Klan.
     Mencken, H. L. Methodist Episcopal church (South).
     temperance movements. 1910-33. [locator]
Ku Klux Klan. American Mercury (periodical). editors and editing.
     Mencken, H. L. Methodist Episcopal church (South).
     temperance movements. 1910-33. [locator]
Mencken, H. L. American Mercury (periodical). editors and
     editing. Ku Klux Klan. Methodist Episcopal church (South).
     temperance movements. 1910-33. [locator]
Methodist Episcopal church (South). American Mercury
     (periodical). editors and editing. Ku Klux Klan. Mencken, H.
     L. temperance movements. 1910-33. [locator]
```

Chapter 12. Syntax (Section 12.2.2.1)

• **dates (time) in rotated term syntax : 124**

In these headings, numerical dates indicating time periods are placed at the end of the string of terms. These date terms have not been given lead position in this example, but there is no reason that date terms could not be placed in lead position if they are useful access points.

• **locators in rotated term syntax : 125**

The "[locator]" represents some kind of notation or link that leads the user to the actual document or to a surrogate for it, such as a citation and abstract. We shall be discussing locators later on in chapter 15.

• **rotated term syntax in *America: history and life* : 126**

The IR database producer ABC-Clio uses rotated term syntax in its IR databases *America: history and life* (ABC-Clio 1999a) and *Historical abstracts* (ABC-Clio 1999b). Figure 12.1 illustrates the display of rotated syntax headings in a page from the printed version of *America: history and life* (1995 ed. p. 187).

• **string syntax compared to subject heading syntax; coextensive index headings in string syntax : 127**

These examples illustrate one of the chief differences between string syntax and subject heading syntax — the attempt to create headings coextensive with the content of a documentary unit. In string syntax, all terms associated with a documentary unit are generally included in every heading. (The exceptions are when so many terms are used to describe a documentary unit that they are split into two or more separate strings representing different topical themes.) For this reason, string headings are often longer than subject headings, which are limited to set patterns. Using subject headings, the indexer is often forced to use a number of separate headings in order to indicate the various aspects of a document's content.

• **coextensive index headings and eliminability in string syntax : 128**

The purpose of including all terms in each heading is to provide as complete a description of the documentary unit as possible within the brief scope of an index heading. This more complete description helps achieve the objective of eliminability, as described at the beginning of this chapter. Having all terms in each heading should help searchers decide whether they want to pursue the documentary unit indicated, or to eliminate it from further consideration.

• **clarity of rotated string syntax : 129**

Another defining feature of rotated string syntax is that terms are not placed in a meaningful order, but simply listed in alphabetical order after the lead term. The crucial question is whether this non-meaningful order seriously affects the clarity of the index headings. In the previous section (12.2.1), we cited research by Drabenstott, Simcox and Fenton (1999) that suggests that most searchers do not understand the subtle meanings conveyed by the order of subdivisions in subject headings. Perhaps the order of a relatively small number of terms in an index heading doesn't really matter that much for comprehensibility. More complicated string syntax patterns place great importance on the arrangement of terms within the string, assuming that order of terms does contribute to comprehension. Whether this is actually the case is an open question.

Chapter 12. Syntax (Section 12.2.2.1)

—. Domesticity. Handbooks. Literature. Periodicals. Values. Women. 1800-1916. *10200d*
—. Family. Women. 1980-88. *3316b*
Home Mission Board. Baptists (Southern). Southern Baptist Convention. Tichenor, Isaac Taylor. 1860's-1902. *8074d*
Home of Truth (commune). Communes. Ogden, Marie. Utah (San Juan County). 1933-77. *15969a*
Home ownership. Attitudes. Politics. Quality of life. Social Classes. 1985-91. *11800d*
—. Blacks. 1980. *11737a*
Home ownership (review article). Ontario (Hamilton). Working Class. 1870's-1940's. *819a*
Homeless. Acculturation. Hispanic Americans. Men. Mental Illness. 1994. *15030d*
—. Children. Honduras (Tegucigalpa). Women. 1980's. *3302a*
—. Cities. Community organizing. Social Reform. ca 1980's-92. *11785d*
—. Cities. Folklore. Food. Hair. Kansas (Manhattan). Midwest. 1991-92. *8393a*
—. Dinkins, David. Disability. Housing. New York City. Public Policy. 1970's-80's. *15213d*
—. Economic Conditions. Ethnicity. Mental health. Minnesota (Minneapolis). 1980's. *4233a*
—. Family. Public Welfare. 1988. *3344d*
—. Hospitals. Institutionalization. Mental Illness. New York City. 1991-93. *11980d*
—. New York City. Poor. Public Policy. 1890-1940. *3531a*
—. Women. 1980's. *11770b*
Homeopathy. California (San Francisco). Medicine (practice of). 19c-20c. *13656a*
Homer, Winslow. Drawings. Markets. 1875-85. *14216d*
—. Hemingway, Ernest *(Islands in the Stream)*. Painting. 1920's-50's. *2344a*
Homestead strike. Labor Unions and Organizations. Pennsylvania (Homestead). Steel Industry. 1892. *3647b*
Homesteading and Homesteaders. Alberta. Dower Act (Alberta, 1917). Property rights. Women. 1909-25. *871a*
—. Alberta (eastern). Barr Colony. British Canadians. Saskatchewan Valley, North. Saskatchewan (western). 1900's-20's. *5566b*
—. Arkansas. Hamilton, Mary. Logging camps. Memoirs. Mississippi Delta region. 1880-1914. *37466 12094b*
—. Authors. Consumerism. Daily Life. Kirkland, Caroline M. Michigan. 1830's-40's. *12480a*
—. Autobiographies. Colorado (Colorado Springs area). Missouri. Westhues, Olive Conran. 1911-18. *15778b*
—. Colorado. Pre-emption Act (US, 1820). Scoville, Winifred J. 1888-1901. *12624a*
—. Colorado (Logan, Washington counties). Frontier and Pioneer Life. Women. 1880's-1920's. *12626b*
—. Colorado (northwestern). Interviews. Women. 1890-1950. *4382b 15772b*
—. Diaries. Frontier and Pioneer Life. Oregon (Crook County). Pratt, Alice Day. Teaching. 1910-29. *15958b*
—. Economic Development. Frontier. 1857-93. *10085a*
—. Federal Government. Housing. Local Government. Pennsylvania (Philadelphia). Urban Renewal. 1976-89. *2826a*
—. Frontier and Pioneer Life. Law. Texas. Women. 1845-98. *12379b*
—. Idaho (Boise River Valley). Land. Law. Speculation. 1869-78. *4607a*
—. Kildahl, Harold B. North Dakota (Devil's Lake area). Norwegian Americans. Personal Narratives. 1866-86. *8636a*
—. Letters. Rural life. Stewart, Elinore Pruitt. Wyoming. 1909-20's. *4452b*
—. Missouri (LaForge). Resettlement. 1933-38. *12505a*
—. Swett, Oscar (family). Utah (Greendale area). 1909-70. *12900a*
Homicide. *See* Murder.
Homolovi Ruins State Park. Archaeology. Arizona. Indians. Pueblo Indians (Hopi). 14c. *173b*
Homosexuality. Abortion. Feminism. Political Parties. Prayer. Public Opinion. Public Schools. 1972-88. *11455d*
—. Acquired immune deficiency syndrome Diseases. Literature. Popular Culture. 1980's-91. *7713b*
—. Acquired immune deficiency syndrome. Outing. Press. 1940's-91. *14972a*

—. Actors and Actresses. Androgyny. LeGallienne, Eva. Women. 1915-81. *6812a*
—. Araki, Gregg. Filmmaking. 1987-91. *14909a*
—. Asian Americans. Computer bulletin boards. 1991-94. *15013a*
—. Asian Americans. Interviews. Parents. 1993. *14984a*
—. Asian Americans. Women. 1990. *15001a*
—. Attitudes. Femininity. Sports. Women. 20c. *10933a*
—. Authors. Blacks. Civil Rights. Lord, Audre. 1970's-92. *7576a*
—. Authors. Letters. Race Relations. Smith, Lillian (review article). Snelling, Paula. South. 1930's-61. *15277a*
—. Barnes, Djuna *(Nightwood)*. Censorship. Great Britain. Hall, Radclyffe *(Well of Loneliness)*. Law. Obscenity. 1890's-1950's. *6766a*
—. Berdaches. Indians. Pueblo Indians (Zuñi). Self-perception. We'wha. 1880's-1980's. *5131b 9279b*
—. Biography. Films. *Night and Day* (film). Porter, Cole. 1946. *14879a*
—. Blacks. Hampton, Mabel. New York City. Women. 1907-89. *7900a*
—. Blacks. Hispanic Americans. Minorities. Politics. Rhetoric. 1980's. *14980a*
—. California (San Francisco Bay area). Family. Men. Women. 1980's. *4572b 8734b*
—. California (San Francisco Bay area). Filipino Americans. Mangaoang, Gil. Personal Narratives. Political activism. 1975-90. *15867a*
—. Canada. Civil Service. Domestic Policy. Men. National Security. 1950's-60's. *9538a*
—. Canada. Dance. Indians. Lescarbot, Marc *(Histoire de la Nouvelle-France)*. Sex. Tobacco. 1609. *9127a*
—. Canada. Interviews. Women. 1950's-60's. *13453v*
—. Cannibalism. Melville, Herman. Novels. 1846-50. *6165a*
—. Catholic Church. Law. Medicine (practice of). Quebec (Montreal). 1890-1960. *5482a*
—. Celebrities. Ethics. Journalism. Politicians. 1950's-80's. *3128a*
—. Colleges and Universities. Politics. 1970's-92. *2423b*
—. Colorado. Initiatives. Oregon. Political Campaigns. Race Relations. 1988-92. *2878a*
—. Composers. Griffes, Charles T. Music. New York City. 1900's-20. *10664b*
—. Courts. Decisionmaking. Military Service. Rationality. *Steffan v. Aspin* (US, 1993). 1970's-94. *14783a*
—. Crime and Criminals (organized). Federal Bureau of Investigation. Historical Accuracy. Hoover, J. Edgar (film review). 1950's. *2845v*
—. Curricula. Multiculturalism. New York City. Public Schools. 1992-93. *15161a*
—. Dramatists. Quebec. Social criticism. 1970's-91. *5493a*
—. Duberman, Martin Bauml. Memoirs. Psychotherapy. Social Conditions. 1950's-91. *3312b*
—. Feminism. New Mexico (Albuquerque). Race. Social Classes. Women. 1965-80. *8613a*
—. Fiction. Women. 1969-89. *3198b*
—. Filipino Americans. New York City. 1987-92. *15164a*
—. Films. Mass Media. Scholarship. 1969-92. *3119a*
—. Fuller, Margaret. Literature. Women. 19c. *10126a*
—. Great Britain. Men. Theater. 1940's-91. *3177b*
—. Higher Education. History Teaching. 1993. *4832a*
—. Leftism. Social Classes. 1970's-91. *14743a*
—. Men. Pennsylvania (Philadelphia). Politics. Social Movements. Women. 1960-66. *15236a*
—. Men. Politics. Social Movements. Women. 20c. *2417b 11022b*
—. Military. World War II. 1940's. *6709b*
—. Mitchell, Alice. Newspapers. Psychology. Sexuality. Tennessee (Memphis). Women. 1880-1920. *8321a*
—. Nazism. Sally Bowles (fictional character). 1939-72. *7595b*
—. New York (Buffalo). Women. 1930's-60's. *3576b 7921b 15201b*
—. New York City. Political activism. Puerto Rico. Santiago, Luis (interview). 1970-91. *15997a*
—. Novels. Women. 20c. *14552d*
—. Oregon. Pharr, Suzanne (interview). Referendum. State Politics. 1992. *8774a*

—. Philosophy. Politics. Self-perception. Social Conditions. Women. ca 1980's. *3306b*
—. Science and Society. Sexology. Women. 1880-1988. *14419a*
—. Television programming. Youth. 1970's-80's. *3135a*
—. Women. 20c. *2428b*
Homosexuality (review article). Europe (northwestern). Sex roles. Women. 1750-1990. *13662a*
—. Personal Narratives. 1892-20c. *3252a*
Homosexuals. Acquired immune deficiency syndrome. California (Los Angeles; Silverlake). Death and Dying. Interpersonal Relations. Joslin, Tom. Massi, Mark. ca 1992. *15893v*
—. Acquired immune deficiency syndrome. Political activism. Social organization. Washington (Seattle). 1980's-93. *4671d*
—. Blacks. Discrimination. Military. 1770's-20c. *963a*
—. Cities. Residential patterns. Women. 1970's-80's. *3236a*
—. Courts. Documents. Military. Steffan, Joseph. 1980's. *11265b*
—. Daughters of Bilitis. Social Movements. Women. 1950's-70's. *14977a*
—. Discrimination. Military. 1993. *2705a*
—. Discrimination. Military. Morality. Political power. 1993. *2702a*
—. Domestic Policy. Europe. Military Service. 1993. *2712a*
—. Interpersonal Relations. Women. 1992. *11790d*
—. Military. Politics. Social Conditions. Technology. Tradition. 1945-93. *2701a*
—. Sex roles. Social protest. Violence. Women's Movement. 1970's-93. *14988a*
—. Sex roles. Women. 1980-92. *3255a*
—. Violence. ca 1991. *11772b*
Homosexuals (image). Acquired immune deficiency syndrome. Public Health. Sexuality. 1980's. *11793d*
Honduras (Tegucigalpa). Children. Homeless. Women. 1980's. *3302a*
Hong Kong. Acculturation. Canada. Consumption. Immigrants. Values. 1978-91. *9530a*
—. Asian Canadians. British Columbia (Vancouver). Economic Development. Immigrants. 1980's. *9717a*
—. British Columbia (Vancouver). Chinese Canadians. Immigration. Multiculturalism. Racism. 1980's-92. *923a*
—. Canada. Foreign Relations. 1980's. *9509a*
Honor. Kentucky. McGready, James. Profanity. Revivals. Sectionalism. 1797-1805. *15488a*
Honorary Degrees. *See* Degrees, academic.
Hood, Adrienne D. American history. Museums. Personal Narratives. Surveys. 1993-94. *16047a*
Hoogt, Cornelius W. van der. Colorado. Dutch Americans. Fraud. Holland-American Land and Immigration Company. Immigration. Noordtzij, Maarten. Zoutman, Albertus. 1892-93. *1887a*
Hook, John. Consumer goods. England (London). Retail Trade. Virginia (Bedford County). 18c. *3905d*
Hooper, Harry Bartholomew. Baseball. 1890's-1925. *9982b*
Hoosier National Forest. Indiana (southern). National forests. 1600-1950. *4189b*
Hoover Dam. Construction. Interviews. 1931-36. *4466b 8664b*
Hoover, Herbert C. Commerce Department. Federal Reserve System. Monetary policy. Strong, Benjamin. 1917-28. *10764d*
—. Diaries. Elections (presidential). Joslin, Theodore. Roosevelt, Franklin D. 1932. *6624a*
—. Documents. Politics. Truman, Harry S. 1945-64. *14755b*
—. Foreign Policy. Poland. Politics. 1914-33. *10713b*
—. Industry. Information access. Taylor, Frederick Winslow. Technology. 1900-30. *14445a*
Hoover, J. Edgar. Anticommunism. Blacks. Justice Department (Radical Division). Leftism. Riots. 1919. *10745a*
—. Documents. Federal Bureau of Investigation (Responsibilities Program). 1951-55. *7277b*
Hoover, J. Edgar (film review). Crime and Criminals (organized). Federal Bureau of Investigation. Historical Accuracy. Homosexuality. 1950's. *2845v*
Hopacan (Captain Pipe). American Revolution. Delaware Indians. Fort Detroit. Indians. Speeches. 1775-81. *1317a*

Figure 12.1. Index entries from *America: history and life.*
Reprinted by permission of ABC-CLIO, ©1996.

12.2.2.2. Faceted Syntax (PRECIS, CIFT).

• definition of faceted syntax : 130

Faceted syntax is used when there is a need or desire to have the individual terms or descriptors in an index heading arranged in some meaningful order. Terms are assigned to facet or role categories and these categories are used to determine the order of terms. Here is an example:

```
[location]          England
[key entity]        automobiles
[modifier]          Korean
[action]            sales
[role definer]      effects of/on
[agent, instrument] advertising
```

• examples of faceted syntax : 131

These terms and their categories result in the following headings:

```
England
     Korean automobiles. sales. effects of advertising. [locator]
automobiles. England
     Korean automobiles. sales. effects of advertising. [locator]
Korean automobiles. England
     sales. effects of advertising. [locator]
sales. Korean automobiles. England
     effects of advertising. [locator]
advertising. Korean automobiles. England
     effects on sales. [locator]
```

In the actual displayed index, these headings would be sorted into alphabetical order and merged with other headings. Again, the "[locator]" represents some method for leading the user to the actual document or to a surrogate for the document.

• faceted syntax compared to rotated term syntax : 132

Contrast these "meaningful" headings with those that would be generated by simple rotated term syntax (with terms after the lead term simply arranged in alphabetical order). Do you find the faceted order of terms more meaningful?:

```
advertising. automobiles. effects. England. Korean. sales. [locator]
automobiles. advertising. effects. England. Korean. sales. [locator]
England. advertising. automobiles. effects. Korean. sales. [locator]
Korean. advertising. automobiles. effects. England. sales. [locator]
sales. advertising. automobiles. effects. England. Korean. [locator]
```

• PRECIS as example of faceted syntax : 133

This simple example of faceted indexing is based on a highly developed indexing syntax called PRECIS, for "Preserved Context Indexing System," created under the leadership of Derek Austin for the British National Bibliography (Austin 1984; Dykstra 1985; Richmond 1981).

• role and facet indicators in faceted syntax : 134

As the example illustrates, terms are tagged with a code for their facet or role category in the overall index statement. In our example, "England" falls in the place facet and indicates the location of the topic of a message; "automobiles" falls into the entity (thing) facet and indicates the key entity of interest; "Korean" falls in the attributes facet and serves to modify or characterize the key entity; "sales" is an action that operates on the key entity (the automobiles are sold); "advertising" is another action, but here it plays the role of agent, means or instrument for effecting these sales; and "effects of/on" is a "role definer" that explains the relationship between the action and the agent or instrument. These facet or role categories determine the order of terms in each heading.

• **role definers in faceted syntax : 135**

The role definer feature can be used whenever the standard roles, such as key entity, attribute, action, agent/means are not sufficient to explain the relationships among terms. Role definers are used to indicate such relationships as participation, influence, effects, use, and applications (Austin 1984, p. 147-151).

• **display of faceted index headings : 136**

The examples of faceted syntax headings illustrate the two-level "shunting" display developed by the designers of PRECIS. This display of terms in headings is meant to preserve the original meaningful order and relationship among terms in each heading. As each term is "shunted" into the lead position, the previous lead term is shunted to the right to form a "qualifier" for the lead term. The terms remaining on the second, indented level are called the "display."

• **137**

Comparing the second and third faceted syntax headings with the first heading, when "automobiles" and "Korean automobiles" (in both forms to provide maximum access) are shunted to the lead position, the previous lead term "England" is shunted to the right to serve as a "qualifier" for these new lead terms. The remainder of the string remains in the "display" on the second line.

• **138**

A slightly different order of facets or categories is followed when the agent/instrument term ("advertising") takes the lead position. The action and any role definer remains in the display (second line), rather than moving up to the qualifier (first line following the lead term).

• **faceted syntax in specialized domains : 139**

The roles and categories defined in PRECIS and similar faceted systems are very generic, designed for the entire universe of subjects. When faceted syntax is used for indexing in particular subject areas or domains, the facets or roles tend to be much more specific to the subject area or domain. For example, the Modern Language Association of America uses the following facets and roles for indexing documents relating to literature and literary study (Modern Language Association of America 1997):

- specific literatures
- performance media
- languages
- periods
- individuals (real)
- anonymous works
- groups/movements
- genres
- works
- features
- literary techniques

Chapter 12. Syntax (Section 12.2.2.2)

- themes/motifs/figures
- influences (recipients)
- sources
- processes
- types of scholarship
- methodological approaches
- theories
- devices/tools
- disciplines
- scholars

• **examples of faceted index headings from *MLA international bibliography*** : 140

Here is an example of faceted syntax indexing from the Modern Language Association's *MLA international bibliography* (Modern Language Association of America 1999, 1981 ed.) one of the leading IR databases in the humanities:

```
[literature]              English literature.
[genre]                   short story.
[period]                  1900-1999.
[author]                  Forster, E. M.
[work]                    "Dr. Woolacott."
[stylistic technique]     symbolism.
[theme]                   salvation; homosexuality.
```

• 141

In the headings generated from these terms, the order of terms (descriptors) is determined by the order of their facets and roles as listed just above. The order of facets and roles in subheadings is therefore fixed and stable, creating a regularity in the displayed index that is absent in simple rotated term syntax. These subheadings are also more uniform than those in the more generic PRECIS-like faceted syntax illustrated in the previous example.

```
homosexuality
    English literature. short story. 1900-1999.
        Forster, E. M. "Dr. Woolacott." symbolism. treatment of
                salvation; HOMOSEXUALITY. [locator]
salvation
    English literature. short story. 1900-1999.
        Forster, E. M. "Dr. Woolacott." symbolism. treatment of
                SALVATION; homosexuality. [locator]
symbolism
    English literature. short story. 1900-1999.
        Forster, E. M. "Dr. Woolacott." SYMBOLISM. treatment of
                salvation; homosexuality. [locator]
```

Note that the subheadings for each of these entries is exactly the same in content and order of terms. Each important term becomes the lead term, one at a time, but the lead term is also kept in its original location, where it is displayed in all capital letters, so that its position in the context of the entire string can be readily ascertained.

Chapter 12. Syntax (Section 12.2.2.2)

• 142

Also, note that the facet and role categories used here for arranging terms in headings are exactly the same as the categories identified in the subject scope for the MLA Bibliography, as discussed in the chapter 2 on subject scope.

• 143

Again, these headings would be placed in their alphabetical positions after being merged with other headings in the index. See a portion of a *MLA international bibliography* index in figure 12.2 (Modern Language Association of America 1999, 1997 ed., p. 775). This faceted indexing system is called CIFT (Contextual Indexing and Faceted Taxonomic access system) and was developed for the Modern Language Association by James D. Anderson in 1978-79 (1979, 1980).

• role definers in faceted syntax : 144

Like PRECIS (an example of a general faceted syntax indexing system), the MLA's CIFT indexing system (an example of a discipline-specific faceted syntax indexing system) uses role definers as necessary to specify the role of particular terms. "Treatment of" is a role definer used in indexing string for E. M. Forster's "Dr. Woolacott" (illustrated above) to indicate the treatment of a theme in literature. Other role definers used in CIFT (where they are called "role indicators" include (Modern Language Association of America 1997):

- application in
- application of
- applied to
- compared to
- influence of
- influence on
- relationship to
- role in
- role of
- sources in
- theories of
- treatment in

• faceted syntax compared to rotated term syntax : 145

Before we leave faceted indexing, compare the headings for symbolism and the treatment of homosexuality and salvation in E. M. Forster's short story "Dr. Woolacott" produced by the MLA CIFT faceted indexing system (illustrated above) with the headings that would be created by simple rotated term syntax:

```
homosexuality. "Dr. Woolacott." English literature. Forster, E.
        M. short story. salvation. symbolism. 1900-1999. [locator]
salvation. "Dr. Woolacott." English literature. Forster, E. M.
        homosexuality. short story. symbolism. 1900-1999. [locator]
symbolism. "Dr. Woolacott." English literature. Forster, E. M.
        homosexuality. short story. salvation. 1900-1999. [locator]
```

Chapter 12. Syntax (Section 12.2.2.2)

HOMOSEXUALITY
English literature. Novel. 1900-1999.

Argentinian literature. Novel. 1900-1999.
  Denevi, Marco. *Rosaura a las diez*. Treatment of concealment of HOMOSEXUALITY. 2-14391.
Argentinian literature. Poetry. 1800-1899.
  Hernández, José. *Martín Fierro*. Treatment of eroticism; HOMOSEXUALITY. 2-14074.
Argentinian literature. Prose and short story. 1900-1999.
  Borges, Jorge Luis. Treatment of Wilde, Oscar; Whitman, Walt; HOMOSEXUALITY. 2-14253 (1-5747).
Argentinian literature. Short story. 1900-1999.
  Borges, Jorge Luis. "La forma de la espada." Treatment of HOMOSEXUALITY. 2-14287.
Australian literature. Novel. 1900-1999.
  Jolley, Elizabeth. *The Well*. Treatment of HOMOSEXUALITY compared to Hall, Radclyffe: *The Well of Loneliness*. 1-6868.
Brazilian literature. Theater. 1900-1999.
  Relationship to HOMOSEXUALITY; transsexual performers. Dissertation abstract. 2-13879.
Chilean literature. Novel. 1900-1999.
  Allende, Isabel. *La casa de los espíritus*. Treatment of gender; HOMOSEXUALITY. 2-14716.
  Thomson, Augusto. *La pasión y muerte del cura Deusto*. Relationship to HOMOSEXUALITY. 2-14834.
Cuban literature. Fiction. 1900-1999.
  Piñera, Virgilio. Relationship to marginality. Treatment of HOMOSEXUALITY. 2-15263.
Cuban literature. Novel. 1900-1999.
  Arenas, Reinaldo. *Otra vez el mar*; *El color del verano*. Role of exile. Treatment of HOMOSEXUALITY. 2-15181.
  Montero, Mayra. *La última noche que pasé contigo*. Treatment of eroticism; racism; popular music; HOMOSEXUALITY; tourism compared to Carpentier, Alejo. 2-15240.
Cuban literature. Prose. 1800-1999.
  Casal, Julián del. "A través de la ciudad: El centro de dependientes." Treatment of HOMOSEXUALITY. Application of theories of Céspedes, Benjamín de: *La prostitución en La Habana*; Giralt, Pedro: *El amor y la prostitución*. 2-15054.
Dramatic arts. Film.
  Treatment of bisexuality; HOMOSEXUALITY in Hitchcock, Alfred: *Strangers on a Train*; Anger, Kenneth: *Fireworks*. 4-372.
  Treatment of cross-dressing by heterosexual actors; relationship to HOMOSEXUALITY of drag queen. 4-787.
  Treatment of family; HOMOSEXUALITY in Livingston, Jennie: *Paris Is Burning*; relationship to American novel. 4-1184 (1-9729).
  Treatment of HOMOSEXUALITY. 4-822.
  ——; father-son relations in Iglesia, Eloy de la: *Los placeres ocultos*; *El diputado*. 4-1351.
  ——; pornography in Almodóvar, Pedro: *Matador*; *La ley del deseo*. 4-1256.
  ——; relationship to patriarchy in Hermosillo, Jaime Humberto: *Doña Herlinda y su hijo*. 4-576.
  —— in Cuba in Gutiérrez Alea, Tomás: *Fresa y chocolate*. 4-292.
  —— in Gutiérrez Alea, Tomás: *Fresa y chocolate*. 4-648, 4-1350.
  —— in Iglesia, Eloy de la: *El diputado*; Almodóvar, Pedro: *La ley del deseo*. 4-1365.
  —— in Miró, Pilar: *Gary Cooper que estás en los cielos*; Werther, *El pájaro de la felicidad*. 4-921.
  Treatment of paranoia; voyeurism; relationship to HOMOSEXUALITY in Hitchcock, Alfred: *Rear Window*. 4-1306.
Dramatic arts. Film. Film adaptation.
  Documentary technique. Treatment of HOMOSEXUALITY; reality; relationship to anxiety of audience in film adaptation of Bernhard, Sandra: *Without You I'm Nothing* by Boskovich, John compared to Livingston, Jennie: *Paris Is Burning*; Dunye, Cheryl: *Janine*; *She Don't Fade*. 4-1550 (1-10252).
  Treatment of gender; HOMOSEXUALITY in film adaptation of Gunter, Archibald Clavering: *A Florida Enchantment* by Drew, Sidney. 4-1476 (1-8363).
  ——; HOMOSEXUALITY in film adaptation of Shakespeare, William: *Much Ado about Nothing* as romantic comedy film by Branagh, Kenneth Charles. 4-1517 (1-1469).
Dramatic arts. Film. Film genres. Comic film in United States.
  Treatment of HOMOSEXUALITY; relationship to repression. 4-1859.
Dramatic arts. Film. Film genres. Documentary film.
  Cinéma vérité. Treatment of HOMOSEXUALITY in Smith, Jack: *Flaming Creatures* as underground film. 4-1932.
Dramatic arts. Film. Film genres. Documentary film by Southern American filmmakers.
  Treatment of HOMOSEXUALITY; relationship to region; community in Riggs, Marlon T.: *Tongues Untied*; Spiro, Ellen: *DiAna's Hair Ego*; *Greeting from Out Here*. 4-1877.
Dramatic arts. Film. Film genres. Horror film.
  Relationship to HOMOSEXUALITY in United States. Dissertation abstract. 4-1989.
  Treatment of vampire; relationship to HOMOSEXUALITY; gender compared to horror fiction (1800-1999). 4-1987 (1-3044).
Dramatic arts. Film. Film genres. Science fiction film.
  Treatment of repression of HOMOSEXUALITY; identity; relationship to postmodernism. 4-2082.

Dramatic arts. Film. Yiddish language literature.
  Relationship to HOMOSEXUALITY. 4-1235.
Dramatic arts. Film and videotape.
  Role of women. Camp; relationship to feminism; HOMOSEXUALITY. 4-1148.
Dramatic arts. Film in United States.
  Treatment of American identity (1945-1997); relationship to HOMOSEXUALITY; communism compared to American novel. Application of queer theory. 4-1058 (1-9717).
Dramatic arts. Television.
  Treatment of HOMOSEXUALITY; relationship to stereotypes in *thirtysomething*. Queer theory. 4-2405.
Dramatic arts. Television and radio in United States. 1900-1999.
  And journalism. Treatment of HOMOSEXUALITY. 4-2217 (1-9914).
Egyptian literature. Drama. 1200-1299: Mamluk dynasty period.
  Ibn Dāniyāl, Shams al-Din Muḥammad. *Al-Mutayyam wa-l-dā'ī' al-yutayyim*. And Ṣafadī, Khalīl ibn Aybak al-: *Law'at al-shāki wa-dam'at al-bāki*. Treatment of HOMOSEXUALITY. 2-18875.
English Caribbean literature. 1900-1999.
  Treatment of HOMOSEXUALITY; national identity compared to Spanish American literature. Dissertation abstract. 1-7374 (2-14008).
English Caribbean literature. Fiction. 1900-1999.
  Relationship to HOMOSEXUALITY; colonialism. Biographical approach. Treatment in Thomas, H. Nigel: *Spirits in the Dark*. 1-7382.
English literature. 1500-1699.
  Relationship to eroticism; HOMOSEXUALITY. Review article. 1-934.
English literature. 1600-1699.
  Treatment of HOMOSEXUALITY; especially lesbianism; Sappho; Virgin Mary. Cultural historical approach. 1-2016.
English literature. 1900-1999.
  Forster, E. M. Relationship to Bloomsbury Group; HOMOSEXUALITY in fraternal organizations at Cambridge University. 1-4801.
  Strachey, Lytton. Relationship to modernism; HOMOSEXUALITY. Dissertation abstract. 1-5327.
English literature. Drama. 1500-1599.
  Shakespeare, William. Role of HOMOSEXUALITY in adaptation (1640-1701). 1-1329.
English literature. Comedy. 1500-1599.
  Shakespeare, William. *Measure for Measure*. Treatment of Vincentio, Duke of Vienna (character); relationship to HOMOSEXUALITY. 1-1435.
  ——. *Much Ado about Nothing*. Treatment of gender; HOMOSEXUALITY in film adaptation by Branagh, Kenneth Charles. 1-1469 (4-1517).
  ——. Treatment of friendship; HOMOSEXUALITY in male-male relations compared to Marlowe, Christopher: *Edward II*; Fletcher, John: *The Two Noble Kinsmen*. Dissertation abstract. 1-1411.
English literature. Tragedy. 1500-1599.
  Shakespeare, William. *Coriolanus*; *Troilus and Cressida*. Treatment of rape; violence; HOMOSEXUALITY compared to Marlowe, Christopher: *Edward II*; Jonson, Ben: *Sejanus*. 1-1622.
  ——. *Hamlet*. Role of Oedipal conflict; relationship to HOMOSEXUALITY. Psychoanalytic approach. 1-1662.
  ——. *King Lear*. Treatment of HOMOSEXUALITY of James I of England, VI of Scotland in folio edition. 1-1707.
English literature. Drama. 1500-1699.
  Treatment of homosociality; HOMOSEXUALITY; cross-dressing. 1-1008.
English literature. Drama. 1500-1599: Renaissance.
  Marlowe, Christopher. *The Massacre at Paris*. Treatment of HOMOSEXUALITY of Henri III, King of France compared to L'Estoile, Pierre Taisan de: *Mémoires-Journaux*. 1-1210 (2-821).
English literature. Drama. 1900-1999.
  Orton, John Kingsley. Treatment of working class; HOMOSEXUALITY; relationship to intellectuality. Dissertation abstract. 1-5143.
English literature. Drama and poetry. 1500-1599: Renaissance.
  Marlowe, Christopher. Treatment of HOMOSEXUALITY; sodomy. Theories of Bray, Alan: *Homosexuality in Renaissance England*. 1-1201.
English literature. Fiction. 1900-1999.
  Maugham, W. Somerset. Relationship to HOMOSEXUALITY; exoticism. 1-5111.
English literature. Musical composition: song cycle. 1900-1999.
  Britten, Benjamin. *Seven Sonnets of Michelangelo*. Treatment of myth; relationship to HOMOSEXUALITY. Sources in Michelangelo. Dissertation abstract. 1-4513 (2-9024).
English literature. Novel. 1800-1899.
  Dickens, Charles. *David Copperfield*. Relationship to HOMOSEXUALITY. 1-3609.
  Eliot, George. *Daniel Deronda*. Relationship to Zionism; HOMOSEXUALITY compared to Herzl, Theodor: *Altneuland*. 1-3706 (2-5951).
English literature. Novel. 1900-1999.
  Bartlett, Neil. *Who Was That Man?*; *Ready to Catch Him Should He Fall*. Pastiche. Treatment of HOMOSEXUALITY as subculture; relationship to lesbian and gay studies. 1-4485.
  Forster, E. M. *Howards End*; "The Machine Stops." Relationship to HOMOSEXUALITY. Treatment of otherness. Psychoanalytic approach; biographical approach. 1-4819.
  ——. *Maurice*. Treatment of tolerance of HOMOSEXUALITY. 1-4823.
  ——. *A Passage to India*. Treatment of India as the other; relationship to HOMOSEXUALITY. 1-4829.

Figure 12.2. Index entries from the *MLA international bibliography*.
Reprinted by permission of the Modern Language Association of America, © 1998.

Chapter 12. Syntax (Section 12.2.2.2)

• 146

Do you find the faceted syntax heading easier to understand than the simple rotated term headings? Does it matter that the simple rotated string does not distinguish between themes in a short story (treatment of homosexuality, salvation) on the one hand and attributes or actions (such as homosexuality or salvation) that could be attributed to the author, E. M. Forster?

• clarity of index headings : 147

Three of the five criteria suggested by Timothy Craven for effective index headings (section 12.2) are collocation, predictability, and clarity. Clarity relates to the comprehensibility of index headings, for example, whether the faceted index headings previously displayed are more or less easy for users to understand compared to rotated term syntax headings.

• collocation of index headings : 148

Collocation of headings relates to the co-location or gathering together of closely related headings in displays. Headings are often scanned or browsed in the company of many other headings presented in some meaningful arrangement. Often this arrangement is alphabetical, first by the main or lead term, then by subsequent terms.

• collocation in rotated term syntax : 149

Let us compare the collocation of headings on the same topic in the sample index page from *America: history and life* (figure 12. 1, using the simple rotated term syntax) with the collocation of headings on the same topic in the *MLA international bibliography* (figure 12.2, using faceted syntax).

• 150

Look at the headings under the lead term "Homosexuality" in figure 12.1. These headings are arranged in alphabetical order based on the second term in each heading (e.g., Abortion, Acquired immune deficiency syndrome, etc.) and if necessary, subsequent terms in heading (e.g., because there are two subheadings beginning with "Acquired immune deficiency syndrome," these headings are then arranged by the next term, "Diseases" and "Outing" respectively).

• 151

Because the terms in subheadings are simply arranged in alphabetical order, there is no uniform pattern for the kinds of terms that will determine the arrangement of headings under the same lead term. Thus, searchers interested in homosexuality among Blacks will find a possibly relevant heading placed under:

```
Homosexuality.
—. Authors. Blacks. ...
```
but also under:
```
Homosexuality.
—. Blacks. ...
```

• 152

Searchers interested in homosexuality in Great Britain will find possibly relevant headings under:

```
Homosexuality.
—. Barnes, Djuna (Nightwood). Censorship. Great Britain. ...
```
and
```
Homosexuality.
—. Great Britain. ...
```

Chapter 12. Syntax (Section 12.2.2.2)

• 153

Searchers interested in Homosexuality in New York City will find possibly relevant headings under:

```
Homosexuality.
—. Blacks. Hampton, Mabel. New York City. ...

Homosexuality.
—. Composers. Griffes, Charles T. Music. New York City. ...

Homosexuality.
—. Curricula. Multiculturalism. New York City. ...
```
and
```
Homosexuality.
—. New York City. ...
```

• 154

The only way to find all possibly relevant headings on some aspect of homosexuality is to scan and examine all of the subheadings up to the alphabetic point where the secondary term of interest is placed as the first term in the subheading, because it is impossible to predict where terms for the aspects of interest will fall in the sequence of terms within headings. So, for homosexuality among blacks, one must scan all headings until "Blacks" is the first term in the subheadings. Because terms in subheadings are arranged in alphabetical order, no term for Blacks will occur in any subsequent subheadings. If your aspect of interest falls late in the alphabet, the only solution is to scan all headings. Try finding all the subheadings including the term "Women" for example.

• collocation in faceted syntax : 155

Now, compare the collocation of headings under "homosexuality" in the *MLA international bibliography* (figure 12.2). Here the lead term "homosexuality" is printed at the top of the page at the right margin. Because terms within headings are arranged in a fixed order by facets, the subheadings are grouped by name of literature, then by genre, then by date or period, then by author, etc. When a category does not apply to a heading, it is simply omitted (as in the subheading "Dramatic arts. Film" where no particular national literature is mentioned). Searchers who are interested in the treatment of homosexuality in English novels of the 20th century can scan the page until they find the subheading "English literature. Novel. 1900-1999." Under this subheading they will find all the entries related to this literature, period, and genre, gathered together in one place and arranged by the next facet category, literary author: "Bartlett, Neil" and "Forster, E. M.," and then, under "Forster, E. M.," by work title, "Howards End," "Maurice," and "A Passage to India." (Note that the headings "English literature. Comedy. 1500-1599" and "English literature. Tragedy. 1500-1599" are out of alphabetical order!)

• predictability of index headings : 156

Thus, the collocation of headings tends to be more regular and predictable when faceted syntax is used, compared to rotated term syntax. However, there is a price to pay, and IR database designers need to decide if the benefit is worth the cost. Rotated term syntax is extremely simple. Index terms are simply assigned and the computer does the rest. In faceted indexing, every term must be assigned to a facet or role category, which adds to the complexity and cost of the indexing operation. The bottom line is which type of display is more helpful to end users (in relation to benefits and costs), and on that question, we have no definitive research.

Chapter 12. Syntax (Section 12.2.2.2.1)

12.2.2.2.1. Converting LCSH to Faceted Syntax.

• **views of Chan (Lois Mai) on faceted syntax for** *Library of Congress subject headings* **: 157**

Lois Mai Chan, one of the most prolific writers on *Library of Congress subject headings*, has said: "Considering the gradual steps the Library of Congress has taken over the years, even a person not familiar with the history of LCSH must conclude logically that LCSH is heading in the direction of becoming a fully faceted vocabulary" (2002).

• **facets of** *Bliss classification* **applied to** *Library of Congress subject headings* **: 158**

Several of Anderson's students have explored this possibility. They scrapped the complex and idiosyncratic LCSH syntax rules that have accumulated over the years and replaced them with the faceted syntax of the Bliss classification, 2d edition (Bliss 1997; Broughton 2001). Here are the Bliss facets, in the order in which they are applied, with slight modification in their labels (e.g., "patient" has been changed to "client"):

- thing/entity
- kind
- part
- property/attribute
- material
- process
- operation
- client
- product
- by-product
- agent/means
- space
- time

• **facets for features of documentary units : 159**

To these, the following feature facets were added:

- approach (author's methodological approach, point of view, etc.)
- format
- medium
- audience

• **coextensive index headings using faceted syntax for** *Library of Congress subject headings* **: 160**

This faceted syntax allows catalogers to create headings that are more frequently coextensive with the content of a message. Thus one comprehensive heading (or string of terms) could often be used instead of several separate and unconnected headings.

• **examples of faceted syntax for** *Library of Congress subject headings* **: 161**

Take, for example, the work *Black Baptists and African missions: the origins of a movement, 1880-1915*, by Sandy D. Martin (Macon, GA: Mercer, c1989). To indicate the subject content of this work, the following LCSH headings could be used, but they cannot be combined into one comprehensive heading according to current syntax rules:

Chapter 12. Syntax (Section 12.2.2.2.1)

```
West Africans — Missions — History — 19th century.
African American Baptists — Southern States — History — 19th century.
National Baptist Convention of the United States of America — Missions
      — Africa, West — History — 19th century.
Carey, Lott — Contributions in missions.
```
• 162

In contrast, here are the same LCSH descriptors (main headings and subdivisions) merged into a single string using faceted syntax. In accordance with standard practice with faceted indexing, role indicators may be inserted within angle brackets to clarify the relationship between descriptors:

```
West Africans. Missions <to>. <by> African American Baptists: National
      Baptist Convention of the U.S.A.; Carey, Lott. <from> Southern
      states. <to> Africa, West. 19th century.
```
• 163

This comprehensive LCSH heading would appear in the alphanumeric subject catalog under each descriptor, providing significantly more direct access than current LCSH syntax allows. For example, this comprehensive heading could be found under the following additional headings, compared to current LCSH practice: Missions; History; 19th century; Southern states; and Africa, West. Here is the complete list of headings under which this faceted heading could be found:

```
19th century
Africa, West
African American Baptists
Carey, Lott.
Missions
National Baptist Convention of the U.S.A.
Southern States.
West Africans
```

• categorization of multiple index headings using facets : 164

As we saw in section 12.2.1 on subject heading syntax, one of the biggest challenges for effective browsing is to provide users with an overview or summary of the kinds of headings available under each main heading. Without such a summary, users are often confronted with hundreds of subheadings, forcing them to browse through tens of computer screens. Facets can be used to summarize the kinds of topics available in relation to each main heading. For example, Under the heading "Africa, West," the following display can be presented, based on facets:

```
Africa, West
      Please choose from the following categories of headings.
            Africa, West, in relation to:
                  Entities/things (persons, institutions, objects,
                  artifacts, etc.)
                  Properties/attributes
                  Processes/Operations/Events
                  Space/Environments/Places
                  Time
```
• 165

When users choose entities/things, they would see a list of persons, institutions, objects, artifacts, and other entities, including: African American Baptists; Carey, Lott; National Baptist Convention of the U.S.A.; and West Africans. When they choose any of these headings, they

Chapter 12. Syntax (Section 12.2.2.3)

would see the complete string of descriptors for any documentary unit relating to both "Africa, West" and the entity chosen.

• 166

Note that "Africa, West" reflects a former pattern of inverted headings once preferred by LCSH.

• 167

When users choose processes/operations/events, they would see "Missions." When they choose Space/Environments/Places, they would see "Southern States." When they choose Time, they would see "19th century."

• testing of faceted syntax for *Library of Congress subject headings* : 168

What is needed now is extensive testing of this type of faceted syntax for LCSH, including usability studies focusing on users and also on catalogers. How readily would catalogers take to this new system? Indexers for the Modern Language Association's *MLA international bibliography* have been using faceted indexing for more than twenty years. When it was first introduced, it took some getting used to! After catalogers get used to this faceted approach, would the quality of their cataloging improve? Would productivity increase? These are questions for future research, for future dissertations!

12.2.2.3. Ad Hoc String Syntax (NEPHIS).

• definition of ad hoc string syntax : 169

Ad hoc string syntax provides a means for coding natural language statements so that a computer program can convert them into meaningful index headings. The statements can be already existing, such as document titles, or they can be created as part of the indexing process. The coding tells the computer how to break up the statement into individual terms, how to arrange these terms within headings, and which terms to place in lead position as main terms. "Ad hoc" (Latin for "to this") means that each statement is encoded specifically for the particular instance at hand — each string is custom made.

• ad hoc string syntax compared to faceted syntax : 170

The difference between this approach and faceted string syntax is that in faceted syntax, individual terms are placed in facet or role categories (or are tagged with category codes) and this category data is used by the computer algorithm to create headings or strings of terms. In ad hoc string syntax, the string already exists and must be coded (on an ad hoc basis) to tell the computer how to rearrange the terms into multiple headings.

• ad hoc string syntax compared to natural language syntax : 171

Later, we shall discuss the much simpler natural language syntax systems called "KWIC," "KWAC" and "KWOC," which involve little or no human coding of individual strings of text. You will want to compare the merits of these two approaches, with respect to clarity, predictability, collocation, eliminability, succinctness (Craven's five criteria for index headings, section 12.2), and also cost.

• NEPHIS as example of ad hoc string syntax : 172

As an example of ad hoc string syntax, we will use NEPHIS (Nested Phrase Indexing System), developed by Timothy Craven (1986).

• notation in NEPHIS : 173

NEPHIS uses 4 symbols to encode natural language statements with instructions for the computer algorithm that creates NEPHIS index headings:

Chapter 12. Syntax (Section 12.2.2.3)

- @ is used to turn off a heading that otherwise would be produced.
- < and > are used to identify phrases (one or more words) that should be kept together. One such phrase may be "nested" within another, hence the name of this syntax system. Each bracketed phrase becomes the lead term in a heading, unless it is turned off with a leading @.
- ? is used to indicate a connective, usually a preposition, that connects phrases and must be dropped or rearranged when the subsequent phrase is the lead term. (This '?' has nothing to do with a question. Craven may have chosen it because it hardly ever occurs in an index heading.)

● examples of NEPHIS coding : 174

Here is an example:

- Title or statement (existing or created in advance of coding):

    effects of advertising on sales of Korean automobiles in England

- Coded statement:

    @effects? of <advertising>? on <sales? of <Korean <automobiles>>? in <England>>

● examples of NEPHIS index headings : 175

Based on this coding, the computer will produce the following headings. In an index, these headings would be arranged in alphabetical order with other headings, and each of them would be followed by some link or locator leading to the actual document:

```
advertising
    effects on sales of Korean automobiles in England [locator]
sales
    of Korean automobiles in England. effects of advertising
            [locator]
Korean automobiles
    sales in England. effects of advertising [locator]
automobiles
    Korean -. sales in England. effects of advertising [locator]
England
    sales of Korean automobiles. effects of advertising
            [locator]
```

● explanation of NEPHIS syntax algorithm : 176

Here is a detailed explanation of how the headings are produced by the NEPHIS computer algorithm. For clarity, here is the coded string again:

```
@effects? of <advertising>? on <sales? of <Korean <automobiles>>? in
<England>>
```

(0) The first term in the statement automatically becomes the lead term in a heading unless it is turned off by a @. Because our statement has an @ in front of "effects," the heading that would have begun with "effects" is eliminated.

(1) The next term, indicated by the first pair of brackets (< ... >), is "advertising." So it becomes a lead term. The preceding term, "effects" becomes the first term in the subheading. The connective that precedes the lead term, marked by the preceding ?, is dropped, so that we have:

```
advertising
    effects on sales of Korean automobiles in England [locator]
```

(2) Our second phrase, marked by the second pair of opening and closing brackets (< ... >), is "sales of Korean automobiles in England." This is a complex phrase that includes two separate embedded or nested phrases (also marked with opening and closing brackets) and two connectives, each indicated by a preceding ?. The first connective, "? of" becomes a breaking point for formatting the heading, so that the term before the connective goes into the lead position, fol-

lowed immediately in the subheading by the rest of the complex phrase. Next comes the preceding phrase, "effects of advertising." So we have:

```
sales
     of Korean automobiles in England. effects of
              advertising [locator]
```

(3) Our third phrase is "Korean automobiles," so this phrase becomes the lead term. It is followed by the other parts of the larger phrase within which "Korean automobiles" is embedded, first by the part that precedes it ("sales"), then by the part that follows it ("in England"). The connective ("of") that immediately precedes the lead term is dropped, and so is the connective ("on") that precedes "sales." (Preceding connectives are always dropped unless the phrase following the connective is attached directly to a preceding phrase!) Next comes the phrase that precedes the complex phrase in which "Korean automobiles" falls ("effects of advertising"). So we have:

```
Korean automobiles
     sales in England. effects of advertising [locator]
```

(4) Our next term, "automobiles" is nested within the larger term "Korean automobiles." This is an adjective-noun combination, without intervening connective. When the main term, "automobiles," goes in the lead position, it is immediately followed by the preceding term, which is following by a hyphen and a full stop (period), to indicate that it is connected directly to the preceding term. As in the third heading, the parts of the larger phrase that precede and follow the lead term and its connected adjective come next, followed by the phrase that precedes the complex phrase containing "automobiles." So we have:

```
automobiles
     Korean -. sales in England. effects of advertising
              [locator]
```

(5) "England" is our last term. It goes into the lead position. As before, it is followed by the other terms within its larger phrase ("sales of Korean automobiles"). Next comes the terms that appear in the preceding phrase ("effects of advertising"). So we have:

```
England
     sales of Korean automobiles. effects of advertising
              [locator]
```

• use of NEPHIS for book indexes : 177

NEPHIS or other types of string indexing syntax can be used in a variety of types of index. NEPHIS has been found to be a useful tool for back-of-the-book indexes, especially for authors who want to index their own books and for other novice indexers. Such beginning indexers typically have little or no experience in formulating appropriate headings for indexes. Frequently, they ignore the need for syntax, using too many single term headings, with no context. This results in too many locators under single headings, such as:

```
United States 33, 44-45, 50, 53, 60-67, 70, 72, 75-79, 80,
     83, 86, 90-100, 121-123, 144-147, 149, 155-158, 160-
     171, 175, 188, 201, 222-223.
```

• 178

Such a long list of locators is a definite turn-off for most users, who have no interest in checking all these locations to see if they have anything to do with their interests. What is lacking in this example are additional terms for each entry showing what is going on in relation to the United States. For example, the above entries might be converted to:

Chapter 12. Syntax (Section 12.2.2.3)

```
United States
     1st Congress, 1789-1791. taxation policies. 33
     Act to Prevent Pernicious Political Activities. 44-45
     Adjutant-General's Office. political patronage. 50
     administrative and political divisions. maps. 53
     aerial photographs. use in weather forecasting. 60-67
     Afro-Americans. historiography. attitudes of white
           historians. 70
     Agency for International Development. role in Vietnam War.
           72
     AID Mission in Vietnam. Office of Provincial Operations.
           impact on strategy in Vietnam War. 75-79
     Air Force Academy. history. role in Vietnam War. 80
     Air Force.
         Afro-Americans. role in Vietnam War. 83
         Women. role in Vietnam War. 86
     Alaska. Sitka. status as former Russian capital. 90-100
     American Indian Religious Freedom Act. 121-123
     Americans with Disabilities Act of 1990. implementation in
           New Jersey. 144-147
     anti-slavery movements. impact on presidential elections.
           149
     armed forces. gays. government policy. 155-158
           executive order of President William Clinton. 160-171
     Army. history.
         civil war, 1861-1865. sources. 175
         history. Mexican War, 1846-1848. 188
         Punitive Expedition into Mexico. 201
         Spanish-American War, 1898. 222-223
  (These examples are based in part on subject entries in the Rutgers
University Libraries catalog.)
```

• 179

Using a syntax system like NEPHIS, the novice indexer can concentrate on making intelligible statements about the content or features of each paragraph (or other documentary unit), such as:

- taxation policies of the 1st Congress (1789-1991) of the United States
- political patronage in the Adjutant-General's Office in the United States
- use of aerial photographs of the United States in weather forecasting
- attitudes of white historians toward the historiography of Afro-Americans in the United States

• 180

These statements can be edited to conform to indexing conventions (such as the deletion of articles), then codes to guide computer manipulation can be added.

• 181

A computer program can convert the resulting statements into multiple headings, with access under every key term. In this way, the indexer is relieved of the need to individually formulate multiple headings.

• 182

In addition to the entries under "United States" that were listed above, these sample statements would also result in the following headings:

```
Adjutant-General's Office
    United States -. political patronage. 50
aerial photographs
    of United States. use in weather forecasting. 60-67

Afro-Americans
    in United States. historiography. attitudes of white
        historians. 70
attitudes
    of white historians toward historiography of Afro-Americans
        in United States. 70
Congress (1789-1991)
    United States -. 1st -. taxation policies. 33
historians
    white -. attitudes toward historiography of Afro-Americans
        in United States. 70
historiography
    of Afro-Americans in United States. attitudes of white
        historians. 70
political patronage
    in United States Adjutant-General's Office. 50
taxation policies
    of 1st United States Congress (1789-1991). 33
weather forecasting
    use of aerial photographs of United States. 60-67
white historians
    attitudes toward historiography of Afro-Americans in United
        States. 70
```

• objectives of string syntax : 183

In short, using a string syntax like NEPHIS helps to accomplish two desirable objectives: It encourages meaningful statements with multiple terms to provide context for index headings, and it produces multiple headings, with direct access under every important term.

• impact of syntax on size of indexes : 184

An index with syntax is also a longer index than one without syntax. Chapter 18 deals with ways to estimate the length of indexes when space is limited (as is common for print-on-paper back-of-the-book indexes). However, an index with syntax and context under headings is always better than an index with little or no syntax, even if it means fewer headings.

12.2.3. Relational Syntax.

• views of Farradane (Jason) on relational indexing : 185

In the 1950s and 1960s, Jason Farradane, a leading British information scientist, developed an indexing syntax he called "relational indexing." His syntax was based on a matrix of relationships based on psychological theories of how the mind assesses relationships among phenomena. The matrix has two dimensions, one representing increasing degrees of association (the horizontal dimension) and the other increasing degrees of discrimination (the vertical dimension). In Farradane's words, "The analysis of thinking shows that the mind has basically two main 'mechanisms' for interconnecting concepts: association and discrimination. Each mechanism develops into three fairly well-defined states ...." (1980b, p. 269).

Chapter 12. Syntax (Section 12.2.3)

• relational indicators in relational syntax : 186

Here is Farradane's relational matrix (Farradane 1980b, p. 270):

```
                              associative mechanisms
                              ========================================
                              awareness      temporary      fixed
                                             association    association
===========================================================================
       -->    concurrent      1   /0         4   /*         7   /;
        |     concept-        concurrence    self-          association
        |     ualization                     activity
        |
        |     non-            2   /=         5   /+         8   /(
discrim-      distinct        equivalence    dimen-         appurtenance
inatory       concept-                       sional
mechanisms    ualization
        |
        |     distinct        3   /)         6   /-         9   /:
        |     concept-        distinct-      action         functional
       -->    ualization      ness                          dependence
                                                            (causation)
===========================================================================
```

• notation for relational syntax : 187

Farradane gave each of these nine relationships a number and a notational symbol (which can be called a "relator". The numbers 1-9 were intended for encoding relationships for computer manipulations, including negations of relationships using numbers 10-18, although negations of relationships "are rarely required" (Farradane 1980b, p. 269). The notational symbols were used to indicate particular relationships between concepts when their terms were linked in displayed index strings. Here are some examples, all from Farradane (1980b):

    chemistry /0 encyclopedia.

An encyclopedia of chemistry. The relationship between "chemistry" and "encyclopedia" is nothing more than concurrence /0 — "a happening together in time or place" (Webster's 1966, p. 304).

    tortoise /+ speed
        /)
    hare /+ speed /= 40 km/hr

The dimensional /+ relator is used for "position in space or time, temporary states, and certain temporary properties" (Farradane 1980b, p. 271), including speed. The distinctness /) relator can be used for a comparison between two distinct phenomena or entities. Here we have a comparison /) of the speed of a tortoise with the speed of a hare, which equals /= 40 kilometers per hour.

    man /* walking; bird /* migrating

These two separate strings illustrate the use of the self-activity /* relator to indicate intransitive actions associated with the entity performing the action.

    gift /- receiving /; child

The action /- relator is used between an action (e.g., receiving) and the object of the action. The agent or tool of an action can be expressed with the association /; relator. Thus we have a gift being received by a child.

Chapter 12. Syntax (Section 12.2.3)

The same relators can be used for "a storm causes damage to a house" (Farradane 1980b, p. 315):

```
house /- damaging /; storm
```

```
water    /-    purifying
   /;          /(
impurities /- precipitating
```

Here we have the purification of water (action /-) by means of precipitating impurities (another action /-). The impurities are associated /; with water. Impurities are not an intrinsic property or part of water, so the appurtenance /(relator would be inappropriate (Farradane 1980b, p. 271-272). But precipitating is a kind of purification, so the appurtenance /(relator is used to indicate the genus-species relationship between them.

```
information /- gathering    |elites     |
                    /; |               | /; behavior
               chemistry   |non-elites |    /-
                                         measuring
                                            /;
                                   sociometric techniques
```

Here we have the gathering of information (action /-) by elites and non-elites (association /; indicating agent). "The elites and non-elites are in the field of (associated with) chemistry" (Farradane 1980b, p. 316), so they are also linked to chemistry with the association /; relator. The behavior associated with /; these elites and non-elites is measured (action /-) by means of sociometric techniques (association /;). The self-activity /* relator is not used to connect the elites and non-elites with their behavior because it is not currently going on, but is past behavior, so has become an association /; rather than self-activity /* (Farradane 1980b, p. 273).

One last example:

```
                              information theory
documents                            /:
    /)    /; information /- measuring /; measures
surrogates
```

This string represents the use of measures derived from information theory (functional dependence /: for derivation or cause and effect) for measuring (association /; for tool or means) information (object of action /-) which is associated /; with surrogates of documents. The surrogates are a substitute for, and therefore distinct /) from, documents (Farradane 1980b, p. 317).

• use of relational syntax : 188

Farradane's relational indexing never became popular, perhaps because it proved to be too difficult for indexers and for searchers to categorize particular relationships by means of his relational matrix. Indexing theorists interested in defining relationships among concepts moved on, for the most part, to newer faceted syntax system such as PRECIS.

• display of relational syntax : 189

Although relational syntax could be used in simple linear strings for headings to be displayed in alphabetical indexes, it was really intended for computer searches in which not only terms are matched but also relationships between them. Thus it is an example of precoordinate syntax designed for postcoordinate searching techniques. Most syntax designed for postcoordinate term matching search techniques will be addressed in section 12.3.

12.2.3.1. Syntagmatic Relationships.

In the 1990s, Rebecca Green renewed calls for more careful and detailed specification of roles and relationships among terms in indexing for message content description (1995a, 1995b, 1995c, 1997; Green & Bean 1995). She contends that IR databases cannot be fully effective without some method for systematically incorporating "syntagmatic" relationships among concepts, or the terms that represent those concepts, in the description of messages or texts.

• definition of syntagmatic relationships : 190

Syntagmatic relationships are those that exist because of circumstance or context. They exist because persons or circumstances bring two or more phenomena together to play special or unusual roles, in contrast to "paradigmatic roles and relationships," which are constant and exist because of the nature of phenomena and the concepts that describe them. For example, the parental/child relationship between a mother and a son is part of the definition of the role of "mother" and the role of "son." Similarly, the teacher/student relationship is a constant part of the meaning of the role "instructor," professor" or "teacher" on the one hand and the role "pupil" or "student" on the other.

• syntagmatic relationships and thematic roles : 191

Thus syntagmatic relationships and roles are those that are special or unusual, not constant or part of the meaning of a concept or term. The relationship between two or more concepts (or the terms that represent them) is based on the roles that each concept plays in a message. As a way of defining and summarizing these roles, Green (1995a) presents a "a default relationship inventory" based on Filmore's (1971) table of thematic roles in human language communication. Here is that list, slightly modified, with an explanation and example for each case of role. The examples are Green's:

Case (type of role)	Use and Example
Agent	Instigator of an event. E.g., *Sadie* asked the young man to the dance.
Counter-agent	Force or resistance against which an action is carried out. E.g., They sailed against the *wind*.
Instrument	Stimulus or immediate physical cause of an event. E.g., He cut his finger with a *knife*.
Experiencer	Entity that experiences or undergoes the effect of an action. E.g., The dancing pleased the *king*.
Object; Patient	Entity that moves or changes or whose position or existence is being considered. E.g., The *door* was shut.

Chapter 12. Syntax (Section 12.2.4)

```
Result                      Entity that comes into existence as
                            a result of an action. E.g., The
                            workman dug a *hole*.

Source                      Place from which something moves.
                            E.g., They drove from *Tel Aviv* to
                            Jerusalem.

Goal                        Place toward which something moves.
                            E.g., The drive from Tel Aviv to
                            *Jerusalem*.
```

This list could be augmented by roles identified in faceted indexing, such as action and attribute (see 12.2.2.2).

• frame-based structures in indexing : 192

Green points out that simple Boolean combination indicates nothing more than the simple co-occurrence of two or more concepts. Similarly, links among terms can be added to indicate participants in particular situations, but links also do not indicate particular roles or relationships. Role indicators can be used to indicate the roles of particular concepts and the terms that represent them, as in faceted indexing. But Green advocates the use of comprehensive frames in which all roles and all participants would be identified at once. She gives the example of commercial exchanges, in which the buyer, the seller, the goods, and money need to be specified. She concludes (1995a, p. 335): "There is little question that document retrieval functions (e.g., indexing, searching) would be significantly complicated by the use of a frame-based structure for representing syntagmatic relationships," but "the benefits will come to overshadow the costs."

12.2.4. Classification Syntax.

• classified displays versus alphabetical displays : 193

The varieties of syntax surveyed thus far (with the possible exception of relational syntax) have all been designed for alphabetical (or alphanumeric) displays of index headings. The only fundamental difference between indexes based on these types of index heading syntax versus indexes based on classification systems is the arrangement of headings (Anderson 1988). Classification systems arrange headings for display not in alphabetical order but in some kind of relational order. Actually, some classification systems, such as the *Library of Congress classification* (Library of Congress 2004), make frequent use of alphabetical displays, but these displays are placed within a larger framework of relational display. Relational arrangements are designed to bring together closely related topics. Here we shall summarize the syntax used in classification systems. Classification systems as methods for arranging displayed indexes will be treated in much more detail in chapter 17.

• classified displays on the world-wide web; classification systems for searching : 194

There has been an explosion of interest in classification as a means for displaying the content of large websites or of listings of websites on the world-wide web (Dodd 1996). This renaissance of classification comes after nearly a century of minimal interest in classification for information retrieval. For the century or so preceding the world-wide web, classification in the context of information retrieval was used largely for marking and parking library materials on shelves or for arranging citations and abstracts in indexing and abstracting services (A&I services). Displayed classifications could be used for browsing in printed A&I services, such as the *MLA international bibliography, Chemical abstracts, Psychological abstracts,* and similar disciplinary A&I

services, because these classifications were relatively shallow and brief. The overall classification system could be presented in a few printed pages, scannable by searchers and comprehended with relative ease. In contrast, full library classification systems, such as the *Dewey decimal classification* (Dewey 1996) in four volumes and the *Library of Congress classification* (Library of Congress 2004) in more than 30 volumes, were very difficult to scan at the detailed level of actual application.

- **display of classification systems in hypertext : 195**

The availability of hypertext on the world-wide web has drastically changed the browsability of complex classification systems. Whereas in the print medium with its locked-in-place linear presentation, searchers can quickly get bogged down in detail within particular classes before moving on to the next more general class, hypertext is able to present classification displays in stages, level by level, so that users are able to choose only those paths through the classification system that interest them. At the highest level of a classification system, it is possible to obtain an overview of an entire collection or IR database, then to pursue any particular class into greater and greater detail. This strong capability for both overview and zooming in to greater detail has made classification systems extremely useful and popular in dealing with the masses of documentary units on the world-wide web and in large IR databases.

- **classification captions versus index headings : 196**

Headings in classification systems are usually called "captions," but they are essentially the same thing as headings, or strings of terms, in alphabetical subject headings or string indexing systems. Older classification systems, such as the *Library of Congress classification* and the *Dewey decimal classification* construct complex captions in much the same way as subject heading syntax. Indeed, Melvil Dewey published the first edition of his classification system in 1876, the very same year that Charles Ammi Cutter (1876) laid down the fundamental principles that are still followed in subject heading syntax. Newer classification schemes, often called "faceted classifications," are much more like the more modern faceted indexing systems, discussed in section 12.2.2.2.

- **syntax in *Dewey decimal classification* : 197**

The process of constructing a complex heading or caption in the *Dewey Decimal classification* (DDC) is very similar to the process of constructing a complex heading in *Library of Congress subject headings* (LCSH). First, an appropriate main heading is sought. In LCSH, these headings are in the main list of headings (the large red volumes of the printed list); in DDC these captions are in volumes 2 and 3 of the printed classification. In both systems, some main headings will have one or more subdivisions (or subclasses) built into the main list, and the cataloger or classifier will select the most appropriate set of main heading plus subdivisions available.

- **198**

Next, in both LCSH and DDC, the cataloger and classifier will add further subdivisions to more fully describe the topic and form of the documentary unit. In DDC, there are often instructions to add elements to the main heading from headings (captions) found elsewhere in the main list, such as the name of a particular industry when the main heading describes women workers in the context of labor economics. Sometimes instructions will tell the classifier to add a subheading from a special table, such as a listing of ethnic and national groups or of geographic names. In addition, the DDC classifier may freely apply a "standard subdivision" to any heading chosen from the main list or constructed according to instructions in the main list. Similarly, in LCSH, the cataloger can choose from a long list of "free-floating subdivisions" and add them to main headings (plus any subdivisions) found in the main list of headings.

Chapter 12. Syntax (Section 12.2.4)

• 199

Thus, the headings or captions in both LCSH and DDC are built up, one at a time, term by term or class caption by class caption, by choosing main headings (or captions) and enumerated subdivisions (or subclasses) from a main list, then adding additional subdivisions according to fairly complex rules that have accumulated over the past century. The only fundamental difference between these two systems is how the resulting headings or captions are arranged for display.

• analytico-synthetic classification syntax : 200

Both LCSH and DDC are highly synthetic, in the sense that headings or captions are built up with a variety of elements from various lists. These systems are often called "analytico-synthetic" systems, because first the topic is analyzed into its component elements, then a comprehensive heading or caption is synthesized (placed together) from corresponding headings or captions.

• syntax in *Library of Congress classification* : 201

The *Library of Congress classification* (LCC) is modeled after a more ancient pattern, in which there is much less synthesis and much more enumeration of pre-coordinated captions in its main schedules. Hence LCC is often called an enumerative classification. This is why it takes more than 30 volumes to present the full *Library of Congress classification*, whereas the much more synthetic *Dewey decimal classification* needs only four volumes. The DDC can be just as detailed as LCC in many areas, but its highly synthetic nature means that the same topics or aspects of topics are not enumerated over and over again as they frequently are in LCC. Classification systems prior to DDC tended to be much more enumerative than analytico-synthetic.

• syntax in faceted classifications : 202

Modern faceted classifications tend to be completely analytico-synthetic (Vickery 1966). Whereas in DDC, many captions are precoordinated in the main schedules, fully faceted classifications have no precoordinated captions. Instead, they consist of facets, from which terms are taken and combined in an agreed-upon order, called the "citation order of facets."

• syntax in *MLA international bibliography* classification : 203

The Modern Language Association of America uses such a fully faceted classification system for arranging the main entries (citations plus notes) in the printed *MLA international bibliography* (Modern Language Association of America 1999). This classification is based on the very same facets used in the MLA's CIFT indexing system (section 12.2.2.2; Anderson 1979, 1980; Modern Language Association of America 1997). To illustrate this classification, here are the primary facets used for the classification of documentary units dealing with literature (Modern Language Association America 1999, 1997 ed.):

- specific literatures
- periods
- individuals (real)
- genres
- works

• 204

The citation order of these facets displayed in the printed *MLA international bibliography* is the order listed here. Thus, all documentary units dealing with specific literatures are first given the descriptor (term or heading) for that literature. Those documentary units not dealing with a particular literature are given a "general literature" descriptor. Next, if a particular period is dealt with, the appropriate period descriptor is assigned. If a particular person or writer is dealt with, his or her descriptor is assigned. If a particular genre is dealt with, its descriptor is assigned. And if a particular literary work is dealt with, its descriptor is assigned.

• arrangement of indexes versus classifications : 205

This process is exactly the same as that used in faceted indexing. In fact, at the MLA, the same indexing process results in both alphabetical index displays and classified displays. Descriptors (or terms) are assigned, and their facet or role categories are indicated. The categories determine the order of descriptors within the string of terms, but then these strings (complete headings) are arranged and displayed in very different orders in alphabetical displays as compared to relational classified displays.

• 206

In the alphabetical displays, headings are arranged according to the alphabetical order of the terms in headings, beginning at the left and working character by character to the right. Thus a heading for "homosexuality" (a theme in literature) may be right next to "homography," "homonymy," and "homophone" (linguistic phenomena) and very near "Homer" (the ancient Greek writer). In the relational classified display, these headings will be grouped and displayed according to the facets to which they belong and relate to. "Homosexuality" as a theme in literature will fall under the literatures in which it is treated or under literature in general, if no particular literature is mentioned; "homography," "homonymy," and "homophone" will fall under linguistics as general phenomena, but also under particular languages when these attributes relate to particular languages. "Homer" will fall under ancient Greek literature.

• 207

Thus, in relational classification displays, all headings are first grouped within the facet of the first term before moving on to the next term and its facet. This means that all headings for particular literatures are first grouped together within these literature categories before considering the facets for period, persons, genres, or works.

• classified arrangements of index headings within facets : 208

Within facets, headings may be arranged in alphabetical order, but usually this is the last choice for arrangement in classification schemes, used only when no "relational" order can be agreed upon. Much more common arrangements are hierarchical (with broad topics coming before narrow topics), chronological, or geographical (grouping by continent or region).

• hierarchical arrangement in classification : 209

An example of hierarchical arrangement within a facet is the DDC arrangement of languages (Dewey 1876-1996, 1996 ed. v. 1, table 6). First languages are arranged by language family, based on current understandings from the field of historical linguistics. These families include Indo-European, Hamito-Semitic (including Arabic and Hebrew), Altaic (including Hungarian), Uralic (including Turkish), and many others. There is no "natural" order among these families. Perhaps linguists could suggest their relative ages and they could be arranged in the chronological order of their earliest development, or they could be arranged in alphabetical order, but DDC chooses to arrange them according to potential interest among its users. Most people in the United States speak and study Indo-European languages, so that family is placed first, followed by Hamito-Semitic, Altaic, and Uralic. (Within the DDC, many languages are also arranged by place of origin rather than by, or in addition to, language family.)

Chapter 12. Syntax (Section 12.2.4)

• 210

Within Indo-European language, the same criteria of potential interest is used, so that among the Indo-European language families, Germanic comes first, and within the Germanic language, West Germanic (English, Dutch, German) comes before North Germanic (the Scandinavian languages) and East Germanic, because the English language belongs to West German. Next come the Romance languages (French, Spanish, Portuguese, etc.), Latin, Greek, the Slavic languages, and finally the Indo-European families of potentially less interest. Greek gets a rather prominent place, ahead of Russian, because of traditional interest in the classics, in contrast to modern Greek! We will deal with these arrangement issues in more detail in chapter 17 (Arrangement of displayed indexes).

• facet arrangement in *MLA international bibliography* classification : 211

As a final example of the arrangement of classification headings, here are a few headings selected from the classified section of the *MLA international bibliography* (Modern Language Association of America 1999, 1997 ed.):

```
British and Irish literatures
    English literature
        [periods]
        1800-1899
        1900-1999
            [persons]
            Ford, Ford Madox (1873-1939)
            Forster, E. M. (1879-1970)
                [genres]
                Novel
                    [works]
                    Howards End (1910)
                    A Passage to India ((1924)
                        [citation and notes]
    Irish literature
    Scottish literature
    Welsh literature
Breton literature
Commonwealth literature
    Australian literature
    Canadian literature
    New Zealand literature
English Caribbean literature
    Antiguan literature
    Barbadian literature
    Dominica (W.I.) literature
    Grenadian literature
    Guyanese literature
    Jamaican literature
    St. Kitts literature
    St. Lucian literature
    Trinidad and Tobago literature
American literature
```

Chapter 12. Syntax (Section 12.2.4)

```
European literature
    Central European literature
        French literature
            [periods]
            1800-1899
            1900-1999
                [persons]
                Gide, André (1869-1951)
                    [genres]
                    Novel
                        [works]
                        L'Immoraliste (1902)
                            [citation and notes]
        German literature
        Netherlandic literature
        Czech literature
        Slovak literature
        Hungarian literature
        Polish literature
    Northern European literature
    Southern European literature
    Latin American literature
```

• role of notation in classification systems : 212

Some classification schemes use a system of notation to represent headings or captions. Such notations are used in all library classifications to facilitate the arrangement of documents on shelves. The notation, whether consisting only of numerals (as in DDC) or in mixed alphanumeric characters (as in LCC) are brief and succinct representations of assigned captions. They are designed to preserve the preferred order of classification categories and captions, and they can serve as part of "call number" addresses for locating particular documents on shelves.

• 213

It is important to understand that classifications are not arranged according to their notation. Notations are assigned after the preferred order is determined. Notations are used to preserve the preferred order, not to create it. The preferred order is based on relationships among facets (and the preferred citation order of facets), and within facets, by the preferred ordering of headings within the facet, whether hierarchical (broad before narrow), chronological, geographical, or alphabetical.

• 214

Notations are not needed when classification systems are used in fixed media, where classified items can't fall out of order. Thus it is possible to use library classifications, such as the DDC, in printed bibliographies or on websites without the accompanying notation.

• syntax and facet indicators in *Universal decimal classification* : 215

The *Universal decimal classification* (UDC) is an important classification system, widely used for indexing and for the arrangement of documents in Europe and other parts of the world (British Standards Institution 1963; Gilchrist and Strachan 1990). It began as an expansion of the *Dewey decimal classification*, but over time it became more fully faceted in its organization, permitting users to freely combine topics from any part of the classification, and also to determine their own preferred citation order of facets. (In contrast, DDC presents a fixed predetermined order of facets in every class or subclass, and topics can be combined from various parts of the main classes only when specific instructions are given to do so.) In general, topic notations from the various facets are separated by the "relation sign" : (colon). When topics in non-

Chapter 12. Syntax (Section 12.2.4.1)

contiguous classes are simply treated together in a documentary unit (as opposed to being in a relationship), the somewhat weaker connective sign + can be used, or the/(slash) can be used to indicate a series of consecutive notations (from the first number to the last). In addition, in order to identify certain facets, the UDC has developed special facet codes. They include (British Standards Institution 1961, p. 10-25):

```
=  ...          for language
(0 ...)         for form of presentation
(1 ...) to (9 ...)   for place
(= ...)         for race and nationality (ethnicity)
"..."           for time
.00 ...         for point of view
```

• examples of notation in *Universal decimal classification* : 216

Using these notational symbols, topic notations such as the following examples can be built up (Bose 1990, p. 127-128):

```
061.3(41-44):323.118(680)"1968"
```

This notation represents the conference 061.3 of the British Commonwealth (41-44) in relation to : apartheid 323.118 in South Africa (680) in 1968 "1968".

```
631.586.001.5(540)"1971/1981"(047.1)
```

This notation represents dry farming 631.586 from the point of view of research .001.5 in India (540) covering 1971-1981 "1971/1981" in the form of progress reports or reviews (047.1).

notational symbols in *Universal decimal classification* compared to relational syntax : 217

These facet codes in UDC can be compared to the notational symbols used by Farradane in his relational syntax to indicate particular relationships between terms (see section 12.2.3).

12.2.4.1. Chain Syntax.

• definition of chain syntax : 218

Chain indexing is based on a syntactic technique (chain syntax) to create alphabetical index headings from classification headings (captions) that have been arranged in a non-alphabetical relational classified order. (As we have seen, the criteria used to create a classified arrangement may expressed by a preferred citation order of facets and within facets, hierarchies or chronologies or geographic groupings, etc.)

• alphabetical indexes for classified arrangements : 219

The advantage of relational classified arrangements is that related headings are close together (zebras may be located near antelopes because both are mammals, for example). The disadvantage of relational classified arrangements is that unless the user knows the logic of the arrangement, particular headings may be hard to locate. Therefore, every relational classified arrangement needs to have an alphabetical index to provide direct alphanumeric access to headings, with links to their location in the relational classified arrangement.

• creation of chain indexes from classified arrangements : 220

Chain syntax is a method of converting a relational classified arrangement of headings to an alphabetical one. The indexing itself has already been done, and documents have already been associated with headings. Chain syntax is used to produce a secondary alphabetical index to the primary relational classified index, rather than an index to the original documents directly.

• examples of chain indexes : 221

Consider the following simple example, based on the *Dewey decimal classification*. First we have headings (captions) arranged in classified order, beginning with broad disciplinary area (the social sciences), followed by a particular discipline (economics). Under economics we have a general operation of concern to economists (public finance), followed by a more particular operation (taxation). To find entries under taxation, the user would have to find the social sciences, locate economics among all the social sciences, find public finance among all the operations of concern to economists, and within public finance, find taxation. Our example is unrealistic because none of the other social sciences are listed, and under economics, only public finance is listed. In the real world of the *Dewey decimal classification*, the classified array would typically be much much fuller. (See more comprehensive examples in section 17.3.1.)

```
300     social sciences
330         economics
336             public finance
336.2               taxation
```

• 222

To create the chain index, we create chains of caption terms for each heading, followed by the class notation, which will serve as the locator to lead back to the entry we want. In each of these chains, we include every preceding caption term to which our particular caption term is subordinate. The order of these caption terms is the reverse of their order in the classification schedule. For this example, we come up with:

```
social sciences. 300
economics. social sciences. 330
public finance. economics. social sciences. 336
taxation. public finance. economics. social sciences. 336.2
```

• 223

These new headings can stand as they are, or they can be edited to remove redundant terms. For example, if we agree that just about everyone knows that economics is a social science, then we might remove the term "social science" following "economics" in each chain. We would then have:

```
social sciences. 300
economics. 330
public finance. economics. 336
taxation. public finance. economics. 336.2
```

• 224

These headings would be sorted in alphabetical order and would be merged with the thousands of other headings created for the chain index. Now, someone interested in taxation could go to the alphabetical chain index, look directly under "taxation," and find the locator "336.2." This locator would take them to the place in the classified index where the full entries for documents on taxation are listed.

12.2.5. Natural Language Syntax.

• natural language text as source for index headings : 225

In most of the syntax systems we have discussed thus far, human indexers select terms or create (or at least encode) statements based on their analysis of the meaning, purpose, features, and content of a documentary unit. In contrast, natural language syntax is applied to statements,

Chapter 12. Syntax (Section 12.2.5)

or segments of text, that already exist. Most commonly, it is applied to titles of documents. (Among the string syntax systems, ad hoc string syntax, such as NEPHIS, can be applied to natural language text or titles, but frequently, it is used to encode statements created by indexers.)

• **document titles as basis for index headings : 226**

Some might argue that titles of documents do not consist of natural language, because titles are created according to special rules for the special purpose of characterizing a document, or at least calling attention to it. But for our purposes, titles are not created for the specific purpose of creating index headings, and therefore we can consider them a variety of natural language.

• **effectiveness of natural language syntax : 227**

How effective are indexes based on manipulation of natural language segments? The ultimate answer requires sophisticated testing of actual retrieval successes and failures and the assessment of satisfaction of real users using real indexes to resolve real problems or needs. But short of that, we know that such indexes are widely used. Prominent and profitable examples are the many publications (citations indexes, current contents publications, etc.) of the Institute for Scientific Information (1961-2004, 1969-2004, 1976-2004). Their indexes use permuted syntax, which we will discuss in the next section, but they are based, for the most part, on the titles of documents.

• **natural language syntax in digital libraries : 228**

Natural language syntax has been used as well to create browsable displayed indexes in modern digital libraries. A important example is the "Keyphind" phrase browser used in the New Zealand Digital Library (section 8.3.8).

• **effectiveness of natural language syntax : 229**

Most would agree that the effectiveness of a displayed index depends primarily on three elements: (1) The quality of the complete index heading (including all terms or subheadings) as a representation of the content, meaning, purpose, and/or features of a documentary unit; (2) the adequacy of the access provided to this statement and its collocation with related entries; and (3) the quality of the cross-references that link alternative vocabulary to the access terms used in the entry headings and that link these heading terms with other terms that are related hierarchically or in other ways.

• **criteria for evaluation of natural language syntax : 230**

If this be true, then we should evaluate indexes using natural language syntax on the basis of these three essential aspects. The third of these, the links among terms, will be treated later in chapter 13 on vocabulary management. Natural language syntax indexes have traditionally skimped on this requirement for good indexes, but there is no inherent reason that they should lack vocabulary management. Natural language syntax indexes can incorporate good vocabulary management, in the form of cross-reference structure, that is just as adequate as that provided by any other type of index.

• **adequacy of titles as indexable matter : 231**

The first of these requirements, the quality of the statement in the index heading, will obviously depend on the quality of the natural language statement or title. These can be quite good, as brief summaries of the content, purposes, meaning, and features of a documentary unit. They can also be quite worthless for this purpose. Witness the famous article by Vannevar Bush on the future of information retrieval, entitled: "As We May Think" (1945). At the outset we can say that natural language syntax should only be used when titles or other text segments are adequate expressions of a documentary unit's content, purpose, meaning, and/or features. Suffice it to say at this point, that many such statements crafted by human analysts specifically for indexes have proven to be less than adequate, so it is inappropriate to disqualify natural language syntax on grounds that natural language statements are never adequate.

• adequacy of collocation in natural language syntax : 232

The second feature, the adequacy of access and collocation with related entries, is the result of syntactic features, so we shall evaluate the most common examples of natural language syntax on these grounds in the following sections.

• natural language syntax in keyword indexes : 233

The most common examples of natural language syntax are KWIC (Key Word In Context) indexes, KWOC (Key Word Out of Context) indexes, and KWAC (Key Word Alongside Context) indexes.

12.2.5.1. KWIC Indexes.

• definition and example of KWIC indexes : 234

In KWIC (Key Word In Context) indexes, a separate heading is created for every keyword in a text segment. In the index display these keywords are arranged in alphabetical order down the middle of the index column, with the original text that surrounds the keyword preserved on both sides of the keyword. Here are KWIC headings for the title "Encyclopedic Dictionary of Library and Information Science":

```
      science. encyclopedic    DICTIONARY of library and information    [locator]
      information science.     ENCYCLOPEDIC dictionary of library and   [locator]
      tionary of library and   INFORMATION science.  encyclopedic dic-  [locator]
      clopedic dictionary of   LIBRARY and information science.    en-  [locator]
      brary and information    SCIENCE.  encyclopedic dictionary of li- [locator]
```

Each of these headings would be followed by a locator for the documentary unit represented. They would be merged with hundreds or thousands of other entries for other documentary units.

• evaluation of KWIC index syntax : 235

Access is good, because direct access is provided under every important word in the text segment, and access can be further improved with the addition of cross references linking synonymous, equivalent, narrower, possibly broader, and other related terms (as will be discussed later on in chapter 13 on vocabulary management). For example, someone looking for "librarianship" should be referred to entries beginning with "library and information science."

• collocation in KWIC indexes : 236

The effectiveness of collocation, the co-location (or locating together) of closely related headings, gets a middle-level grade. From our example, we see that such collocation is entirely dependent on the word order in the original statement, so that we will have entries on "information science" falling together, but entries on "library science" will be separated from our "library and information science" entries.

• 237

Also, unless keywords are actually changed, synonymous or essentially equivalent key words will not fall together — for example, "lawyer" and "attorney." These collocation problems will apply to all natural language indexes unless a form of vocabulary control is imposed.

• format of KWIC indexes : 238

A chief complaint about KWIC indexes is the unconventional presentation format, with the lead term displayed down the middle of the column, rather than at the left as is customary for displayed indexes. The KWOC and KWAC formats, which are discussed next, were created in response to this complaint.

12.2.5.2. KWOC Indexes.

• definition and example of KWOC indexes : 239

KWOC (Key Word Out of Context) indexes were designed to more closely imitate the traditional index format in which the lead terms appear at the left of headings, rather than down the middle of the column or page. The headings for the encyclopedic dictionary would be:

```
dictionary
    encyclopedic dictionary of library and information science. [locator]
encyclopedic
    encyclopedic dictionary of library and information science. [locator]
information
    encyclopedic dictionary of library and information science. [locator]
library
    encyclopedic dictionary of library and information science. [locator]
science
    encyclopedic dictionary of library and information science. [locator]
```

• word pairs and phrases in KWOC indexes : 240

This format might look nicer than the KWIC format at first glance, but it sacrifices a very important attribute — the preservation of word pairs and longer phrases. In the KWOC format, we lose the direct access to phrases such as "information science" and "library and information science," getting instead the rather meaningless word combinations: "information/ encyclopedic ..." and "library/encyclopedic ... ." This is a serious drawback for this format.

12.2.5.3. KWAC Indexes.

• definition and example of KWAC indexes : 241

KWAC (Key Word Alongside Context) indexes were developed to preserve word pairs and longer phrases, while at the same time presenting the index in a traditional format with the lead term in a heading appearing at the left of a column. The headings for this same encyclopedic dictionary would be:

```
dictionary
    of library and information science. encyclopedic - [locator]
encyclopedic
    dictionary of library and information science. [locator]
information
    science. encyclopedic dictionary of library and - [locator]
library
    and information science. encyclopedic dictionary of - [locator]
science.
    encyclopedic dictionary of library and information - [locator]
```

• word pairs and phrases in KWAC indexes : 242

Here word pairs and phrases beginning with the lead word are preserved for collocation and searching, but words preceding the keyword are no longer contiguous. Compare this "science" heading with the "science" heading in the KWIC index. There, in the KWIC heading, the words immediately to the left of the lead term tell us what kind of science we are dealing with:

```
library and information    SCIENCE. encyclopedic dictionary of ...
```

12.2.6. Permuted Syntax.

• **word pairs in natural language syntax : 243**

One of the problems with the natural language syntax described in the previous section was that some important word combinations could be lost because of the vagaries of natural language style. Thus in our example, the term "library science" got subsumed in the longer phrase "library and information science."

• **244**

In the title "Indexing for information retrieval: the design of indexes for textual databases" the words "design" and "databases" are widely separated, so that a person interested in "database design" or "database indexes" or "information retrieval databases" might not find this document when browsing a displayed natural language syntax index, or finding it might not be as direct as it could be.

• **definition of permuted syntax : 245**

Permuted syntax was developed to avoid these problems by providing direct access to every two-word pair in the original indexing statement (a document title or a statement prepared by an indexer) or a set of index terms, regardless of whether or not these two words appear together in the original statement or set of index terms. Direct access is provided to every keyword (every word not on a stop list), and each access word is linked to every other word that occurs in the same index statement or set of terms.

• **permuted syntax versus natural language syntax : 246**

Permuted syntax is not listed under natural language syntax because it can be used with any set of terms, no matter how they are selected or generated. Thus it can be used with the words found in natural language segments, such as titles, or with descriptors selected from controlled vocabularies by human indexers.

• **multi-word phrases in permuted syntax : 247**

In principle, permuted syntax could be used to create all possible combinations of three or four or more words occurring in index statements or sets of terms, but because the number of unique permuted headings expands very quickly (exponentially) as the number of words in each heading increases, more than two words is not generally practical.

• **example of permuted syntax : 248**

Permuted headings for our continuing example "Encyclopedic dictionary of library and information science" would be:

```
dictionary
    encyclopedic   [locator]
    information    [locator]
    library        [locator]
    science        [locator]
encyclopedic
    dictionary     [locator]
    information    [locator]
    library        [locator]
    science        [locator]
```

```
information
    dictionary      [locator]
    encyclopedic    [locator]
    library         [locator]
    science         [locator]
library
    dictionary      [locator]
    encyclopedic    [locator]
    information     [locator]
    science         [locator]

science
    dictionary      [locator]
    encyclopedic    [locator]
    information     [locator]
    library         [locator]
```

• 249

Each two-word pair would be followed by a locator for the documentary unit represented. As pointed out, the permuted entries permit searches for every two-word combination, such as "library science" and "information science," as well as "science [of] information" and "science [of] library."

• nonsensical index headings in permuted indexes : 250

Automatic permutation also creates nonsensical pairs, such as "encyclopedic science," and also misleading pairs, such as "science information" and "science library," but the proponents of permuted indexes contend that such "false drops" or false combinations do little harm. Users rarely pay any attention to the nonsensical ones. The misleading combinations (like "science library," "science information") are more problematic, but proponents believe that the extra access provided is worth the price of these misleading headings. Indeed, these false drops are no different, in principle, than the false drops created by combinations of unrelated terms in electronic search systems based on word or term matching algorithms.

12.2.7. Ad Hoc Syntax.

• definition of ad hoc syntax : 251

Ad hoc syntax refers to syntax that is developed on a case by case basis (ad hoc = Latin "to this"). It is generally used for one-time indexing projects, as opposed to ongoing indexing operations, such as regularly updated IR databases or indexing and abstracting services. Ongoing projects more commonly use indexing syntax systems that create consistent index heading patterns over time. Ad hoc string syntax (section 12.2.2.3) is a modern version of ad hoc syntax. In ad hoc string syntax, a single string is used to represent each documentary unit and a computer algorithm is used to create multiple index headings from this same string, with each of these headings conveying the same information. In contrast, in traditional ad hoc syntax, each separate heading is created separately, and different ad hoc headings for the same documentary unit often convey different (and incomplete) information.

• examples of ad hoc syntax : 252

The most common example of ad hoc syntax is that used in most back-of-the-book indexes. Indexers who create the detailed indexes to individual books rarely use a pre-established system of syntax, but rather put terms together as they see fit for the particular situation. Because such a

Chapter 12. Syntax (Section 12.2.7)

book index is a one-time operation, there is no need to record practice for the sake of long-term consistency, although good indexers attempt to maintain consistency throughout a single index.

• characteristics of ad hoc syntax : 253

The actual syntax used in a one-time indexing project can resemble any of the syntax patterns already discussed, but the most common pattern is subject heading syntax (section 12.2.1).

• elements of ad hoc syntax : 254

Ad hoc syntax generally consists of a main heading, followed by a subheading or modifier to provide context or qualification for the main heading. To repeat the admonition stressed previously in our discussion of string indexing, no one wants to find a main heading like "computers," with no contextual subheading or modification, followed by tens if not hundreds of undifferentiated locators. Instead, a main heading like "computers" should be modified with appropriate subheadings, such as:

```
computers
    compared with abacus
    for management
    in hospitals
    management of
```

• guidelines for ad hoc syntax: prepositions in ad hoc syntax : 255

The National Information Standards Organization (NISO) *Guidelines for indexes and related information retrieval devices* (Anderson 1997a, p. 22) recommends that prepositions be kept to a minimum in subheadings, so that one would use:

```
clothing
    rationing
```

rather than:

```
clothing
    rationing of
```

The contention is that the first combination of clothing and rationing is perfectly clear, making the "of" at the end of "rationing" redundant.

• 256

But prepositions must be used to clarify relationships if confusion or ambiguity is possible, as in the previous examples of:

```
computers
    for management
```

as opposed to:

```
computers
    management of
```

• cross references in ad hoc syntax : 257

The heading "computers" also needs a cross reference to related headings. Such a cross reference might look like this:

Chapter 12. Syntax (Section 12.2.7)

```
computers   144, 195
==========================================================
| Used for electronic digital calculators. See          |
| also narrower terms microcomputers;                   |
| minicomputers; mainframe computers; IBM PC            |
| computers; Apple Macintosh computers; IBM clone       |
| computers. See also related terms: computer           |
| programming, computer algorithms. See also            |
| broader terms: information technology.                |
==========================================================
    compared with abacus   208
       for management   160
       in hospitals   155
       management of   23
```

• placement of cross references in ad hoc syntax : 258

Cross references, like those displayed just above, need to be set off from the actual entries (headings plus locators) that will lead directly to documentary units. Putting cross references inside a box, or using some other graphic design features to set them apart, should help prevent users from confusing cross references with entry headings. A continuing controversy in indexing is where these cross references should be displayed: immediately after a main heading, as above, or at the very end of the entry array (after all the subheading entries under a main heading), as in:

```
computers   144, 195
       compared with abacus   208
       for management   160
       in hospitals   155
       management of   23
==========================================================
| The term "computers" is used for electronic digital   |
| calculators. See also narrower terms microcomputers;  |
| minicomputers; mainframe computer; IBM PC computers;  |
| Apple Macintosh computers; IBM clone computers. See   |
| also related terms: computer programming, computer    |
| algorithms. See also broader terms: information       |
| technology.                                           |
==========================================================
```

• 259

Displaying cross-reference alternatives to the main heading first, before subheadings, has the advantage of alerting searchers to other, perhaps better, possibilities before they waste time in scanning subheadings under a less-than-appropriate main heading. In some indexes, subheadings can be quite numerous. They can stretch on for a column, a page, a screen full or more. Some index users may never see the cross references to other terms if they are placed at the end of a long list of subheadings.

• explanatory cross references : 260

On the other hand, you don't want users to miss the entries with subheadings because of the cross references. Cross references need to be worded and designed in such a way that they are seen to be advisory or optional, not mandatory! We don't want users to think they are commands to go elsewhere, like the "see" or "use" references that link un-used terms to used terms. Expanded explanation might be helpful, such as "If you are interested in COMPUTERS, you may ALSO want to check the NARROWER TERMS: ..."

In these cross reference examples, the first note is really a kind of scope note, defining the main heading term by showing the user what other terms it is used for. Elsewhere in the index, a "see" or "use" cross reference would lead the user from the "used for" term to the term that is used in its place:

```
electronic digital calculators
     See [or Use]: computers
```

(Cross references are part of vocabulary management, which will be discussed in more detail in chapter 13.)

12.2.7.1. Combining Ad Hoc Syntax with Systematic Syntax.

• examples of ad hoc and systematic syntax in *Psychological abstracts* : 262

In some displayed indexes, the main headings or lead terms in entries are standardized, controlled vocabulary terms, but the subheadings are created on an ad hoc basis freely by indexers with no concern about standardization of terms or syntax. The subject index in *Psychological abstracts* is a good example. The subheadings are designed to provide context for the lead term or main heading. They read like titles, but in the case of *Psychological abstracts*, they conform to a pattern that places primary topics first, followed by features such as research subjects, places, and methodological approaches. These subheadings function like mini-abstracts. Figure 12.3 illustrates entries from *Psychological abstracts*. Note for example the last entry in the left column:

```
Homosexual Parents — Serials
    ...
    psychological well being & family relationships & formation of
        friendships & intimate relationships, 17-35 yr olds raised in
        lesbian families, England, longitudinal study, 36675
```

• combinations of systematic syntax and citations : 263

In other displayed indexes, main headings and subheadings may be standardized but are followed by titles, or complete citations to documents. Titles may in turn be supplemented with explanatory terms or phrases if they are not clear. These titles and explanatory phrases provide additional context for the main and subheadings. This practice is used in H.W. Wilson Company indexes, such as *Readers' guide to periodical literature*. See examples in figure 12.4. Note the expansion of the title in the first entry under "Homosexuality and politics":

```
"Barney Fag" [D. Armey's slur against B. Frank]
```

• examples of placement of cross references : 264

Note also the placement of cross references immediately after main headings, before subheadings, in both *Psychological abstracts* and *Readers' guide*. In *Psychological abstracts*, these cross references are incorporated into the main heading:

```
Homosexuality [See Also Bisexuality, Lesbianism, Male
    Homosexuality] — Serials
```

Chapter 12. Syntax (Section 12.2.7.1)

strict firearms control law & homicide by firearms vs other methods, 1969-85, Canada, 19665
substance abuse & intoxication & homicidal behavior, murderers, 25536
suicide & homicide rates, 15-24 yr olds, test of R. Easterlin & M. Shapiro's cohort hypothesis, 29487
suicide & murder as result of reversal of fortune & exposure of illegal activity, 55 yr old corporate executive, 21659
sunlight duration & atmospheric & geomagnetic activity, rate of violent vs nonviolent suicide & homicide, 1979-87, Belgium, 25500
symptomatology & stress & attitudes toward crime & criminals & coping responses, college students in community victimized by serial killer, 17740
themes & cross cultural similarities in homicides between sexual intimates, adults, 1988-90, Australia, implications for response to regional & ethnic patterns in prevention, 17756
uncharacteristic violence resulting in murder of wife, male 65 yr old with congenital subarachnoid cyst, case report, 2488
unemployment & homicide & suicide rates, 1940-84, 9850
validity of repressed memories & accuracy of their recall through hypnosis, 50 yr old male on trial for murdering his wife, case report, 31455
violence & social support & posttraumatic stress, battered females charged with actual vs attempted homicide of abusive partner vs seeking mental health clinic services, 9941
weather features, criminal homicide rates, 8 yr study, 40834
workplace related injury deaths & homicides, health care workers, 1980-90, US, 30868
Homicide [See Also Genocide, Infanticide]—Books
Homicide in families and other special populations, 33620
Overkill: Mass murder and serial killing exposed, 9955
Homicide [See Also Genocide, Infanticide]—Chapters
Children who survive after one parent has killed the other: A research study, 21809
Homicidal behavior, 29675
Homicide and US regional culture, 33621
Legal self-defense for battered women, 31462
Lethal confrontational violence among young men, 29572
Murderous guilt, 26325
Murderousness in relationship to psychotic breakdown (madness), 43873
Prediction of homicide of and by battered women, 44122
Seeing and thinking sociologically, 36684
Serial murder, 5941
Homing (Animal) [See Animal Homing]
Homographs—Serials
trait anxiety & social desirability, interpretative bias favoring threat on homophone task, medical students, 13427
Homonyms—Serials
subjective familiarity of 40 English homophonic word & name pairs, adults, 24039
understanding of homonyms, 3 yr olds, 32624
Homophobia [See Homosexuality (Attitudes Toward)]
Homosexual Liberation Movement—Serials
parallels between disability politics & gay pride movement, personal as political & force of collective power, 9267
use of collective action frames of women's movement for community responses to violence against gays & lesbians, invisibility of gender in gay & lesbian movements, 13259
Homosexual Parents—Serials
best interest & judicial discrimination in child custody law, homosexual parents, Canada, 3907
division of labor & relationship satisfaction & child's psychosocial adjustment, lesbian couples with 4-9 yr olds, 17297
homophobia vs sex & sexual orientation of parent, reactions to child custody judgment, college students, Canada, 28930
parenting issues & mediation as alternative to courts in adoption & child custody, gay couples, 27524
parents' relationship quality & parenting skills & child's cognitive functioning & behavioral adjustment, lesbian vs heterosexual parents & their 3-9 yr olds, 17278
psychological well being & family relationships & formation of friendships & intimate relationships, 17-35 yr olds raised in lesbian families, England, longitudinal study, 36675

Homosexuality [See Also Bisexuality, Lesbianism, Male Homosexuality]—Serials
age at seroconversion & incidence of & progression toward AIDS, HIV infected heterosexual vs bisexual or homosexual adults, France, 21959
biblical perspectives on homosexuality, 5222
biological perspective on development & psychopathology of sexual orientation, research review, 29015
brief counseling for gay & lesbian adjustment issues, 2610
choice RT task with interference of sexually explicit vs neutral stimuli, assessment of sexual preferences, heterosexual vs homosexual male vs female adults, 24952
demographic & biographical & disorder characteristics & problems, disabled 19-29 yr olds with homosexual orientation, Poland, 36840
developmental considerations in & obstacles to provision of child welfare services, gay & lesbian youths, 10968
evidence for & Christian assessment of biological basis of homosexuality, 43594
fixation & regression in psychoanalytic theory of homosexuality, 17277
food related attitudes, risk for development of eating disorders, heterosexual males vs females vs lesbians vs gay males, 33677
heterosexual homosexual distinction as inhibition to diversity of sexual experiences & limitation to totality of personhood, 32917
history of US military policy to exclude homosexual soldiers, 19555
homosexuality, research review, 17279
Hurdles activity & role playing in homosexuality education, attitudes & beliefs about coming out, college students & professional personnel, 21156
issues & problems & social responsibility in cross cultural anthropological research on same sex eroticism & sexual intolerance, 5226
issues in homosexual orientation, commentary, 17270
issues of gay or lesbian or bisexual identity development & work environment heterosexism in career counseling, 7708
legal case characteristics & sentencing, homosexual vs heterosexual child molesters, 35375
median age of death from AIDS vs non-AIDS causes, homosexual vs heterosexual males vs females, 1858-1993, review of obituaries & other sources, 24941
melancholic identification & formation of gender character & bodily ego, commentary on conference presentation, 33116
melancholic identification & formation of gender character of ego & grief over loss of homosexual attachments, conference presentation, 33104
melancholic identification & formation of gender characters & bodily ego & grief over loss of homosexual attachments, reply to commentary on conference presentation, 33103
MMPI & California Psychological Inventory profiles & selection rates & job performance, gay & lesbian vs heterosexual law enforcement applicants, 11810
moral significance & human meaning of homosex, 17295
nature of being in closet & coming out & practice of outing, homosexuals, 17273
partner age preferences in newspaper personal advertisements, heterosexual vs homosexual males vs females, 43635
path analysis of standard behavioral & biological theories of homosexuality etiology, 17305
perceived emotional & tangible support for entry into treatment centers, 20-68 yr old homosexual vs heterosexual alcoholic African American females, 14955
perceived physical attractiveness of males vs females depicted as homosexual vs heterosexual, nonhomophobic male vs female college students, 5232
prevalence of homosexuality based on sexual behavior & attraction, 16-50 yr olds, US & UK & France, 40295
prevalence of symptoms of homophobia, implications for rehabilitation counselors, 3361
privacy & ethics issues in outing, homosexuals, 17292
psychodynamic perspective on biological & genetic factors in homosexuality & alcoholism & obesity, 21331
public discussion of homosexuality, distress & psychosexual functioning, gay & lesbian youths, letter, 28741

Figure 12.3. Index entries from *Psychological abstracts*.
Reprinted by permission of the American Psychological Association, ©1996.

HOMOSEXUALITY—See also—*cont.*
    Lesbianism
    Outing of homosexuals
    Parents of gays
    Press and homosexuality
    United States—Armed Forces—Homosexuals
    United States. Navy—Homosexuals
    Washington (State). National Guard—Homosexuals

Ball gowns and tiaras: what the gay establishment can learn from drag queens. M. Musto. *Utne Reader* p40-2 Ja/F '95
Cloth spirit: remembering loved ones through their wardrobes. J. Green. *Utne Reader* p44-6 S/O '95
Dying of the light [AIDS and homosexuality; cover story] M. Decter. il *National Review* v47 p36-7+ N 27 '95
The fatal mistakes of AIDS education. W. Odets. *Harper's* v290 p13-17 My '95
From baths to worse [gay club scene in Los Angeles] R. D. Foster. il *Los Angeles* v40 p76-81 Ja '95
God and gays in the Republican Party. K. Hetter. il *U.S. News & World Report* v118 p38 My 29 '95
Having my lox and being Pope too. M. Richler. il *Saturday Night* v109 p46 D '94/Ja '95
Human and civil rights for gays and lesbians. V. J. Genovesi. il *America* v172 p15-20 Ap 22 '95
My fiancé says he's gay. S. Forsyth. il *Mademoiselle* v101 p50+ Je '95
Out in the burbs [gay culture] L. M. Markowitz. il *Utne Reader* p22+ Jl/Ag '95
A second wave [increase in AIDS infections] D. Ramos. *The New Republic* v212 p29 Je 5 '95
Virtually normal [interview with A. Sullivan] M. Marvel and I. Sischy. il pors *Interview* v25 p132-5 S '95

    Bibliography
Pride of presence. M. Sanborn. il *Publishers Weekly* v242 p28-30+ Je 19 '95

    Genetic aspects
Bisexual bugs [added DNA changes fruit fly behavior; research by Ward F. Odenwald and Shang-Ding Zhang] J. Travis. il *Science News* v148 p13-14 Jl 1 '95
Gay genes, revisited [research of Dean H. Hamer and Simon LeVay posits that male homosexuality is linked to a gene on the X chromosome] J. Horgan. il *Scientific American* v273 p26 N '95
Is there a 'gay gene'? [research by Dean Hamer on X chromosomes of brothers] T. Watson and J. P. Shapiro. il *U.S. News & World Report* v119 p93-4+ N 13 '95
Nature plus nurture [research on transsexual brains and gay genes] S. Begley. il *Newsweek* v126 p72 N 13 '95
New evidence of a "gay gene" [research by Dean Hamer on X chromosomes in brothers] A. Toufexis. il *Time* v146 p95 N 13 '95
NIH's "gay gene" study questioned [ORI investigation of D. H. Hamer] E. Marshall. por *Science* v268 p1841 Je 30 '95
Search for a gay gene [DNA transplant causes male fruit flies to display homosexual behavior; research by Ward Odenwald and Shang-Ding Zhang] L. Thompson. il *Time* v145 p60-1 Je 12 '95
X chromosome again linked to homosexuality [research by Dean H. Hamer] J. Travis. *Science News* v148 p295 N 4 '95

    History
Friends of Dorothy [D. Dean] H. Als. il pors *The New Yorker* v71 p88-95 Ap 24 '95

    Study and teaching
    See Gay studies

    Periodicals
See Gay periodicals

    Study and teaching
See Gay studies

    Canada
Index on same-sex rights. J. Fisher. il *The Canadian Forum* v73 p48 Ja/F '95

    Great Britain
    History
Obscenity: a celebration [O. Wilde] W. Koestenbaum. il *The New York Times Magazine* p46-7 My 21 '95

    Greece
    History
'An army of lovers': the Sacred Band of Thebes. L. Crompton. bibl il map *History Today* v44 p23-9 N '94

    India
Out of India. J. Seabrook. *Utne Reader* p47-8 Ja/F '95

    Russia (Republic)
Pink dawn. A. Husarska. *The New Republic* v212 p11-12 Ja 2 '95

HOMOSEXUALITY AND CHRISTIANITY
    See also
      Church work with homosexuals
      Gay bishops
      Gay deacons
      Homosexuals Anonymous Fellowship Services
      Ordination of homosexuals
Cheap shots [interview with A. Sullivan] B. Roehr. *The Christian Century* v112 p837-8 S 13-20 '95
Fatigue on the right [Colorado Springs evangelicals' political activism that helped produce anti-gay amendment may have peaked] J. Impoco. il *U.S. News & World Report* v119 p48-9 O 23 '95
The gay movement and aggressive secularism. D. R. Carlin, Jr. *America* v173 p12-16 S 23 '95
How America went gay. C. W. Socarides. *America* v173 p20-2 N 18 '95
Human and civil rights for gays and lesbians. V. J. Genovesi. il *America* v172 p15-20 Ap 22 '95
In defense of gay politics: confessions of a pastoralist. D. Toolan. il *America* v173 p18-21 S 23 '95
Love thy gay neighbor. R. E. Burns. *U.S. Catholic* v60 p2 My '95
Mel White. S. Hollandsworth. il por *Texas Monthly* v23 p123+ S '95
Mind's eye [Catholic League's stance against Gay Pride Parade in New York City and its rhetoric in light of Supreme Court decision against gays in Boston's St. Patrick's Day Parade] D. T. Wackerman. il *America* v173 p5 Jl 15-22 '95
My censorship—and ours [religious groups fight sex ed and homosexuality in Fairfax County, Va. public schools] M. Tax. il *The Nation* v260 p374+ Mr 20 '95
Presbyterians consider same-sex unions. *The Christian Century* v112 p534-5 My 17 '95
Showdown in Des Moines [gay school board member J. Wilson loses re-election bid following opposition by the religious right] A. M. Stan. *Mother Jones* v20 p42 N/D '95
Starting a college gay-studies course [Montana College of Mineral Science and Technology course objected to by fundamentalist Christian minister] H. Gonshak. *The Education Digest* v60 p49-52 Ja '95

    History
Same-sex unions: what Boswell didn't find [cover story] P. L. Reynolds. *The Christian Century* v112 p49-54 Ja 18 '95

HOMOSEXUALITY AND EMPLOYMENT
Sexual orientation showing up in paychecks. N. Folbre. il *Working Woman* v20 p15 Ja '95

HOMOSEXUALITY AND JUDAISM
Sodomy and scripture: a message to Michael Lerner. S. Tucker. *The Humanist* v55 p39-40 Ja/F '95

HOMOSEXUALITY AND MUSIC
    See also
      Gay composers
      Queer punk rock

HOMOSEXUALITY AND POLITICS
    See also
      Gay congressmen
      Gay politicians
      Log Cabin Republicans (Organization)
"Barney Fag" [D. Armey's slur against B. Frank] *The New Republic* v212 p9 F 20 '95
Candace Gingrich. B. Frank. por *Esquire* v124 p52 Ag '95
Cash the check, Bob [R. Dole's rejection of campaign contribution by Log Cabin Republicans] J. Leo. il *U.S. News & World Report* v119 p43 S 18 '95
The contagion of prejudice [Cobb County Coalition formed to protest anti-gay resolution] P. O'Toole. il *Glamour* v93 p160-3+ Jl '95
Contract on gays [Contract with the American Family] G. Rotello. *The Nation* v260 p872-3 Je 19 '95
Disoriented [constitutionality of Colorado's anti-gay rights amendment] J. Rosen. *The New Republic* v213 p24-6 O 23 '95
The gay movement and aggressive secularism. D. R. Carlin, Jr. *America* v173 p12-16 S 23 '95
"Gay rights"—for or against? *Glamour* v92 p92 N '94
Gay rights issues bust out all over [Supreme Court will consider challenge to Colorado's anti-gay constitutional amendment] K. Hetter. il *U.S. News & World Report* v119 p71+ O 2 '95
Gingrich: Newt's gay sister gets out front. M. Isikoff. il por *Newsweek* v125 p24 Mr 13 '95
How America went gay. C. W. Socarides. *America* v173 p20-2 N 18 '95
In defense of gay politics: confessions of a pastoralist. D. Toolan. il *America* v173 p18-21 S 23 '95
Judgment by the press [New York times' treatment of gay rights case in Cincinnati, Ohio] *National Review* v47 p16 Jl 31 '95
Mind's eye [Catholic League's stance against Gay Pride Parade in New York City and its rhetoric in light of Supreme Court decision against gays in Boston's St. Patrick's Day Parade] D. T. Wackerman. il *America* v173 p5 Jl 15-22 '95
My censorship—and ours [religious groups fight sex ed and homosexuality in Fairfax County, Va. public schools] M. Tax. il *The Nation* v260 p374+ Mr 20 '95
No more rights turns [Supreme Court to hear Colorado anti-gay rights case] J. Leo. il *U.S. News & World Report* v119 p34 O 23 '95
With the Lesbian Avengers in Idaho [fighting anti-gay ballot initiative] S. Pursley. il *The Nation* v260 p90+ Ja 23 '95

    Anecdotes, facetiae, satire, etc.
Hypocrites and sepulchers. K. Clinton. il *The Progressive* v59 p35 Jl '95

Figure 12.4. Index entries from *Readers' guide to periodical literature.* Reprinted by permission of the H. W. Wilson Company, © 1995.

12.2.8. Syntactic Cross References.

• necessity for syntactic cross references : 265

In the examples of string indexing described in section 12.2.2, each set of terms — each complete heading — is generally entered under every significant term. But entry under every key term is not the usual pattern for more traditional subject headings and many examples of ad-hoc syntax. For example, the subject heading:

```
United States — History — Civil War, 1861-1865 — Bibliography
```

is not also entered under civil war, bibliography, or history.

• examples of syntactic cross references : 266

Therefore, cross references are needed from these terms to the established heading:

```
History
===========================================================
| See also names of countries, regions, cities,           |
| other places and topics followed by the                 |
| subdivision "— history," e.g., United States —          |
| History; Piano — History.                               |
===========================================================


Civil war
===========================================================
| See also names of countries followed by the             |
| subdivisions "History — Civil war," e.g.,               |
| Spain — History — Civil war; United States              |
| — History — Civil war                                   |
===========================================================
```

• 267

LCSH (Library of Congress 2003, 1999 ed.) uses specific "use" references for civil wars rather than the general see-also reference just illustrated:

```
Civil War, U.S., 1861-1865
    USE
        United States — History — Civil War, 1861-1865
Spanish Civil War and theater
    USE
        Spain — History — Civil war, 1936-1939 — Theater and the war
```

But there is no LCSH cross reference from "Civil war" to the Spanish civil war, or to any other civil wars.

• definitions of syntactic cross references : 268

Such cross references are needed whenever the syntax system does not provide access points under every important term. These cross references may be called "syntactic cross references," because they augment syntactic patterns when the syntax limits the number of access terms.

12.3. Postcoordinate Syntax for Non-Displayed Indexes.

• precoordinate syntax versus postcoordinate syntax : 269

One big difference between the syntax used in displayed indexes and the syntax used with non-displayed indexes is the point (in time) when the syntax is used or implemented. Syntax

Chapter 12. Syntax (Section 12.3)

used for headings in displayed indexes obviously must be implemented before the index is produced and presented for display. Because such syntax is implemented prior to display (and prior to any searching), it is often called "precoordinate" syntax. Terms are "coordinated" prior to ("pre") publication.

• characteristics of non-displayed indexes : 270

In contrast to a displayed index, the searcher rarely sees the complete non-displayed index. In fact such an index to documentary units may not actually exist as a separate entity prior to a search. It can indeed be created "on the fly" based on options and procedures made available to a searcher. These options and procedures must be considered part of the documentary unit indexing system, because without them the index is inaccessible. Search options and procedures make it possible for the searcher to submit terms describing desirable documents, and for these terms to be matched against terms associated with documentary units and/or documentary records.

• use of inverted files for non-displayed indexes : 271

In some systems, searchable terms are copied from of documentary unit records and placed in separate files, sometime called "inverted files," and then search terms are matched by the search algorithm against these files instead of the full, original records. But from the point of view of the user, it doesn't matter. All this is internal to the system and is not seen by the user.

• definition of inverted files : 272

Actually, the traditional term "inverted file" doesn't make much sense. The idea is that the original file of documentary unit records is the "direct file." It may be arranged on the basis of some key criteria, such as principal author, or simply creation date. When descriptors or terms are pulled from records in this "direct file," and then rearranged in some other order, for example, alphabetically by the term or descriptor, with links back to the original documentary record, this new file was called an "inverted file," because the arrangement was different than that of the "direct file." The arrangement was somehow "inverted." (See the more formal definition of "inverted file" in the glossary.)

• definition of postcoordinate syntax : 273

Because users can combine terms at the time of search, after indexing (if any!) has taken place and after the indexing system has been put into place, the syntax for the non-displayed indexes used in such systems is often called "postcoordinate," meaning that term combination or coordination takes place after ("post") the presentation of the database and its searching system.

• postcoordinate syntax used with precoordinate syntax : 274

Although the focus of this section is on postcoordinate syntax, it is possible, and often beneficial, to use postcoordinate syntax techniques to search index headings that have been created using precoordinate syntax, such as subject headings in library online public access catalogs (OPACs) or Medical subject headings (MESH) in medical IR databases. Farradane's relational syntax (section 12.2.3) is an example of precoordinate syntax that was designed primarily for postcoordinate searching.

• links in postcoordinate syntax : 275

Precoordinate headings or strings of terms can help to prevent "false drops" in postcoordinate searching — the retrieval of items based on term associations that don't actually exit. The individual terms are associated with the documentary unit, but not with each other. Lancaster (1991, p. 172) gives the example of a documentary unit dealing with:

```
Middle East ... Political Leaders
Public Opinion, Telephone Surveys, United States, Attitudes ...
United States, Foreign Aid ... [etc.]
```

Chapter 12. Syntax (Section 12.3)

If these sets of terms were linked (precoordinated) in advance and postcoordinate searches are limited to terms within precoordinated sets of terms, or higher weights are given to terms occurring together in such precoordinated sets of terms, then the false drops, or false associations, such as "United States" and "Political Leaders," or "Middle East" and "Public Opinion" could be avoided.

• vocabulary lists versus non-displayed indexes : 276

As noted in section 11.1, many IR databases using postcoordinate syntax do permit users to see lists of terms. It is important to keep in mind that these lists of terms are not indexes to documentary units. They are simply lists of terms that are found in documents or that have been assigned to documents.

• 277

Sometimes these lists of terms are called indexes, which is O.K. What is important to realize is that they are indexes to terms, not indexes to (indicators of) documentary units. The complete index to documentary units (whether displayed or non-displayed) will consist of, or at least permit, the combination of multiple terms in order to describe and point to particular documentary units.

• absence of syntax in vocabulary lists : 278

The reason why this is an important distinction is that for an index to effectively retrieve documents, it must be possible to search for combinations of terms simultaneously. There is no syntax in these lists of single terms. The syntax for combining terms resides in the search system, not in these lists. Therefore, the search system, along with the terms in or assigned to documents, constitutes the information retrieval indexing system.

• definition of non-displayed indexes : 279

To repeat, for non-displayed indexes, the complete indexing system consists of the terms in documentary units or in documentary records and the search system that provides the capability for combining these terms into a search statement. The search statement, consisting of one or more terms, plays the same role in non-displayed indexes as the heading, with its main heading and subheading combinations, plays in a displayed index. Figure 12.5 compares the attributes of displayed and non-displayed documentary unit indexes with simple term indexes.

Chapter 12. Syntax (Section 12.3)

Major components	Displayed documentary unit indexes	Non-displayed documentary unit indexes	Vocabulary lists
1. Terms describing documentary units.	Terms reside in precoordinate index headings.	Terms reside in doc. units, in IR database records, and/or in inverted files of terms.	Terms reside in doc. units, in IR database records, and/or in inverted files of terms.
2. Syntax for combining terms to create doc. unit descriptions.	Syntax is used to combine terms to create index headings prior to the presentation of the index (pre-coordination).	Syntax is used to combine terms to create search statements at the time of the search (post-coordination).	No syntax. Only single terms are displayed for later use in search statements.
3. Vocabulary management for synonymous, equivalent, narrower, broader, & related terms.	Cross references are integrated into the display of the index.	Display of vocabulary information & options should be integrated into the search interface.	Usually none, but vocabulary information can be integrated into the displayed vocabulary list.
4. Links from documentary unit descriptions to documentary units.	Printed locators (numbers or citations) in printed indexes; hypertext links in electronic displayed indexes.	Hypertext links from retrieved records to documentary units.	Hypertext links may be included, but without syntax, so no way to refine search results. Usually terms must be moved to a search window.
5. Search interfaces to enable searchers to use the index.	Index headings in searchable arrays: alphabetical, alphanumeric, relational/classified. In electronic media, often displayed in stages.	Search screens inviting search terms, syntax options, vocabulary options; retrieval screens displaying records.	Term browsers. Ideally searchers can select terms to be added to the non-displayed index search window.

Figure 12.5. Comparison of key attributes of displayed and non-displayed documentary unit indexes versus simple vocabulary lists. The major components are based on the NISO *Guidelines for indexes and related information retrieval devices* (Anderson 1997a, p. 8).

Chapter 12. Syntax (Section 12.3.1)

• **major types of syntax for non-displayed indexes: exact match and best match syntax : 280**

For non-displayed indexes, there are two major approaches for the combination of terms: (1) exact match syntax using boolean operators (AND, OR, NOT) to create combinations on the basis of boolean logic; and (2) best match syntax using terms with weights (indicating importance) to rank documents according to predicted relevance to a query, based on relationships between query terms and index terms generated from documentary units or their records. Exact match (boolean) syntax usually demands an exact match between search terms and document terms. Best match (weighted term) syntax does not require an exact match. It seeks instead the best match among available documents and ranks documents on the basis of the predicted quality of the match.

12.3.1. Exact Match (Boolean) Syntax.

• **definition of exact match syntax : 281**

Exact match syntax for electronic matching of terms in non-displayed indexes requires that terms associated with documentary units match exactly the requirements of the search statement. (Note however that the requirements of the boolean OR operator permit terms linked with OR to be either present or absent.) Only documentary units whose terms match search statements exactly (within the leeway provided by search syntax options such as truncation, proximity ranges, and stemming) are retrieved.

• **history of exact match syntax : 282**

Exact match (boolean) syntax existed prior to the widespread availability of computers. It formed the basis of pre-computer postcoordinate search systems based on optical coincidence (the peek-a-boo system described in section 5.1.3) and the mechanical sorting of edge-notched or punched cards. It was perfectly natural for this exact match (boolean) post-coordinate syntax to be implemented in the first computer-based search systems. The first step in almost all automation efforts typically consists of implementing automatic methods for performing the procedures already in place.

• **283**

Exact match (boolean) syntax quickly became the de facto standard method for combining terms for term-matching searches. It was the first method to receive widespread implementation. Since then many established vendors resisted the investment required for adding, or changing to, alternative "best match" syntactic methods. (Many have resisted the addition of browsable displayed indexes with precoordinate syntax as well!) Similarly, many searchers have resisted exploring "best match" options because they are used to, and comfortable with, the now "traditional" exact match (boolean) approach. Recently, however, the best match approach has become the dominant syntax for term matching searches on the worldwide web. Web search engines typically include exact match (boolean) syntax as an option, but the default option is usually best match (weighted term) syntax.

• **syntactic operators in exact match syntax : 284**

With exact match (boolean) syntax, search terms are combined using the operators AND, OR, and NOT. All terms linked with the AND operator must be present in the documentary unit or its record, or else the documentary unit is rejected. (This, after all, is the very essence of the "exact match" approach!) Terms preceded by NOT must not be present; if they are, the document will be rejected. Terms preceded by the OR operator may be present. If they are, the document will be retrieved, but if they are not, the document will not be rejected.

Chapter 12. Syntax (Section 12.3.1)

• examples of exact match syntax : 285

Here is an example of an exact match (boolean) syntax search statement:

```
[(United States) OR Spain OR Russia OR (Soviet Union) OR USER OR Yugo-
slavia OR Bosnia OR England OR Mexico OR (El Salvador)] AND (civil war)
AND history AND bibliography
```

The use of parentheses indicates that the enclosed words constitute a single term. The use of square brackets indicates that the following AND links all the terms within the brackets as a set. Different systems will use different techniques for these "nesting" purposes.

• impact of exact match syntax : 286

An exact match (boolean) search divides an IR database into two distinct and separate sets. Every document either matches or does not match the search statement.

• absence of ranking in exact match syntax : 287

In a purely exact match (boolean) search, all retrieved documents are equal. There is no way to rank documents on the basis of predicted relevance. This is not a problem if only a few documents are retrieved, but as our IR databases get larger and larger, and as the capability of searching multiple databases simultaneously grows, our retrieved sets will continue to get larger and larger. Will users be willing to comb through hundreds or even thousands of un-ordered documents?

• methods for arrangement of retrieved documentary units : 288

Document sets may, of course, be ordered by various other criteria, such as authors, classification captions and/or notation, dates, or descriptors, but most of these arrangements will not necessarily serve to guide the user to the documents that potentially are the most useful or the most relevant.

• narrowing of searches with exact match syntax : 289

When a exact match (boolean) search retrieves too many documents, the usual solution is to narrow the search by adding more requirements, such as language or publication date. Or additional topic or aspect terms may be added, such as "history" in our example above.

• 290

But these additions can be self-defeating, eliminating the possibly "perfect" document that may be an eye-witness account of a civil war (indexed as "personal narrative" rather than "history") or perhaps the "perfect" document is slightly older than the cut-off date, or maybe it is in Spanish when "only English" has been added to the search requirements.

• disadvantages of exact match syntax : 291

A fundamental problem with exact match (boolean) syntax is that no "maybes" are permitted. When a user searches a displayed index, the user is constantly making judgments about the possible relevance of documentary units represented. Some may seem to be obvious choices, others may be obvious rejects, but others may be "maybes," which can be saved for possible examination later. With exact match (boolean) syntax, the "maybes" are rejected out of hand, and are lost to the searcher.

• meaning of syntactic operators in exact match syntax : 292

Another problem with exact match (boolean) syntax is that untrained users often find boolean operators difficult to use because the meaning of the operators is not exactly the same as the equivalent words in natural language.

Chapter 12. Syntax (Section 12.3.2)

• 293

For example, a user who wants to do a comparative study of a number of civil wars around the world might ask a librarian for documents on "civil wars in, say, the United States and Russia and England and Spain and El Salvador and Nicaragua and Yugoslavia."

• 294

If this search were translated directly into an exact match (boolean) search, using AND in all cases, it is unlikely that any documents would be retrieved, unless there was a document on civil wars in all of these countries. What the user likely has in mind are separate documents on these wars, which could be used as the basis of her/his analysis.

• 295

Despite these problems, sometimes exact match (boolean) is the perfect syntax for a search when the requirements are well and precisely defined, and the searcher wants nothing but documents that share every attribute of the search statement (or at least those attributes combined with AND).

• alternative options for syntax for non-displayed indexes : 296

In line with the growing consensus that users need a wide range of options, designers can include exact match (boolean) syntax as an option, but they can also provide access to best match (weighted term) searching as well.

12.3.2. Best Match (Weighted Term) Syntax.

• definition of best match syntax; vector space and probabilistic models : 297

Best match syntax refers to a growing variety of electronic term-matching methods that apply various techniques for predicting potential relevance of documentary units in response to a search statement and then ranking documentary units according to calculated "relevance" scores. Because the most common approaches are based on some method of assigning weights to terms (search terms, index terms or both), this type of syntax can be called "weighted term syntax." Particular models of best match syntax include the vector space model and the probabilistic model. Term weighting techniques are discussed in more detail in chapter 8 on analysis methods, section 8.3.5.

• language model for best match syntax : 298

A newer model for best match syntax is called the "language model." Instead of trying to predict relevance, it aims to predict index terms from the linguistic text of documentary units. The difference in practice is slight. If terms in a search statement match the predicted index terms, then the documentary unit will be returned to the searcher. The major difference is theoretical (Sparck Jones 2001). Remember the discussion about the differences between the vector space model and the probabilistic model in section 8.3. There too, the differences relate mostly to underlying theoretical models, not to implementation or practice.

• 299

Best match syntax uses term frequency data to indicate potential importance, in an effort to permit electronic term-matching systems to approximate the attributes of natural human searching. Rather than dividing a database or collection into two mutually exclusive sets (retrieved and non-retrieved), the best match method re-orders the documents of the entire database (or of a designated subset of the database) on the basis of predicted relevance (or, in the language model, on the basis of the similarity of predicted index terms to search terms). This re-ordering process resembles the process that searchers use in making selections from a displayed index. Searchers typically make preliminary judgments about entries and documents, rejecting some, but considering others as possibly useful, and perhaps listing them as first choice, second choice, third choice, and so on. Following a search they can examine the first choice first. If that is sufficient, fine; if not, they can move on to the second choice, third choice, and so on.

• ranking in best match syntax : 300

The computer algorithms that rank retrieved documents vary widely and are the focus of a major proportion of information science research. In all likelihood, they will continue to improve.

• examples of best match syntax : 301

Here are some very simple examples of best match syntax to illustrate the basic idea behind this approach.

• 302

If we take the search statement that was illustrated above with exact match (boolean) syntax, we enter the terms simply as a list, without any operators:

```
United States
Spain
Russia
Soviet Union
USSR
Yugoslavia
Bosnia
England
Mexico
El Salvador
civil war
history
bibliography
```

• 303

Weights may be indicated by searchers, by indexers, or by computer algorithm. The simplest approach does not require the searcher to provide any weights. The system would check every documentary unit or document record, and would list first those documentary units or records that have every search term, then those that have all but one, then those that have all but two, and so on. Documentary units in the same rank could be arranged by term frequency data. The searcher can then check documentary units as they are listed, checking as few or as many as needed to satisfy the information need or interest.

• 304

In our example, documents on several of the countries, but not on their civil wars, might be listed before documents on civil wars in one or two of the countries. In other words, at this simple level, a document having the terms:

```
United States
Spain
Russia
Soviet Union
USSR
Yugoslavia
Bosnia
England
Mexico
El Salvador
=============
score = 10
```

would rank ahead of a document having the terms:

```
civil war
United States
Spain
Russia
=============
score = 4
```

because, counting every term as equal, the first document has a score of 10 and the second has a score of only 4.

This second document could be a comparative study of three famous civil wars, and might be just what the user is hoping for.

To improve the ranking procedure, searchers can add weights to search terms in order to indicate the primary importance of the idea "civil war" and the aspects of "history," and "bibliography" as follows, using an arbitrary scale such as 1-10 for weights:

```
Weights for search terms
    1   United States
    1   Spain
    1   Russia
    1   Soviet Union
    1   USSR
    1   Yugoslavia
    1   Bosnia
    1   England
    1   Mexico
    1   El Salvador
    10  civil war
    5   history
    5   bibliography
```

Here are the new scores of our retrieved documents:

```
Document 1, with search term weights
    1   United States
    1   Spain
    1   Russia
    1   Soviet Union
    1   USSR
    1   Yugoslavia
    1   Bosnia
    1   England
    1   Mexico
    1   El Salvador
    ===============
    score = 10

Document 2, with search term weights
    10  civil war
    1   United States
    1   Spain
    1   Russia
    =============
    score = 13
```

Weights can also be attached to terms in documentary units or assigned during the indexing process. Weights can be assigned either by human indexers or by computer algorithms that calculate weights based on term frequencies within documentary units, document records, and the entire IR database. In human indexing, the indexer can indicate the relative importance of terms, so that a document on the Spanish civil war, which includes some comparative discussion of the civil wars in the United States and Russia, might be given the following terms and weights:

```
Document 2, with index term weights
    10  civil war
    10  Spain
    5   Russia
    5   United States
    ==============
    score = 30
```

Now, in a search, the weights of index terms can be combined with the weights of search terms to increase the score for documents that are most likely to be most relevant. Many methods can be used for combining search and index term weights. For our example, we will simply multiply them. The new score for this second document in our current search might then be:

```
Document 2, with combined search and index term weights
    Search                  Index
    weights                 weights
        10  civil war       x 10 from index term weight = 100
        1   Spain           x 10 from index term weight =  10
        1   Russia          x  5 from index term weight =   5
        1   United States   x  5 from index term weight =   5
                                                        ==============
                                                        score = 120
```

Chapter 12. Syntax (Section 12.3.2)

• 310

Before, with only search term weights, the irrelevant document that happened to discuss ten different countries, but not their civil wars, was separated from a highly relevant document on the civil wars in three of the countries by only 3 points. But now, by combining index term weights with the search term weights, the separation is increased to 70 points. (For our example, we will assume that each country term was assigned an indexing weight of 5.)

```
Document 1, with combined search and index term weights
   Search                Index
   weights               weights
      10 civil war       x 0 from index term weight
                             (term NOT assigned!)   =  0
       1 United States   x 5 from index term weight =  5
       1 Spain           x 5 from index term weight =  5
       1 Russia          x 5 from index term weight =  5
       1 Soviet Union    x 5 from index term weight =  5
       1 USSR            x 5 from index term weight =  5
       1 Yugoslavia      x 5 from index term weight =  5
       1 Bosnia          x 5 from index term weight =  5
       1 England         x 5 from index term weight =  5
       1 Mexico          x 5 from index term weight =  5
       1 El Salvador     x 5 from index term weight =  5
                                                      =============
                                              score =  50
```

• 311

In this simple example, we have merely multiplied search term weights and index term weights, but they could be combined in any number of more sophisticated ways. How best to combine search and index term weights is a research topic of extreme interest and competition, especially among designers of the growing numbers of search engines on the worldwide web.

• **automatic methods for term weighting : 312**

Among the methods used for automatically assigning weights to search and index terms are the following (discussed in greater detail in section 8.3 on automatic analysis methods and section 8.3.4 on counting words).

- calculating the frequency of a term in the document — the more often the term occurs, the higher its weight, based on the assumption that frequency of occurrence is related to the importance of the idea represented by the term in the document.

- automatic stemming, removing common endings from words, like the final "s" or "es" in order to increase the weights of frequently occurring terms. If "s" and "es" were removed from every word, then "index" and "indexes" would count as the same term, increasing the weight for "index."

- comparison of document term frequencies to database or collection frequencies. This procedure is based on the idea that a term that appears in every document or in most or many documents in a database or collection is not a very good term for distinguishing among documents for the purpose of ranking documents on the basis of predicted relevance. Such a term might be "libraries" in a database dealing with librarianship.

- checking terms against a thesaurus, so that "attorney" and "lawyer" could increase the weight for a combined "attorney/lawyer" term.

- identifying word pairs or phrases and using these phrases instead of, or in addition, to single words. If single words only are used, the term "civil war" would be split into "civil" and "war." But civil wars are not exactly "civil," in the sense of "civil discourse," so confusion could result.

Lots of terms require two or more words to be meaningful, such as "information science," "venetian blind," etc.

- clustering terms on the basis of frequent co-occurrence, then using these clusters of terms and their combined weights instead of individual terms and their weights. This procedure can help deal with synonyms and equivalent terms, because terms like "lawyer" and "attorney" are likely to belong to the same cluster. It can also help to avoid the confusion of homographs — words which have several different meanings, such as "mercury" — a Roman god, a planet, a mineral element, or an automobile — or to distinguish between wars that are "civil" and dialogue or debate that is "civil," even though both meanings come from the same semantic root (Latin for "citizen"). This is because homographs with different meanings will tend to be members of different clusters.

12.4. Our Examples.
12.4.1. A Book Index.

• ad hoc string syntax for book indexes : 313

Our print-on-paper book index will use ad hoc string syntax based on the NEPHIS system, as described in section 12.2.2.3. The indexer will create a brief statement describing the content of each paragraph and will insert NEPHIS coding symbols. The actual index entries will be generated by a NEPHIS computer program. These entries will be sorted into alphabetical order (again by a computer program) and will then be edited by the human indexer. The human indexer will also insert cross references: See references from un-used synonyms or essentially equivalent terms to used terms and see-also references from used terms to related used terms, including narrower terms and broader terms.

• documentary units and locators for book indexes : 314

Below are sample index statements and the entries that would be generated from them for paragraphs in section 12.2.2.3 on ad hoc string syntax. Because we want the index to serve also in the electronic version of the book, the locators attached to each entry are not the usual page numbers, but paragraph numbers, each preceded by the chapter number 12. The reason for this is that pages are an artifact of the printed book format, which consists of paper leaves bound together along one edge of the leaves. Each side of a leaf constitutes a page. There are no pages in the electronic text. (Of course, they could be artificially imposed, but there is no reason to do this for most texts. The only exception are art books in which the page is formatted in a special artistic manner.) Unless pages are artificially imposed, an index tied to page numbers would be useless in the electronic medium. In contrast, the paragraph is an element of the text itself, so paragraphs travel with the text into whatever medium is used for recording the text.

• pages versus paragraphs as documentary units : 315

This issue of pages versus paragraphs as the appropriate documentary unit for indexing applies not only to electronic media. It also applies to different printings or publications of the very same text in paper media. The same text is often formatted differently, in terms of page breaks, in different printings or publications. An index tied to page numbers in one printing or publication cannot be easily used in a different one, with different pagination. It is for this reason that the NISO *Guidelines for indexes and related information retrieval devices* (Anderson 1997a, p. 26) urges indexers to prefer paragraphs as documentary units to which index entries point, instead of the traditional pages.

Chapter 12. Syntax (Section 12.4.1)

• examples of index statements for ad hoc string syntax : 316

a. Sample index statement for paragraphs in 12.2.2.3.

Note that cross references do not refer to particular paragraphs, but link terms within the index, so they have no associated paragraph number.

```
Paragraph         Coded NEPHIS Index strings
number or
section

sec.
12.2.2.3          ad hoc string syntax <@: sec. 12.2.2.3>

169               @definitions? of <ad hoc string syntax>
170               ad hoc string syntax? compared to <faceted syntax?
                      compared to>
171               ad hoc string syntax? compared to <natural language syntax?
                      compared to>
172               NEPHIS? as example of <ad hoc string syntax>
173               notation? in <NEPHIS>
174               examples? of <NEPHIS coding>
175               examples? of <NEPHIS index headings>
176               @explanation? of <NEPHIS syntax algorithm>
177               @use? of <NEPHIS> for <book indexes>
178-182           [no index strings]
183               objectives? of <string syntax>
184               @impact? of <syntax>? on <size? of <indexes>>

cross             entries? see: <@index entries>
references        Nested Phrase Indexing System? see: <@NEPHIS>
                  syntax? see also: <@ad hoc string syntax; ad hoc syntax; chain
                      syntax; classification syntax; faceted syntax; natural
                      language syntax; permuted syntax; postcoordinate syntax;
                      precoordinate syntax>
```

• examples of index headings based on ad hoc string syntax : 317

b. Unsorted entries generated for each paragraph

These NEPHIS strings were converted by the NEPHIS computer algorithm into the following un-sorted index entries. Later on, they would be merged with similar entries from the rest of the book and sorted into alphabetical order. The human indexer must then do a final edit of the compiled and sorted index to fix any inconsistencies, add additional cross references, and remove redundant entries.

```
For the section:
   ad hoc string syntax : sec. 12.2.2.3

For paragraph 169:
   ad hoc string syntax
       definitions : 12.169

For paragraph 170:
   ad hoc string syntax
       compared to faceted syntax : 12.170
   faceted syntax
       compared to ad hoc string syntax : 12.170
```

Chapter 12. Syntax (Section 12.4.1)

For paragraph 171:
   ad hoc string syntax
      compared to natural language syntax : 12.171
   natural language syntax
      compared to ad hoc string syntax : 12.171

For paragraph 172:
   NEPHIS
      as example of ad hoc string syntax : 12.172
   ad hoc string syntax
      NEPHIS : 12.172

For paragraph 173:
   Notation
      in NEPHIS : 12.173
   NEPHIS
      notation : 12.173

For paragraph 174:
   Examples
      of NEPHIS coding : 12.174
   NEPHIS coding
      examples : 12.174

For paragraph 175:
   Examples
      of NEPHIS index headings : 12.175
   NEPHIS index headings
      examples : 12.175

For paragraph 176:
   NEPHIS syntax algorithm
      explanation : 12.176

For paragraph 177:
   NEPHIS
      use for book indexes : 12.177
   book indexes
      use of NEPHIS: 12.177

For paragraph 183:
   Objectives
      of string syntax : 12.183
   string syntax
      objectives : 12.183

For paragraph 184:
   Syntax
      impact on size of indexes : 12.184
   size
      of indexes. impact of syntax : 12.184
   indexes
      size. impact of syntax : 12.184

Chapter 12. Syntax (Section 12.4.1)

```
Cross references
   entries
         see: index entries
   Nested Phrase Indexing System
         see: NEPHIS
   syntax
         see also: ad hoc string syntax; ad hoc syntax; chain syntax;
            classification syntax; faceted syntax; natural language
            syntax; permuted syntax; postcoordinate syntax; precoordinate
            syntax
```

• examples of index headings based on ad hoc string syntax : 318

c. Sample index entries for paragraphs 12.169-184 sorted into alphabetical order; identical headings and subheadings consolidated (but see-references omitted)..

```
ad hoc string syntax : sec. 12.2.2.3
   compared to faceted syntax : 12.170; natural language syntax :
         12.171
   definitions : 12.169
   NEPHIS : 12.172
book indexes
   use of NEPHIS for : 12.177
examples
   of NEPHIS coding : 12.174; NEPHIS index headings : 12.175
faceted syntax
   compared to ad hoc string syntax : 12.170
indexes
   size. impact of syntax : 12.184
natural language syntax
   compared to ad hoc string syntax : 12.171
NEPHIS
   as example of ad hoc string syntax : 12.172
   notation : 12.173
   use for book indexes : 12.177
NEPHIS coding
   examples : 12.174
NEPHIS index headings
   examples : 12.175
NEPHIS syntax algorithm
   explanation : 12.176
notation
   in NEPHIS : 12.173
objectives
   of string syntax : 12.183
size
   of indexes. impact of syntax : 12.184
string syntax
   objectives : 12.183
syntax (see also: ad hoc string syntax; ad hoc syntax; chain syntax;
      classification syntax; faceted syntax; natural language syntax;
      permuted syntax; postcoordinate syntax; precoordinate syntax)
   impact on size of indexes : 12.184
```

• display of book indexes in electronic media : 319

This same NEPHIS-based index can be made available with an electronic version of our book. The display of this index in electronic media should be quite different, following patterns suggested by Drabenstott and Vizine-Goetz (1994), discussed in section 12.2.1 on subject heading syntax and also in section 17.2 on alphanumeric arrangement in hypertext displays. For electronic browsing, only the main headings will be displayed at first. Subheadings will be displayed only when a particular main heading is chosen.

• syntax for full-text searching of books in electronic media : 320

An electronic edition of our book could also offer two syntactic approaches to full-text searching: best match syntax based on term frequency weighting; and exact match syntax based on boolean operators. The display or presentation of these options will be discussed in chapter 19 on search interfaces.

12.4.2. An Indexing and Abstracting Service.

• 321

Our indexing and abstracting service makes use of automatic indexing for all documents, reserving human intellectual analysis and indexing only for selected documents judged to be the most important based on evidence of high use or high demand.

a. Comprehensive searches.

• comprehensive searches in indexing and abstracting services in electronic media : 322

For comprehensive searches involving all documents, searchers may use automatic indexing, with the choice of exact match (boolean) or best match (weighted term) syntax. A wide range of search options will be available with each type of syntax, such as user-defined stop lists, user-regulated automatic stemming, truncation, term proximity requirements, targeted searching by term location, and clustering.

• user-defined stop lists : 323

The user-defined stop list gives searchers the opportunity to review the default stop list and to delete any terms which they do NOT want eliminated from their searches, either permanently (until changed) or for a single search. Searchers may also add terms to their personal stop list. Stop lists were discussed in section 8.3.3.

• user options for automatic stemming : 324

Users may use or reject automatic stemming, which automatically removes common suffixes from terms. If they opt for stemming, they can review the default algorithms and choose to delete any that they do not wish to use. Common stemming procedures, for example, will delete the final 's,' 'es,' 'ed,' 'er,' 'or,' and 'ing' from all words. Experienced searchers may choose to eliminate particular stemming procedures from their personal search profile. For example, they may want to preserve the 'ing' ending, in order to distinguish "indexing" from "index," "indexes," "indexer," and "indexers." Stemming was discussed in section 8.3.6.

• use of truncation : 325

Truncation is the capability of ad hoc stemming for a particular search, performed by the searcher. A searcher may turn off all automatic stemming, but in a particular search, may use the truncated form "index?," which would match any term beginning with "index," such as "index," "indexing," "indexes," "indexer," and "indexers." (Our vocabulary management thesaurus would enable us to match the variant form "indices" as well. See our discussion of vocabulary management in chapter 13.)

• use of proximity requirements : 326

Term proximity requirements permit a searcher to require that two or more terms be contiguous or close to each other, perhaps in the same sentence or paragraph, or within a certain number of words. For example, we could require "information" and "science" to be contiguous. We can even require that "information" precedes "science," so that we don't retrieve items on "science information."

• targeted searches : 327

Targeted searching allows the searcher to specify the parts of texts or text records to be searched. This is analogous to permitting the searcher to define the indexable matter of the documents in the database. The searcher may require terms to be in document titles, or in abstracts, or in first paragraphs, or last paragraphs, or in lead sentences (the first sentence of any paragraph), or in captions to illustrations or tables. These techniques may help to increase the precision of the search by limiting retrieval to documents where particular terms represent more central themes, as opposed to peripheral comments.

• use of clustering : 328

Once one or more useful documents have been identified, users may ask for clusters of documents using a wide variety of criteria and thresholds, such as vocabulary similarity, assigned index term similarity (for important documents only), bibliographic coupling (similarity in cited references), co-citation (similarity in subsequent citation patterns), authors, affiliations, etc. These techniques were discussed in section 8.3.11.

• comprehensive searches based on automatic indexing in print media : 329

Comprehensive searches in the printed version of our indexing and abstracting service will rely on KWIC indexes based on titles and abstract sentences. KWIC displays can also be made available for browsing in the electronic version of the A&I service. To illustrate this syntax and format, we will use some topic sentences from selected paragraphs. Here are the titles and sentences that we will use in our sample KWIC index:

- An earlier title of our book: *Indexing for Information Retrieval: The Design of Indexes for Textual Databases*
- Section 1.1. Purpose.

Ever since humankind learned how to record messages on portable long-lasting media — clay tablets, papyrus, much later paper and more recently various electronic media — we have devised ways to describe and organize these messages so that they could be found, used and enjoyed later on.

- Section 1.2. Assumptions.

This book assumes that the index designer is confronted with an information retrieval problem and that the designer knows quite a bit about this problem.

- Section 1.3. Terminology.

We begin by defining some key terms that will be used throughout this book.

- Section 1.4. Standards and Codes of Practice.

Since the beginning of librarianship, millennia ago, improvements in practice have come about mainly through the development of new and better standards of practice.

- Section 1.5. Types of IR databases.

The NISO standard identifies more than 30 types of indexes used for information retrieval.

• examples of KWIC indexes in print media : 330

These natural, pre-existing text segments will result in the following index entries, which have been sorted into alphabetical order, first by the keyword in the middle of the page (just to the right of the spatial division between the two columns), then by words to the right of the keyword, then by words to the left of the keyword:

Chapter 12. Syntax (Section 12.4.2)

	Assumptions.	: 001.2
be used throughout this	book.	: 001.3
This	book assumes that the index design	: 001.2
le long-lasting media --	clay tablets, papyrus, much later	: 001.1
Standards and	Codes of Practice.	: 001.4
at the index designer is	confronted with an information ret	: 001.2
Types of IR	Databases.	: 001.5
n of Indexes for Textual	Databases	: 000
We begin by	defining some key terms that will	: 001.3
we have devised ways to	describe and organize these messag	: 001.1
formation Retrieval: The	Design of Indexes for Textual Data	: 000
k assumes that the index	designer is confronted with an inf	: 001.2
val problem and that the	designer knows quite a bit about t	: 001.2
about mainly through the	development of new and better stan	: 001.4
ctronic media -- we have	devised ways to describe and organ	: 001.1
nd more recently various	electronic media -- we have devise	: 001.1
could be found, used and	enjoyed later on.	: 001.1
es so that they could be	found, used and enjoyed later on.	: 001.1
Ever since	humankind learned how to record me	: 001.1
The NISO standard	identifies more than 30 types of i	: 001.5
rianship, millennia ago,	improvements in practice have come	: 001.4
is book assumes that the	index designer is confronted with	: 001.2
Types of	Indexes.	: 001.5
Retrieval: The Design of	Indexes for Textual Databases	: 000
es more than 30 types of	indexes used for information retri	: 001.5
	Indexing for Information Retrieval	: 000
	information retrieval. SEE ALSO: IR	
ypes of indexes used for	information retrieval.	: 001.5
er is confronted with an	information retrieval problem and	: 001.2
Indexing for	Information Retrieval: The Design	: 000
Types of	IR Databases.	: 001.5
e begin by defining some	key terms that will be used throug	: 001.3
em and that the designer	knows quite a bit about this probl	: 001.2
ssages on portable long-	lasting media -- clay tablets, pap	: 001.1
Ever since humankind	learned how to record messages on	: 001.1
Since the beginning of	librarianship, millennia ago, impr	: 001.4
ord messages on portable	long-lasting media -- clay tablets	: 001.1
media.	SEE ALSO particular media	
	such as PAPER, PAPYRUS, CLAY	
	TABLETS, etc.	
on portable long-lasting	media -- clay tablets, papyrus, mu	: 001.1
ently various electronic	media -- we have devised ways to d	: 001.1
nd learned how to record	messages on portable long-lasting	: 001.1
cribe and organize these	messages so that they could be fou	: 001.1
inning of librarianship,	millennia ago, improvements in pra	: 001.4
The	NISO standard identifies more than	: 001.5
sed ways to describe and	organize these messages so that th	: 001.1
ets, papyrus, much later	paper and more recently various el	: 001.1
g media -- clay tablets,	papyrus, much later paper and more	: 001.1
ow to record messages on	portable long-lasting media -- cla	: 001.1
Standards and Codes of	Practice.	: 001.4
and better standards of	practice.	: 001.4
nia ago, improvements in	practice have come about mainly th	: 001.4
s quite a bit about this	problem.	: 001.2
an information retrieval	problem and that the designer know	: 001.2
	Purpose.	: 001.1
humankind learned how to	record messages on portable long-l	: 001.1

Chapter 12. Syntax (Section 12.4.2)

```
xes used for information    retrieval.                          : 001.5
nted with an information    retrieval problem and that the des  : 001.2
Indexing for Information    Retrieval: The Design of Indexes    : 000
                The NISO    standard identifies more than 30 t  : 001.5
                            Standards and Codes of Practice.    : 001.4
opment of new and better    standards of practice.              : 001.4
ng-lasting media -- clay    tablets, papyrus, much later paper  : 001.1
                            Terminology.                        : 001.3
gin by defining some key    terms that will be used throughout  : 001.3
he Design of Indexes for    Textual Databases                   : 000
                            Types of IR Databases.              : 001.5
hat they could be found,    used and enjoyed later on.          : 001.1
media -- we have devised    ways to describe and organize thes  : 001.1
```

b. Selective searches (most important documents only).

• **selective searches in indexing and abstracting services : 331**

Users who choose to limit their searches to those documents judged to be most important may use all of the syntactic options for electronic searches just described for comprehensive searches, or they may browse a displayed alphabetical index or a faceted classification based on descriptors assigned by human indexers. Syntax used for index headings in both the alphabetical and the classified displays will be illustrated here, but the arrangement and display of these indexes will be treated later in chapter 17 on the arrangement of displayed indexes and chapter 19 on the search interface.

• **faceted syntax in indexing and abstracting services : 332**

Headings displayed in both the alphabetical and faceted classified displays use faceted syntax, as described in section 12.2.2.2. The facets are based on the subject scope of the database, which were laid out in section 2.5.2. Here they are again:

Topical facets

- entities or things:
    - persons, both individuals and groups. Groups should be indexed on the basis of important characteristics. Users of services, for example, may be characterized by occupation, objectives, level of experience, gender, age, ethnicity, sexual orientation, etc.
    - institutions and organizations, both particular ones by name, but also types. Libraries, for example, should be indexed according to attribute categories such as public, school, academic, special, etc.
    - artifacts. Chief among these will be texts and documents and the tools and other equipment and structures that make them available — catalogs, indexes, databases, shelving, furniture, buildings, etc.
    - natural objects. These will have less importance in the "artificial" (i.e., human created) world of information. Important exceptions may be various pests that attack documents.
    - abstract entities. In addition to the institutions and organizations, with their own subfacet just above, these include the theories and disciplines that contribute to our understanding of information phenomena.
- constituent materials. The materials from which artifacts are created or of which naturally occurring objects consist are generally of little interest for most of library and information science. A notable exception is the sub-field of conservation and preservation, which is concerned with the long-term viability of document media and the impact of the constituent elements in ink, pa-

per, film, and electronic media. Library architecture is of course concerned with building materials and the components of furniture.

• attributes or properties. All attributes or properties relating to relevant entities, materials, operations, processes, events, places and time periods should be noted.

• operations, processes, events. All operations, processes, and events relating to library and information science should be noted. These include human information behavior, searching, browsing, collection development, document acquisition, cataloging and indexing, reference and information services, management of these operations, conservation and preservation, building and collection maintenance, on-going evaluation, research, and of course IR database design.

• places. Whenever entities or operations, processes and events are associated with a particular place or type of place, it will be noted.

• times. Likewise, whenever entities or operations, processes and events are associated with a particular time or time period, it will be noted.

In addition, for index headings, we add the following facets:

• agents, instrumentalities (note that this is a facet based on the role played by an element in the analysis, rather than on its fundamental type, kind, or nature. Any of the preceding facet elements can play the role of an agent or instrumentality — means, method, cause — of an operation, process, or event).

Feature facets (features of messages, as opposed to topics)

• methodological approaches to topic (when significant attention is focused on methods of studying or treating a topic). These are operations used by the creator of the message to create results. Generally speaking, these methods are not the topic of a message, but the means used to create results, or the message itself. This facet may also be used for points of view or biases.

• unusual text formats or media (e.g., review article, bibliography)

• unusual audience intended (e.g., for children, for language learners)

• indexing worksheet for faceted syntax in indexing and abstracting services : 333

c. indexing worksheet

These facets are represented in the record format for each documentary unit, along with fields for descriptive and evaluative information and an abstract. In turn, this record format (to be discussed later on in chapter 20) will be reflected in the indexing worksheet, which will be available to indexers as a computer screen or on paper, as follows:

```
tag and field name
================================================================
rec\ record number or identifier
ind\ indexer, analyst
aut\ authors & author affiliations
tit\ titles (main, subtitles, etc.)
cit\ citation (this would be broken down into separate fields for every
     bibliographic element, e.g., journal title, volume, issue,
     pages; or edition, place, publisher, date, pagination, size,
     illustrations, ISBN, etc., etc.)
```

Chapter 12. Syntax (Section 12.4.2)

```
not\ non-topical notes about the text (topical information will go into
     abstract)
abs\ abstract
     use\ evidence of use or importance, e.g., citations to reviews,
     citing
works, circulation figures, etc.
com\ user comments — comments on the document contributed by database
     users.

[Indexing facets]

ent\ entities/things
prt\ constituent parts or materials
att\ attributes, properties
opp\ operations, processes, events
agt\ agents, means, causes
pla\ places
tim\ times
app\ approaches to, treatment of topic
frm\ unusual formats, media
aud\ unusual intended audience
loc\ locator
```

• examples of faceted syntax in indexing and abstracting services : 334

d. Examples of indexing

If we imagine the major sections of this book as periodical articles or book chapters that might be included in our indexing and abstracting service database as important documents, we could index them as follows. We include only those indexing fields that are used in each case. It is very rare that all fields will be used for any single message. As with NEPHIS, a "@" may be used to indicate a descriptor that should not become a lead term, e.g., "@types" in the indexing for section 1.5.

```
The book as a whole
   ent\ information retrieval databases.
   opp\ design.
   loc\ 2435.
   Note: The locators for all of these sample entries are hypothetical. In
   an electronic index, the locator is usually not even visible except as
   a hypertext link. In a print database, it could be a number that leads
   to a numbered sequence of citations plus abstracts. The nature and va-
   riety of locators will be discussed in chapter 15. Here, we focus on
   the creation of index headings from descriptors assigned to facets.

Section 1.3. Terminology.
   ent\ information retrieval databases.
   att\ terminology.
   frm\ definitions.
   loc\ 2435.1.3.
   Note that this section consists, predominantly, of definitions, but
   definitions are NOT the topic of the section. Rather, "definitions" de-
   scribes the format of the treatment of the topic.

Section 1.4. Standards and codes of practice.
   ent\ information retrieval databases.
   att\ standards.
   loc\ 2435.1.4.
```

Section 1.5. Types of IR databases.
   ent\ information retrieval databases.
   att\ @types.
   loc\ 2435.1.5.

Section 1.6. IR databases versus other types of databases.
   ent\ databases.
   att\ @types: information retrieval databases; concrete entity
          and event databases.
   opp\ comparison.
   loc\ 2435.1.6.

Part 2. Design principles and options.
   ent\ information retrieval databases.
   opp\ design.
   loc\ 2435.pt.2.

Chapter 2. Subject scope and domain.
   ent\ information retrieval databases.
   att\ subject scope; subject domain.
   opp\ description.
   agt\ facets.
   loc\ 2435.2.

Chapter 3. Documentary scope.
   ent\ information retrieval databases.
   att\ documentary scope.
   loc\ 2435.3.

Chapter 4. Documentary domain.
   ent\ information retrieval databases.
   att\ coverage domain.
   loc\ 2435.4.

Chapter 5. Display media.
   ent\ information retrieval databases.
   att\ display media; codes; symbols.
   loc\ 2435.5.

Chapter 6. Documentary units.
   ent\ information retrieval databases.
   att\ documentary units.
   loc\ 2435.6.

Chapter 7. Indexable matter.
   ent\ information retrieval databases.
   att\ indexable matter.
   loc\ 2435.7.
Chapter 8. Analysis and indexing methods.
   ent\ information retrieval databases.
   prt\ indexes.
   opp\ generation.
   agt\ analysis methods: human indexing; automatic indexing.
   loc\ 2435.8.

Chapter 12. Syntax (Section 12.4.2)

```
Chapter 9. Exhaustivity.
   ent\ information retrieval databases.
   prt\ indexes.
   att\ exhaustivity.
   loc\ 2435.9.

Chapter 10. Specificity.
   ent\ information retrieval databases.
   prt\ indexes: vocabulary.
   att\ specificity.
   loc\ 2435.10.

Chapter 11. Displayed and non-displayed indexes.
   ent\ information retrieval databases.
   prt\ indexes.
   att\ displayed indexes; non-displayed indexes.
   opp\ comparison.
   loc\ 2435.11.
Chapter 12. Syntax.
   ent\ information retrieval databases.
   prt\ indexes.
   att\ syntax: precoordinate syntax; postcoordinate syntax.
   opp\ comparison.
   loc\ 2435.12.
```

• generation of faceted index headings for indexing and abstracting services : 335

e. generation and format of headings

Computer programs will take the indexing illustrated above and generate headings under each term as the main heading or lead term, with all other terms in each record displayed in subheadings to provide context for the lead term.

• format for faceted index headings in indexing and abstracting services : 336

For our index heading format, we will use a three-level style arranged as follows. Terms are placed and arranged in each entry according to their facet category:

```
lead term
    entities. parts. attributes.
        operations. agents. places. times. approaches.
                formats. audience. locator.

NOTE: The deeper indent on the fourth line indicates that this is a
  "wrap-around" or "turn-over" line, a continuation of the 3rd level.
```

When a particular entity or part (but not attribute) is the lead term, it will drop out of the second level. When the lead term is repeated in the string, it is placed in italics.

• display of faceted index headings in indexing and abstracting services : 337

The displayed headings will look like the following examples in print media; in electronic media they will be displayed in stages following patterns suggested by Drabenstott and Vizine-Goetz (1994), discussed in section 12.2.1 on subject heading syntax, and later in more detail in section 17.2. For electronic browsing, only the main headings will be displayed at first. Subheadings will be displayed only when a particular main heading is chosen. Also, in the electronic version, users will have the choice between browsable alphabetical or relational classified displays (section 17.3).

Chapter 12. Syntax (Section 12.4.2)

```
================================================================
```
analysis methods
    information retrieval databases. indexes.
        generation. *analysis methods:* human indexing; automatic
            indexing. 2435.8.
automatic indexing
    information retrieval databases. indexes.
        generation. analysis methods: human indexing; *automatic*
            indexing. 2435.8.
codes
    information retrieval databases. display media;
        codes; symbols. 2435.5.
comparison
    databases. types: information retrieval databases;
        concrete entity and event databases.
      comparison. 2435.1.6.
    information retrieval databases. indexes. displayed
        indexes; non-displayed indexes.
      comparison. 2435.11.
    information retrieval databases. indexes. syntax:
        precoordinate syntax; postcoordinate syntax.
      comparison. 2435.12.
concrete entity and event databases
    databases. types: information retrieval databases;
        concrete entity and event databases.
      comparison. 2435.1.6.
coverage domain
    information retrieval databases. *coverage domain.*
      2435.4.
databases
    types: information retrieval databases; concrete entity
        and event databases.
      comparison. 2435.1.6.
definitions
    information retrieval databases. terminology.
      definitions. 2435.1.3.
description
    information retrieval databases. subject scope; subject domain.
      description. facets. 2435.2.
design
    information retrieval databases.
      design. 2435.
display media
    information retrieval databases. *display media;*
      codes; symbols. 2435.5.
displayed indexes
    information retrieval databases. indexes. *displayed*
      indexes; non-displayed indexes.
      comparison. 2435.11.
documentary domain. SEE: coverage domain.
documentary scope
    information retrieval databases. *documentary scope.*
      2435.3.
documentary units
    information retrieval databases. *documentary units.*
      2435.6.

Chapter 12. Syntax (Section 12.4.2)

exhaustivity
    information retrieval databases. indexes. *exhaustivity*.
        2435.9.
facets
    information retrieval databases. subject scope; subject domain.
        description. *facets*. 2435.2.
generation
    information retrieval databases. indexes.
        generation. analysis methods: human indexing; automatic
            indexing. 2435.8.
human indexing
    information retrieval databases. indexes.
        generation. analysis methods: *human indexing*; automatic
            indexing. 2435.8.
indexable matter
    information retrieval databases. *indexable matter*.
        2435.7.
indexes
    information retrieval databases.
        generation. analysis methods: human indexing; automatic
            indexing. 2435.8.
    information retrieval databases. displayed indexes; non-
        displayed indexes.
    comparison. 2435.11.
    information retrieval databases. exhaustivity. 2435.9.
    information retrieval databases. syntax: precoordinate syntax;
        postcoordinate syntax.
    comparison. 2435.12.
    information retrieval databases. vocabulary. specificity. 2435.10.
information retrieval databases
        design. 2435.pt.2.
    coverage domain. 2435.4.
    databases. types: *information retrieval databases*;
        concrete entity and event databases.
    comparison. 2435.1.6.
    display media; codes; symbols. 2435.5.
    documentary scope. 2435.3.
    documentary units. 2435.6.
    indexable matter. 2435.7.
    indexes.
        generation. analysis methods: human indexing; automatic
            indexing. 2435.8.
    indexes. displayed indexes; non-displayed indexes.
        comparison. 2435.11.
    indexes. exhaustivity. 2435.9.
    indexes. syntax: precoordinate syntax;
        postcoordinate syntax.
    comparison. 2435.12.
    indexes: vocabulary. specificity. 2435.10.
    standards. 2435.1.4.
    subject scope; subject domain.
        description. facets. 2435.2.
    terminology.
        definitions. 2435.1.3.
    types. 2435.1.5.

```
non-displayed indexes
    information retrieval databases. indexes. displayed
        indexes; non-displayed indexes.
    comparison. 2435.11.
postcoordinate syntax
    information retrieval databases. indexes. syntax:
        precoordinate syntax; postcoordinate syntax.
    comparison. 2435.12.
precoordinate syntax
    information retrieval databases. indexes. syntax:
        precoordinate syntax; postcoordinate syntax.
    comparison. 2435.12.
specificity
    information retrieval databases. indexes: vocabulary.
        specificity. 2435.10.
standards
    information retrieval databases. standards. 2435.1.4.
subject domain
    information retrieval databases. subject scope; subject domain.
        description. facets. 2435.2.
subject scope
    information retrieval databases. subject scope; subject domain.
        description. facets. 2435.2.
symbols
    information retrieval databases. display media;
        codes; symbols. 2435.5.
syntax
    information retrieval databases. indexes. syntax:
        precoordinate syntax; postcoordinate syntax.
    comparison. 2435.12.
terminology
    information retrieval databases. terminology.
        definitions. 2435.1.3.
vocabulary
    information retrieval databases. indexes.
        specificity. 2435.10.
=====================================================================
NOTE: Remember, this small sample index has entries for only a small number of
documents (our book as a whole plus 16 sections, for a total of 17 documentary
units). In a real database index, these entries would be dispersed among thou-
sands of other entries.
```

• purpose of displayed indexes in indexing and abstracting services : 338

The purpose of this displayed index is to help users explore information possibilities even if they are unclear on exactly what they are looking for. The idea is that seeing examples of the kinds of topics available will help clarify information needs or desires.

12.4.3. A Full-Text Encyclopedia/Digital Library.

• 339

Our full-text encyclopedia/digital library will receive the same kind of indexing, using the same syntax, as our indexing and abstracting service, but all articles will receive human indexing, because all articles have already been refereed and chosen on the basis of their relevance and importance, in the judgment of the editors.

Chapter 12. Syntax (Section 12.4.3)

• **search options for electronic encyclopedias and digital libraries : 340**

Thus, users may browse displayed indexes, or they may choose electronic searches using either best match or exact match syntax. Electronic searches may be directed to the full text of articles, or limited to indexer-assigned descriptors and equivalent terms from the thesaurus. (The thesaurus and other aspects of vocabulary management will be discussed in chapter 13.)

• **hypertext links in electronic encyclopedias and digital libraries : 341**

In addition to these two basic approaches to indexing and searching (postcoordinate and precoordinate), our encyclopedia/digital library will also feature hypertext links, just like a well-designed paper encyclopedia. Within each article, every term (whether preferred, equivalent or variant term) that is associated with one or more other articles (based on the human indexing of those articles) will be highlighted, so that a user may click on the term and go directly to the linked articles. In addition, see-also references will be appended to the article, based on thesaurus relations between the main topic or topics of the article and other article topics. (These term relationships will be discussed in chapter 13 on vocabulary management.)

• **user suggested cross-references : 342**

Later, as users travel from article to article, these paths will be recorded in selected installations, including the internet. Cross-reference links will be added based on high-frequency connections indicated by the traffic patterns of users.

• 343

These references can be called "user suggestions":

```
Use patterns also suggest the following related articles, in which you
may be interested: [list of additional article titles that the user may
select.]
```

Chapter 13. Vocabulary Management

Contents of Chapter 13
13.1. The Vocabulary Problem.
13.2. Research on Vocabulary Issues.
13.3. Vocabulary Solutions.
13.3.1. Syndetic Structure in Displayed Alphabetical Indexes.
13.3.2. Indexing Thesauri.
13.3.2.1 Examples of Indexing Thesauri.
13.3.3. End-User Thesauri.
13.3.3.1. Compiling an End-User Thesaurus.
13.3.3.1.1. Sources of Terms.
13.3.3.1.2. Selecting Terms.
13.3.3.1.3. Categorizing Terms.
13.3.3.1.4. Bound Terms Versus Elemental Descriptors.
13.3.3.1.5. Term Relationships.
13.3.3.1.6. Variant Forms and Equivalent Terms.
13.3.3.1.7. Homographs.
13.3.3.1.8. Thesaurus Displays.
13.3.4. Co-Occurrence Term Clustering.
13.3.5. Ontologies.
13.4. Our Examples.
13.4.1. A Book Index.
13.4.2. An Indexing and Abstracting Service.
13.4.3. A Full-Text Encyclopedia/Digital Library.

13.1. The Vocabulary Problem.

• 1

There is near universal agreement that vocabulary is a major problem area in information retrieval, and therefore it is an important issue in the design of effective IR databases as well.

• richness of human language : 2

The problem stems from the enormous richness of human language, which is the most common tool used for describing information needs or desires on the one hand, and the most common tool used for describing the content, meaning, purpose, or features of messages, texts and documents on the other, even when those items are not themselves composed of human language (such as musical scores, mathematical formulae, photographs, paintings, other images, sound and dance performances, or three-dimensional objects — sculpture, architecture, design). Of course, a large proportion of messages sought by searchers also consist of texts representing human language.

• categories of information needs and desires : 3

We can categorize searches in response to information needs or desires in the following way:

• searches for known items with known vocabulary : 4

1. Searches for known items with known vocabulary. The seeker knows exactly what message, text, or document s/he wants and what to call it (how to describe it) in the language of the database(s) being used. This also implies that the seeker knows exactly what database(s) to use as well! If the database is well-constructed, this user should not encounter vocabulary problems.

• searches for known items with unknown vocabulary : 5

2. Searches for known items but without known vocabulary. The seeker knows exactly what message, text, or document s/he wants, but does not know what to call it, or how to describe it, in the language of the database(s) being used. S/he may also be faced with the problem of finding an appropriate IR database. This user could be aided by a display of vocabulary, with links from alternative forms. Even a search for a known author can be problematic. In preparing this chapter, Anderson did a search for A. Steven Pollitt in the *Library literature and information science* database. No hits were found, because this database entered this author as "Pollitt, A.S."! (To the credit of this database, it did direct him to the browsable list of terms used in the database, and there he was able to find "Pollitt, A.S."!) In another search in another database, Anderson was seeking a citation to one of his own papers, which he knew was in the database, but he could not find any entries under his own name, because the database had changed his name from "James D. Anderson" to "Anderson, J.D." — a form he has never used, and a form that conflates his rather common name with hundreds or thousands of other persons! A third example is an important author on indexing, abstracting and vocabulary management. His full name is Frederick Wilfrid Lancaster, but he generally uses "F. W. Lancaster." His name is currently listed in the Research Libraries Group (RLG) Union Catalog (RLIN — Research Libraries Information Network, 23 Oct. 2000) in the following ways:

```
Lancaster, F. W.
Lancaster, F. Wilfred
Lancaster, F. Wilfrid
Lancaster, F. Wilfried
Lancaster, Frederick Wilfred
Lancaster, Frederick Wilfrid
```

• 6

Thus, vocabulary problems are not limited just to topical terms. All terms, including names of persons, names of places, and names of companies are often affected. The pharmaceutical firm Hoffmann LaRoche has appeared in databases in many different forms, including:

```
Hoffmann La Roche Co
Hoffmann La Roche Inc
Hoffmann La Roche, Inc
Hoffmann Laroche Inc
Hoffmann Laroche, Inc
Hoffmannf La Roche Co
Hoffmannla Roche Company
Hoffmannla Roche F Co
Hoffmannla Roche Inc
Hoffmannlaroche And Company
Hoffmanlaroche Chemical Works
Hoffmanlaroche Inc
(These headings are also from RLIN: the RLG Union Catalog, 18 January
2001, displayed via the Eureka interface).
```

• 7

The official heading for one of the principal Hoffmann-La Roche companies in the national Name Authority File is: Hoffmann-La Roche, inc. [sic, lower case "inc."] (The national Name Authority File is a thesaurus of names of persons and corporate bodies and titles of works maintained by the Library of Congress and other large libraries.) The headings with "Hoffmannla"

Chapter 13. Vocabulary Management (Section 13.1)

displayed above reflect treatment of the hyphen — in those headings it has simply been eliminated — not replaced with a space. Subject or author searches in the RLG Union Catalog via the staff interface for "Hoffmann La Roche" result in zero hits (as of 18 January 2001). The same search via the Eureka interface will retrieve author entries, but no subject entries. As noted in section 8.3.1 on automatic word indexing, the hyphen can be especially problematic.

• searches for unknown items with known vocabulary : 8

3. Well-defined searches for unknown items with known vocabulary. The seeker does not have a particular message, text or document in mind, but has a well-defined interest and knows how to describe this interest in the language of the database(s) being used. Nevertheless, a well-designed thesaurus or vocabulary management interface might be effective in alerting the user to closely associated terms used in one or more databases — terms of which s/he may not be aware. For example, a person searching for messages about "marriage" in a library catalog might be helped by knowing that the Library of Congress also uses separate subject headings for special types of marriage, such as "child marriage," "polyandry," "polygamy," and "same-sex marriage."

• searches for unknown items with unknown vocabulary : 9

4. Well-defined searches for unknown items with unknown vocabulary. The seeker has a well-defined interest, but does not know how to describe it in the language of the database(s) being used or which databases might be most appropriate! Here a well-designed thesaurus or similar vocabulary management tool should be able to inform the user of terms that are used for her/his interest in a variety of databases. It might also indicate in which database such terms occur most frequently. S/he should be able to begin the search with her/his own terms, which should be linked via the vocabulary management system to the terms used in relevant databases.

• searches for unknown items with unknown vocabulary and vague concepts : 10

5. Vague searches for unknown items with unknown vocabulary. The seeker has only a vague idea of what s/he needs or wants, and certainly doesn't know what to call it, or how to describe it in the language of any IR database. S/he also is "at sea" regarding the best IR database for her/his purposes. Here the user needs an effective tool for browsing the vocabulary of one or more databases at the highest (most generic) conceptual level, in order to choose broad areas of possible interest and then to work down into particular areas where her/his concepts of interest might be found.

• searches of exploration : 11

6. Just looking for something interesting. The seeker has no particular need or desire, except to explore to see what's available. S/he will be interested in finding interesting IR databases to explore. This user also needs a broad-based browsing mechanism through which s/he can explore all the possibilities provided by one or more databases. (We assume that such users are interested in finding interesting or entertaining or useful messages, texts, or documents. Otherwise, they shouldn't be using an IR database. Guiding users to appropriate types of databases is itself a problem for us to tackle! We will need to find ways to make clear what kinds of services our IR databases are designed to provide — that is, the location of messages, texts, and documents!)

• continua of information seeking situations : 12

These seekers and their information seeking situations can be placed on at least two continua of situations, one relating to the extent to which a known item (message, text or document) is being sought, and another relating to the extent to which the interest, need, or desire is well understood and well described (and if the latter, the extent to which searchers know the vocabulary of the IR database(s) they choose to use). Vocabulary management tools need to support all of these users, in whatever situation they find themselves.

13.2. Research on Vocabulary Issues.

• research on information seeking; views of Belkin (Nicholas J.) on anomalous states of knowledge : 13

Several researchers have studied and described these user situations. Our Rutgers colleague Nicholas Belkin is justly famous for articulating the rather uncomfortable "anomalous state of knowledge (ASK)" in which information seekers find themselves when they suffer a knowledge gap and therefore don't know exactly how to describe what it is that they do not know! (Belkin, Oddy, & Brooks 1982a, 1982b).

• views of Furnas (George W. et al.) on variability of vocabulary : 14

Furnas et al. (1987) have demonstrated that even when seekers have a fairly good idea of what they are looking for and what they want (in terms of topic), their use of vocabulary will vary considerably. In their experiments, human subjects were asked to name common word-processing tasks and to find recipes for every-day foods or dishes or want ads for common household items. In quite common domains such as these, Furnas et al. found that two persons were likely to agree on a term for a given concept less than 20% of the time. They also suggest that in order to accommodate 80% of user term choices, IR systems need to provide an average of 15 "aliases" or alternative names for concepts.

• vocabulary of users compared to *Library of Congress subject headings* : 15

In a library-oriented study modeled on that of Furnas et al. (1987), Collantes (1995) studied the "degree of agreement in naming objects and concepts" by students and librarians compared to the terms actually used by the Library of Congress in its subject headings system. She found the same kind of dispersion of terminology as Furnas et al.

• views of Bates (Marcia) on variability of vocabulary : 16

Marcia Bates has repeatedly described this terminological problem in the context of library catalogs and IR databases, based on her own research and that of others: "Even in controlled vocabulary environments there is an enormous range of terms used by both searchers and indexers for any one topic (1986, 1989). ... [E]ven the most popular term is likely to be used by only a minority of searchers" (1990, p. 26-27).

• variability of vocabulary among searchers and indexers : 17

The importance of vocabulary unpredictability is now widely accepted. In an overview of vocabulary problems, Chen, Ng, Martinez & Schatz (1997) declare that "in information science, indexing and search uncertainty have been recognized as the primary sources of information retrieval problems. ... Because of the indeterminism involved in indexing and searching, an exact match between the searcher's term and those of the indexer is unlikely (Chen & Dhar 1987)" (p. 17).

• 18

Saracevic et al. (1988a, b, c) demonstrated that similar variability exists among expert intermediary searchers working on behalf of end users. Study after study indicates that information seekers, searchers, and indexers agree on terms about 25% of the time. Most of this variability appears to be due to differences in choices of terms, the remainder to differences in perception or conceptualization of topics or features (Iivonen 1994a, b).

Chapter 13. Vocabulary Management (Section 13.3)

• variability of vocabulary in full-text sources : 19

Keyword searching of full text is no panacea, because the same variability found among abstracters, indexers and searchers is just as common among authors who create texts. In a landmark study of retrieval from full-text databases, Blair and Maron (1985) declared that "vocabulary problems make high recall impossible in full-text databases." Based on their experimental work, Furnas et al. (1987) and Gomez, Lochbaum & Landauer (1990) advocate an "unlimited aliasing" strategy (in which every concept can have an unlimited number of names or "aliases"). They found that "searcher success is markedly improved by greatly increasing the number of names per object." By "object" they mean concept in a search.

13.3. Vocabulary Solutions.

• 20

Solutions currently in use, or suggested, to assist searchers with vocabulary problems include:

1. Syndetic structure (cross references) integrated into displayed browsable alphabetical indexes based on subject headings, string indexing, or other types of index headings.

2. Indexing thesauri designed to guide the assignment of terms by indexers. Indexing thesauri can be helpful to searchers as well, especially if they include a large lead-in vocabulary (un-used terms) leading to the preferred terms actually used in one or more databases. Lists of subject headings can be used in a similar way, especially if syndetic cross-reference structure is well developed. Many indexing thesauri exist. Some are not made available to end users, but many others are available. Often, though, they are separate databases, not integrated with search interfaces. One challenge is how to make them easily accessible within the search interface and to display useful vocabulary information in the context of a search.

3. End-user or searching thesauri, designed for searchers rather than indexers. Instead of aiming to control the terminology used by indexers, the purpose of an end-user or searching thesaurus is to help searchers find useful terminology. In the words of Marcia Bates, "the philosophy of control ... is that vocabulary control shall consist of grouping term variants around a concept and making it easy for searchers to select and search on those variations without having to key them in, rather than eliminating the variation" (1990, p. 27). The challenge of merging end-user thesauri with search interfaces is similar to the challenge for indexing thesauri.

4. Co-occurrence term clustering. Here computer programs are used to compile lists of terms that occur together most frequently in various contexts. The most frequently co-occurring terms are likely to include terms closely related to the term with which a searcher begins, from which the searcher can select likely terms to improve a search.

5. Ontologies, which attempt (or claim) to raise the level of more traditional thesauri to the realms of virtual reality. This new name for vocabulary tools comes from the branch of philosophy devoted to the study of "being" or "existence." The term comes into information science and information retrieval via artificial intelligence and knowledge engineering, where expert knowledge is used to describe a portion of reality (of being!). These detailed descriptions of "what is" (real world knowledge) are thought to have potential for automatic identification, description, or translation of useful texts.

Chapter 13. Vocabulary Management (Section 13.3)

• research on solutions for vocabulary problems : 21

While there is a fair amount of research documenting the vocabulary problems faced by searchers (and indexers), there is relatively little research that actually assesses the impact of the various solutions proposed. While authors like Bates (1986, 1989, 1990) and Anderson & Rowley (1992) have advocated end-user or searcher thesauri, few if any have actually been constructed, must less tested for efficacy using rigorous research methods.

• views of Bates (Marcia) on variability of vocabulary : 22

Bates did guide the development or adaptation of a thesaurus for online searching of a "very large records management database" (1990). Arguing for effective display of vocabulary, she reminds us that "It has long been a staple of psychological research that recognition of terms is much easier than recall — in the psychological sense of recall from memory. ... Most of us can identify good terms from a list of related ones far faster and in greater numbers than we can think up such terms on our own" (p. 27).

• experimental research on end-user thesauri : 23

One of the few experiments involving the impact of an end-user thesaurus was performed by Finnish researchers, who tested the impact of a "searching thesaurus" made available to users of a full-text journalism database (Kristensen & Jarvelin 1990). Overall, the use of the end-user thesaurus improved retrieval results in most instances.

• field research on use of thesauri : 24

There is a larger body of research assessing the actual use by searchers of existing thesauri, which are largely those designed more for indexers than for searchers. Examples include Fidel's 1991 study of searchers, in which she examined their searching styles, including the extent to which they used controlled vocabularies. Lauren Harrison's dissertation at Rutgers took a similar approach, examining the use of thesauri by searchers in a large pharmaceutical firm (1998). Dubois (1984) is one of many researchers who advocates this kind of field research, based on actual users using actual tools. Dubois sees a "controlled vocabulary or structured thesaurus as a semantic map, serving just as useful a purpose as a geographical map. Both maps use certain symbols and conventions to represent an area, whether of knowledge or of land" (p. 64).

• 25

The results of studies of actual searcher behavior suggest that expert searchers make much use of thesauri, so if one can assume that such searchers know what they are doing, one can assume they find thesauri to be valuable aids in effective searching.

• integration of thesauri with search interfaces : 26

A growing area of work involves efforts to integrate thesauri and the vocabulary information they can provide into search interfaces. Among the leaders in this effort are A. Steven Pollitt and colleagues (Pollitt & Ellis 1994; Smith & Pollitt 1996; Pollitt, Smith & Braekevelt 1997; Pollitt 1998). Similar work has been pursued by Jones and Hancock-Beaulieu (1994). Their thesis is that while, "in principle, the 'knowledge' encoded in a thesaurus can be exploited in many ways to help users clarify their information needs and enhance query performance, ... attempts to automate this process via AI [artificial intelligence] techniques face many practical difficulties. In the short term it may be more useful to improve support for direct *interactive* use of thesauri." To this end, they work toward "an interface for thesaurus navigation and query enhancement" (p. 366).

• combining thesauri and co-occurrence lists : 27

Shapiro and Yan (1996) report on a prototype system that is designed to improve query formulation and expansion by displaying terms and semantic knowledge (term relationships) from

Chapter 13. Vocabulary Management (Section 13.3)

publicly available thesauri. Schatz, Johnson, Cochrane and Chen (1996) have expanded this approach to include not only thesauri based on expert human knowledge, but also computer-generated co-occurrence lists, which display terms in frequency order, based on how often they occur together in text.

• **mapping of search terms to controlled vocabulary : 28**

Buckland, Chen, Chen, Kim, Lam, Larson, Norgard and Purat (1999) have worked on systems for "mapping entry vocabulary to unfamiliar metadata vocabularies" — that is, guiding users, based on the terms of their initial search query, to appropriate terms in the various controlled vocabularies that pertain to relevant databases.

• **interaction with multiple controlled vocabularies : 29**

The ability for users to interact with multiple vocabularies depends on standards for interoperability — so that a single search interface can search and interact with multiple different vocabulary tools. Mike Taylor (1999) reviews work on technical standards for communication and navigation with remote thesauri. An invitational conference on electronic thesauri (Milstead 1999), sponsored by the National Information Standards Organization and other interested organizations, has called for producers of thesauri, ontologies, and other vocabulary tools to agree on basic principles for terminological description, so that vocabulary data can be shared across tools, databases, systems and platforms.

• **display of thesauri for searching : 30**

The basic approach for integrating one or more thesauri (or other controlled vocabulary or vocabulary management resources) into a search interface has been the design of display techniques that make vocabulary information available to users in the context of searches. In the work of Pollitt et al., interface displays have presented vocabulary from one or more facets or categories chosen by the user from a thesaurus or a classification system (such as the *Dewey decimal classification*). When tied to a particular database (or databases), the number of postings can be indicated (that is, the number of documents associated with each term). Searches can be narrowed by choosing terms in two or more facets simultaneously, with the resulting postings shown. Ideally, a searcher should be able to select terms in such a display and apply them directly to a search in one or more databases.

• **work of Pollitt (A. Steven, et al.) on display of thesauri for searching : 31**

Here is an example of Pollitt et al.'s work, illustrated by a hypothetical search for documents on therapies for the treatment of degenerative diseases using the EMTREE thesaurus and a 300,000-record subset of the EMBASE database (Pollitt, Smith, & Braekevelt 1997). EMBASE is the electronic version of the Elsevier medical IR database *Excerpta medica*. EMTREE is the thesaurus for this database.

• **facets in EMTREE thesaurus : 32**

The EMTREE thesaurus, like many modern thesauri, is structured around the basic facets of the fields it covers. Examples of facets for medicine include diseases, therapies, drugs, parts of the body, and types of persons (by age, sex, ethnicity, etc.).

• **dynamic postings in faceted relational classified displayed indexes : 33**

In this example, the user has selected the disease facet. Within the disease facet, the user selects degenerative disease. A list of degenerative diseases is shown, along with postings. The postings shown in this first display indicate the total number of documents dealing with degenerative diseases in general and with particular degenerative diseases. However, as soon as the therapy facet is added in the second display, all the postings are adjusted dynamically to indicate just the documents that deal with both degenerative disease and therapy. Note that the total postings for these two categories drop to 1074 in the second display, whereas degenerative disease alone had 3135 postings.

```
degenerative disease

3135 degenerative disease
1297 ... alzheimer disease
 242 ... arthrosis
 101 ... creutzfeldt jakob disease
  25 ... friedreich ataxia
  64 ... gonarthrosis
  41 ... hip arthrosis
 224 ... keratosis
 350 ... osteoarthritis
 721 ... parkinson disease
  29 ... pick presenile dementia
   3 ... prion disease
  72 ... retina degeneration
  63 ... senile dementia
  14 ... senility
   5 ... spondylarthrosis
   5 ... tapetoretinal degeneration
   6 ... vitreoretinal degeneration
  79 ... wilson disease
```

• 34

A careful reader may add up all the postings for the types of degenerative disease and notice that they add up to 3341, rather than 3135. This difference is due to the situation that some documents will treat more than one disease, so that they will be posted under more than one disease descriptor.

• 35

Now the searcher adds a view of the therapy facet from EMTREE. The "top term" in this display, "therapy" is selected (and highlighted). As noted, with dynamic postings, the postings associated with degenerative diseases are immediately adjusted to show the joint postings for the two top terms (1074), but the postings for each particular degenerative disease term are also adjusted to indicate just the joint postings for the disease AND therapy (either therapy in general or one of the particular therapies), and also for each particular therapy AND degenerative disease. Degenerative diseases not associated with the term "therapy," such as "prion disease," drop out of the display:

```
therapy                              degenerative disease

1074 therapy                         1074 degenerative disease
   4 ... acupuncture                  262 ... alzheimer disease
  46 ... biological therapy            96 ... arthrosis
   7 ... cancer therapy                22 ... creutzfeldt jakob disease
   1 ... computer assisted therapy      3 ... friedreich ataxia
  26 ... conservative therapy          23 ... gonarthrosis
   8 ... counseling                    14 ... hip arthrosis
  10 ... detoxification               183 ... keratosis
   3 ... disease control              158 ... osteoarthritis
 817 ... drug therapy                 360 ... parkinson disease
   2 ... emergency treatment            3 ... pick presenile dementia
  18 ... intensive care                 9 ... retina degeneration
   2 ... lavage                        22 ... senile dementia
```

Chapter 13. Vocabulary Management (Section 13.3)

```
 65 ... maintenance therapy              3 ... senility
  2 ... nonsurgical invasive therapy     3 ... spondylarthrosis
  4 ... palliative therapy               2 ... vitreoretinal degeneration
 41 ... patient care                    39 ... wilson disease
 46 ... physical medicine
 30 ... prophylaxis
 31 ... radiotherapy
 55 ... rehabilitation
  9 ... substitution therapy
  6 ... supplementation
```

• 36

Now, in the therapy facet window, the searcher selects (clicks on, highlights) "drug therapy," so now only types of drug therapy are displayed, in association with degenerative diseases. Again, postings are adjusted to show the number of postings for documents relating to drug therapy AND degenerative disease. Degenerative disease terms which do not co-occur with drug therapies drop out of the display:

```
drug therapy                            degenerative disease

817 drug therapy                        817 degenerative disease
  1 ... adjuvant therapy                190 ... alzheimer disease
  1 ... antibiotic therapy               49 ... arthrosis
  3 ... anticoagulant therapy            14 ... creutzfeldt jakob disease
  1 ... antimicrobial therapy             1 ... friedreich ataxia
  2 ... bone marrow suppression          13 ... gonarthrosis
  3 ... chelation therapy                 8 ... hip arthrosis
  1 ... chemoprophylaxis                 86 ... keratosis
  7 ... chemotherapy                    114 ... osteoarthritis
  3 ... drug choice                     302 ... parkinson disease
  2 ... drug combination                  2 ... pick presenile dementia
113 ... drug comparison                   5 ... retina degeneration
  7 ... drug indication                  17 ... senile dementia
  1 ... drug intermittent therapy         1 ... senility
  3 ... drug megadose                     2 ... spondylarthrosis
 19 ... drug mixture                     34 ... wilson disease
  3 ... drug monitoring
  1 ... drug program
  2 ... drug surveillance program
  7 ... drug withdrawal
  1 ... fibrinolytic therapy
  3 ... hormonal therapy
  2 ... photodynamic therapy
  1 ... phytotherapy
 27 ... placebo
  1 ... psychopharmacotherapy
  6 ... puva
  1 ... self medication
  1 ... sympathetic blocking
```

• 37

Finally, the user selects "alzheimer disease" in the list of degenerative diseases, so that the display shows only this disease and the drug therapies that co-occur in document indexing with this disease:

Chapter 13. Vocabulary Management (Section 13.3.1)

```
drug therapy                              degenerative disease

190 drug therapy                          190 alzheimer disease
  1 ... anticoagulant therapy
  1 ... chelation therapy
  2 ... chemotherapy
 25 ... drug comparison
  1 ... drug indication
  2 ... drug megadose
  2 ... drug monitoring
  1 ... drug withdrawal
  3 ... hormonal therapy
  9 ... placebo
```

• 38

At any point, the user can highlight descriptors in both views and ask for documents or document surrogates to be displayed. For example, by selecting "hormonal therapy" and "alzheimer disease," then asking for documents, the 3 documents associated with both of these descriptors would be displayed.

• 39

We now turn to particular approaches to vocabulary management.

13.3.1. Syndetic Structure in Displayed Alphabetical Indexes.

• definition of syndetic structure : 40

Cross references, or syndetic structure, have been an integral part of displayed alphabetical subject indexes since the advent of subject heading systems in the second half of the 19th century. They are also used in all well-designed back-of-the-book indexes and in name indexes for authors, places, and corporate bodies. "Syndetic" comes from the Greek "syn" (together, as in "synthesis") and "dein" (to bind). Hence syndetic structure is the structure of links that serve to bind together into a cohesive whole the connected topics of an index that have been dispersed and scattered by arranging their headings in alphabetical order. For example, an alphabetical index will disperse the names of animals from anteaters to zebras. The syndetic structure will link all these names to broader headings (such as "mammals," "vertebrates," and eventually "animals") so that a searcher can find all the particular animals listed in an index.

• role of syndetic structure : 41

Syndetic structure also binds together different headings for the same (or essentially the same) concept (such as "attorney," "lawyer"). It also points to different concepts bearing the same name ("mercury": a god, an automobile brand, a planet, a chemical element). And it can point to narrower or subordinate concepts ("motor vehicles: see also narrower terms: automobiles, trucks, buses"). Sometimes it points to broader or superordinate concepts ("motor vehicles: see also broader: term vehicles"). And it can point to other related terms ("teeth: see also related terms: dentistry, dental hygiene, tooth brushes").

• subject headings versus terms in syndetic structure : 42

Syndetic structure has traditionally been associated with headings in library catalogs (such as *Library of Congress subject headings*) or in back-of-the-book indexes. Thus, in our discussion of syndetic structure, we refer to links between and among headings. However, newer terminology for syndetic cross references uses the word "term" instead of "heading." The word "term" is the most general term (word) for any kind of descriptive word or phase, including descriptors, captions, keywords and headings.

Chapter 13. Vocabulary Management (Section 13.3.1)

• **types of syndetic structure; types of cross references : 43**

Traditional types of syndetic cross references have included see and see-also references:

• **equivalent-term cross references : 44**

See references (also called equivalent-term cross references) link unused headings to preferred (used) synonymous or equivalent headings, e.g.:

```
Gay marriage
    see
        Same-sex marriage
```

• **see-also references : 45**

See-also references link headings to related headings, generally headings for narrower topics and non-hierarchically related topics (that is, topics that are not narrower, part of, or broader than the initial topic). For example:

```
Marriage
    see also
        Arranged marriage
        Astrology and marriage
        Beast marriage
        Betrothal
        Bisexuality in marriage
        Bride price
        Child marriage
        Common law marriage
        Communication in marriage
        Companionate marriage
        Commuter marriage
        Concubinage
        Courtship
        Cross-cousin marriage
        Deaf — Marriage
        Divorce
        Domestic relations
        Elopement
        Endogamy and exogamy
        Family
        Free love
        Group marriage
        Handicapped — Marriage
        Home
        Honeymoons
        Intermarriage
        Marital status
        Marriages of celebrities
        Married people
        Mate selection
        Matrimonial advertisements
        Mentally handicapped — Marriage
        Polyandry
        Polygamy
        Posthumous marriage
        Remarriage
        Same-sex marriage
        Sex in marriage
        Teenage marriage
        Temporary marriage
```

Chapter 13. Vocabulary Management (Section 13.3.1)

```
Weddings
Wives — Effect of husband's employment on
Woman-to-woman marriage
and subdivision "Marriage" under names of individual persons.
```

• **narrower-term cross references; related-term cross references : 46**

This long list of related headings, compiled from *Library of Congress subject headings* authority records in the RLIN (Research Libraries Information Network) database, includes both narrower headings (types of marriage, such as "arranged marriage," "beast marriage," "child marriage," and "same-sex marriage") and related headings, which clearly do not refer to types of marriage, but to concepts related to marriage, such as "betrothal" and "bisexuality in marriage."

• **omission of see-also references : 47**

But this long list of *Library of Congress subject headings* related to "Marriage" does not include subdivisions under the heading "Marriage," such as "Marriage — Annulment," "Marriage — Parental consent," and "Marriage — Religious aspects," or "Marriage" followed by place names, such as "Marriage — United States." A complete list of related headings would also include "Marriage" with all its subdivisions.

• **purpose of syndetic structure : 48**

This long list of related headings illustrates one of the principal purposes of syndetic structure. It would be next to impossible for a user (or even a cataloger) to remember or to think of these particular related headings, yet with a display of these options, it might be fairly easy for a user to decide if any of these headings are of any interest.

• **cross references in OPACs : 49**

Ideally, in an online library catalog (OPAC — Online Public Access Catalog), these cross references would be presented as hypertext links, so that users could simply click on headings of interest. If a user clicked on "Woman-to-woman marriage," they might see the *Library of Congress subject headings* scope note: "Here are entered works on a traditional institution in certain societies, in which one woman marries another with no sexual relationship between them." This would help to clarify the difference between this heading and "Same-sex marriage."

• **postings data in cross references : 50**

Postings data is very useful in cross references, to let the user know how many items are listed under a particular heading. Some OPACs routinely include such postings information in cross references.

• **cross references and syndetic structure in thesauri : 51**

Recently, the Library of Congress adopted the standard cross reference structure developed for indexing thesauri during the 1960s, including the now fairly standard thesaurus notations:

```
USE = "see" or "go to" or "search under"
UF  = "used for"
BT  = "broader term(s)"
RT  = "related term(s)"
NT  = "narrower term(s)"
```

• **UF as notation for un-used terms : 52**

UF (used for) indicates synonymous or equivalent headings for which the designated preferred heading is used, e.g.:

Chapter 13. Vocabulary Management (Section 13.3.1)

```
Same-sex marriage
     UF   Gay marriage
          Homosexual marriage
          Lesbian marriage
          Same-sex unions
```

• 53

This means that "Same-sex marriage" is used for "Gay marriage," "Homosexual marriage," "Lesbian marriage," and "Same-sex unions."

• UF as instruction for creation of equivalent-term cross references : 54

The UF notation serves as an instruction to make use (or see) references (equivalent-term cross references) from each of the un-used UF headings to the preferred heading. Thus the UF instruction just above should result in the following use references, which would be placed in their appropriate alphabetical positions in a displayed alphabetical index:

```
Gay marriage        USE   Same-sex marriage
Homosexual marriage USE   Same-sex marriage
Lesbian marriage    USE   Same-sex marriage
Same-sex unions     USE   Same-sex marriage
```

• form of equivalent-term cross references in OPACs : 55

The implementation of these cross references will vary according to the design of the particular OPAC. The authorized heading "Same-sex marriage" could be a hypertext link, so that the user need only click on it. In other designs, any of these headings could be used. Instead of sending a user to the preferred heading "Same-sex marriage," all of the equivalent (UF) headings would be linked, so that each of them would lead to the same catalog entries. In this case, the OPAC should display a notice that explains:

```
"Same-sex marriage" is the heading used for: Gay marriage; Homosexual
marriage; Lesbian marriage; Same-sex unions.
```

Such an explanatory note is often helpful for searchers who wonder why what they got was not what they asked for exactly!

• NT as notation for narrower terms; narrower-term cross references : 56

NT "narrower term(s)" usually indicates only hierarchically subordinate headings or headings for parts of the item referred to. However, after the Library of Congress moved from the old format for syndetic structure, in which narrower headings and related headings were listed together in see-also references, it has not been able to completely distinguish between these two categories of headings. Consequently, many so-called NT (narrower terms) in *Library of Congress subject headings* are not really narrower in the usual sense.

• narrower terms versus related terms versus in syndetic structure

• narrower terms versus related terms in thesauri : 57

In the following list from *Library of Congress subject headings*, the headings marked with an asterisk (*) should probably be listed as RT (related terms):

```
Marriage
     NT   Arranged marriage
          *Astrology and marriage
          Beast marriage
          *Bisexuality in marriage
          *Bride price
          Child marriage
          Common law marriage
```

309

Chapter 13. Vocabulary Management (Section 13.3.1)

```
*Communication in marriage
Companionate marriage
Commuter marriage
*Concubinage
Cross-cousin marriage
Deaf — Marriage
*Divorce
*Domestic relations
Elopement
Endogamy and exogamy
*Free love
Group marriage
Handicapped — Marriage
Intercountry marriage
Intermarriage
*Marital status
Marriages of celebrities
*Married people
*Mate selection
*Matrimonial advertisements
Mentally handicapped — Marriage
Polyandry
Polygamy
Posthumous marriage
Remarriage
Same-sex marriage
*Sex in marriage
Teenage marriage
Temporary marriage
*Weddings
*Wives — Effect of husband's employment on
Woman-to-woman marriage
```

• 58

On the other hand, human language and the concepts represented by human terms do not always fit nicely into categories, and the proper categorization of some of these terms could be debated. Is sex part of marriage? If so, then perhaps "sex in marriage" and "bisexuality in marriage" might be seen as in a "whole-part" relationship with marriage and therefore they could qualify as narrower headings. "Communication in marriage" and perhaps "domestic relations" could surely be defended in a similar way. Are mate selection and weddings a part of marriage? Perhaps, but most people would probably make a distinction between marriage and concubinage, while divorce is almost the opposite of marriage. Married people are participants in marriage, but it's hard to see them as part of the process or status of marriage, in the sense of species (kind or type) or instance. Perhaps one could argue that they are part of marriage, although that's stretching the usual meaning of the whole-part relationship, which usually refers to geographic relations (Paris is part of France) or constitutive elements (wrists are parts of the human body). These considerations are typical of challenges facing a thesaurus editor who attempts to chart the relationships among terms in a thesaurus.

• translation of notation for thesauri into natural human language : 59

Thesaural notation such as NT, BT, RT should never be used in cross references designed for end users. These short-hand notations are really instructions to catalogers or indexers (or to OPAC systems) to make cross references. The previous example should be displayed as:

Chapter 13. Vocabulary Management (Section 13.3.1)

```
Marriage
    See also narrower terms:
            Arranged marriage
            *Astrology and marriage
            ... [etc.]
```

Sometime users interpret these suggested see-also references more as commands that they must follow, rather than optional suggestions to consider. To ensure that they interpret these cross references properly, it may be wise to use more explanation, such as:

```
Marriage
    You may also want to check the following narrower terms:
            Arranged marriage
            *Astrology and marriage
            ... [etc.]
```

• BT as notation for broader terms; broader-term cross references : 61

The *Library of Congress subject headings* lists only two headings as BT (broader terms) for "Marriage":

```
Marriage
    BT  Love
        Sacrament
```

Marriage is considered a sacrament only in some Christian churches, and perhaps in other religions. We can all hope that love is involved, but it's hard to see "Marriage" as a kind of "love." A more appropriate broader heading might be "Social institutions" or perhaps "Family institutions."

As with NT references, the cross reference for end users should read something like:

```
Marriage
    You may also want to check the following broader terms:
            Love
            Sacrament
```

• RT as notation for related terms; related-term cross references : 64

The *Library of Congress subject headings* lists the following headings as RT (related terms) for "Marriage":

```
Marriage
    RT  Married life
        Matrimony
        Nuptiality
        Wedlock
        Betrothal
        Courtship
        Family
        Home
        Honeymoons
```

As noted previously, in a more carefully constructed syndetic structure, the headings marked with an asterisk (*) in the list of narrower headings above would be moved to this list.

As with the NT and BT cross references, for the end user the RT cross reference should read:

Chapter 13. Vocabulary Management (Section 13.3.1)

```
Marriage
    You may also want to check the following related terms:
       Married life
       Matrimony
       Nuptiality
           ... [etc.]
```

• general see-also references : 67

The *Library of Congress subject headings* continues to use general see-also references along with the new style thesaural references (USE, BT, RT, NT). These are references to types or categories of headings rather than to particular headings, e.g.:

```
Marriage
    See also subdivision Marriage under names of individual persons.
```

• cross references in library catalogs : 68

The conventional wisdom has been that library catalogs need all the see or use references specified by the *Library of Congress subject headings*. The *Anglo-American cataloguing rules* also call for similar see references for many names of persons, corporate bodies, places, and titles.

• 69

There is some disagreement regarding see-also references. Some argue that see-also references for narrower, broader, or related headings should only fall under headings that have documents posted to them. They don't like the idea of saying "see also" from a heading where there are no postings!

• 70

However, we argue that if there are no document postings attached to a heading, then it is even more important to point to related, narrower, or broader headings. Thus, if you have no documents related to marriage in general, then it will certainly be helpful to include see-also references to headings for types of marriage and headings related to marriage for which you do have postings (that is, for topics on which you do have documents!).

• 71

Another long tradition has been to include see and see-also references only to headings which have postings. No one wants to select a suggested heading, only to find nothing there!

• 72

However, some OPAC routinely include all the see and see-also references suggested by *Library of Congress subject headings* and the national Name Authority File (for names of persons, corporate bodies, places and titles). But the number of postings are included for each heading. If the postings are zero, e.g., "Marriage, see also the narrower term: Beast marriage (0)," then the user will know that "Beast marriage" is a legitimate heading, but the particular library has no documents posted to that heading. The information that a library, or an IR database, has no documents on a particular topic is often useful.

• omission of cross references in OPACs : 73

See and see-also references were standard parts of card catalogs. It is ironic that many libraries, when they converted their card catalogs to OPACS, dropped all syndetic structure, providing no cross references whatsoever for their users. Greenberg (1997) has documented this sorry situation, which she calls "stagnation," and also signs of "progress" as some libraries move to restore "reference structures" (i.e., syndetic structure) to OPACs. Similar information, along with calls for reform and the improvement of "reference structures" can be found in an important report of an American Library Association committee (Association of Library Collections and

Chapter 13. Vocabulary Management (Section 13.3.2)

Technical Services. Subcommittee on Subject Relationships/Reference Structures 1999). (It is unfortunate that this ALA committee abandoned the traditional term "syndetic structure," which has only one meaning, in favor of the very vague term "reference structures"!)

• impact of omission of cross references : 74

What has been the impact of so many OPACs forcing users to search without syndetic structure? Does searching really become more effective with the restoration of cross references? While the answer may seem obvious, from a logical point of view, it is important to verify the actual impact through research into actual human information seeking behavior. This is a rich area for research, but little has been done to document or verify the real impact of syndetic structure (or its lack) on real users, with real needs or desires. The cost of syndetic structure is significant, so it would be good to have empirical verification of the positive impact of such investment.

• proposal for research on syndetic structure : 75

One type of investigation that could help us assess the actual impact of syndetic structure on users would be to measure the impact of a slowly growing syndetic structure (cross-reference) thesaurus on the search results of users of a library OPAC. Such research could take place in a library whose OPAC has no cross references. The investigator could collect all search terms that do not match catalog headings and therefore lead nowhere — so called dead-end or no-result searches.

• 76

Every such no-match term would be added to the OPAC as a cross reference, with a link to the closest available subject heading (conceptually speaking). The hypothesis suggests that over time, a significant number of equivalent-term links would be established, and, over time, the number of no-match, dead-end or no-result searches would diminish. A more complex research design could also include see-also references to narrower, related, and broader headings.

• 77

Would such an end-user thesaurus actually lead to better searches and more satisfied searchers? That's the tougher question, which we will leave to the researcher to tackle. (See also the similar proposal by Landauer (1985) to collect vocabulary directly from users in section 13.3.3.1.2.)

13.3.2. Indexing Thesauri.

• 78

Indexing thesauri, designed to guide indexers in the selection of terms for describing messages, texts, and documents, can also assist searchers if they are made available and displayed in useful ways . They are especially valuable when presented as an integral component of a search interface, whether the interface is designed to support browsing or electronic term-matching searches of non-displayed indexes.

• 79

Indexing thesauri, focusing on the control and organization of single-concept terms, began to be popular in the 1950s and 1960s. According to Krooks and Lancaster (1993), "the majority of the basic problems of thesaurus construction had already been solved by 1967."

Chapter 13. Vocabulary Management (Section 13.3.2)

• **source of term "thesaurus" : 80**

The term "thesaurus" is based on the Greek word for "treasure." The term was adopted by Peter Mark Roget (1779-1869), the compiler of the first modern classified "treasury" of words designed to bring together terms with similar meanings as an aid for writers. It is somewhat ironic that the main objective of Roget's thesaurus (and its modern successors) is almost exactly the opposite that of the modern information retrieval thesaurus. While Roget's thesaurus helps writers identify the best term for their particular purpose (an objective that BOTH types of thesauri share!), its main purpose is often seen as encouraging and facilitating variety in expression, something prized in many contexts. The information retrieval thesaurus aims to control or compensate for such variety — to bring together the many terms that might be used to describe essentially the same, or closely related topic, to facilitate searching.

• **books on construction of thesauri : 81**

There is a large literature on the construction of thesauri. Some of the most important works are:

- Aitchison, Jean; Gilchrist, Alan; Bawden, David (1997). *Thesaurus construction and use: a practical manual.* 3rd ed. London: Aslib, c1997. xvi, 212 p. ISBN 0851423906.

- Lancaster, F. Wilfrid (1986). *Vocabulary control for information retrieval.* 2nd ed. Arlington, VA: Information Resources Press; 1986. xvii, 270 p. ISBN 0878150536.

- National Information Standards Organization (1993). *Guidelines for the construction, format, and management of monolingual thesauri.* Bethesda, MD: NISO Press; c1994. xii, 69 p. ANSI/NISO Z39.19-1993. ISBN 1-880124-04-1.

- Soergel, Dagobert (1974). *Indexing languages and thesauri: construction and maintenance.* Los Angeles: Melville Pub. Co.; 1974. xliii, 632 p. (A Wiley-Becker & Hayes series book). ISBN 0471810479.

• **thesauri for full-text IR databases : 82**

Milstead, herself the author of an important indexing thesaurus in the field of library and information science (1994), has written on the role of "Thesauri in a full-text world" (1997).

• **views of Soergel (Dagobert) on construction of thesauri : 83**

Soergel, in perhaps the most comprehensive treatment of thesauri (1974), written before modern electronic thesaurus construction programs became common, provided a checklist of compilation procedures (p. 364-368). Here it is, with some modifications and additional commentary:

1. Select sources for the collection of terms, such as glossaries, dictionaries, textbooks, treatises and items to be indexed.

2. Assign an abbreviation to each important source (for citing source or authority in term records).

3. Select terms.

4. Transfer terms with all information to thesaurus records. See Soergel's suggested term record card below. Remember, cards such as this were used in the pre-computer age. It is still useful to consider this record card in terms of the information Soergel considers to be important! Similar information could, of course, be placed into thesaurus database record fields.

5. Sort terms into alphabetical order (by main term on record card).

6. First round of merging: merge information for identical terms, when the same terms have been selected from different sources.

Chapter 13. Vocabulary Management (Section 13.3.2)

7. Second round of merging: sort terms conceptually (as opposed to alphabetically), then merge information and terms representing the same concept. Steps 8-15 are part of this process of sorting terms conceptually in order to locate different terms for the same concept. Once such terms are found, one term will be selected as the main (preferred) term. The other terms become non-preferred terms and should be listed as synonymous or equivalent terms on the record card for the main term.

8. Define broad subject fields and sort terms into these broad fields.

9. Define subfields within each broad subject field and sort terms into these subfields.

10. Work out detailed classified structure; select preferred terms; merge information for terms representing same concept.

11. Produce preliminary version of classified index (the conceptually-ordered listing of terms).

12. Improve classificatory structure.

13. Produce improved version of classified index; distribute among subject experts.

14. Discuss classified index with subject experts; refine selection of descriptors.

15. Assign notational symbols (to maintain classified order of terms).

16. Make systematic search for additional cross references (ST, ET, BT, NT, RT etc. — see record card for these abbreviations).

17. Revise all entries in the working file as follows:

   a. Formulate standardized abbreviation.

   b. Standardize form of main terms.

   c. Standardize terms in BT, NT, RT fields to be identical to the corresponding main terms on the main term record cards. One of the principal advantages of modern electronic thesaurus construction programs is that they help maintain these reciprocal relations, ensuring that the form of a term is identical as a BT, NT, or RT and an MT (main term). Include classification notation with BT, NT, and RT terms.

   d. Improve classificatory structure.

   e. Create USE/UF references. In the final thesaurus display, every synonymous and equivalent term becomes a UF term in a standard thesaurus display, meaning that the MT (main term) is UF (used for) the listed synonymous or equivalent terms. For each of these UF terms, a USE reference must be generated, e.g.:

   ```
   attorney: USE lawyer
   ```

18. Produce the main part of the thesaurus in list-form (i.e., in alphabetical order by MT — main term).

19. Check inverse cross references and insert where necessary. (Again, this is making sure that reciprocal BT, NT, and RT terms are listed in both MT (main term) records and in the records where they are BT, NT, or RT terms. Modern thesaurus construction programs can do this automatically.)

20. Insert modifications in the manuscript; duplicate and distribute among subject experts.

21. Review the whole thesaurus. Consult with subject experts.

22. Insert modifications.

23. Produce alphabetical index (e.g., in KWIC format to locate preferred terms by any word within them).

24. Check homographs and cross references using alphabetical index.

Chapter 13. Vocabulary Management (Section 13.3.2)

25. Reproduce test version of the thesaurus.
26. Test the thesaurus by indexing and retrieval experiments. Insert modifications.
27. Duplicate or print the user version of the thesaurus.
28. The end, but not really — for a good thesaurus, all work must continue!

• card format for term records for thesauri : 84

Soergel's Thesaurus Record Card

```
==================================================================
01. hierarchical level: 0 1 2 3 4 5 6  | 02. type: DS OP NP EL CH
---------------------------------------|--------------------------
03. Subject field:                     | 10. MT.
---------------------------------------|
05. Notation:                          |
---------------------------------------|--------------------------
12. Standard abbr. (AB):               | 46. Related terms (RT):
---------------------------------------|
20. Spellings variants (incl. abbr.)   |
                                       |
                                       |
---------------------------------------|
30. Synonymous terms (ST), incl.       |
    equivalent terms (ET):             |
                                       |--------------------------
                                       | 50. Translations (TR):
                                       |
                                       | French:
                                       |
                                       | German:
                                       |
                                       | Russian:
                                       |
                                       | Spanish:
---------------------------------------|--------------------------
4. Classification:                     | 60. Definition, scope note (SN):
42. Category (CA):                     |
---------------------------------------|
44. Broader terms (BT):                |
                                       |
                                       |
                                       |
                                       | 65. Sources/authorities (AU):
                                       |
---------------------------------------|--------------------------
45. Narrower terms (NT):               |70. Unspecified relation (UN):
                                       |
                                       |
                                       |
                                       |--------------------------
                                       |81. Editor/Date:
                                       |
==================================================================
```

Chapter 13. Vocabulary Management (Section 13.3.2)

Notes for the record card:

Each field has its own numerical notation; some numbers are skipped in case new fields need to be added later on.

01. When terms are later sorted into hierarchies, based on BT and NT descriptors, each term will fall at a particular hierarchical level. Noting this level here will help a typist in compiling the hierarchical display. This is now done automatically by computer programs!

02. These codes indicate the current status of the main term in field 10: DS=descriptor (authorized term); OP=other preferred term (but not adopted as as an authorized descriptor); NP=non-preferred term; EL=eliminate term; CH=change term information.

03. In order to find different terms indicating the same, or essentially the same concept, terms must be sorted conceptually. The subject field is the first large category for conceptual sorting. For faceted thesauri, these first level categories will be the main facets.

05. Later, when cards are sorted into final conceptual order, a notation can be assigned to maintain this order. Cards can then be sorted by notation when the classified display of terms is being prepared. Such a notation could resemble the decimal notation used by the *Dewey decimal classification*, e.g., entities could be assigned notations in the 100-400s, attributes in the 500-600s, actions in the 700s, places in the 800s, and times in the 900; or it could resemble the notation used by the *Library of Congress classification*, with BA-FZ used for entities, GA-HZ used for attributes, JA-LZ used for actions, MA-MZ used for places and PA-PZ used for times.

10. This is the main term for this card. All the information on the card will relate to this term.

12. A standard abbreviation for a term is often helpful to indexers, who can use it to save time. Later, before an index is prepared for users, most abbreviations would be expanded to the full standard form. (Abbreviations can be the standard form when they are better known, as with acronyms such as "radar" and "Unesco.")

20. Variant spellings go here (as well as variant abbreviations).

30. Synonymous and equivalent terms go here.

4/42. This field can be used for finer categorization within the broad subject field, noted in field 03.

44. Broader terms go here.

45. Narrower terms go here.

46. Related terms go here.

50. If the thesaurus is to be multilingual, than the equivalent terms in others languages go here.

60. A definition of the term, if needed, or a scope note explaining the usage of the term in the indexing language, goes here.

65. Here is recorded the source of the term, or the authority for the definition/scope note.

70. Any terms whose relationship to the main term has not yet been determined can go here.

81. The name or initials of the thesaurus editor, plus the date, go here.

• **computer programs for construction of thesauri : 85**

Milstead (1990) has described and compared modern thesaurus construction software. A current website, maintained by Leonard Will (2003, www.willpower.demon.co.uk/thessoft.htm) lists and describes currently available software.

Chapter 13. Vocabulary Management (Section 13.3.2.1)

13.3.2.1 Examples of Indexing Thesauri.

• 86

Three excellent examples of indexing thesauri are the *Unesco thesaurus* (Unesco 1977, 2nd ed. 1995), *Thesaurus eurovoc* (European Communities 1995), and the ASIS thesaurus of information science and librarianship (Milstead 1994). Both the Unesco and Eurovoc thesauri have detailed introductions, which cover such topics as purpose, history, principles of construction, sources of terms, structure of the thesaurus, semantic relationships, presentation, and guidelines for use. The Unesco and Eurovoc thesauri are multilingual, whereas the ASIS thesaurus is monolingual, English only. Here we will describe these thesauri in terms of the displays they provide in print form. The *Unesco thesaurus* is also available on the world-wide web at http://www.ulcc.ac.uk/unesco/index.htm, courtesy of the University of London Computer Center.

• *Unesco thesaurus* (1977) : 87

The first edition of the *Unesco thesaurus* (1977) presented its terminology in four displays. The main display included records for all preferred authorized terms plus USE references for lead-in non-authorized terms, such as:

```
Independent schools
    USE Private education
```

• term records in *Unesco thesaurus* (1977) : 88

Here is the Unesco (1977) record for "Index languages":

```
Index languages Z50 *X02 *X50
    SN  An 'artificial language' used by documentation
        systems for purposes of indexing. (Wersig 15-10)
    UF  Documentary languages
        Indexing languages
        Retrieval languages
    NT  Controlled languages
        Free language systems
        Natural language systems
    BT  Language varieties
    TT  Languages
        Philology
    RT  Document description
        Index language compilation
        Index language elements
        Information processing
        Information retrieval
        Information storage devices
        Linguistics
```

• classification notation in *Unesco thesaurus* (1977) : 89

The notations "Z50 *X02 *X50" indicates the three locations where the concept represented by the term "indexing languages" falls in the classified display of the terminology. The primary location, which will be illustrated below, is indicated by Z50; notations preceded by an asterisk indicate secondary locations.

• notation in *Unesco thesaurus* (1977) : 90

The two letter codes represent the following:

```
SN = scope note. The authority or source of the term and/or definition
     is given in parenthesis.
```

Chapter 13. Vocabulary Management (Section 13.3.2.1)

```
UF = used for (followed by synonymous or equivalent terms that the main
     preferred authorized term is "used for."
NT = narrower term(s)
BT = broader term(s)
TT = top term(s) of the hierarchies in which the main term falls. If
     there is no TT, then the main term is the top term of a hierarchy.
RT = related term(s)
```

• KWIC display in *Unesco thesaurus* (1977) : 91

The KWIC display allows users to find every authorized preferred term containing any particular word. Here is the segment of the KWIC display for the word "index," "indexes," and "indexing":

```
                  Shelf as  index
                            Index entries
                            Index language codes
                            Index language compilation
                            Index language elements
                            Index language order
                            Index language vocabularies
                  Concepts  (index language)
             Interpolation  (index language)
                            Index languages
  Automatic generation of   index languages
                            Index terms
            File guidance   (index)
          File maintenance  (index)
           File management  (index)
          File organization (index)
                    Filing  (index)
                            Indexers
                            Indexes
    Alphabetical subject    indexes
               Articulated  indexes
                    Author  indexes
                      Book  indexes
                     Chain  indexes
                  Citation  indexes
                Classified  indexes
              Computerized  indexes
                Coordinate  indexes
                Cumulative  indexes
                      KWAC  indexes
                      KWIC  indexes
                      KWOC  indexes
         Manual coordinate  indexes
                      Name  indexes
                Periodical  indexes
                  Permuted  indexes
            Pre-coordinate  indexes
                    PRECIS  indexes
                   Printed  indexes
  Punched card coordinate   indexes
                  Relative  indexes
                   Rotated  indexes
                   Subject  indexes
                     Title  indexes
```

Chapter 13. Vocabulary Management (Section 13.3.2.1)

```
          Visible  indexes
         Rotation  (indexes)
Alphabetico-classed  indexes/catalogues
                  Indexing
      Associative  indexing
           Author  indexing
        Automatic  indexing
         Citation  indexing
            Depth  indexing
             Name  indexing
       Relational  indexing
          Subject  indexing
            Title  indexing
                  Indexing consistency
                  Indexing exhaustivity
  Abstracting and  indexing services
                  Indexing specificity
Statistical linguistics (indexing)
```

Note: It is not clear why the qualifier "(index)" is used with the terms "File guidance," "File maintenance," "File organization," and "Filing," while the qualifier "(indexes)" is used with the term "Rotation." The former terms clearly apply to operations; the later term may be used to indicate rotated term indexes — that is, a kind of index.

• hierarchical displays in *Unesco thesaurus* (1977) : 92

Each authorized preferred term falls in at least one hierarchy and sometimes more than one. The top term (TT) indicates the name of the hierarchy. Some hierarchies in this *Unesco thesaurus* are quite small, such as:

```
Immunization
 . Vaccination
```

• 93

Other thesauri would group such small hierarchies into larger hierarchies, such as:

```
Actions/operations
 . Medical actions/operations
 . . Immunization
 . . . Vaccination
```

• 94

Here is a portion of the "index language elements" hierarchy:

```
Index language elements
 . Cross-references
 . Index language codes
 . . Call numbers
 . . Notation
 . . . Alphabetic notation
 . . . Expressive notation
 . . . . Hierarchical notion
 . . . Mixed notation
 . . . Mnemonic notation
 . . . Numeric notation
 . . . Ordinal notation
 . . . Retroactive notation
 . . Reference codes
```

Chapter 13. Vocabulary Management (Section 13.3.2.1)

```
. Index language order
. . Citation order
. . Collocation
. . Filing order
. . . Alphabetization
. Index language vocabularies
. . Blank words
. . Concepts (index language)
. . . Isolates
. . Index terms
. . . Abbreviations
. . . . Acronyms
. . . Bound terms
. . . Compound terms
. . . Homographs
. . . Identifiers
. . . . Proprietary names
. . . Subject headings
. . . Synthesised terms
. . Lead-in terms
. . Modifier terms
. . . Qualifiers
. . . Sub-headings
. Precision oriented devices
. . Compound terms
. . Coordination (concept)
. . . Post-coordination
. . . Pre-coordination
. . Link indicators
. . Operator systems
. . . Relational indexing
. . Role indicators
. . Vocabulary specificity
. . Weights
. Recall oriented devices
. . Hierarchical relations
. . . Polyhierarchical relations
. . . Subordination
. . . . Narrower terms
. . . Superordination
. . . . Broader terms
. . Non-hierarchical relations
. . . Part-whole relations
. . . Related terms
. . Terminological control
. . . Synonym control
. . . Wordform confounding
. . . . Truncation
. Scope notes
. Term interrelations
. . Semantic relations
. . . Classes (terms)
. . . . Main classes
. . . Equivalence relations
. . . . Synonyms
. . . . . Quasi-synonyms
. . . Facet analysis
```

Chapter 13. Vocabulary Management (Section 13.3.2.1)

```
. . . Graphic displays
. . . Hierarchical relations
. . . . Polyhierarchical relations
. . . . Subordination
```

• relational displays in *Unesco thesaurus* (1977) : 95

The first edition of the *Unesco thesaurus* (1977) also displayed its vocabulary in a detailed enumerative classification. Each concept represented by a preferred authorized term was listed (enumerated) in one or more classes where it fit conceptually. The purpose was to provide the user with an overall view of the entire scope of the thesaurus, and within the classification, more detailed views of each constituent field or discipline.

• 96

Here is the outline of the classification for "information libraries and archives":

```
Z            INFORMATION LIBRARIES AND ARCHIVES

             Summary

Z08          Information
Z10          Information transfer
Z15          Information materials
Z15.01/59        Bookform materials
Z15.60/99        Non-book materials
Z18          Bibliology
Z20/84       Library and information science
Z24              Information/library history
Z26              Information/library research
Z28              Information/library philosophy, policy and development
Z30              Information/library planning and administration
Z32              Information/library facilities
Z34              Information/library personnel
Z36              Information/library profession
Z38              Information/library training
Z40/56           Information/library operations
Z42                  Library housekeeping operations
Z45/56               Information processing
Z48                      Document description
Z50                      Index languages
Z52                      Information storage devices
Z54                      Information retrieval
Z56                      Information systems evaluation
Z58              Information/library stock
Z60/70           Information/library systems
Z62                  Libraries
Z65                  Information services
Z68                  Information systems
Z72          Information use
Z73/75       Library use promotion
Z85/99       Archives
Z92              Records management
Z93              Archive operations
Z95/97           Records
Z98              Archive agencies
```

Chapter 13. Vocabulary Management (Section 13.3.2.1)

• 97

And here is the detailed classification of Index languages. Terms preceded by an asterisk (*) are cross-references to primary locations within the classification:

```
Z50             Index Languages
                (By basic type)
    Z50.01/15   Controlled languages
    Z50.05          Classification systems
                        (By specificity)
    Z50.05.10           Broad classification systems
    Z50.05.15           Close classification systems
                        (By basic type)
    Z50.05.20           Hierarchical classification systems
                            UF Enumerative classification systems
                               Monohierarchical classification systems
                            List individual systems alphabetically, e.g.
    Z50.05.20D              Dewey Decimal Classification
    Z50.05.20L              Library of Congress Classification
    Z50.05.30/40        Analytico-synthetic classification systems
                            UF Polyhierarchical classification systems
                               Synthetic classification systems
                            List individual systems, alphabetically, e.g.
    Z50.05.30U              UDC
                                UF Universal Decimal Classification
                        (By facet systems)
    Z50.05.40           Faceted classification systems
                            List individual systems alphabetically, e.g.
    Z50.05.40B              Bliss Classification System
    Z50.05.40C              Colon classification
    Z50.07          Alphabetical subject headings lists
    Z50.08          Term lists
    Z50.08.20           Uniterms
    Z50.10          Thesauri
                        UF Descriptor languages
    Z50.10.10           Alphabetical thesauri
    Z50.10.30           Systematic thesauri
    Z50.10.40           Classification/thesaurus systems
    Z50.10.50           Compressed vocabularies
    Z50.10.60           Macrothesauri
    Z50.10.65           Microthesauri
    Z50.10.70           Monolingual thesauri
    Z50.10.72           Multilingual thesauri
    Z50.12          Authority lists
    Z50.14          Switching languages
    Z50.16      Natural language systems
    Z50.18      Free language systems
                (By index language element)
    Z50.26/94 Index language elements
                    *Linguistics X02/54
    Z50.27          Recall oriented devices
                        *Hierarchical relations Z50.56
                        *Terminological control Z50.48
    Z50.28          Precision oriented devices
                        *Compound terms Z50.35.40
                        *Coordination Z50.74
                        *Link indicators Z50.77
                        *Operator systems Z50.62
```

Chapter 13. Vocabulary Management (Section 13.3.2.1)

...

• *Unesco thesaurus* (1995) : 98

The 2nd edition of the *Unesco thesaurus* (1995) merged the formerly separate KWIC display with the alphabetical display of term records. It also dropped the hierarchical displays and the detailed enumerative classification, opting instead for a series of "microthesauri" for relatively narrow topical areas.

• microthesauri in Unesco *thesaurus* (1995) : 99

For browsing and navigation, microthesauri are grouped into the following 7 major categories, representing the major disciplinary domains of the *Unesco thesaurus*, plus a separate microthesaurus for places:

```
1  Education
2  Science
3  Culture
4  Social and human sciences
5  Information and communication
6  Politics, law and economics
7  Countries and country groupings
```

• 100

If you pick one of these categories, you can browse through the major subdivisions, e.g., for 5. Information and communication:

```
5.   Information and communication
5.05 Information sciences
5.10 Communication research and policy

5.15 Information management
5.20 Information industry
5.25 Documentary information systems
5.30 Information sources
5.35 Documentary information processing
5.40 Information technology (software)
5.45 Information technology (hardware)
```

• 101

Here is the microthesaurus for 5.35 Documentary information processing, in which you see the term records for the terms that fall within this microthesaurus:

```
5.35 Documentary information

Acquisitions
    UF Accessions
    UF Acquisitions policy
    NT1 Book selection
        UF Book ordering
        UF Document selection
        UF Journal screening
    NT1 UNESCO coupons
        UF Book coupons

Information dissemination
    NT1 Book distribution
    NT1 Dissemination of knowledge
    NT1 International circulation of materials
    NT1 Selective dissemination of information
```

Chapter 13. Vocabulary Management (Section 13.3.2.1)

```
        UF Interest profiles
        UF SDI

Information processing
    UF Documentary information processing
    UF Information handling
    UF Information storage and retrieval
    UF Information work
    UF Information/library operations
    NT1 Cataloguing
        UF Bibliographic description
        UF Centralized cataloguing
        UF Cooperative cataloguing
        UF Descriptive cataloguing
        NT2 Bibliographic control
    NT1 Documentary analysis
        UF Information analysis
        NT2 Abstracting
        NT2 Indexing
            UF Concept analysis
            UF Subject indexing

Information retrieval
    UF Bibliographic searches
    UF Literature searches
    UF Retrospective searches
    NT1 Online searching
        UF Online information retrieval
        NT2 Search strategies

Library circulation
    UF Library loan services
    NT1 Interlibrary loans
        UF External loans
    NT1 Periodical circulation

Records management
    UF Records disposal
    UF Records disposition
    NT1 Archive records preservation
    NT1 Records appraisal
        UF Selective retention
```

• display of multiple hierarchical levels in *Unesco thesaurus* (1995) : 102

Also new to the 2nd edition of the *Unesco thesaurus* (1995) is the display of several levels of hierarchy within term records. In the first edition, only one level of BT or NT terms were shown in each term record. Now two or three levels are shown. Compare this new record for "Indexing languages" with the record from the 1st edition, shown above:

```
Indexing languages
    MT  5.05 Information sciences
        FR Language d'indexation
        SP Lenguaje de indizacio@'n
    SN  An artificial language used by documentation systems
        for purposes of indexing.
    UF  Documentary languages
    UF  Retrieval languages
```

Chapter 13. Vocabulary Management (Section 13.3.2.1)

```
NT1 Authority lists
NT1 Controlled languages
    NT2 Classification systems
        NT3 Subject headings
NT1 Terminological control
NT1 Thesauri
    NT2 Thesaurus compilation
RT  Information retrieval
RT  Linguistics
RT  Terminology
```

• **term records in *Unesco thesaurus*** (1995) : 103

Gone is the former TT for top terms of hierarchies. Gone also are notations from the detailed enumerative classification. Instead you now have "MT 5.05 Information sciences," indicating the number and name of the microthesaurus (MT). New also are the equivalent terms in French and Spanish. Note the two additional levels of narrower terms displayed under the NT1 Controlled languages. The numbers following the NT notation indicate the hierarchical level.

• ***Eurovoc thesaurus*** : 104

The *Thesaurus eurovoc* (European Communities 1995) — commonly called the "Eurovoc thesaurus" — uses displays very similar to those of the 2nd edition of the *Unesco thesaurus*.

• **term records in *Eurovoc thesaurus*** : 105

Here is a thesaurus record for "marine environment," in which the microthesaurus "5211 natural environment" is named, followed by two levels of broader terms, two levels of narrower terms, and a related term. One difference from the *Unesco thesaurus* is that terms, except proper nouns, are all lower case, as advocated by the NISO guidelines (Anderson 1997a). Unesco continues to begin all descriptors with a capital letter.

```
marine environment
    MT    5211 natural environment
    BT1   aquatic environment
      BT2   physical environment
    NT1   littoral
    NT1   sea-bed
      NT2   continental shelf
      NT2   inshore grounds
    RT    marine life
```

• 106

And here is the thesaurus record for "marital status." Another difference between the *Unesco thesaurus* and the *Eurovoc thesaurus* is apparent here. Whereas the *Unesco thesaurus* prefers plural forms for countable nouns, such as "persons" and "parents," the *Eurovoc thesaurus* prefers singular forms. Plural forms for such terms are customary in the United States.

```
marital status
    MT    2806 family
    UF    family status
    NT1   cohabitation
    NT1   divorced person
    NT1   married person
    NT1   separated person
    NT1   single parent
    NT1   unmarried person
    NT1   widowed person
    RT    civil status
    RT    matrimonial law
```

Chapter 13. Vocabulary Management (Section 13.3.2.1)

• 107

We criticized some of the narrower terms used in *Library of Congress subject headings* under "marriage," because some of them were not truly narrower, in a hierarchical or whole part sense (see 13.3.1). Here too, one could argue with some of the narrower terms for "marital status." "Cohabitation" is the activity of cohabiting; it is not the name of a status. All the other narrower terms are kinds of persons — and persons are not statuses. What has happened here is that the thesaurus editors have chosen to use "cohabitation" to stand for "cohabiting person" and also for the "status of cohabiting person." Similarly, "divorced person" stands as well for "status of divorced person." Such conflation of concepts is fairly common in controlled vocabularies. (One could also argue that none of the "statuses" listed as narrower terms under "marital status" are types of marital status — in fact they are alternatives to the status of marriage, but "marital status" is commonly used to indicate the whole range of "married," "non-married," "formerly married," and perhaps "sort-of married"!)

• microthesauri in *Eurovoc thesaurus* : 108

Like the *Unesco thesaurus*, the microthesauri of the *Eurovoc thesaurus* are grouped into the major disciplinary domains covered by the thesaurus, plus a category for the European Communities:

```
04   politics
08   international relations
10   European Communities
12   law
16   economics
20   trade
24   finance
28   social questions
32   education and communications
36   science
40   business and competition
```

• 109

The domain of "28 social questions" is divided into nine separate microthesauri:

```
2806   family
2811   migration
2816   demography and population
2821   social framework
2826   social affairs
2831   culture and religion
2836   social protection
2841   health
2846   construction and town planning
```

• 110

The microthesaurus "2806 family" contains expanded thesaurus records relating to families, not only types of families and parts of families, but also activities and methods used by or in families. In these microthesaurus term records, each of the top-level records are expanded to include not only several levels of narrower terms, but also the related terms pertaining to narrower terms. When a related term falls in another microthesaurus, the number for that microthesaurus is given after the term. Compare the last record shown below for "marital status" with the main thesaurus record for the same term illustrated above:

2806 family

artificial reproductive techniques
          RT   bio-ethics (2826)
          RT   descendant
          RT   private law (1206)
          RT   trade in organs (2826)
  NT1 surrogate mother
  NT1 test tube fertilization

family
          RT   household (2816)
  NT1 breadwinner
  NT1 dependant
          RT   custody
          RT   maintenance obligation
  NT1 family by marriage
  NT1 family policy
          RT   birth policy (2816)
          RT   family benefit (2836)
          RT   maternity benefit (2836)
    NT2 family protection
          RT   care of mothers and infants (2841)
  NT1 head of household
          RT   household (2816)
  NT1 large family
          RT   birth policy (2816)
          RT   home help (2836)
  NT1 one-parent family
          RT   single parent
  NT1 relationship
    NT2 abandoned child
          RT   child protection (2826)
    NT2 adopted child
          RT   adoption of a child
    NT2 natural child
    NT2 only child
    NT2 orphan

family law
          RT   private international law (1231)
          RT   private law (1206)
  NT1 adoption of a child
          RT   adopted child
  NT1 custody
          RT   children's rights (1236)
          RT   dependant
  NT1 descendant
          RT   artificial reproductive techniques
          RT   nationality (1231)

  NT1 divorce
          RT   divorced person
  NT1 emancipation
  NT1 guardianship

Chapter 13. Vocabulary Management (Section 13.3.2.1)

```
    NT1   judicial separation
                RT   separated person
    NT1   maintenance obligation
                RT   dependant
                RT   divorced person
                RT   law of obligations (1211)
    NT1   marriage
                RT   marriage rate (2816)
                RT   married person
                RT   mixed marriage (1231)
                RT   nationality (1231)
    NT1   matrimonial law
                RT   marital status
    NT1   parental authority
                RT   children's rights (1236)
    NT1   parental responsibility
    NT1   surname

family planning
                RT   demographic policy (2816)
    NT1   birth control
                RT   birth policy (2816)
                RT   births (2816)
       NT2   abortion
          NT3   illegal abortion
          NT3   therapeutic abortion
       NT2   contraception
                RT   women's movement (0431)
       NT2   sterilization

marital status
                RT   civil status (1211)
                RT   matrimonial law
    NT1   cohabitation
    NT1   divorced person
                RT   divorce
                RT   maintenance obligation
                RT   single person (2816)
    NT1   married person
                RT   marriage
    NT1   separated person
                RT   judicial separation
                RT   single person (2816)
    NT1   single parent
                RT   one-parent family
    NT1   unmarried person
                RT   single person (2816)
    NT1   widowed person
                RT   single person (2816)
                RT   survivor's benefit (2836)
```

Chapter 13. Vocabulary Management (Section 13.3.2.1)

• ASIS thesaurus : 111

The *ASIS thesaurus of information science and librarianship*, compiled by Jessica L. Milstead and published in 1994, is a good example of a modern thesaurus covering a single disciplinary domain, in contrast to the much broader subject scopes of the *Unesco thesaurus* and the *Eurovoc thesaurus*.

• display of ASIS thesaurus : 112

The *ASIS thesaurus* uses the more traditional displays of the 1st edition of the *Unesco thesaurus*: an alphabetical display of term records, hierarchy displays, and a KWIC display of terms sorted by every significant keyword in every term.

• facets in ASIS thesaurus : 113

A major difference between the *ASIS thesaurus* versus the Unesco and Eurovoc thesauri is the use of a comprehensive facet list, which includes the top terms of all hierarchies. There are no small "orphan" hierarchies, as we saw in the first edition of the *Unesco thesaurus*. Thesaurus facets tend to be more rigorously defined than the conceptual groupings displayed in microthesauri.

• 114

The top hierarchical terms, representing the main facets of the *ASIS thesaurus* are:

```
activities and operations
buildings and facilities
communications media
document types
fields and disciplines
hardware, equipment, and systems
knowledge, information, etc.
natural functions and events
networks
organizations
persons and informal groups
physical media
product and service providers
qualities
research and analytic methods
sectors of the economy
sociocultural aspects
```

• 115

The "activities and operations" facet is divided by domain:

```
business and management operations
communications activities
computer operations
educational and psychological activities
general activities
information and library operations
socioeconomic activities
technical and manufacturing operations
```

• 116

"Information and library operations" consist of:

```
access to resources
arrangement
bibliographic control
bibliography
```

Chapter 13. Vocabulary Management (Section 13.3.2.1)

```
book collection
database leasing
document delivery
document handling
document retrieval
documentation
genealogy
information dissemination
information flow
information production
information resources management
information retrieval
information seeking
information services
information transfer
information use
knowledge engineering
library services
navigation
organization of information
output reformatting
photocopying
preservation of library materials
relevance judgments
```

• 117

"Organization of information" consists of:

```
cataloging (bibliographic)
classification
database design
facet analysis
index language construction
indexing
relevance ranking
subject analysis
```

• 118

"Indexing" consists of:

```
assignment indexing
automatic indexing
book indexing
database indexing
derivative indexing
manual indexing
name indexing
periodical indexing
probabilistic indexing
string indexing
subject indexing
```

• 119

And finally, "subject indexing" consists of:

```
chain indexing
generic posting
multilingual subject indexing
postcoordinate indexing
```

331

Chapter 13. Vocabulary Management (Section 13.3.3)

```
PRECIS
precoordinate indexing
```

13.3.3. End-User Thesauri.

• end-user thesauri versus indexing thesauri : 120

End-user thesauri, also called "searching thesauri" in contrast to "indexing thesauri," are intended to guide and assist searchers, as opposed to indexers. Rather than focusing only on the indexing of particular IR databases, they are meant to organize and display the vocabulary of their subject scope and domain in order to improve search performance in any IR database or across multiple databases.

• differences between indexing thesauri versus end-user thesauri : 121

The principal difference between end-user thesauri versus indexing thesauri is that end-user thesauri do not designate particular terms as preferred, but rather they attempt to organize and display the vocabulary as it is actually used within the subject scope and domain of the thesaurus. Thus, in principle, the vocabulary of an end-user thesauri will be much larger than a typical indexing thesaurus, and it will include a greater variety of word forms and parts of speech, even misspellings.

• lead-in terms in end-user thesauri : 122

Remembering the research of Furnas et al. (1987), which suggested the need for as many as fifteen different ways to express a given concept in order to accommodate 80% of the terms that users will bring to an IR database, the aim for an end-user thesaurus is to encompass the entire vocabulary of its users. All such terms will be "lead-in" terms — terms that will lead the user into the thesaurus.

• gathering terms in end-user thesauri : 123

Even though no particular term is designated as "authorized" or "preferred," it is necessary to have a gathering place for all terms that can be considered equivalent or synonymous for a given concept. For this purpose, it is convenient to choose one term to name the concept, and also the record in which all these terms will be gathered. Much like an indexer thesaurus, all lead-in terms that are equivalent or synonymous to the gathering term will lead users to the gathering term record, and there they will find all synonymous, equivalent, variant, narrower, related, and broader terms. They can then choose to use all of these terms in a search, or to select particular relevant terms.

• examples of end-user thesauri : 124

The concept of end-user thesauri has yet to be fully realized in practice. Thus we are unable to point to any published or widely available examples. Instead, we will illustrate the idea of an end-user thesaurus by walking through the steps that might be used to compile such a thesaurus for the field of IR database design — the subject scope of this book. These steps are similar to those used for an indexer thesaurus (as listed in section 13.3.2 from the work of Dagobert Soergel), except for the special effort to include the entire vocabulary of users and texts within a subject domain.

Chapter 13. Vocabulary Management (Section 13.3.3.1)

13.3.3.1. Compiling an End-User Thesaurus.
13.3.3.1.1. Sources of Terms.

• 125

The first step in compiling a thesaurus is to identify sources of terms for the thesaurus. For an end-user thesaurus, the best source of terms are user queries. After all, the whole purpose of an end-user thesaurus is to match the vocabulary of users to the vocabulary of IR databases and the vocabulary of the texts they are seeking.

• 126

The second best sources are the texts containing potential answers to queries. This is because our overall goal is to link queries with answers. To do this, we must incorporate the vocabulary of both our users and our authors — the people who create the messages with useful answers or responses to queries.

• 127

The third best source are expert human indexers. Human indexers develop an understanding of a field and a grasp of useful terminology. They should be encouraged to provide new terms, and the terms they suggest should certainly be incorporated into a thesaurus.

• 128

The fourth principal source for terms are existing linguistic reference tools, such as other thesauri, dictionaries, glossaries, handbooks, etc. These sources are the least important because once published, terminological reference works have a tendency to begin aging at once. They are often the most removed from the actual "conversations" that users and authors are carrying on about the concepts that interest them. Nevertheless, to the extent that such tools do indeed include important vocabulary for a particular subject scope and domain, then certainly their terms should be included.

• procedures for compilation of end-user thesauri : 129

Once terms are gathered from searchers, texts, indexers, and reference sources, end-user thesaurus editors face the same kinds of challenges as editors of more traditional indexing thesauri. However, the optimum solutions may not be the same. These challenges include: sorting and categorizing terms to create useful hierarchies and/or microthesauri; deciding between bound terms vs. elemental descriptors; determining useful term relationships; finding all important variant forms and equivalent terms; identifying and distinguishing homographs; designing helpful displays for end-user browsing and searching; and testing and validating the resulting thesaurus.

13.3.3.1.2. Selecting Terms.

• 130

To the extent possible, the end-user thesaurus should contain the terms actually being used by searchers. This means we need to find ways to collect these terms directly from users. Some OPAC programs (online public access catalogs) permit libraries to collect terms from searches. Web search engines may do this routinely. Terms from searches can be matched against a growing end-user thesaurus to see if they are already included. If they are not, they can be routed to a thesaurus editor.

Chapter 13. Vocabulary Management (Section 13.3.3.1.2)

• search statements as source of terms for end-user thesauri : 131

When search statements consist of long phrases or sentences, rather than isolated terms, some natural-language processing needs to be performed (either by humans or by algorithm) to identify multi-word terms, such as "information science" or "birth control." (See for example section 8.3.8 on phrase identification.)

• views of Landauer (Thomas K.) on users as source of terms for end-user thesauri : 132

Landauer (1985) has also urged the use of end-user terminology. He writes:

"For several years our research group has been studying the words people use when referring to various types of objects and operations (Furnas, Landauer, Gomez, & Dumais 1983; Gomez & Lochbaum 1984). ... The problem is that these 'access' words are largely 'inaccessible,' with an untutored person guessing the required word only about 10%-15% of the time. While there are many possible approaches to the problem, a simple optimal strategy in fact exists: given a table of data where each cell contains the frequency with which people apply every possible word to each object in a system, the optimal strategy simply looks in the table for a user's word to find the maximum frequency cell associated with it. This cell indicates what object is most frequently meant by that word. If the most-likely object does not satisfy the user, the system can offer the object associated with the next highest cell, etc. This strategy leads to a successful match in the first three offerings as much as 80-90% of the time — a dramatic improvement over the usual 10-15% hit rate. ...

"Consider the advantages of such a system. It collects the data from exactly the right subjects .... It uses the real targets, and the real motivations" (p. 131).

• 133

Landauer is using the term "object" for the item or concept the searcher wishes to name and about which s/he desires some response or information. The same end-user word could be used for different items or concepts — what we call a homograph — the same word (or "graph") representing different concepts (such as "race" for ethnicity or a sports contest). Similarly, different end-user words can be used to represent the same item or concept — what we call equivalent terms (such as "car" and "automobile").

• 134

We can illustrate Landauer's table as follows:

```
Users' search terms:          01        02        03      ...
                     ==================================
Concepts or items    A  |  1  |   3   |   5   |
indicated by terms   B  |  3  |   5   |   0   |
with frequency       C  |  9  |   9   |   7   |
scores               D  |  0  |   7   |   2   |
                     E  |  7  |   0   |   1   |
                     F  |  9  |   1   |   3   |
                     ... |     |       |       |
                     ==================================
```

• 135

Users' search terms are represented by 01, 02, 03, etc., across the top of the table. Concepts or items named by these search terms are represented by A, B, C, D, etc. displayed along the side of the table. Each cell within the table indicates the frequency that a particular search term has been used to indicate a particular concept.

When a searcher asks for 02, s/he is first shown concept (or item) C because C has the highest frequency of correspondence with term 02 (9). If the user rejects C, s/he is shown D next (with score 7), and if D is rejected, then B (with score 5), and so on.

Term 01 has been used most frequently (9) to indicate both concepts C and F. Therefore term 01 can be considered a homograph, indicating two different concepts (or items) with equal frequency.

On the other hand, both 01 and 02 have been used at frequency 9 to indicate concept C. Therefore, they are equivalent terms for this concept.

Such an interactive thesaurus would keep track of the number of times users who begin with a particular term select a particular concept (or item). This data would be used to create or update the frequency data for concepts or items associated with particular terms. If an end-user term is new and not yet in the thesaurus, the user is asked to suggest another term. If eventually the user hits upon the concept or item s/he is looking for in the thesaurus, all the unsuccessful terms that s/he first used can be linked to the sought concept or item. In the words of Landauer:

> "There are several failures, followed (with luck) by a hit. The important thing to notice is that this trail of failures has a lot of information in it. The terms in the unsuccessful attempts are *prima facie* good candidate keywords for the ... [user's desired object, operation, or concept]" (p. 131).

The user can be asked to confirm that the failed terms should indeed be linked to the successful term and its concept/item.

• selection of terms from texts for end-user thesauri : 141

The second most important source of terms for an end-user thesaurus are the texts contained in or represented in IR databases. Modern thesaurus construction software should be capable of pulling in terms from the full text of document titles, abstracts, and even the full text of documents or documentary units.

We shall illustrate one approach to the compilation of an end user thesaurus by pulling in terms from a section of this book. The actual terms in the text will be the starting point, but as compilation proceeds, other terms — broader, narrower, and other related terms — will be added by a thesaurus editor.

• identification of phrases from full text for end-user thesauri : 143

It is usually wise to do some preliminary processing of natural language text before submitting it to a thesaurus program. If no processing is done, the program will treat every word as a single term, so that multi-word terms will be decomposed. "Information science" will become "information" and "science." "Birth control" will become "birth" and "control." "John F. Kennedy" will become "John," "F.," and "Kennedy." Many of these single word terms will lose most if not all of any significance that they may have had as part of multi-word terms.

Therefore, it is prudent to link multi-word terms by using an automatic syntactic parsing program or by having a human being insert term links.

Chapter 13. Vocabulary Management (Section 13.3.3.1.2)

• 145

To illustrate the compilation of thesaurus terms from natural language, we will be using text from section 1.2 (Definitions). Here is the definition for "documentary unit," with multi-word terms linked using the equal sign (=):

documentary=unit. A "documentary=unit" is the portion of a document that can be directly retrieved by an IR=database. Documentary=units may be complete documents, such as complete books, or complete periodical=articles. Or they may be parts of complete documents — chapters=in=books, or paragraphs or charts or diagrams or illustrations in periodical=articles. This same variety in the size of documentary=units applies to all media. An IR=database for videotapes, for example, might retrieve only complete videotapes (so that the documentary=unit is the complete tape), or it might be able to retrieve individual=frames or short sequences=of=frames, in which cases, either the individual=frames, or the short sequences=of=frames, constitute the documentary=units. In all cases, the documentary=unit is the unit that is analyzed for indexing (either by machine=algorithm or by human=inspection). Consequently, the "documentary=unit" is also called the "unit=of=analysis." "Bibliographic=unit" has also been used for this concept, indicating the unit described and retrievable via a bibliography. Small documentary=units have also been called "information=units," but one should hope that all documentary=units will be informative!

• phrases from full text for end-user thesauri : 146

The following multi-word terms were identified and linked:

```
bibliographic=unit
chapters=in=books
documentary=unit
documentary=units
human=inspection
individual=frames
information=units
IR=database
machine=algorithm
periodical=articles
sequences=of=frames
unit=of=analysis
```

• 147

If "unit=of=analysis" had not been linked, its meaning would be completely lost in the individual terms "unit" and "analysis." For a complete thesaurus of the terminology used in this book, the text of the entire book could be processed in this manner.

• indexers as source of terms for end-user thesauri : 148

A thesaurus-construction program should, of course, also permit the addition of formal descriptors from database records (terms used by indexers) and also terms directly suggested by indexers or editors. And of course, thesaurus editors should also be able to add terms from glossaries, textbooks, other thesauri, and similar sources. Terms from such existing terminological lists can be entered one by one, from lists, or in the form of texts, as illustrated by our "documentary=unit" definition example.

13.3.3.1.3. Categorizing Terms.

• 149

Hundreds of words and phrases can be pulled in from even small texts or a small number of database records. If very large numbers of terms are entered into a thesaurus program from multiple records or texts, terms could be ranked by frequency for priority processing.

• 150

The task facing the compiler of the thesaurus is sorting all these terms into broad conceptual categories. These categories can represent the major facets or aspects of the subject scope and domain of an IR database. In turn, these categories may become the main facets or hierarchies of the thesaurus. But first, the thesaurus editor needs to go through several rounds of refinement, sorting terms into sub-categories and making distinctions about broader and narrower terms.

• 151

For example, on the first round of sorting or categorizing, all geographical terms can be placed into a single "places" category, but later, these places can be sorted by continent, nation, province or state, district or country, city or town, etc. Some place terms may be names of generic types of places, rather than particular places, so these will need to be sorted by type or kind as well. The particular place names, after sorting, can produce a hierarchical array of places, from very large places to very small. Names of types of places can also create a kind of environmental hierarchy. (For examples of these sorts of hierarchies, take a look at table 2, Geographic areas, in the *Dewey decimal classification* (Dewey 1996). Within table 2, category 1 is for generic places. Ancient places are placed in category 3. Modern places, including extraterrestrial places, fall into categories 4-9.)

• stop list terms in end-user thesauri : 152

As texts or user search statements are matched against a thesaurus, only those terms not already in the thesaurus will be routed to the thesaurus editor for acceptance and sorting. At the very beginning, however, on the first round of term acquisition from full-text sources, the initial terms will include all of the most commonly used non-substantive words that are usually found in stop lists. Even before conceptual sorting, the thesaurus editor needs to sort these in-coming terms into three groups: stop list terms (terms of no substantive significance); terms to discard (because they are outside the subject scope and domain of the thesaurus); and substantive terms to be added to the thesaurus. The stop list is treated as a separate thesaurus category or hierarchy (even though it most likely will not be structured into a real hierarchy with broader and narrower levels). Once a term is added to the thesaurus stop list, all future occurrences of that term will match the original term and it will not again appear on a list of new terms to be considered for integration into the thesaurus. In contrast, if a term is discarded, it will reappear the next time it is encountered in a text. Generally speaking, if in doubt, a term should be added to the stop list. It can always be removed from the stop list for integration into substantive hierarchies later. An alternative is to create a fourth initial category for "terms under consideration."

• 153

If an acceptable existing stop list is available, it can be loaded into the thesaurus in advance, thereby blocking the appearance of all of its stop list terms.

• sorting of terms for end-user thesauri : 154

After stop list and discard terms are marked or removed, sorting and categorization of the remaining terms can begin.

Chapter 13. Vocabulary Management (Section 13.3.3.1.3)

• **facets for end-user thesauri : 155**

When beginning a new thesaurus, it is generally best to sort all terms into the broad categories or facets that reflect the principal interests of the potential users of the thesaurus. In the words of Dagobert Soergel (1985), "A properly designed facet frame captures the essential conceptual structure of a field and is instrumental in eliciting the concepts to be included in the index language, in assisting in the analysis of a search topic, and in the analysis of an entity in indexing" (p. 397).

• **primary facets for end-user thesauri : 156**

Facets and facet analysis were discussed in chapter 2 on subject scope and domain. We can begin our sorting with a very generic set of primary facets — a starting point until more detailed facets are identified. Here is such a generic list, based on Ranganathan's basic PMEST categories (Personality = things; Matter = attributes; Energy = actions; Space = places; and Time).

```
1. things/entities: including persons/institutions/texts
2. properties/attributes
3. operations/processes/events
4. places
5. times/eras
6. stop list words
```

• **term records for end-user thesauri : 157**

As soon as a term is added to the thesaurus as a candidate term, it is placed in a thesaurus record. A typical thesaurus record includes the following fields:

```
rec\  Record number
des\  Descriptor or term
sor\  Source of term
scn\  Scope note
eqv\  Synonymous or equivalent terms
var\  Errors or variant forms
nrt\  Narrower terms
brt\  Broader terms
rlt\  Related terms
```

• **field tags for term records : 158**

The three letter tags on the left, followed by a back slash, are tags used to identify thesaurus record fields. Each thesaurus construction software program will have its own way of identifying these or similar fields.

• **initial categorization of terms for thesauri : 159**

The process of initial concept sorting is performed by simply assigning one (or more) of the broad initial primary facet terms as a broader term in each term's thesaurus record. This process is analogous to the physical sorting of concept cards into conceptual piles, as was done formerly when thesauri were compiled using a card for each term. (See the description of this physical sorting in section 13.3.2.)

• **size of categories in thesauri : 160**

After initial categorization of terms into broad primary facets, these large categories must be further broken down into sub-categories for the purpose of locating different terms for the same concepts, and also for creating useful displays of terms for scanning and browsing by end users. Criteria for what constitutes useful displays (and therefore, useful categories) must be based on assessments of utility for users. These are qualitative, subjective judgments, not subject to rigorous criteria of right, wrong, or correct. For any particular vocabulary, there are many possible displays. The objective is to create displays that help the user get an overview of the field and to

Chapter 13. Vocabulary Management (Section 13.3.3.1.3)

navigate effectively from one conceptual area to another. Also, for display purposes, sorting into sub-categories should continue until each sub-category has no more than 20-30 terms — the number of terms that can be scanned on a single computer screen.

• **categories of entities in end-user thesauri : 161**

In our exemplar end-user thesaurus, for example, we can subdivide the large "things/entities" category by types of entity, reflecting major categories of entities or things within the scope of this book, as follows:

- artifacts, products, tools
- computers
- disciplines
- institutions, organizations
- persons
- systems
- messages, texts, documents
- other (miscellaneous) things/entities

• 162

There is some duplication or overlap here. Computers, of course, are artifacts, but separate sub-categories of special importance can usefully be pulled out of larger groups and given their own categories. Similarly, messages, texts, and documents are also artifacts, and disciplines are social institutions, but both of these categories may have special significance for the scope and domain of this thesaurus. The "other (miscellaneous)" category can be used for terms that don't seem to fit elsewhere. Later, after studying these "other/miscellaneous" terms, we may be led to create new categories.

• **categories of operations and processes in end-user thesauri : 163**

Similarly, our "operations/processes/events" facet can be subdivided into the following categories. Compare these to the similar types of "activities and operations" used in the ASIS thesaurus, described above in section 13.3.2.1:

- business operations/processes/events
- computer operations/processes/events
- conceptual operations/processes
- generic operations/processes/events
- human behavior/processes/events
- information organization operations/processes/events
- information retrieval/processes/events
- communication operations/processes/events
- mathematical operations/processes/events
- political operations/processes/events
- research operations/processes/events
- social operations/processes/events

Chapter 13. Vocabulary Management (Section 13.3.3.1.4)

• definition of categories in thesauri : 164

An immediate reaction to this list might be: "what is meant by this category?" or "these categories don't seem to be mutually exclusive." For example, conceptual operations are often examples of human behavior, and many communication operations are also conceptual operations.

• 165

The definitions of categories are based in part on the terms that have been placed in them. What is meant by "conceptual operations," for example, is determined, at least in part, by the terms placed in that category, e.g., association, cognition, cognitive processes, concept analysis, decision making, discovery, education, invention, knowledge representation, modeling, perception, planning, scholarship, thinking, understanding, writing, etc. Category terms can be displayed whenever needed. In addition, the general meaning of a category can be described in a scope note.

• categories in thesauri not mutually exclusive : 166

Thesaurus categories are often not mutually exclusive, and some terms can usefully fall into more than one category. Our thesaurus, for example, might put "knowledge representation" in categories for "conceptual operations" and for "information organization operations." The aim in categorization is to create displays that will be useful to users. As already stated, there are many ways to display the vocabulary of any field. Our criteria must be "useful," "evocative," rather than necessarily "correct."

• merger of conceptually similar term records : 167

As we pursue this conceptual sorting, we may discover that we have two separate records for essentially the same concept. It is only though this process of separating and grouping by concept that we can find different terms representing conceptually similar or identical ideas. Once found, the records for identical or essentially the same concepts should be merged into a single record. The equivalent, variant, narrower, broader, and related terms from both records will be combined into a single new record. One or the other of the concept terms from the earlier records can be chosen to represent the new concept — to be the gathering term for all the terms related to the concept.

• sorting of terms in end-user thesauri : 168

The actual process of category subdivision, or sorting terms into sub-categories, is carried out by replacing a previous "broader term" by a narrower "broader term" in the thesaurus records. An early hierarchical display will list, for example, all the terms initially classed as "operations/processes/ events" as a single undifferentiated list of terms in the "operations/processes/events" hierarchy. Using this list, the thesaurus editor can open the record for each term and replace the broader term "operations/processes/events" with new broader terms, such as "information organization operations/ processes/events," "computer operations/processes/events," "conceptual operations/processes/events," etc. These new subordinate gathering terms can be integrated into the overall thesaurus structure by listing them as narrower terms in the record for the category term "operations/processes/events."

13.3.3.1.4. Bound Terms Versus Elemental Descriptors.

• 169

What constitutes a term or descriptor in an end-user or search thesaurus? Thesaurus experts have long debated the appropriate nature of terms in a thesaurus, some advocating a goal of listing only "single concept, elemental terms," while others champion the admission and use of

Chapter 13. Vocabulary Management (Section 13.3.3.1.4)

bound terms as found in the vocabulary within the subject scope and domain covered by the thesaurus.

• views of standards for thesauri on bound terms : 170

The *International standard for monolingual thesauri* (International Organization for Standardization 1986) says, "it is a general rule that terms in a thesaurus should represent simple or unitary concepts as far as possible, and compound terms should be factored (i.e. split) into simple elements, except when this is likely to affect the users' understanding" (quoted in Aitchison and Gilchrist 1987, p. 24). The American National Standard *Guidelines for the construction, format, and management of monolingual thesauri* (National Information Standards Organization 1993) acknowledges that "the establishment of procedures for dealing consistently with compound terms is one of the most difficult areas in the fields of thesaurus construction and indexing" (p. 11).

• 171

Few would object to the decomposition of "workload of dentists in Scotland" into "workload," "dentists," and "Scotland" (example in Aitchison and Gilchrist 1987, p. 24). But what about "philosophy of education," "history of science," "library science," "information science," "library school," "school library," or "birth control"? Thesaurus standards and textbooks provide guidelines for making these decisions, but there are no clear criteria or rules. In an end-user search thesaurus, the emphasis should be on user warrant — actual linguistic behavior of users or potential users. If multi-word phrases are treated as terms by users — that is, if they consistently or very frequently appear in the same form, then they should be listed as terms in the thesaurus. If "information science" is always (or almost always) "information science," then it should be considered a single term. However, if it is just as often expressed as the "science of information," then it may not be an established term warranted by usage and can be split into two terms "information" and "science."

• 172

Our preference is to err on the side of bound terms. One early version of our exemplar thesaurus had the term "prototype fuzzy query processors." This of course could have been broken down into "prototypes," "fuzzy queries," and "processors," (and "fuzzy queries" could be factored into "fuzziness" and "queries") but by keeping the original term together, as it appeared in the text from which it was drawn, it can be listed together with similar complex terms in displays of narrower or related terms under "prototypes" (giving users an array of specific prototypes to choose from); under "fuzziness," illustrating instances of this attribute; under "queries" (leading users to procedures applied to queries); and under "processors" (illustrating a wide range of processing applications).

• 173

Actually, the question is not whether to factor (split) or decompose a bound term that represents a compound or complex concept into its component concepts, but whether to list compound/complex terms as well as their more elemental parts. In the case of the "prototype fuzzy query processors" example, the complex bound term is listed under each of its more elemental factors. (A compound bound term is generally one with two conceptual components, such as "information science" or "birth control." A complex bound term is then one with more than two components, such as "reinforced concrete foot bridges" or "African American female fiction writers.")

Chapter 13. Vocabulary Management (Section 13.3.3.1.5)

• impact of bound terms on size of thesauri : 174

The main argument against bound or compound terms is that they increase the size of the vocabulary. The main arguments in their favor is that they reflect the actual vocabulary of users and authors and, perhaps more importantly, that they help prevent false drops — the retrieval of irrelevant documentary units that are associated with search terms. For example, if "library schools" and "school libraries" are factored (split) into "libraries" and "schools," then a search for library schools, using the factored terms "libraries" and "schools" will also retrieve documents on school libraries. If "library schools" and "school libraries" were maintained as separate terms, such false drops could be avoided. Both terms, "school libraries" and "library schools" are certainly justified by user warrant — warranted through common usage by potential thesaurus users.

13.3.3.1.5. Term Relationships.

• 175

The display of relationships among terms based on the relationships among the concepts they represent is a hallmark of the modern information retrieval thesaurus. The role of such relationships, and which ones are useful, has long been a topic of debate.

• term relationships in thesauri : 176

The standard relationships recommended by the NISO thesaurus standard (National Information Standards Organization 1993) include:

- Equivalence, which encompasses synonyms, lexical variants, and quasi-synonyms.
- Hierarchical, which encompasses generic (broader and narrower), whole-part, and instance relationships.
- Associative, which include relationships between overlapping and mutually exclusive sibling terms within the same hierarchy, derivational relationships, and relationships between concept terms in different hierarchies.

• examples of term relationships in thesauri : 177

Here are examples of these standard relationships, taken from the NISO standard (p. 13-20):

• equivalence relationships in thesauri : 178

- Equivalence relationships
  - Synonymous:
    - sweat = perspiration;
    - salt = sodium chloride;
    - photocopies = Xeroxes;
    - subways = undergrounds.
  - Lexical Variants:
    - online/on-line;
    - pediatrics/paediatrics;
    - mice/mouse;
    - International Federation for Documentation/FID.
  - Quasi-synonyms:
    - wetness/dryness (antonyms);
    - REM sleep vs. rapid eye movements.

Chapter 13. Vocabulary Management (Section 13.3.3.1.5)

Note: In addition to these types of equivalence relationships, many IR databases will declare terms that are clearly narrower in scope to be equivalent to a broader term in order to reduce the size of the vocabulary. For example, various brands or types of automobiles might be declared to be equivalent to "automobiles," e.g., Jeeps = (USE) automobiles; convertibles (automobiles) = (USE) automobiles; jalopies = (USE) automobiles.

• **hierarchical relationships in thesauri : 179**

- Hierarchical relationships
  - Generic relationship:
    - rodents > rats.
  - Whole-part relationship:
    - nervous system > central nervous system > brain;
    - Canada > Ontario > Toronto;
    - science > biology > botany;
    - armies > divisions (military) > battalions > regiments.
  - Instance relationship:
    - mountain regions > Alps, Himalayas;
    - state capitals > Albany, Trenton.

• **associative relationships in thesauri : 180**

- Associative relationships
  - Overlapping siblings:
    - ships/boats (can be precisely defined to distinguish, but often used loosely as equivalents that are interchangeable).
  - Mutually exclusive siblings:
    - roses/daffodils (these relationships are often not displayed because they are considered obvious, and therefore, redundant).
  - Derivational relationships:
    - mules/donkeys;
    - mules/horses (because mules are derived from a donkey plus a horse; in contrast, the relationship between donkeys and horses is the same as roses and daffodils, just above).
  - Concept terms in different hierarchies:
    - mathematics/mathematicians (disciplines/practitioners);
    - botany/plants (disciplines/objects studied);
    - hunting/hunters (operations/agents);
    - temperature control/thermostats (operations/instruments);
    - plants/herbicides (objects/counteragents);
    - inflammation/anti-inflammatory agents (processes/counteragents);
  - weaving/cloth (actions/products);
    - harvesting/crops (actions/targets);
    - poisons/toxicity (objects or substances/properties);
    - death/bereavement (causal dependence).

Chapter 13. Vocabulary Management (Section 13.3.3.1.5)

• more detailed term relationships in thesauri : 181

Some experts in vocabulary management have advocated the specification of more detailed relationships among concepts and terms. Some examples follow.

• views of Farradane (Jason) on term relationships : 182

Several decades ago, Jason Farradane developed an indexing system called "relational indexing" (summarized in Farradane 1980b and discussed previously in section 12.2.3 on relational syntax). His relationships were based, he claimed, on the fundamental relationships used in the human mind to organize concepts:

- concurrence
- equivalence
- distinctness
- self-activity (agent & activity)
- dimension (object or action/dimensions)
- action (action & object)
- association
- appurtenance
- functional dependence.

• views of Diener (Richard) on term relationships : 183

Based on Farradane's work as well as earlier theories of the Scottish philosopher David Hume and the Classification Research Group (U.K.), Richard Diener (1984), while a doctoral student at Rutgers, suggested the following relationships as key:

- concurrence
- hierarchy (broader)
- hierarchy (narrower)
- equivalence
- distinctness
- action/object (transitive)
- action/agent (intransitive)
- causation
- time-space/object or action
- object or substance/property (constant)
- object or substance/property (variable)
- object or substance/material
- object or substance/quality/quantity.

• views of Wang, Vandendorpe, and Evens on term relationships : 184

About the same time, Wang, Vandendorpe, and Evens (1985) tested the efficacy of an even larger list of 43 "lexical-semantic relations":

```
Parts and Wholes
    part-whole, e.g., horn <part of> cow
    head-organization, e.g., chief <head of> tribe
    personnel-object, e.g., police <equipped with> gun
    count-mass, e.g., lump <piece of> sugar
```

Chapter 13. Vocabulary Management (Section 13.3.3.1.5)

```
    set-element, e.g., flock <set of> sheep
    substance, e.g., ski <made of> wood
    provenance, e.g., milk <comes from> cow

Collocation Relations
    typical agent, e.g., conqueror <agent of> to conquer
    typical object, e.g., loser <object of> to beat
    typical result, e.g., hole <result of> to dig
    typical instrument, e.g., needle <instrument of> to sew
    typical experiencer, e.g., lover <experiencer of> to love
    typical source, e.g., earth <source of> to sprout
    typical location, e.g., kitchen <location of> to bake
    habitat-object, e.g., Africa <home of> hyena
    characteristic sound, e.g., bark <sound of> dog
    preposition-object, e.g., on <preposition for> list
    queuing, e.g., Monday <precedes> Tuesday
    special copula (linking) verb, e.g., to fall <is linked to>
            victim
    destroying verb, e.g., to correct <destroys> mistake
    prepare for use verb, e.g., to lay <prepares> table
    deterioration verb, e.g., to decay <deterioration> tooth
    increase verb, e.g., to mount <increase> tension
    decrease verb, e.g., to shrink <decrease> cloth

Paradigmatic Relations
    male term, e.g., drake <male of> duck
    female term, e.g., lioness <female of> lion
    offspring-parent, e.g., kitten <child of> cat
    cause-action effected, e.g., to send <causes> to go
    verb-adjective, e.g., to redden <becomes> red
    process noun-verb, e.g., death <is process of> to die
    adjective-noun, e.g., solar <is adjective for> sun
    adjective-verb, e.g., combustible <is adjective for> to burn
    verb-adjective, e.g., to neighbor <is to be> near
    irregular imperative, e.g., fire! <imperative for> to shoot
    perfect-infinitive, e.g., went <past tense for> to go
    past participle-infinitive, e.g., gone <past participle for>
            to go
    plural-singular, e.g., men <plural of> man

Taxonomy and Synonymy
    taxonomy, e.g., lion <is an> animal
    synonymy, e.g., speedy <is same as> fast

Antonymy Relations
    complementarity, e.g., single <is complement of> married
    antonymy, e.g., hot <is opposite of> cold
    converseness, e.g., to buy <is converse of> to sell
    reciprocal kinship, e.g., husband <is reciprocal of> wife
```

• views of ALA ALCTS Subject Analysis Committee on term relationships : 185

In 1995, the Subject Analysis Committee of the Association of Library Collections and Technical Services (ALCTS), a division of the American Library Association, appointed a special committee (Subcommittee on Subject Relationships/Reference Structures) to investigate relationships among concepts and terms in subject indexing/cataloging, with special emphasis on the use of such relationships in syndetic structures, which they called reference structures. (It is unfortunate that they, and others, have begun to use the term "reference structures" in place of the classic term "syndetic structures" or the more common term "thesaural (or thesaurus) relationships," or the plain "term relationships" or "concept relationships." When I first saw "reference structures," I thought it referred to structures for the provision of reference services. After all, "reference" is a well-established term for a major emphasis in librarianship — Anderson).

• compilation of term relationships by Michel (Dee) and Kuhr (Pat) : 186

As part of this ALCTS committee's work, Dee Michel, with the assistance of Pat Kuhr, compiled a list of 165 relationships worthy of consideration. Here is their taxonomy of these subject relationships (Association of Library Collections and Technical Services. Subcommittee on Subject Relationships/Reference Structures 1999, Appendix B):

```
Note: Asterisks (*) following a relationship term in the taxonomy indi-
cates that the term was considered by some sources to be hierarchical
and by other sources to be associative. These relationships are listed
twice, in two different categories.

ASSOCIATIVE RELATIONSHIPS

    Combined ideas
    Conceptually related terms
    Contiguity
        Definition-based contiguity
        Empirical knowledge-based contiguity
    Definitional associative relationships
    Different hierarchy associative relationships
        Environmental relationships
            Abstract environmental relationships
                Discipline/object studied pairs
                Entity/framework pairs
                Entity/school of thought pairs
                Field of endeavor/practitioner pairs
            Concrete environmental relationships
                Entity/environment pairs
                Entity/place pairs
                Position in time and space
                Process/environment of application pairs
            Through situation
                Situation or condition/what may occur pairs
        Etymologically related associative relationships
        Process issue relationships
            Entity/counteragent pairs
                Process/counteragent pairs
                Thing/counteragent pairs
            Indirect object
            Instigator/process pairs*
            Agent/process pairs*
            Entity/counteragent pairs*
            Instrument/goal pairs*
            Instrument/process pairs*
            Intransitive verb situations*
            Process/counteragent pairs*
        Method/product pairs
        Process/method pairs
```

Chapter 13. Vocabulary Management (Section 13.3.3.1.5)

```
    Process/property pairs*
        Process/property of entity pairs*
        Property/process performed on it pairs*
    Process/recipient pairs
        Action/target pairs
        Entity/process pairs
        Process/entity processed pairs
        Process/product pairs
    Producer/product pairs
    Product/material pairs
Property issue associative relationships
    Entity/device for measurement pairs
    Entity/entity pairs
    Entity/measure pairs
    Process/property pairs
        Process/property of entity pairs
        Property/process performed on it pairs
    Property/property as attribute pairs
    Thing considered as attribute of another thing
    Thing/application pairs
    Thing/property pairs
        Physical or intrinsic property
        Temporary or variable property
        Temporary state
        Thing/abstract property pairs
Meaning overlap associative relationships
    Extrasemantic relationships
    Used somewhat interchangeably
Same hierarchy associative relationships
    Causal relationships
        Dependency relationships
            Entity/predecessor pairs
            Possible cause/effect pairs
            Processes in sequence
        Genetic predecessor relationships*
        Influencing relationships
            Agent/process pairs*
            Entity/counteragent pairs*
                Process/counteragent pairs*
                Thing/counteragent pairs*
            Instrument/goal pairs*
            Instrument/process pairs*
            Intransitive verb situations*
            Process/counteragent pairs*
        Process/method pairs
        Raw material/product pairs
    Closely related siblings
        Closely related genealogical siblings
        Definitionally related siblings
        Frequently interchangeable siblings
        Meaning overlap siblings
        Substitutes
    Considered as relationships
    Coordinate ideas
        Coordinates with no broader term
            Parts of equations*
```

Chapter 13. Vocabulary Management (Section 13.3.3.1.5)

```
    Entity studied in mutual relationship to another entity
            Parts of equations*
        Partitive relationships*
            Composition partitive relationships*
                Comprehensive partitive relationships*
                Intrinsic partitive relationships*
            Whole/part pairs*
                Non-physical whole/part pairs*
                Physical whole/part pairs*
                    Anatomical whole/part pairs*
                        Anatomical organ whole/part pairs*
                        Anatomical system whole/part pairs*
                    Artifact whole/part pairs*
                    Geographic whole/part pairs*
                Topic inclusion*
                    Discipline/subdiscipline pairs*
                Whole/attachment pairs*
                Whole/integral part pairs*
                Whole/piece pairs*
                Whole/segmental part pairs*
                Whole/systemic part pairs*
                    Anatomical system whole/part pairs*
        Persons interacting in a special context
        Property/property pairs
        Reciprocals
        Similarity
    Scope issues
        Generic terms
        Noun not true broader term
        Polysemes
        Scope noted term and other possible meanings
    Unspecified associative relationships
```

EQUIVALENCE RELATIONSHIPS

```
    Different lexical term variants
        Dialectical variants
        Different root synonyms
        Generic/trade name pairs
        Popular/technical term pairs
            Eponym/descriptive pairs
            Medical/common term pairs
        Style and diction variants
        Superseded synonyms
        Translation equivalents
        Variant names for emergent concepts
        Variation in formality
    Lexical variants
        Orthographic variants
            Acronyms and abbreviations
            Omitted components
            Spacing and punctuation variants
            Spelling variants
```

Chapter 13. Vocabulary Management (Section 13.3.3.1.5)

            Stem equivalents
                Derivational suffix variants
                    Adjective/noun pairs
                        Common language derivational suffix variants
                    Infinitive/gerund pairs
                        Scientific language derivational suffix variants
                    Verb/noun pairs
                Plural/singular pairs
                    Irregular plural/singular pairs
                    Regular plural/singular pairs
            Syntactic variants
                Inversion variants
                Phrase variants
    Quasi-synonyms
        Antonyms
            Complementary antonyms
            Conversive antonyms
            Near antonyms
            Scalar antonyms
                Complements on a scale
                Unequivalent opposites
            Very loose antonyms
        BT/NT issue relationships
            Elements of compound terms
            General to specific 'See' references
            Generic posting
            Near synonyms
        Synonyms
            Absolute synonyms
            Cognitive synonyms
            Contextual synonyms
            Plesionyms
            Same referent synonyms
            Same sense synonyms
            True synonyms

HIERARCHICAL RELATIONSHIPS

    Class/instance pairs
    Genus/species pairs
    Non-inclusion hierarchical relationships
        Genealogical relationships
        Generic predecessor relationships*
        Organizational reporting
    Partitive relationships*
        Composition partitive relationships*
            Comprehensive partitive relationships*
            Intrinsic partitive relationships*
        Whole/part pairs*
            Non-physical whole/part pairs*
            Physical whole/part pairs*
                Anatomical whole/part pairs*
                    Anatomical organ whole/part pairs*
                    Anatomical system whole/part pairs*
                Artifact whole/part pairs*
                Geographic whole/part pairs*
            Topic inclusion*

Chapter 13. Vocabulary Management (Section 13.3.3.1.5)

```
Discipline/subdiscipline pairs*
Whole/attachment pairs*
Whole/integral part pairs*
Whole/piece pairs*
Whole/segmental part pairs*
Whole/systemic part pairs*
    Anatomical system whole/part pairs*
```

• **research on term relationships in thesauri : 187**

Willetts (1975) explored the use of Farradane's relationships, as well as others suggested by the British Classification Research Group, in ten thesauri. She focused on "affinitive relationships," most often called "related terms" (as opposed to broader and narrower terms). Molholt (1990), one of the principal architects of the *Art and architecture thesaurus* (1990, 1994), has also addressed the nature of the "related term" relationship.

• **attitudes of users toward term relationships in thesauri : 188**

The large numbers of distinct relationships that some theorists have suggested have never been widely adopted. Most of them are not clearly apparent to indexers or to searchers, and therefore they can be quite difficult to identify and use. This has been true both in indexing syntax (see section 12.2.3) and in thesauri. The consensus among thesaurus makers and users, as reflected in national and international standards, is that all relationships should be subsumed into just three types: equivalence, hierarchical ("broader" and "narrower"), and other (for other related or associated terms).

• **hierarchical relationships versus associative relationships in thesauri : 189**

Even the distinction between hierarchical and non-hierarchical (i.e., merely associated or related) concepts, although perhaps clear in theory, is not always easy (or useful) in practice. Our "Prototype fuzzy query processors" can be used to illustrate this issue.

• **term relationships in hierarchical displays in thesauri : 190**

While "prototype fuzzy query processors" are clearly "prototypes" as well as "processors," they are NOT "fuzziness," nor are they "queries," and purists would properly insist that the relationship between "prototype fuzzy query processors" and "fuzziness" or "queries" be listed as "related" rather than hierarchical or "narrower/broader." One problem with this approach is that related terms are often absent from hierarchical displays, yet hierarchical displays are one of the most useful working displays for thesaurus editors as they structure vocabularies and for end users as they explore terms and concepts.

• **display of term relationships in thesauri : 191**

Some newer thesauri are getting around this problem by including related terms within hierarchical displays. The *Eurovoc thesaurus*, illustrated above in section 13.3.2.1, has replaced hierarchical displays with microthesauri, in which related terms are displayed along with narrower terms.

• **term relationships during compilation of thesauri : 192**

Some thesaurus construction software include only broader and narrower terms in hierarchical displays. For this reason, at least in the initial compilation of a thesaurus, it is useful to treat all term relationships as hierarchical (broader/narrower or whole/part or class/member/instance). After each pass at sorting or categorizing terms, a hierarchical display can be generated which will include all terms sorted into a particular category. The terms in each category can then be re-sorted, or re-categorized into yet another level of subordinate categories. If terms were tagged as related, rather than broader or narrower terms, at this early stage of classification, they could be lost from the hierarchical display as produced by some thesaurus construction programs.

Chapter 13. Vocabulary Management (Section 13.3.3.1.5)

• 193

Once sorting and categorization has taken place, term relationships which are not strictly hierarchical may be converted to associative or related.

• attitudes of users toward term relationships in thesauri : 194

However, unless related terms are included in hierarchical or microthesaurus displays, as in the *Eurovoc thesaurus*, some end users will likely find a simple display of all related terms together (both hierarchical — BT/NT — and other related terms) to be more helpful as they work to refine a search. From such a display, they can make their own decision as to which terms might be useful and should be added to their search. (It is perhaps ironic that this return to a combined listing of all related terms, whether broader, narrower, or merely associated, is exactly where subject heading syndetic structure was before the *Library of Congress subject headings* adopted the more "modern" BT, NT, and RT relationships!)

• hierarchical relationships versus associative relationships in thesauri : 195

In the examples of hierarchical (broader and narrower) displays both in the syndetic structure of subject headings (section 13.3.1) and in indexing thesauri (section 13.3.2.1), we noted at times a loose definition of broader and narrower. Purists insist that narrower terms must pass the "is a" test, or clearly be a part of or an instance of the item represented by the broader term. For example, a chair "is a" kind of furniture. An ankle is "part of" a human body. But, among the examples of syndetic structure, both "Bride price" and "Divorce" were listed as narrower terms to "Marriage." Neither "Bride price" nor "Divorce" are kinds of marriage (they don't pass the "is a" or "part of" or "instance of" tests), and it's rather a stretch to say they are "part of" marriage, in the usual sense of the "whole/part" relationships, as in "human body/ankle." In the Eurovoc microthesaurus for "family," narrower terms for "family" include "large family" and "one-parent family," which are clearly kinds of families. They also include "head of household" and "breadwinner," which can be considered "parts of" a family. But "family policy"? It's clearly related, but it does not appear to pass any rigorous text for hierarchical or whole/part relationships.

• views of Cutter (Charles Ammi) on role of principles in cataloging : 196

We are reminded of Charles Ammi Cutter's (1904, p. 6) famous advice to catalogers: "The convenience of the public is always to be set before the ease of the cataloger .... When these habits [of the public] are general and deeply rooted, it is unwise for the cataloger to ignore them, even it they demand a sacrifice of system and simplicity."

• 197

Applied to end-user thesauri, it may well be more useful to our users to broaden the usual definition of "narrower" to include all terms indicating kinds of, parts of, instances of, and closely associated topics in relation to a term chosen by the user. This is a question worthy of careful research and investigation.

• 198

In contrast to what may be useful in displays for humans, there is renewed interest in detailed relationships in more carefully structured vocabulary management tools for machine manipulation, now called "ontologies," which will be discussed later in section 13.3.5.

• 199

Finally, designers and compilers of end-user thesauri must decide what relationships among concepts and terms to record in term records. At the moment, based on the available evidence, we recommend the following relationships:

- equivalent terms
- broader terms

- narrower terms
- other related terms (associative terms)

• 200

In displays for users, all categories of relationships should be included. Thus in hierarchical displays, equivalent and related terms should be displayed along with narrower terms.

13.3.3.1.6. Variant Forms and Equivalent Terms.

• 201

In the process of sorting or categorizing terms, the thesaurus editor will come across different terms that have essentially the same meaning (e.g., lawyer and attorney) and variant forms of the same term (e.g., index, indexes, indices). At some point, such equivalent and variant forms should be combined into a single record, so that the end user can easily find together all the terms that mean essentially the same thing.

• gathering terms in end-user thesauri : 202

For this purpose, one term is chosen to be the gathering term to name or represent the concept; equivalent terms are placed in the equivalent terms field; and variant forms, both for the gathering term and for equivalent terms, are placed in a variant terms field. Please note that different thesaurus construction software may have different names for these fields!

• gathering terms versus preferred terms in thesauri : 203

In indexing thesauri, the gathering term is usually called a preferred term or descriptor. It is the term that is designated for use in indexing. But an end-user thesaurus is not designed to guide indexing. Rather it is designed to gather and display terms related to concepts — thus the term "gathering term" rather than "preferred term" or "descriptor." The term "descriptor" is generally used to mean a term that is a preferred term authorized for indexing in a particular indexing language.

• choice of gathering terms in end-user thesauri; choice of preferred terms in indexing thesauri : 204

The choice of a gathering term (or a preferred term in an indexing thesaurus), e.g., "attorney" versus "lawyer" is, in the final analysis, somewhat arbitrary. The choice should favor the most-used term, if that is possible to determine. But the only function of a gathering term in an end-user search thesaurus is to serve as a "hitching post" around which to gather equivalent, variant, broader, narrower, and other related terms. Access to the thesaurus and through it to IR databases will be available through all terms, regardless of which term is selected to serve as a gathering term for a particular concept.

• equivalent terms versus variant terms in end-user thesauri : 205

The operational difference between the "equivalent" and "variant" fields is that terms in the equivalent field get entries in alphabetical displays, while variant terms do not. This means that any variant form that should get an entry in vocabulary displays should be placed in the equivalent terms field. An example might be "indices," which is sufficiently different from the gathering term "indexes" to merit a separate entry.

• 206

In contrast to indices, it's probably not necessary to have a separate entry for "index," so if "indexes" is the gathering term, "index" can be placed in the variant term field.

Depending on the type of display, entries for equivalent terms may take the form of "go to," "use," or "see" cross references, leading from the equivalent term to the gathering term, for example:

```
indices
     GO TO
          indexes
```

• 208

In such a cross reference, the gathering term "indexes" can take the form of a hypertext link to its record, so that the user need only select or click on "indexes" to move to that term and its record. An alternative is simply to take the user to the gathering term record whenever an equivalent term is chosen.

• 209

The advantage of the explicit "go to" reference is that it tells the user that the gathering term is "indexes." Some users get confused when they choose one term (indices) and they are taken to another term (indexes) without explanation. This may seem obvious, but sometimes equivalent terms are not quite so "equivalent." Not all attorneys are lawyers, nor are all lawyers attorneys, so if a thesaurus editor decides that nevertheless these concepts are so similar that they will be merged into a single conceptual record, then it's a good idea to inform the user that this is the case. Of course, the user can be informed even if an explicit "go to" reference is not used.

• used for terms versus equivalent terms in end-user thesauri : 210

In some thesauri (and in some thesaurus construction software), the equivalent term field is called the "used for" field, but this is inappropriate for an end-user thesauri, because all terms are usable and are, in fact, used. The terminology "used for" and "use" should be limited to indexer thesauri, rather than end-user thesauri. (But even in indexing thesauri, the term "used for" and UF can be confusing. It is not uncommon for users of thesauri to get confused about which term is "used for" which. After all, narrower terms are listed after an NT; broader terms are listed after a BT; and related terms are listed after an RT. So why shouldn't the terms after a UF be "used for" terms — terms to be used for the concept that the thesaurus record represents? Perhaps the notation UT, for "un-used terms" might be better.)

13.3.3.1.7. Homographs.

• 211

As terms are sorted and categorized, it will also become apparent that some terms stand for two or more very different concepts, e.g., "mercury" can refer to a Roman god, a metallic element, a planet, or an automobile; "term" can refer to a word or phrase used in indexing and also to a period of time, as in a term of office or a prison sentence or a division of the academic year; "sentence" can refer to a verbal phrase or to a criminal penalty; "bibliography" is both a process and a result of that process (as are many "-tion" words — e.g., translation, citation); "race" can refer to a speed contest or to the broadest of ethnic groupings; "port" is a fine wine from Portugal and also a harbor; and so on. When such instances occur, separate records should be established for each concept, and the gathering term should be qualified, e.g., mercury (god); mercury (element); mercury (planet); translation (operation), translation (product). In each such record, the unqualified term should be listed as an equivalent term, so that any reference to "mercury" will lead to the equivalent gathering terms "mercury (god)," "mercury (element)," "Mercury (automobile)," and/or "mercury (planet)," providing an opportunity to choose among these alternatives.

13.3.3.1.8. Thesaurus Displays.

• search options in end-user thesauri : 212

Examples of thesaurus displays have been presented throughout this chapter. Ideally, a user should be able to locate useful displays in an end-user thesaurus either through direct term searches, or through browsing.

• browsable indexes for end-user thesauri : 213

Users should be able to browse both alphabetical and relational classified displayed indexes. The alphabetical display should include all gathering and equivalent terms. When a user chooses a term, the record for the conceptual gathering term would be displayed. All related terms (broader, narrower, and other related terms) would be hyperlinked, so that the user could choose any of these terms to continue exploring terminology.

• relational displays in end-user thesauri : 214

The relational classified displayed index would begin with a display of the top facet or subject-scope category terms for the thesaurus, as illustrated previously for indexing thesauri (section 13.3.2.1). The user could choose any of the main thesaurus facets or categories, then move down hierarchies of terms until the most detailed levels are reached, which might be in the form of microthesauri.

• searching with end-user thesauri : 215

At any point, when a user finds an interesting or useful term, s/he should be able to add that term, and any (or all) of its equivalent, variant, broader, narrower, or related terms to a search statement. It is convenient to give the user the options of either adding all associated terms, or choosing particular terms.

• 216

After collecting terms for a search statement, the user should be able to send the search statement to one or more IR databases.

• 217

Alternatively, the user should be able to move from an interesting term in the end-user thesaurus to browsable alphabetical or relational classified indexes for a particular IR database, and then choose to see brief records, such as index headings based on indexing strings (strings of descriptors) and/or titles. When choosing this option, the user could be shown a list of IR databases using a particular term. The user could then select one of these IR databases and move directly to its displayed browsable indexes.

13.3.4. Co-Occurrence Term Clustering.

• 218

Term clustering based on co-occurrence has proven to be a very useful technique for gathering related terms to display to a searcher, from which s/he may select additional terms to augment or refine a search statement or to move elsewhere in a browsable displayed index. An early example, Tamas E. Doszkocs' Interactive Dictionary, was illustrated and discussed in section 8.3.10 in the context of automatic indexing.

- research on clustering of terms for vocabulary management : 219

More recent examples, including research and experimentation with clustering as a tool for automatically creating vocabulary management tools, is described in Chen, Ng, Martinez and Shatz (1997) and Schutze and Pedersen (1997).

- clustering terms for vocabulary management : 220

A simple example of clustering to facilitate vocabulary management is routinely offered in Ovid search interfaces for medical databases (Diakoff 2000). Searchers often want to use standard MeSH (Medical Subject Heading) descriptors for searching databases produced by the U.S. National Library of Medicine, but they don't want to bother finding the authorized terminology in MeSH volumes. All they need to do is to enter a keyword search and ask for MeSH terms that co-occur with these keyword terms. A list of MeSH terms, ranked according to the frequency of co-occurrence with the initial keyword search statement, will be displayed, from which the user may choose the most appropriate MeSH terms and insert them into a search query.

13.3.5. Ontologies.

- definitions of ontologies : 221

"Ontology" or "ontologies" is a new term in information science, imported from philosophy by way of artificial intelligence and knowledge engineering.

- 222

A standard philosophical definition is: "the branch of metaphysics dealing with the nature of being or reality." It comes from the Greek "ontos" which means "being" or "existence" (Webster's 1966, p. 1025, 1026); "-ology" simply means "science" or "study of," as in "biology" — the study of life.

- 223

The *Oxford English dictionary* (1989) definition, cited by Soergel (1999), is very similar: "The science or study of being; that department of metaphysics which relates to the being or essence of things, or to being in the abstract." Soergel continues by saying that "Part of such a study is a classification of things that are into basic types, often starting with *living vs. nonliving entities*. Thus, the term *ontology* assumed the additional meaning of a shallow classification of basic categories. ... [S]o eventually *ontology* was used to designate any classification, particularly in the communities of linguistics, AI, and software engineering. Indeed, once these communities increased their awareness that there is not only a problem of classification but also of terminology, 'ontologies' included lead-in vocabularies as well, and became full-fledged thesauri."

- 224

FOLDOC: The Free On-line Dictionary of Computing (1999) provides the following definitions of "ontology":

"1. <philosophy> A systematic account of Existence.

"2. <artificial intelligence> (From philosophy) An explicit formal specification of how to represent the objects, concepts and other entities that are assumed to exist in some area of interest and the relationships that hold among them.

"For AI systems, what "exists" is that which can be represented. When the knowledge about a domain is represented in a declarative language, the set of objects that can be represented is called the universe of discourse. We can describe the ontology of a program by defining a set of representational terms. Definitions associate the names of entities in the universe of discourse (e.g., classes, relations, functions or other objects) with human-readable text describing what the names mean, and formal axioms that constrain the interpretation and well-formed use of these terms. Formally, an ontology is the statement of a logical theory.

"A set of agents that share the same ontology will be able to communicate about a domain of discourse without necessarily operating on a globally shared theory. We say that an agent commits to an ontology if its observable actions are consistent with the definitions in the ontology. The idea of ontological commitment is based on the Knowledge-Level perspective.

"3. <information science> The hierarchical structuring of knowledge about things by subcategorising them according to their essential (or at least relevant and/or cognitive) qualities. See subject index. This is an extension of the previous senses of "ontology" (above) which has become common in discussions about the difficulty of maintaining subject indices" (1997-04-09).

• ontologies versus thesauri : 225

As implied by FOLDOC's second definition, ontologies are generally seen as tools for machine manipulation, rather than for human inspection and browsing, and this difference may become the distinction between an IR (information retrieval) thesaurus versus an IR ontology, but the distinction is still very fuzzy, as is the usage of the term. Because "ontology" is a new word in information science, and carries a certain cachet, many people are now calling any thesaurus or classification an ontology, and a new term for "information scientist" or "information architect" is "ontologist." Literally, an "ontologist" is one who studies being, or reality, which is not inappropriate for indexers or catalogers or classifiers!

• views of Hjerppe (Roland) on ontologies versus knowledge organization systems : 226

This machine versus people orientation is suggested also by Roland Hjerppe (1996) in his keynote address to the Fourth International ISKO Conference (International Society for Knowledge Organization) in Washington, DC:

"What are then the differences between formal ontologies and systems for knowledge organization? One of the main differences is that formal ontologies are designed and built using strict representation formalisms, for use mainly by software entities, grounded, i.a. [inter alia, among other things], in logical theory, whereas systems for knowledge organizations have been built using semi-natural language, for use by people. Since software agents do not have any understandings of terms or concepts of the kinds that humans have, not having grown up in the world and in that process, i.a., acquired a language, there has been a need to replace that understanding with formalism and logic" (p. 18).

• views of Sowa (John) on categories in ontologies : 227

At the same conference Roberto Poli (1996) presented a paper on "Ontology for knowledge organization." In his introduction (p. 313), he quotes John Sowa as saying: "The first step in designing a database, a knowledge base, or an object-oriented system is to select an appropriate collection of ontological categories" (Sowa 1995). Apart from the use of the term "ontological," this assertion is exactly the theme of chapter 2 of this book, on the subject scope and domain specification of IR databases!

• views of Poli (Roberto) on categories in ontologies : 228

Poli identifies a number of such basic ontological categories, structured into "at least five ontological levels of the inanimate physical world, of the animate physical world, of the psychological world, of the social world and of the ideal world" (p. 315).

Chapter 13. Vocabulary Management (Section 13.3.5)

• 229

Poli continues:

"In general, we may distinguish the general categories, which hold for all the ontological levels, from the regional categories, which apply only to certain levels. The general categories comprise, for example, object, event, substratum, substance, form, relation, determination, dependence, structure, part, whole, unity, multiplicity, dimension, continuum, discrete, internal, external, identity, diversity, possibility, actuality, necessity, change.

"Examples of regional categories are the following. For the material world: space, time, cause, situation, reciprocal action, dynamic structure, dynamic equilibrium, becoming. For the animate world: organic structure, adaptation, end-directedness, material exchange, self-regulation, life of the species, degeneration of the species. For the psychological world: act, content, consciousness, unconsciousness, pleasure, displeasure. For the social world: social system, family, community, conflict, class, institution, integration. For the ideal world: the categories of the activities and products of knowledge, art and faith.

"These lists are obviously provisional and their purpose is purely exemplary."

• categories and term relationships in thesauri versus ontologies : 230

Compare these categories to those suggested earlier for thesauri by Farradane, Diener, Wang et al., and the ALCTS subcommittee in section 13.3.3.1.5 on term relationships, and to the facets and categories discussed in chapter 2.

• weak structures in ontologies : 231

On the other hand, the structure of some ontologies can be quite simple. Iwazume, Takeda and Nishida (1996) use a "weakly structured" ontology for their efforts to capture information from the internet. "Weakly structured ontologies have only one type of associative relation between terms" (p. 262). Compare this single "associative relation" type with the suggestion in section 13.3.3.1.5 (term relationships in end-user thesauri) that some users may be best served by a simple ranked list of related terms. Co-occurrence clustering (section 13.3.4) is also based on the idea of a single, simple relationship measured by frequency of co-occurrence.

• views of Vickery (Brian C.) on ontologies : 232

Vickery (1997) provides an excellent overview of the current status of ontologies in the world of information science and information retrieval, citing and describing several examples. He too cites Sowa, who describes an ontology as "a catalogue of everything that makes up a [possible] world, how it is put together, and how it works ... a catalogue of concept and relation types" (Sowa 1983).

• ontologies for machine translation; conceptual levels in ontologies : 233

One of the examples cited by Vickery is "Mikrokosmos," an ontology designed to aid in machine translation. This ontology has about 4,500 concepts represented, from many domains. Here are the top conceptual levels (Vickery 1997, p. 280):

```
All
    Object
        Physical
        Mental
        Social
    Event
        Physical
        Mental
        Social
```

Chapter 13. Vocabulary Management (Section 13.4)

```
Property
    Attribute (a property of an Object or Event)
    Relation (a relation between Objects and/or Events)
```

• ontologies for business : 234

Another ontology cited and described by Vickery (1997, p. 282) is "Enterprise," "a collection of terms and definitions relevant to business enterprises. It is intended as a communication medium between people, between people and computer systems, and between systems. It contains about 100 defined terms, with added non-preferred synonyms and borderline terms. The defined terms are listed in five groups": Activities and processes; Organisation; Strategy; Marketing; and Time. The terms within these categories are not hierarchical "is-a" species; rather they are clusters of associated terms. Thus, under "activities and processes," one finds not only actions such as "execute," "planning," and "resource-allocation," but also agents ("doer," "activity-owner"), products or results of action (such as "plan") and attributes (such as "task-begin," "task-end," "capability," and "skill").

• compilation of ontologies : 235

Vickery includes a section on "building ontologies," which reads very much like our section on compiling an end-user thesaurus in section 13.3.3.1. Steps include (citing Uschold and Gruninger 1996): domain definition, collection of concept terms "by scanning the literature of the domain, and by consulting domain experts," grouping terms, noting synonyms, creating cross references, and producing definitions.

• views of Vickery (Brian C.) on ontologies : 236

Vickery concludes by summing up (p. 284-285):

"... we can describe an ontology as a schedule, in some form that may involve the use of semantic categories, of concepts significant in a particular domain (that may be as wide as the universe of knowledge), together with a definition or scope note for each concept, and mechanisms for displaying its relationship to other concepts.

"The analogy with bibliographic classification and thesauri is obvious, although there are equally obvious differences because the uses intended for ontologies are not the same as for classification and thesauri. ...

"In conclusion: this new development of tools at the "knowledge level" shows once again the growing understanding of the importance of semantic analysis in information processing."

13.4. Our Examples.

13.4.1. A Book Index.

• 237

Our book index must serve both a traditional print-on-paper book, and also the same text published electronically, perhaps on a computer disk, a CD-ROM, or on the world-wide web.

(a) The printed book.

• vocabulary management for book indexes in print media : 238

The printed book will have a fairly traditional back-of-the-book index, except that entries will be keyed to paragraphs rather than pages. As noted in chapter 6 on documentary units, pages are artifacts of physical format of the printed book. They are not normally associated with texts themselves, and therefore pages do not normally travel with the text into electronic media. In contrast, paragraphs are attributes of narrative language texts, and therefore they are present in such texts regardless of medium.

Chapter 13. Vocabulary Management (Section 13.4.1)

• **integration of vocabulary management in book indexes : 239**

For the printed back-of-the-book index, the vocabulary management component must be integrated into the index in the form of see and see-also references. The see references will be placed as independent entries in their alphabetical positions, e.g.:

```
hardware
    for IR databases : 1.205
headings
    see: index headings
hierarchical arrangement
        in classification : 12.209
```

• **equivalent-term cross references for synonymous and equivalent terms in book indexes : 240**

See references are needed from every synonymous or equivalent term of any significance in order to lead the user to the term chosen for that concept.

• **double posting for synonymous and equivalent terms in book indexes : 241**

Sometimes "double posting" is used in a back-of-the-book index as an alternative to a see reference from an unused term to a used term. For example, if a see reference from "attorneys" to "lawyers" takes up just as much space as a duplicate entry under the term "attorneys," then both terms can be used, thereby relieving the user from having to move to the preferred term. In this case, both equivalent terms are used:

```
attorneys
    information seeking behavior : 25, 46, 93.
lawyers
    information seeking behavior : 25, 46, 93.
```

• **242**

The entry under "attorneys" takes up no more vertical space than the see reference:

```
attorneys
    SEE lawyers
```

Therefore the indexer can choose to "double post" these duplicate entries under each equivalent term.

• **equivalent-term cross references for narrower terms in book indexes : 243**

See references are also used from narrower terms to broader terms when an indexer decides the narrower term is too narrow for the index and decides to include every instance of particular narrower topics under the heading for their broader topic. For example, an indexer may choose not to create headings for each type of string indexing syntax (NEPHIS, PRECIS, CIFT, rotated term, etc.) and instead to encompass all of them under the broader heading "string indexing syntax." In this case, each of the narrower terms needs to have a see reference leading to this broader term. This option will be avoided in the index for this book because we have a policy of high specificity, leading, we hope, to high precision searches.

• **terminology in equivalent-term cross references : 244**

"See" or "use" are the traditional directives for cross references from un-used terms to used preferred terms. Some indexers are experimenting with other terms such as "go to" or "search under," or more expansive instructions, such as "for this topic, please go to":

```
hardware
    for IR databases : 1.205
headings
    for this topic please go to: index headings
hierarchical arrangement
        in classification : 12.209
```

Chapter 13. Vocabulary Management (Section 13.4.1)

• see-also references in book indexes : 245

See-also references will be placed in special boxes or windows within entry arrays under main headings. In some book indexes, it may be useful to expand the simple traditional "see also" terminology to try to make it clearer:

```
indexes
      ============================================================
      |  You may also be interested in the following narrower   |
      |  terms:                                                 |
      |                                                         |
      |  ad hoc string syntax; ad hoc syntax; chain syntax;     |
      |  classification syntax; faceted syntax; natural         |
      |  language syntax; permuted syntax; postcoordinate       |
      |  syntax; precoordinate syntax;  relational syntax;      |
      |  rotated term syntax; string syntax; subject            |
      |  heading syntax; subject heading syntax                 |
      ============================================================
syntax
    absence in vocabulary lists : 12.278
    among variables in IR research : 8.14
    as essential attribute of indexes : 12.5
    definitions : 12.1
    examples : sec. 12.4
    for book indexes : sec. 12.4.1; digital
            libraries : sec. 12.4.3; displayed
            indexes versus non-displayed indexes
            : 11.9; electronic encyclopedias :
            sec. 12.4.3; full-text searching of
            books in electronic media : 12.320;
            index headings : Chapter 12;
            indexing and abstracting services :
            sec. 12.4.2; non-displayed indexes
            (alternative options : 12.296;
            major types : 12.280); search
            statements : Chapter 12; string
            indexing : sec. 12.2.2
    impact on precision : 12.3; examples :
            12.4; on size of indexes : 12.184
    in Dewey decimal classification : 12.197;
            faceted classifications : 12.202;
            index headings compared to search
            statements : 12.1, 6; Library of
            Congress classification : 12.201;
            Library of Congress subject
            headings : 12.20 (history : 12.21);
            Modern Language Association
            classification : 12.203; Universal
            decimal classification : 12.215
    postcoordinate - : sec. 12.1
    precoordinate - : sec. 12.1-12.2
    principles in subject heading systems :
            12.108
    role in indexing : 12.2
    versus specificity : sec. 10.7
```

Chapter 13. Vocabulary Management (Section 13.4.1)

• application of thesauri to book indexes : 246

These displayed cross references could be generated from a thesaurus for the book index (described below in the section on the electronic book). It is unusual for a back-of-the-book index to have its own thesaurus, but if there is one for an electronic book index, we could take advantage of it to generate see and see-also references for the printed index. The more traditional approach to see and see-also references in a back-of-the-book index is for the indexer simply to compose them during the indexing process.

• 247

If a thesaurus is used, all lead terms (main headings) in the displayed index can be matched against the thesaurus, and every term linked to a lead term as an equivalent, narrower, broader, or related term can be pulled into the displayed index as a lead-in term for a cross reference leading back to the original lead term (main heading) in the index.

• 248

For example, our index will have the lead term "thesauri." In the book thesaurus, "thesauri" might have the BT (broader term) "vocabulary management tools"; the narrower term "end-user thesauri" and also narrower terms for particular thesauri, such as "Unesco thesaurus" and "Eurovoc thesaurus"; and related terms for "syndetic structure" and "ontologies."

• 249

These terms within the thesaurus record for "thesauri" would generate the following see-also references for the back-of-the-book index. (These examples use the more traditional brief form "see also" rather than the more explanatory phrase used in the previous example just above.) These see-also references would be placed in their alphabetical positions, according to the lead-in term for each reference:

```
vocabulary management tools
      SEE ALSO NARROWER TERM thesauri
end-user thesauri
      SEE ALSO BROADER TERM
            thesauri
Unesco thesaurus
      SEE ALSO BROADER TERM
            thesauri
Eurovoc thesaurus
      SEE ALSO BROADER TERM
            thesauri
ontologies
      SEE ALSO RELATED TERM
            thesauri
syndetic structure
      SEE ALSO RELATED TERM
            thesauri
```

(b) The electronic book.

• vocabulary management for indexes in electronic books : 250

The displayed index that is provided with the printed book can also be made available for users of the electronic version of our book for on-screen browsing. In the electronic version of the displayed index, users can simply point to and click on a cross-reference term, and the program will take them directly to the preferred term.

Chapter 13. Vocabulary Management (Section 13.4.2)

• presentation of see-also references in displayed indexes in electronic media : 251

The electronic displayed index will be presented in stages, showing one level of heading at a time. In the initial presentation, only the lead terms will be displayed. When a user selects a lead term, all subheadings (or index heading strings) under that heading will be displayed, along with see-also references to narrower, broader, and related terms. The presentation of displayed indexes, including see-also references, in electronic media, will be a primary focus of chapter 19 on the search interface.

• non-displayed indexes for electronic books : 252

Users of the electronic book will also have access to a non-displayed index that they may search electronically. For this index, there will be an electronic thesaurus. It will be compiled from the indexing terms assigned by the human indexer to each paragraph of the book. These terms will be sorted and given broader, narrower, related, and equivalent terms in the manner described earlier in this chapter for compiling an end-user thesaurus (section 13.3.3.1).

• presentation of suggestions for vocabulary management for searches in non-displayed indexes : 253

When the user keys in a search term, a window will display the thesaurus record for that term (if it has a record). This window will be similar to the see-also window under the term "syntax" in the displayed index just above, except that suggested terms will be grouped by relationship (narrower terms, related terms, broader terms, equivalent terms). The user will have the option of adding any term in the thesaurus window to the search, or of replacing the original term with terms from the thesaurus window, or of moving to a new thesaurus window for any narrower, broader, or related terms in the original thesaurus window.

• 254

Users will also have the option of browsing the thesaurus using either hierarchical or alphabetical displays, and tagging thesaurus terms for a search.

• 255

They also, of course, have the option of ignoring the thesaurus all together!

• 256

Examples of thesaurus vocabulary management information integrated into electronic search screens will be shown in chapter 19 on the search interface.

13.4.2. An Indexing and Abstracting Service.

• 257

The vocabulary management component for our indexing and abstracting service will be similar to that for our book. Our indexing and abstracting service has the following indexes:

(a) print displayed index based on human indexing for high use documents.

(b) print displayed index based on automatic indexing for all documents.

(c) electronic displayed index based on human indexing for high use documents.

(d) electronic displayed index based on automatic indexing for all documents.

(e) electronic non-displayed index for all documents.

• vocabulary management for indexing and abstracting services in print media : 258

In the displayed print index for high use documents, cross references from synonymous and equivalent terms and to narrower, broader, and related terms will be generated from the thesaurus for the A&I service. They will be displayed in the index within special windows or boxes, similar to the see-also references for the term "syntax" shown above for the book index.

Chapter 13. Vocabulary Management (Section 13.4.2)

• **see-also references for equivalent terms in automatic indexing : 259**

Cross references in the print displayed index based on automatic indexing will be similar, except that the relationship among equivalent terms will be different. In the index based on human indexing, one preferred term is chosen for each concept, so that equivalent terms for the same concept normally result in see or use references from the un-used term to the used term (unless double posting is used!).

• 260

In automatic indexing, all equivalent terms are equal; none are preferred over the others; all can be used, so that equivalent terms will result in see-also references rather than see or use references. We could have terms under both "librarianship" and "library science", so under each, we need a cross reference that reminds users to "see also" the other term, e.g.:

```
librarianship
     SEE ALSO EQUIVALENT TERM
          library science

library science
     SEE ALSO EQUIVALENT TERM
          librarianship
```

• 261

In cross references in the electronic displayed index, users may point to or click on a target term, and go directly to that term.

• **vocabulary management for non-displayed indexes for indexing and abstracting services in electronic media : 262**

The vocabulary management component for the electronic non-displayed index will be similar to that described above for the electronic book. A master thesaurus will be maintained based on descriptors chosen by indexers as well as the full text of selected high-use documents and on the surrogate records for other documents (titles, notes, and abstracts). When a user keys in a term for a search, a thesaurus window will appear suggesting additional or alternative terms for the search. The user may select any of these terms to add to the search or to replace initial terms, or the user may explore thesaurus records for any of the displayed terms. A user may also choose to limit a search to descriptors only, rather than keywords, thereby confining search results to selected high-use documents.

• **suggestions for vocabulary management for multiple terms in search statements : 263**

Often an electronic search will include multiple terms. In this case the user will be shown a list of terms, with vocabulary management suggestions displayed for the first one. If users would like similar vocabulary management suggestions for the other terms, they can highlight or select each of the other terms one at a time.

• **optional status of suggestions for vocabulary management : 264**

At the same time, initial results of the search should be shown as well, so that users know that they can ignore vocabulary management information if it is not needed. The goal is to make the opportunity for vocabulary management suggestions clear and make it as easy to use as possible, but, at the same time, not to force users to make use of it.

• 265

Examples of displays of vocabulary management information will be illustrated and discussed in chapter 19 on the search interface.

13.4.3. A Full-Text Encyclopedia.

• 266

Our full-text encyclopedia also has both displayed and non-displayed electronic indexes, so its vocabulary management components will be similar to those described for the electronic book and for the electronic indexing and abstracting service, just above. A comprehensive thesaurus will be created for all terms in the encyclopedia, so that cross references can be incorporated into the alphabetical displayed index in their alphabetical positions. Thesaurus information will also be made available to users of the electronic index through thesaurus windows.

• 267

In addition, terms within articles will be hyperlinked to articles related to the concept represented by these terms. See-also references will also be placed at the beginning of articles and sections of articles.

Chapter 14. Surrogates

Contents of Chapter 14
14. Surrogates
14.1. Purpose of Surrogates.
14.2. Guidelines and Standards for Surrogates.
14.3. Selected Readings on Abstracts and Abstracting.
14.4. Surrogates for Machine Searching.
14.5. Our Examples.
14.5.1. A Book Index.
14.5.2. An Indexing and Abstracting Service.
14.5.3. A Full-Text Encyclopedia/Digital Library.

• definitions of surrogates : 1

A surrogate is a representative. A surrogate judge stands in the stead of a deceased person. A surrogate mother takes the place of one who is not able to carry a fetus to birth. A message/text/document surrogate stands in the place of the original full text containing the message of interest. Just as a surrogate judge in no way duplicates all aspects or characteristics of a deceased person, or similarly, a surrogate mother is not an exact duplicate of the future parent of a child, a message/text/document surrogate represents only certain key aspects of a message, text, or documentary unit. Henceforth, in accord with the usual vocabulary, we shall use the term "document surrogate" rather than "message surrogate" or "text surrogate." After all, the document contains the text, which represents the message in question.

• 2

A document surrogate is a brief representative of a full documentary unit. Its nature and content will depend on the nature and content of the full documentary unit and the needs of users.

• content of surrogates : 3

Surrogates for language-based documents usually consist of a brief description of (or citation to) the document (e.g., author, title, publisher, or source). For non-language-based messages, it can be the creator and/or performer, a title or name of the message (painting, sculpture, performance) and a brief description of the object or event (as opposed to its content). When more information is desirable in the surrogate, a more detailed description or abstract of the message (the content or meaning) can be added, or a "thumb-nail" picture of the text, such as a painting or sculpture or map. Surrogates should also include any indexing descriptions of the documentary unit.

• display versus content of surrogates : 4

This chapter focuses on the content and uses of full, complete surrogates. Chapter 15 addresses locators, which are an essential component of all surrogates. Chapter 16 deals with the display of surrogates, especially the staged display beginning with very brief surrogates and progressing to the complete surrogate.

• size, content, format of surrogates : 5

The size, content, and format of surrogates vary considerably, depending on circumstances. For example, surrogates can be quite brief when the documentary units to which they refer are included within the database. A prominent example is back-of-the-book indexes in which the surrogate is nothing more than an index heading plus a locator (such as page or paragraph num-

Chapter 14. Surrogates

ber). In large full-text databases or digital libraries, fuller surrogates are useful to help users preview documentary units so that they can choose the ones they actually want to see or use.

• **types of abstracts : 6**

Most larger surrogates contain an abstract. In their classic text on abstracting, Borko and Bernier (1975) describe a variety of types of abstracts (p. 13-20):

- By authorship:
  - author-prepared abstracts;
  - subject-expert & professional abstractor-prepared abstracts.
- By purpose:
  - informative abstracts;
  - descriptive or indicative abstracts;
  - critical abstracts (or reviews);
  - modular abstracts (which could include an annotation followed by indicative, informative, and critical modules).
- By form:
  - telegraphic abstracts (in the highly abbreviated style of old-fashioned telegraphs!);
  - statistical or tabular abstracts;
  - structured abstracts (not mentioned by Borko and Bernier, but increasingly popular). These abstracts contain bold-faced subheadings such as "Background" or "Context," "Aims" or "Objective," "Participants," "Design" or "Method," "Interventions," "Setting," "Outcome Measures," "Results," "Conclusions," and "Comments" (Hartley & Sydes 1996; Hartley 2000). Some of these exemplar headings came from guidelines from the American Medical Association for structured abstracts, which may be seen at: http://jama.ama-assn.org/info/auinst_abs.html.

• **alternatives to abstracts : 7**

Borko and Bernier (1975) also discuss alternatives to abstracts (p. 21-24):

- Extracts (selection of verbatim sentences from texts by computer algorithm);
- Terse literatures (condensations), including:
  - Terse conclusions;
  - Terse explanations;
  - Terse intentions;
  - Terse organizations of data;
  - Terse admonitions (terse conclusions with warning);
  - Terse advocacy;
  - Ultraterse literatures ("one-thousandth or less of the original number of words," p. 23).

Chapter 14. Surrogates (Section 14.1)

14.1. Purpose of Surrogates.

• views of Greene (Stephan et al.) on purpose of surrogates : 8

Stephan Greene et al. (2000) have summarized the role and purpose of surrogates. Among their purposes are:

- creating "comprehensible, predictable, and controllable environments in which they [i.e. users] can rapidly and safely explore and use information." ("Safely" may refer to avoiding the risk of missing or losing valuable information!) (p. 380).

- enabling users "to make decisions about what objects to examine next" (p. 381).

- in browsing, to "provide an important alternative to primary objects as they take far less time to examine and provide enough semantic cues to extract gists and allow users to assess the need for further processing of other surrogates and the primary objects" (p. 381).

- "In digital libraries and archives, surrogates are crucial for browsing large distributed collections" (p. 381).

- "Well-designed surrogates help exploit human perceptual strengths while not exceeding cognitive limitations" (p. 381).

- "An effective preview is an information surrogate that communicates to the user, at the appropriate time, sufficient information about the primary object it represents to support users in making a correct judgment about the relevance of that object to the user's information need" (p. 381).

14.2. Guidelines and Standards for Surrogates.

• 9

Greene et al. (2000) also suggest some guidelines for the design and creation of useful surrogates (p. 386). Their suggestions are in quotes, followed by commentary:

- "Use salient surrogates." "Salient" comes from the Latin "salire," to leap, and here means "standing out from the rest; noticeable; conspicuous; prominent" (Webster's 1966, p. 1286). The point is that surrogates should concentrate on what "stands out" or "leaps out" in the original message, text, or documentary unit.

- "Leverage data types (use visual surrogates for visual data, etc.)" Here the emphasis is on making clear to users the kind of message represented. Thumbnail representations can be much more effective here than words — a small representation of a map or photograph or painting, for example.

- "Use multiple surrogates. This supports different user styles and experiences." In chapter 16, we shall discuss the use of a variety of surrogate views, of various sizes and styles, for various purposes and stages of a search. Typically, these multiple views are based on a single full surrogate. In contrast to different views of the same surrogate, Green et al. suggest that the same message may deserve different surrogates aimed at different users, depending on user characteristics — the kinds of messages users may be seeking, as well as user styles, experience, and objectives. For example, a user seeking illustrations may be better served with a surrogate containing thumbnail images, whereas a user seeking answers to questions will prefer some summary answers or results. It is the rare IR database, however, that creates multiple surrogates for the same documentary unit, representing different aspects or points of view for different situations.

- "Use surrogates to inform users about the size, extent, and availability of collections or objects." Surrogates need to characterize not only content of messages, but important features, such as size, format, language, intellectual level, and quality or appropriateness for various uses. Copy-

Chapter 14. Surrogates (Section 14.2)

right restrictions or other terms of availability and use are also frequently important. Additional aspects will be appropriate for visual images — color, medium, style, etc. O'Connor (1985) discusses the desirable features of surrogates for film and video recordings.

• standards for surrogates : 10

There are many official and unofficial standards for creating document surrogates, especially citations and abstracts. Important examples include:

American National Standards Institute (1977). *ANSI Z39.29-1977 American National Standard for bibliographic references.* New York: American National Standards Institute; c1977. 92 p. Revision approved in 2003. See National Information Standards Organization (2004?) below.

American Psychological Association (1994). *Publication manual of the American Psychological Association.* 4th ed. Washington, DC: American Psychological Association; c1994. xxxii, 368 p. ISBN 1557982430.

Anderson, James D. (1997a). *Guidelines for indexes and related information retrieval devices.* Bethesda, MD: NISO Press; 1997. vii, 53 p. (NISO Technical Report; 2. ISSN: 1081-8006). ISBN 1-880124-36-X. These NISO guidelines include sections on surrogates and locators.

Anglo-American cataloguing rules (2002). Prepared under the direction of the Joint Steering Committee for Revision of AACR, a committee of the American Library Association, the Australian Committee on Cataloguing, the British Library, the Canadian Committee on Cataloguing, Chartered Institute of Library and Information Professionals, the Library of Congress. 2nd ed., 2002 revision. Ottawa: Canadian Library Association; Chicago: Library Association; 2002. Loose-leaf with multiple pagings. "AACR2" is the principal international standard for creating surrogates for library catalogs, used in most English-speaking countries, and in many others.

The Chicago manual of style (1993). 14th ed. Chicago: University of Chicago Press; c1993. ix, 921 p. ISBN 0226103897.

Gibaldi, Joseph (1999). *MLA handbook for writers of research papers.* 5th ed. New York: Modern Language Association of America; 1999. xvii, 332 p. ISBN 0873529758.

National Information Standards Organization (1997b). *ANSI/NISO Z39.14-1997 Guidelines for abstracts: an American national standard.* Approved November 27, 1996 by the American National Standards Institute. Bethesda, MD: NISO Press, c1997. viii, 14 p. (National information standards series. ISSN 1041-5653). ISBN: 1-88012-431-9.

National Information Standards Organization (2004?). *Z39.29-200x Bibliographic references.* Bethesda, MD: NISO Press; 2004? "This standard has been approved by the voting members and is being readied for publication." — www.niso.org, 4-14-2004.

• standards for identification of authors : 11

Guidelines like the *Chicago manual,* the *MLA handbook,* and the *Publication manual of the American Psychological Association* (popularly known as the "APA manual" or "APA style") are examples of standards that were not created to facilitate information retrieval but to cite references in research papers and books. A primary goal, especially in the APA manual, is to save space in published articles. Every character costs money! Thus the APA manual tells the user to reduce the forenames of authors to initials only. This unauthorized shortening of author names violates all information retrieval and cataloging standards, where the identification of an author is a key goal. This practice leads to confusion among many authors having common names. "James D. Anderson" is common enough, but when it is reduced, without the author's permission, to "J. D. Anderson," it is even more common, referring willy-nilly to hundreds or thousands of different authors. This practice should not be followed in any database designed for the identification and retrieval of messages, texts, or documents.

Chapter 14. Surrogates (Section 14.3)

• 12

The only acceptable practice is to cite persons by the names that they themselves use in their publications and are known by, as mandated by the Anglo-American Cataloguing Rules and advocated by the NISO guidelines for indexes and other information retrieval devices (Anderson 1997a). The NISO standard for bibliographic references (National Information Standards Organization 1979) comments as follows on this issue: "For personal authors, record the name(s) as given on the work. ... The first-named author must always be recorded. However, consideration of space, cost, or local regulations may require omission of other names or exclusive use of initials for given names" (p. 31). This last sentence is an acknowledgment of the demand by some publishers to sacrifice effective information retrieval in order to save money on space. To repeat, it is totally unacceptable in any database whose purpose is information retrieval!

• 13

Library standards go even further and call for the creation of unique headings for every author. If two authors have the same name, then dates of birth or death, or other qualifications should be added to distinguish among different persons (*Anglo-American cataloguing rules* 2002).

14.3. Selected Readings on Abstracts and Abstracting.

• 14

The NISO standard on abstracts (National Information Standards Organization 1997b) includes a good bibliography of "selected readings." It is now available without charge via the world-wide web: www.niso.org/standards/ (accessed 9 Oct. 2003).

• 15

In addition to general works on abstracts and abstracting, the bibliography has special sections on quality, guidelines, cognitive processes, structure and content, standards, and the role of abstracts in information retrieval.

14.4. Surrogates for Machine Searching.

• role of surrogates in data mining; in knowledge discovery : 16

The emphasis of this chapter has been creating surrogates for human examination. But there is also growing interest in creating effective surrogates for machine searching and "data mining" — the "mining" for useful data from digital libraries, the world-wide web, and other IR databases by means of sophisticated searching algorithms. Some of this work was summarized in a special issue of *Library trends* on "Knowledge discovery in bibliographic databases" (1999). Several examples of "metadata" — data about data — are examined as aids to such machine searching. (If you agree that knowledge resides only in the minds of humans — and other creatures, then "data mining" is a better term than "knowledge discovery." What is intended is the discovery of messages and texts that represent potentially useful knowledge, and that, after analysis and synthesis, may result in new knowledge, in the minds of users!)

• role of Dublin core metadata in surrogates : 17

The Dublin core — to be discussed in some detail in chapter 20 on record format — is an example of a surrogate schema that was designed precisely to encourage creators of webpages to include metadata, such as titles, keywords, content descriptions, authors, sources, format descriptions, and geographic coverage data. This metadata constitutes a surrogate designed primarily for machine analysis in machine searching, data mining, and knowledge discovery, as opposed to human examination. The effort to persuade webpage creators to include such metadata surrogates is no different, in principle, than the long tradition of expecting authors of periodical articles to include an abstract and, in many cases, keywords, for their articles.

14.5. Our examples.
14.5.1. A Book Index.

• 18

A book and its index constitute a full-text database, regardless of whether the medium of presentation is print on paper or electronic. In either case, the documentary units to which index headings or terms point are contained within the database, making it possible to have very brief surrogates, consisting of nothing more than an index heading or term (depending on syntax and presentation mode) and locators for documentary units (usually pages or paragraphs). For indexes displayed for browsing, a full index heading of several terms should be used. For non-displayed indexes used for electronic term-matching searches, surrogates generally consist of individual descriptors or terms plus a link to the documentary unit.

• 19

As noted in chapter 6 on documentary units, pages are, in the majority of cases, artifacts of the paper medium, not of the text that is encoded on those pages, and therefore, our book index will refer to paragraphs, not pages. Paragraphs, after all, are elements of language prose text, regardless of medium! Therefore, the actual surrogate in our displayed book index will be nothing more than an index heading plus a paragraph locator. For the print index, the paragraph locator will consist of a chapter number plus paragraph number. For the displayed browsable index in electronic media, the locator can be a hypertext link. For our electronic non-displayed indexes, our surrogates will consist of single terms or descriptors, plus a link to the relevant paragraph(s). In such electronic non-displayed indexes, the locator (or link) is not generally visible to the user. (More details about our locators will be provided in the next chapter, along with methods for numbering paragraphs in print media.)

• 20

In chapter 16 on surrogate displays, the possibility of fuller surrogates for electronic books will be discussed (section 16.1.1).

14.5.2. An Indexing and Abstracting Service.

• 21

Our A&I service is mostly a reference database. Only documents judged to be especially important are included in the electronic version of the database as full text. Therefore, we have rather large surrogates for all documents. Even for full texts included within the database, it is often more convenient to view a summary surrogate for the document than the full text. The summary may provide all the information one needs, in a much more concise way, or it may persuade the user that the full-text is not a useful document after all, saving time and energy.

• contents of surrogates in indexing and abstracting services : 22

Our surrogate for each document will consist of:

(a) a full citation, based on the NISO standard for bibliographic citations (National Information Standards Organization 2004?).

(b) a structured informative abstract (when possible); otherwise a structured descriptive or indicative abstract, composed according to the NISO standard for abstracts (National Information Standards Organization 1997b).

Informative abstracts include the purpose, methodology, results, and especially the conclusions of investigations, rather than just describing the investigation. Some documents have no results or conclusions. Examples may include review articles, general discussions, letters, narratives, biographies and bibliographies. For these types of documents, descriptive or indicative abstracts should be included.

The structured format provides for headings for various aspects of the message, such as "Background," "Aims," "Method," "Results," "Conclusions," and "Comments." Abstracts for messages without results can have similar headings. A literature review, for example, could have headings for "Sources" and "Selection criteria."

(c) A list of index descriptors assigned by human indexers. This applies only to "important" documents, because only important documents receive human indexing.

• role of keywords in surrogates in indexing and abstracting services : 23

All documents are indexed automatically based on terms (keywords) in their citations and abstracts, so there is little point in listing these terms separately in the surrogate, unless we are able to employ advanced automatic indexing techniques to select the most important key descriptors or phrases for a text based on frequency, co-occurrence, or natural language processing. The most important keywords or phrases could be regularized by matching them against a thesaurus. If we adopt such a way to pinpoint the most important terms, then these key terms should be listed in a separate part of the surrogate.

14.5.3. A Full-Text Encyclopedia/Digital Library.

• 24

Like our book, our encyclopedia/digital library is "full text," so our surrogates can be brief — just index headings plus locators. And because this is an electronic resource, the locators can be invisible. All searches can take the user directly to articles or texts.

• 25

However, as in the case of our indexing and abstracting service, it may be helpful to display a fuller surrogate before taking a user to the full article. A fuller surrogate might help a user select which articles they wish to peruse.

• 26

Our encyclopedia articles are written in such a way that the initial paragraph(s) serve as an abstract or summary of the entire article. All index terms (descriptors) assigned to each article are listed immediately following the introductory paragraph(s), along with any see-also references to related articles, so that this opening section can serve the same summarizing function as the surrogate in the A&I service.

Chapter 15. Locators

Contents of Chapter 15
15.1. Our Examples.
15.1.1. A Book Index.
15.1.2. An Indexing and Abstracting Service.
15.1.3. A Full-Text Encyclopedia/Digital Library.

• definition of locators : 1

Locators are devices that link or lead a user from a surrogate to a message, text, and documentary unit or to a larger surrogate. Locators locate the desired item. Locators are essential elements for all surrogates. Full surrogates were discussed in the previous chapter. The staged display of surrogates will be discussed in the next chapter.

• external locators : 2

IR databases use both internal and external locators. External locators are used to locate messages, texts, and documentary units outside of the database. These locators consist of citations or identifiers with enough information to permit location of items in libraries, bookstores, or other document depositories, including the world-wide web. Citations consist of identifying, descriptive data such as author, title, journal or publisher, date, numbering, pagination. An identifier can be a unique identifying number or notation, such as an International Standard Book Number (ISBN), which by itself can identify a particular book, of the International Standard Serial Number (ISSN), which uniquely identifies a periodical or other ongoing resource.

• 3

Standards and guidelines for citation-style external locators were discussed in the previous chapter on surrogates.

• internal locators : 4

Internal locators are used within an IR database, to lead from an index heading or partial surrogate to a fuller surrogate, or from a surrogate to full text. In print databases, internal locators are usually numbers that can be used to locate a fuller surrogate or documentary unit. When IR databases are presented in electronic media, internal locators are usually hypertext links.

• internal locators for indexing and abstracting services : 5

Indexing and abstracting services in print form typically will use numerical locators in their indexes for authors, subjects, and features (such as chemical registry numbers or affiliations). These numerical locators can be used to locate full surrogates, often with abstracts, in a section that is classified for browsing, so that similar or related surrogates are grouped together.

• visible locators; invisible locators : 6

In print IR databases, locators, both internal and external, have always been, of necessity, visible. In electronic IR databases, most internal locators are invisible hypertext links. (Of course the link is marked or highlighted to indicate that it is a link, but there is no visible linking or locator number or notation as in print media.) Most external locators in electronic IR databases continue to be visible, but there are movements afoot to create hypertext links between IR databases and electronic publications and document depositories, such as electronic journals, digital libraries, publisher's collections, or the world-wide web.

• locators in book indexes : 7

Chapter 15. Locators

In back-of-the-book indexes, the traditional locator has been the page number, attached to an index heading. As noted elsewhere in this book, there is growing interest in using locators that will take readers directly to paragraphs, rather than pages. Pages are artifacts of books printed on leaves of paper. When the same text is presented in a digital form, such pages usually disappear, making an excellent index tied to pages completely useless. Paragraphs, in contrast, are elements of prose or narrative language text, so that paragraphs travel with such text from print to digital media.

• **methods for numbering of paragraphs** : 8

A challenge for book design is how to number paragraphs so that index entries may refer directly to paragraphs rather than pages. Options include:

- numbering paragraphs on pages, then using both page and paragraph numbers, such as: 35.4, which would indicate the fourth paragraph on page 35. The disadvantage of this approach is that it still relies on page numbers, which will disappear if the text is moved to a digital format, or will change if the text is republished in a different print format with a different pagination. The advantage is that this can be done without actually printing a number next to each paragraph.

- numbering paragraphs for the entire text in one sequence. Using this method, the paragraph numbers must be attached to the paragraph. The disadvantage of this approach is that in a long book, the paragraph numbers can get quite large.

- numbering paragraphs within segments of the text. In a multivolume text, paragraphs could be numbered within each volume. Locators would include both the volume number and the paragraph number, as in: 1.367, 2.578. However, volumes are also artifacts of the print medium and may not travel with the text into a digital medium. A better alternative is to number paragraphs within chapters, because chapters are elements of a text. In this book, paragraphs are numbered within chapters, so that index locators include a chapter number and a paragraph number, such as: 8.123, 12.87.

• **indication of ranges of locators** : 9

It is not uncommon for several contiguous documentary units to be associated with the same index heading. In such cases, rather than listing each locator separately, a range of locators is indicated. The NISO guidelines (Anderson 1997a) cautions against abbreviated locator numbers in ranges, to avoid possible confusion. Here are some examples:

- listing all locators: 25, 26, 27, 28.
- listing a range of locators: 25-28.
- abbreviating a range: 20-5, 103-12, 1014-27 (to be avoided unless numbers are very long, e.g., 100026-28).

• 10

Some indexing experts make a distinction between listing a sequence of contiguous locators (25, 26, 27, 28) and a range of locators (25-28). They use separate locators (25, 26, 27, 28) when the topic is treated separately on each page (or paragraph), while they use a range (25-28) when the treatment is continuous across several pages or paragraphs. Most indexes do not make this fine distinction, and it is unlikely that users are aware of the difference.

• **locators as indicators of postings** : 11

In print IR databases, visible locators have also served to indicate the number of documentary units associated with a particular index heading. This is called the number of postings. (The number of documentary units posted to, or associated with, a particular index heading.) This was especially true for page or paragraph numbers in back-of-the-book indexes and surrogate num-

Chapter 15. Locators

bers in subject indexes in indexing and abstracting services. The user could tell at a glance whether there was only one, or many items, associated with a particular index heading.

• indicators of postings for hypertext locators : 12

In electronic media, with invisible hypertext locators, the user has lost this valuable information about the number of items associated with a particular index heading. Therefore, many IR databases have begun to record the number of postings with every index heading. This is very useful information, helping the user to visualize available resources.

• locators for nonbook media : 13

Locators are needed to pin-point documentary units within many types of media other than books, for example, sound recordings, films and videos, maps, and collections or sets of objects (slides, photographs, etc.). If items within a collection, such as individual slides, are numbered, then these numbers can be used as their locators. But when elements within a larger documentary unit are not generally numbered, such as frames within a video or film, playing time can be used as a locator. Playing time was formerly often used for sound recordings as well, but with compact disks, individual items (songs, movements, etc.) are usually numbered and directly accessible. Some documentary units have specialized traditional locator systems. For example, parts of earth maps can be indicated and located using standard longitudes and latitudes.

• locators for webpages : 14

The usual locators for webpages have been URLs, uniform resource locators. (At first, these were called "universal resource locators," but according to the CNET glossary (CNET Networks 2001), "universal ... was deemed by most to be too ambitious, and the more frequently used "uniform" was instated by the now-defunct URI Working Group.")

• instability of URLs : 15

But URLs are often very unstable, changing whenever a page moves within a website or from one website to another. There have been many initiatives seeking to provide more stable locators for electronic resources and, in addition, to provide the means for linking directly to them via digital networks. In 1999, the National Information Standards Institute (NISO), the National Federation of Abstracting and Indexing Services (NFAIS), the Digital Library Federation (DLF), and the Society of Scholarly Publishers (SSP) sponsored a special invitational workshop to explore "linkage from citations to electronic journal literature" (National Information Standards Organization 1999).

• locators for digital resources : 16

Among the possible solutions discussed at the NISO et al. workshop were the Digital Object Identifier (DOI), the SICI (Serial Item and Contribution Identifier), and the PII (Publisher Item Identifier). The following summary of the the PII and the SICI initiatives is based primarily on Paskin (1997). Norman Paskin is the director of the International DOI Foundation (IDF), whose website <http://www.doi.org> is the primary source for the subsequent description of the DOI.

• Publisher Item Identifier (PII) : 17

PII: Publisher Item Identifier. Introduced in 1995 by a consortium of scientific publishers, the PII is a seventeen-character string used to identify items without regard to format. It identifies the "semantic content" only, with "no separate identifiers for the same document in different media." The seventeen characters begin with one to indicate "source publication type," then ten characters based on an ISBN or an ISSN plus two characters for a year, then five digits to identify the item, and finally a single check digit. The ISBNs or ISSNs plus year digits are used to generate a unique identifier.

• examples of Publisher Item Identifier (PII) : 18

Here is an example:

S0165380696004038

S indicates an item from a serial.

01653806 is taken from the ISSN 0165-3806.

96 are two year digits.

00403 is the item number.

8 is a check digit.

• Serial Item and Contribution Identifier (SICI) : 19

SICI: Serial Item and Contribution Identifier. First defined in 1991 by the Serials Industry Advisory Committee, the SICI was revised in the mid-1990s and is now described in an official NISO standard: ANSI/NISO Z39.56-1996. It is a variable-length notation that can be used to identify both print and electronic serial publications and their components. It consists of three segments, one for an item (e.g., an issue of a serial), one for a contribution to the item (e.g., a particular article), and a final control segment. It has three different formats, one to identify a serial issue; one to identify a particular contribution based on its physical appearance; and one to identify a contribution "without a physical appearance," such as a contribution "in the production process, or in electronic final form." The control segment is used to indicate which format is being used; it can also include a "Medium/Format Identifier (MFI)."

• examples of Serial Item and Contribution Identifier (SICI) : 20

Here are examples, taken from the NISO standard (National Information Standards Organization 1996b), with fictitious data:

For a serial item (issue):

1234-5679(19950221)1:2:3<>1.0.TX;2-P

The elements are:

The ISSN for the serial: 1234-5679

The date of the issue: 1995,02,21, i.e., 21 Feb. 1995

Numbering, e.g., series 1, volume 2, number 3.

There is nothing inside <>, which is reserved for a contribution.

1 indicates SICI format 1 for a serial issue

0 indicates no "Derivative Part Indicator," such as a table of contents or an abstract.

TX is a "Medium/Format Identifier," e.g., text.

2 indicates that this is version 2 of the SICI

-P is a check character.

For a contribution (article):

1234-5679(19950221)1:2:3<123:ABCDEF>2.0.TX;2-A

The first part of this code is the same as the previous example, except that now a contribution is indicated within the <>.

123 indicates location (page number).

ABCDEF is a title code based on the words in a title, such as "Analyzing brief cataloging description exception files." (This made-up title is not from the NISO standard!)

2 indicates SICI format 2 for a contribution.

Chapter 15. Locators

The remainder of this notation — 0.TX;2-A — is the same as the first example, even though the final check character is now an A.

• 21

Here are two examples for real publications, also from the standard:

Forbes January 1, 1996 vol. 157 no. 1

    0015-6914(19960101)157:1<>1.0.TX;2-V

Hutheesing, Nikhil, "Keeping the seats warm" *Forbes* January 1, 1996 vol. 157 no. 1 p. 62.

    0015-6914(19960101)157:1<62.KTSW>2.0.TX;2-F

• Digital Object Identifier (DOI) : 22

DOI: Digital Object Identifier. Originally called the Uniform File Identifier, the DOI project was initiated by the American Association of Publishers as a means for identifying individual digital objects or copyrighted works in digital form. "A DOI differs from a URL because it identifies an object, not the place where the object is located" (International DOI Foundation 2001). Like the SICI, the DOI (or at least its syntax) is now described in a NISO standard, ANSI/NISO Z39.84-2000 (National Information Standards Organization 2000).

• components of Digital Object Identifier (DOI) : 23

Much like the ISBN, the DOI has two parts, a prefix and a suffix. The prefix is assigned to a publisher or content producer by a "Registration Agency." At least initially, all prefixes begin with "10." The suffix is a number for a particular item assigned by the publisher or content producer. A suffix can be assigned to any object of any size, ranging from a complete book to a particular chart or song or melody. It may be assigned to any "file type," such as language text, audio, video, image, or software.

• resolution of Digital Object Identifier (DOI) : 24

To function, the DOI must be linked to the object it represents. This is done by means of a "distributed central directory," where the DOI is linked to metadata describing the object, including location information.

• examples of Digital Object Identifier (DOI) : 25

Here is an example of a DOI from the NISO standard (National Information Standards Organization 2000):

    10.1006/rwei.1999.0001

The 10 is a Directory Code, assigned by a Maintenance Agency. Currently, the directory code is 10 for all DOIs.

1006 is the Registrant's Code — the code for the publisher or producer.

The rest of the DOI, after the slash (/) is the item number assigned by the registrant.

• 26

Many other identifying initiatives are under way. Here is a brief listing, as identified in Green & Bide (1997).

• Book Item and Component Identifier (BICI) : 27

BICI: Book Item and Component Identifier. The BICI is modeled after the SICI, described above, but will be for chapters and other parts of books (such as maps, illustrations, bibliographies or entries in directories and encyclopedias). The book's ISBN would be used instead of the serial's ISSN.

Chapter 15. Locators

• Common Information System (CIS) : 28

CIS: Common Information System. The CIS has been devised by the International Confederation of Authors and Composers' Societies and the International Federation of Phonograph Industries to integrate and standardize a number of identifier systems used mainly in the world of music, such as the CAE, ISMN, and ISRC, which are listed next.

• Compositeur, Auteur, Editeur (CAE) : 29

CAE: Compositeur, Auteur, Editeur. Coming from Europe, with a French title, the CAE is a number that "identifies the creators and publishers of music and literary texts." There are plans to extend it to visual, audiovisual and plastic arts, and to rename it the "Interested Party (IP) number" (Green and Bide 1997).

• International Standard Music Number (ISMN) : 30

ISMN: International Standard Music Number. This identifies published editions of printed music.

• International Standard Recording Code (ISRC) : 31

ISRC: International Standard Recording Code. This is for individual sound recordings, such as individual music tracks on CDs.

• International Standard AudioVisual Number (ISAN) : 32

ISAN: International Standard AudioVisual Number. This is similar to the ISRC, but is designed for individual films or television programs.

• International Standard Work Code (ISWC) : 33

ISWC: International Standard Work Code. This notation was created for musical compositions — the underlying works or messages — as opposed to any particular printed or recorded expressions of works. There is interest in extending this beyond music to other types of works. An initial alphabetic character indicates the type of work, e.g., T (tune) for music. L could be used for literature. The initial letter is followed by 9 digits for the work plus a check digit. The code can be assigned to any element, for example, a complete opera or a single aria within it.

• Uniform Resource Names (URN) : 34

URN: Uniform Resource Names. URNs are a project of the Internet Engineering Task Force (IETF) to create unchanging (persistent!) names for internet resources, in contrast to the ever-changing URLs. The URN would name the item, not its location, which is the purpose of the URL. (This effort is similar to the DOI, described previously.)

• Persistent Uniform Resource Locator (PURL) : 35

PURL: Persistent Uniform Resource Locators. In the meantime, OCLC has developed the PURL, which is an unchanging identifier that points to a resolution database, maintained by OCLC, which will track changing URLs for particular webpages. OCLC encourages other agencies to begin offering PURL services as well (Weibel, Jul & Shafer 2001).

• locators in libraries : 36

Locators in libraries lead from catalog surrogates to the documentary units within the library, such as books, serials, video tapes, films, etc. The most frequently used locator in libraries is called the "call number," because before open-stack libraries became popular, one used the "call number" to call for the book (Comaromi 1981, p. 9).

• call numbers in libraries : 37

Call numbers in libraries typically consist of a classification notation and a "book number" for the particular item, which of course need not be a book, but could be any kind of message medium — film, video, sound recording, etc.

Chapter 15. Locators

• book numbers in call numbers; work marks in call numbers : 38

The book number generally consists of an author number — often an alphabetic letter followed by a series of numbers — and a work mark, one or more alphabetic letters representing a particular work by an author.

• views of Lehnus (Donald J.) and Comaromi (John P.) on book numbers : 39

Donald J. Lehnus (1980) and John P. Comaromi (1981) have written two of the most comprehensive books on book numbers, their history and use.

• classification notation in call numbers : 40

The classification notation — the first part of the library locator or call number — is drawn from the classification scheme used for arranging books (such as Dewey Decimal Classification (DDC), Library of Congress Classification (LCC), Universal Decimal Classification (UDC), Bliss Classification (BC), National Library of Medicine Classification, Superintendent of Documents Classification (SuDocs) — for U.S. government publications, etc.).

• examples of call numbers in libraries : 41

Here are some examples, representing both the DDC and the LCC, all taken from Comaromi (1981, p. 66-67, 96, 109), slightly modified and with added commentary:

```
613.25    The Bethesda weight loser diet, by Marilyn Lewis
L675
              613.25 is the DDC notation for dieting.
              L675 is an author number for Marilyn Lewis in this class
                 (it may be different in other classes).

613.25    The Arlington weight loser diet, by Marilyn Lewis
L675ar
              This is a second book by the same author. A work mark,
                 "ar" has been added to represent this book. This
                 means that these books will be out of order on the
                 shelves, but the first book didn't need a work mark
                 at the time it was cataloged because it was the first
                 book by this author in this class.
              Some libraries might give it a work mark anyway in order
                 to preserve alphabetical order!

613.25    Let them eat cake: a critique of the Arlington diet, by
L675ary       Sue Franklin.

              Here a "y" has been added to indicate that this work is a
                 commentary or criticism of the preceding book. The
                 author number does not represent the author of the
                 book, but the author of the book that is being criti-
                 cized! In this way, the critical book will be shelved
                 next to the book being criticized.

613.25    The Arlington weight loser diet, 2nd edition, by Marilyn
L675ar2       Lewis.

              The 2 following the work mark "ar" indicates
                 the 2nd edition.

613.25    Same book as immediately above, but a second copy.
L675ar2
c.2
```

```
HN 64 .N38      Poverty and riches by Scott Nearing
HN 64 .N4       Social adjustment by Scott Nearing
HN 64 .N44      Social sanity by Scott Nearing
```

These are Library of Congress call numbers. The HN 64 stands for "social reform literature in the United States 1801-1945." In most cases, LCC does not use work marks attached to author numbers within classes. Instead, each separate work gets a separate "book number," arranged so that the books will be in alphabetical order. Hence here we have .N38, .N4, and .N44.

• development of cutter numbers by Cutter (Charles Ammi) : 42

Note that book or author numbers use decimal numbers, so that .N4 comes after .N38. The procedure of combining an initial alphabetic letter with a decimal number in order to maintain an alphabetical sequence was developed by Charles Ammi Cutter in the 19th century. Such numbers are often called "cutter numbers" in his honor! Creating these numbers is often called "cuttering."

```
HD          Laws governing the manufacture of surgical instruments in
9999            England, by John King.
.S9722
G65
```
    HD stands for industries; 9999 for miscellaneous industries and trades in alphabetical order.
    .S9722 stands for surgical instruments by place.
    G6 stands for Great Britain, and the 5 for the author John King. He doesn't get his own author number because LCC does not permit more than two "cutter numbers."

• local nature of call numbers in libraries : 43

The same book may have a different call number in a different library, even if the classification notation is the same. That's because each book number (author number with possible work mark) is built up to place the book in its proper place in a particular class of items in a particular library. These are not uniform item identifiers that are the same everywhere, such as the International Standard Book Number (ISBN).

15.1. Our Examples.

15.1.1. A Book Index.

• chapter and paragraph numbers as locators : 44

For the index in our printed book, locators are numbers that lead directly to chapters, sections, or paragraphs in the text. Chapter and section locators include "chap." and "sec.," e.g., "chap. 15," "sec. 15.1.2." Paragraph locators consist of a chapter number plus a paragraph number within the chapter. The elements are separated by a full stop, e.g., 12.164, which indicates paragraph number 164 in chapter 12. Chapter and section numbers are displayed at the top of every page, while paragraph numbers are displayed along the right margin.

• paragraph numbers as locators : 45

An alternative would have been to number paragraphs continuously throughout the book, but it was thought that in a book as large as this, the paragraph numbers would become too long toward the end of the book and become unwieldy.

Chapter 15. Locators (Section 15.1.2)

• 46

As indicated previously (sections 6.1; 6.5.1), the paragraph is used as the basic documentary unit for our book index instead of the traditional page. In most cases the page is an artifact of the book format and the paper medium, not of the text itself, and therefore the page does not usually travel with the text into electronic media. A further advantage is that the paragraph represents a unit of message development and presentation in language prose. In traditional writing style, each paragraph presents a topic or a variation of a topic. Therefore, the paragraph, rather than the page, is the better documentary unit for book indexes.

• locators for indexes in electronic books : 47

For our book indexes in electronic media, our locators could be hypertext links without visible paragraph numbers. Internal links could connect displayed index headings or keywords and descriptors directly to text paragraphs or intermediate surrogates. However, if we preserve the visible chapter, section, and paragraph numbers in our electronic indexes, then these indexes can be used to locate chapters, sections, or paragraphs in the printed book as well. Therefore, we will keep them. Nevertheless, these visible locators will also be hypertext links so that in electronic media, a click will take the user to the text, or if preferred, to an intermediate surrogate (see section 16.1.1).

• 48

In both our displayed and non-displayed electronic indexes, searches will lead initially to brief surrogates consisting of the full index heading for the paragraph plus its locator (chapter and paragraph number). Users can then click on the locator to go immediately to a particular paragraph, or can use the numerical locators to find the paragraph in the printed book.

• browsing of indexes in electronic books : 49

Users of our electronic displayed indexes have the option of browsing a single alphabetical index or separate hierarchies representing the main topical categories of the book. In the initial browsing mode, only single descriptors are displayed. Only when a descriptor is chosen are full index headings displayed with chapter and paragraph locators.

• postings in indexes in electronic books : 50

Consequently, in the displays of single descriptors, both in the alphabetical and the faceted browsable displays, postings information is substituted for locators. In a similar way, in electronic term-matching searches, postings are displayed for each term in a search statement. (If Boolean syntax is used, postings for the combined statement is also provided. Such combined postings are not possible for weighted term syntax searches, because retrievals are presented in ranked order and users have the option of considering as many retrievals as they wish!)

• 51

Thus, postings information is provided for single terms and descriptors, while visible locators are provided for full indexing headings.

15.1.2. An Indexing and Abstracting Service.

• 52

Like our book example, our A&I service is presented in both electronic and print media, thus the same argument for preserving visible locators in the electronic indexes applies here, as well.

• internal locators for indexing and abstracting services in print media : 53

Internal locators will lead from author, subject, and feature indexes to full surrogates in our print A&I service. These locators will consist of a section number and an abstract number. The section number will represent the major classes of library and information science, where abstracts are grouped for browsing. Abstracts will be numbered sequentially within these sections.

• **internal locators for indexing and abstracting services in electronic media : 54**

The same internal locators will be used in our electronic indexes, but they will be displayed only with full index headings after a single descriptor is chosen in a browse search (in either the alphabetical index or the faceted displays) or after an electronic term-matching search is conducted. (Only the most important documents receive human indexing and thus have full index headings. When less important documents are retrieved via a term-matching search, the title is used in place of an index heading for the brief initial surrogate.) By displaying numerical locators, the electronic indexes may be used for locating surrogates in both the print and the electronic version of the A&I service database. In the electronic A&I service, these visible locates will also be hypertext links.

• **postings for indexing and abstracting services in electronic media : 55**

As in our electronic book indexes, postings will be presented at the early stages of all searches, before index headings (or titles) are displayed.

• **external locators for indexing and abstracting services : 56**

For both our print and electronic A&I services, external locators will consist of full citations, based on the guidelines of the NISO standard for bibliographic references (National Information Standards Organization 2004?). These citations include such additional locators as ISBNs, ISSNs, and URLs as appropriate.

15.1.3. A Full-Text Encyclopedia/Digital Library.

• 57

Our encyclopedia/digital library is presented only in electronic media, so here all locators can be internal hypertext links without visible numerical locators. Postings will be provided at each stage of a search — for individual descriptors, whether in an alphabetical or faceted browse display or in an electronic term-matching search — and also for initial surrogate displays (consisting of full index headings).

Chapter 16. Surrogate Displays

Contents of Chapter 16
16.1. Our Examples.
16.1.1. A Book Index.
16.1.2. An Indexing and Abstracting Service.
16.1.3. A Full-Text Encyclopedia/Digital Library.

• 1

Surrogates are almost always displayed in stages in both print and electronic IR databases. The purpose is to provide to users only what is useful at a particular stage of a search. How and when to display surrogates is a key element of interface design, which is the main topic of chapter 19. The content and structure of complete surrogates was the topic of chapter 14. Locators as essential elements of all surrogates was addressed in chapter 15. Here we focus on what portions of surrogates to display in various situations.

• staged display of surrogates in print media : 2

For example, in a print-medium indexing and abstracting service, only the names of authors (sometimes accompanied with titles of documentary units, but often not) are displayed in author indexes. A locator leads from this very partial display to the full surrogate elsewhere in the A&I service. Similarly, only topical or subject headings are displayed in subject indexes.

• staged display of surrogates in electronic media : 3

The same principle should govern the display of brief initial surrogates in electronic media. The portion of the full surrogate displayed at any stage of the search should relate directly to the type and purpose of the search.

• display of surrogates for subject searches; for author searches in electronic media : 4

Thus, for a topical or subject search, the brief surrogate should contain topical or subject information directly related to search terms. If human indexing is used, then a full index heading containing all (or the most important) descriptors assigned to the documentary unit can be displayed. This full topical or subject-oriented index heading will provide context for the descriptor of primary interest. For an author search, authors should be the first element displayed. For image searches, a thumbnail of retrieved images should be included in the initial display.

• research on display of surrogates : 5

One of the few research articles that focuses directly on alternative displays of surrogates (Thomas 2001) is based on a 1997 dissertation at the University of Pittsburgh. The article is densely detailed and still reads very much like a dissertation, but it contains useful conclusions based on empirical research that support the contention that displays should be tailored to the task at hand (p. 42):

"The primary objective [of this research] was to explore the effect that layout and content might have on a typical information retrieval task."

"... it was found that alterations to the content of particular screens — in this case, enhancing the content of the brief display — has a significant effect on the behavior of the experiment participants. Participants who used brief display screens that contained more topically oriented data elements resorted to full display screens significantly fewer times than did those using standard, citation-oriented brief displays. This finding is important because it suggests that — for topically oriented tasks, at least — brief catalog displays might be redesigned to include more fields with

Chapter 16. Surrogate Displays

subject-rich content (e.g., MARC 520 and 6xx fields [i.e., summary and subject heading fields]). Such a redesign would presumably reduce both the number of screens that users would need to view and the complexity of those screens. This might, in turn, simplify the user's task of finding wanted items in the catalog."

• display of full surrogates : 6

Users should always have the option of moving from an initial partial surrogate display to a display of the full surrogate. In a full-text database, users should also have the option of skipping the full surrogate and moving directly to the full text, but frequently, especially in searches with many retrievals, users may find it easier and more efficient to peruse surrogates before choosing full texts.

• unified surrogates : 7

The display of the full surrogate is sometimes called the unified display, because all elements of the full surrogate are brought together in a single full (unified!) display. Unfortunately, some IR databases do not make a full unified display available. For example, in some print IR databases, the index headings or descriptors are not displayed with the fullest surrogate. This is unfortunate because the indexing headings or descriptors provide a much more succinct description of the content of a documentary unit than an abstract or summary. Most electronic IR databases do make full unified surrogates available, but unfortunately not all do — and some full-text IR databases don't make any surrogates available!

• options for display of surrogates : 8

In electronic databases, users should be provided options for tailoring surrogate displays, both brief displays and full unified displays. Default initial surrogate displays might consist of a single line of data — e.g., only the full topical subject index heading (for a subject search) or only the author plus title (for an author search). A title search should provide the title first, followed by the author. Such brief displays can provide more entries (brief surrogates) on a single browsable screen.

• 9

However, if a user would like to see authors and titles combined with subject index headings, they should have that option.

• 10

Similarly, if they wish to see an intermediate surrogate, such as a full citation without an abstract, they should be able to request this kind of display as well.

• format options for display of surrogates : 11

Thus designers of electronic IR databases will need to formulate default displays, not only with respect to the amount of information to provide, but also various formatting options. But experienced and frequent users should have the option of changing the format of displays as well as the amount and arrangement of information.

• 12

For example, the default display of a unified full surrogate may consist of full headings for each field in the surrogate, such as:

Chapter 16. Surrogate Displays

```
Descriptors:
Classification:
Summary:
Title:
Authors:
Journal:
Numbers:
Date:
Pages:
Image:
Abstract:
```

• 13

However, an experienced user may prefer to see only record structure tags, such as:

```
des\
cls\
sum\
tit\
aut\
jnl\
num\
dat\
pag\
img\
abs\
```

Record tags are briefer, so that the display will take up less space, but many tags will make sense only to experienced searchers.

• 14

Default displays generally display only those fields with data, but some users may prefer to see all fields, whether they are used or not. The absence of data in particular fields can be informative to experienced searchers.

• order of fields in display of surrogates : 15

Similarly, an experienced searcher may prefer a different ordering of fields within a surrogate. They may want the more traditional display that puts citation information first, or they may prefer a more topically-oriented display that puts topical fields (descriptors, classification notation and caption, and/or summary) first.

• display of surrogates in libraries : 16

In libraries, catalogers or other librarians, or adventuresome students of library and information science, might prefer to see surrogates in the form of underlying MARC records, rather than in formatted displays that might look like an old catalog card or a display with field captions. Here are three display options for the same library surrogate. The formatted and MARC displays come from the online catalog of Rutgers University Libraries:

• International Standard Bibliographic Description (ISBD) : 17

International Standard Bibliographic Description (ISBD) display:

Chapter 16. Surrogate Displays

```
Svenonius, Elaine.
     The intellectual foundation of information organization / Elaine
Svenonius. — Cambridge, Mass. ; London : MIT Press, c2000.
     xiv, 255 p. ; 24 cm. — (Digital libraries and electronic publish-
ing).
     Contents: 1. Information Organization — 2. Bibliographic Objec-
tives — 3. Bibliographic Entities — 4. Bibliographic Languages — 5.
Principles of Description — 6. Work Languages — 7. Document Languages —
8. Subject Languages:
Introduction, Vocabulary Selection, and Classification — 9. Subject
Languages: Referential and Relational Semantics — 10. Subject-Language
Syntax.
     1. Information organization. 2. Bibliography—Methodology. 3. Cata-
loging.
```

• formatted display of surrogates : 18

Formatted display with field headers:

```
Personal author: Svenonius, Elaine.
Title: The intellectual foundation of information organization / Elaine
          Svenonius.
Publication info: Cambridge, Mass. ; London : MIT Press, c2000.
Physical descrip: xiv, 255 p. ; 24 cm.
Series: Digital libraries and electronic publishing
Contents: 1. Information Organization — 2. Bibliographic Objectives —
          3. Bibliographic Entities — 4. Bibliographic Languages — 5.
          Principles of Description — 6. Work Languages — 7. Document
          Languages — 8. Subject Languages: Introduction, Vocabulary
          Selection, and Classification — 9. Subject Languages: Ref-
          erential and Relational Semantics — 10. Subject-Language
          Syntax.
Subject: Information organization.
Subject: Bibliography—Methodology.
Subject: Cataloging.
```

• display of MARC records : 19

MARC record display:

```
     000:      : am a0p
     001:      : 99041301
     003:      : DLC
     005:      : 20000527151605.9
     008:      : 990722s2000 mau b 001 0 eng
     010:      : 99041301
     020:      : 0262194333 (hc : alk. paper)
     040:      : DLC|cDLC|dDLC|dOrLoB|dOrLoB-B
     050: 00: Z666.5|b.S92 2000
     082: 00: 025.3|221
     100: 1 : Svenonius, Elaine.
     245: 14: The intellectual foundation of information organization
/|cElaine Svenonius.
     260:      : Cambridge, Mass. ;|aLondon :|bMIT Press,|cc2000.
     300:      : xiv, 255 p. ;|c24 cm.
     440:   0: Digital libraries and electronic publishing
     504:      : Includes bibliographical references (p. [199]-243) and index.
     505: 00: |g1.|tInformation Organization —|g2.|tBibliographic Objec-
tives —|g3.|tBibliographic Entities —|g4.|tBibliographic Languages —
```

Chapter 16. Surrogate Displays

```
|g5.|tPrinciples of Description —|g6.|tWork Languages —|g7.|tDocument
Languages —|g8.|tSubject Languages: Introduction, Vocabulary Selection,
and Classification —|g9.|tSubject Languages: Referential and Relational
Semantics —|g10.|tSubject-Language Syntax.
 650:  0: Information organization.
 650:  0: Bibliography|xMethodology.
 650:  0: Cataloging.
```

Details about the MARC record and its tags may be found at the MARC homepage: http://lcweb.loc.gov/marc/. MARC will be discussed in more detail in chapter 20 on record format.

• order of fields in display of surrogates : 20

Notice that in all of these traditional library displays, topical information is displayed last. If a user is engaged in a subject search (rather than an author-oriented or known-item search for a particular author or a particular document), then it would be good to rearrange the fields in these displays so that topical information is displayed first:

International Standard Bibliographic Description (ISBD) display (rearranged with topical fields first):

```
    1. Information organization. 2. Bibliography—Methodology. 3. Cata-
        loging.
    Contents: 1. Information Organization — 2. Bibliographic Objec-
        tives — 3. Bibliographic Entities — 4. Bibliographic Lan-
        guages — 5. Principles of Description — 6. Work Languages —
        7. Document Languages — 8. Subject Languages: Introduction,
        Vocabulary Selection, and Classification — 9. Subject Lan-
        guages: Referential and Relational Semantics — 10. Subject-
        Language Syntax.Svenonius, Elaine.
The intellectual foundation of information organization / Elaine
        Svenonius. — Cambridge, Mass. ; London : MIT Press, c2000.
    xiv, 255 p. ; 24 cm. — (Digital libraries and electronic publish-
        ing).
```

• formatted display of surrogates : 21

Formatted display with field headers (rearranged with topical fields first):

```
    Subject: Information organization.
    Subject: Bibliography—Methodology.
    Subject: Cataloging.
    Contents: 1. Information Organization — 2. Bibliographic Objectives —
        3. Bibliographic Entities — 4. Bibliographic Languages — 5.
        Principles of Description — 6. Work Languages — 7. Document
        Languages — 8. Subject Languages: Introduction, Vocabulary
        Selection, and Classification — 9. Subject Languages: Ref-
        erential and Relational Semantics — 10. Subject-Language
        Syntax.
    Personal author: Svenonius, Elaine.
    Title: The intellectual foundation of information organization / Elaine
        Svenonius.
    Publication info: Cambridge, Mass. ; London : MIT Press, c2000.
    Physical descrip: xiv, 255 p. ; 24 cm.
    Series: Digital libraries and electronic publishing
```

Chapter 16. Surrogate Displays (Section 16.1)

• display of surrogates based on automatic indexing : 22

For most types of simple routine automatic indexing of full text, there are entirely too many terms for a useful surrogate display of documentary unit keywords, whether in a brief topical or subject-oriented display or as part of a unified display. In the simplest forms of automatic indexing, every term is a "keyword" except those on a stop list. It is not very helpful to list every non-stop-list term in a documentary unit, or even every non-stop-list term in an abstract (there can be hundreds), in a surrogate display.

• 23

However, more advanced techniques in automatic indexing include methods for selecting the most important keywords or phrases. In chapter 8, an example of automatic phrase identification for a digital library was illustrated (section 8.3.8). Twelve key phrases were identified for each documentary unit. These key phrases would certainly be appropriate for a unified surrogate display, and indeed, they served as the basis for initial topical displays for topical searches in the digital library.

16.1. Our Examples.
16.1.1. A Book Index.

• display of surrogates in printed books : 24

In a typical print medium back-of-the-book index, index headings constitute brief topical subject surrogates for documentary units, such as pages or paragraphs. The locator, a page or paragraph number, will take the reader to the documentary units indicated.

• display of surrogates in tables of contents : 25

Similarly, a typical table of contents for a printed book consists of a display of surrogates for larger documentary units, such as whole chapters and possibly sections within chapters. This book, for example, offers the reader three tables of contents with different levels of surrogate display. The first table of contents displays only chapter titles. The second adds a brief summary statement for each chapter, and the third table of contents includes all section headings.

• 26

The title or caption for each chapter or section serves as a surrogate for that chapter or section, and locators (chapter and section numbers) will lead the reader to particular chapters and sections.

• unified surrogates for printed books : 27

Unified surrogates are very rare in printed books. They would consist of all the index headings associated with a particular documentary unit (page or paragraph). For larger units of text, unified surrogates would consist of the titles or captions for the documentary unit and its parts (such as a chapter and its sections), plus all the index headings for the entire unit. These could be arranged to form a complete outline of the larger unit.

• display of surrogates in electronic books : 28

Our electronic book could display surrogates for paragraphs in the same manner as our printed book, relying on the full index heading to represent each paragraph, and chapter and section titles to represent chapters and sections in the full table of contents. The electronic book would also have the second table of contents with brief descriptive summaries. In each case, hypertext locators would take the user directly to the text of the documentary unit (paragraph, chapter, or section).

For users of the electronic book's non-displayed index (for term-matching searches), retrieved paragraphs would be represented with the full index heading, just as they are in a browse search.

• intermediate surrogates for electronic books : 30

However, it might be nice to provide an expanded surrogate for retrieved paragraphs, especially when the same index heading (in a browsable display) or the same search statement (in a term-matching search) retrieves several paragraphs. These intermediate surrogates could be displayed, and the user could use them to select which paragraph to choose.

• topic sentences as intermediate surrogates for electronic books : 31

The expanded surrogate could consist of the first sentence of each paragraph. This first sentence is often called the "topic sentence" because it should introduce the scope of the paragraph. For example, if a user is looking for a definition of "syndetic structure" they would retrieve:

```
definitions. of syndetic structure : 12:38; 13:39
```

But if the surrogate were expanded to include the topic sentence of each paragraph, the user would see:

```
definitions. of syndetic structure :
   12:38.  A key element in LCSH is the "syndetic" structure, which
           consists of cross-reference links between headings.
   13:39.  Cross references, or syndetic structure, have been an
           integral part of displayed alphabetical subject in-
           dexes since the advent of subject heading systems in
           the second half of the 19th century.
```

• 32

The first topic sentence indicates that the definition is given in the context of Library of Congress Subject Headings (LCSH), while the second topic sentence indicates a slightly more generic definition.

• 33

The same type of surrogate display could be used with the full-text electronic index. An electronic keyword search might retrieve ten, twenty, thirty, or even more paragraphs. These could be ranked according to predicted relevance and both the index heading (based on human indexing) and the topic sentence could be displayed for each paragraph. Such ranked listings could also include a predicted relevance score, from 100% to 0%. The user could then select which paragraphs to actually view.

16.1.2. An Indexing and Abstracting Service.

• 34

Our indexing and abstracting service will display brief surrogates in much the same way as our book.

• display of surrogates in print media : 35

In the printed version of the A&I service, each displayed index will display an appropriate segment from the full surrogate, with a locator number that will take the user to the full surrogate.

Chapter 16. Surrogate Displays (Section 16.1.3)

• **display of surrogates for subject searches in print media : 36**

Thus the subject index will display the subject index heading based on human indexing. Because human indexing is invested only in more important documents, there is also a keyword index, which includes surrogates for less important documents. The keyword index uses a KWIC format (see chapter 12 on indexing syntax, section 12.4.2) to display both document titles and sentences from abstracts.

• **display of surrogates for author searches in print media : 37**

The author index displays surrogate segments consisting of authors' names (last name, forenames), followed by titles of documents with which they are associated.

• **display of surrogates in tables of contents : 38**

The table of contents will display the major facets or categories of the A&I service, within which the full surrogates are displayed.

• **display of surrogates in electronic media : 39**

The display of surrogates for our electronic A&I service will be similar to our electronic book. Retrieved documents found via our browsable displayed indexes, both alphabetical and faceted, will be represented with their index heading based on human indexing. Browsable indexes, and their surrogates, are limited to the more important documents.

• **40**

Searches based on term-matching in the non-displayed index will display index headings for the more important documents. For less important documents, titles will be displayed. Unless the user requests an alternative display order, these brief surrogates will be arrayed in order of predicted relevance, with a predicted relevance score (ranging from 100% to 0%). The user can move from selected brief surrogates to the full unified surrogate, or directly from the brief surrogate to the full text, if available (for more important documents).

• **41**

Full surrogates will be formatted to reflect the nature of the search. Surrogates retrieved via a topical browse or electronic search will display topical fields first. Surrogates retrieved via an author or title search will display authors and titles first.

16.1.3. A Full-Text Encyclopedia/Digital Library.

• **42**

All articles in our electronic encyclopedia/digital library receive human indexing, so for subject searches, the brief surrogate for each article will be the full index heading. When the same index heading represents more than one article, then the surrogate will be augmented with the title of the article and the opening sentence.

• **43**

For author searches, the brief surrogate will be the full name of the author (last name, then forenames) plus the title of the article.

Chapter 17. Arrangement of Displayed Indexes

Contents of Chapter 17
17.1. Alphanumeric Displays.
17.2. Alphanumeric Arrangement in Hypertext Displays.
17.3. Relational Classified Displays.
17.3.1 Display of Dewey Decimal Classification in Hypertext.
17.3.2. Constructing and Displaying a Faceted Classification.
17.3.2.1. Display of Faceted Classification in Print Media.
17.4. Our Examples.
17.4.1. A Book Index.
17.4.2. An Indexing and Abstracting Service.
17.4.3. A Full-Text Encyclopedia/Digital Library.

• **purpose of displayed indexes : 1**

Index displays are absolutely essential in print databases, because they provide the means for accessing, inspecting and browsing terms and headings that represent topics and features of documentary units. Index displays can also be very helpful in electronic environments, permitting users to browse and select from among displayed precoordinated headings.

• **psychological advantages of displayed indexes : 2**

Psychological research has long confirmed that human beings find it easier to recognize relevant terms than to recall them directly from their memories. This is especially true for topics or areas with which searchers are not familiar. Effective index displays can show options for a search that otherwise may not occur to a user. Effective vocabulary management displays (see chapter 13) can be very helpful for displaying search options and alternatives as well.

• **options for arrangement of displayed indexes : 3**

Indexes can be displayed in two fundamentally different ways — alphanumerically, based on the letters and numerals that make up index headings, or relationally, whereby headings representing similar or related topics or features are grouped together based on closeness of relationship, with narrower subordinate headings being displayed after broader superordinate headings.

• **relational classified displays; definition of classification : 4**

Relational displays are often called classified displays, and indeed they can be based on established classification systems, such as the Universal Decimal Classification (UDC), the Dewey Decimal Classification (DDC), the Library of Congress Classification (LCC), and many others. However, in a narrow strict sense, classification means nothing more than placing items into classes. In this sense, classification and indexing are essentially the same operations. In indexing (indicating), we assign terms to, or extract terms from, a document, and in so doing, we place that document in classes with all other documents having those same terms.

• **5**

Regardless of whether we call it "indexing" or "classification," after the indexing (the assignment or extraction of terms) and/or the classing (placing documents into classes) has been done, the crucial question is how to arrange these classes (or the terms or headings or captions that represent the classes) in a display that is useful and meaningful to users.

Chapter 17. Arrangement of Displayed Indexes (Section 17.1)

• advantages of alphanumeric displays : 6

The best possible solution to the arrangement of index headings or classes is to provide both alphabetical (or alphanumeric) displays and relational classified displays. Alphanumeric access, whether through electronic searches of non-displayed indexes or via alphanumeric displays, appears to be best when users know what they are looking for and know what to call it. The advantage of a displayed alphanumeric index over electronic alphanumeric searching is that small variations in the format of terms are less problematic in a displayed index. A user interested in "ground water" may not know whether it should be expressed as "groundwater," "ground-water," or "ground water." In searching for "IR databases," should "IR" be spelled out? Should singular or plural forms be used? Scanning an alphanumeric display can often help lead the user to the preferred term for a desired concept, especially if vocabulary management has been integrated into the display (see chapter 13)..

• advantages of relational classified displays : 7

A relational classified display is often useful when a user wants to get an overview, either of the entire database or collection, or of a subset of the database or collection. This approach is also useful when users only have vague ideas about what they are looking for. A relational classified display should show users what is available in various categories of interest.

• alphanumeric displays versus relational classified displays : 8

The interplay between alphanumeric and relational classified displays (as well as with electronic term-matching searches) will be a major topic in chapter 19 on interface design. In the IR database interface, all search options need to be brought together in one place, and these options need to be made as clear as possible to users, so that they can choose the approach that is most beneficial to them.

17.1. Alphanumeric Displays.

• problematic nature of alphanumeric displays : 9

At first glance, alphanumeric order may appear to be straightforward and non-problematic, but instead, it is an area of extreme disagreement among information professionals. It is also an example of an area where strongly held opinions are not based on empirical research into the most effective methods of alphanumeric arrangement. In fact, this is a problem on which there is almost no relevant research. The design of useful research on this question is itself problematic. The fact that there is no consensus on how to arrange indexing headings in an alphanumeric array means that we, as a profession, simply do not know how to do it! This problem was discussed briefly in chapter 1 (section 1.4) as an example where standards have not succeeded in achieving consensus or resolving problems. Here the issues are laid out with a little more detail.

• 10

This fact that the library and information professions, in effect, do not know how to effectively arrange index headings in an alphanumeric display is really quite amazing, when one considers that until the computer burst upon the scene, alphanumeric arrays were the principal means for accessing many information retrieval databases for at least a hundred years.

• 11

How many important entries have been lost simply because users thought they were dealing with a simple straightforward alphanumeric list, when in reality it was a highly structured list based on obscure sorting principles like those advocated by the Library of Congress? This is not a trivial matter. For a physician looking for a key reference on some disease, finding it may mean the difference between life or death.

Chapter 17. Arrangement of Displayed Indexes (Section 17.1)

● **controversies in alphanumeric arrangement; roman numerals in alphanumeric arrangement : 12**

The major controversies stem from a conflict between symbols versus concepts — whether arrangements should be based on the actual characters (alphabetic letters, numbers, punctuation) in a heading, or the meaning of the heading. The classic example is roman numerals. "XXVI" means "twenty-six." But "XXVI" consists of the alphabetic characters X, V, and I. Should it be arranged on the basis of those characters, in their normal alphabetic sequence, or according to its meaning?

● 13

The specific controversies include whether to consider the space and various punctuation marks as sorting characters; the treatment of numerals, abbreviations, initialisms, and initial articles; and whether to group headings on the basis of criteria other than alphanumeric characters. Depending on the choices adopted, radically different arrangements can result, and a user who does not understand rather esoteric principles of arrangement can easily miss a sought-after entry by a great distance.

● **standards for alphanumeric arrangement : 14**

In discussing controversies in alphanumeric arrangement, four important but unofficial standards will be cited. Each has been issued by an important information organization, yet each adopts radically different solutions for certain controversies. It should be noted that none of these "standards" has been adopted by any official standards-setting body, such as NISO, the National Information Standards Organization in the United States, so even though they are called "standards," none of them have achieved that official status. They are all unofficial standards. As a result, there are no official uniform standards for alphanumeric arrangement in the United States! The four most important unofficial standards are:

- ALA: American Library Association (1980), Filing Committee. *ALA filing rules*. Chicago: American Library Association; 1980. ix, 50 p.
- LC: Library of Congress (1980). *Library of Congress filing rules*. Prepared by John C. Rather and Susan C. Biebel. Library of Congress. Processing Services. Washington, DC: Library of Congress, Cataloging Distribution Service; 1980. 111 p.
- NISO-1: "Alphanumeric arrangement," in Anderson, James D. (1997a). *Guidelines for indexes and related information retrieval devices*. Bethesda, MD: NISO Press; 1997: 32-35. vii, 53 p. (NISO technical report; 2).
- NISO-2: Wellisch, Hans H. (1999). *Guidelines for the alphabetical arrangement of letters and sorting of numerals and other symbols*. Bethesda, MD: NISO Press; c1999. vi, 20 p. (NISO technical report; 3).

Anderson (1982) discussed the new ALA and LC rules soon after they appeared. The main issues are summarized here.

● **spaces in alphanumeric arrangement : 15**

If the space is considered to be a sorting character, the arrangement is called "word-by-word" as opposed to "letter-by-letter." In word-by-word arrangement, "New York" will come before "Newark." Headings beginning with the same word, such as "New," will fall together in the arrangement before longer words that begin with the letters, such as "news" or "newt." In letter-by-letter arrangements, "Newark" will come first, before "New York," and longer words beginning with "new" will be intermingled among headings beginning with the word "New." ALA, LC, and both NISO standards are in agreement on this issue, all calling for word-by-word arrangement, but many reference tools, IR databases, and back-of-the-book indexes ignore the space in their alphanumeric arrangements.

Chapter 17. Arrangement of Displayed Indexes (Section 17.1)

• punctuation in alphanumeric arrangement : 16

ALA, LC, and NISO-2 each distinguish between punctuation marks which should be considered as equivalent to a space because they usually mark divisions between words, or at least word segments. Examples include the hyphen, dash and slash (NISO-2, p. 11), as opposed to punctuation marks that do not usually by themselves divide words or word segments and therefore should be ignored, such as the period (full stop), comma, semi-colon, colon, parentheses, square brackets, angle brackets, braces (curved brackets), apostrophe, quotation marks (single or double), exclamation mark, and question mark. ALA puts the period (full stop) in the first category (to be considered equivalent to a space), but in all four of these standards, multiple spaces (or the equivalent) are to be treated as a single space, so this difference affects only "words" with internal periods, such as initialisms. According to NISO-2, "N.A.T.O." and "NATO" will be placed next to each other, but the ALA standard would separate them!

• 17

NISO-1 fails to distinguish between these two classes of punctuation, suggesting that all punctuation marks should be equivalent to a space (p. 32). LC states that "punctuation as such has no place in the collating sequence of characters considered in filing arrangement. A mark of punctuation is taken into account, however, in two situations: 1) when it signals the end of an element or field and indicates the need for subarrangement ...; and 2) when it serves as the sole separator between two discrete words, e.g., Mott-Smith; 1951/1982; 1:3) and so must be treated as equivalent to a space. The second situation dictates that a hyphen will always be treated as a space."

• numbers in alphanumeric arrangement : 18

Older standards called for numbers to be arranged as if they were written out in words in the language of the text, whereas modern standards call for numbers to be arranged in numerical order, preceding alphabetic letters. But even here, there is disagreement about whether arrangement should be based on the actual characters present in a number or on the numerical meaning of the characters. For example, should "1/4" be placed with ".25" because their numerical meaning is the same, or should it be arranged on the basis of the characters "1", "/" and "4"? Both ALA and LC prefer the latter approach, treating the "/" as a space, while both NISO standards prefer the former. LC and ALA also ignore the meaning of decimals following integers, so that 1.3 is arranged as if it were 1+space+3. Both NISO standards call for arranging decimal numbers by their value. Roman numerals are usually arranged by their numerical value rather than on the basis of their alphabetic letters. All four standards agree on Roman numerals!

• abbreviations; acronyms in alphanumeric arrangement : 19

There is a growing consensus that abbreviations should be arranged based on the actual spelling of the abbreviation, not on the basis of the full form, so that "St. Louis" will not be arranged as if it were "Saint Louis." Acronyms (words created from initials or syllables, such as "radar," "scuba," or "Unesco") have always been arranged as spelled. Thus NATO would not be arranged as if it were North Atlantic Treaty Organization. In every case of such alternative placements, cross-references are essential to guide users to headings that they may miss.

• initialisms in alphanumeric arrangement : 20

Initialisms can be problematic because there is no standard form for presenting them. "ALA" can also appear as "A.L.A." or "A L A." All standards except NISO-2 treat periods or full stops (.) as a space, so that "A.L.A." and "A L A" would fall at the very beginning of the "A's" in the alphanumeric arrangement, but "ALA" would come much later, just before "Alabama"! Accord-

Chapter 17. Arrangement of Displayed Indexes (Section 17.1)

ing to NISO-2, however, "A.L.A." and "ALA" would fall together, but would be separated from "A L A."

• non-alphanumeric criteria in alphanumeric arrangement : 21

One of the most controversial practices is arranging headings on the basis of non-alphanumeric criteria — criteria that have nothing to do with the actual symbols or characters in the heading. LC, for example, continues to insist that headings beginning with the same word should not be arranged simply on the basis of the subsequent word, which most users might expect, but should first be grouped on the basis of the nature of the entity represented and the form of the heading. Thus, when headings begin with the same word, persons must come before places; places must come before things (corporate bodies or topics); and things must come before titles of documents. Even headings for persons are not in a single alphanumeric sequence. Headings that begin with a forename must come in a separate sequence before headings that begin with a family name. This means that a title like "Paris after the war" will come long after a person named "Paris, Virginia," or an entry for "Paris (France)." ALA and both NISO standards reject this "structured" arrangement.

• subject headings in alphanumeric arrangement : 22

Similarly, LC will arrange subject headings beginning with the same word not in simple alphanumeric order, but in separate sequences according to the nature of the heading and its subdivisions. After a main heading without any subdivisions, headings are grouped in the following separate sequences: (1) the heading with chronological subdivisions; (2) the heading with general form and topical subdivisions; (3) the heading with geographic subdivisions; (4) longer subject headings beginning with the same word(s), including first (4a) types of the main heading and their subdivisions — that is, the main heading modified by an inverted adjective (e.g., Missions, Canadian); then (4b) qualified main headings and their subdivisions — e.g., Missions (Canon law); and finally (4c) longer phrases beginning with the same word or words and their subdivisions — e.g., Missions and literature.

• 23

These non-alphanumeric principles are rarely explained to users. Indeed, many professional librarians are completely unaware of them!

• 24

For this reason, both NISO standards urge a minimum number of exceptions to strict arrangement on the basis of characters present, including the space. Most punctuation is ignored, while hyphens, dashes, and slashes are treated as spaces. Multiple spaces, or their equivalent, are considered a single space. Exceptions to strict character arrangement include: arranging Roman numerals and fractions by value rather than by the actual alphabetic characters (for Roman numerals) or separate numerals (for fractions); ignoring initial articles unless they are part of the names of persons (Le Guin, Ursula K.) or places (El Paso, The Dalles); considering the meaning of the decimal point (unlike the full stop or period) in determining the value of numbers. NISO-2 does not recommend an exception for initial articles. If a heading or title begins with "A," "An," or "The," NISO-2 would arrange it by these words.

• ampersand in alphanumeric arrangement : 25

The ampersand (&) is a special problem in alphanumeric arrangement. LC and NISO-2 place it after a space, but before the lowest number. NISO-1 treats it as a space. And ALA recommends ignoring it altogether, but allows for an option of arranging it as if spelled out in the language of the text. Both NISO standards also have an option for arranging it as if it were spelled out.

Chapter 17. Arrangement of Displayed Indexes (Section 17.1)

• examples of alphanumeric arrangement : 26

To illustrate the effect of some of these principles, here are four brief alphanumeric sequences, each arranged according to our four unofficial standards. Pretend you absolutely must find five headings: the titles "3/4 of an ounce," "A.L.A. takes a stand," "Charles and the wise men," and "The African experience," and the subject heading "Missions and Christian union." Pretend also that the alphanumeric index or catalog you are consulting consists not just of these few headings, but of hundreds of thousands, or even millions, of headings:

ALA arrangement

```
.8 gram took me to jail [title]
1.3 acres. [title]
3/4 of an ounce [title]
10:00 a.m. [title]
XX century cyclopedia and atlas. [title]
1001 nights. [title]
1066 and all that. [title]
1984. [title]
A.L.A. takes a stand. [title]
The African experience. [title]
African foods. [title]
ALA and LC. [title]
Charles II, King of England. [forename]
Charles II, King of England. [title]
Charles III, Emperor of Germany [forename]
Charles (airplane). [topical heading]
Charles (Ala.). Police Department. [place name]
Charles, Allen. [family name]
Charles and the wise men. [title]
Charles, Duke of York. [forename]
Charles, (Va.). Municipal Court. [place name]
Charles, Virginia [family name]
Charles (yacht). [topical heading]
Missions — African influences
Missions, American
Missions and Christian union
Missions around the world [title]
Missions — Asia
Missions (canon law)
Missions, Tamil
Missions — Theory
Missions to Buddhists
Missions to Mormons
Missions — United States
```

LC arrangement

```
.8 gram took me to jail [title]
1.3 acres. [title]
3/4 of an ounce [title]
10:00 a.m. [title]
CZ century cyclopedia and atlas. [title]
1001 nights. [title]
1066 and all that. [title]
1984. [title]
A.L.A. takes a stand. [title]
The African experience. [title]
```

Chapter 17. Arrangement of Displayed Indexes (Section 17.1)

```
African foods. [title]
ALA and LC. [title]
Charles II, King of England. [forename]
Charles III, Emperor of Germany [forename]
Charles, Duke of York. [forename]
Charles, Allen. [family name]
Charles, Virginia [family name]
Charles (Ala.). Police Department. [place name]
Charles (Va.). Municipal Court. [place name]
Charles (airplane). [topical heading]
Charles (yacht). [topical heading]
Charles II, King of England. [title]
Charles and the wise men. [title]
Missions — African influences
Missions — Theory
Missions — Asia
Missions — United States
Missions, American
Missions, Tamil
Missions (canon law)
Missions and Christian union
Missions to Buddhists
Missions to Mormons
Missions around the world [title]
```

NISO-1 arrangement

```
3/4 of an ounce [title]
.8 gram took me to jail [title]
1.3 acres. [title]
10:00 a.m. [title]
XX century cyclopedia and atlas. [title]
1001 nights. [title]
1066 and all that. [title]
1984. [title]
A.L.A. takes a stand. [title]
The African experience. [title]
African foods. [title]
ALA and LC. [title]
Charles II, King of England. [forename]
Charles II, King of England. [title]
Charles III, Emperor of Germany [forename]
Charles (airplane). [topical heading]
Charles (Ala.). Police Department. [place name]
Charles, Allen. [family name]
Charles and the wise men. [title]
Charles, Duke of York. [forename]
Charles, (Va.). Municipal Court. [place name]
Charles, Virginia [family name]
Charles (yacht). [topical heading]
Missions — African influences
Missions, American
Missions and Christian union
Missions around the world [title]
Missions — Asia
Missions (canon law)
Missions, Tamil
```

Missions — Theory
Missions to Buddhists
Missions to Mormons
Missions — United States
```

### NISO-2 arrangement

```
3/4 of an ounce [title]
.8 gram took me to jail [title]
1.3 acres. [title]
10:00 a.m. [title]
XX century cyclopedia and atlas. [title]
1001 nights. [title]
1066 and all that. [title]
1984. [title]
African foods. [title]
ALA and LC. [title]
A.L.A. takes a stand. [title]
Charles II, King of England. [forename]
Charles II, King of England. [title]
Charles III, Emperor of Germany [forename]
Charles (airplane). [topical heading]
Charles (Ala.). Police Department. [place name]
Charles, Allen. [family name]
Charles and the wise men. [title]
Charles, Duke of York. [forename]
Charles, (Va.). Municipal Court. [place name]
Charles, Virginia [family name]
Charles (yacht). [topical heading]
Missions — African influences
Missions, American
Missions and Christian union
Missions around the world [title]
Missions — Asia
Missions (canon law)
Missions, Tamil
Missions — Theory
Missions to Buddhists
Missions to Mormons
Missions — United States
The African experience. [title]
```

17.2. Alphanumeric Arrangement in Hypertext Displays.

• 27

The ALA, LC and NISO rules discussed in the previous section were created for single sequences of headings in print displays, such as card catalogs, print-on-paper reference works, or back-of-the-book indexes.

• 28

Modern OPACs (online public access catalogs) and electronic IR databases are typically presented in hypertext formats, which make alternative alphanumeric presentations not only feasible, but highly desirable.
```

Chapter 17. Arrangement of Displayed Indexes (Section 17.2)

• **staged display of alphanumeric indexes in hypertext : 29**

In hypertext, alphanumeric displays are much more effective if they are presented in stages. These stages can reflect some of the structured approaches advocated in the previous section by the Library of Congress. Staged presentation has been advocated for the display of subject headings in OPACS for many years by experts such as Karen Drabenstott and Diane Vizine-Goetz (1994). Their recommendations are discussed in the section 12.2.1 on subject heading syntax. A similar approach was presented by the Subcommittee on the Display of Subject Headings in Subject Indexes in Online Public Access Catalogs of the Subject Analysis Committee of the Cataloging and Classification Section of the Association for Library Collections and Technical Services (American Library Association 1992) and was also recommended by participants in the Library of Congress conference on "The future of subdivisions in the Library of Congress Subject Heading system" (Conway 1992). The suggestions of the LC conference were also discussed in section 12.2.1 on Library of Congress subject headings.

• **visual limitations of hypertext displays : 30**

A disadvantage of electronic hypertext displays is that they are typically presented via comparatively small electronic screens, where only a limited number of headings can be viewed at one time — many fewer than in a large two-page spread in a print-on-paper indexing and abstracting service.

• **advantages of hypertext displays : 31**

But a major advantage of hypertext displays is that it is very easy to permit users to follow a selected path of headings and subheadings in which, at each stage, they are presented with relatively few choices. Whereas a print-on-paper display has only a single sequence of headings, the hypertext display can have many sequences, and for each sequence, it is easy to display a more limited (more manageable) number of choices to the user.

• **goals of alphanumeric displays in hypertext; scrolling in hypertext displays : 32**

A goal of all hypertext displays is "no scrolling" and no "below the fold" index headings. Both of these phrases express the same idea — that users should be able to see at a glance all available choices. "Below the fold" refers to the traditional truth regarding front-page stories in newspapers. The stories at the top half of the page, "above the fold" will garner a lot more attention than the stories on the lower half of the page, the "below the fold" stories.

• **33**

A general exception to this rule is the display of a complete alphanumeric index. It is impossible to display a complete alphanumeric index of any size in a small window, unless a "fisheye" technique is used. The expectation is that users understand how an alphanumeric index works and they will use the techniques provided to move quickly to the section of the alphanumeric index in which they are interested. But once they choose a heading in an alphanumeric index, then the "no scrolling" and "no below the fold" headings comes into play in full force.

• **fish-eye menu displays : 34**

Fisheye menu displays have been developed by the Human-Computer Interactions Lab of the University of Maryland (Bederson 2000). The fisheye menu permits display of a very long list of headings, but only the section of interest is in legible type. Before and after the section of interest, the list is in very small type. Displays of this type are useful because they make it clear that there are thousands of choices to which the user can move on demand.

Chapter 17. Arrangement of Displayed Indexes (Section 17.2)

• examples of alphanumeric displays in hypertext;
display of subject headings in hypertext : 35

Below are examples of alternative display approaches, using an array of Library of Congress subject headings. First, 271 subject headings from the Rutgers University Libraries OPAC are displayed in the traditional fashion just as they have been displayed on cards in card catalogs for 100 years or more. This is also the way they were displayed in the Rutgers OPAC when they were copied in 1998. A newer Rutgers OPAC is similar, except that all the punctuation, such as dashes, commas, and parentheses, have been removed! (www.libraries.rutgers.edu/iris.html).

• 36

Our sample topic "homosexuality" is not a big topic in the Rutgers University Libraries. 271 is not a particularly large number of headings beginning with the same term. Many topics have hundreds more, where the problems illustrated here are compounded enormously. Check, for example, such headings as "art," "United States," or "women."

• 37

The number at the right of each heading indicates the number of postings — the number of bibliographic records for documentary units linked to the heading in the library catalog. In a typical OPAC, only ten to twenty lines are displayed on a single screen, depending on interface design features of the particular OPAC and screen size, so it is very difficult for a user to get an overview of what is available. Here, a space has been added after every tenth heading. The Rutgers University Library OPAC displays up to thirteen subject headings per screen. At thirteen headings per screen, it would take twenty-one screens to scan this entire list. Few users would have the patience to slog through twenty-one screens to get an overview of what any library has on a single topic!

```
================================================================
Homosexuality.                                               50+
Homosexuality -- abstracts.                                    1
Homosexuality -- Addresses, essays, lectures.                 16
Homosexuality -- Addresses, essays, lectures -- Abstracts.     1
Homosexuality -- America -- History.                           1
Homosexuality and art.                                         9
Homosexuality and art -- Bibliography.                         1
Homosexuality and art -- New Zealand.                          1
Homosexuality and art -- United States.                        3
Homosexuality and Christianity.                                2
Homosexuality and Christianity -- Bibliography.                1
Homosexuality and Christianity -- History.                     1
Homosexuality and Christianity -- Periodicals.                 2
Homosexuality and education -- England.                        1
Homosexuality and education -- Great Britain.                  1
Homosexuality and education -- United States.                  7
Homosexuality and literature.                                 26
Homosexuality and literature -- Addresses, essays, lectures.   1
Homosexuality and literature -- Bibliography.                  2
Homosexuality and literature -- England -- History -- 16th centur>   4
Homosexuality and literature -- England -- History -- 17th centur>   3
Homosexuality and literature -- England -- History -- 19th centur>   1
Homosexuality and literature -- England -- History -- 20th centur>   3
Homosexuality and literature -- England -- Oxford -- History -- 1>   1
Homosexuality and literature -- Europe.                        1
Homosexuality and literature -- France.                        1
Homosexuality and literature -- France -- History -- 19th century>   1
Homosexuality and literature -- France -- History -- 20th century>   3
```

Chapter 17. Arrangement of Displayed Indexes (Section 17.2)

```
Homosexuality and literature -- Great Britain.                              2
Homosexuality and literature -- Great Britain -- Colonies -- Hist>          1
Homosexuality and literature -- Great Britain -- History.                   2
Homosexuality and literature -- Great Britain -- History -- 19th >          5
Homosexuality and literature -- Great Britain -- History -- 20th >          3
Homosexuality and literature -- Greece -- History.                          1
Homosexuality and literature -- History -- 20th century.                    5
Homosexuality and literature -- Latin America.                              2
Homosexuality and literature -- New Zealand.                                1
Homosexuality and literature -- Periodicals.                                3
Homosexuality and literature -- Rome.                                       1
Homosexuality and literature -- Scotland -- History -- 19th centu>          1
Homosexuality and literature -- Spain.                                      1
Homosexuality and literature -- United States.                              5
Homosexuality and literature -- United States -- History.                   1
Homosexuality and literature -- United States -- History -- 19th >          5
Homosexuality and literature -- United States -- History -- 20th >          4
Homosexuality and music.                                                    2
Homosexuality -- Argentina.                                                 1
Homosexuality -- Asia.                                                      1
Homosexuality -- Asia -- Cross-cultural studies.                            1
Homosexuality -- Australasia -- Cross-cultural studies.                     1
Homosexuality -- Australia -- Sydney (N.S.W.)                               1
Homosexuality -- Biblical teaching.                                        11
Homosexuality -- Bibliography.                                             13
Homosexuality -- Bibliography -- Methodology.                               1
Homosexuality -- Boise, Idaho.                                              1
Homosexuality -- Brazil -- History.                                         1
Homosexuality -- Brazil -- Moral and ethical aspects.                       1
Homosexuality -- Brazil -- Social aspects.                                  1
Homosexuality -- California -- Los Angeles (County)                         1
Homosexuality -- Case studies.                                              1
Homosexuality -- Cases, clinical reports, statistics.                       1
Homosexuality -- China.                                                     1
Homosexuality -- Collections.                                               1
Homosexuality -- Congresses.                                                3
Homosexuality -- Cross-cultural studies.                                    2
Homosexuality -- Denmark.                                                   1
Homosexuality -- Dictionaries.                                              2
Homosexuality -- Drama.                                                     4
Homosexuality -- Drama -- Directories.                                      1
Homosexuality -- Early works to 1800.                                       1
Homosexuality, Ego-Dystonic -- therapy.                                     1
Homosexuality -- England -- History.                                        2
Homosexuality -- England -- London.                                         2
Homosexuality -- Europe.                                                    1
Homosexuality -- Europe -- History.                                         6
Homosexuality -- Family relationships.                                      1
Homosexuality -- Fiction.                                                  10
Homosexuality -- Film catalogs.                                             1
Homosexuality -- France -- 18th century -- History -- Sources.              1
Homosexuality -- France -- History.                                         3
Homosexuality -- France -- History -- 19th century.                         1
Homosexuality -- France -- History -- 20th century.                         1
Homosexuality -- France -- Paris.                                           1
Homosexuality -- Genetic aspects.                                           1
Homosexuality -- Germany.                                                   1
```

401

Chapter 17. Arrangement of Displayed Indexes (Section 17.2)

```
Homosexuality -- Germany -- Addresses, essays, lectures.                   1
Homosexuality -- Germany -- History -- Addresses, essays, lecture>         1
Homosexuality -- Government policy -- Germany (East)                       1
Homosexuality -- Government policy -- Germany -- History -- 20th >         2
Homosexuality -- Government policy -- History.                             1
Homosexuality -- Government policy -- United States.                       1
Homosexuality -- Great Britain.                                            6
Homosexuality -- Great Britain -- Addresses, essays, lectures.             1
Homosexuality -- Great Britain -- Case studies.                            1
Homosexuality -- Great Britain -- History.                                 2
Homosexuality -- Great Britain -- Juvenile literature.                     1
Homosexuality -- Great Britain -- Public opinion.                          1
Homosexuality -- Greece.                                                   3
Homosexuality -- Greece -- Bibliography.                                   1
Homosexuality -- Greece -- History.                                        1
Homosexuality -- Gt. Brit.                                                 1
Homosexuality -- History.                                                 11
Homosexuality -- History -- 19th century.                                  1
Homosexuality -- History -- 20th century.                                  1
Homosexuality -- History -- Cross-cultural studies.                        1
Homosexuality -- History -- Miscellanea.                                   1
Homosexuality in art.                                                      6
Homosexuality in art -- Bibliography.                                      1
Homosexuality in art -- United States.                                     1
Homosexuality in folklore.                                                 1
Homosexuality in literature.                                              47
Homosexuality in literature -- Addresses, essays, lectures.                6
Homosexuality in literature -- Bibliography.                               3
Homosexuality in literature -- Europe.                                     1
Homosexuality in literature -- Periodicals.                                2
Homosexuality in literature -- Study and teaching (Secondary)              1
Homosexuality in literature -- United States.                              1
Homosexuality in motion pictures.                                         28
Homosexuality in motion pictures -- Addresses, essays, lectures.           1
Homosexuality in motion pictures -- Encyclopedias.                         1
Homosexuality in radio -- Great Britain -- Encyclopedias.                  1
Homosexuality in religion.                                                 1
Homosexuality in television.                                               1
Homosexuality in television -- Great Britain.                              1
Homosexuality in television -- Great Britain -- Encyclopedias.             1
Homosexuality in television -- United States.                              1
Homosexuality in the Bible.                                                5
Homosexuality -- Japan -- History.                                         1
Homosexuality -- Juvenile literature.                                      1
Homosexuality -- Latin America.                                            1
Homosexuality -- Law and legislation.                                      4
Homosexuality -- Law and legislation -- Canada.                            2
Homosexuality -- Law and legislation -- Europe.                            1
Homosexuality -- Law and legislation -- France.                            1
Homosexuality -- Law and legislation -- Germany.                           2
Homosexuality -- Law and legislation -- Great Britain.                     2
Homosexuality -- Law and legislation -- Great Britain -- Addresse>         1
Homosexuality -- Law and legislation -- Great Britain -- History.          1
Homosexuality -- Law and legislation -- Greece.                            2
Homosexuality -- Law and legislation -- New Jersey.                        1
Homosexuality -- Law and legislation -- Scotland -- History.               1
Homosexuality -- Law and legislation -- United States.                    12
```

Chapter 17. Arrangement of Displayed Indexes (Section 17.2)

```
Homosexuality -- Law and legislation -- United States -- Addresse>    1
Homosexuality -- Law and legislation -- Washington (State)            1
Homosexuality -- Legal status, laws, etc. -- United States -- Bib>    1
Homosexuality -- Literary collections.                                4
Homosexuality, Male.                                                 20
Homosexuality, Male -- Addresses, essays, lectures.                   2
Homosexuality, Male -- Bibliography.                                  1
Homosexuality, Male -- Caribbean Area -- History -- 17th century.     2
Homosexuality, Male -- Case studies.                                  1
Homosexuality, Male -- China -- History.                              1
Homosexuality, Male -- Costa Rica.                                    1
Homosexuality, Male -- Cross-cultural studies.                        1
Homosexuality, Male -- England.                                       2
Homosexuality, Male -- England -- History.                            1
Homosexuality, Male -- England -- History -- 17th century.            2
Homosexuality, Male -- Europe -- History.                             1
Homosexuality, Male -- Fiction.                                       1
Homosexuality, Male -- France -- History.                             1
Homosexuality, Male -- Germany.                                       2
Homosexuality, Male -- Germany -- History.                            2
Homosexuality, Male -- Germany -- History -- 20th century.            1
Homosexuality, Male -- Government policy -- Germany -- History -->    1
Homosexuality, Male -- Great Britain.                                 1
Homosexuality, Male -- Great Britain -- History -- 19th century.      3
Homosexuality, Male -- Great Britain -- History -- 20th century.      1
Homosexuality, Male -- Greece.                                        3
Homosexuality, Male -- Greece -- History.                             4
Homosexuality, Male -- History.                                       6
Homosexuality, Male -- History -- Addresses, essays, lectures.        1
Homosexuality, Male, in literature.                                   9
Homosexuality, Male -- Indonesia -- Irian Jaya.                       2
Homosexuality, Male -- Islamic countries.                             1
Homosexuality, Male -- Italy -- Florence -- History.                  1
Homosexuality, Male -- Japan -- History.                              1
Homosexuality, Male -- Law and legislation -- Greece -- History.      1
Homosexuality, Male -- Melanesia -- Addresses, essays, lectures.      1
Homosexuality, Male -- Mexico -- Guadalajara.                         1
Homosexuality, Male -- New York (N.Y.) -- History -- 20th century>    1
Homosexuality, Male -- North America.                                 1
Homosexuality, Male -- Papua New Guinea.                              2
Homosexuality, Male -- Poetry.                                        2
Homosexuality, Male -- Psychological aspects.                         3
Homosexuality, Male -- Psychology.                                    1
Homosexuality, Male -- Rome.                                          1
Homosexuality, Male -- Rome -- History.                               2
Homosexuality, Male -- Social aspects -- England.                     1
Homosexuality, Male -- South Africa.                                  1
Homosexuality, Male -- United States.                                 7
Homosexuality, Male -- United States -- Addresses, essays, lectur>    1
Homosexuality, Male -- United States -- Case studies.                 1
Homosexuality, Male -- United States -- Handbooks, manuals, etc.      1
Homosexuality, Male -- United States -- History.                      1
Homosexuality, Male -- United States -- Psychological aspects.        2
Homosexuality -- Middle East -- History.                              1
Homosexuality -- Miscellanea.                                         3
Homosexuality -- Moral and ethical aspects.                           8
Homosexuality -- Moral and religious aspects.                         1
```

Chapter 17. Arrangement of Displayed Indexes (Section 17.2)

```
Homosexuality -- Mythology.                                            3
Homosexuality -- Netherlands.                                          1
Homosexuality -- New Jersey -- Periodicals.                            2
Homosexuality -- New Jersey -- Societies, etc.  -- Directories.        1
Homosexuality -- North America.                                        1
Homosexuality -- Oceania -- Cross-cultural studies.                    1
Homosexuality -- Papua New Guinea.                                     1
Homosexuality -- Periodicals.                                          6
Homosexuality -- Periodicals -- Directories.                           1
Homosexuality -- Personal narratives.                                  3
Homosexuality -- Philosophy.                                           3
Homosexuality -- Physiological aspects.                                1
Homosexuality -- Poetry.                                               4
Homosexuality -- Political aspects.                                    3
Homosexuality -- Political aspects -- Great Britain.                   1
Homosexuality -- Political aspects -- United States.                   3
Homosexuality -- popular works.                                        1
Homosexuality -- Psychological aspects.                               12
Homosexuality -- Psychological aspects -- Juvenile literature.         1
Homosexuality -- Psychological aspects -- Statistics.                  1
Homosexuality -- Public opinion.                                       2
Homosexuality -- Public opinion -- Great Britain.                      1
Homosexuality -- Quotations, maxims, etc.                              1
Homosexuality -- Religious aspects.                                   10
Homosexuality -- Religious aspects -- Catholic Church.                12
Homosexuality -- Religious aspects -- Catholic Church -- Addresse>     1
Homosexuality -- Religious aspects -- Catholic Church -- Periodic>     1
Homosexuality -- Religious aspects -- Christianity.                   37
Homosexuality -- Religious aspects -- Christianity -- Addresses, >     1
Homosexuality -- Religious aspects -- Christianity -- History.         3
Homosexuality -- Religious aspects -- Comparative studies.             2
Homosexuality -- Religious aspects -- Judaism.                         3
Homosexuality -- Religious aspects -- Lutheran Church.                 1
Homosexuality -- Religious aspects -- Lutheran Church in America.      1
Homosexuality -- Religious aspects -- United Methodist Church (U.>     1
Homosexuality -- Research -- Social aspects.                           1
Homosexuality -- Rome.                                                 1
Homosexuality -- Rome -- Bibliography.                                 1
Homosexuality -- Services for -- New Jersey -- Directories.            1
Homosexuality -- Slang.                                                1
Homosexuality -- Social aspects.                                       2
Homosexuality -- Social aspects -- Europe.                             1
Homosexuality -- Social aspects -- Italy.                              1
Homosexuality -- Social aspects -- Statistics.                         1
Homosexuality -- Southern States -- Case studies.                      1
Homosexuality -- Spain -- History.                                     1
Homosexuality -- Spain -- Valencia -- History -- 16th century.         1
Homosexuality -- Spain -- Valencia -- History -- 17th century.         1
Homosexuality -- Spain -- Valencia -- History -- 18th century.         1
Homosexuality -- Statistics.                                           1
Homosexuality -- Taiwan.                                               1
Homosexuality -- Terminology.                                          2
Homosexuality -- U.S.                                                  1
Homosexuality -- United States.                                      50+
Homosexuality -- United States -- Addresses, essays, lectures.         2
Homosexuality -- United States -- Bibliography.                        1
Homosexuality -- United States -- Case studies.                        2
```

Chapter 17. Arrangement of Displayed Indexes (Section 17.2)

```
Homosexuality -- United States -- Directories.                       1
Homosexuality -- United States -- Drama.                             1
Homosexuality -- United States -- History.                           8
Homosexuality -- United States -- History -- 20th century.           1
Homosexuality -- United States -- Miscellanea.                       1
Homosexuality -- United States -- Moral and ethical aspects.         3
Homosexuality -- United States -- Periodicals.                       1
Homosexuality -- United States -- Personal narratives.               5
Homosexuality -- United States -- Philosophy.                        1
Homosexuality -- United States -- Psychological aspects.             2
Homosexuality -- United States -- Public opinion.                    1
Homosexuality -- United States -- Public opinion -- Addresses, es>   1
Homosexuality -- United States -- Public opinion -- History -- 20>   1
Homosexuality -- United States -- Religious aspects -- Catholic C>   1
Homosexuality -- United States -- Religious aspects -- Christiani>   1
================================================================
```

• staged display of alphanumeric indexes in hypertext : 38

In contrast to this very long single level display, here is an example of a staged display that is much more appropriate for hypertext. In this single screen display, users can get an overview of all the available headings, and they can choose which type of heading to pursue:

```
============================================================
Homosexuality [SELECT one of the following choices]
      general works [50+]
      special formats or forms of treatment [50+]
      special literary or linguistic treatment [20+]
      special moral and religious aspects [30+]
      special places [50+]
      special political & legal aspects [40+]
      special psychological & medical aspects [20+]
      special social aspects [20+]
Homosexuality & other topics, e.g., art, Christianity [10+]
Homosexuality in cultural expressions, e.g., in art, folklore [10+]
Homosexuality: special types, e.g., Ego-Dystonic, Male [10+]
============================================================
```

If users select "special formats or forms of treatment," they will get:

```
============================================================
Homosexuality: special formats or forms of treatment:
      Abstracts [1]
      Bibliography [14]
      Case studies [1]
      Collections [1]
      Congresses [3]
      Dictionaries [2]
      Early works to 1800 [1]
      Film catalogs [1]
      History [13]
      Juvenile literature [1]
      Miscellanea [3]
      Periodicals [6]
      Personal narratives [3]
      Philosophy [3]
      Popular works [1]
      Statistics [1]
```

Chapter 17. Arrangement of Displayed Indexes (Section 17.2)

If users select "special literary or linguistic treatment," they will get:

```
===============================================================
Homosexuality: special literary or linguistic treatment:
        Addresses, essays, lectures [17]
        Drama [5]
        Fiction [10]
        Literary collections [4]
        Mythology [3]
        Poetry [4]
        Quotations, maxims, etc. [1]
        Slang [1]
        Terminology [2]
===============================================================
```

If users select "special moral and religious aspects," they will get:

```
===============================================================
Homosexuality: special moral and religious aspects:
        Biblical teaching [11]
        Moral and ethical aspects [8]
        Moral and religious aspects [1]
        Religious aspects [10]
        Religious aspects — Catholic Church [14]
        Religious aspects — Christianity [41]
        Religious aspects — Comparative studies [2]
        Religious aspects — Judaism [3]
        Religious aspects — Lutheran Church [1]
        Religious aspects — Lutheran Church in America [1]
        Religious aspects — United Methodist Church [1]
===============================================================
```

If users select "special places," they will get a geographical list. In this case, it might be useful to abandon the alphanumeric approach and to group by continent, region, and country. In a long display of places, the first display could be limited to continents:

```
===============================================================
Homosexuality: special places:
        America [1]
            Latin America [1]
                Argentina [1]
                Brazil [3]
            North America [1]
                United States [50+]
                    California [1]
                    Idaho [1]
                    New Jersey [3]
                    Southern States [2]
        Asia [2]
            China [1]
            Japan [1]
            Taiwan [1]
        Australasia [1]
            Australia [1]
            Oceania [1]
            Papua New Guinea [1]
```

Chapter 17. Arrangement of Displayed Indexes (Section 17.2)

```
        Europe [7]
            Denmark [1]
            England [4]
            France [7]
            Germany [3]
            Great Britain [13]
            Greece [5]
            Netherlands [1]
            Rome [2]
            Spain [4]
        Middle East [1]
==================================================================
```

If users select "special political & legal aspects," they will get:

```
==================================================================
Homosexuality: special political & legal aspects:
    Government policy [5]
    Law and legislation [32]
    Legal status, laws, etc. [1]
    Political aspects [7]
    Public opinion [3]
==================================================================
```

If users select "psychological & medical aspects," they will get:

```
==================================================================
Homosexuality: special psychological & medical aspects:
    Cases, clinical reports, statistics [1]
    Genetic aspects [1]
    Physiological aspects [1]
    Psychological aspects [14]
==================================================================
```

If users select "special social aspects," they will get:

```
==================================================================
Homosexuality: special social aspects:
    Cross-cultural studies [2]
    Family relationships [1]
    Public opinion [3]
    Research — Social aspects [1]
    Services for — New Jersey — Directories [1]
    Social aspects [4]
    Social aspects — Statistics [1]
==================================================================
```

If users select "Homosexuality & other topics," they will get:

```
==================================================================
Homosexuality & other topics:
    and art [14]
    and Christianity [6]
    and education [9]
    and literature [50+]
    and music [2]
```

Chapter 17. Arrangement of Displayed Indexes (Section 17.2)

```
        and national socialism [2]
        and psychoanalysis [4]
================================================================
```

If users select "Homosexuality in cultural expressions," they will get:

```
================================================================
    Homosexuality in cultural expressions:
        in art [8]
        in folklore [1]
        in literature [50+]
        in motion pictures [30]
        in radio [1]
        in religion [1]
        in television [4]
        in the Bible [5]
================================================================
```

If users select "Homosexuality: special types," they will get:

```
================================================================
    Homosexuality: special types:
        Ego-Dystonic [1]
        Female: see lesbianism [hypertext link] [50+]
        Male [50+]
================================================================
```

• display of subject headings in hypertext : 39

All of the examples shown thus far in this section are based on Library of Congress subject headings, a system designed in the 19th century for card catalogs (see section 12.2.1).

• display of string indexing in hypertext : 40

More modern syntax for displayed index headings, such as string indexing (also discussed in section 12.2.2) typically are more consistent in using single-concept descriptors. In hypertext displays, the first level of display can be limited to these single-concept descriptors. Here is a brief example based on entries from *America: history and life* (ABC-Clio 1999a). Note the presence of a few compound headings such as "History teaching," "Hogs and Hog raising," and "Homesteading and Homesteaders":

```
================================================================
    ...
    History Teaching [69]
    Hitchcock, Alfred [2]
    Hitchcock, Edward [1]
    Hitler, Adolf [4]
    Hmong [1]
    Ho Chi Minh [1]
    Hoaxes [1]
    Hockey [3]
    Hoffbauer, Charles [1]
    Hoffman, Abbie [1]
    Hoffman, Bob [1]
    Hoffman, Howard S. [1]
    Hoffmeister, P. M. [1]
    Hofmann, Hans [1]
    Hofmann, Mark W. [1]
    Hofmann, Otto [1]
```

Chapter 17. Arrangement of Displayed Indexes (Section 17.2)

Hofstadter, Richard (*Age of Reform: From Bryan to FDR*). [1]
Hoge, Moses [1]
Hogs and Hog Raising [1]
Hohenberger, Frank M. [1]
Hohokam culture. [8]
Holbrook, Stewart. [1]
Holden, William Curry (obituary) [1]
Holiday, Billie [1]
Holidays [1]
Holiness movement [3]
Holland-American Land and Immigration Company [1]
Hollins College [1]
Holloway, Josepine Groves [1]
Holly, Buddy [1]
Holme, Thomas [1]
Holmes, E. Burton [1]
Holmes, John W. [1]
Holmes, Oliver Wendell (1809-94) [1]
Homes, Oliver Wendell (1841-1935) [3]
Homes, Oliver Wendell (1841-1935; "Path of the Law") [1]
Homes, Oliver Wendell (1841-1935; review article) [1]
Holt, Daniel M. [1]
Holt, Homer Adams [1]
Holy Cross Mission [1]
Holy Cross-Faith Memorial School [1]
Holy Family Church [1]
Holy Roman Empire [1]
Holy war (concept) [1]
Homan, George B. [1]
Home care [4]
Home (concept) [4]
Home Economics [7]
Home Mission Board [1]
Home of Truth (commune) [1]
Home ownership [2]
Home ownership (review article) [1]
Homeless [10]
Homeopathy [1]
Homer, Winslow [2]
Homestead strike [1]
Homesteading and Homesteaders [17]
Homicide: See Murder [hypertext link] [43]
Homolovi Ruins State Park [1]
Homosexuality [53]
Homosexuality (review article) [1]
Homosexuals [14]
Homosexuals (image) [1]
Honduras (Tegucigalpa) [1]
Hong King [4]
Honor [1]
Honorary Degrees [1]
Hood, Adrienne D. [1]
Hoogt, Cornelius W. van der [1]
Hook, John [1]
Hooper, Harry Bartholomew [1]
Hoosier National Forest [1]
Hoover Dam [1]

Chapter 17. Arrangement of Displayed Indexes (Section 17.2)

```
Hoover, Herbert C. [5]
Hoover, J. Edgar [2]
Hopacan (Captain Pipe) [1]
   ...
================================================================
```

• visual resolution of print displays : 41

By way of comparison, all of the above headings, plus all but twelve of the full index entries under them, are displayed on a single two-page spread in the 1999 print edition of *America: history and life* (p. 186-187). Page 187 is illustrated in full in section 12.2.2.1 on rotated string syntax. (The first 12 entries under "History Teaching" are displayed on the previous page, 185). The display of so many full entries on two pages is evidence of the far greater visual resolution possible in print media. There is no way that so many full entries could be displayed on a single electronic screen, which is precisely why in hypertext, it is essential to display browsable displays in stages!

• display of index headings in hypertext media : 42

In hypertext media, the full headings should only be displayed when a user selects a particular heading. Thus, if a user selects "Homosexuals," then the following display of full headings would be appropriate:

```
================================================================
HOMOSEXUALS. Acquired immune deficiency syndrome. California (Los Ange-
     les; Silverlake). Death and Dying. Interpersonal Relations. Jos-
     lin, Tom. Massi, Mark. ca 1992. 15893v
—. Acquired immune deficiency syndrome. Political activism. Social or-
     ganization. Washington (Seattle). 1980's-93. 4671d
—. Blacks. Discrimination. Military. 1770's-20c. 963a
—. Cities. Residential patterns. Women. 1970's-80's. 3236a
—. Courts. Documents. Military. Steffan, Joseph. 1980's. 11265b
—. Daughters of Bilitis. Social Movements. Women. 1950's-70's. 14977a
—. Discrimination. Military. 1993. 2705a
—. Discrimination. Military. Morality. Political power. 1993. 2702a
—. Domestic Policy. Europe. Military Service. 1993. 2712a
—. Interpersonal Relations. Women. 1992. 11790a
—. Military. Politics. Social Conditions. Technology. Tradition. 1945-
     93. 2701a
—. Sex roles. Social protest. Violence. Women's Movement. 1970's-93.
     14988a
—. Sex roles. Women. 1980-92. 3255a
—. Violence. ca 1991. 11772b
================================================================
```

• staged display of index headings in hypertext : 43

The syntax of these headings have only one level, but nevertheless, if there are two many headings to display easily on a single screen, the first display of headings could be limited to only the first term coming after the lead term. Only if a user selected that term would the full strings be displayed. If this option were implemented, the previous display would look like this:

Chapter 17. Arrangement of Displayed Indexes (Section 17.2)

```
=================================================================
HOMOSEXUALS. Acquired immune deficiency syndrome. [2]
-. Blacks. [1]
-. Cities. [1]
-. Courts. [1]
-. Daughters of Bilitis. [1]
-. Discrimination. [2]
-. Domestic Policy. [1]
-. Interpersonal Relations.
-. Military. [1]
-. Sex roles. [2]
-. Violence. [1]
=================================================================
```

• staged display of faceted index headings in hypertext : 44

Faceted index headings are frequently displayed in two or more levels. Here is a hypertext display based on faceted headings from the 1997 edition of the *MLA international bibliography* (Modern Language Association of American 1999). The printed page with these headings was displayed in section 12.2.2.2 on faceted syntax.

```
=================================================================
HOMOSEXUALITY
    Argentinian literature. Novel. 1900-1999. [1]
    Argentinian literature. Poetry. 1800-1899. [1]
    Argentinian literature. Prose and short story. 1900-1999. [1]
    Argentinian literature. Short story. 1900-1999. [1]
    Australian literature. Novel. 1900-1999. [1]
    Brazilian literature. Theater. 1900-1999. [1]
    Chilean literature. Novel. 1900-1999. [2]
    Cuban literature. Fiction. 1900-1999. [1]
    Cuban literature. Novel. 1900-1999. [2]
    Cuban literature. Prose. 1800-1899. [1]
    Dramatic arts. Film. [12]
    Dramatic arts. Film. Film adaptation. [3]
    Dramatic arts. Film. Film genres. Comic film in United States. [1]
    Dramatic arts. Film. Film genres. Documentary film. [1]
    Dramatic arts. Film. Film genres. Documentary film by     Southern
    American filmmakers. [1]
    Dramatic arts. Film. Film genres. Horror film. [2]
    Dramatic arts. Film. Film genres. Science fiction film. [1]
    Dramatic arts. Film. Yiddish language literature. [1]
    Dramatic arts. Film and videotape. [1]
    Dramatic arts. Film in United States. [1]
    Dramatic arts. Television. [1]
    Dramatic arts. Television and radio in United States. 1900-1999. [1]
    Egyptian literature. Drama. 1200-1299: Mamluk dynasty period. [1]
    English Caribbean literature. 1900-1999. [1]
    English Caribbean literature. Fiction. 1900-1999. [1]
    English literature. 1500-1699. [1]
    English literature. 1600-1699. [1]
    English literature. 1900-1999. [2]
    English literature. Comedy. 1500-1599. [3]
    English literature. Drama. 1500-1599. [1]
    English literature. Drama. 1500-1599: Renaissance. [1]
    English literature. Drama. 1900-1999. [1]
    English literature. Drama and poetry. 1599-1599: Renaissance. [1]
```

Chapter 17. Arrangement of Displayed Indexes (Section 17.3)

```
English literature. Fiction. 1900-1999. [1]
English literature. Musical composition: song cycle. 1900-1999. [1]
English literature. Novel. 1800-1899. [2]
English literature. Novel. 1900-1999. [4]
English literature. Tragedy. 1500-1599. [3]
   ...
```

• 45

But even this first level display is too long for a single screen (without scrolling), so it would be better to increase the number of levels, displaying only the first term in the initial display after the term "Homosexuality" is selected. However, if there is only one heading with the same first term, then the full first level can be displayed:

```
HOMOSEXUALITY
     Argentinian literature. [4]
     Australian literature. [1]
     Brazilian literature. [1]
     Chilean literature. [2]
     Cuban literature. [4]
     Dramatic arts. [26]
     Egyptian literature. [1]
     English Caribbean literature. [2]
     English literature. [22]
        ...
```

• 46

Finally, the full heading can be displayed, after a series of selections by the user:

```
HOMOSEXUALITY
     English literature. Novel. 1900-1999. [4]
          Bartlett, Neil. Who Was That Man?; Ready to Catch Him Should He
               Fall. Pastiche. Treatment of HOMOSEXUALITY as subculture;
               relationship to lesbian and gay studies. 1-4485.
          Forster, E. M. Howards End; "The Machine Stops." Relationship to
               HOMOSEXUALITY. Treatment of otherness. Psychoanalytic
               approach; biographical approach. 1-4819.
          — Maurice. Treatment of tolerance of HOMOSEXUALITY. I-4823.
          — A Passage to India. Treatment of India as the other;
               relationship to HOMOSEXUALITY. I-4829.
```

• 47

Now, the user can move from these headings to full surrogates, or perhaps even to full texts.

17.3. Relational Classified Displays.

• alphanumeric displays versus relational classified displays : 48

Relational classified displays are designed to arrange and display topical descriptors or headings based on relationships between and among the topics represented. This contrasts with alphanumeric arrangement, which is based solely (or mostly!) on the characters (alphabetic letters and numerals) in headings. Thus, an alphanumeric display will put "antelopes" at one end of a

Chapter 17. Arrangement of Displayed Indexes (Section 17.3)

display, and "zebras" at the other, but most relational classified displays would bring them close together, because both are animals, and both are mammals.

• **definition of classification : 49**

Literally, classification simply means the creation of classes, and placing objects or concepts into these classes. At this level, there is no difference between indexing on the one hand and classification or classifying on the other. In indexing, terms are extracted or assigned to a message, and in so doing, the indexer creates a class for the concept named by the term and links the message to this class. The process is exactly the same when a message is classified.

• **classification versus indexing : 50**

In the concept of indexing, there is no clear indication of how the resulting index terms or headings should be arranged for consultation, but there is a common expectation that index terms should be arranged in some alphanumeric order. Similarly, there is an expectation that the classes created in classification should be arranged in an order other than alphanumeric. The common dictionary definition of "classification" suggests a "systematic" arrangement (Webster's 1966).

• **51**

Because the systematic arrangement of classes resulting from classification are usually based on relationships among these classes, we use the term "relational classification." We want to emphasize the idea that relationships among classes is key to their arrangement for display and discovery.

• **syntax in classification : 52**

Classifications (classification schemes, classification systems) in the domain of library and information science are controlled vocabularies indicating concepts and relationships. Their syntax — their rules for combining concepts and terms into complex classes — was discussed in chapter 12, which covered the syntax of all kinds of indexing languages, including classification schemes (see section 12.2.4).

• **display of classification : 53**

In this section, we focus on the display of classifications, and also on the creation of new classifications for IR databases displayed in hypertext media, such as those on the world-wide web.

• **literature on classification : 54**

There is an enormous literature on classification, with authors stretching back to ancient philosophers and now including many anthropologists and sociologists interested in the pervasive human activity of classifying, as well as library and information scientists, interested in classification for message display and discovery. Here is a sampling of this rich literature:

- Anderson, James D. (1988). Indexing and classification: file organization and display for information retrieval. In: Weinberg, Bella Hass, ed. *Indexing: the state of our knowledge and the state of our ignorance:* proceedings of the 20th annual meeting of the American Society of Indexers; 1988 May 13; New York, NY. Medford, NJ: Learned Information; 1989: 69-83. x, 134 p. ISBN 0-938734-32-6.

- Bean, Carol A.; Green, Rebecca (2001). *Relationships in the organization of knowledge.* Dordrecht, Netherlands; Boston: Kluwer Academic Publishers; c2001. ix, 232 p. (Information science and knowledge management; v. 2). ISBN 0-7923-6813-4.

- Beghtol, Clare (1986). Bibliographic classification theory and text linguistics: aboutness analysis, intertextuality and the cognitive act of classifying documents. *Journal of documentation.* 42: 84-113; 1986 June.

Chapter 17. Arrangement of Displayed Indexes (Section 17.3)

- Bliss, Henry Evelyn (1997). *Bliss bibliographic classification.* 2d ed. Edited by J. Mills and Vanda Broughton, with the assistance of Valerie Lang and Colin Neilson. London; Boston: Butterworths; London; New York: Bowker-Saur; 1977-[continuing].

- Bose, H. (1990). *Universal Decimal Classification: theory and practice.* 2nd rev. and enl. ed. New Delhi: Sterling Publishers; New York: distributed by Apt Books; viii, 192 p. ISBN 8120707168.

- Bowker, Geoffrey C.; Star, Susan Leigh (1999). *Sorting things out: classification and its consequences.* Cambridge, MA: MIT Press, c1999. xii, 377 p. (Inside technology).

- Bowker, Geoffrey C.; Star, Susan Leigh (1998). *How classifications work: problems and challenges in an electronic age* [special issue]. Library trends. 47(2): 185-337; 1998 Fall.

- Bowker, Geoffrey C. (1998). *The kindness of strangers: kinds and politics in classification systems* [example of International classification of diseases]. Library trends. 47(2): 255-292; 1998 Fall.

- British Standards Institution (1961). *Universal Decimal Classification.* Prepared by the B.S.I. under the auspices of the International Federation for Documentation (F.I.D.) and with the concurrence of the Lake Placid Club Education Foundation, New York. B.S. 1000A (F.I.D. No. 289) Abridged English ed. 025.45, 3rd ed., rev. London: British Standards Institution; 1961. 254 p.

- British Standards Institution (1963). *Guide to the Universal Decimal Classification (UDC).* B.S. 1000 C: 1963, (F.I.D. No. 345). London: British Standards Institution; c1963. 128 p.

- Chan, Lois Mai (1996). *Dewey Decimal Classification: a practical guide.* 2d ed. Albany, NY: Forest Press; 1996.

- Chan, Lois Mai (1999). *A guide to the Library of Congress Classification.* 5th ed. Englewood, CO: Libraries Unlimited; 1999.

- Coates, Eric (1988). The role of classification in information retrieval: action and thought in the contribution of Brian Vickery. *Journal of documentation.* 44: 216-225; 1988 Sept.

- Dahlberg, Ingetraut (1978). A referent-oriented, analytical concept theory for INTERCONCEPT. *International classification.* 5(3): 143-151; 1978.

- Dahlberg, Ingetraut (1981). Conceptual definitions for INTERCONCEPT. *International classification.* 8(1): 16-22; 1981.

- Foskett, A. C. (1984). Better dead than read: further studies in critical classification [Augmented title: presented at a colloquium held by the Graduate School of Library and Information Science, UCLA, June 1982]. *Library resources and technical services.* 28: 346-359; 1984 Oct.

- Gilchrist, Alan; Strachan, David, ed. (1990). *The UDC: essays for a new decade.* London: Aslib, the Association for Information Management, c1990. vi, 97 p. ISBN 0-85142-265-9.

- *Knowledge organization:* official quarterly journal of the International Society for Knowledge Organization. Formerly International Classification. Includes frequent bibliographies of recent literature.

- Kwasnik, Barbara H. (1989). *The influence of context on classificatory behavior.* 1989. xiv, 250 leaves. Thesis (Ph. D.)—Rutgers University; 1989.

- Kwasnik, Barbara H. (1999). The role of classification in knowledge representation and discovery. *Library trends.* 48(1): 22-47; 1999 Summer.

- Langridge, D. W. (Derek Wilton) (1992). *Classification: its kinds, elements, systems and applications.* London; New York: Bowker-Saur; in association with Wagga Wagga, New South Wales: Centre for Information Studies, Charles Sturt University; c1992. 84 p. (Topics in library and information studies). ISBN 0-86291-622-4.

Chapter 17. Arrangement of Displayed Indexes (Section 17.3)

- Lincoln, Bruce (1989). *Discourse and the construction of society: comparative studies of myth, ritual, and classification.* New York: Oxford University Press; 1989. ix, 238 p.

- McIlwaine, Ia (1997). The Universal decimal classification: some factors concerning its origins, development, and influence. *Journal of the American Society for Information Science.* 48: 331-339; 1997 Apr.

- Miksa, Francis L. (1984). *The development of classification at the Library of Congress.* University of Ill. at Urbana-Champaign. Graduate School of Lib. & Information Science; 1984. 78 p.

- Miksa, Francis L. (1989). *The DDC, the universe of knowledge, and the post-modern library.* Albany, NY: Forest Press, a Division of OCLC Online Computer Library Center; 1998. vii, 99 p. ISBN 0-910608-64-4.

- Olson, Hope Alene (1998). Mapping beyond Dewey's boundaries: constructing classificatory space for marginalized knowledge domains [examining Dewey decimal classification for bias]. *Library trends.* 47(2): 233-254; 1998 Fall.

- Ranganathan, S. R. (Shiyali Ramamrita, rao sahib) (1965). *The Colon classification.* New Brunswick, NJ: Graduate School of Library Service, Rutgers, the State University; 1965. 289 p. (Artandi, Susan, ed. Rutgers series on systems for the intellectual organization of information; v. 4).

- Richmond, Phyllis A. (1988). Precedent-setting contributions to modern classification [American view of Vickery's accomplishments]. *Journal of documentation.* 44: 242-249; 1988 Sept.

- Satija, Mohinder Partap (1988). Classification: some fundamentals, some myths, some realities. *Knowledge organization.* 25(1/2): 32-35.

- Satija, Mohinder Partap (1992). Ranganathan and classification: a chronology 1924-1992. *International classification.* 19(1): 3-6; 1992.

- Svenonius, Elaine (1992). Ranganathan and classification science. *Libri.* 42: 176-183; 1992 July/Sept.

- Thomas, Alan R. (1995). Blissful beliefs: Henry Evelyn Bliss counsels on classification. *Cataloging and classification quarterly.* 19(3/4): 17-22; 1995.

- Vickery, Brian Campbell (1966). *Faceted classification schemes.* New Brunswick, NJ: Graduate School of Library Service, Rutgers the State University; 1966. 108 p. (Artandi, Susan, ed. Rutgers series on systems for the intellectual organization of information; v. 5).

- Vickery, Brian Campbell (1991). Eric de Grolier's "big book" on classification [published in 1956, its opinions are still valid]. *International classification.* 18(3): 170; 1991.

- Wiegand, Wayne A. (1988). The "Amherst method": the origins of the Dewey decimal classification scheme. *Libraries and culture.* 33(2): 175-194; 1998 Spring.

- **research on classification : 55**

Sociologists and anthropologists have always been interested in classification, especially folk classifications, because they so clearly emulate the dominant attitudes of a culture. Scholars in library and information science have long recognized the same phenomena in classifications used in libraries and IR databases. They replicate the dominant hegemonic attitudes of the culture in which they were created.

- **research on relational classified displays in hypertext : 56**

What is largely missing from the literature of classification research — what we badly need — is research that focuses on determining the best kinds of classifications for browsable displays on the world-wide web and other hypertext media. A. Steven Pollitt (see section 13.3 and his entries in the Bibliography) has been doing design work on the hypertextual display of faceted classifications and thesauri, while Marti Hearst has recently begun conducting usability studies of faceted classified displays on the web (Hearst et al. 2002). Hearst calls faceted displays "matrix views," treating each facet as a dimension in a multidimensional matrix. Thus, one of her examples, an architectural website, has a people dimension, a locations dimension, a structure types dimension, a materials dimension, a periods dimension, and a style dimension.

• role of relational classified displays in information retrieval : 57

As noted in section 12.2.4 on the syntax of classification, classification was largely ignored in library and information science in the United States during the 100 years preceding the advent of the world-wide web. Classification was rarely used for information retrieval. It was used for "marking and parking" books on library shelves. These books were discovered in most cases via alphanumeric catalogs, but once found, the expectation was that closely related books would be nearby, thanks to the classification system in use. Relatively shallow classifications were also used during this period in printed indexing and abstracting services for browsing the major sections of their subject scopes.

• 58

The problem with classification for initial browsing and message discovery was the great difficulty in displaying the complex classifications used in libraries. There was no easy way to guide users through the thousands of classes in the Dewey Decimal Classification or the more than thirty volumes of the Library of Congress Classification. Both of these popular classification systems provide summaries of their detailed schedules of classes, but workable, practical user-accessible links between these summaries and specific classes with explanatory headings or captions were missing. And without the names of classes (the headings and captions), it really isn't possible to browse a classification.

• display of classification in hypertext : 59

Hypertext has changed all that! Hypertext is ideal for displaying classification because hypertext can support the multiple levels of detail inherent in complex classification schemes, and it can permit users to follow only those pathways through the classification that interest them.

• relational classified displays on world-wide web : 60

With the advent of the world-wide web, classification has become a hot topic again. Hanne Albrechtsen has called classification the "Sleeping Beauty of library and information science" (Star and Bowker 1998, p. 185). The Sleeping Beauty of classification has been kissed by Prince(ss) Hypertext and now classification is wide awake and flexing its muscles!

• traditional classification versus faceted classification for hypertext displays : 61

Hypertext-based IR databases are now using both traditional classifications, such as the Dewey Decimal Classification, and newer faceted classifications for displaying their contents. Traditional classification schemes were designed for one-dimensional displays, such as a sequence of books on shelves, or a listing on static media, such as paper. Most traditional classifications are fixed and inflexible in the way that they arrange facets — the major attributes or aspects of topics. The Universal Decimal Classification is an exception — it is much more fully faceted than other traditional classifications, and the arrangement of facets is not fixed. This is one of the primary advantages of faceted classifications: that the arrangement of facets is not fixed and can be left to users to decide what is best for them (Anderson 1990). This option — letting users choose the combination of major facets according to their interests — was included in Anderson's design for the Modern Language Association of America's new International Bibliography in 1980, but so far it has not been implemented by the vendors of that IR database. (More on faceted classification is coming in section 17.3.2.)

Chapter 17. Arrangement of Displayed Indexes (Section 17.3.1)

• **advantages of traditional classification : 62**

The main advantage of traditional classification schemes, most notably the Dewey Decimal Classification and the Library of Congress Classification in the United States, is that these have been used in libraries for the past century and are widely known by library users. OPACs are essentially obligated to use the same classification system for relational classified displays in the OPAC as is used for the arrangement of library materials on its shelves.

17.3.1 Display of Dewey Decimal Classification in Hypertext.

• **notation and captions for classification : 63**

Classification schemes like the Dewey Decimal Classification (DDC) and the Library of Congress Classification (LCC) consist of captions or headings representing classes of messages and notation that can be used to represent these classes.

• **role of classification captions; notation for classification : 64**

Classification notation by itself means nothing unless a user has memorized its meaning. The DDC's 973 means nothing unless a user has learned that 9 means history, 7 means North America, and 3 means United States, thus 973 represents the history of the United States. Similarly, HQ76 means nothing unless a user of the LCC has leaned that H represents the social sciences, Q represents "The Family. Marriage. Women," and 76 represents homosexuality. (Apparently the 19th century creators of the LCC believed all sex occurred in the context of the family, marriage and women, so even male homosexuality is classed here!)

• **65**

The purpose of classification notation is to maintain the desired order of classes on shelves and to serve as locators (call numbers) leading users to particular classes and particular messages. But for browsing classification schemes, it is essential to include the captions that describe the content (and meaning) of classes.

• **66**

Libraries have traditionally posted only the most broad-level captions on their shelves — the captions for the major divisions of a classification scheme, such as "religion," "psychology," "social sciences," "sociology," etc. Rarely have libraries provided captions more detailed than these. Users were not expected to attempt detailed topical browsing in the stacks — they were expected to first find what they were looking for in alphanumeric library catalogs, then to use the classification notation to find the related class in the stacks.

• **display of *Dewey decimal classification* in hypertext : 67**

But traditional classification schemes can provide options for browsing, as long as the meaning (the caption) for each class is displayed. Hypertext makes such browsable displays possible. Here we illustrate an example of how the DDC might be displayed in hypertext for effective browsing, starting from the top level and working down to quite specific classes. A user could enter this sequence of displays at any point by searching for a particular term or caption via an alphanumeric index or electronic search.

• **role of notation in display of classification : 68**

In these browsable displays, notation is not needed to maintain the desired order of captions. The browsable display could dispense with notation all together, only providing users with call numbers when they decide to pursue a particular message. But since notation is so important in libraries, and so frequently associated with a classification like DDC (indeed, its name is based on its decimal-style notation), we will include notation in our displays.

Chapter 17. Arrangement of Displayed Indexes (Section 17.3.1)

• postings in display of classification : 69

As browsing continues, it's very useful to include the number of postings for each class — that is, the number of messages contained within that class. However, there are two very different posting figures that could be displayed: the number of messages in an entire class, including all its subdivisions; or the number of messages that fall within a broad class, but not in any narrower subdivision. In the following display, we shall include both — the first number will include all messages in a class and all its subdivisions; the second number will include only those messages in the named class itself. In this hypothetical display, all postings are of course "made up"!

• display of *Dewey decimal classification* in hypertext : 70

Our opening display begins with DDC's ten main classes:

```
=================================================================
[Select any heading for more information]
000   generalities [50,000 : 75] (including fields that relate to
         many other disciplines or knowledge in general, such as
         data processing, computer science, bibliography, library
         and information science, journalism)
100   philosophy & psychology [100,000 : 24]
200   religion [200,000 : 50]
300   social sciences [500,000 : 200]
400   language [50,000 : 150]
500   natural sciences & mathematics [400,000 : 25]
600   technology (applied sciences) [200,000 : 15]
700   the arts — architecture, fine and decorative arts, music,
         recreation [300,000 : 27]
800   literature & rhetoric [200,000 : 75]
900   geography & history [200,000 : 45]
=================================================================
```

The user selects 300 social sciences:

```
=================================================================
The social sciences: [Select any heading for more information]
300     social sciences [500,000 : 200]
301-307    sociology & anthropology [150,000 : 10]
310        collections of statistics [100 : 5]
320        political science [70,000 : 300]
330        economics [80,000 : 300]
340        law [25,000 : 100]
350        public administration, military science [30,000 : 5]
360        social problems & services [50,000 : 50]
370        education [59,000 : 100]
380        commerce, communications, transportation [25,000 : 20]
390        customs, etiquette, folklore [10,900 : 50]
[back] for previous screens
=================================================================
```

The "previous screens" option will display a window listing previous screens viewed, from which the user may select a particular previous screen to return to.

The user selects political science:

Chapter 17. Arrangement of Displayed Indexes (Section 17.3.1)

```
===================================================================
political science:
[Select any heading for more information]
320      political science [70,000 : 300]
   .1            the state [300 : 100]
   .3            comparative government [2700 : 100]
   .4            structure and functions of government [3000 : 100]
   .5            political ideologies [3000 : 100]
   .6            policy formulation [1000 : 500]
321         forms of state [1000 : 100]
322         relation of state to social groups [5,000 : 200]
323         relation of state to its residents [5,000 : 200]
324         electoral process [4,000 : 200]
325         international migration [5,000 : 200]
326         slavery & emancipation [10,000 : 500]
327         international relations [10,000 : 1000]
328         legislation [10,000 : 1000]
329         practical politics [10,000 : 1000]
[back] for previous screens
===================================================================
```

The user selects political ideologies:

```
===================================================================
political ideologies:
[Select any heading for more information]
320      political science [70,000 : 300]
   ...
   .5            political ideologies [3000 : 100]
   .51              liberalism [50]
   .52              conservatism [50]
   .53              collectivism and fascism [2500 : 100]
   .54              nationalism [100]
   .55              religiously oriented theories and ideologies [100]
   .56              racism [100]
   .57              anarchism [100]
[back] for previous screens
===================================================================
```

The user selects collectivism and fascism:

```
===================================================================
collectivism and fascism:
[Select any heading for more information]
320      political science [70,000 : 300]
   ...
   .5            political ideologies [3000 : 100]
   ...
   .53              collectivism and fascism [2500 : 100]
   .531                socialism [250]
   .532                communism [2000 : 200]
                         [SEE ALSO communism as an economic
                                   system]
   .532 2                  Marxism-Leninism [1800]
   .533                fascism [250]
[back] for previous screens
===================================================================
```

Chapter 17. Arrangement of Displayed Indexes (Section 17.3.1)

Cross references to related headings in different relational arrays can and should be integrated into these displays. In the previous screen, if the users selects "SEE ALSO communism as an economic system," the display should move directly to communism within the context of economics, rather than political science. But instead, the user chooses previous screens:

```
===============================================================
previous screens:
[Select a heading to return to that screen]
The social sciences: [500,000 : 200]
political science: [70,000 : 300]
political ideologies: [3000 : 100]
collectivism and fascism: [2500 : 100]
===============================================================
```

The user returns to the social sciences, then picks economics:

```
===============================================================
economics:
[Select any heading for more information]
330 economics [80,000 : 300]
331     labor economics [20,000 : 500]
332     financial economics [10,000 : 500]
333     land economics [5,000 : 500]
334     cooperatives [5,000 : 500]
335     socialism & related systems [10,000 : 1000]
336     public finance [10,000 : 500]
338     production [10,000 : 500]
339     macroeconomics [10,000 : 500]
[back] for previous screens
===============================================================
```

The user chooses socialism & related systems:

```
===============================================================
socialism & related systems:
[Select any heading for more information]
335       socialism & related systems [10,000 : 1000]
  .02         utopian systems and schools [100]
  .1        systems of English origin [100]
  .2        systems of French origin [100]
  .3        systems of American origin [100]
  .4        Marxian systems [8,000 : 1000]
  .5        democratic socialism [300]
  .6        fascism [1000: 500]
  .7        Christian socialism [100]
  .8        other systems [100 : 100]
  .9        voluntary socialist and anarchist communities [100]
[back] for previous screens
===============================================================
```

The user chooses Marxian systems:

Chapter 17. Arrangement of Displayed Indexes (Section 17.3.2)

```
===============================================================
Marxian systems:
[Select any heading for more information]
335       socialism & related systems [10,000 : 1000]
    ...
    .4        Marxian systems [8,000 : 1000]
    .41           philosophic foundations, economic
                      concepts, aims [1000: 100]
    .411              philosophic foundations [500 : 100]
    .411 2                dialectical materialism [200]
    .411 9                historical materialism [200]
    .412              economic concepts [500]
    .42           early period [1000 : 500]
    .422              communism (1848-1875), Communist manifesto [250]
    .423              scientific socialism (1875-1917) [250]
    .43           communism (Marxism-Leninism). Soviet
                      communism [6000 : 1000]
    .433              Trotskyite doctrines [100]
    .434              national variants as schools of thought
                          [290: 900]
    .434 4                Yugoslav communism, Titoism [200]
    .434 5                Chinese communism, Maoism [800]
    .434 7                Cuban communism, Castroism [1000]
    .437              comparative studies [2000]
[back] for previous screens
===============================================================
```

This is the screen that the user could have come to directly if s/he had chosen that "SEE ALSO communism as an economic system" cross-reference back in the political science screens. The "communism" terms would be highlighted when this screen was shown in response to choosing the cross-reference.

17.3.2. Constructing and Displaying a Faceted Classification.

• faceted classification : 71

In this section, we will illustrate the creation of a new faceted classification for library and information science (LIS).

• role of facets in classification;
enumerative classification versus faceted classification : 72

All classification schemes or systems are based on facets, or basic aspects, of topics. The difference between more traditional enumerative classification and faceted classification is how the facets are used. In an enumerative classification (like, for example, the Dewey Decimal Classification or the Library of Congress Classification), the order of facets is fixed — both the order in which facets are displayed in arrays (vertical sequences) and also the order in which facets are considered, or combined, in compound or complex classes (horizontal combinations reflected in captions and notation). Often, within classes and subclasses, the order of facets is determined by the designers of the classification scheme on a case by case basis, so that there is no consistency in facet order across classes. Thus, for example, in the Dewey Decimal Classification, literature is classified first by the culture-related facets of language and nationality, then by genre, then by period, but music is classified first by instruments, and the "fine arts" are classified first by medium/operation (painting, drawing, sculpture, etc.). Whereas nationality is a primary facet in literature, it is a "low level" facet in the other arts. Furthermore, some facets cannot be combined with the primary facets. For example, the theme facet in literature (what literature is about) cannot be combined with language, nationality, genre, and period when a particular writer is involved. Similarly, in painting, individual painters are classed only by place or country. The iconography or genre facets may not be combined with the place or nationality facets for individual painters. None of these restrictions would apply in a non-enumerative faceted classification.

• flexibility of facet order in faceted classification : 73

In a faceted classification, the facets for place, nationality, form, medium, style, instruments or equipment, actions, operations, processes, events, movements, persons, themes, etc. would be kept separate, so that they can be combined freely and in any order. The great advantage of this capability for modern electronic browsing systems is that users can choose the facets of greatest interest to them and create their own browsable classifications, combining facets as they choose. Facet order is no longer fixed. We saw an example of this faceted approach in chapter 13, in a discussion on the display of thesauri, using medical facets from the EMTREE thesaurus (section 13.3).

• citation order of facets for relational classified displays in print media;
citation order of facets for shelf arrangement : 74

However, when a faceted classification is displayed in a static medium, such as paper, or is used to arrange items in a single linear one-dimensional sequence, like books on shelves, the facets must be displayed (or "cited") in some consistent order. The order selected is called the "citation order of facets." We will illustrate this procedure later when we use our faceted classification of LIS to create a single, linear, fixed display sequence.

• determination of facets for classification : 75

The first step in creating any classification, including a faceted classification, is to determine what the facets should be. What are the categories of topics and features of primary interest to the targeted user community? When an IR database already has a well defined subject scope, these facets should already be defined. The subject scope should include all the important facets of interest.

• facets for classification of literature : 76

When Anderson was involved in the creation of a faceted classification (and indexing) system for the Modern Language Association of America (Anderson 1979, 1980), he relied heavily on the many divisions or special interest groups of that large academic association to identify key facets. These divisions represent the primary interests of the members of the MLA. Members of each division were surveyed to determine the focus of their primary research and scholarly interest. For some literary scholars, for example, it turned out that a primary interest was the methodological approaches used in the study of literature, rather than the more traditional aspects of nationality, language, genre or period. This meant that the new classification needed a special facet for methodological approaches, to include such methods as psychological, psychoanalytic, feminist, Marxist, etc. (The final list of facets for the MLA classification and its CIFT indexing system have been displayed and discussed in several previous chapters, including chapter 2 on subject scope and chapter 12 on syntax. See sections 2.1 and 12.2.2.2.)

• special interest groups as sources of facets for library and information science;
special interest groups of American Society for Information Science and Technology : 77

For a serious classification of LIS, we would want to take a similar approach. We would want to visit (metaphorically if not literally — e.g., by consulting their publications and reviewing their activities and programs) the various professional associations (American Library Association, American Society for Information Science and Technology, Special Libraries Association, Music Library Association, Map Library Association, Law Library Association, and many more), and also their special interest groups or divisions. For example, ASIST (The American Society for Information Science and Technology) has the following SIGs (Special Interest Groups) (www.asis.org 2001):

- Arts and Humanities
- Automated Language Processing
- Bioinformatics
- Classification Research
- Computerized Retrieval Services
- Digital Libraries
- Education for Information Science
- History and Foundations of Information Science
- Human-Computer Interaction
- Information Analysis and Evaluation
- Information Architecture
- Information Generation and Publishing
- Information Needs, Seeking and Use
- Information Policy
- International Information Issues
- Knowledge Management
- Library Automation and Networks
- Management
- Medical Informatics
- Metrics
- Scientific and Technical Information Systems
- Technology, Information, and Society
- Visualization, Images, and Sound

• **Classification Research SIG of American Society for Information Science and Technology : 78**

Each of these SIGs has a mission statement, or description of interests, and these statements can be used as an indication of important areas of interest. As an example, here is the mission statement for the ASIST SIG/CR (Classification Research):

"SIG/CR studies the fundamental principles, underlying processes, and analytic constructs of classification schemes and procedures by humans or automata. It is concerned with organizing information, and includes indexing, index construction, indexing language [sic], thesaurus construction, terminology, classification of information in any form, and testing and evaluating the effectiveness of these products. It is also concerned with the ability to develop abstractions from perceived reality. Theoretical emphases include cognition, grouping and organization of groupings, and linguistics."

• **special interest groups of American Library Association : 79**

The other major organizations in LIS have similar groups. Thus, the American Library Association includes the Association for Library Collections and Technical Services, which includes the Cataloging and Classifications Section, which includes the Subject Analysis Committee.

Chapter 17. Arrangement of Displayed Indexes (Section 17.3.2)

• **facets for library and information science : 80**

The facets for our classification of LIS were laid out in the subject scope for our indexing and abstracting service for library and information science in section 2.5.2. To the best of our ability, these facets reflect the interests of the members of the LIS professions. These major facets and some of their more important subfacets are:

- Participants & Agencies — including persons, groups, organizations, institutions, companies, libraries, and archives.

- Reference & Retrieval Resources — including (1) access resources such as IR databases, indexes, catalogs; and (2) message/text/document collections and resources in all media and formats.

- Tools & Equipment — including computers, buildings, furniture.

- Operations, Processes & Events — including human information behavior, searching, collection development, acquisition, cataloging, indexing, reference & information services, conservation & preservation, building & collection maintenance, administration & management, and design, evaluation & research.

- Disciplines & Related Theories: the sciences, applied sciences/technology, social sciences, history, humanities, arts, law, etc.

- Places

- Times

- [Attributes] Our attributes will be dispersed into the facets or subfacets where they apply, so that, for example, personal attributes or characteristics (such as ethnicity, gender, etc.) will be found with our persons subfacet and attributes of our reference and retrieval resources (such as format, medium, language) will be found in that subfacet.

• **arrangement of topics within facets : 81**

Once facets have been identified, the next job is to arrange topics within facets. One option is alphanumeric arrangement, but alphanumeric arrangement defeats the purpose of a classification — the bringing together of related topics. Thus, we shall attempt a relational classified grouping of subfacets and topics within each facet. The purpose of our arrangements of topics within facets is to provide our users with convenient overviews of what is available. There is usually no "natural order" of topics. Our aim should be to divide topics up in such a way that no category has more members than can be conveniently viewed on a single computer screen (without scrolling!). This means from 10-20 topics within each category level. Within each category, the arrangement should be as helpful as possible. If no helpful arrangement can be determined, then alphanumeric arrangement within a category is always an option.

• **arrangement of facets for persons; for groups; for institutions : 82**

Our major facet of "Participants & Agencies" includes individual persons, groups of persons, and institutions, including associations, companies, libraries and archives. Our first breakdown of this facet could be as follows:

- Individual persons:
    - <by name> — in alphanumeric order!
- Individuals and groups of persons
    - <by characteristics>
        - <by role or occupation>: users, professionals, paraprofessionals, vendors, librarians, information scientists, archivists, catalogers, indexers, bibliographers, etc.

Chapter 17. Arrangement of Displayed Indexes (Section 17.3.2)

      <by age>

      <by gender and gender identity>

      <by ethnicity>

      <by sexual orientation>

      <by health and abilities status>

      <by religion>

      <by educational level>,

      etc., etc.

- Individual institutions

      <by name> — in alphanumeric order

- Institutions

      <by type>, e.g.,

            libraries <also by type: public, academic, special, etc.>

            archives <also by type>

            governments and government agencies <by level: central/federal, state/provincial, county, municipal, etc.>

            non-profit, non-governmental organizations

            businesses <by industry>

            etc.

                                          • arrangement of facets for ethnicities : 83

Some of our subfacet categories could be quite large, depending on the collection of messages to be indexed and classified. If there is a special emphasis on ethnic (or cultural) characteristics of library users, we might need a very complete classification of ethnicities. The Dewey Decimal Classification has a separate table for ethnicities (its Table 5), with thousands of categories. We might usefully borrow its descriptors and arrangement (with appropriate permission, of course!). DDC's table 5 is organized in the following ethnocentric manner, giving prominence to North Americans and Europeans:

```
—1   North Americans
—2   British, English, Anglo-Saxons
—3   Germanic peoples
—4   Modern Latin peoples (French, Walloons, Catalans)
—5   Italians, Romanians, related groups
—6   Spanish and Portuguese (including Latin Americans)
—7   Other Italic peoples (Ancient Romans)
—8   Greeks and related groups
—9   Other racial, ethnic, national groups
—91  Other Indo-European peoples (South Asians,
        Iranians, Celts, Slaves, Balts)
—92  Semites (Hebrews, Israelis, Jews; Arabs,Ethiopians)
—93  Non-Semitic Afro-Asiatic peoples
—94  Peoples of North and West Asian origin; Dravidians
        (Turkic peoples; Finno-Ugrians, Hungarians, etc.)
—95  East and Southeast Asian peoples (Chinese, Japanese, Koreans,
        Burmese, etc.)
—96  Africans and people of African descent
—97  North American native peoples
```

Chapter 17. Arrangement of Displayed Indexes (Section 17.3.2)

```
—98  South American native peoples
—99  Australian & Southeast Asian native peoples
—999 Miscellaneous peoples [!]: Basques, Chechens, etc.
```

• arrangement of facets for databases : 84

Within our large facet for "Reference & Retrieval Resources," we have a subfacet for "access resources" such as IR databases, indexes, catalogs, etc. Within this facet, IR databases might be arranged as follows:

- IR databases
    - \<by type\>
        - A&I services
        - back-of-the-book indexes
        - bibliographies
        - digital libraries
        - library catalogs
        - card catalogs
        - OPACs
    - \<by data models\>
    - \<by parts/aspects\>
        - \<by subject scope\>
        - \<by subject domain\>
        - \<by documentary scope\>
        - \<by documentary units\>
- indexes
    - \<by type\>
        - displayed indexes
            - alphanumeric indexes
            - relational classified indexes
        - non-displayed indexes
        - \<indexes for types of messages\>
            - book indexes
            - film indexes
            - periodical indexes
            - slide indexes
            - video indexes
            - webpage/website indexes
        - \<by parts/aspects\>
            - \<by syntax\>
            - \<by media\>
            - \<by codes/symbols\>
            - \<by language\>

Chapter 17. Arrangement of Displayed Indexes (Section 17.3.2)

<by specificity of indexing vocabulary>
<by exhaustivity of indexing>
etc., etc.

• **arrangement of facets for document collections : 85**

Also within our "reference and retrieval resources" facet we have a subfacet for message/text/document collections and resources. These can be arranged by media (print, video, film, digital, etc.), by format and genre (books, pamphlets, broadsheets and broadsides; photographs, slides, filmstrips, films; poetry, drama, fiction, novels, short stories; etc.), and of course by discipline and topic. They can also be arranged by text type (language text, musical text, visual text, performance text). And language texts can be arranged by language.

• **arrangement of facets for languages : 86**

The classified relational arrangement of languages was briefly discussed in section 12.2.4. Here we add more detail. There are thousands of human languages, as well as artificial or created languages (such as indexing languages, programming languages, etc.) The traditional classification of natural human languages illustrates the principle of ethnocentricity: When there is no obvious best order for categories, arrange them in the order of potential interest to your clientele. The arrangement of ethnicities by the DDC illustrated above is an example of ethnocentric arrangement. The DDC provides ways for other cultures to move their topics of primary interest to "the head of the line!"

• **arrangement of facets for language families : 87**

Natural human languages are traditionally arranged by language families that reflect the historical development of languages as identified by historical linguists. Prominent language families include:

- Afro-Asiatic (Hamito-Semitic) — which includes Arabic and Hebrew.
- Indo-European — including languages long spoken from India to Europe.
- Sino-Tibetan languages — including Chinese.
- Ural-Altaic — including Korean, Turkish, Hungarian, Estonian, and Finnish.

• **88**

These language families, of course, could be arranged in alphabetical order, and if we only include a few major families, then it doesn't make much difference in a hypertext display. In static displays (e.g., for books on shelves or listings in print on paper), however, where all subdivisions in each broad category are displayed before you reach the next broad category, it makes an enormous difference. If all Afro-Asiatic languages were displayed first before users reached any Indo-European languages, they would have to wade through or navigate around all the Berber languages, Chadic languages, Coptic language, Cushitic languages, Egyptian language, Hamitic languages, and Omotic languages, as well as the more familiar Semitic languages.

• **arrangement of facets for Indo-European languages : 89**

Similarly, we must decide on the arrangement of the Indo-European languages. Again, they could be arranged in alphabetical order. But even in a hypertext display, there are 17 subfamilies listed by the Library of Congress Subject Headings under Indo-European languages. If we listed them alphabetically, we would begin with Albanian, Anatolian languages, Armenian, Baltic languages, Celtic languages before we reach Germanic languages, which includes English.

Chapter 17. Arrangement of Displayed Indexes (Section 17.3.2)

• 90

Therefore, it may be more helpful to list first those subfamilies of greater potential interest to our users:

- Germanic languages — which includes English(!), as well as German, Dutch, and the Scandinavian languages.
- Italic languages (Romance languages) — French, Spanish, Portuguese, Italian, Romanian.
- Greek
- Slavic languages — Russian, Croatian, Serbian, Czech, Polish.

• arrangement of facets for Germanic languages : 91

To finish our classification of language, how should the Germanic languages be arranged? *Library of Congress subject headings* simply lists them in alphabetical order: Afrikaans, Danish, Dutch, English, Frisian, German, Gothic, Low German, Norwegian, Scots, and Swedish. The *Dewey decimal classification* groups them into East Germanic, North Germanic, and West Germanic, and it lists West Germanic first, because that includes not only Dutch and Frisian, but English. Then comes East Germanic (German), followed by North Germanic (the Scandinavian languages).

• arrangement of facets for places : 92

Our place facet might include both places by general characteristics (such as mountains, oceans, or areas of low economic development) and named geographic places and entities (such as the Rocky Mountains). Focusing on geographic places, how might they best be arranged? We could, of course, put all places in one large alphabetical sequence, so that the following places would fall together:

```
Aachen, Germany
Aba, Zaire
Abakan, Russia
Abashiri, Japan
```

• 93

Such an arrangement would not be conducive to browsing. It would serve only persons who know what places they wanted, and such persons should be using an alphanumeric displayed index or electronic search options. Browsers will be better served with a series of hierarchies for continents, regions, countries, major divisions, minor divisions, cities, and towns, such as:

```
North America (with other continents)
    United States (with the other countries of North America)
        Northeast (in order to divide the country into 4 regions
                    of approximately 12-13 states each)
            New Jersey (along with 12-13 other states in the
                        Northeast)
                Middlesex County (along with New Jersey's 12
                                    other counties)
                    New Brunswick (along with the other
                                    cities and townships of
                                    Middlesex County).
```

• arrangement of facets by other facets : 94

It is often useful to arrange one facet by another facet. For example, one may want to arrange libraries by place. In a hypertext environment, this can be problematic if a faceted classification has a separate place facet, because if it does, the user can choose to combine the library facet (or subfacet) with the place facet on their own to create the desired display. Similarly, in a static dis-

Chapter 17. Arrangement of Displayed Indexes (Section 17.3.2)

play (print on paper or the arrangement of items on a shelf), the library subfacet and the place facet should be combined by the rules of facet citation order (see section 17.3.2.1).

• 95

On the other hand, it is quite legitimate and common to arrange one facet by another facet as long as the resulting categories or descriptors pass the facet "is a" test, that is, that every member of the resulting subfacet is truly a member of the main facet. For example, in the following example, the various places are not libraries, so they violate the "is a" test:

- libraries
    - \<by place\>
        - Africa
        - Asia
        - Australia
        - Europe
        - North America
        - South America

• 96

But in this next example from the persons facet, all the resulting descriptors do indeed refer to types of persons. Africans are persons.

- persons
    - \<by ethnicities\>
        - Africans
        - African Americans
        - Europeans
            - French
    - \<by occupation\>
        - barbers
        - computer scientists
        - librarians

• display of faceted classification : 97

When we have arranged all our facets and subfacets, we are ready to display our classification. Such a faceted classification is designed for a hypertext display, beginning with our list of facets. See them displayed on a webpage in figure 2.5 (paragraph 2.95). Here they are listed in a tabular format. Note that the wording has been slightly modified for display to users. The list of facets listed earlier was for professionals like you! Users may select two or three facets to browse simultaneously, just as was done with medical facets in section 13.3.

• postings for categories versus postings for descriptors : 98

The numbers following each facet category represent postings — the number of documentary units in each facet category. Double postings are used. The first number represents inclusive comprehensive postings for the facet — the total number of documentary units in the facet, including all subordinate categories; the second number represents only those documentary units in the facet category at the top level. These are documentary units that discuss the entire facet, so that they are indexed with the name of the facet. Thus, there are 10,000 documentary units indexed with terms from the Participants & Agencies facet, but only 25 of these are indexed with the top-level term "participants and agencies."

• dynamic postings in faceted relational classified displayed indexes : 99

As soon as a user selects more than one facet, dynamic postings take effect. As the user combines facets and descriptors, all postings are adjusted to indicate only the postings that apply to all of the facets or descriptors chosen. In effect, the selection of facets and descriptors within facets acts like a boolean AND search statement. (Dynamic postings were also illustrated in section 13.3 in displays taken from the EMTREE thesaurus.)

```
================================================================
              MAJOR FACETS OF LIBRARY & INFORMATION SCIENCE
        (Select up to 3 of these facets to browse simultaneously.
            Click on category boxes, then click on BROWSE!)

 [] Participants & Agencies (10,000:25): persons, groups,
         organizations, institutions, companies, libraries, archives.
 [] Reference & Retrieval Resources (3,750:5): access resources
         (information retrieval databases, indexes, catalogs);
         information resources in all media and formats.
 [] Tools & Equipment (3,000:10): computers, buildings, furniture,
         etc.
 [] Operations, Processes & Events (11,000:10): human information
         behavior, searching, collection development, acquisition,
         cataloging, indexing, reference & information services,
         conservation & preservation, building & collection maintenance,
         administration & management, design, evaluation & research.
 [] Disciplines & Related Theories (2,670:100): the sciences,
         applied sciences/technology, social sciences, history,
         humanities, arts, law, etc.
 [] Places (2,275:0): by type; by name.
 [] Times (1,225:0): by centuries, decades, years
================================================================
```

• 100

Our hypothetical user chooses to browse three facets: (1) Reference & Retrieval Resources; (2) Operations, Processes & Events; and (3) Disciplines & Related Theories. In these illustrations an asterisk (*) indicates chosen categories. In hypertext, selections would be highlighted. Because postings are dynamic, as soon multiple facets are chosen, all postings are adjusted to indicate the number of documentary units that share postings in all of the chosen facets. Thus, in the next display, comprehensive postings for the three chosen facets drop to 500. In the following display, when videotapes, technical services and sciences are chosen, the total number of postings drops to 10, indicating that there are only ten documentary units dealing with videotapes, technical services, and the sciences. Finally, when "cataloging" is chosen in the operations facet, then all postings in other facets show the number of documentary units that fall into the cataloging category and into each category in the other facets.

Chapter 17. Arrangement of Displayed Indexes (Section 17.3.2)

*Ref. & Retrieval Resources[500:5])	*Operations, Processes, Events[500:10]	*Disciplines & Related Theories [500:10]

access resources[200:50]
   IR databases[100:50]
   library catalogs[100:50]
information resources
      [300:50]
   print resources[50:20]
   videotapes[50:50]
   film resources[50:30]
   audio recordings[50:20]
   digital resources[50:10]
	human information
	   behavior[50:25]
	public services
	   [50:10]
	technical services
	   [200:50]
	maintenance[50:25]
	administration[100:50]
	research & develop-
	   ment[50:20]
		disciplines
		   [450:10]
		humanities
		   [50:20]
		social sciences
		   [100:25]
		sciences[150:10]
		technologies
		   [50:10]
		professions [50:10]
		arts[50:10]
		interdisciplinary
		   theories [50:5]

• 101

Now our hypothetical user selects "videotapes" in column 1; "technical services" in column , and "sciences" in column 3, resulting in the following display:

Ref. & Retrieval Resources[10:0]	Operations, Processes, Events[10:0]	Disciplines & Related theories [10:0]

information resources
      [10:0]
   *videotapes[10]
	*technical services
	   [10:2]
	   collection develop-
	     ment[1]
	   acquisitions[0]
	   cataloging[2]
	   classification[2]
	   indexing[1]
	   vocabulary manage-
	     ment[2]
	   materials process-
	     ing[0]
	   preservation[0]
		Disciplines[10:0]
		   *sciences[10:2]
		     mathematics[0]
		     astronomy[0]
		     physics[2]
		     chemistry[0]
		     earth sciences[2]
		     life sciences[4]

• 102

Note that some categories now have zero postings. Should we still display them? Probably yes, because the user can still choose them and also choose different information resources and different disciplines, which would then change all the postings.

• 103

Finally our user selects "cataloging" and "life sciences," so that our display becomes:

Chapter 17. Arrangement of Displayed Indexes (Section 17.3.2)

```
===============================================================================
Ref. & Retrieval              Operations, Processes,   Disciplines &
Resources[4:0]                Events[4:0]              Related theories
                                                       [4:0]
===============================================================================
information resources         technical services       Disciplines[4:0]
      [4:0]                         [4:0]                sciences[4:0]
   *videotapes[4]                *cataloging[4:0]          *life sciences[4:0]
                                   descriptive                paleontology[0]
                                      cataloging[0]          biology[4:0]
                                   subject cata-                 botany[0]
                                      loging[4]                  zoology[0]
                                                                 ecology[0]
                                                                 biochemistry[0]
                                                                 genetics[2]
                                                                 sexology[3]
===============================================================================
```

If you are wondering why the two postings for genetics and the three postings for sexology add up to four postings for biology, it is because one documentary unit has postings for both genetics and sexology. Thus there are three documentary units posted to sexology and two to genetics, but only four separate documentary units. See the index headings for these documentary units below.

At any point, the user has the option to ask the IR system to "show documents." This option will display topical index headings, consisting of strings of descriptors. Indeed the best systems will always show a few strings in a display window at the bottom of the screen, along with an option to see more headings. The great advantage of showing index heading strings immediately and dynamically as the user explores the classification is that the user is given an immediate indication of the kinds of messages available in each combination of facets, subcategories, or descriptors. Such immediate gratification can be very reassuring and useful!

Here are hypothetical topical index headings that match our users last specification: videotapes; subject cataloging; and life sciences. Life sciences has no postings to the broad descriptor "life sciences," but there are postings to two subordinate descriptors: genetics and sexology, so index headings with these descriptors are displayed. If there were index headings with the descriptor "life sciences," then they would take precedence over the strings with subordinate descriptors. After each string the number of postings is indicated (1 in each of these cases, but in some cases several documentary units could have the same index heading), plus options for full surrogates (abstract) or full text.

Our index strings use the CIFT faceted syntax (see section 12.2.2.2):

1 cd-roms; films; videotapes. <on> genetics. subject cataloging. classification. <by> National Library of Medicine. [1] [abstract] [full text]

2 films; sound recordings; videotapes. <on> genetics; sexology. subject cataloging. <using> Library of Congress subject headings. [1] [abstract] [full text]

3 sexology. subject cataloging. training. <using> videotapes. [1] [abstract] [full text]

Chapter 17. Arrangement of Displayed Indexes (Section 17.3.2.1)

4 videotapes. <on> sexology. descriptive cataloging; subject cataloging. <using> AACR2. MARC records. [1] [abstract] [full text]

• 108

Note that in strings 1, 2, and 4, the videotapes (and other media) are the objects being cataloged, but in string 3, the videotapes play the role of an agent or means for training. This difference is indicated by the ordering of terms in the strings and also by the use of role indicators within angle brackets.

17.3.2.1. Display of Faceted Classification in Print Media.

• citation order of facets : 109

As noted previously, in static media such as paper (as opposed to dynamic hypertext media) or for arranging items in a single linear sequence in files or on shelves, a decision must be made about the order of facets — the "citation order of facets." This will determine the order in which facets will be displayed in arrays (vertical displays) or arranged in files or on shelves. It will also determine the order in which facets are considered and combined to create compound and complex classes. For these purposes, we will cite our facets in the following order:

> thing. kind. part. property. material. process. operation. user. product. by-product. agent/means. space. time.

• citation order of facets in *Bliss bibliographic classification* : 110

This citation order of facets is based directly on that used by the *Bliss bibliographic classification* (BC), with one modification. The BC citation order of facets is (Bliss Classification Association 2001): thing. kind. part. property. material. process. operation. patient. product. by-product. agent. space. time. We have changed "patient" to "user," and we have clarified that "agent" may also include "means" (methods).

• role facets versus type facets in citation order of facets : 111

Several of these facets represent roles rather than distinct types of phenomena based on their inherent nature. For example, items from our participants & agencies facet could play the role of things which are experiencing a process or to which some operation is applied, but frequently, they will play the role of user or agent.

• 112

Similarly, items from our reference and retrieval resources facet could play the role of things, but often they will play the role of agent or product.

• 113

For example:

> children. Asian. female. cognitive development. encouragement. <by> children's librarians.

versus:

> books. picture books. Chinese language. cataloging. <for> immigrants: children. <using> Library of Congress Subject Headings; <by> library school students.

In the first string, children are the "thing" experiencing the process of cognitive development, as well as the operation of encouragement by the agent children's librarians. In the second example, books are the thing being acted upon (cataloging), but the users who benefit (we hope) from this operation are children. *Library of Congress subject headings* and library school students are agents. Another example:

Chapter 17. Arrangement of Displayed Indexes (Section 17.3.2.1)

medicine (discipline). literature. indexing; abstracting. Medline database. <using> Medical Subject Headings (MeSH); structured abstracts; <by> computer analysis; intellectual analysis.

Here, the operation of indexing and abstracting is applied to the literature of medicine, resulting in the product Medline. MeSH and structured abstracts are agents; computer analysis and intellectual analysis are means.

• 114

These last two examples illustrate that the "agent/means" facet can include tools and means or methods as well as personal or organizational agents. Thus, in the last example the "product" Medline results from the indexing and abstracting of the medical literature using the agents of MeSH and structured abstracts by means of both computer and intellectual analysis.

• notation for classification : 115

Notation is used with classification in order to maintain the conceptual, relational order of classes. When classification resides in fixed media, notation is not needed. Many classifications used on the world-wide web do not use notation; similarly, many classifications in print-on-paper media also function without notation. But when classification is used to arrange discrete items, such as books on a shelf or cards in a file, a notation is required to keep them in the order determined by the classification.

• types of notation for classification : 116

There are several types of notation:

- pure notation — only one type of character is used, such as only numerals only in the notation for the Dewey Decimal Classification.

- mixed notation — different types of characters are used, such as the alphabetic letters and numerals in the notation for the Library of Congress Classification.

- enumerative notation — which simply enumerates the order of classes, with no indication of elements within classes. The Library of Congress Classification notation is enumerative, similar to the numbering of houses on a street.

- expressive notation — which expresses the components of a class. The Dewey Decimal Classification uses notation which is synthesized from the elements of compound and complex classes, resulting often in very long notations, but experienced librarians can "read" these notations to find out a lot about the class that is represented. The notation used for the Universal Decimal Classification is even more expressive, using a variety of punctuation marks to indicate facets. See examples of UDC notation in section 12.2.4.

- retroactive notation — in which facet notation begins with the last facet in classification displays. Additional facets are added working backwards (or upwards) in the classification display (hence the name "retroactive notation"). The result is that the more general and simple classes will be placed before the more specific and complex classes. Retroactive notation is complex and difficult to create, but a user need only follow normal alphabetical or numerical order to use it. And the resulting notations are much shorter that the long expressive notations used by DDC and UDC. We shall illustrate retroactive notation as we apply it to our faceted classification of LIS. Our notation is modeled on that of the *Bliss bibliographic classification*, which also uses retroactive notation.

• retroactive notation for classification of library and information science : 117

Here are our facets for LIS, arranged in an order opposite to the citation order of facets noted above, so that the more general facets (such as time and place) come first:

Chapter 17. Arrangement of Displayed Indexes (Section 17.3.2.1)

A. time.

B. space (place).

C. agent (means).

D. by-product.

E. product.

F. user (patient).

G. operation.

H. process.

J. raw material.

K. property.

L. part.

M. kind.

N. thing.

• 118

To illustrate how this retroactive notation works, we need to assign some notation to some of our facets, to serve as examples. Like the notation of the *Bliss bibliographic classification*, a space is placed after each grouping of three letters to make reading easier:

```
A.   Time.
AB.  BCE (BC) years, preceded by '-'; e.g., AB-2000 = 2000 BCE.
AC.  CE (AD) years, for years 0001-1499, using 4 digits in all cases.
AJ.  16th century; AJ by itself = 16th century; AJ1584 = the year
         1584; AJ1580-1590 = the decade of the 1580s.
AK.  17th century.
AL.  18th century.
AM.  19th century.
AN.  20th century.
AP.  21st century.

B.   Space (places).
BB.  Generic places, environments.
BC.  Specific geographical places.
BD.    North America.
BE.       United States.
BEC          Northeast.
BEC N           New Jersey.
BEC NM              Middlesex County.
BEC NN                  New Brunswick.
BF.    Central America.
BG.    South America.
BH.    Europe.
BHJ.      Western Europe.
BHM.         France.
BK.    Africa.
BQ.    Asia.
BV.    Australia.
BX.    Isolated islands.
BY.    Antarctica.
```

Chapter 17. Arrangement of Displayed Indexes (Section 17.3.2.1)

C. Agents.
CC. persons (add notation F).
CD. theories.
CE. methods.
CF. disciplines.
CG.   humanities.
CGL.   literature.
CH.   social sciences.
CJ.   sciences.
CJK.   mathematics.
CJL.   astronomy.
CJM.   physics.
CJN.   chemistry.
CJP.   earth sciences.
CJQ.   life sciences.
CJQ R.   paleontology.
CJQ S.   biology.
CJQ T.   botany.
CJQ U.   zoology.
CJQ V.   ecology.
CJQ W.   biochemistry.
CJQ X.   genetics.
CJQ Y.   sexology.
CK.   technologies.
CL.   professions.
CM.   arts.
CN. tools.
CNN.   cataloging tools.
CNN P.   Anglo-American Cataloguing Rules.
CNN Q.   Library of Congress Subject Headings.
CNP.   computers.
CNQ.   furniture.

D. By-products.

E. Products.

F. Users (persons).
FG. by gender.
FH. by sexual orientation.
FJ. by age.
FK. by ethnicity.
FL. by occupation.
FM. by educational level.

G. Operations.
GH. human information behavior.
GJ. public services.
GK. technical services.
GKL.   collection development.
GKM.   acquisitions.
GKN.   cataloging.
GKN P.   descriptive cataloging.
GKN Q.   subject cataloging.
GKP.   classification.
GKQ.   indexing.
GKR.   vocabulary management.

Chapter 17. Arrangement of Displayed Indexes (Section 17.3.2.1)

```
GKS.    materials processing.
GKT.    preservation.
GL.     maintenance.
GM.     administration.
GN.     research & development.

H.  Processes.

J.  Raw materials.

K.  Properties.

M.  Kinds.
MN. Formats.
MP. Languages.
MQ. Afroasiatic (Hamito-Semitic) (which includes Arabic and Hebrew).
MQQ.        Semitic.
MQR.        Arabic.
MQS.        Hebrew.
MR. Indo-European.
MRR. Germanic languages.
MRR S.      English.
MRS. Italic (Romance) languages.
MRS T.      French.
MRS U.      Spanish.
MR. Slavic languages.
MRA.        Russian.
MS. Sino-Tibetan languages.
MX. Ural-Altaic (which include Korean, Turkish, Hungarian, Estonian,
            Finnish).

MZ. Disciplines as "kind" of Reference & Retrieval Resources (see.
        CF/CM — add notation directly to MZ).

N.  Reference & Retrieval Resources.
NN. access resources.
NP.     IR databases.
NPQ.        digital libraries.
NPR.        indexing and abstracting services.
NPX.        numerical databases.
NPY.        fact databases.
NQ.     library catalogs.
NR. information resources.
NS.     print resources.
NT.     videotapes.
NU.     film resources.
NV.     audio recordings.
NW.     digital resources.
```

• 119

Now we can synthesize some notations from strings of terms, to illustrate the ordering of complex classes in our classification. Remember, the rule for retroactive notation is that terms are combined in reverse order, according to the value of the notation. That is, the term that comes last in the alphanumeric arrangement of the notation is placed first in the synthesized notation for any compound or complex class. The result will be that general classes will come before more detailed classes, and that the ordering of facets in complex classes will correspond to the citation order of facets that we chose as preferred:

```
AM. Library and information science (LIS) in the 19th century.
BHM AM. LIS in 19th century France.
CHE. Application of social scientific methods to LIS. Social science is
     represented by CH; methods by CE; we can drop the first C in CE
     because that's the same C (for agents) that is in the notation
     CH.
```

We know that the E represents a new topic because E comes before H in alphabetical order. Every time an earlier letter appears in retroactive notation (earlier in alphabetical order), it represents a new topic! E is also the notation for products. We know this can't be the product E, because if a product were involved, its E notation would come first, before the C for agent. Our E in this notation must be the E within the C facet.

```
GKN QCN PNQ. Subject cataloging with computerized Library of Congress
     Subject Headings (LCSH). Subject cataloging is GKN Q; computers
     are CNP; LCSH is CNNQ. After we use CNP (agents. tools. com-
     puters), we don't have to repeat the CN in CNN Q (agents. tools.
     cataloging tools. LCSH). Because of retroactive (backward) addi-
     tion of notation, NQ cannot come from the thing class (N) because
     if things were involved in a primary way (as the object of sub-
     ject cataloging), the N notation would have to precede the G no-
     tation! Similarly, NQ cannot stand for CNQ (furniture) because if
     it were in the string, it would have to precede computers (CNP)!
     Retroactive notation reduces the repetition of notation, with the
     results that overall notation is shorter.
NPQ MZC JQY. Digital libraries in sexology. NPQ for digital libraries;
     MZC JQY for sexology.
NWM ZCJ QY. Digital resources in sexology. NW for digital resources;
     MZC JQY for sexology.
NWM ZCJ QYG KNQ CNP NQ. Subject cataloging of digital resources in sex-
     ology using computerized Library of Congress Subject Headings. NW
     for digital resources; MZC JQY for sexology; GKN QCN PNQ for sub-
     ject cataloging as above.
```

17.4. Our Examples.

17.4.1. A Book Index.

• alphanumeric arrangement of book indexes : 120

Our printed book has a back-of-the-book index which, as tradition demands (with good reason), is arranged in alphanumeric order based on the index headings. Our arrangement will be based on the order recommended by NISO-1, the NISO Technical Report *Guidelines for indexes and related information retrieval devices* (Anderson 1997a), except that we will follow NISO-2 (Wellisch 1999) when it comes to the treatment of punctuation (see section 17.1).

• 121

These guidelines are a good compromise between rigid character-by-character arrangement (which would put the Roman number XXX in the "X" section of the alphabet), and excessive "meaning" arrangement (which forces users to know the meaning and spelling of abbreviations). There will be no categorical arrangement based on the nature of referents, such as persons, places, things, or titles of messages/texts.

Chapter 17. Arrangement of Displayed Indexes (Section 17.4.2)

• **display of alphanumeric indexes in printed books : 122**

As is the custom for printed books, full headings, including subheadings and cross references, will be displayed. Because print-on-paper media cannot support hypertext, indexes cannot be displayed in stages, as recommended for electronic media.

• **relational classified displays for printed books : 123**

Our printed book also has a rather detailed table of contents, which also constitutes an index. (It meets all the definitional requirements of an index as an indicating device that leads to messages!) The table of contents is arranged to reflect the order of topics in the book. It is hoped that these topics are arranged in a rational and sensible order, reflecting their mutual relations.

• **arrangement of displayed indexes for electronic books : 124**

The electronic version of our book will feature a displayed, browsable alphanumeric index. It will use the same alphanumeric order as the printed book, and the same table of contents will serve as a kind of relational classified index.

• **hypertext indexes for electronic books : 125**

For the electronic version of our book, both the table of contents and the alphanumeric index will be displayed as hypertext. Both indexes will be displayed in stages. For example, the table of contents will display first only chapter headings. Once a chapter heading is selected, then its primary sections will be displayed. Once a primary section is selected, its subsections will be displayed.

• **126**

Similarly, for the alphanumeric index, at first, only lead terms or main headings will be displayed. Once a heading or lead term is selected, cross references and subheading strings will be displayed.

• **postings in displayed indexes for electronic books : 127**

Because all headings are hypertext, the user may go directly from any heading to the appropriate portion of the text. Instead of paragraph or page numbers, postings will indicate the number of paragraphs related to each heading.

17.4.2. An Indexing and Abstracting Service.

• **displayed indexes for indexing and abstracting services in print media : 128**

Our printed A&I service has two displayed alphanumeric subject indexes, one for human indexing of high-use documents and one for automatic indexing of all documents. Both will be arranged in accordance with NISO-1 plus NISO-2 for punctuation, the same NISO recommendations as our printed book (Anderson 1997a; Wellisch 1999). Locators will lead to surrogates that are arranged according to our faceted relational classification of LIS, as described just above in section 17.3.2.1.

• **displayed indexes for indexing and abstracting services in electronic media : 129**

Our electronic indexing and abstracting service will use the same options for the display of indexes as our electronic book. The displayed alphanumeric indexes will use the arrangement recommended by the NISO-1 indexing standard (Anderson 1997a), with the NISO-2 punctuation exception (Wellisch 1999). Users may also browse a relational classified index based on our faceted classification, choosing up to three facets to browse simultaneously.

• **display of results for electronic searches : 130**

Users of the electronic non-displayed index will have the results of their searches displayed either in ranked order according to predicted relevance, or in relational classified order based on the faceted classification. The retroactive notation used for our faceted classification will determine the arrangement of the relational classification. Users who select a best match search will get the ranked order display; users who select an exact match search will get the relational classified display. (Or they may select other arrangements, such as by date of creation or publication, author, title, or topic string).

• 131

Sophisticated users may choose to combine a relational classified display with relevance-ranked retrieval. They will need to specify how many records they wish to deal with. (Remember that in ranked retrieval, every search retrieves the entire database, but the database is re-arranged according to predicted relevance based on the search, so that users may decide how much recall and how much precision they want. The more recall they select, the greater the number of messages that will be displayed in the relational classification; the more precision they select, the fewer the messages that will be displayed in the relational classification.)

• 132

Once ranked-retrieval enthusiasts specify the number of messages they want to deal with (say 200), then these 200 messages (or rather, their brief surrogates) can be displayed in relational classified order, with the headings from the classification providing context for the messages. Within each classification category, messages can be arranged by rank.

17.4.3. A Full-Text Encyclopedia/Digital Library.

• 133

Our full-text electronic encyclopedia/digital library shares all the display options of our electronic indexing and abstracting service. Users may browse a faceted relational classification (up to three facets simultaneously) or they may browse an alphanumeric index (also arranged according to the recommendations of NISO-1 plus NISO-2 for punctuation; see section 17.1). The relational classification will be similar to the faceted classification for LIS illustrated in section 17.3.2.

• 134

Users may also avail themselves of electronic best-match or exact match searches of the full-text of the encyclopedia, in which cases, their retrievals will be displayed in ranked order, or in relational classified order, as described for our indexing and abstracting service.

Chapter 18. Size of Displayed Indexes

Contents of Chapter 18
18.1. Our Examples.
18.1.1. A Book Index.
18.1.2. An Indexing and Abstracting Service.
18.1.3. A Full-Text Encyclopedia/Digital Library.

• size of indexes for printed books : 1

The size of indexes is most often a concern for creators and publishers of indexes for print-on-paper monographs — often called back-of-the-book indexes. Frequently these indexes are allocated a pre-determined amount of space — a limited number of pages at the end of a book. The number of pages is often determined by the number of remaining pages in the last signature (set of pages) in a book rather than any consideration of how long or how detailed the index ought to be! The publisher, concerned about the cost of production and the impact of book price on potential sales, often resists the idea of adding an entire set of pages just to accommodate a few more pages of an index. The size of indexes is also a concern for producers of any other type of printed index, such as printed indexing and abstracting services. The longer the index, the more paper will be needed and the higher the cost of production. Size is less of an issue for indexes in electronic media because the cost of storage and transmission has been going down over time as the technologies for digital storage and communication have matured.

• determination of size of indexes : 2

Determining the size of an index in advance, at the planning stage, is a very complicated matter because it involves so many factors — indeed, most of the factors we have been discussing in this book. The principal factors include:

• the number of documents to be indexed (unless the index is for a single document, such a back-of-the-book index).

• the size of the document(s) to be indexed.

• the size and number of documentary units to which the index will refer (paragraphs or pages in the case of a back-of-the-book index).

• the exhaustivity of indexing.

• the specificity of the indexing language.

• the type of syntax used for combining terms.

• the length of typical headings (the number of terms in typical headings).

• the extent and style of vocabulary management: the number and length of cross-references; the preference for cross-references versus double entry for alternative terms or access points.

• the size of document surrogates and/or locators.

• type font and size.

• page size and format; number and width of columns.

• estimation of size of indexes : 3

One approach to estimating the size of a contemplated index is to actually create a sample index for a few documentary units, and then to extrapolate to the complete index based on the number of documentary units.

• merging of index headings in displayed indexes : 4

In making such an estimate, it is important to remember that duplicate headings and subheadings are usually merged in displayed indexes. But if there are too many duplicate entries, then further detail should be added so that no user is confronted with more than five locators under any heading or subheading (in accordance with the NISO guidelines, Anderson 1997a).

• 5

Take, for example, the following three hypothetical entries:

```
NEPHIS strings
   creation of multiple index entries : 31
NEPHIS strings
   editing : 32
NEPHIS strings
   creation of multiple index entries : 34
```

• 6

When these separate entries are sorted into alphabetical order, the duplicate elements are merged. These headings all have the same main heading, "NEPHIS strings," so these duplicate headings are printed (or displayed) only once, with the subheadings indented and displayed underneath. The subheading for the first and third entries are identical, so they are merged, and the locators for these entries are listed in numerical order at the end of the merged subheading. The three merged and compacted entries now take up a lot less space and look like this:

```
NEPHIS strings
   creation of multiple index entries : 31, 34
   editing : 32
```

This merging of entries reduces the original six lines to only 3, a 50% reduction.

• 7

We shall attempt to estimate the size or length of the back-of-the-book index for our printed book. After the back-of-the-book index is completed, according to the design specifications included in this book, we can see how accurate our estimate turned out to be!

18.1. Our Examples.

18.1.1. A Book Index.

• estimation of size of book indexes : 8

For our back-of-the-book displayed index, we are using the paragraph as our documentary unit. Our calculation of index size is based on the sample index that we created in section 12.4.1. Until the book is finished, we won't know the actual number of documentary units, so for this exercise, we will use the number of 2,000. (A preliminary index was compiled for chapters 1-12 plus introductory matter. This first half of the book has 1246 paragraphs!)

• 9

Our overall estimate of index size can be based on the following factors:

- estimated number of documentary units (paragraphs): 2,000.

- estimated number of NEPHIS term strings per documentary unit: .75. (Most paragraphs will get one string; a very few may require more than one string; and some will get no index heading string at all because they discuss the same topic as a previous paragraph. For our sample index based on 16 paragraphs, there are a total of 12 strings, resulting in the average figure of .75.)

Chapter 18. Size of Displayed Indexes (Section 18.1.1)

- estimated number of number of entries per documentary unit: 1.375. (In NEPHIS indexing, the string of terms used to describe a documentary unit is entered under every keyword unless a keyword is turned off. Although turned-off keywords, preceded by an "@," don't get an entry as a main heading, they do get entries as subheadings. On the other hand, duplicate keywords are merged as main headings and often as subheadings. Such merging should be limited, however, so that no entry has more than 5 locators. For our sample of 16 paragraphs, there are a total of 26 keywords that resulted in 22 index entries, with an average of 1.375 entries per paragraph.)

- size/length of entries per documentary unit: 2.25 lines. (After the 22 sample entries were merged, they occupy 35 65-character lines, not counting cross references. If we reduce line width to 50 characters, these same entries occupy 36 lines. If we reduce type to a legible 8 point size and use a small font, such as Times, we can get 50 characters to the line, more or less, in a three column format on 8-1/2-by-11-inch pages. A smaller format book would use only two columns. When we divide 36 lines by 16 documentary units, we get the figure 2.25 lines per documentary unit.

- total length of index: 4500 lines, or 21.4 pages. (We multiply our 2.25 lines per documentary unit by the number of documentary units, 2,000, resulting in a total of 4500 lines. Then we divide these 4500 lines by 210 lines per page. This 210 figure is based on assumptions of 8 pt. Times type in three columns, with 70 lines of type in each column, and therefore 210 lines per page.)

- upper-case versus lower-case letters. Upper-case letters take up more space than lower-case letters. We are following the NISO indexing guidelines (Anderson 1997a, section 6.2.3) recommendation to use only lower-case letters except for proper nouns.

- cross-references. This estimate includes no cross references, which we know are absolutely essential for a good index. We can increase the number of pages by 20% (4.28 pages), to 25.68 pages, for approximately 450 cross-references, assuming two lines per cross-reference (4.28 pages x 210 lines = 898.8 lines, divided by 2 = 449.4 cross references, rounded off to 450. Some see-also references will require more than two lines, such as the see-also reference under "syntax" in section 12.4.1.

- total estimate. Based on these factors, we estimate a an index requiring approximately 26 pages.

• accuracy of estimation of size of book indexes : 10

How accurate is our estimate? Not very accurate! A preliminary index based on chapters 1-12 of the book plus front matter, without any cross references or any final editing, came to 24 pages. If we double that to 48 pages and add 20% (9.6 pages) for cross references (57.6 pages), then subtract 7.6 pages for final editing, we come to a more realistic estimate of 50 pages.

• problems with estimation of size of book indexes : 11

The large error in our preliminary estimate illustrates the difficulty of extrapolating from a very small sample. Most likely the NEPHIS strings in our sample were shorter than usual. But the main source of our error was not in the procedure itself, but the fact that such an estimate is not intended as a prediction, but as a guideline.

• estimation of size of book indexes as guideline for indexing : 12

If an indexer uses the parameters discussed above to estimate the size of an index, and the estimate fits within the allocated space, then the indexer needs to treat the estimate parameters as a guideline for creating the index. Thus if we estimate that, on average, .75 of the paragraphs would get index entries, then we should try to apply this ratio to our indexing. Approximately 25% of our paragraphs should not get separate entries, but should be subsumed under the entry for the previous paragraph.

Chapter 18. Size of Displayed Indexes (Section 18.1.1)

• 13

Similarly, our estimate is based on an average of 1.375 entries per paragraph. This means that many NEPHIS strings should have only one lead term indicated, while a minority of strings might have two or even three, so that the overall average would be close to 1.375.

• relationship of size of indexes to document size : 14

Based on the size of the raw index for the first twelve chapters, we now estimate that the total index will be 50 pages long. Is this too long for an index for a book of say 500 pages? (Formatted pages through chapter 12 came to 294 pages.) Most back-of-the-book indexes are much smaller than 10% of the length of the book, but an index with the kind of detail that we propose does not appear to be unreasonable for a book whose very topic is information retrieval. We shall wait and see how accurate our revised estimate turns out to be, and then what our publisher is willing to support.

• reduction of size of book indexes : 15

If we need to reduce the size of our index, there are several steps we can take:

• Reduce the number of NEPHIS strings per documentary unit. We can't save much space here, because very few paragraphs get more than one string. However, some paragraphs don't get a separate index string when the topic is the same as the previous paragraph. For a series of contiguous paragraphs on the same topic, our index will lead the reader to the first of these paragraph.

• Reduce the number of keywords per string. This can result in major savings of space by reducing the number of separate entries per documentary unit. We can do this either by reducing the length of the NEPHIS strings, or simply by deleting entries under some keywords.

• permuted index headings versus cross references in book indexes : 16

• Replacing entries with cross references. We can replace sequences of entries with a single cross reference. This is done fairly easily for multi-word terms, like "ad hoc string syntax." With the most generous provision of permuted headings, duplicate entries would fall under three versions of this term:

```
ad hoc string syntax
string syntax
    ad hoc -.
syntax
    string -. ad hoc -.
```

We could eliminate all the entries under the second and third permutations by replacing them with the following cross-references:

```
string syntax, ad hoc -.
    see: ad hoc string syntax
syntax, string -. ad hoc -.
    see: ad hoc string syntax
```

• type size for displayed indexes in print media : 17

• Reduce type size. The NISO guidelines (Anderson 1997a, section 8.2.1) recommend that type be no smaller than 6 points. We are using 8 point type, so we could reduce it as much as two points.

• run-in layout versus indented layout for book indexes : 18

• Compress entry layout. Our current sample index uses an "indented layout" (a separate indented line for each subheading), except at the third level, when subheadings are merged into a single "run-in layout" paragraph to save space (subheadings are listed one after another in a single hanging-indented paragraph). In the following hypothetical entries, for example, the subheadings at the third level, following "ad hoc -." are merged into a single "run-in" paragraph.

Chapter 18. Size of Displayed Indexes (Section 18.1.2)

```
syntax
   string -.
      ad hoc -. NEPHIS as example : 33; reference to Craven
            (Timothy) : 33; role in conversion of natural
            language statements into index entries : 31;
            compared to faceted string syntax : 32
      faceted - compared to ad hoc string syntax : 32
```

We could save additional space by using the "run-in" format at the second level as well. The NISO guidelines (Anderson 1997a, section section 8.2.5) prefer indented over run-in subheadings because "users can scan them more quickly and can therefore understand them more easily. However, where economy dictates space-saving measures, run-in subheadings are preferable to shortening the index." So, if necessary, we could convert the following hypothetical entries, which take up 9 lines:

```
string syntax
   ad hoc -.
      compared to faceted string syntax : 32
      NEPHIS as example : 33
      reference to Craven (Timothy) : 33
      role in conversion of natural language statements into
            index entries : 31
   advantages for indexes : 35
   faceted - compared to ad hoc string syntax : 32
```

to a run-in format that takes only 6 lines, a savings of 1/3 of the lines. We trust you will agree, however, that the compression of subheadings makes the index much denser and harder to scan.

```
string syntax
   ad hoc -. (compared to faceted string syntax : 32; NEPHIS as
      example : 33; reference to Craven (Timothy) : 33; role in
      conversion of natural language statements into index en-
      tries : 31); advantages for indexes : 35; faceted - com-
      pared to ad hoc string syntax : 32
```

- Final editing of the formatted index. When the final index is typeset and formatted, and still exceeds the allowable space, the indexer can choose to eliminate or merge entries until the index does fit.

18.1.2. An Indexing and Abstracting Service.

• 19

We shall not attempt a size estimate for our printed indexing and abstracting service. The number of documents that would be indexed for each monthly and annual issue is still unknown. Furthermore, because it will come out on a monthly basis, if the monthly issues are too long, we can make the kind of adjustments described just above on a month to month basis.

• 20

We also attempt no estimate for the length or size of our indexes for the electronic indexing and abstracting service for two reasons:

- size is not a major issue for electronic media.
- our indexes do not have separate existence, apart from the database as a whole. They are compiled as needed from the records for documents included in the database.

18.1.3. A Full-Text Encyclopedia/Digital Library.

• 21

Similarly, it makes no sense for us to worry about the size of the indexes for our full-text electronic encyclopedia/digital library. All the indexes are embedded, in one way or another, in the database itself — in the records for each article or in the text of the article. Even the displayed indexes do not have separate existence. When a displayed index is called for, it is compiled from the records for the documentary units. Between updates, it may be convenient to maintain the displayed index as a separate file, and as such it can be said to occupy space. However, this space is not a costly commodity as it is in paper media.

Chapter 19. Search Interface

Contents of Chapter 19
19.1. Print on Paper Interfaces.
19.2. Electronic Interfaces.
19.3. Computer Interface Research: Human Computer Interaction.
19.4. Our Examples
19.4.1. A Book Index.
19.4.2. An Indexing and Abstracting Service.
19.4.3. A Full-Text Encyclopedia/Digital Library.

• importance of search interfaces : 1

The most important element for all IR databases is the way in which their content and access options are presented to the user. Database presentation has earned the relatively new name "search interface." We use it in the broadest sense, not only for electronic interfaces for electronic searches, but also for browsing in both electronic and print media. All IR databases, regardless of medium, must present their content and their access options to users, so all have search interfaces.

• search interfaces for print media; human-computer interaction : 2

The principles of effective display for information searching have been under development and scrutiny for centuries for paper (and paper-like) media. Such principles are relatively new for electronic media. In the electronic digital arena, a whole new discipline has developed, "human-computer interaction" (HCI), whose major focus is on the computer interface through which humans interact with computers. Within this field, interfaces for electronic IR databases are a major component.

• impact of search interfaces : 3

If search interfaces are ineffective, then all the design features we have been discussing throughout this entire book are for naught! "A database is perceived first through its interface and search engine. Not even the most informative, reliable, and accurate database can be successful if its software component is not intuitive and user-friendly" (Jacsó 2002, p. 7).

• 4

This truth is echoed by Schulze (2001, p. 119):

"The single most crucial role of the user interface is to communicate the value of the system to the user. From the user's perspective, the interface is the system. A good interface directs the user's attention to important information, makes it obvious what a user needs to do, and provides help and guidance throughout the information-seeking process. If the interface fails to accomplish these objectives, the user may perceive the overall system as a failure — no matter how well its functionality was designed. What information professionals can, and should, do is draw relevant knowledge from cognate disciplines such as HCI so as to enhance their ability to provide useful, efficient, and timely access to information."

Chapter 19. Search Interface (Section 19.1)

19.1. Print on Paper Interfaces.

• 5

Printed IR databases became increasingly important after the invention of printing with movable type. Specialists in graphic design have focused on the effective design of reference books in general and indexing and abstracting tools in particular.

• search interfaces for indexing and abstracting services in print media : 6

Let's review the typical interface between user and database for a printed indexing and abstracting service. First, the user approaches the service on the library shelves. Immediately they get an impression of its size. The printed version of *Chemical abstracts* comes in 2 volumes each week, for a total of 104 weekly volumes per year. In addition, 6-month indexes come in 55 volumes each, for a total of 214 volumes a year (based on an estimate for the total number of volumes for 2002 from www.cas.org). Even if libraries bind some of these volumes together, they constitute one of the largest indexing and abstracting services ever, and its size is immediately apparent. *Sociological abstracts* extends to five large bound volumes in a typical year. The *MLA international bibliography* of the Modern Language Association of America is squeezed into two large volumes (something it can do because it does not include abstracts). The *Bibliography of the history of art* comes in five volumes a year, or six volumes if you include both the French and the English subject index. *Historical abstracts* comes in eight volumes per year, bound into four volumes at Rutgers University. *Information science abstracts* comes in nine slim volumes per year, bound into three volumes at Rutgers. *Library literature* fits into one modestly sized annual volume.

• tables of contents for indexing and abstracting services : 7

The user will typically open the first volume of an annual (or longer period) cumulation and find a table of contents at the front of the volume. If abstracts are provided, these are generally arranged in accordance with a relational classification for the discipline(s) covered. The table of contents will lay out at least the major divisions of the classification, which serve as an overview of the content of the IR database. The indexes will also be listed for such features as authors, subjects, journals and other sources, and possibly for titles of works.

• 8

Here, for example, are the table of contents for several typical A&I services:

• table of contents for *Abstracts in anthropology*;
indexing and abstracting services for anthropology : 9

Abstracts in anthropology, volume 43, number 1, 2001

```
Linguistics
    Historical
    Psycholinguistics
    Sociolinguistics
    Theoretical linguistics
Cultural anthropology
    Applied anthropology, social policy
    Arts
        Dance, folklore, graphic arts, music
Cultural ecology
Economics
    Theory, technology, political economy, colonialism,
        development
```

Chapter 19. Search Interface (Section 19.1)

Ethnohistory
Kinship
    Family organization, marriage
Medical anthropology
Minorities
    Ethnicity, class differentials, sex roles
Political structure and process, law
Psychological anthropology
Social organization
Sociocultural change
    Culture contact, migration, modernization
Symbol systems
    Religion, ritual, world view
Theoretical, methodological and general
Urban studies
Author index
Subject index
Periodicals abstracted in this issue

● table of contents for *Historical abstracts*; indexing and abstracting services for history : 10

Historical abstracts, part A: modern history abstracts (1450-1914), volume 47, 1996

Users' guide
List of abbreviations
Bibliographic entries
Subject index
Author index
List of abstracters (see annual index)
List of periodicals (see annual index)
Part I: General
1. General bibliography
2. Methodology and research methods
3. Historiography
    General
    Philosophy of history
    Tributes and commemoration
4. Archives, libraries, institutes, and museums
5. Societies and meetings
6. Teaching and study of history
Part II: Topics
1. General
2. International relations
3. Wars and military history
4. Political history
5. Social and cultural history
    General
    Social history
    Intellectual history and the arts
6. Economic history
7. Religions and churches
8. Science and technology
Part II: Area or Country
Section 1. Africa and the Middle East
    Africa
        East and East Central Africa
        North Africa

Chapter 19. Search Interface (Section 19.1)

```
        South and South Central Africa
        West and West Central Africa
        Islands off the African Coast
    Middle East
        Afghanistan
        Arabia
        Cyprus
        Egypt
        Ottoman Empire
        Persia (Iran)
```
...

• table of contents for *Sociological abstracts*;
indexing and abstracting services for sociology : 11

Sociological abstracts, volume 46, number 1, February 1998

```
0100 methodology and research technology
0103 methodology (conceptual & epistemological)
0104 research methods/tools
0105 statistical methods
0161 models: mathematical & other
0188 computer methods, media, & applications
0200 sociology: history and theory
0202 of professional interest (teaching sociology)
0206 history & present state of sociology
0207 theories, ideas, & systems
0267 macrosociology: analysis of whole societies
0285 comparative & historical sociology
0300 social psychology
0309 interaction with (small) groups (group processes,
        space use, leadership, coalitions, & teamwork)
0312 personality & social roles (individual traits,
        social identity, adjustment, conformism, & deviance)
0373 cognitive/interpretive sociologies, symbolic
        interactionism, & ethnomethodology
0394 life cycle & biography
0400 group interactions
0410 social group identity & intergroup relations
        (groups based on race & ethnicity, age, &
        sexual orientation)
0491 refugees
0500 culture and social structure
0513 culture (kinship, forms of social organization,
        social cohesion & integration, & social
        representations)
0514 social anthropology
0600 complex organization
0621 jobs, work organization, workplaces, & unions
0623 military sociology
0624 bureaucratic structure/organizational sociology
0665 social network analysis
0671 sociology of business & entrepreneurism
0674 voluntary associations/philanthropy
0700 social change and economic development
0749 market structures & consumer behavior
0770 capitalism/socialism — world systems
0800 mass phenomena
```

Chapter 19. Search Interface (Section 19.1)

```
0826 social movements
0827 public opinion
0828 communication
0829 collective behavior
0842 sociology of leisure/tourism
0850 popular culture
0868 transportation systems & behaviors
0869 sociology of sports
0900 political sociology/interactions
0911 interactions between societies, nations, & states
0925 sociology of political systems, politics, & power
0989 welfare state
0995 nationalism
1000 social differentiation
1019 social stratification/mobility
1020 sociology of occupations & professions
1022 generations/intergenerational relations
1100 rural sociology and agriculture
1200 urban sociology
1300 sociology of language and the arts
1330 sociology of language/sociolinguistics
1331 sociology of art (creative & performing)
1375 sociology of literature
1400 sociology of education
1500 sociology of religion
1600 social control
1636 sociology of law
1653 police, penology, & correctional problems
1700 sociology of science
1772 sociology of technology
1800 demography and human biology
1837 demography (population studies)
1844 human biology/sociobiology
1864 genetic engineering/reproductive biotechnology
1900 the family and socialization
1938 sociology of the child
1939 adolescence & youth
1940 sociology of sexual behavior
1941 sociology of the family, marriage, & divorce
1976 socialization
1977 birth control (abortion, contraception, fertility,
       & childbearing)
1978 sociology of death & dying
2000 sociology of health and medicine
2045 sociology of medicine & health care
2046 social psychiatry (mental health)
2079 substance use/abuse & compulsive behaviors (drug
       abuse, addiction, alcoholism, gambling, eating
       disorders, etc.)
2100 social problems and social welfare
2143 social gerontology
2147 sociology of crime
2148 social work & welfare services
2151 juvenile delinquency
2187 social service programs/delivery systems
2190 victimology (rape, family violence, & child abuse)
2192 sociological practice (clinical & applied)
```

Chapter 19. Search Interface (Section 19.1)

```
2200 sociology of knowledge
2252 history of ideas
2300 community/regional development
2317 sociology of communities & regions
2400 polity, planning, forecasting
2454 planning & forecasting
2460 social indicators
2462 policy sciences
2496 negotiation, dispute settlements
2499 sociology of ethics & ethical decision making
2500 radical sociology
2555 Marxist & radical sociologies
2580 critical sociology
2600 environmental interactions
2681 disaster studies
2682 social geography
2697 famine, hunger, & malnutrition
2700 studies in poverty
2793 homelessness
2800 studies in violence
2884 terrorism
2898 genocide
2900 feminist/gender studies
2959 feminist studies
2983 sociology of gender & gender relations
author index
source index
subject index
```

• table of contents for *Information science abstracts*; indexing and abstracting services for information science : 12

Information science abstracts, volume 36, number 9, 2001

```
Information science and documentation
1.1 Primary and secondary sources
1.2 Education for information work
1.3 Professional and organizational aspects
1.4 Socioeconomic aspects
1.5 International aspects
Research methods
2.1 Definitions, theoretical considerations
2.3 Bibliometrics
2.6 Psychological aspects, cognition
2.8 Mathematics, logic
Information generation and promulgation
3.1 Writing and recording
3.3 Publicity
3.4 Meetings, personal interchange
3.5 Instruction
3.6 Technology transfer
3.7 Publishing
3.8 Copying, printing
3.11 Communications and telecommunications systems
3.13 Office communication and automation
Information recognition and description
4.2 Computer languages
4.5 translation and dictionaries
```

Chapter 19. Search Interface (Section 19.1)

```
4.6 directories
4.7 Classification, indexing, and thesauri
4.9 Pattern and character recognition
Information processing and control
5.1 File design, building, and updating
5.2 Computer systems (general)
5.6 Software and programming
5.8 Graphics and displays
5.9 System interfacing
5.10 Security considerations
5.11 Searching and retrieval
Information systems and applications
6.1 Networks, regional systems, consortia
6.2 Bibliographic search services, databases
6.4 Audio-visual and non-print media
6.6 Life sciences and biomedicine
6.7 Social sciences and humanities
6.8 Business, commerce, and industry
6.9 Management information systems and decision support
6.11 Government
Libraries and information services
7.1 Planning, Administration
7.2 Automation
7.3 Collection development and preparation
7.4 Collection management and preservation
7.5 circulation control
7.6 Interlibrary lending and resource sharing
7.7 User services, assistance, and orientation
7.9 School libraries and media centers
7.11 Archives and museums
Author index
Subject index
Titles abstracted
```

• **search options in print media IR databases : 13**

The table of contents lays out the search options to the user: browse the classified display of citations and abstracts, or search the alphanumeric indexes for a topic or an author or other feature, depending on the indexes provided. Chemical Abstracts, for example, provides separate indexes for authors, topics, patents (by patent number), chemical substances, and chemical formulas.

• **use of enumerative classification in indexing and abstracting services in print media : 14**

Notice that all of the classifications just displayed are of the traditional enumerative variety (discussed in chapter 17 on the display of indexes, both alphanumeric and relational). None of them identify or display facets in any consistent order, nor do users have any options for rearranging the citation order of facets. Enumerative classifications are fixed; they are not manipulable. They are typically used in fixed, static media, such as print on paper.

• **preference for alphanumeric indexes in print media : 15**

Also, as we noted in chapter 17, the use of relational classified indexes in print-media IR databases has generally been limited to rather shallow classifications for browsing through displays of abstracts or citations. Alphanumeric indexes have been the primary means for more detailed searching in printed IR databases. Some print IR databases do not use relational classifications at all. Examples include the many indexing services published by the H.W. Wilson Company, including the famous *Readers' guide to periodical literature*, and the more specialized *Humanities index, Social sciences index*, and many others.

• **standards for display of indexes : 16**

Because of the greater emphasis on alphanumeric displays in print media, guidance for the display of indexes has almost entirely focused on alphanumeric indexes and catalogs during the era of print media dominance. The NISO guidelines for indexes (Anderson 1997a) builds on this tradition, providing special sections on the following aspects of display (section numbers refer to sections in the guidelines, not in this book):

- Integration of vocabulary management information in displayed indexes (6.8.1) — including the location of see-also references (6.8.1.3).
- Use of scope and history notes (6.8.3) — to explain the use of particular terms and headings.
- Syntax in displayed indexes (7.2) — listing ten varieties of syntax, all for alphabetical indexes.
- Locators in displayed indexes (7.4) — including their types, the display of multiple locators after merged identical headings, punctuation, and emphasis for certain locators.
- Typography (8.2.1) — size, use of different typefaces (bold, italic, small capitals, etc.), and use of graphic features such as boxes, shadings, and icons.
- Arrangement of entries (8.2.2) — including a brief mention of relational classified displays!
- Treatment of recurring elements (8.2.3) — the merging of repetitive headings or subheadings.
- Vertical spacing (8.2.4) — use of blank lines between sections for clarity, making it easier for a user to locate sections.
- Entry layout (8.2.5) — dealing with choices between indented versus run-in layout, also mentioned briefly in section 18.1.1. (Run-in layout is sometimes called "run-on" or "paragraph style.")
- Running headlines (8.2.6) — with the name of an index on the top of every page.
- Guidewords (8.2.7) — terms at the top left and top right of two-page spreads informing the user of the content of the two pages.
- Columns (8.2.8) — maximum number, minimum width.
- Continuation lines (8.2.9) — handling entries that extend from the bottom of one column to the top of the next, especially when an entry extends from one page to the next.

• **vocabulary management in printed indexes : 17**

It has long been standard practice to integrate vocabulary information into the index proper, so a user has both index headings and guides to alternative or preferred headings in the same sequence.

• **problems with see-also references : 18**

One problem that was discovered in recent research (Liddy & Jorgensen 1993; Jorgensen & Liddy 1994, 1996) on actual use of printed indexes by students and other typical users is confusion in the minds of some users about the purpose of see-

also references. Some users appear to take them as commands to go elsewhere, rather than suggestions to consider other options. In other words, they do not see the crucial distinction between the traditional "see" or "use" references on the

one hand (which are commands to use other, established headings) and optional "see also" references on the other hand (which list other headings that they might want to consider).

Chapter 19. Search Interface (Section 19.1)

• terminology of see-also references : 19

Traditionally, see-also references have been as brief and succinct as possible, to save space. The "also" in "see also" is supposed to indicate that the reference is only a suggestion. Some designers are taking a little more space to make this clearer, as in: "you may also want to check the narrower terms (broader terms, related terms)," etc.

• placement of see-also references : 20

Related to this confusion is a continuing controversy as to where see-also references ought to be placed in a printed index display. Some experts want them at the very end of a sequence of entries — to be considered only after all subheadings have been considered; others insist that they must be placed at the very beginning of a sequence of subheadings so that they are not lost, and to alert the user to other options before they waste a lot of time examining subheadings under the first heading.

• 21

Here is an example of the problem: Suppose someone turns in a printed index to the heading "homosexuality." Under this main heading, there may be hundreds of entries, distributed under many subheadings. (In the actual sample drawn from the Rutgers University Libraries OPAC and illustrated in section 17.2, there were 271 separate headings beginning with the term "homosexuality.")

• 22

The Library of Congress suggests the following see-also references for the general heading "homosexuality":

```
BT  Sexual orientation
RT  Bisexuality
NT  Astrology and homosexuality
    Gay bars
    Homosexuality, Male
    Lesbianism
```

• 23

The first NT (narrower term) reference may seem a little idiosyncratic — of all the relations between homosexuality and other topics, why this one? It is because of term order. In the array of headings under "homosexuality" displayed in section 17.2, there are several "homosexuality and ..." headings. But in the case of "homosexuality and astrology," "astrology" comes first, so we must alert our users to this fact.

• 24

We might also quibble about whether "gay bars" should really be a narrow term for "homosexuality." It certainly fails the traditional "is a" test (gay bars are not a form of homosexuality!). "Gay bars" really should be a related term! But these problems are not the point here; they are discussed in sections 12.2.1 and 13.3.1.

• terminology in see-also references : 25

If these see-also references were placed at the end of the 271 headings beginning with "homosexuality," most users would never see them. If they have any usefulness at all, they must be displayed at the beginning of the array. They must also be translated into normal English. We must never use secret symbols (like BT, RT, NT) in our public indexes and catalogs!

• 26

The standard translation of these see-also references has been:

```
homosexuality
    SEE ALSO
        BROADER TERM:
            sexual orientation
        RELATED TERM:
            bisexuality
        NARROWER TERMS:
            Astrology and homosexuality
            Gay bars
            Homosexuality, Male
            Lesbianism
```

• 27

As noted above, research has shown that these brief references can be confusing, so some designers suggest some additional clarification, along the lines of something like:

```
homosexuality
        You may also want to check the following headings,
        which indicate similar topics:
        BROADER TERM:
            sexual orientation
        RELATED TERM:
            bisexuality
        NARROWER TERMS:
            Astrology and homosexuality
            Gay bars
            Homosexuality, Male
            Lesbianism
```

• 28

In addition, the NISO indexing guidelines (Anderson 1997a, section 6.8.1.3) suggest that such see-also references be set off in some way so that they are not confused with subheadings. For example, they could be enclosed in a box of some sort:

```
Homosexuality.                                                    50+
    ==============================================================
    | You may also want to check the following headings, which |
    | indicate similar topics:                                 |
    |                                                          |
    |         BROADER TERM:                                    |
    |             sexual orientation                           |
    |         RELATED TERM:                                    |
    |             bisexuality                                  |
    |         NARROWER TERMS:                                  |
    |             Astrology and homosexuality                  |
    |             Gay bars                                     |
    |             Homosexuality, Male                          |
    |             Lesbianism                                   |
    ==============================================================
Homosexuality -- abstracts.                                        1
Homosexuality -- Addresses, essays, lectures.                     16
Homosexuality -- Addresses, essays, lectures -- Abstracts.         1
Homosexuality -- America -- History.                               1
Homosexuality and art.                                             9
Homosexuality and art -- Bibliography.                             1
Homosexuality and art -- New Zealand.                              1
Homosexuality and art -- United States.                            3
Homosexuality and Christianity.                                    2
```

Chapter 19. Search Interface (Section 19.1)

. . .

• repetition of recurring elements in indexes : 29

In the example above, based on *Library of Congress subject headings,* the recurring element "homosexuality" is repeated over and over again because these headings were designed for 3x5 inch cards. In order to file cards, the entire heading was required on every card. Printed indexes in books have long done away with this unnecessary, and indeed distracting, repetition. It is indeed ironic that modern OPACS continue this ancient card-based practice!

• 30

If this display did not repeat recurring elements over and over again, it would look like this:

```
Homosexuality.                                                     50+
       ================================================================
       | You may also want to check the following headings, which |
       | indicate similar topics:                                 |
       |                                                          |
       |       BROADER TERM:                                      |
       |           sexual orientation                             |
       |       RELATED TERM:                                      |
       |           bisexuality                                    |
       |       NARROWER TERMS:                                    |
       |           Astrology and homosexuality                    |
       |           Gay bars                                       |
       |           Homosexuality, Male                            |
       |           Lesbianism                                     |
       ================================================================
Homosexuality.                                                     50+
    -- abstracts.                                                   1
    -- Addresses, essays, lectures.                                16
    -- Addresses, essays, lectures -- Abstracts.                    1
    -- America -- History.                                          1
  and art.                                                          9
       -- Bibliography.                                             1
       -- New Zealand.                                              1
       -- United States.                                            3
  and Christianity.                                                 2
       ... [etc., etc.]
```

• placement of see-also references : 31

Many of the subdivisions under "homosexuality" have their own see-also references. These should be displayed in a similar manner, directly after the first instance of the subheading. For example:

```
Homosexuality                                                      50+
      ...
   -- Law and legislation.                                           4
         ========================================================
         | You may also want to check the following             |
         | heading, which indicates a similar topic:            |
         |                                                      |
         |     BROADER TERM:                                    |
         |         Sex and law                                  |
         ========================================================
   -- Law and legislation.                                           4
        -- Canada.                                                   2
        -- Europe.                                                   1
        -- France.                                                   1
```

```
                            -- Germany.                           2
```
• 32

In the last two examples, we have repeated the heading or subheading before and after the see-also reference box. Do you think this makes the display clearer?

• see-also references from unused headings : 33

Another controversy is whether indexes or catalogs should include see-also references from authorized headings under which there are no entries. Some designers and indexers object to having a reference that reads "see also ..." from a heading that has no entries. On the other hand, when there are no entries under a heading, then it's all the more important to include such see-also references!

• 34

For example, your user looks up "vertebrates." There are no entries under "vertebrates" in your index or catalog. But your library or database does have lots of material on particular kinds of vertebrates, just not on vertebrates in general. Then, wouldn't it be all the nicer to have the following see-also reference?

```
            vertebrates
                see also the narrower terms: amphibians; birds; fishes;
                      mammals; reptiles
```

19.2. Electronic Interfaces.

• problems and advantages of search interfaces for electronic IR databases : 35

The environment for interfaces for electronic digital IR databases is entirely different from the interfaces for print databases, with different capabilities (and limitations) for the display of indexes and for performing searches. On the one hand, electronic interfaces introduce new levels of flexibility and the availability of ever more sophisticated machine processing and computation to aid in searching. Graphical user interfaces (GUI) can also take advantage of all sorts of visual features to highlight and illustrate search options and content.

• 36

On the other hand, one of the biggest challenges in electronic interfaces is to find ways to present an overall idea of the scope and nature of a database, its content, how it is structured and how it may be searched. Related to this is the relatively small screen size for search interface display, compared to the much larger visual space afforded by the typical two-page spread in print media. In a printed display, hundreds of entries can be clearly displayed on a single two-page spread, whereas the typical electronic screen display is often limited to ten or twenty entries.

• separation of search interfaces from content of IR databases : 37

Access to electronic IR databases is further complicated by the fact that many IR databases are not presented directly to users by the database producers, but by intermediary vendors. It is the database vendor who provides the search interface. As a result, the very same IR database can be presented to different user groups via entirely different interfaces. An IR database may have a sophisticated vocabulary management thesaurus, but whether this vocabulary assistance is integrated with the search or browsing interface is entirely up to the vendor, not the IR database producer.

Chapter 19. Search Interface (Section 19.2)

• **faceted classification of *MLA international bibliography*** : 38

To cite just one example, since the early 1980s, the Modern Language Association of America has used a faceted classification and indexing system for its IR database, the largest in the world covering literature, language, and folklore. But to our knowledge, no vendor has ever implemented the browsable features of this indexing and classification system. They have not provided access to browsable alphanumeric indexes, with full index headings. Nor have they made available the browsable classification facets, so that users can select and combine facets of interest to create classifications tailored to their needs, as described in section 17.3.2.

• **comparison of print interfaces versus electronic interfaces** : 39

When a user approaches a print database, the very first impression provides immediate information on the size and scope of the database. The database may consist of a single volume, thick or thin, or it may consist of hundreds of volumes in many sections of shelving, like a complete set of the printed *Chemical abstracts* database.

• 40

Immediately, users get an idea of what they are dealing with. When there are many volumes, they are generally arranged in some systematic way, which should be immediately apparent. Often, volumes are arranged by year, or groups of years, and by type of index (authors, subjects, titles, chemicals, etc.), and by sections of the alphabet (A-G, H-M, N-S, T-Z, etc.). Users can pick a desired volume. If they choose to check out the table of contents, they often get an overview of the database, in terms of the kinds of indexes available and the search options. They may be shown an overview of a relational classification that is used to group surrogates. Most users skip detailed introductions on "how to search," preferring to jump right into the index that they think is most appropriate.

• 41

As a search begins, users begin getting feedback which is fairly clear, even if it consists of a frustrating inability to get anywhere, or a failure to find anything of interest. When this happens, the cause of the difficulty is usually fairly obvious — "I just can't figure this system out," or "none of these citations have anything to do with what I am looking for." It is clear that if the user wants to pursue the search, some help is needed, either from instructions in an introduction, or from someone who can explain the various parts of the indexing system or perhaps suggest an entirely different database.

• 42

Compare this to an electronic IR database, where it is often not at all clear what the problem is — "Am I still connected?" "Am I logged on?" "Is the computer working properly?" "What database am I in?" "What do all these strange icons mean?" "How do I initiate a search?" "How do I quit a search?" — These kinds of problems rarely if ever occur in print media. Take quitting, for example. Everyone knows how to shut a book and put it back on the shelf, or just leave it on a table!

• 43

So the biggest challenge for electronic IR databases and their search interfaces is how to present an effective overview of what is available, how it can be accessed, and how to get in and out of the various options.

Chapter 19. Search Interface (Section 19.3)

19.3. Computer Interface Research: Human Computer Interaction.

• 44

The interface between humans and computers is so important that a whole new discipline has grown up to focus on it: human computer interaction, or HCI for short. HCI draws from computer science, information science, cognitive psychology, and other related disciplines to focus on how humans and computers can most effectively interrelate across the spectrum of activity in which computers now participate.

• 45

A subset of HCI studies focus on information retrieval interactions. Marchionini and Komlodi (1998) summarized this literature in the 1998 *Annual review of information science and technology*.

• taxonomy of interface design guidance : 46

Kemp and Buckner (1999) have surveyed much of the literature offering "design guidance for hypermedia design" and have used it to create a "taxonomy" of design recommendations. Newer IR database interfaces are almost always hypertextual, so the guidance literature they cite is generally quite relevant to our purposes. Their use of the word "taxonomy" is interesting, and is analogous to its use by the Modern Language Association of America (MLA). In a narrower sense, "taxonomy" is often used, as in biological taxonomies, for a classification within a facet, such as a taxonomy of plants or animals. Here, as in the MLA case, it is simply used with the same sense as "classification." The Kemp and Buckner classification includes phenomena from several facets (entities, operations, attributes), arranged in a traditional enumerative fashion. This is not a faceted classification in which each facet is developed separately for later combination.

• definitions of taxonomy : 47

The term "taxonomy" comes from the Greek for arrangement or division (taxis) and law (nomos). Thus it refers to rules of division and arrangement. Such rules are much more uniform and strict in the division and arrangement within a facet, so the traditional use of this term for classification within a single facet is still appropriate. Thus, the rules for zoological taxonomic classification are often rather narrowly focused on physical characteristics (back-bones or not, resulting in vertebrates versus invertebrates) and ancestry/evolution. The "rules" for classifying the design literature are much less specific.

• literature of interface design guidance : 48

In analyzing the literature of design guidance, Kemp and Buckner point out two characteristics worth remembering (p. 148): (1) guidelines "may be contentious or totally wrong"! and (2) "experimental data is in short supply." In other words, most guidelines are based on expert knowledge and opinion (the source of guidance in librarianship for millennia!) rather than on experimental HCI or information science research that seeks to verify the impact of design variations through actual study of use.

• 49

The following summary emphasizes guidelines that tend to reinforce the "expert knowledge" of this book's authors!

• views of Hearst (Marti A.) on search interfaces and visualization : 50

Marti Hearst (1999b) provides an excellent overview of the field of HCI with respect to search interfaces and the visualization of information in the context of information retrieval. She begins with some basic design principles:

Chapter 19. Search Interface (Section 19.3)

- Offer informative feedback. For information retrieval, this will include "feedback about the relationship between their query specification and documents retrieved, about relationships among retrieved documents, and about relationships between retrieved documents and metadata describing collections" (p. 259).

- Reduce working memory load (that is the load on the human memory!). This includes providing "browsable information that is relevant to the current stage of the information access process" (p. 259).

- Provide alternative interfaces for novice and expert users. Here she treats the tradeoff between "simplicity versus power" (p. 259).

• visualization of information : 51

Hearst focuses on two aspects of information visualization: the first is the use of windows, menus, icons, dialog boxes and similar visual devices to illustrate interface options and procedures. The second is the visualization of the information content within the IR database itself, especially of "very large information spaces."

• overviews of information content : 52

Hearst discusses a variety of attempts to provide overviews of IR database content:

- **Category or directory overviews:** these include the kinds of directories now popular on web search sites, such as Yahoo! These also include the more carefully faceted approaches illustrated in section 13.3 for browsing faceted thesauri and in section 17.3.2 for browsing faceted classifications.

- **Clustering techniques:** Here documents are clustered based on similarities with respect to some attribute, such as reference citations, terminology, or metadata (indexing terms). Topical terms are used to characterize clusters. Users can select interesting clusters and recluster their contents into a new set of clusters. This technique, called "scatter/gather" browsing has been tested by Hearst in a study mentioned in section 8.3.11 on clustering as a technique of automatic indexing (Hearst 1999a). Documents are scattered into clusters by a clustering algorithm, then clusters are regathered by user selection, and these selected clusters are rescattered, to create clusters of greater refinement.

- **Graphical overviews:** Graphical illustrations of information space have attracted lots of attention, but so far they have not proven to be effective. Hearst's assessment is that "although intuitively appealing, graphical overviews of large document spaces have yet to be shown to be useful and understandable for users. In fact, evaluations that have been conducted so far provide negative evidence as to their usefulness" (p. 274).

• examples of search interfaces : 53

Hearst includes many current examples of IR search interfaces. Her chapter is highly recommended! In addition, McKiernan (1997-1999) has maintained a webpage at Iowa State University in which he lists projects, research, products and services related to "visual browsing in web and non-web databases."

• impact of cognitive abilities on visualization : 54

Hearst (1999b) points out that the design of effective search interfaces is complicated by the variety of human abilities and preferences: "From the viewpoint of user interface design, people have widely differing abilities, preferences, and predilections. Important differences for information access interfaces include relative spatial ability and memory, reasoning abilities, verbal aptitude, and (potentially) personality differences. Age and cultural differences can contribute to acceptance or rejection of interface techniques. An interface innovation can be useful and pleasing for some users, and foreign and cumbersome for others" (p. 261).

Chapter 19. Search Interface (Section 19.3)

• views of Allen (Bryce L.) on visualization and cognitive abilities : 55

The impact of cognitive abilities on the effectiveness of visualization techniques is the focus of a paper by Bryce Allen (1997). He writes in his abstract: "The idea of obtaining subject access to information by being able to visualize an information space, and to navigate through that space toward useful or interesting information, is attractive and plausible. However, this approach to subject access requires additional cognitive processing associated with the interaction of cognitive facilities that deal with concepts and those that deal with space. This additional cognitive processing may cause problems for users, particularly in dealing with the dimensions, the details, and the symbols of information space. Further, it seems likely that different cognitive abilities are associated with conceptual and spatial cognition. As a result, users who deal well with subject access using traditional conceptual approaches may experience difficulty in using visualization and navigation" (p. 63).

• icons versus words : 56

Apart from spatial images, different people react differently to visual and verbal symbols. Anderson, for example, finds icons often meaningless, whether they are on the dashboard of a new car or on a search interface. He likes to say that humans spent millennia learning how to represent speech in writing. Before that we could only use pictures. So why now, with the richness of speech and writing, should we revert to confusing pictures?

• 57

Of course, pictures can be worth a thousand (or ten thousand) words when the object of interest is inherently visual, such as a painting or architectural marvel!

• views of Raskin (Jef) on icons : 58

Anderson's iconic idiosyncrasies are echoed by the interface designer Jef Raskin ("creator of the Apple Macintosh project"):

"Icons, those familiar little pictures used to identify buttons and other objects, are a shibboleth of modern interface design. ... Icons contribute to visual attractiveness of an interface and, under the appropriate circumstances, can contribute to clarity; however, the failings of icons have become clearer with time. ... *Instead of icons explaining, we have found that icons often require explanation* [emphasis in original]. If you wanted to obscure or to encode an idea to keep it from prying eyes, substituting icons for the words might not be a bad start. ... In every study that considered the question, icons were demonstrated to be more difficult to understand than were labels, especially at first viewing, which contradicts one of the most frequently cited reasons for using icons, namely, comprehensibility for beginners" (Raskin 2000, p. 168-170).

• views of Raskin (Jef) on interfaces for experts versus novices : 59

Raskin disagrees with Hearst on the advantages of separate interfaces for experts versus novices. He writes on the "myth of the beginner-expert dichotomy":

"This dichotomy is invalid. As a user of a complex system, you are neither a beginner nor an expert, and you cannot be placed on a single continuum between these two poles. You independently know or do not know each feature or each related set of features that work similarly to one another. You may know how to use many commands and features of a software package; you may even work with the package professionally, and people may seek your advice on using it. Yet you may not know how to use categories of commands in that same package" (Raskin 2000, p. 69).

• 60

Raskin is especially critical of interfaces that change automatically after some degree of use: "most attempts to make interfaces adaptive are ill-advised; whenever a system changes automati-

Chapter 19. Search Interface (Section 19.3)

cally, even if the change is as small as, say, a reordered set of items on a menu, your expectations are upset and your habituation is frustrated" (Raskin 2000, p. 69-70).

• customization of interfaces : 61

However, there is general consensus that frequent users, who desire to do so, should have the option of customizing search interfaces to conform to their own preferences. For example, they might change the default electronic search mode from best-match (weighted term) to exact match (boolean). It would be nice if they could opt for labels instead of (or in addition to) icons! For the display of results of electronic searches, they might specify arrangement by date or topic (index heading) rather than predicted relevance.

• views of Head (Alison J.) on customization of interfaces : 62

Head (1997), author of *Design wise: a guide for evaluating the interface design of information resources* (1999), includes the capability of permitting users to customize an interface as one of the attributes that "empower users": "users can customize the interface with special function keys, shortcuts, screen colors, and rate of information delivered per screen" (p. 23).

• views of Peters (Ronnie) on search interfaces : 63

Back in 1992, Ronnie Peters, an art director for a computer communications firm, laid out some of the issues involved in "designing for the computer screen." She writes:

"Designing for the computer screen poses new challenges for the designer. While some of the issues are new such as time, motion, and sound, other aspects such as the readability of typography, the separation and combination of image and type, and the general issues associated with projecting the three-dimensional world onto a two-dimensional surface are part of a complex design tradition. When designing for this new medium, the designer is faced with the problem of organizing a large amount of information in a small area and must establish the most orderly arrangement of information, determine the hierarchic scale of importance, arrange the easiest accessibility of information, and design the appearance accordingly" (Peters 1992, p. 147).

• size of computer screens : 64

Regarding the size of the computer screen, she writes:

"The computer screen for ease of navigation and accessibility is the best place to store information, but it is also the computer's most limited resource. The amount of storage space required on the computer memory is rapidly becoming smaller, but the delivery platform, the computer screen, is increasing in both size and resolution at a much slower pace. The limited space of the computer screen and the coarseness of the resolution leave little room for embellishment and decoration" (Peters 1992, p. 152).

• decoration in search interfaces : 65

Regarding decoration, Peters has blunt words: "Any notion that design for the computer screen is merely decorative is a misunderstanding. Good computer screen design does not decorate; it clarifies" (1992, p. 136).

• views of Nielsen (Jakob) on scrolling : 66

In addition to specialized HCI journals, more general computer science and information science periodicals pay a lot of attention to search interfaces for IR databases. In 1999, the *Communications of the ACM* (Association for Computing Machinery) published Jakob Nielsen's "User interface directions for the web." His best advice is to avoid forcing your user to scroll! "Scrolling must be avoided on navigation pages. Users need to be able to see all their options at the same time and links below the window border when the page comes up ('below the fold' in Jared Spool's newspaper analogy) are much less likely to be chosen than the top links" (Nielsen 1999, p. 67). We must remember this when we display browsable classification categories. All the categories should fit on a typical computer screen. (Nielsen has written many books relating to interface design, including *Designing exceptional websites: secrets of an information architect.* Indianapolis: New Riders; 1999; *Designing web usability*. Indianapolis: New Riders; 2000; and with Jeff Johnson, *GUI bloopers: don'ts and dos for software developers and web designers.* San Francisco: Morgan Kaufmann; 2000.)

• views of Shneiderman (Ben) on search interfaces : 67

One of the most famous and widely quoted authorities on IR interface design and information visualization in digital media is Ben Shneiderman, who for many years led the Human-Computer Interaction Laboratory at the University of Maryland in College Park. We take as our most overriding principle his famous mantra, here quoted from the third edition of his influential book *Designing the user interface* (1998, p. 523):

"There are many visual design guidelines. The central principle might be summarized as this *visual-information-seeking mantra*:

```
Overview first, zoom and filter, then details on demand
Overview first, zoom and filter, then details on demand
Overview first, zoom and filter, then details on demand
Overview first, zoom and filter, then details on demand
Overview first, zoom and filter, then details on demand
Overview first, zoom and filter, then details on demand
Overview first, zoom and filter, then details on demand
Overview first, zoom and filter, then details on demand
Overview first, zoom and filter, then details on demand
Overview first, zoom and filter, then details on demand
Overview first, zoom and filter, then details on demand
Overview first, zoom and filter, then details on demand
```

"Each line represents one project in which I found myself rediscovering this principle and therefore wrote it down as a reminder."

• 68

Shneiderman explains his (our!) mantra as follows (1998, p. 524):

"Overview: Gain an overview of the entire collection [e.g., of the database or digital library].

"Zoom: Zoom in on items of interest.

"Filter: Filter out uninteresting items.

"Details-on-demand: Select an item or group and get details when needed."

To these basic tasks, he adds:

"Relate: View relationships among items.

"History: Keep a history of actions to support undo, replay, and progressive refinement.

"Extract: Allow extraction of subcollections and of the query parameters."

We close this survey of HCI interface design research and advice with the quote that Shneiderman uses to open his section on "information visualization" (1998, p. 522):

"Grasping the whole is a gigantic theme. Arguably, intellectual history's most important. Ant-vision is humanity's usual fate; but seeing the whole is every thinking person's aspiration" — David Gelernter, *Mirror worlds*, 1992.

Chapter 19. Search Interface (Section 19.4)

19.4. Our Examples

• guidelines for search interfaces : 69

We shall try to illustrate the application of interface design principles summarized in the previous section to our sample IR databases. But before we discuss our three on-going examples, we offer the guidelines we give to our students for electronic search interface displays, along with some examples of their work:

• design features for opening screens for IR databases : 70

a. **The opening screen.** This screen should provide an overview of the content and access options for the IR database, without scrolling! It should include:

a.1. The database title.

a.2. A brief statement describing the purpose of the database, its documentary scope and domain, and its subject domain (primary audience).

a.3. An overview of the topical content, expressed in terms of the major facets (categories or aspects) included in the subject scope. Each facet label (and icon if used) should be accompanied with a few sample topics to help define the meaning and content of the facet. Each facet heading should include the number of postings included in that facet (the number of messages that are indexed with terms included in the facet).

a.4. A clear indication of at least three access options. These options are related to earlier design decisions discussed in this book, such as:

a.4.1. Browsing two or three topical (or feature) facets simultaneously (sections 13.3, 17.3.2).

a.4.2. Browsing one or more alphanumeric indexes for subjects, authors, titles, or other features (section 17.2).

a.4.3. Performing an immediate keyword search. This option can be indicated with an open box, inviting keywords (section 12.3).

a.4.4. Opting for a more sophisticated electronic search, e.g., an "advanced search" (sections 8.3, 12.3).

a.4.5. Choosing to do a key phrase browse, based on phrase co-occurrence in message documents (section 8.3.8).

• examples of opening screens for IR databases : 71

Figures 19.1-19.9 illustrate opening screen designs by our students. Remember, these are design sketches. Our students are not professional designers. These are intended to guide designers, who should incorporate the essential aspects illustrated in these examples:

• Figure 19.1, the opening screen for an "Art image database" by Minsoo Park (2001), includes a summary of topics illustrated in paintings, as well as features of paintings, such as style, color, and genre.

• Figure 19.2, the opening screen for an IR database on lesbian studies by Melissa Hoffman (2001), is perhaps a little crowded. Nevertheless, search options are well-displayed in the left menu bar, and the key facets are nicely laid out, with illustrative examples of content, in the "Browse Subject Index" window, which might be better labeled the "Browse Subject Categories" window! It is not clear what the "Alphabetical Index" is, in relation to the Subject Index and the Author or Title Index.

• Figure 19.3 illustrates the opening screen for an IR database on symbols of the United States by Veronica Meyer (2001). In the navigation bar at the there top is an option to "browse by symbol,"

Chapter 19. Search Interface (Section 19.4)

but how that would work has not been resolved. Creating a browsable display of symbols will depend on identifying salient features of symbols (such as shapes) and working out a meaningful classification for these features.

- Figure 19.4 shows the opening screen for an IR database on web development resources, by Matthew Brown (2001).

- Figure 19.5 shows the opening screen for "Opera for Smarties Online," a design by J. Fernando Peña (2000). Postings should be added to each facet category.

- Figure 19.6 is the opening screen for Robert Rittman's "Desire: Database of Ethnic Studies for Information Retrieval" (2000). It's probably too crowded, but includes options for an alphanumeric browse of a key-word-in-context index based on document titles and abstracts. Postings for categories are needed here as well.

- Figure 19.7, the opening page for Jennifer Schroth's environmental database (2000), points to browsable alphanumeric indexes for authors, titles, subjects and a merged comprehensive index. Her categories could also benefit from postings data.

- Figure 19.8 shows the opening screen for Enola Romano's "Reptile House" database (2000), designed for students, who would benefit from postings data with her categories.

- Figure 19.9 shows the opening screen for Elizabeth Pregill's "Symbolist Movement" database (2001).

• design features for display of browsable facets : 72

b. The faceted browse page. If users select two or three facets to browse, they come to this page, on which facets are displayed in two or three columns. The display of browsable faceted relational indexes was discussed and illustrated in sections 13.3 and 17.3.2.

b.1. In most cases, facets should be displayed by means of hierarchies or trees such that at each level, all choices can be displayed without scrolling.

b.2. Each term or heading within a facet should include information on the number of postings associated with that term or heading. Often, two postings figures are useful: (1) the total postings for that term and all subordinate terms and (2) the number of messages that are linked to the particular term itself. Thus "Animals (3000:200)" would indicate that 3000 messages relate to animals in general or to specific animal categories or species, while 200 messages relate to animals in general (see section 17.3.2).

b.3. Users should be provided immediate feedback, with a window showing at least two or three very brief surrogates. These surrogates should reflect the type of search, so for topical facet browses, they should consist of a topical index heading. With each brief (one line) surrogate, users should have the options of going immediately to a fuller surrogate, or even to the full text (in full-text databases). The display of surrogates was discussed in chapter 16.

• examples of display of browsable facets : 73

Figures 19.10-19.11 illustrate the display of browsable facets in IR database designs by Rutgers students:

Figure 19.10 illustrates the display of browsable facets for purpose, people & groups, and events in Eric J. Johnson's design for a specialized IR database for a collection of historical playing cards in the Cotsen Children's Library at Princeton University (2003).

Figure 19.11 illustrates the display of browsable facets for occupations, ethnic groups, and geographic places in Lori A. Rowland's design for an IR database for the *Journal of Women's history* (2003).

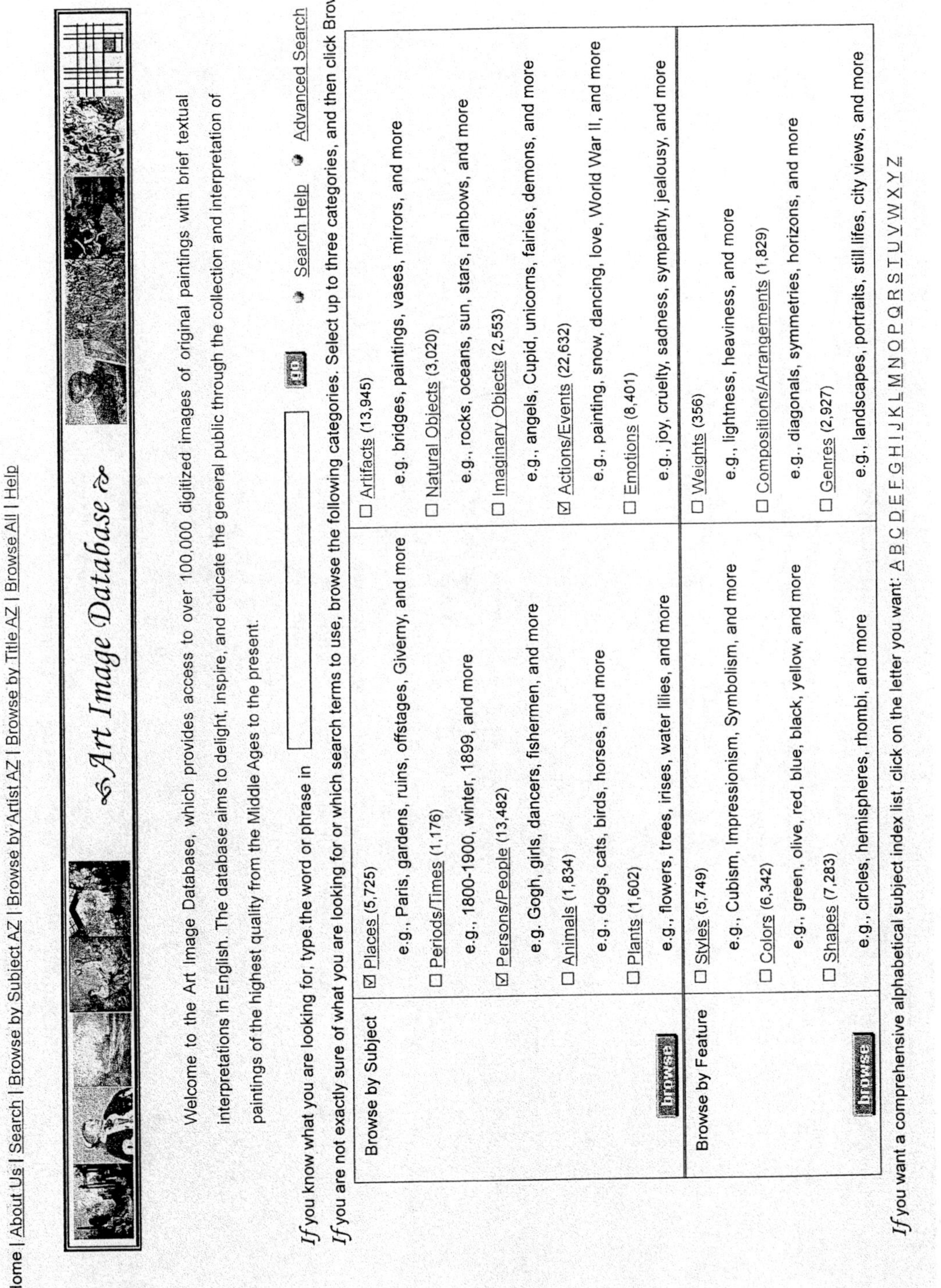

Chapter 19. Search Interface (Section 19.4)

Home | About Us | Search | Browse by Subject AZ | Browse by Artist AZ | Browse by Title AZ | Browse All | Help

Art Image Database

Welcome to the Art Image Database, which provides access to over 100,000 digitized images of original paintings with brief textual interpretations in English. The database aims to delight, inspire, and educate the general public through the collection and interpretation of paintings of the highest quality from the Middle Ages to the present.

If you know what you are looking for, type the word or phrase in [   ]   • Search Help   • Advanced Search
If you are not exactly sure of what you are looking for or which search terms to use, browse the following categories. Select up to three categories, and then click Browse.

Browse by Subject		
☑ Places (5,725)		☐ Artifacts (13,945)
e.g., Paris, gardens, ruins, offstages, Giverny, and more		e.g., bridges, paintings, vases, mirrors, and more
☐ Periods/Times (1,176)		☐ Natural Objects (3,020)
e.g., 1800-1900, winter, 1899, and more		e.g., rocks, oceans, sun, stars, rainbows, and more
☑ Persons/People (13,482)		☐ Imaginary Objects (2,553)
e.g., Gogh, girls, dancers, fishermen, and more		e.g., angels, Cupid, unicorns, fairies, demons, and more
☐ Animals (1,834)		☑ Actions/Events (22,632)
e.g., dogs, cats, birds, horses, and more		e.g., painting, snow, dancing, love, World War II, and more
☐ Plants (1,602)		☐ Emotions (8,401)
e.g., flowers, trees, irises, water lilies, and more		e.g., joy, cruelty, sadness, sympathy, jealousy, and more

[Browse]

Browse by Feature		
☐ Styles (5,749)		☐ Weights (356)
e.g., Cubism, Impressionism, Symbolism, and more		e.g., lightness, heaviness, and more
☐ Colors (6,342)		☐ Compositions/Arrangements (1,829)
e.g., green, olive, red, blue, black, yellow, and more		e.g., diagonals, symmetries, horizons, and more
☐ Shapes (7,283)		☐ Genres (2,927)
e.g., circles, hemispheres, rhombi, and more		e.g., landscapes, portraits, still lifes, city views, and more

[Browse]

If you want a comprehensive alphabetical subject index list, click on the letter you want: A B C D E F G H I J K L M N O P Q R S T U V W X Y Z

Figure 19.1. Opening screen for an "Art image database" by Minsoo Park (2001).

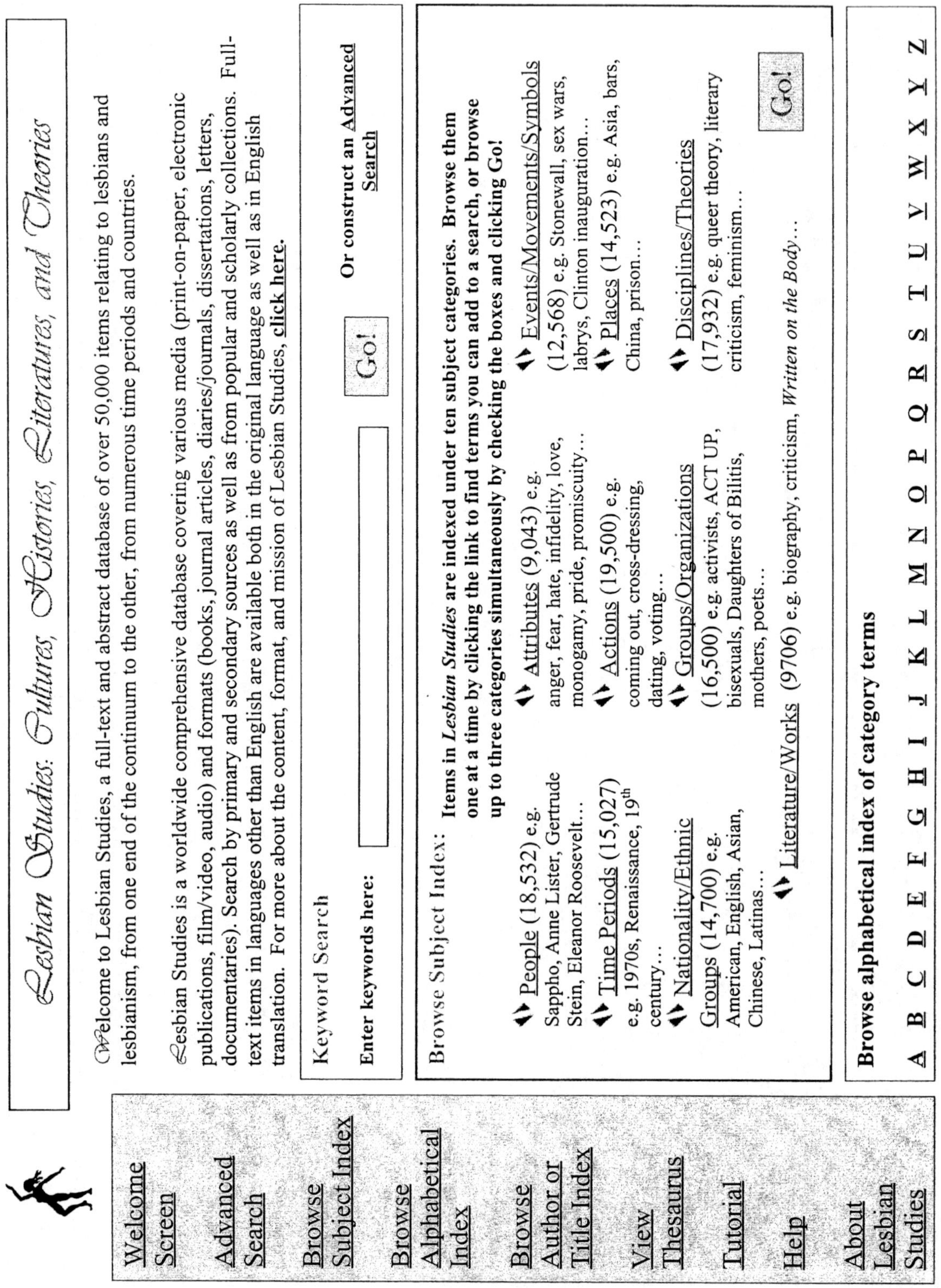

Chapter 19. Search Interface (Section 19.4)

Lesbian Studies: Cultures, Histories, Literatures, and Theories

Welcome to Lesbian Studies, a full-text and abstract database of over 50,000 items relating to lesbians and lesbianism, from one end of the continuum to the other, from numerous time periods and countries.

Lesbian Studies is a worldwide comprehensive database covering various media (print-on-paper, electronic publications, film/video, audio) and formats (books, journal articles, diaries/journals, dissertations, letters, documentaries). Search by primary and secondary sources as well as from popular and scholarly collections. Full-text items in languages other than English are available both in the original language as well as in English translation. For more about the content, format, and mission of Lesbian Studies, **click here**.

Keyword Search

Enter keywords here: [   ] Go!   Or construct an <u>Advanced Search</u>

Browse Subject Index: Items in *Lesbian Studies* are indexed under ten subject categories. Browse them one at a time by clicking the link to find terms you can add to a search, or browse up to three categories simultaneously by checking the boxes and clicking Go!

▼ <u>People</u> (18,532) e.g. Sappho, Anne Lister, Gertrude Stein, Eleanor Roosevelt...

▼ <u>Time Periods</u> (15,027) e.g. 1970s, Renaissance, 19th century...

▼ <u>Nationality/Ethnic Groups</u> (14,700) e.g. American, English, Asian, Chinese, Latinas...

▼ <u>Attributes</u> (9,043) e.g. anger, fear, hate, infidelity, love, monogamy, pride, promiscuity...

▼ <u>Actions</u> (19,500) e.g. coming out, cross-dressing, dating, voting...

▼ <u>Groups/Organizations</u> (16,500) e.g. activists, ACT UP, bisexuals, Daughters of Bilitis, mothers, poets...

▼ <u>Literature/Works</u> (9706) e.g. biography, criticism, *Written on the Body*...

▼ <u>Events/Movements/Symbols</u> (12,568) e.g. Stonewall, sex wars, labrys, Clinton inauguration...

▼ <u>Places</u> (14,523) e.g. Asia, bars, China, prison...

▼ <u>Disciplines/Theories</u> (17,932) e.g. queer theory, literary criticism, feminism...

Go!

Browse alphabetical index of category terms

A B C D E F G H I J K L M N O P Q R S T U V W X Y Z

- <u>Welcome Screen</u>
- <u>Advanced Search</u>
- <u>Browse Subject Index</u>
- <u>Browse Alphabetical Index</u>
- <u>Browse Author or Title Index</u>
- <u>View Thesaurus</u>
- <u>Tutorial</u>
- <u>Help</u>
- <u>About Lesbian Studies</u>

Figure 19.2. Opening screen for an IR database on lesbian studies by Melissa Hoffman (2001).

Chapter 19. Search Interface (Section 19.4)

BROWSE A-Z Subject Index   BROWSE CATEGORY   ADVANCED Search   ABOUT USA   HELP
Browse by Symbol   Browse by Author   Browse by Title

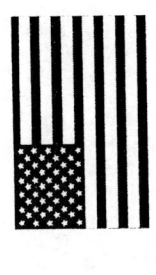

WELCOME TO USA

UNDENIABLE SYMBOLS of AMERICA

This database has over 100,000 articles, books, videos, speeches and songs about the symbols that represent the United States of America. This Database is for those conducting scholarly research as well as those who want to know more about what makes America the country it is.

If you know what you are looking for, please type it here:

[   ]

OR Browse by CATEGORY:

Click on a gold star to select a category. A selected category will turn the star blue. You may select up to three categories.

★ PEOPLE (48,000) : (George Washington, Benjamin Franklin...)
★ OBJECTS/ARTIFACTS (18,000) : (Apple Pie, American Flag...)
★ MONUMENTS/STRUCTURES (32,000) :(Lincoln Memorial, White House...)
★ SPORTS (11,000) : (Baseball, Softball...)
★ SONGS (10,000) : (Star Spangled Banner, America the Beautiful...)
★ ANIMALS (9,000) : (Bald Eagle...)
★ OATHS (9,000) : (Pledge of Allegiance, Presidential Oath...)
★ EVENTS (32,000) : (World War II, Vietnam War...)
★ ORGANIZATIONS/GROUPS (20,000) : (VFW, NASA...)
★ SPEECHES (18,000) : (Gettysburg Address, FDR's Pearl Harbor Speech...)
★ GOVERNMENT DOCUMENTS/ LAWS (46,000) : (Constitution, Declaration of Independence...)

OR Browse our A-Z Subject Index:

1,2,3.... A B C D E F G H I J K L M N O P Q R S T U V W X Y Z

Figure 19.3. Opening screen for an IR database on symbols of the U.S.A. by Veronica Meyer (2001).

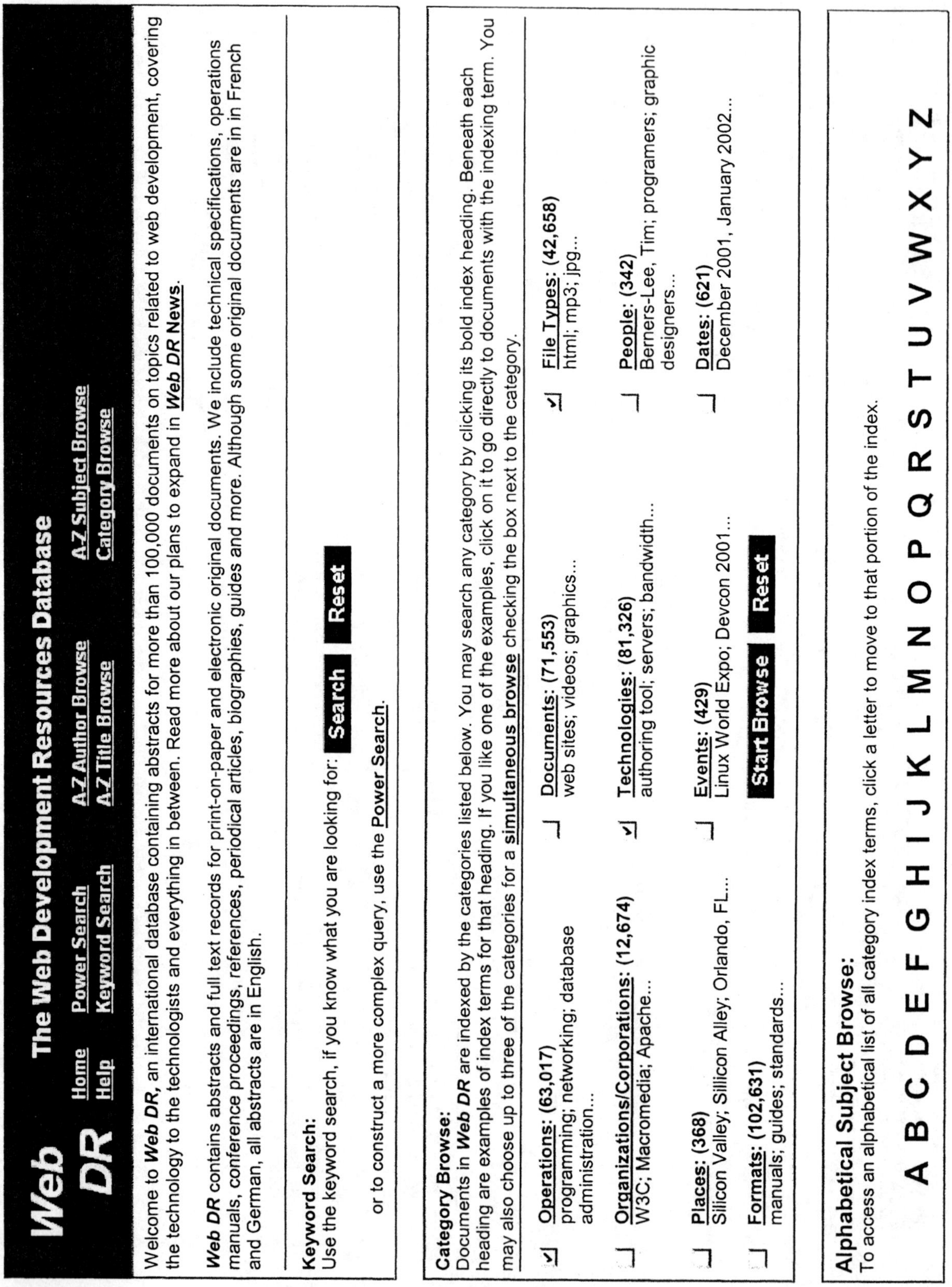

Chapter 19. Search Interface (Section 19.4)

Web DR — The Web Development Resources Database

Home | **Power Search** | **A-Z Author Browse** | **A-Z Subject Browse**
Help | **Keyword Search** | **A-Z Title Browse** | **Category Browse**

Welcome to *Web DR*, an international database containing abstracts for more than 100,000 documents on topics related to web development, covering the technology to the technologists and everything in between. Read more about our plans to expand in *Web DR News*.

Web DR contains abstracts and full text records for print-on-paper and electronic original documents. We include technical specifications, operations manuals, conference proceedings, references, periodical articles, biographies, guides and more. Although some original documents are in French and German, all abstracts are in English.

Keyword Search:
Use the keyword search, if you know what you are looking for: [Search] [Reset]

or to construct a more complex query, use the **Power Search**.

Category Browse:
Documents in *Web DR* are indexed by the categories listed below. You may search any category by clicking its bold index heading. Beneath each heading are examples of index terms for that heading. If you like one of the examples, click on it to go directly to documents with the indexing term. You may also choose up to three of the categories for a **simultaneous browse** checking the box next to the category.

- ☑ **Operations:** (63,017)
  programming; networking; database administration…
- ☐ **Organizations/Corporations:** (12,674)
  W3C; Macromedia; Apache…
- ☐ **Places:** (368)
  Silicon Valley; Silicon Alley; Orlando, FL…
- ☐ **Formats:** (102,631)
  manuals; guides; standards…
- ☐ **Documents:** (71,553)
  web sites; videos; graphics…
- ☑ **Technologies:** (81,326)
  authoring tool; servers; bandwidth…
- ☐ **Events:** (429)
  Linux World Expo; Devcon 2001…
- ☑ **File Types:** (42,658)
  html; mp3; jpg…
- ☐ **People:** (342)
  Berners-Lee, Tim; programers; graphic designers…
- ☐ **Dates:** (621)
  December 2001, January 2002…

[Start Browse] [Reset]

Alphabetical Subject Browse:
To access an alphabetical list of all category index terms, click a letter to move to that portion of the index.

A B C D E F G H I J K L M N O P Q R S T U V W X Y Z

Figure 19.4. Opening screen for an IR database on web development resources by Matthew Brown (2001).

Chapter 19. Search Interface (Section 19.4)

HOME ABOUT US BROWSE SUBJECT CATEGORIES BROWSE ALPHA-SUBJECT INDEX SEARCH DATABASE HELP

OPERA FOR SMARTIES ONLINE

Welcome to Opera for Smarties Online (OSO)! OSO is the Web's most complete resource on opera and its creators, interpreters, and critics. Over 100,000 scholarly journal articles (most in full-text) and books in many languages are indexed, as well as opera scores, libretti, plot synopses, and recordings and reviews. OSO is updated quarterly, so visit frequently!

(To learn more about our policies for selecting items for the OSO database, go to About Us.)

Browse Subject Categories

Select up to three of the categories below and browse them simultaneously by clicking Browse.

- ☐ **Composers** (Mozart, Verdi, Wagner, Britten...)
- ☐ **Librettists** (Striggio, da Ponte, Boito, Maeterlinck...)
- ☐ **Performers and Conductors** (Farinelli, von Bülow, Caruso, Toscanini...)
- ☐ **Schools and Movements** (Romantic, Impressionistic, French, Verismo...)
- ☐ **Composition and Musical Expression** (arias, leitmotifs, recitatives, cabalettas....)
- ☐ **Operas** (*Don Giovanni*, *Aida*, *Carmen*, *The Ring*...)
- ☐ **Opera Characters and Roles** (Figaro, buffoons, Tosca, femmes fatales...)
- ☐ **Opera Themes** (love, infidelity, promiscuity, liberation...)
- ☐ **Opera Settings** (Greece, Seville, Valhalla, Paris...)
- ☐ **Time Periods** (mythical, 17th century, 1890-1905, 1945-...)

BROWSE

Browse Alpha-Subject Index

Look at OSO's comprehensive alphabetical index of subjects by clicking Browse.

BROWSE

Quick Search

[   ]

Type keyword(s) without punctuation
(For more advance search options, go to Search Database.)

SEARCH

J. Fernando Peña—Final Project (Anderson), May 6, 2000

Figure 19.5. Opening screen for "Opera for Smarties Online" by J. Fernando Peña (2000).

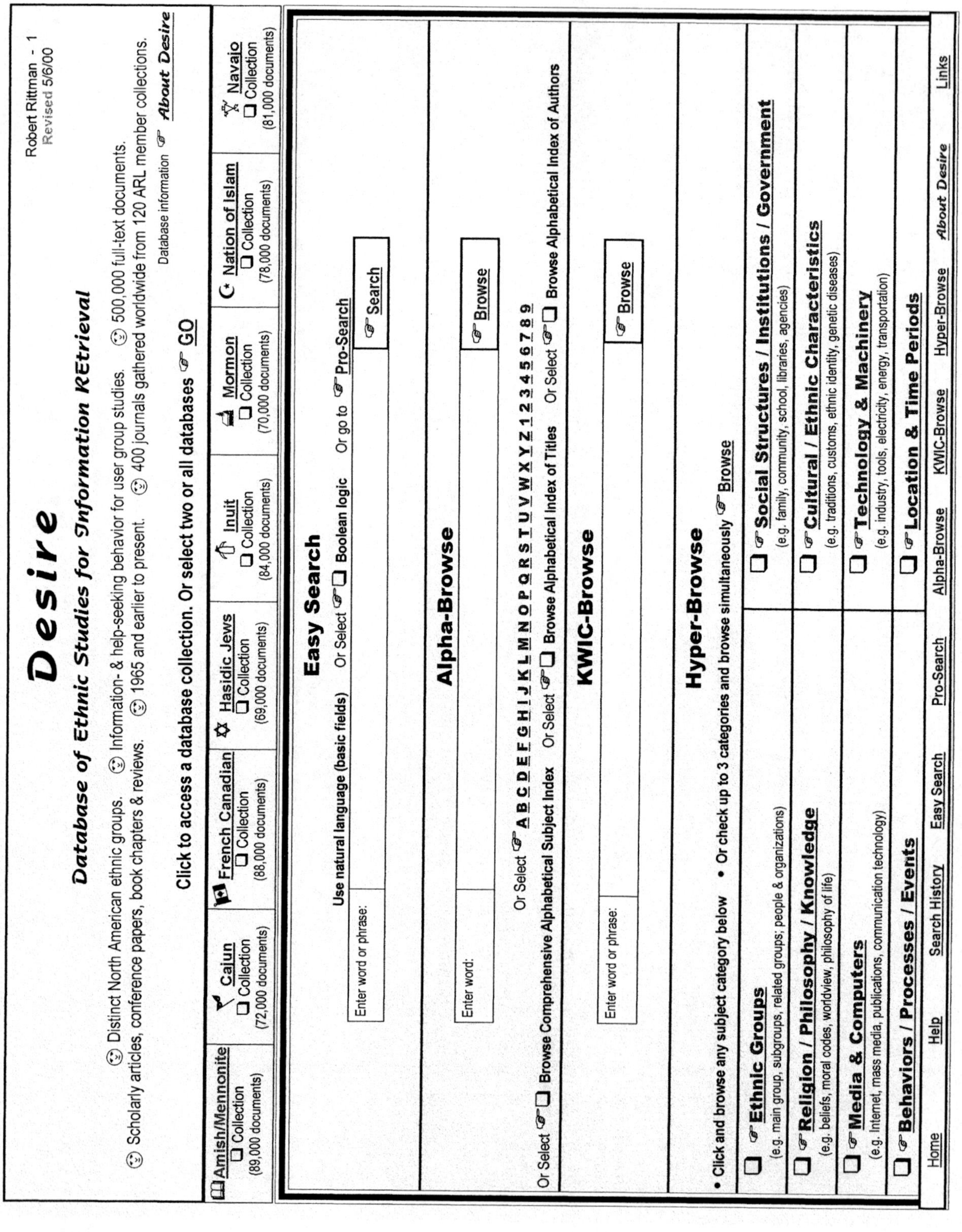

Chapter 19. Search Interface (Section 19.4)

Figure 19.6. Opening screen for "Desire: Database of Ethnic Studies for Information Retrieval" by Robert Rittman (2000).

Chapter 19. Search Interface (Section 19.4)

Home	About Us	Keyword Search	Browse A-Z Author Index	Browse A-Z Title Index	Browse A-Z Subject Index	Browse Comprehensive A-Z Index	Browse Categories	Exit Database

DB&S Environmental Database

Welcome to the DB&S Environmental Database. This database contains either full text or abstracts of over 200,000 journal and newspaper articles, government documents, books, maps and audio/visual materials from 1965 – the present dealing with federal and state environmental rules, regulations, standards and problems, along with people, agencies, organizations and companies in the environmental field.

[   ]   Search

(Keyword Search)

Browse an Alphabetical Listing by choosing one of the following Indexes:

Browse A-Z Author Index	Browse A-Z Title Index	Browse A-Z Subject Index	Browse Comprehensive A-Z Index

Browse up to three categories below simultaneously. Just select the box next to the category or categories you want to browse, then click on the GO button below.

☐ **People**
   (ex. Attorneys, Epidemiologists, Toxicologists)

☐ **Agencies/Organizations**
   (ex. ATSDR, DEP, USEPA)

☐ **Associations**
   (ex. American Bar Association, NJICLE)

☐ **Natural Elements**
   (ex. Air, Forests, Soil, Water)

☐ **Chemicals/Pollutants**
   (ex. Arsenic, Cadmium, Carbon, PCBs)

☐ **Actions**
   (ex. Construction, Incineration, Preservation)

☐ **Processes**
   (ex. Erosion, Pollution, Contamination)

☐ **States**
   (ex. New Jersey, New York, Pennsylvania)

☐ **Legislative Policies/Acts**
   (ex. CERCLA, Clean Air Act, Clean Water Act)

☐ **Diseases/Conditions**
   (ex. Anemia, Birth Defects, Cancer)

GO

Figure 19.7. Opening page for an environmental database by Jennifer Schroth (2000).

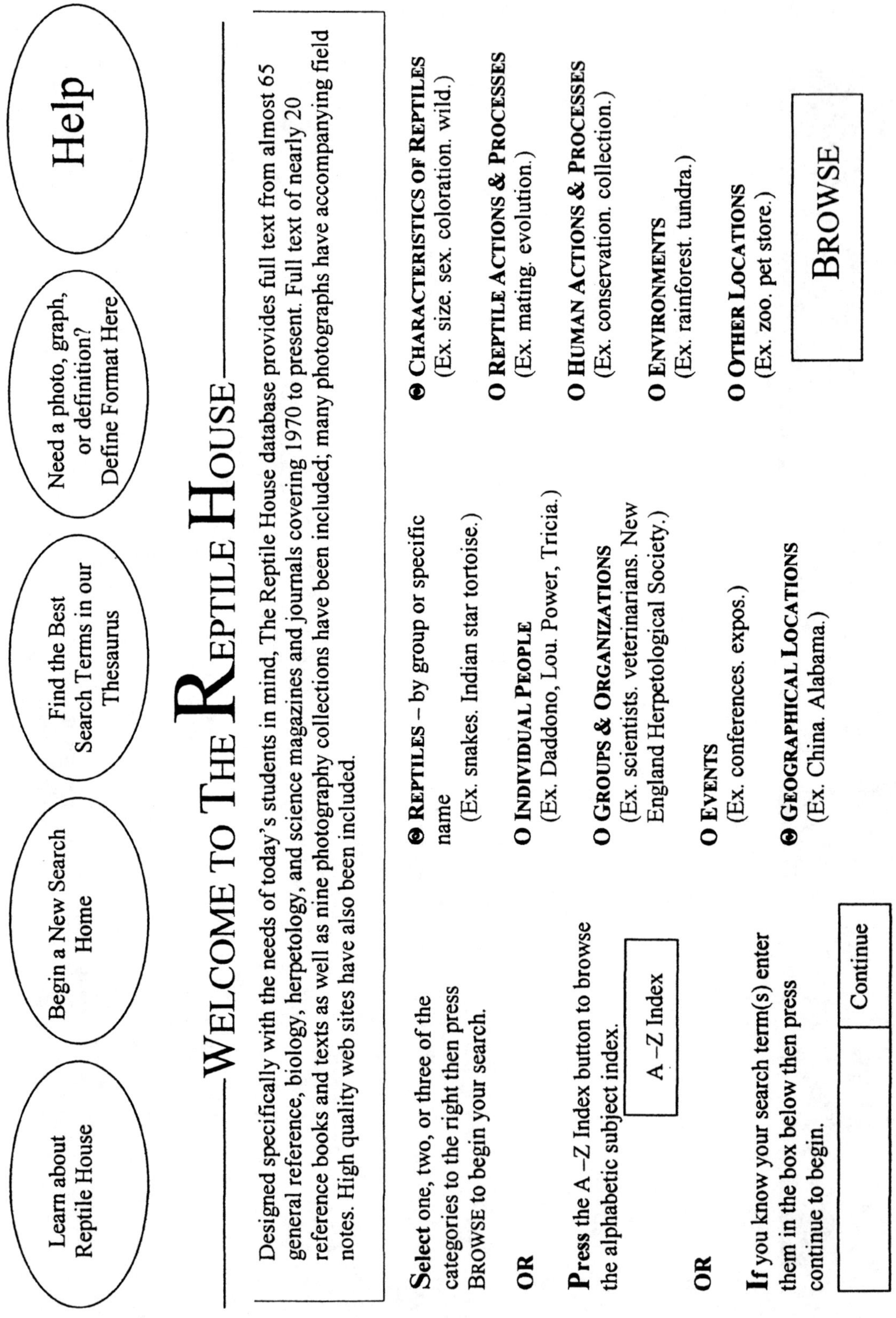

Chapter 19. Search Interface (Section 19.4)

(Learn about Reptile House) (Begin a New Search Home) (Find the Best Search Terms in our Thesaurus) (Need a photo, graph, or definition? Define Format Here) (Help)

WELCOME TO THE REPTILE HOUSE

Designed specifically with the needs of today's students in mind, The Reptile House database provides full text from almost 65 general reference, biology, herpetology, and science magazines and journals covering 1970 to present. Full text of nearly 20 reference books and texts as well as nine photography collections have been included; many photographs have accompanying field notes. High quality web sites have also been included.

Select one, two, or three of the categories to the right then press BROWSE to begin your search.

OR

Press the A–Z Index button to browse the alphabetic subject index.

[A–Z Index]

OR

If you know your search term(s) enter them in the box below then press continue to begin.

[   ]

[Continue]

- ◉ **REPTILES** – by group or specific name
  (Ex. snakes. Indian star tortoise.)
- ○ **INDIVIDUAL PEOPLE**
  (Ex. Daddono, Lou. Power, Tricia.)
- ○ **GROUPS & ORGANIZATIONS**
  (Ex. scientists. veterinarians. New England Herpetological Society.)
- ○ **EVENTS**
  (Ex. conferences. expos.)
- ◉ **GEOGRAPHICAL LOCATIONS**
  (Ex. China. Alabama.)
- ◉ **CHARACTERISTICS OF REPTILES**
  (Ex. size. sex. coloration. wild.)
- ○ **REPTILE ACTIONS & PROCESSES**
  (Ex. mating. evolution.)
- ○ **HUMAN ACTIONS & PROCESSES**
  (Ex. conservation. collection.)
- ○ **ENVIRONMENTS**
  (Ex. rainforest. tundra.)
- ○ **OTHER LOCATIONS**
  (Ex. zoo. pet store.)

[BROWSE]

Figure 19.8. Opening page for "Reptile House" database by Enola Romano (2000).

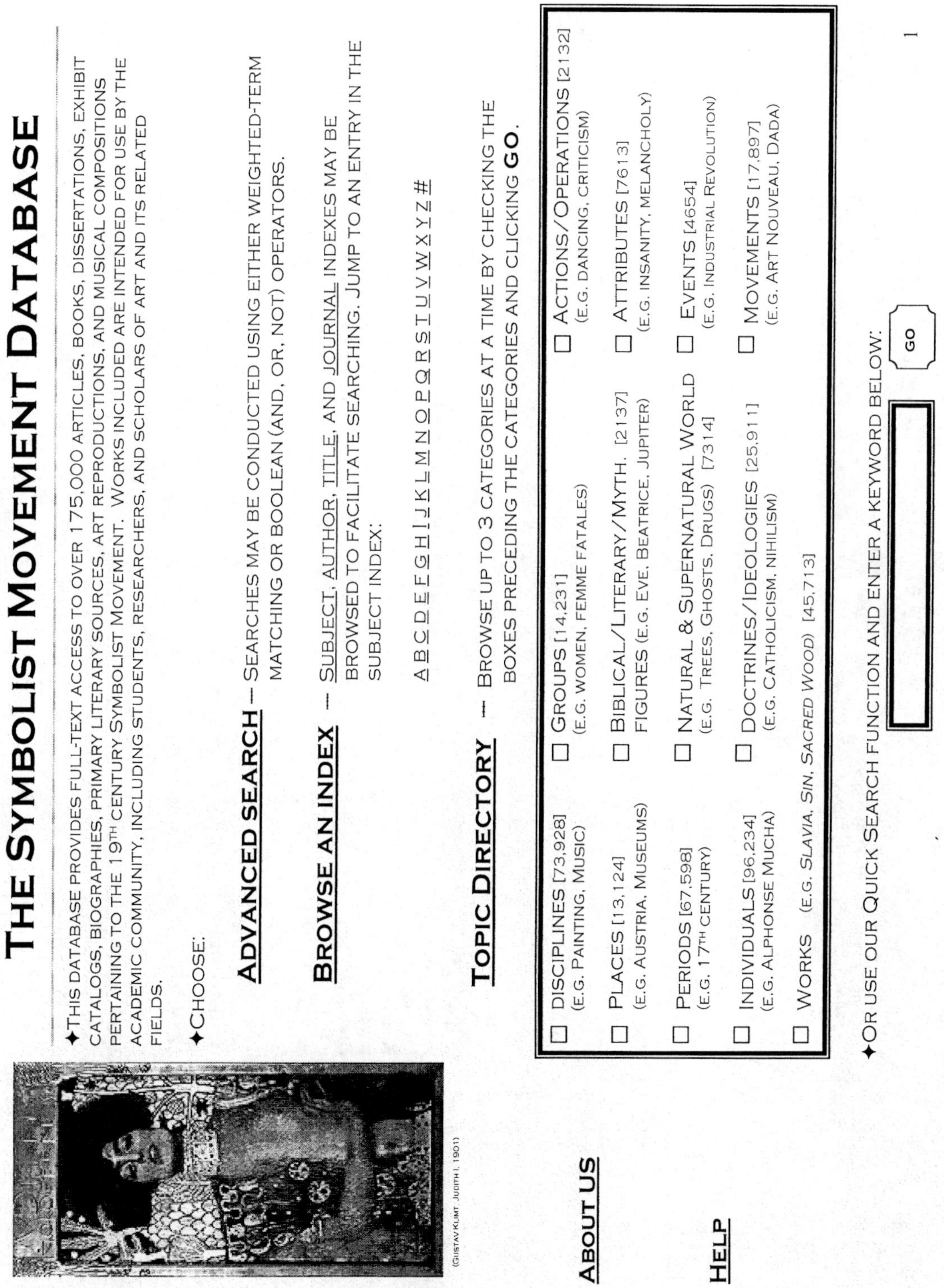

Chapter 19. Search Interface (Section 19.4)

WELCOME TO
THE SYMBOLIST MOVEMENT DATABASE

♦ THIS DATABASE PROVIDES FULL-TEXT ACCESS TO OVER 175,000 ARTICLES, BOOKS, DISSERTATIONS, EXHIBIT CATALOGS, BIOGRAPHIES, PRIMARY LITERARY SOURCES, ART REPRODUCTIONS, AND MUSICAL COMPOSITIONS PERTAINING TO THE 19TH CENTURY SYMBOLIST MOVEMENT. WORKS INCLUDED ARE INTENDED FOR USE BY THE ACADEMIC COMMUNITY, INCLUDING STUDENTS, RESEARCHERS, AND SCHOLARS OF ART AND ITS RELATED FIELDS.

♦ CHOOSE:

ADVANCED SEARCH — SEARCHES MAY BE CONDUCTED USING EITHER WEIGHTED-TERM MATCHING OR BOOLEAN (AND, OR, NOT) OPERATORS.

BROWSE AN INDEX — SUBJECT, AUTHOR, TITLE, AND JOURNAL INDEXES MAY BE BROWSED TO FACILITATE SEARCHING. JUMP TO AN ENTRY IN THE SUBJECT INDEX:

A B C D E F G H I J K L M N O P Q R S T U V W X Y Z #

TOPIC DIRECTORY — BROWSE UP TO 3 CATEGORIES AT A TIME BY CHECKING THE BOXES PRECEDING THE CATEGORIES AND CLICKING **GO**.

☐ DISCIPLINES [73,928] (E.G. PAINTING, MUSIC)
☐ PLACES [13,124] (E.G. AUSTRIA, MUSEUMS)
☐ PERIODS [67,598] (E.G. 17TH CENTURY)
☐ INDIVIDUALS [96,234] (E.G. ALPHONSE MUCHA)
☐ WORKS (E.G. SLAVIA, SIN, SACRED WOOD) [45,713]
☐ GROUPS [14,231] (E.G. WOMEN, FEMME FATALES)
☐ BIBLICAL/LITERARY/MYTH. [2137] FIGURES (E.G. EVE, BEATRICE, JUPITER)
☐ NATURAL & SUPERNATURAL WORLD (E.G. TREES, GHOSTS, DRUGS) [7314]
☐ DOCTRINES/IDEOLOGIES [25,911] (E.G. CATHOLICISM, NIHILISM)
☐ ACTIONS/OPERATIONS [2132] (E.G. DANCING, CRITICISM)
☐ ATTRIBUTES [7613] (E.G. INSANITY, MELANCHOLY)
☐ EVENTS [4654] (E.G. INDUSTRIAL REVOLUTION)
☐ MOVEMENTS [17,897] (E.G. ART NOUVEAU, DADA)

[GO]

♦ OR USE OUR QUICK SEARCH FUNCTION AND ENTER A KEYWORD BELOW:

(GUSTAV KLIMT, JUDITH, 1901)

ABOUT US

HELP

Figure 19.9. Opening screen for "Symbolist Movement" Database by Elizabeth Pregill (2001).

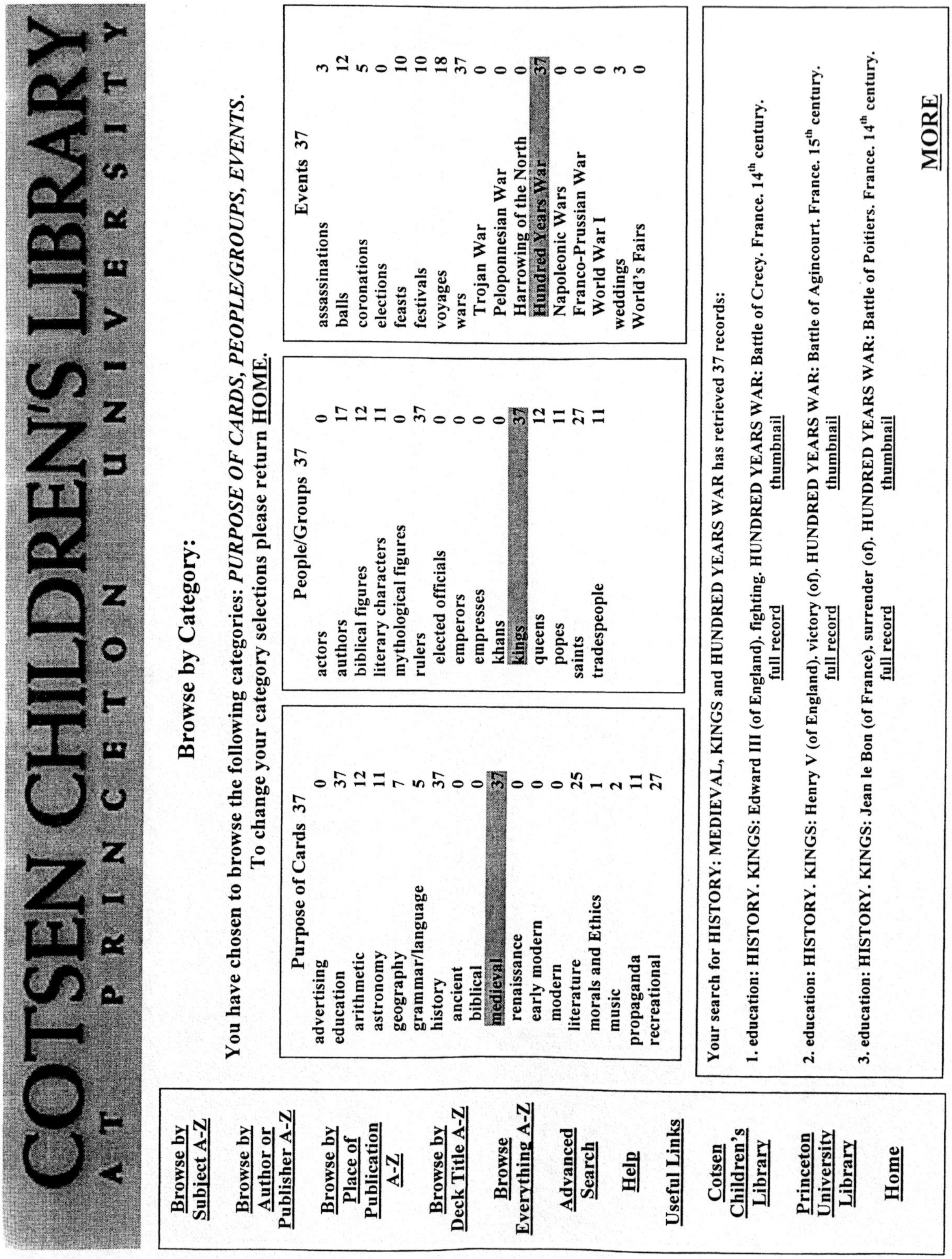

Chapter 19. Search Interface (Section 19.4)

Figure 19.10. Browsable facets for historical playing cards (Eric J. Johnson, 2003).

Chapter 19. Search Interface (Section 19.4)

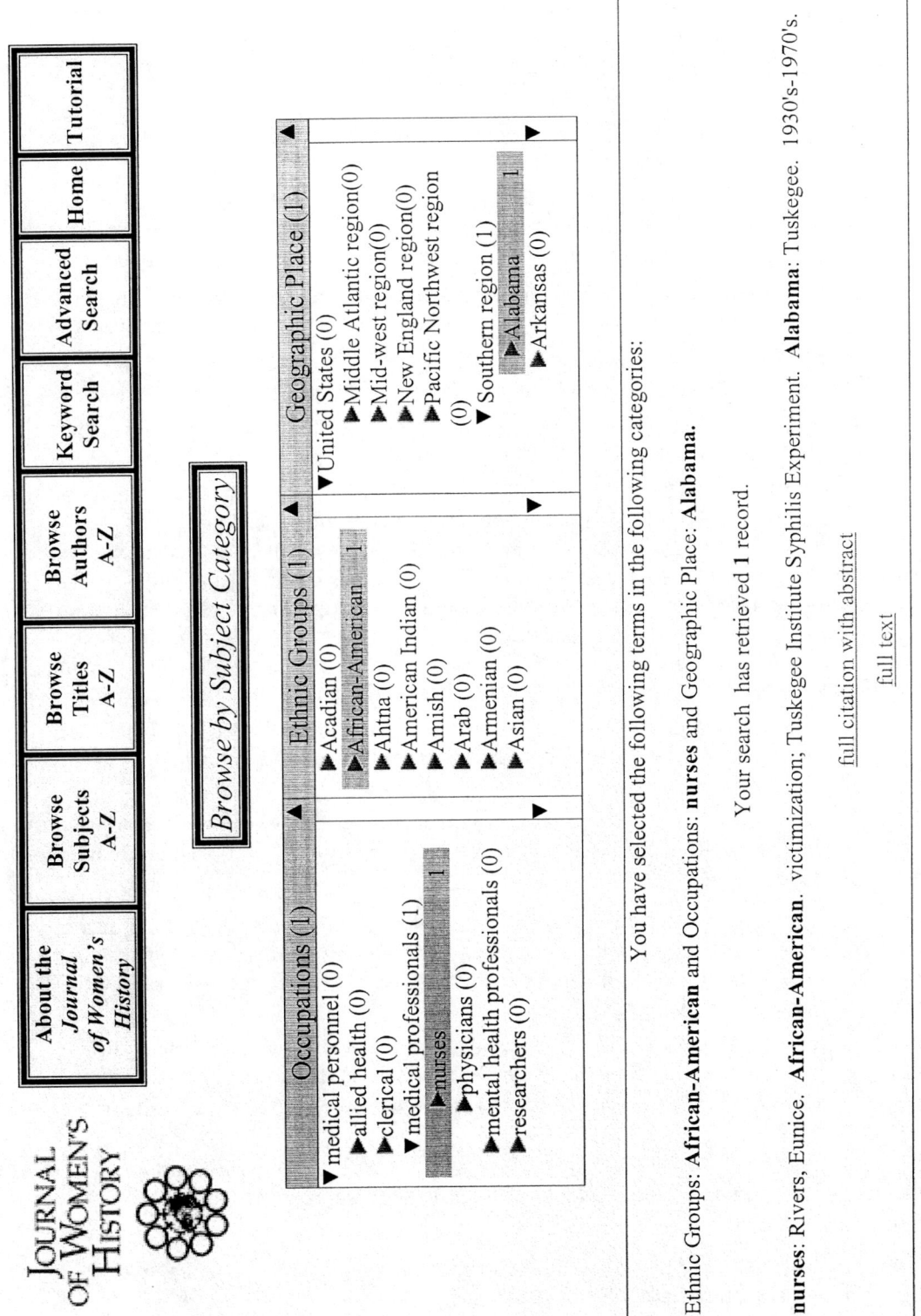

Figure 19.11. Browsable facets for women's history (Lori A. Rowland, 2003).

Chapter 19. Search Interface (Section 19.4)

• design features for display of browsable alphanumeric indexes : 74

c. The alphanumeric subject index browse page. If users select the option to browse the alphanumeric subject index, they come to this page. Similar pages will support browsing of other alphanumeric indexes for such features as authors, titles, formats, media, etc. The display of alphanumeric indexes in hypertext was discussed in section 17.2.

c.1. Alphanumeric indexes can be quite large, so scrolling cannot be avoided, but it can be facilitated with various browsing techniques, such as:

c.1.1. The option to move immediately to entries beginning with letters or numbers typed on a keyboard, so that if users type "n" the index pointer moves immediately to the beginning of the "N" entries; if they type "na," the pointer moves immediately to the "NA" entries, and so on.

c.1.2. The option to perform a string search within the index, to find each successive heading containing a string of characters of interest, e.g., a string search on "language" would take users to each successive heading containing the word "language," such as "natural language processing."

c.1.3. A scroll bar, to facilitate rapid movement up and down the index.

c.1.4. A fish-eye display, in which the entire index is visible, but only the portion of direct interest is actually readable (Bederson 2000).

c.2. The index should be displayed as described in section 17.2 on the display of alphanumeric indexes in hypertext. In the opening display, only the lead terms of index headings are displayed. As soon as a term is selected, users should be shown the subheadings that fall under that lead term and vocabulary information for the lead term. The subheadings can consist of full or partial strings of descriptors assigned to messages, accompanied with postings data if they refer to more than one message, or, if they indicate a single message, with options to move immediately to a fuller surrogate or full text. If more than one message is indicated, then the next display could include fuller surrogates, to include such features as authors and titles and/or brief summary.

Vocabulary information should display options for related, broader or narrower terms that users might prefer. By selecting any such term, the index display should move immediately to that term.

• examples of display of browsable alphanumeric indexes : 75

Figures 19.12-19.13 illustrate the display of browsable alphanumeric indexes in IR database designs by Rutgers students:

Figure 19.12 illustrates a browsable alphanumeric index in Eric J. Johnson's design for a historical playing cards database. As soon as the user selects the lead term "kings," vocabulary management information is displayed beneath that term, and brief surrogates for possibly relevant records and cards are displayed to the right.

Figure 19.13 illustrates a browsable alphanumeric index in Lori A. Rowland's women's history IR database design. As in figure 19.12, as soon as the user selects the lead term "social work," vocabulary information for that term is displayed, and brief surrogates for results are displayed to the right.

• design features for electronic searches : 76

d. The electronic search page. Users selecting the advanced search option would come here. They would be offered such options as:

d.1. Selecting searchable features by which to limit or focus a search, such as authors, titles, controlled topical vocabulary, languages, formats, media, etc.

d.2. Changing the search algorithm, e.g., changing from a default algorithm, such as best match (weighted term, vector space, probabilistic) to exact match (boolean), as described in sections 8.3 and 12.3.

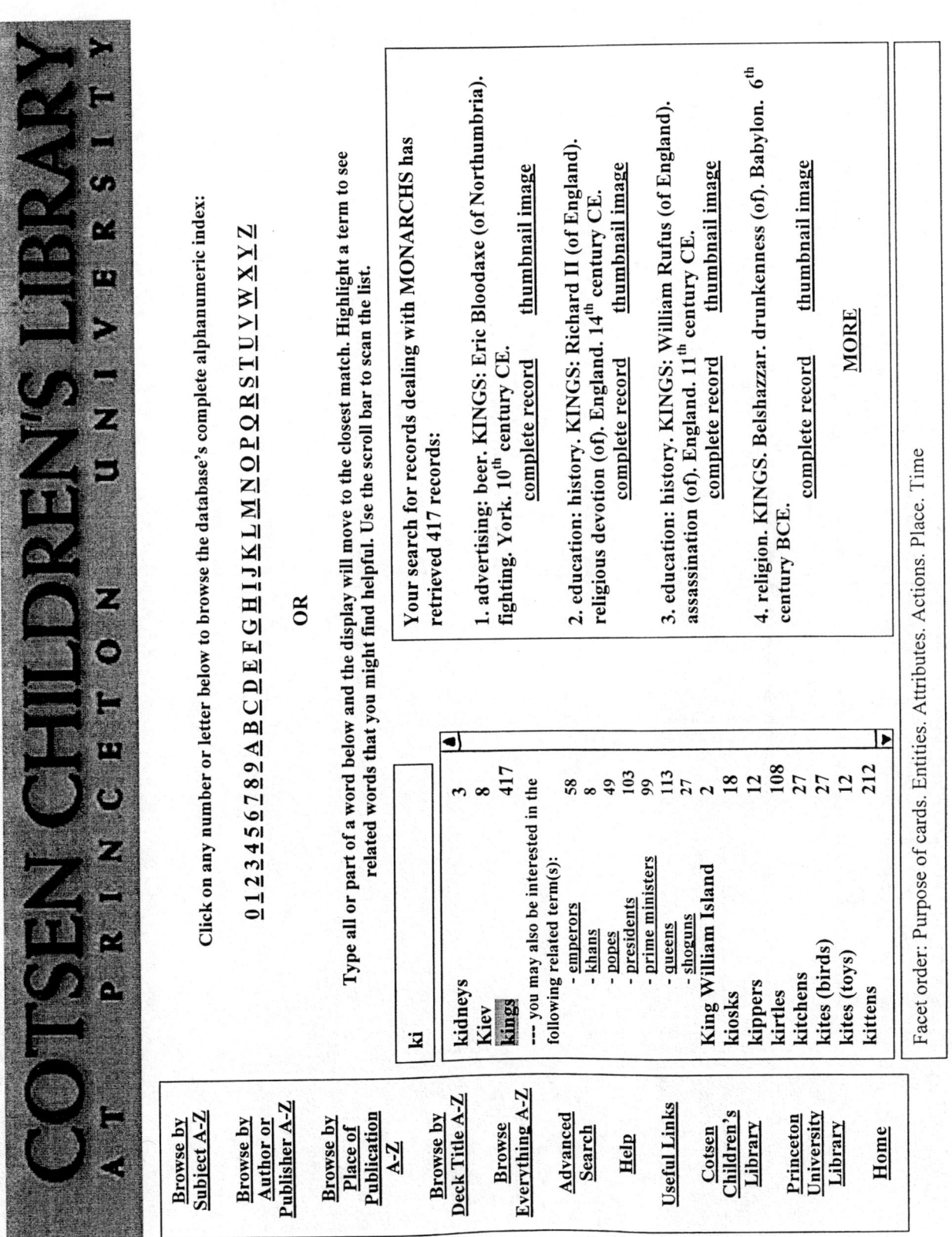

Figure 19.12. Browsable alphanumeric index for historical playing cards (Eric J. Johnson, 2003).

Chapter 19. Search Interface (Section 19.4)

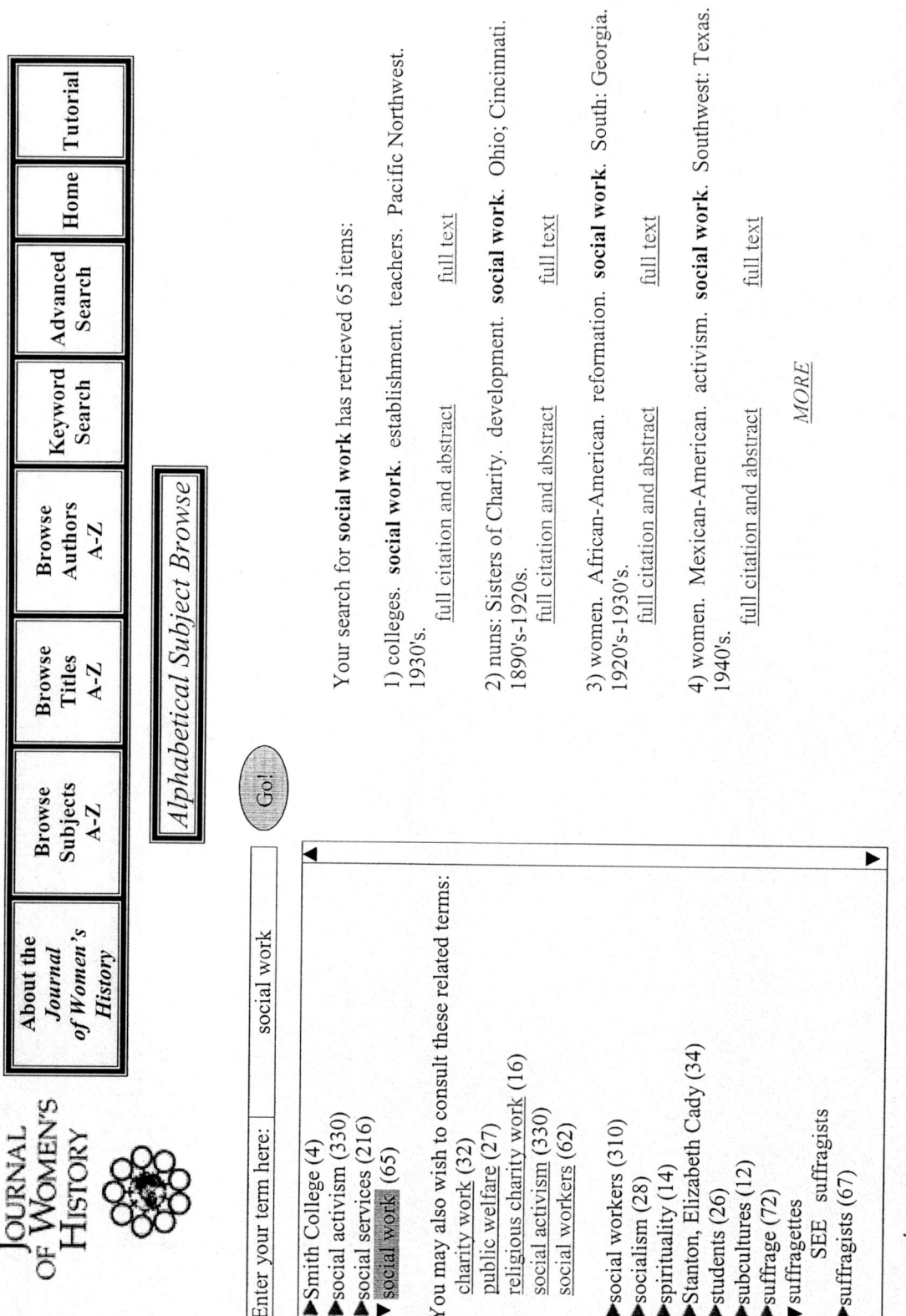

Figure 19.13. Browsable alphanumeric index for women's history (Lori A. Rowland, 2003).

Chapter 19. Search Interface (Section 19.4)

d.3. Additional search features: stemming (selecting various stemming algorithms), truncation, weighting, proximity criteria, etc. (sections 8.3, 12.3).

d.4. Changing the default display of retrieved matches, e.g., from a ranked list based on predicted relevance to classified or alphabetical by topic headings, or by author, or by title, or by date, etc. Changing default brief surrogate to fuller surrogate, etc. (See chapter 16 on surrogate displays).

• examples of options for electronic searches : 77

Figures 19.14-19.15 illustrate interface displays for advanced electronic searches in IR database designs by Rutgers students:

Figure 19.14 illustrates advanced electronic search options in Eric J. Johnson's design for a historical playing cards database.

Figure 19.15 illustrates similar options in Lori A. Rowland's women's history IR database design.

• design features for display of electronic search results;
for display of vocabulary information for electronic searches : 78

e. Electronic search results page. Here results from an electronic search are displayed, but also vocabulary suggestions are offered for possible search modification.

e.1. Users are provided immediate feedback on their search, with displays of brief surrogates, with options to move directly to fuller surrogates and/or full-text. For each retrieved message, they may have the option to find "more like this." A clustering algorithm would seek other documentary units with similar characteristics related to the initial search. Thus, for a topical search, index terms and highly weighted key words or phrases could be used. In addition, reference citations could be considered, as in bibliographic coupling or co-citation. In the spirit of customization, advanced users could be given the option of choosing attributes to consider. (See section 8.3.11.)

e.2. Users are also provided with vocabulary options, in case they want to refine their search:

e.2.1. For each term in the search statement users are shown any available vocabulary information, such as: related terms (based on thesaural relationships or co-occurrence clustering), narrower terms, and/or broader terms. For each of these new terms, users have the option to add it to the search statement, or to explore additional terms associated with the new term. How all this is presented clearly is a design challenge!

e.2.2. If users choose to add additional terms to their search statement, they also must be able to delete or edit previous terms.

• examples of display of electronic search results;
of vocabulary information for electronic searches : 79

Figures 19.16-19.17 illustrate the display of results from advanced electronic searches, along with vocabulary assistance, in IR database designs by Rutgers students:

Figure 19.16 illustrates the display of results (on the left) and vocabulary assistance (on the right) in Eric J. Johnson's design for a historical playing cards database. Users have the option of exploring additional search terms related to each of their original search terms, then adding new terms to the search statement and/or deleting any of the original terms.

Figure 19.17 illustrates the display of results (at the top) and vocabulary assistance (at the bottom) in Lori A. Rowland's women's history IR database design. Vocabulary assistance options are similar to those in figure 19.16.

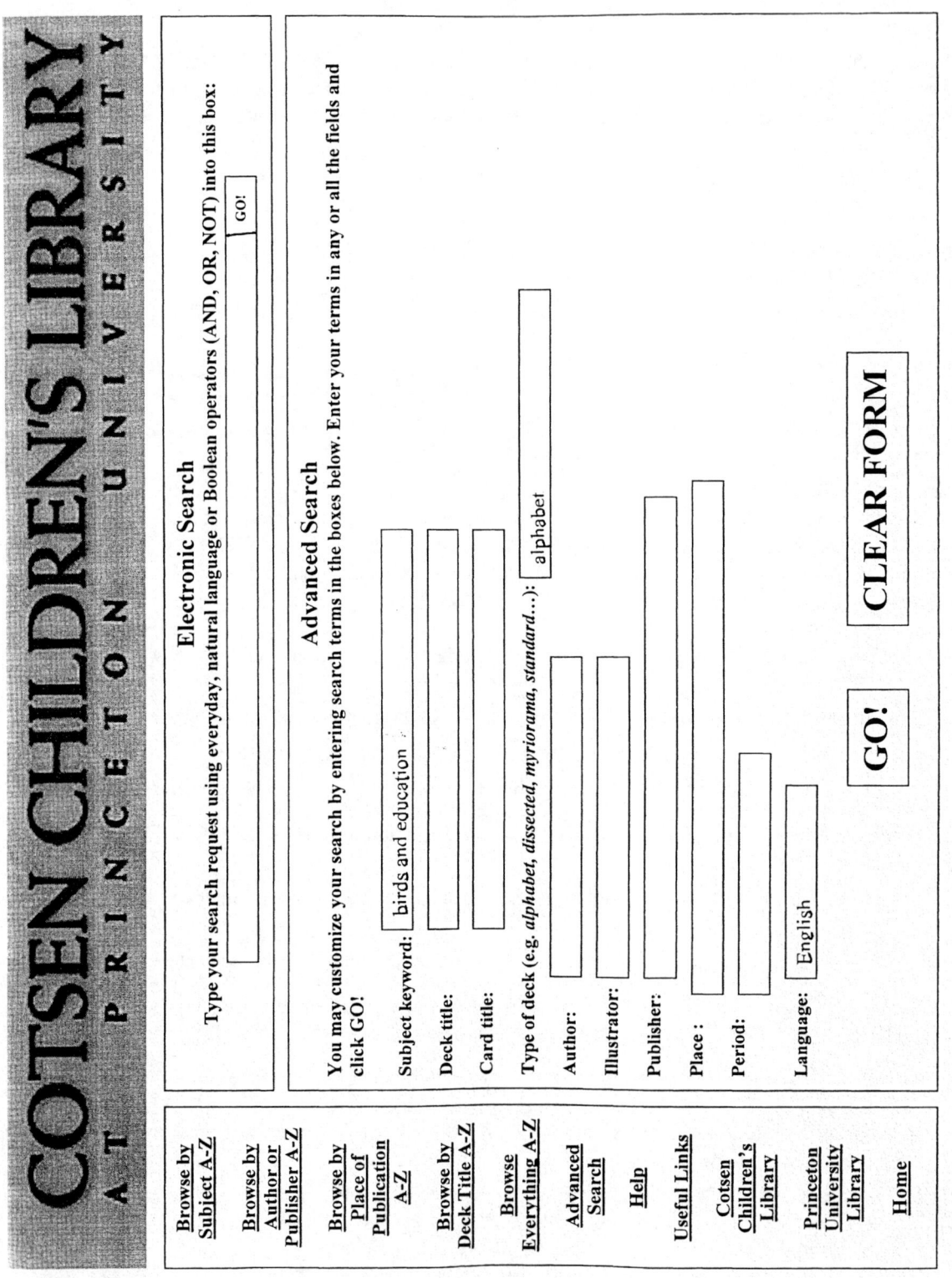

Figure 19.14. Advanced electronic search options for historical playing cards (Eric J. Johnson).

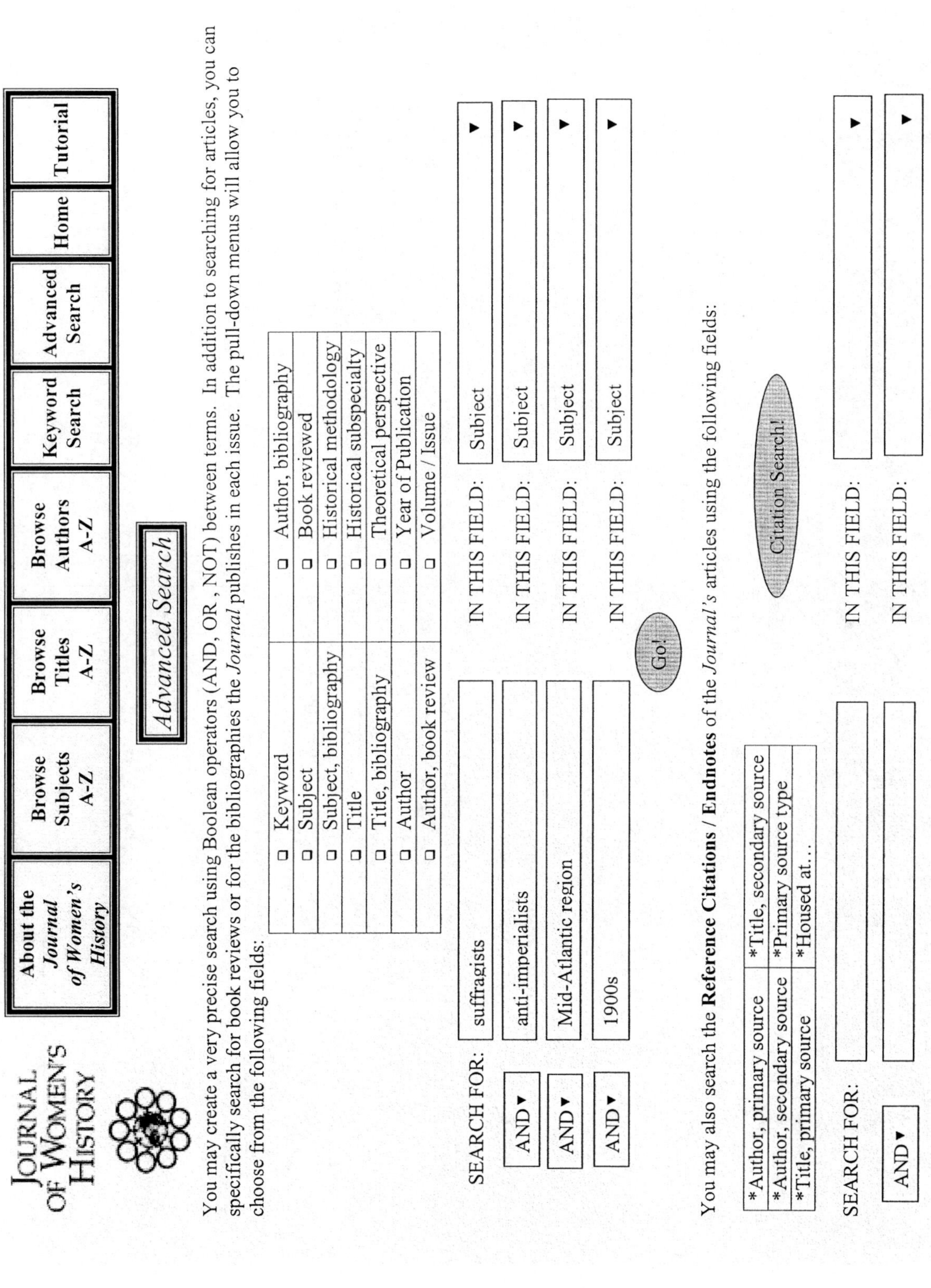

Chapter 19. Search Interface (Section 19.4)

| About the *Journal of Women's History* | Browse Subjects A-Z | Browse Titles A-Z | Browse Authors A-Z | Keyword Search | Advanced Search | Home | Tutorial |

JOURNAL OF WOMEN'S HISTORY

Advanced Search

You may create a very precise search using Boolean operators (AND, OR, NOT) between terms. In addition to searching for articles, you can specifically search for book reviews or for the bibliographies the *Journal* publishes in each issue. The pull-down menus will allow you to choose from the following fields:

☐ Keyword	☐ Author, bibliography
☐ Subject	☐ Book reviewed
☐ Subject, bibliography	☐ Historical methodology
☐ Title	☐ Historical subspecialty
☐ Title, bibliography	☐ Theoretical perspective
☐ Author	☐ Year of Publication
☐ Author, book review	☐ Volume / Issue

SEARCH FOR: | suffragists | IN THIS FIELD: | Subject ▼
AND ▼ | anti-imperialists | IN THIS FIELD: | Subject ▼
AND ▼ | Mid-Atlantic region | IN THIS FIELD: | Subject ▼
AND ▼ | 1900s | IN THIS FIELD: | Subject ▼

Go!

You may also search the **Reference Citations** / **Endnotes** of the *Journal's* articles using the following fields:

*Author, primary source	*Title, secondary source
*Author, secondary source	*Primary source type
*Title, primary source	*Housed at…

Citation Search!

SEARCH FOR: | | IN THIS FIELD: | ▼
AND ▼ | | IN THIS FIELD: | ▼

Figure 19.15. Advanced electronic search options for women's history (Lori A. Rowland).

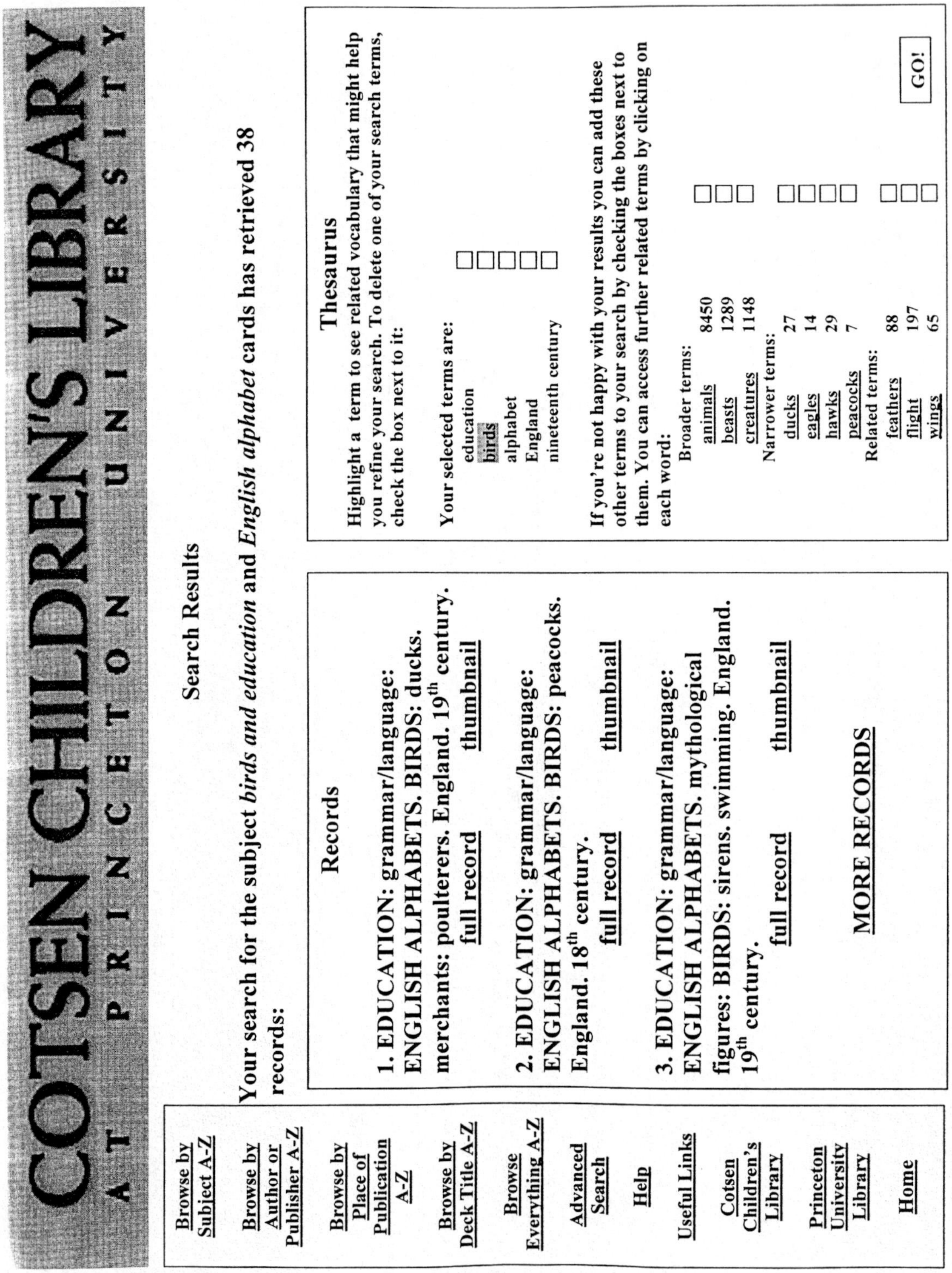

Chapter 19. Search Interface (Section 19.4)

COTSEN CHILDREN'S LIBRARY
AT PRINCETON UNIVERSITY

Browse by Subject A-Z

Browse by Author or Publisher A-Z

Browse by Place of Publication A-Z

Browse by Deck Title A-Z

Browse Everything A-Z

Advanced Search

Help

Useful Links

Cotsen Children's Library

Princeton University Library

Home

Search Results

Your search for the subject *birds and education* and *English alphabet* cards has retrieved 38 records:

Records

1. EDUCATION: grammar/language: ENGLISH ALPHABETS. BIRDS: ducks. merchants: poulterers. England. 19th century.
   full record   thumbnail

2. EDUCATION: grammar/language: ENGLISH ALPHABETS. BIRDS: peacocks. England. 18th century.
   full record   thumbnail

3. EDUCATION: grammar/language: ENGLISH ALPHABETS. mythological figures: BIRDS: sirens. swimming. England. 19th century.
   full record   thumbnail

MORE RECORDS

Thesaurus

Highlight a term to see related vocabulary that might help you refine your search. To delete one of your search terms, check the box next to it:

Your selected terms are:
    education ☐
    <u>birds</u> ☐
    alphabet ☐
    England ☐
    nineteenth century ☐

If you're not happy with your results you can add these other terms to your search by checking the boxes next to them. You can access further related terms by clicking on each word:

Broader terms:
    <u>animals</u> 8450 ☐
    <u>beasts</u> 1289 ☐
    <u>creatures</u> 1148 ☐
Narrower terms:
    <u>ducks</u> 27 ☐
    <u>eagles</u> 14 ☐
    <u>hawks</u> 29 ☐
    <u>peacocks</u> 7 ☐
Related terms:
    <u>feathers</u> 88 ☐
    <u>flight</u> 197 ☐
    <u>wings</u> 65 ☐

GO!

Figure 19.16. Advanced electronic search results and vocabulary assistance for historical playing cards (Eric J. Johnson, 2003)

Chapter 19. Search Interface (Section 19.4)

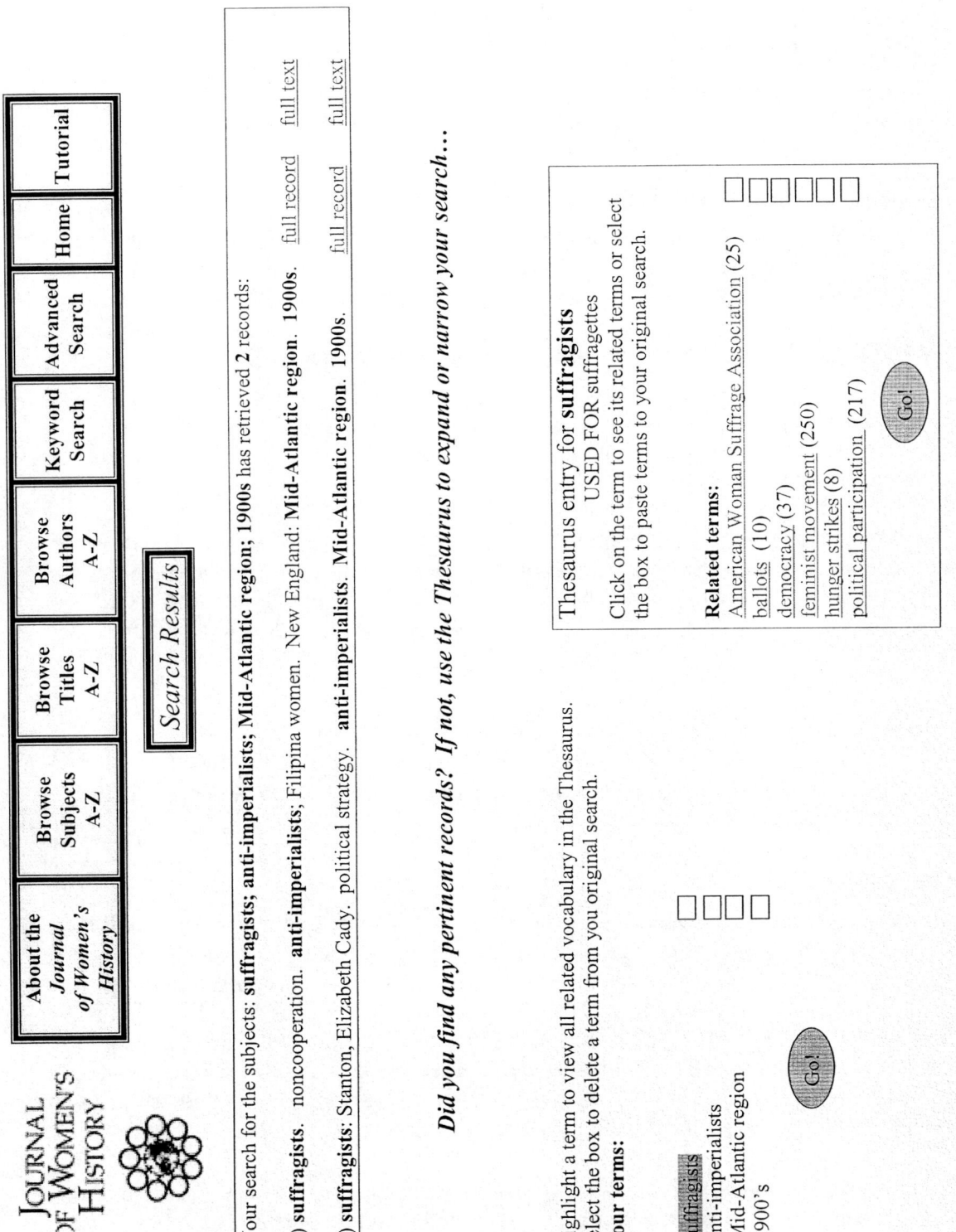

Figure 19.17. Advanced electronic search results and vocabulary assistance for women's history (Lori A. Rowland, 2003).

Chapter 19. Search Interface (Section 19.4.1)

• design features for surrogate displays : 80

f. Surrogate displays. An IR database needs a minimum of two surrogate displays, one very brief, and one full. Many IR databases will also provide options for intermediate displays, e.g., including a citation and brief summary, as opposed to a full abstract with index terms. Examples of brief surrogates are displayed in figures 19.10-19.17.

f.1. As described in chapter 16 on surrogate displays, each surrogate should be tailored to the type of search. Thus, the briefest displays for a topical search should consist of topical information, such as index headings, as opposed to authors or title. On the other hand, authors should be included in the briefest display for an author search.

f.2. Similarly, the arrangement of information in fuller surrogates should also relate to the kind of search, so that for a topical search, topical information (indexing terms or heading, brief summary, abstract) will precede non-topical information, such as authors, title, citation.

• examples of surrogate displays : 81

Figures 19.18-19.19 illustrate the display of full surrogates in IR database designs by Rutgers students:

Figure 19.18 illustrates the display of a full surrogate in Eric J. Johnson's design for a historical playing cards database. Note that topical information is displayed first in the form of a string of topical descriptors, then an abstract. This is because this surrogate was retrieved in a topical search.

Figure 19.19 illustrates the display of a full surrogate in Lori A. Rowland's women's history IR database design. As in figure 19.18, topical information is provided first (a string of descriptors, then an abstract), because this surrogate was retrieved in a topical search. In an author search, the first element displayed should be the author, followed by the title and other document information.

19.4.1. A Book Index.

• 82

Our book index can be presented in both print-on-paper and electronic digital hypertext media.

• interface designs for book indexes in print media : 83

a. Print-on-paper edition.

The presentation of indexes in the print-on-paper book will be quite traditional. There will be three tables of contents — the first a brief overview displaying only chapter titles, the second adding brief narrative summaries of each chapter, and the third listing all chapter subheadings. A separate list of figures will also be provided. The body of the book will consist of the main text, followed by the glossary, the bibliography, and finally the alphabetical index. The bibliography will serve as an index to discussions of topics related to cited works. Citations will be listed in alphabetical order (by personal or corporate author, or title if there is no author), and each citation will conclude with references to the sections where the work is cited and discussed.

• 84

The alphanumeric index will look fairly traditional as well, except that we will use special boxes to enclose "see-also" references, with wording designed to indicate that the headings listed within the box are merely optional suggestions to consider, not commands to go elsewhere. We will make a special effort to avoid entries devoid of context (i.e., headings consisting of only one term), and also too many identical entries (headings with many locators listed after them).

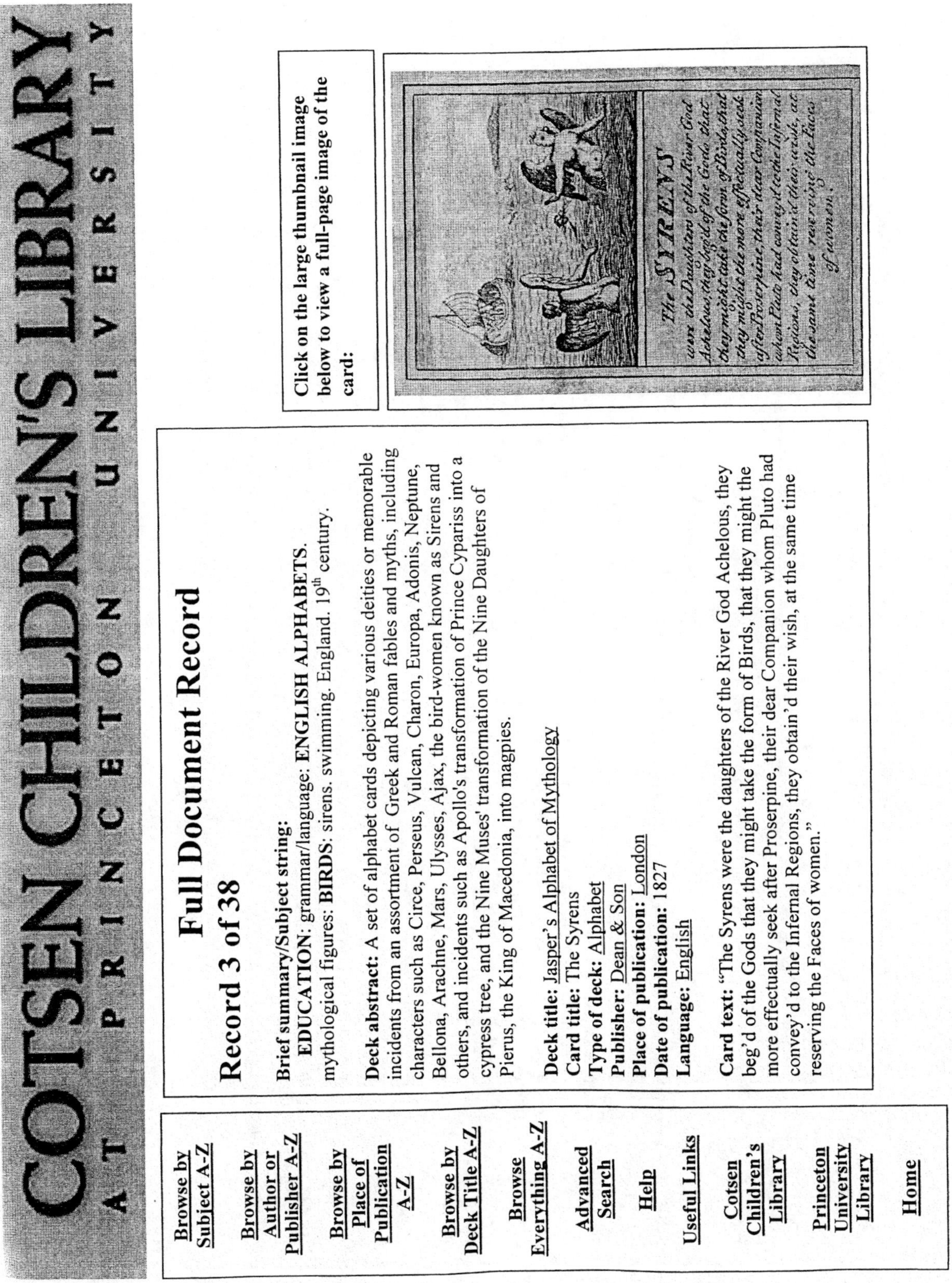

Chapter 19. Search Interface (Section 19.4.1)

COTSEN CHILDREN'S LIBRARY AT PRINCETON UNIVERSITY

Full Document Record

Record 3 of 38

Click on the large thumbnail image below to view a full-page image of the card:

Brief summary/Subject string:
EDUCATION: grammar/language: ENGLISH ALPHABETS. mythological figures: BIRDS: sirens. swimming. England. 19th century.

Deck abstract: A set of alphabet cards depicting various deities or memorable incidents from an assortment of Greek and Roman fables and myths, including characters such as Circe, Perseus, Vulcan, Charon, Europa, Adonis, Neptune, Bellona, Arachne, Mars, Ulysses, Ajax, the bird-women known as Sirens and others, and incidents such as Apollo's transformation of Prince Cypariss into a cypress tree, and the Nine Muses' transformation of the Nine Daughters of Pierus, the King of Macedonia, into magpies.

Deck title: Jasper's Alphabet of Mythology
Card title: The Syrens
Type of deck: Alphabet
Publisher: Dean & Son
Place of publication: London
Date of publication: 1827
Language: English

Card text: "The Syrens were the daughters of the River God Achelous, they beg'd of the Gods that they might take the form of Birds, that they might the more effectually seek after Proserpine, their dear Companion whom Pluto had convey'd to the Infernal Regions, they obtain'd their wish, at the same time reserving the Faces of women."

Browse by Subject A-Z
Browse by Author or Publisher A-Z
Browse by Place of Publication A-Z
Browse by Deck Title A-Z
Browse Everything A-Z
Advanced Search
Help
Useful Links
Cotsen Children's Library
Princeton University Library
Home

Figure 19.18. A full surrogate in a historical playing cards IR database (Eric J. Johnson, 2003).

Chapter 19. Search Interface (Section 19.4.1)

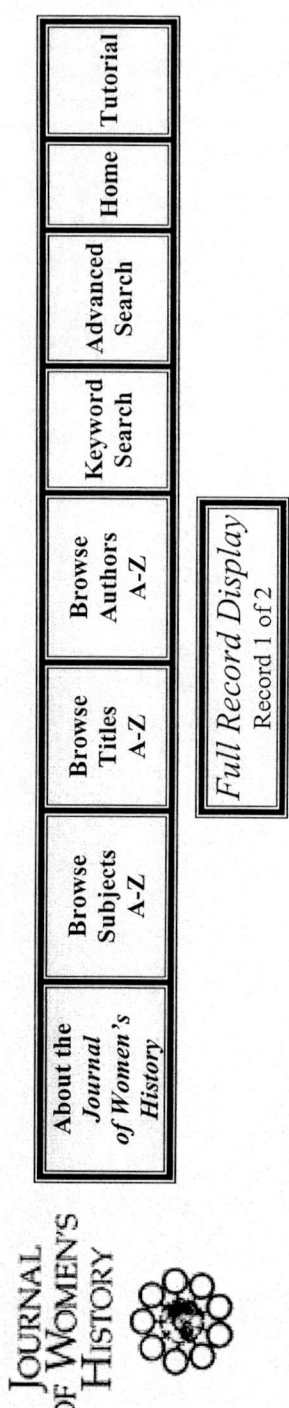

Figure 19.19. A full surrogate in a women's history IR database (Lori A. Rowland, 2003).

Chapter 19. Search Interface (Section 19.4.1)

• locators for documentary units in book indexes : 85

As we specified in section 6.5.1 on documentary units, our index entries will be linked to paragraphs, rather than pages. In addition, index headings will be placed at the right margin of text pages, next to their documentary units to act as glosses on the text of the paragraph. These glosses are meant to facilitate browsing for topics. Some index headings will lead to sections and to entire chapters as well.

• 86

Thus the printed book would provide "unified displays" of documentary units, complete with index terms (see chapter 16 on surrogate displays).

• interface designs for book indexes in electronic media : 87

b. The electronic edition.

Our electronic book could open with a welcoming screen that might look something like this type-script diagram. (Simple type-script or even pen and pencil diagrams can be used to convey essential design aspects to professional graphic and web-page designers):

```
=========================================================================
[help] [table of contents] [alphabetical index] [advanced search] [the authors]

INFORMATION RETRIEVAL DESIGN: Principles and Options for Information
Description, Organization, Display, and Access in Information Retrieval
Databases, Digital Libraries, Catalogs, and Indexes       _____
by James D. Anderson & José Pérez-Carballo (c) 2004      |_____|
                                                          [Keyword SEARCH!]

     Prefatory material                  Displayed versus non-displayed
     Introduction/background                         indexes
         Standards                       Syntax
         Types of databases              Vocabulary management
     Design principles/options           Surrogation
         Documentary scope               Surrogate displays
         Subject scope & domain          Locators
         Documentary domain              Arrangement of displayed indexes
         Display media                   Size of displayed indexes
         Documentary units               Search interface
         Indexable matter                Record format
         Analysis & indexing methods     Full-text display
         Exhaustivity                    Implementation/evaluation
         Specificity                     Glossary
=========================================================================
```

• 88

The options across the top of the screen will take the user directly to:

• help screens for persons wanting details about how the electronic book and its indexes work.

• a full table of contents, with all subdivisions under the main headings that are listed on the opening screen. Users may scroll down this full table of contents, or may do keyword searches. By clicking on a heading, they will go to the beginning of the text in the selected section.

• the alphabetical index, which will be presented in stages, first with the display of main headings, then with subheadings and vocabulary guidance, with options to move directly to the text associated with particular headings (see section 17.2).

• an electronic search interface for advanced searches of the full text.

• information about the authors!

Chapter 19. Search Interface (Section 19.4.2)

• 89

Users who choose an electronic search may have their results displayed either in rank order of predicted relevance, or according to the detailed table of contents, which serves as a relational classification of the topics in the book.

• 90

Users who click on any of the categories displayed on the opening screen will go a table of contents for its chapter or section. There, they can select documentary units of interest, either beginning at the top of the chapter or with any section within the chapter.

19.4.2. An Indexing and Abstracting Service.

• 91

Our indexing and abstracting service also comes in both print-on-paper and electronic media.

• interface designs for indexing and abstracting services in print media : 92

a. The print version.

The print format will be fairly traditional, at least in outward appearance.

• 93

A summary table of contents will list the following sections:

• A classification of library and information science. This relational classification is used to arrange the abstracts of documents judged to be most important. (See section 17.3.2 for a description of this classification.)

• Alphabetical subject index to important documents. This index leads users to the most important abstracts in the previous section.

• Other abstracts. The documents represented in this section receive only automatic indexing based on titles and abstracts. Their surrogates are arranged alphabetically by author. There are see-also references under authors for documents included in the "important abstracts" section. The surrogates consist of full bibliographic citations and abstracts (when available), but no index entries, because the automatically generated keyword-in-context index is based directly on the titles and abstracts.

• Alphabetical keyword-in-context (KWIC) index to all abstracts. (See an example of this index in section 12.4.2.)

• interface designs for indexing and abstracting services in electronic media : 94

b. The electronic version.

The opening screen for our electronic indexing and abstracting service might look something like this (illustrated in a preliminary version, in typescript):

Chapter 19. Search Interface (Section 19.4.2)

```
===============================================================================
                [Help] [Advanced search] [Browsable subject index]
                [Author, Title, Journal indexes] [Background]
                                                 _____
BLISTER: Bibliography of Library & Information  |                      |
Science & Technology: Evaluation & Research            [Keyword SEARCH!]

An indexing and abstracting service providing access to 20,000 scholarly & pro-
fessional journal articles, monographs, multimedia & web resources, disserta-
tions, and proceedings, 1981-2004. Choose Advanced search, Browsable subject in-
dex, Author, Title, Journal indexes, or browse detailed displays of primary cate-
gories below (Click on category boxes, then click on BROWSE CATEGORIES!):

[] Participants & Agencies (10,000:25): persons, groups, organizations,
      institutions, companies, libraries, archives.
[] Reference & Retrieval Resources (3,750:5): access resources (information
      retrieval databases, indexes, catalogs); information resources in all
      media and formats.
[] Tools & Equipment (3,000:10): computers, buildings, furniture, etc.
[] Operations, Processes & Events (11,000:10): human information behavior,
      searching, collection development, acquisition, cataloging, indexing,
      reference & information services, conservation & preservation, building
      & collection maintenance, administration & management, design,
      evaluation & research.
[] Disciplines & Related Theories (2,670:100): the sciences, applied sciences/
      technology, social sciences, history, humanities, arts, law, etc.
[] Places (2,275:0): by type; by name.
[] Times (1,225:0): by centuries, decades, years
===============================================================================
```
• 95

The options across the top of the screen will take the user directly to:

• help screens for persons wanting details about how the this A&I service is organized and the various access options available, and how they work.

• a full table of contents, with brief descriptions of each section and option.

• the full classification, with all subdivisions (as described in section 17.3.2. Within the classification, users can do keyword searches to find class captions containing particular words. Users can move from the classification to particular documents.

• the alphabetical index to high-use documents (described in section 12.4.2), which will be presented in stages (as described in section 17.2), first with the display of main headings, then with subheadings and vocabulary guidance, with options to move directly to abstracts and the full text associated with particular headings.

• an advanced electronic search screen.

• information about how this A&I service is compiled, including its domain; how high-use documents are selected; and how indexing and classing of high-use documents are done.

• 96

Figure 19.20 illustrates a later version of this opening page, implemented in HTML coding. It could use a quick keyword search box near the top of the screen!

Chapter 19. Search Interface (Section 19.4.2)

| Help | Keyword search | Browsable subject index | Author, Title, Journal indexes | Background |

BLISTER: Bibliography of Library & Information Science & Technology: Evaluation & Research

An indexing and abstracting service providing access to 200,000 scholarly & professional journal articles, monographs, multimedia & web resources, dissertations, and proceedings, 1981-2004. Choose Keyword search, Browsable subject index, Author, Title, Journal indexes, or browse detailed displays of primary categories listed below (highlight category headings, then click Browse Categories:

Participants & Agencies	Reference & Retrieval Resources	Tools & Equipment	Operations, Processes & Events	Disciplines & Related Theories
persons, groups, organizations, institutions, companies, libraries, archives.	access resources (information retrieval databases, indexes, catalogs); information resources in all media and formats.	computers, buildings, furniture, etc.	human information behavior, searching, collection development, acquisition, cataloging & indexing, reference & information services, conservation & preservation, building and collection maintenance, administration & management, design, evaluation & research.	the sciences, applied sciences / technology, social sciences, history, humanities, arts, law, etc. **Places** by type; by name. **Times** by centuries, by decades, by years.

Figure 19.20. Hypothetical opening page for an indexing and abstracting service in library and information science.

Chapter 19. Search Interface (Section 19.4.3)

• 97

Users who choose an electronic search may have their results displayed in rank order of predicted relevance, or, if they choose to restrict their search to high use documents, results can be displayed according to the classification of library and information science, which serves to place retrieved documents in a broader relational context.

• 98

Users may select up to three categories displayed on the opening screen to browse simultaneously, as described in sections 13.3 and 17.3.2.

19.4.3. A Full-Text Encyclopedia/Digital Library.

• 99

Our full-text encyclopedia/digital library of library and information science comes only in electronic media. Its opening screen will look something like this (illustrated in type-script). Postings data should be added!

```
================================================================================
       [help] [authors] [alphabetical index] [Advanced search] [About WELIS]

            WELIS: WORLD ENCYCLOPEDIA OF LIBRARY AND INFORMATION SCIENCE
         A select collection of 400 articles on the world of messages, texts,
     images, media, operations, technology, people and institutions related to the
        selection, organization, storage, preservation, communication, dissemination,
              and retrieval of vital and entertaining and enlightening information.

Browse up to 3 of the categories below simultaneously,    |_____|
or browse the alphabetical index, or do a keyword search.   [Keyword SEARCH!]

[ ] messages, texts, images, media      [ ] buildings, furniture, equipment
[ ] institutions & collections          [ ] disciplines
[ ] groups and persons                  [ ] theories, research methods
[ ] tools and technology                [ ] attributes, properties
[ ] databases, indexes, catalogs,       [ ] operations, processes, events
       reference works                  [ ] places    [ ] historic periods
[ ] codes and standards                 [BROWSE CATEGORIES]
================================================================================
```

• 100

The options across the top of the screen will take the user directly to:

• help screens for persons wanting details about how the encyclopedia/digital library is organized and the various access options available, and how they work.

• an alphabetical listing of authors of encyclopedia articles. By selecting any particular author, the user will see a list of articles prepared by that author and some biographical information.

• the alphabetical index (described in section 12.4.3), which will be presented in stages (as described in section 17.2), first with the display of main headings, then with subheadings and vocabulary guidance, with options to move directly to the articles associated with particular headings.

• an electronic search screen.

• information about how this encyclopedia was compiled and is continuously updated, including the selection of topics, articles, and authors.

Chapter 19. Search Interface (Section 19.4.3)

• 101

Users who choose an electronic search may have their results displayed either in rank order of predicted relevance, or according to the classification of library and information science, which serves to place retrieved documents in a broader relational context.

• 102

Users who choose to browse up to three of the categories displayed on the opening screen will go directly to displays of the categories in columns. By selecting headings within each of the categories, they will narrow their selection of topics, with headings for relevant articles displayed in a results window. From these brief surrogates, they can go directly to articles or to parts of articles.

Chapter 20. Record Format

Contents of Chapter 20
20.1. The MARC Format for Cataloging Data.
20.2. Record Format for the *MLA International Bibliography*.
20.3. Record Format for ABC-CLIO.
20.4. Record Format for a Class IR Database.
20.5. The Dublin Core Record Format for Internal Metadata.
20.5.1. Dublin Core Qualifiers.
20.5.2. Dublin Core Example.
20.6 Other Metadata Schemas.
20.7. Our Examples.
20.7.1. A Book Index.
20.7.2. An Indexing and Abstracting Service.
20.7.3. A Full-Text Encyclopedia/Digital Library.

• 1

After the basic overall design of a IR database has been completed, or at least sketched out, an appropriate record format can be designed to contain all the important data concerning individual documentary units.

• purpose of record formats : 2

The record format defines the way that data is tagged or labeled and stored in electronic computer-readable media. Such electronic records are not generally displayed directly to end users, unless specifically requested. Rather they are used to generate the various displays that are especially designed for the end user (such as those described in chapter 16 on surrogate displays).

• principles for design of record formats : 3

The general principle to follow in setting up a record format is that every element of data that will be important for the implementation of any database display or search feature should be separately identified. Each of these elements will have a separate field (or subfield) in the record, and each of these fields will have a name or caption, which is abbreviated or represented by some type of tag, label or notation.

20.1. The MARC Format for Cataloging Data.

• definition of metadata : 4

One of the most widely used record formats for data about messages (now often sporting the fashionable name "metadata") is the MARC (MAchine-Readable Cataloging) format. The "meta" of "metadata" comes from the Greek for "along with" or "over," so literally, "metadata" is "along with" data or "over" data, which now means "data about data" or, more accurately, data about messages, texts, and documents. Until recently, there were separate MARC formats for various media and document formats, but now all these MARC formats have been integrated into a single massive format (through format integration). Still, however, there are separate versions of MARC in various countries, such as USMARC, CAN/MARC (Canada) and UKMARC (United Kingdom). "There are currently more than twenty different MARC formats, mostly identified by country .... To allow exchange between these formats an international format,

Chapter 20. Record Format (Section 20.1)

UNIMARC, was developed by the International Federation of Library Associations in 1977" (Olson & Boll 2001, p. 6).

• examples of MARC formats for books : 5

Here is a MARC record for Hans Wellisch's *Indexing from A to Z,* from the Research Libraries Information Network (RLIN), the bibliographic database of the Research Libraries Group (RLG):

```
ID:DCLC9546720-B           RTYP:c      ST:p    FRN:    MS:c  EL:     AD:10-31-95
CC:9110   BLT:am   DCF:a   CSC:        MOD:    SNR:    ATC:          UD:05-19-01
CP:nyu    L:eng    INT:    GPC:        BIO:    FIC:0   CON:b TOC:
PC:s      PD:1995/         REP:        CPI:0   FSI:0   ILC:          II:1
   010       9546720
   020       082420882X
   040       DLC$cDLC$dDLC
   050 00    Z695.9$b.W45 1995
   082 00    025.3$220
   100 1     Wellisch, Hans H.,$d1920-
   245 10    Indexing from A to Z /$cHans H. Wellisch.
   250       2nd ed., rev. and enl.
   260       New York :$bH.W. Wilson,$c1995, c1996.
   300       xxix, 569 p. ;$c23 cm.
   504       Includes bibliographical references (p. [505]-523) and index.
   650  0    Indexing.
```

• fields in MARC formats : 6

The MARC format consists of fixed fields for data of fixed length (shown across the top of the Wellisch record), and variable length fields. There are hundreds of fields and subfields. Variable length fields are labeled with a three-digit tag. Within these fields, subfields are marked with a delimiter and an alphanumeric code (a, b, c, ... or 1, 2, 3). In this display, the subfield delimiter is a "$", but the actual delimiter is a special character not found in many character sets (a vertical line with two cross-bars). The $ is used in its place in may displays. In a similar MARC display in chapter 16, the subfield delimiter is a vertical line (|), but without the cross-bars. Only the fields actually used in this sample record are illustrated, as follows (going left to right for the initial fixed fields). Some of the fixed fields shown here are unique to RLIN:

Fixed fields:

ID: record identifier (an RLIN field); the initial "DCLC" indicates that this record came from the Library of Congress.

RTYP: Record type (an RLIN field); c=cataloging data only.

ST: status of record in RLIN (an RLIN field); p=production record, fully indexed.

FRN: fuller record notification (an RLIN field); no longer used.

MS: MARC record status; c=corrected or revised.

EL: encoding level; blank=full level.

AD: add date; date the record was added to the database.

CC: cataloging category (an RLIN field); 9110=Anglo-American Cataloguing Rules, 2d edition (ACCR2), full level cataloging, full level of content designation (item in hand), Library of Congress MARC record.

BLT: bibliographic level and type; a=language material (type), m=monographic item (level).

DCF: descriptive cataloging form; a=AACR2.

Chapter 20. Record Format (Section 20.1)

CSC: cataloging source; blank=national bibliographic agency, such as the Library of Congress.

MOD: modified record; blank=not modified.

SNR: series numbering (an RLIN field); blank=not a series, or numbering not specified.

ATC: Analysis treatment codes (an RLIN field for analytics, i.e. parts of a larger document separately cataloged or indexed); blank=not applicable, not used

UD: update date.

CP: place of publication; nyu=New York State, United States.

L: language; eng=English.

INT: target audience (intellectual level); blank=unspecified.

GPC: government publication; blank=not a government publication.

BIO: biography; blank=not a biographical work.

FIC: literary form (fiction); 0=not fiction.

CON: nature of contents; b=bibliographies.

TOC: type of control (for archival materials).

PC: type of date [of publication]; s=single known/probable date.

PD: publication date(s).

REP: form of item (for reproductions); blank=not a reproduction.

CPI: conference publication; 0=not a conference publication.

FSI: festschrift; 0=not a festschrift.

ILC: illustrations; blank=no illustrations.

II: index; 1=index present.

Variable length fields:

010: Library of Congress Control Number (LCCN).

020: International Standard Book Number (ISBN), without the hyphens!

040: cataloging source; $c=transcribing agency; $d=modifying agency. In this record, all are DLC, the Library of Congress.

050 00: Library of Congress Classification notation; after the 3-digit tag are two "indicators"; the first 0=item in Library of Congress (LC); second 0=notation assigned by LC; the subfield code $b precedes the author number and date.

082 00: Dewey Decimal Classification (DDC) notation; first indicator 0=full edition of DDC used; second indicator 0=assigned by LC; subfield code $2 precedes the edition (20th edition of DDC).

100 1: main entry heading — personal name, for the primary author; the indicator 1=surname; subfield code $d precedes author's birth date.

245 10: title statement; after the "/" and the subfield code $c comes the "statement of responsibility," i.e., the author(s) and or other responsible parties; the first indicator 1=title access required; the second indicator 0=no initial article, so do not skip any characters in sorting or arranging this title (if the title began with "The," this indicator would be 4=skip "the" plus the following space).

250: edition statement.

260: publication, distribution (imprint); the subfield code $b precedes the publisher; the subfield code $c precedes the date.

Chapter 20. Record Format (Section 20.1)

300: size (number of pages and height in centimeters); the subfield code $c precedes the height.

504: a note about the bibliography and index.

650 0: a subject heading; the first indicator is blank=no information about level of subject (primary vs. secondary); the second indicator is used for the source of the heading, in this case 0=Library of Congress Subject Headings.

• MARC formats for authority records; for classification data : 7

In addition to the MARC format for documentary units in all formats and media, there are separate MARC formats for name and subject headings, for classification notation and captions, for community information, and for library holdings. MARC records for name and subject headings are called "name authority" and "subject authority" records. They include the authorized forms for names of persons, corporate bodies, place names, subjects and features (formats, approaches, etc.), along with alternative and related headings, the source of this data, and the library that created the record. These records are stored in "authority files." The National Authority File is maintained by the Library of Congress, with input from other large cooperating libraries.

• examples of MARC formats for name authorities : 8

Here is the National Authority File MARC record for James D. Anderson!

```
ID:NAFL8239766      ST:p     EL:n    STH:a    MS:c    UIP:a    TD:19880428172211
KRC:a    NMU:a    CRC:c    UPN:a    SBU:a    SBC:a    DID:n    DF:04-22-82
RFE:a CSC:    SRU:b    SRT:n    SRN:n    TSS:    TGA:?    ROM:?    MOD:    LCT:
VST:d 05-05-88                 Other Versions: earlier
    040     DLC$cDLC$dDLC
    100 10  Anderson, James D.$q(James Doig),$d1940-
    400 10  $wnna$aAnderson, James Doig,$d1940-
    670     His Directory of courses on indexing in Canada and the United States,
            1976.
    670     LC data base, 4-28-88$b(hdg.: Anderson, James Doig, 1940- ; usage:
            James D. Anderson)
```

• 9

Skipping over the fixed fields (which are analogous to the fixed fields for the book record illustrated above), the 040 field indicates the organizational source of information (the Library of Congress). The 100 field shows the authorized form of name. The subfield code $q precedes a "qualifier" with a fuller form of name that is not used, and the $d precedes the date of birth.

• 10

The 400 field shows an alternative form of name, from which a see reference should be created, so that users who search for "Anderson, James Doig" will be sent to "Anderson, James D. (James Doig)." The preceding subfield code $w is used for codes indicating information about the unused heading. In this case, it indicates that "Anderson, James Doig" is the pre-AACR2 heading. Anglo-American Cataloging Rules, 2nd edition (AACR2) specifies that the name for a person should be the form that the person uses. The previous rules insisted that the name should be the "official" form, i.e., the form on the birth certificate! Thus, under the new AACR2 rules, we use "Twain, Mark" and "Orwell, George," but under the previous rules, we used "Clemens, Samuel Langhorne" and "Blair, Eric"! The 670 fields show the sources of information used to establish this record.

Chapter 20. Record Format (Section 20.1)

• 11

Here is an authority record for Alexander Library, the main social sciences and humanities library at Rutgers University. The main difference between this record and the Anderson record is that names of corporate bodies go in the 110 field, and their alternative (see reference) forms go in the 410 fields. The 510 field indicates that a see also reference should go from "Rutgers University. Library" to "Archibald Stevens Alexander Library." The subfield code $w includes a code indicating that "Rutgers University. Library" is a former name, so the see also reference from "Rutgers University. Library" could read: "search also under the later heading: Archibald Stevens Alexander Library." Under current cataloging rules, documentary units published under the old name will still use that name as an access heading.

```
ID:NAFL8257645      ST:p      EL:n      STH:a      MS:c      UIP:a       TD:19860115081903
KRC:a      NMU:a      CRC:c      UPN:n      SBU:a      SBC:a      DID:n      DF:04-27-82
RFE:a CSC:      SRU:b      SRT:n      SRN:n      TSS:      TGA:?      ROM:?      MOD:      LCT:
VST:d 01-29-86                          Other Versions: earlier
    040     DLC$cDLC$dDLC
    110 20  Archibald Stevens Alexander Library.
    410 20  Central Library (Rutgers University)
    410 20  Alexander Library
    410 20  Rutgers University.$bLibraries.$bArchibald Stevens Alexander Library
    410 20  Rutgers University.$bArchibald Stevens Alexander Library
    510 20  $wa$aRutgers University.$bLibrary
    670     Its Special Collections Dept. A checklist of periodicals ... 1981 (su
            bdiv.)$bCIP t.p. (New Brunswick, N.J.; Archibald Stevens Alexander Libra
            ry, Rutgers University)
    670     NUCMC data from Rutgers Univ. Lib. for Burnett, V.S. Papers, ca. 1924
            -1947$b(name not given)
    670     Phone call to Rutgers Univ. Lib., 12-10-85$b(Rutgers University Libra
            ry renamed Archibald Stevens Alexander Library in 1973; part of Rutgers
            University Libraries [system]; also known as Central Library)
```

• MARC formats as digital communication formats : 12

As a digital communication format, the MARC record is sent and received by libraries and other users as a string of characters, as illustrated in the following example (Furrie 1998):

```
01041cam  2200265 a 45000010020000000003000400020005
0017000240080041000410100024000820200025001060200
0440013104000180017505000240019308200180021710003
2002352450087002672460036003542500012003902600037
0402300002900439500004200468520022000510650003300
730650001200763^###89048230#/AC/r91^DLC^19911106082
810.9^891101s1990####maua###j######000#0#eng##^##$
a###89048230#/AC/r91^##$a0316107514 :$c$12.95^##$a
0316107506 (pbk.) :$c$5.95 ($6.95 Can.)^##$aDLC$cD
LC$dDLC^00$aGV943.25$b.B74 1990^00$a796.334/2$220^
10$aBrenner, Richard J.,$d1941-^10$aMake the team.
$pSoccer :$ba heads up guide to super soccer! /$cR
ichard J. Brenner.^30$aHeads up guide to super soc
cer.^##$a1st ed.^##$aBoston :$bLittle, Brown,$cc19
90.^##$a127 p. :$bill. ;$c19 cm.^##$a"A Sports ill
ustrated for kids book."^##$aInstructions for impr
oving soccer skills. Discusses dribbling, heading,
 playmaking, defense, conditioning, mental attitud
e, how to handle problems with coaches, parents, a
nd other players, and the history of soccer.^#0$aS
occer$vJuvenile literature.^#1$aSoccer.^\
```

These data are almost always formatted, as in the previous illustrations, for display to librarians. It is usually only systems programmers who see the data in this "string" format. The first 24 positions contain a "leader," which includes some of the fixed-field data. Next comes the directory, which consists of a list of all the three digit tags used. These tags are underlined in this illustration to make it easier to see them (but they are not underlined, of course, in the actual MARC format). After each tag, the next four characters specify the length of the field, and the next five characters specify its starting point in the data string. Thus the 245 field (see line 4 of the illustration) is 87 characters long and begins at position 267 in the data string. The directory and each subsequent field ends with a "field terminator," shown here as "^".

• 13

Throughout the rest of this chapter, all record formats will be shown as formatted displays, sometimes called "worksheets" or "workforms" because they are the workforms that indexers or catalogers or their helpers fill out with the metadata about the message, text and document they are indexing or cataloging. In the early days of automation, paper worksheets were often filled out, for later keying into the computer by specialized input staff. But later, as indexers and catalogers became more accustomed to working on computers, workforms were typically filled out directly on the computer.

• websites for MARC formats : 14

Full information can be obtained about the MARC format at the official MARC homepage, maintained by the Library of Congress Network Development and MARC Standards Office: http://www.loc.gov/marc/ (Library of Congress 2003a). Especially recommended is *Understanding MARC bibliographic: machine-readable cataloging:* http://www.loc.gov/marc/umb/ (Furrie 1998).

20.2. Record Format for the MLA International Bibliography.

• record formats for indexing and abstracting services versus MARC formats : 15

The MARC formats are probably the most complex formats for recording metadata about documents, texts, and messages in existence. Over the years, new fields and subfields have been added to accommodate just about every need and desire. The relatively new field 856 for electronic location and access has 26 subfields for such data as host name, password, contact for access assistance, operating system, file transfer mode, and URL.

• 16

Typically, the record formats for indexing and abstracting services are much simpler, providing fields for just one IR database, as opposed to catering to the needs of hundreds of thousands of libraries of varying sizes.

• record formats for literature : 17

Figure 20.1 shows the two-page worksheet (record format) for national literatures used by indexers for the *MLA international bibliography* of the Modern Language Association of America (1997). The MLA has three other worksheets for the other major divisions of its subject scope: general literature (that is, literature in general as opposed to national literatures), folklore, and language and linguistics.

Chapter 20. Record Format (Section 20.2)

MLA BIBLIOGRAPHY WORKSHEET
For NATIONAL LITERATURES

accession no: acc/

indexer: res/   received/completed:

document type: typ/   checked online:

document language: (type 'xx' beneath appropriate abbreviation)	lan/	Eng	Fre	Ger	Ita	Spa	Rus	Other:

document title (and subtitle):   tit/

gloss: glo/

document author(s):   au1/
(include editors, etc. If more than 3,
continue on another sheet):   au2/

au3/

JOURNAL ARTICLE
journal title or acronym: jnl/

publication information: date: dat/

volume: vol/

issue: iss/

pagination: ext/

BOOK ARTICLE
analyzed collection headsheet acc. no.:   cac/

pagination: cpp/

editor(s):   cau/

collection title: cti/

MONOGRAPH OR COLLECTION
publication information: place: pla/

publisher: pub/

date: yr/

pages: pag/

additional title page information: tpa/

series name or acronym: ser/

series number: sno/

ISBN: ibn/

DAI   degree-granting institution: dgi/

Dissertation Abstracts no.:   dan/   dgy/

Figure 20.1. Record format for the *MLA international bibliography and database*. Reprinted by permission of the Modern Language Association of America, © 1997.

Chapter 20. Record Format (Section 20.2)

Subject indexing: give appropriate descriptors.

	specific literatures:	yl/
	performance media:	ya/
	languages (if different from language of national literature):	ul/i
	periods:	ta/
	individuals (real):	ra/
	anonymous works:	ra/
	groups/movements:	qa/i
	genres:	pa/
	works:	na/

Further Description of Literary Topic:

	features:	ma/
	literary techniques:	lk/
	themes/motifs/figures:	la/<tof
	influences (recipients):	kr/<ion
	sources:	ka/<soi
	processes:	ja/

Description of Document Author's Process:

	types of scholarship:	hs/
	methodological approaches:	ha/
	theories:	ga/<apo
	devices/tools:	fa/<uso
	disciplines:	ea/
	scholars:	da/
	general/miscellaneous:	ca/
	special types of documents:	
	bibliography:	ba/
	other:	aa/

Role Indicators   [internal use:]   inu/

< agn against	< dat date	< iof influence of	< thr theories of
< and and	< dsc discusses	< ion influence on	< tin treatment in
< api application in	< dur during	< ofx of	< tof treatment of
< apo application of	< esp especially	< onx on	< tox to
< apt applied to	< fau for (audience)	< ret relationship to	< usi use in
< asx as	< for for	< rin role in	< uso use of
< atx at	< frm from	< rof role of	< wit with
< bet between	< inc includes	< soi sources in	< zot (other—provide desired term, followed by colon)
< byx by	< int into	< stu study example	
< cot compared to	< inx in	< taf to and from	

Figure 20.1. Record format for the *MLA international bibliography and database* (continued). Reprinted by permission of the Modern Language Association of America, © 1997.

Chapter 20. Record Format (Section 20.3)

• fields in record formats for document descriptions : 18

The first half of the worksheet (Figure 20.1) contains the fields for describing the document containing the message. There are separate sections for journal articles, articles or chapters within books or other media, and monographs and collections. There are fields for up to three authors, with a provision for additional authors. The gloss field can be used for any explanatory note that the indexer feels would be helpful.

• fields in record formats for facets of literature : 19

The second page of the worksheet (Figure 20.1 continued) contains the facets for national literatures in the MLA faceted classification and indexing system — CIFT: Contextual Indexing and Faceted Taxonomy (Anderson 1979). There are different sets of facets for each of the major divisions of the *MLA international bibliography* (general literature, national literatures, folklore, language/linguistics), and this is why each section has a separate worksheet. The facets are used for the analysis of message content and features. These facets have been discussed in some detail in sections 2.1 and 2.2 (subject scope) and section 12.2.2.2 (faceted syntax). Note the role indicators at the bottom of the worksheet. Indexers may insert these role indicators to clarify the relationships among descriptors.

20.3. Record format for ABC-CLIO.

• 20

ABC-CLIO, publishers of the indexing and abstracting services for history *American: history and life* and *Historical abstracts* uses a much simpler record format, illustrated in Figure 20.2.

• record formats for rotated term syntax : 21

This record format is only for periodical articles. The major differences between this format and the MLA format is that the ABC-CLIO format includes a field for an abstract but has no indexing facets. Whereas the MLA uses faceted indexing (and classification) and therefore must have facet fields, the ABC-CLIO databases use the much simpler rotated term syntax for its index headings. The descriptors assigned to a message, usually four or five plus a time period, are simply placed in alphabetical order, with the time period coming last. In alphabetical index displays, each descriptor is rotated out of the string of descriptors to become the lead term, one at a time. (See section 12.2.2.1.)

• 22

The message represented in Figure 20.2 has been assigned seven descriptors, including a time period. Two of them appear in the abstract, so they are simply tagged by an editor: "Mencken, H. L." and "Ku Klux Klan." The others are listed in a box at the bottom of the form. The 'X' code indicates topical descriptors, the 'Y' a proper noun or "identifier," in this case the title of a periodical. Abbreviations are used for the topical descriptors, to save key strokes: EDS. for "Editors and Editing," TEMP. for "Temperance Movements," and METHEP (South) for "Methodist Episcopal Church (South)." The time period or "chronologic descriptor" goes in a separate field at the bottom of the worksheet.

Chapter 20. Record Format (Section 20.3)

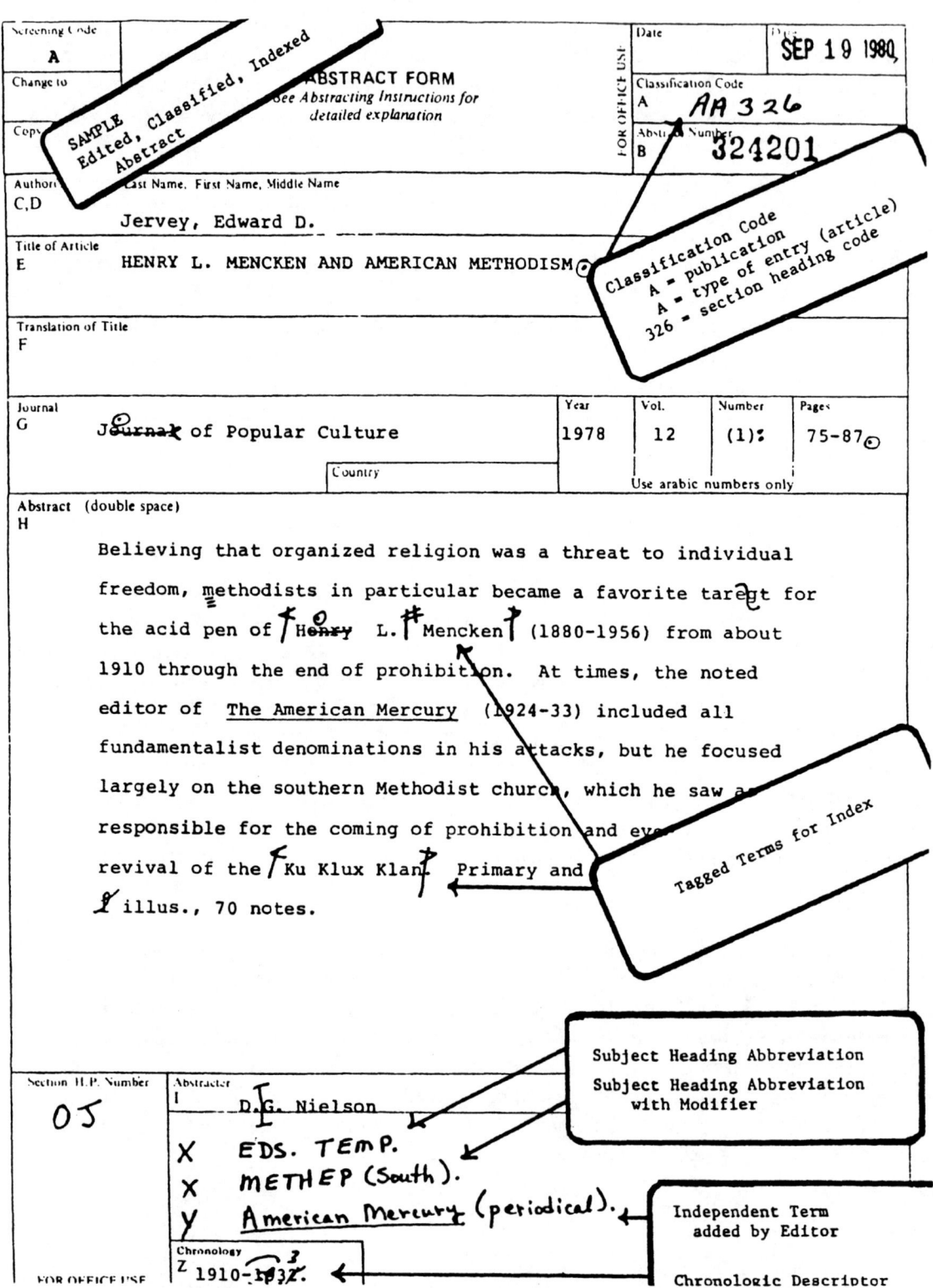

Figure 20.2. Record format for the *American history and life* database (ABC-Clio). Reprinted by permission of ABC-CLIO, © 1980.

20.4. Record Format for a Class IR Database.

• 23

At Rutgers University, masters classes in IR database design have created a small prototype IR database. Here is the record format for that database, illustrated with a list of the fields that comprise the format. The three-character field tags are modeled on those used by the Modern Language Association. Field names following the "\" are limited to 15 characters, so some are abbreviated. Full field names will be used later when these fields are explained. The first three fields are created automatically by the IR database management program for internal purposes:

```
rec\
RNO\
VVV\MAIN_VIEW
sem\Semester
num\Record No.
ind\Indexer
aut\Authors
tit\Titles
cit\Citation
dat\Date of pub
not\Bibliog note
abs\Abstract _ WINDOW
sum\Summary _ WINDOW
ent\Key entity
ird\IRD Doc scope
irs\IRD Subj scope
clt\Clientele
oth\Other entities
prp\Properties
opr\Operations
tls\Tools/means/agt
pla\Places, envirn
tim\Time, period
asp\Other aspects
qua\Quality
aud\Audience
frm\Format, medium
lan\Language
ddc\Dewey Dec class
lcc\LC class
lsh\LC Subj Heading
nph\NEPHIS string
prc\PRECIS string
rf1\docs cited 1
rf2\docs cited 2
rf3\docs cited 3
rf4\docs cited 4
rf5\docs cited 5
```

• 24

Here are brief descriptions of these fields. This record format is determined in part by the requirements of a particular IR database management program, which mandates a tag for each field consisting of three characters followed by a back-slash. Most IR database management programs will specify some special requirements for the record formats that they can manipulate.

Chapter 20. Record Format (Section 20.4)

• 25

These field descriptions are an example of the kind of guidance that IR database producers typically provide to their indexers.

A. Administrative fields:

First come a few fields that are used to manage the record itself, and to indicate who created it and when:

```
rec\
RNO\
VVV\MAIN_VIEW
```

These three fields are for internal IR database management functions. The first two are for internal record identifiers. Sometimes these identifiers change to reflect the sequence of records in a display. Users have options for rearranging the database for browsing and editing records. For example, records could be arranged alphabetically by author or indexer or title or subject descriptors. In each arrangement, a sequential record number is displayed.

The VVV\ field is for managing "views," the option for creating different views in which only certain fields will be displayed. The order of fields may also be changed in different views, so that, for example, topical fields could be displayed before author and title fields.

```
sem\Semester
```

This field is used to record the particular semester in which a record was added to the database.

```
num\Record No.
```

Here the database producer or indexer creates a permanent record number that will always be associated with a particular record. Record numbers are often added in sequence, like the old fashioned accession numbers that libraries used to give to books as they were added to the collection. The record number is useful for calling up a particular record, if you know its record number.

```
ind\Indexer
```

This is the name of the person who created the record.

B. Documentary description fields:

Next come a few fields that describe the message with respect to its creators, its name or title, and where it can be found.

```
aut\Authors
```

Here go the author or authors of the message represented. Multiple authors may be listed. Because index entries may be produced directly from this field (or any other field, for that matter), the names of authors are entered last name first. Multiple authors are separated with semicolons. "Author" may be interpreted broadly to include any person or institution contributing to the creation of a document, such as illustrators, editors, sponsoring bodies, translators, etc. Role indicators, such as (ed.), (tr.), (ill.) may be included for roles such as editor, translator, or illustrator.

```
tit\Titles
```

Main titles, subtitles, alternative titles, etc. go here. Titles or title elements may be separated with colons or semicolons, as appropriate.

The single words that make up bound terms, like "information=science," may be linked with an equal sign, so that they are not separated in automatic indexing or thesaurus construction operations. Some IR database management programs (as well as searching programs) include natural language processing algorithms for identifying word phrases that should be treated as bound terms.

Chapter 20. Record Format (Section 20.4)

cit\Citation

Here we enter an appropriate citation for the document that contains the message and its text. This field merges all citation data together in one big field, in violation of the general principle that every important element be separately identified. Real databases (as opposed to this demonstration class database) would have separate fields for every element of the citation — edition, place, publisher, publication and copyright dates, pagination, illustrations, size (for books), journal title, volume, issue, pagination (for journal articles), etc. Each text format and document medium would necessitate many unique fields. Database producers use these unique fields to remind indexers or catalogers not to forget to include important data!

But because our IR database design course emphasizes data about the content, purpose, meaning and application of messages, in contrast to the publication details of texts and documents, we have not considered it necessary to isolate all of these important data. Compare this general field to the many specific fields included in the MLA and ABC-CLIO record formats (Figures 20.1 and 20.2).

dat\Date of publication

This is an exception to the general merging together of all citation data about particular documents. Because date of publication is often of major interest in searching, we have created a special field for it.

not\Bibliographic note

This field is for any other descriptive data of potential interest about the message, text or document other than data about topics and features for which there are special fields. This is the same as the "gloss, glo/" field in the MLA record format (Figure 20.1).

C. Topical summary fields:

Here we have two fields for narrative summaries of the message — first a longer abstract, followed by a one line, or one sentence summary. In both these fields, equal signs may be used to bind together the words in bound terms, such as "United=States" or "New=Jersey."

abs\Abstract _ WINDOW

Here is placed an abstract of the message. The "WINDOW" note means that the program will automatically open up a word-processing window for this field, to facilitate input and editing.

sum\Summary _ WINDOW

The summary field gets a one line (or one sentence) summary of the content. Like the abstract field, a word-processing window will open up to facilitate input.

D. Topical descriptor fields:

Fields "ent\Key entity" through "lan\language" are for descriptors, described in detail below. In these fields we place single concept descriptors that characterize the main themes or purpose of the message and its features. These can be used for electronic searching, or for creating index headings for displayed indexes, both alphabetical and relational/classified.

Multiple descriptors in each field may be separated by colons or semicolons, depending on their relations. Colons may be used for hierarchically related descriptors, e.g., "New Jersey: New Brunswick," or "citation indexes: Science citation index." Following the *NISO guidelines for indexes* (Anderson 1997a), descriptors should be in lower-case letters; only proper names are capitalized. Following AACR2, titles are not capitalized except for the first word and proper nouns.

These descriptor fields have explicit delimiters for individual descriptors — colons, semi-colons, or a full stop (period) at the end of the field. Therefore, it is not necessary to use the equal sign for binding together the words of a multi-word descriptor (bound term). Binding the words of a

Chapter 20. Record Format (Section 20.4)

bound term is only needed in the free-text fields (title, abstract, summary, etc.) where for automatic indexing each word will be treated as a separate unit unless they are bound together.

E. Faceted indexing and classification fields:

The class database uses facets for indexing and classification. The first set of descriptor fields are for the facets that are used for this purpose.

`ent\Key entity`

The key entity will be the thing, person, group, institution, or text/document that is the object or recipient or experiencer of the main activity or process described in the message. Thus, in a message about cataloging maps, the key entity is "maps." In a message about deteriorating paper, the key entity is "paper." In a message about aging adults, "adults" is the key entity.

`ird\IR database documentary scope`

This database has a special focus on IR databases, so frequently IR databases will be the key entity. This "ird\" field is a special one that is used only for topical descriptors when the key entity consists of IR databases in general, or types of IR databases (e.g., full-text IR databases), or a particular IR database. For example, if we have a message about the IR database *Business periodicals index,* we would put that descriptor in the "ent\" field, and here we could put "periodical articles" to describe the documentary scope of the database.

Note: This field is for document scope descriptors when document scope is treated as a topic of a message. This field is not used to indicate the document type (medium, format) for the message itself. That is a feature, not a topic, and therefore it is considered later in the feature section of the record format.

`irs\IR database subject scope`

This is a second special field to be used only when one or more IR databases are listed as the key entity. In that case, we can describe the subject scope in this field. For example, if the key entity is *Medline,* we could put the descriptors "medicine" and "diseases" here.

Note: This field is for subject scope descriptors when a subject scope is treated as a topic of a message. This field is NOT used to indicate the "subject scope" of the message itself — descriptors for the subject scope of the message itself are placed in their appropriate fields, according to the type of topic, e.g., entity, operation, place, time, etc.

`clt\Clientele`

Here we can list any special clientele that is a topic addressed in the message, for example, the design of IR databases for children or for the visually impaired. This field is not for the target audience of the message itself. Special audiences for messages are features that belong in the appropriate feature field below.

`oth\Other entities`

This field is for any entities, or parts of the preceding entities, that did not fit well in the preceding entity categories.

`prp\Properties & attributes`

Here any important properties or attributes possessed by the preceding entities can be placed. Or, when a property or attribute is the major focus of a message, without regard to any particular entity, that property can go here without any entities being placed in the entity categories. For example, properties or attributes such as "academic freedom" or "editorial independence" might be discussed in a message, without regard to who possesses (or does not possess) these attributes.

`opr\Operations, processes, events`

Chapter 20. Record Format (Section 20.4)

Operations, processes, and events — happenings — go here. Operations may be those that are performed on or experienced by the preceding entities (e.g., cataloging of maps, deterioration of paper). In these examples, "maps" and "paper" are the key entities; "cataloging" and "deterioration" are operations or processes.

tls\Tools, means, agents

This is a "role" field, open to both entities and operations when these play the role of a tool, a means, a method, or an agent for some action, operation, or process. Take, for example, the cataloging of maps by paraprofessionals using the MARC format. The key entity is "maps," the operation is "cataloging," the "MARC format" is a tool, and "paraprofessionals" are agents. This tool and these agents would go in this field: "tls\MARC format; paraprofessionals." Role indicators can be used to clarify roles and relationships, e.g., "tls\<using>MARC format; <by>paraprofessionals."

pla\Places, environments

Here we can list any places or environments that are important in the messages. They can be particular places, e.g., New Brunswick, NJ, or types of places, e.g., densely populated places or deserts.

tim\Time, period

Time periods go here, both particular dates and broad periods.

asp\Other aspects

Here we can place any other topics that do not fit well into the preceding categories.

F. Feature fields:

The next few fields are used for descriptors that characterize important features of a message, text or document, other than the topics addressed by the message.

qua\Quality

Here we can characterize the quality or importance of a message for our clientele with such descriptors as "highest priority," "high priority," "low priority," "difficult," "danger to our business," etc.

aud\Audience

Here we list special and unusual persons for whom a message is particularly designed or aimed. We do not bother to list the usual or expected audience. For example, most messages in this class database are aimed at librarians, information scientists, researchers, practitioners, and students. But when a message is aimed, say, at university presidents (to convince them to spend more on libraries or information retrieval research), or at children, or at the visually impaired, then we should indicate these special audiences.

frm\Format, medium

Here we can name both the format of the text and the medium of the document, because searchers often want to restrict their search to particular formats (books, periodical articles, bibliographies, maps, charts, etc.) and/or media (print, video, film, electronic, world-wide web, etc.).

lan\Language

Language of a message is also important for written texts.

G. Alternative indexing method fields:

Here we can enter alternative indexing data to illustrate how different indexing systems might treat the same message. These are not formal descriptor fields, so all bound terms should be linked with equal signs.

```
ddc\Dewey Decimal Classification
```

This field may contain a DDC notation, followed by a full caption describing the topic represented by the notation. Place a colon after the notation. Separate segments of the caption with semicolons.

```
lcc\Library of Congress Classification
```

Like the DDC field, here we can place an LCC notation, followed by a full caption describing its meaning.

```
lsh\Library of Congress Subject Headings
```

Here we may place one or more LC subject headings. Remember to bind bound terms with equal signs, because this is NOT a formal descriptor field. Separate multiple subject headings with semicolons.

```
nph\NEPHIS strings
```

NEPHIS strings go here. See chapter 12, section 12.2.2.3 for some guidance on creating NEPHIS strings.

```
prc\PRECIS string
```

PRECIS strings go here. PRECIS is a form of faceted indexing — see section 12.2.2.2. If you use this field, you should do some reading on PRECIS. Here are some suggestions:

Austin, Derek (1984). *PRECIS: a manual of concept analysis and subject indexing*. With assistance from Mary Dykstra. 2nd ed. London: British Library, Bibliographic Services Division; c1984. xi, 397 p.

Dykstra, Mary (1985). *PRECIS: a primer*. London: British Library, Bibliographic Services Division; 1985. viii, 262 p.

Richmond, Phyllis A. (1981). *Introduction to PRECIS for North American usage*. Littleton, CO: Libraries Unlimited; 1981. 321 p.

Tonta, Yasar Ahmet. *LCSH and PRECIS in library and information science: a comparative study*. Champaign, Ill.: Graduate School of Library and Information Science, University of Illinois at Urbana-Champaign; c1992. 68 p. (Occasional papers; no. 194).

H. Citation fields:

Here are fields to list a few cited references from messages, in case we want to create a citation index. We have only 5 fields for this purpose, to use as illustrations; in a real situation, we should not limit the number of citation fields. (Actually, our database management program permits the addition of any number of new fields at anytime, without disrupting fields already present in records.)

In these fields, we can enter brief citations, like those used in the citation indexes published by the Institute for Scientific Information: *Science citation index, Social science citation index, Arts and humanities citation index*.

```
rf1\docs cited 1
rf2\docs cited 2
rf3\docs cited 3
rf4\docs cited 4
rf5\docs cited 5
```

Chapter 20. Record Format (Section 20.5)

20.5. The Dublin Core Record Format for Internal Metadata.

• 26

The Dublin Core is one of the more recent record formats proposed. Its purpose is to encourage message, text and document description for documents on the internet and especially the world-wide web. Its name comes from Dublin, Ohio, the home of OCLC (The Online Computer Library Center, Inc.), where the proposal was first discussed among leaders of the library, information, and internet community. They had been called together by OCLC and the National Center for Supercomputer Applications (NCSA) in March 1995. The "Core" refers to the idea that a list of 15 basic elements constitutes a basic core of the metadata that should accompany electronic documents.

• website for Dublin Core; metadata for Dublin Core website : 27

The primary and most authoritative source of up-to-date information about the Dublin Core is the website for the Dublin Core Metadata Initiative, www.dublincore.org/. It is perhaps instructive, regarding the difficulty of persuading resource creators to actually provide comprehensive metadata, that the metadata for this Dublin Core home page was quite skimpy when accessed on 16 April 2002. Many of the 15 core categories are missing, including "creator," "subject and keywords," "publisher," and "type." Here it is:

```
<dc:title>Dublin Core Metadata Initiative (DCMI) Home Page</dc:title>
<dc:description> The Dublin Core Metadata Initiative is an open
forum engaged in the development of interoperable online metadata
standards that support a broad range of purposes and business
models. DCMI's activities include consensus-driven working groups,
global workshops, conferences, standards liaison, and educational
efforts to promote widespread acceptance of metadata standards and
practices.</dc:description>
<dc:date>2001-01-16</dc:date>
<dc:format>text/html</dc:format>
<dc:language>en</dc:language>
<dc:contributor>Dublin Core Metadata Initiative</dc:contributor>
```

• purpose of Dublin Core : 28

The Dublin Core is designed for self-application by message, text, and resource creators and publishers on the internet and world-wide web. All elements are optional, and all are repeatable. The idea is to encourage and facilitate, not to legislate, so everything is voluntary. Thus, the Dublin Core initiative could be compared to CIP: Cataloging in Publication, whereby basic cataloging records appear on the verso of many books published in the United States and the United Kingdom. The principal difference is that with CIP, publishers send data, and sometimes galleys, of their soon to be published books to the Library of Congress (or British Library), and in the United States, it is the Library of Congress that prepares the CIP data. With the Dublin Core, resource creators or publishers are on their own!

• cataloging and indexing by document creators : 29

There is nothing new about asking document creators to describe their own messages and texts. Many publishers of scholarly journals expect authors to describe the content of their articles with descriptors or keywords. The journal *Information processing & managing,* to cite but one example, publishes these keywords just after the abstract, which of course is also metadata!

Chapter 20. Record Format (Section 20.5)

• metadata versus bibliographic records : 30

Some experts have suggested that the term "metadata" should be reserved for data about messages, texts and documents that is embedded within the document itself. This is the expectation for metadata that describes a digital document. But any kind of document — digital, print-on-paper, or of any other medium — can certainly contain its "bibliographic record" within itself, as has long been the practice with CIP (Cataloging in Publication) in printed books. This distinction, between records separate from documents or included in documents, does not seem to be very useful.

• core elements of Dublin Core : 31

Here are the fifteen Dublin Core elements. The titles of the elements are from the Dublin Core Metadata Initiative website, but not the explanations, unless quotations are indicated:

1. **Title** — the name given to the resource by its creator or publisher.

2. **Creator** — the person(s) or organization(s) primarily responsible for the content of the resource, including authors, artists, photographers, illustrators, etc.

3. **Subject and Keywords** — The topic covered by the resource, expressed in keywords, phrases, descriptors, subject headings, or classification notation; terms may be in natural language, from a controlled vocabulary, or both. "Recommended best practice is to select a value from a controlled vocabulary or formal classification scheme."

4. **Description** — a verbal (word-based) description of the content of the resource, including abstract, table of contents, or a "free-text" description. A "reference to a graphical representation of content" may also be used.

5. **Publisher** — the person or corporate body responsible for making the resource available in its present form; the publisher provides access to the resource — makes it public.

6. **Contributor** — other persons or organizations (other than creator) who have contributed to the content of the resource, but whose contributions are secondary to those of the principal creators, e.g., editors, translators, illustrators, conveners, etc.

7. **Date** — "A date associated with an event in the life cycle of the resource. Typically, Date will be associated with the creation or availability of the resource. Recommended best practice for encoding the date value ... follows the YYYY-MM-DD format."

8. **Resource Type** — the category of the resource, in terms of format, genre, etc., such as home page, novel, poem, working paper, preprint, technical report, essay, dictionary. "Recommended best practice is to select a value from a controlled vocabulary (for example, the working draft list of Dublin Core Types ...). To describe the physical or digital manifestation of the resource, use the Format element."

9. **Format** — Here format is used in a special sense to mean the "physical or digital manifestation of the resource." The "digital manifestation" refers to the code and symbols in which the resource is represented, e.g., html, ASCII, Postscript file, executable application, JPEG image, etc. "Typically, format may include the media-type or dimensions of the resource. Format may be used to determine the software, hardware or other equipment needed to display or operate the resource. Examples of dimensions include size and duration. Recommended best practice is to select a value from a controlled vocabulary (for example, the list of Internet Media Types (MIME) defining computer media formats)."

10. **Resource Identifier** — a string of characters and/or numerals used to uniquely identify the resource, e.g., URLs (Universal Resource Locator), DOIs (Digital Object Identifier), ISBNs (International Standard Book Number), etc. Some of these identifiers are discussed in chapter 15 on locators.

11. **Source** — The work, either print or electronic, from which a resource is derived.

12. **Language** — the human language of the content of the resource. Some have suggested that programming languages for executable applications could also be named here. "Recommended best practice for the values of the Language element is ... [to use] a two-letter code (taken from ISO 639 standard ...), followed optionally by a two-letter Country Code (taken from the ISO 3166 standard ...). For example, 'en' for English, 'fr' for French, or 'en-uk' for English used in the United Kingdom."

13. **Relation** — References to related resources.

14. **Coverage** — With respect to place and time: "the extent or scope of the content of the resource. Coverage will typically include spatial location (a place name or geographic coordinates), temporal period (a period label, date, or date range) or jurisdiction (such as a named administrative entity). Recommended best practice is to select a value from a controlled vocabulary (for example, the [Getty] Thesaurus of Geographic Names ...) and that, where appropriate, named places or time periods be used in preference to numeric identifiers such as sets of coordinates or date ranges."

15. **Rights Management** — "Information about rights held in and over the resource. Typically, a Rights element will contain a rights management statement for the resource, or reference a service providing such information. Rights information often encompasses Intellectual Property Rights (IPR), Copyright, and various [other] Property Rights. If the Rights element is absent, no assumptions can be made about the status of these and other rights with respect to the resource."

20.5.1. Dublin Core Qualifiers.

• 32

Within most Dublin Core elements, there are qualifiers that can be used to describe types and sources of data. "Element Refinement" qualifiers specify types of elements. For example, within the description element, two element refinement qualifiers are "Table of Contents" and "Abstract."

• 33

"Element Encoding Scheme" qualifiers indicate a particular scheme used within the element. Thus, in the subject and keywords element, possible qualifiers include: LCSH, MeSH, DDC, LCC and UDC, for *Library of Congress subject headings*, *Medical subject headings*, *Dewey decimal classification*, *Library of Congress classification*, and *Universal decimal classification*, respectively.

• 34

The use of qualifiers is optional. The actual descriptive data (or "value") for the element can just be placed in the element without the use of qualifiers.

20.5.2. Dublin Core Example.

• metadata records using Dublin Core by Joseph (Michael) : 35

Here is an example of a Dublin Core description prepared by a Michael Joseph at Rutgers University for a talk on the Dublin Core on March 10, 1997. It describes a poem called "Co. A, Third Regiment, New Jersey Volunteers," by Dr. J. A. Wamsley. "Type" qualifiers are used to indicate "element refinement" qualifiers, while "scheme" is used to indicate "element encoding scheme" qualifiers. "Scheme=internal" means that the scheme is a local one that is not in general use. In accordance with normal subject cataloging, AACR2 is a scheme used for the establishment of personal and place names as subjects or authors, as well as the formulation of titles.

```
===============================================================
title:       (scheme=AACR2)        Co. A, Third Regiment, New
                                     Jersey Volunteers.
author:      (scheme=internal)
             (type=name)           Wamsley, J. A.
subject:     (scheme=AACR2)        New Jersey. Militia. 3rd Regiment.
subject:     (scheme=AACR2)        Woodbury (N.J.)
subject:     (scheme=AACR2)        Gloucester County (N.J.)
subject:     (scheme=internal)     Sullivan, Dan
subject:     (scheme=internal)     Maul, Ben
subject:     (scheme=internal)     Cunard, Joe
subject:     (scheme=internal)     Ridgway, Frank
subject:     (scheme=internal)     Kearney, Phil
subject:     (scheme=internal)     Stratton, Lucretia
subject:     (scheme=LCSH)         New Jersey — History —
                                     Revolution, 1775-1783 —
                                     Poetry
subject:     (scheme=internal)
             (type=notes)          Includes the names of soldiers in
                                     company, many by last name
                                     only.
description: (scheme=internal)     broadside published between 1900
                                     and 1915
date:        (scheme=NASI.X3.30-1995)
             (type=creation)       19970801 [hypothetical!]
type:        (scheme=freetext)     poem
identifier:  (scheme=url)          http://www.libraries.rutgers.edu/
                                     rulib/njb01023.jpg
source:      (scheme=freetext)     RUL SC/UA NJB. 1900-1910 Wamsley
language:    (scheme=Z39.53)       Eng
coverage:    (scheme=freetext)
             (type=temporal)       18th century New Jersey
===============================================================
```

20.6 Other Metadata Schemas.

• **number of metadata schemas : 36**

There are hundreds of relatively new digitally-oriented metadata schemas being used or under development for digital resources and libraries. Just as traditional indexing and abstracting services tend to create their own record formats reflecting their special needs and customs, now just about every major digital resource or library seems to think it must create its own metadata schema! Grace Agnew, a metadata expert at Rutgers University Libraries, estimated that there were over 1000 metadata schemas in 2002, and the number will continue to grow.

• **isolation versus consensus in metadata schemas : 37**

This "go it alone" tendency is in sharp contrast to more traditional libraries, which worldwide have adopted the MARC format as their standard digital format for library collections metadata. But then libraries have a long history of cooperation and sharing. Most U.S. libraries began relying on Library of Congress cataloging as soon as the Library of Congress began printing catalog cards more than 100 years ago. Through committees of the American Library Association, U.S. libraries have grown used to coming up with standards that all can subscribe to.

Chapter 20. Record Format (Section 20.6)

• interoperability among metadata schemas : 38

Unique record formats for describing messages, texts and documents were never seen as a major problem for traditional indexing and abstracting services, but they used to be published on paper and had to be searched one at a time.

• 39

Now there is great interest in searching digital resources and digital libraries simultaneously, so multiple incompatible metadata schemas are a big roadblock to the goal of "interoperability" — the capability of interacting with multiple resources and multiple metadata schemas at the same time.

• standards for interoperability for metadata schemas : 40

Consequently, standards-setting bodies such as NISO (National Information Standards Organization) in the U.S. and ISO (International Standards Organization) world-wide are working on new standards to at least lead to greater compatibility among metadata schemas, so that fields and elements in one schema can be matched to similar fields and elements in other schemas.

• standards for interoperability for vocabulary data : 41

NISO held a national invitational conference in 1999 to tackle the interoperability challenge among metadata schemes for vocabulary information, as found in thesauri, ontologies, and classification schemes. The purpose was to develop a standard for the description of semantic and syntactic features and relationships, so that vocabulary data can be shared among vocabulary management databases (Milstead 1999).

• Z39.50 standard for information retrieval protocols : 42

NISO also led the development of the Z39.50 standard for "Information Retrieval: Application Service Definition & Protocol Specification." This protocol includes standard definitions for search commands, so that a user of one IR database search interface or online public access catalog (OPAC) can use the commands of that system to query and receive results from another IR database or catalog (Taylor 1999, p. 220; National Information Standards Organization 2002). NISO Z39.50 has also been adopted by ISO as an international standard, ISO 23950.

• examples of metadata schemas : 43

Here are just a few examples of other metadata schemes in use for digital resources:

GILS (Global Information Locator Service): In the United States, this schema began as a "Government Information Locator Service," but soon became international. The U.S. initiative was mandated by the U.S. Paperwork Reduction Act of 1994, which directed federal agencies to provide metadata for their documents. See http://www.gils.net (accessed 27 May 2002). GILS is compatible with NISO Z39.50.

FGDC (Federal Geographic Data Committee) Content Standard for Digital Geospatial Metadata: "Metadata or 'data about data' describe the content, quality, condition, and other characteristics of data. The Federal Geographic Data Committee approved the Content Standard for Digital Geospatial Metadata (FGDC-STD-001-1998) in June 1998" (http://www.fgdc.gov/metadata/metadata.html; accessed 27 May 2002). "The objectives of the standard are to provide a common set of terminology and definitions for the documentation of digital geospatial data. The standard establishes the names of data elements and compound elements (groups of data elements) to be used for these purposes, the definitions of these compound elements and data elements, and information about the values that are to be provided for the data elements" (http://www.fgdc.gov/metadata/contstan.html; accessed 27 May 2002). As such, this might be considered the "Dublin Core" for geospatial data!

VRA (Visual Resources Association) Core Categories for Visual Resources: "The *VRA core categories,* version 3.0, consist of a single element set that can be applied as many times as necessary to create records to describe works of visual culture as well as the images that document them. ... The elements that comprise the core are designed to facilitate the sharing of information among visual resources collections about works and images" (http://www.vraweb.org/vracore3. htm; accessed 27 May 2002).

IMS-IEEE LOM (Instructional Management Systems-Institute of the Electrical and Electronic Engineers Learning Object Meta-data): This schema is being used by DLNET (Digital Library Network for Engineering and Technology): "DLNET has adopted and implemented the IMS-IEEE LOM standard on metadata and content packaging that was designed specifically for engineering and technical resources. DLNET has extended the IMS-IEEE LOM to capture some custom metadata requirements" (http://www.dlnet.vt.edu/DLNET_Resources.jsp#working_ documents "Learning object definition," p. 10; accessed 27 May 2002). See also IMS Global Learning Consortium, Inc. "About IMS" http://www.imsproject.org/aboutims.html (accessed 27 May 2002). IMS-IEEE LOM uses the term "meta-data" with a hyphen because the Metadata Corporation claims a copyright on the term "Metadata"! (http://www.imsproject.org/faqs/ newpage2.cfm?number=7; accessed 27 May 2002).

20.7. Our Examples.
20.7.1. A Book Index.

• fields in record formats for book indexes : 44

Our book index has been created using NEPHIS, the Nested Phrase Indexing System (see sections 12.2.2.3 and 12.4.1). The record format for the print index needs fields only for the chapter number, the section number, the paragraph number and rarely more than one NEPHIS strings, something like this:

```
chapter    chp\
section    sec\
paragraph  par\
string1    st1\
string2    st2\
string3    st3\
string4    st4\
string5    st5\
```

• 45

Most paragraphs will have only one indexing string, but by providing for up to five strings, we can accommodate unusually rich paragraphs (topically speaking!) or extra long paragraphs. Most index headings lead directly to paragraphs within chapters, but a few headings lead to sections and some headings lead to chapters as a whole.

• 46

A filled out record might look like this:

```
chp\12
sec\12.2.2.3
par\184
st1\@impact? of <syntax>? on <size? of <indexes>>
st2\@excessive number? of <locators? in <indexes>>
st3\
st4\
st5\
```

• 47

A record like this would be used to create the kind of index described in section 12.4.1.

For the electronic book, we need a slightly fuller record format, because we want to include the full text of the paragraph in the record (or a link to the paragraph, depending on IR database software specifications). We also include a field for the table of contents heading, so that the record can be called up from the table of contents heading in addition to index entries or free text words. So the record format could look like this:

```
chapter        chp\
section        sec\
paragraph      par\
text           txt\
tab-of-cont    toc\
string1        st1\
string2        st2\
string3        st3\
string4        st4\
string5        st5\
```

And the full record would look something like this:

```
chp\12
sec\12.2.2.3
par\184
txt\An index with syntax is also a longer index than one
    without syntax. Chapter 18 deals with ways to estimate
    the length of indexes when space is limited (as is
    common for print-on-paper back-of-the-book indexes).
    However, an index with syntax and context under headings
    is always better than an index with little or no syntax,
    even if it means fewer headings.
toc\12.2.2.3. Ad Hoc String Syntax (NEPHIS)
st1\@impact? of <syntax>? on <size? of <indexes>>
st2\
st3\
st4\
st5\
```

This is a display of the internal representation of the record. It is not the display meant for the end user. Appropriate displays for the user are treated in chapter 16 on the display of surrogates.

20.7.2. An Indexing and Abstracting Service.

The record format for our indexing and abstracting service must accommodate a somewhat more complicated faceted indexing system, as described in section 12.4.2, and it must also provide for the full description of the document or message represented.

The record format could look something like this:

Chapter 20. Record Format (Section 20.7.2)

```
tag\  field name
==================================================================
rec\  record number or identifier.
ind\  indexer, analyst.
sta\  status. Here we indicate whether this is an "important" document
         that will receive human analysis and indexing. Otherwise it
         will receive only automatic indexing.
aut\  authors & author affiliations. For each author (broadly defined as
         any person or body that participated in the creation of the
         message), special codes can be used to indicate type or role,
         such as "<au>" for author, "<ed>" for editor, "<tr>" for
         translator, "<il>" for illustrator, "<cb>" for corporate body.
         Each author can be followed by an affiliation, with the indi-
         cator "<af>." For example: <au>Anderson, James D., <af>Rutgers
         University; <cb>Ometeca Institute.
tit\  titles (main: subtitles; etc.).
lan\  document language(s).
jnl\  journal title or acronym.
dat\  issue date (see also cdt\ for copyright date; pyr\ for publication
         date, used mostly for books). Journals are notorious for pub-
         lishing issues years late, so the issue date may NOT corre-
         spond to the publication date or the copyright date, in which
         case, all should be used.
vol\  volume number.
iss\  issue number.
ext\  extent, e.g., including paging or other appropriate indication,
         depending on medium.
cti\  collection title — for an article or chapter in a book or on a
         website. The article title goes above in the tit\ field; the
         collection title goes here, with publication information to go
         in the following fields.
pla\  place of publication.
pub\  publisher.
pyr\  year of publication.
cdt\  copyright date.
pag\  pagination or extent — this time for a complete monograph or col-
         lection of separate articles or chapters. The "extent," or
         pagination for the part goes above in the ext\ field.
edt\  edition.
tpa\  other title information.
ser\  series title.
sno\  series number.
not\  non-topical notes about the text (topical information will go into
         abstract).
sum\  brief summary.
abs\  abstract.
use\  evidence of use or importance, e.g., citations to reviews, citing
         works, circulation figures, etc.
com\  user comments — comments on the document contributed by database
         users.

[Indexing facets for topics]

ent\  entities/things.
prt\  constituent parts or materials.
att\  attributes, properties.
opp\  operations, processes, events.
```

Chapter 20. Record Format (Section 20.7.3)

```
agt\ agents, means, causes.
pla\ places.
tim\ times.

[Indexing facets for features]

app\ approaches to, treatment of topic.
frm\ unusual formats, media.
aud\ unusual intended audience.
qua\ quality, importance, etc.
loc\ locator.
```

Return to section 12.4.2 for a description of how the indexing procedures work, and to section 16.1.2 for a brief description on the display of surrogates in our A&I service.

20.7.3. A Full-Text Encyclopedia/Digital Library.

• 52

The record format for our full-text electronic encyclopedia/digital library will be similar to that for our A&I service, but the detailed information about each document will not be necessary, because most documents were originally commissioned and published for the first time as part of the encyclopedia/digital library database. For those articles that are republished from elsewhere, the source information will be recorded as a note in a source field, rather than in the kind of detailed bibliographic fields that were used for the A&I service.

• 53

Here are the fields that we will need. The detailed descriptions of certain fields are not repeated here if they are the same as those used for the A&I service:

```
tag\ field name
===================================================================
rec\ record number or identifier.
ind\ indexer, analyst.
aut\ authors & author affiliations.
tit\ title.
src\ source. Used for articles that were not specially commissioned for
        this encyclopedia/digital library, but were obtained from
        other publications. This is a free-form note that describes
        the source.
    top\ topic — based on displayed index heading string.
sum\ brief summary.
abs\ abstract.
com\ user comments — comments on the article contributed by database
        users.

[Indexing facets]
ent\ entities/things.
prt\ constituent parts or materials.
att\ attributes, properties.
opp\ operations, processes, events.
agt\ agents, means, causes.
pla\ places.
tim\ times.
app\ approaches to, treatment of topic.
```

ct1\ citations. This is a repeatable field for a list of citations to materials that the author used in creating the article, and to which users may refer for further information.
ct2\
ct3\ ... etc.
lk1\ links. This is a repeatable field for hypertext links from this article to other articles in the encyclopedia. The source of the link is indicated as follows: "<en>" for links created by encyclopedia staff; "<us>" for links based on use patterns or user comments. The reason for listing links here is to give the user the opportunity to choose any of these topics (and articles) instead of reading this article. If links were not listed here, users would find them only as they read or scanned the article.
lk2\
lk3\ ... etc.
sa1\ see also references. Here are listed the "see also" references that refer from this article to the most closely related articles. These references are appended to the article in a separate list. See also references are for links that are not made from the body of the text of the article. Therefore they tend to be less closely tied to the content of particular parts of the article, but are related to the article as a whole.
sa2\
sa3\ ... etc.
==

Chapter 21. Full-Text Display

Contents of Chapter 21
21.1 Linear Versus Hypertext Formats
21.2 Encoding Schemas for Digital Texts
21.3 Browsing Full Texts Online
21.4. Our Examples.
21.4.1. A Book.
21.4.2. An Indexing and Abstracting Service.
21.4.3. A Full-Text Encyclopedia/Digital Library.

• 1

This final chapter on the design of IR databases deals with the display of the full text of messages. It applies only to full-text databases — databases that include or are linked to the full texts of the messages that they organize for retrieval. In reference IR databases — all IR databases that do not provide direct access the full text of their messages — the user is referred to other collections or providers, such as libraries (both physical and digital), publishers, government agencies, document delivery services, or websites, etc., for the actual full text. So for reference databases, this section will not apply.

• 2

We place this section last because the display and viewing of the actual text of messages is often the final step in the search and retrieval process. Of course, after examining one or more texts, a user may recast a search and begin again.

• 3

The display of surrogates for texts — index headings, classification captions, locators, citations, abstracts, and other representations — was treated earlier in chapter 15 (for locators) and chapter 16 (for surrogate display). The various surrogates for messages are essential parts of the search apparatus — tools for helping to guide users to the ultimate goal, the full texts of appropriate messages. Thus the display of surrogates is placed much earlier in the design process.

• display of full texts in digital media : 4

Most modern IR databases, including digital libraries, display texts in digital formats that are hospitable to hypertext — that is, text that includes internal hypertext links, as exemplified by well-designed sites on the world-wide web.

21.1. Linear Versus Hypertext Formats.

• 5

Hypertext can be contrasted with traditional text presentations in fixed media, such as printed language texts on paper, images on film or video, and speech or music on various types of sound recordings. Fixed media present text from beginning to end in a single stream. Thus, these are called linear presentations. One great advantage of the book format on the paper medium is that it is relatively easy to skip around from place to place, compared to film, video and some sound-recording media.

Chapter 21. Full-Text Display (Section 21.1)

• interactivity in hypertext : 6

Hypertext is interactive in the sense that a user (a reader or viewer or listener) should have the capability of skipping around from place to place rather freely. Feifer and Tazbaz (1997) are very critical of many texts presented via hypertext media. They focus on "multimedia," which of course usually refers to multiple presentation formats (language text, visual images, sound texts) conveyed via the digital hypertext medium!:

"... most current multimedia is non-interactive and linear. Not only does current multimedia fail to exploit the potential of the technology, it fails to even achieve the interactivity afforded by a traditional book" (p. 51).

• 7

They continue:

"Multimedia [i.e. hypertext digital media!] has the potential to be non-linear and interactive. Multimedia is not necessarily interactive, but it should be. Without interactivity a multimedia title [i.e. text] can just as easily be delivered on a video tape as by the computer. It is a waste to deliver a linear presentation on a computer monitor ...." (p. 52).

• guidelines for hypertext : 8

A primary recommendation of Feifer and Tazbaz is that hypertext must be presented in chunks of "bite-size information." They say:

"... an interactive system should present information in bite-size chunks. Each choice should lead to a single idea or concept. After viewing that information the user should be able to make new meaningful choices" (p. 55).

• conversion of linear text to hypertext : 9

What this means is that if the original text to be conveyed to a user was in a traditional linear format, e.g., a periodical article in a print-on-paper publication or a TV program on videotape, it should, ideally, be converted to an interactive hypertext format for delivery to the user in the digital medium.

• 10

Hart (2000) is especially critical of database producers who are guilty of simply "dumping printed documents online." He says:

"Much of the potential of technologies such as Adobe Acrobat [for .pdf files] has been wasted by communicators who can't or won't even take the time to reformat a vertically oriented document designed for paper to fit on a horizontally oriented computer screen. ... Endless scrolling from the top of a page to the bottom or squinting to view a full page displayed in a miniscule font is inefficient and outright annoying to many readers. Indeed, the very word 'scrolling' speaks eloquently about how badly this design serves our audience, for if scrolls were such a good communication medium, why did we abandon them in favor of bound books?" (p. 8).

• 11

But even when texts are reformatted for digital presentation, often they are not broken up into bite-sized chunks. This is often the case even when hyperlinks are provided to sections, but sections are not divided into separate pages or chunks. The result is that when scrolling is required, before you know it, you have passed into an entirely different part of the document and are lost.

• 12

Cataloger's desktop and *Classification plus,* CD-ROMs from the Library of Congress, are examples of this practice of providing hyperlinks, but not dividing the text up into separate sections. When using the electronic H schedule of the Library of Congress Classification, all the tables for the subdivision of many classes — more than 100 tables in all — are presented in one

Chapter 21. Full-Text Display (Section 21.1)

enormous file. When you are linked to a particular table, if you are not exceedingly careful, before you know it you are in an entirely different table. Each of these tables should have been formatted as a single separate digital page. (The Library of Congress discontinued *Classification plus* in 2002 when it introduced *Classification web*.)

• **constrained hypertext : 13**

Narayanan and Hegarty (1998) point out that the completely free unconstrained hypertext format is not always optimal is certain situations, such as training manuals. They say:

"In a hypermedia manual [i.e., in our terminology, a hypertext manual], different types of descriptions and depictions can be made available as different nodes that are linked together so that the user can move from node to node to view these different displays. The order of traversal of nodes in a hypermedia document can be fully constrained and linear or completely nonlinear and flexible. The challenge to anyone developing an instructional manual ... is to allow the appropriate descriptions and/or depictions to be delivered to the user at the relevant stage of comprehension.

[Note: As explained previously, hypertext versus linear text is not a question of medium, but of format; both can and do exist in all forms of digital media. Thus we use the term "hypertext" rather than "hypermedia."]

• **14**

"Our working hypothesis is that neither a fully constrained, linear presentation of the different descriptions and depictions nor a system that allowed completely flexible traversal of nodes is optimal for instructional manuals. The former is essentially what is currently provided by printed media, and hinders many processes of comprehension by making it difficult to move between textual and pictorial material based on content. The open-ended and unguided nature of the latter means that at any given time, users will have available to them representations that are both relevant and irrelevant to their current state of comprehension, thus reducing the chances of finding the relevant information. Although hyperlinks allow flexible switching between different displays, evidence is mounting that users, especially novices, do not search these media optimally. For example, users can go from node to node haphazardly, get lost and fail to get an overview of how the information in the different displays can be integrated .... Therefore, effective hypermedia design needs to find a mid-point between the two extremes of completely linear presentation and completely hyperlinked displays that can be searched in any order" (p. 289).

• **automatic conversion of linear text to hypertext : 15**

Converting a linear text into hypertext can be done automatically or through detailed human analysis. The different approaches are exactly analogous to the human and machine methods for analysis and indexing discussed in chapter 8. Indeed, analysis for hypertext linking is fundamentally the same as analysis for indexing. Indexing is, after all, pointing or indicating. A hyperlink simply takes the user directly to the message to which it points!

• **16**

Similarly, normal text breaks can be used to divide a text up into appropriate informative chunks or documentary units (see chapter 6). Thus, a normal narrative text can be "chunked" into paragraphs, tables, illustrations and similar distinct sections, with hyperlinks leading to related paragraphs and images.

• **display of full texts in original formats : 17**

On the other hand, if a text has been converted from a linear format in a fixed medium such as print on paper, some users will want to see it in its original form. This is exactly what Adobe Acrobat's .pdf (portable document format) does. It preserves the original format and appearance of a text. Thus, ideally, IR databases will provide both options, permitting users to view a document in its original format, or to view the same text in a chunked and hypertexted format.

21.2. Encoding Schemas for Digital Texts.

• purpose of text encoding schemas : 18

Many schemas have been developed for encoding texts of various formats for electronic digital presentation, analysis and retrieval. Why should texts be encoded? Susan Hockey, formerly head of the Rutgers University Center for Electronic Texts in the Humanities, explains:

"Markup or encoding is necessary for electronic texts. It makes explicit for computer processing things which are implicit to the human reader. It can be used to specify areas or fields of the text to be searched and to identify text which has been retrieved. It can be used to designate 'hot text' for hypertext links and, most obviously, to provide formatting information for display or printing of the text. Attempting to use an electronic text without markup would be like using a bibliographic record where the fields are not delimited in any way" (Hockey 1994).

• examples of text encoding schemas : 19

As examples of text encoding schemas, we shall discuss SGML (Standard General Markup Language), HTML (HyperText Markup Language), XML (eXtensible Markup Language), and TEI (Text Encoding Initiative).

• definitions of text encoding schemas : 20

We begin with definitions from *The free on-line dictionary of computing*, FOLDOC (2002):

• definition of SGML : 21

"**Standard Generalized Markup Language (SGML):** A generic markup language for representing documents. SGML is an International Standard that describes the relationship between a document's content and its structure. SGML allows document-based information to be shared and re-used across applications and computer platforms in an open, vendor-neutral format. SGML is sometimes compared to SQL [Standard Query Language], in that it enables companies to structure information in documents in an open fashion, so that it can be accessed or re-used by any SGML-aware application across multiple platforms.

• ISO standard for SGML : 22

"SGML is defined in 'ISO 8879:1986 Information processing — Text and office systems — Standard Generalized Markup Language (SGML),' an ISO [International Standards Organization] standard ....

• 23

"SGML identifies document elements such as titles, paragraphs, tables, and chapters as distinct objects, allowing users to define the relationships between the objects for structuring data in documents. The relationships between document elements are defined in a Document Type Definition (DTD). This is roughly analogous to a collection of field definitions in a database. Once a document is converted into SGML and the information has been 'tagged,' it becomes a database-like document. It can be searched, printed or even programmatically manipulated by SGML-aware applications" (FOLDOC 2002).

• definition of HTML; tags in HTML : 24

"**Hypertext Markup Language (HTML):** A hypertext document format used on the World-Wide Web. HTML is built on top of SGML. 'Tags' are embedded in the text. A tag consists of a '<,' a 'directive' (case insensitive), zero or more parameters and a '>.' Matched pairs of directives, like '<TITLE>' and '</TITLE>' are used to delimit text which is to appear in a special place or style.

Chapter 21. Full-Text Display (Section 21.2)

• links in HTML : 25

"Links to other documents are in the form: <A HREF="http://machine.edu/subdir/file.html">foo</A>where 'A' and '/A' delimit an 'anchor.' 'HREF' introduces a hypertext reference, which is most often a Uniform Resource Locator (URL) (the string in double quotes in the example above). The link will be represented in the browser by the text 'foo' (typically shown underlined and in a different colour).

• tags in HTML : 26

"Other common tags include <P> for a new paragraph, <B>..</B> for bold text, <UL> for an unnumbered list, <PRE> for preformatted text, <H1>, <H2> .. <H6> for headings.

• international standards body for HTML : 27

"The World-Wide Web Consortium (W3C) is the international standards body for HTML. Home <http://www.w3.org/MarkUp/" (FOLDOC 2002).

• definition of XML : 28

"**Extensible Markup Language (XML):** An initiative from the W3C [The World-Wide Web Consortium] defining an 'extremely simple' dialect of SGML suitable for use on the World-Wide Web. http://www.w3.org/XML/" (FOLDOC 2002).

• definition of TEI : 29

"**Text Encoding Initiative (TEI):** A project working to establish a standard for interchanging electronic text for scholarly research. The TEI has adopted SGML and implemented the TEI standard as an SGML Document Type Definition.

• 30

"The TEI was incorporated as a not-for-profit consortium in December 2000, with host sites in Bergen, Oxford, Virginia, and Providence RI, USA. Home http://www.tei-c.org/" (FOLDOC 2002).

• views of Hockey (Susan) on SGML : 31

Here is Susan Hockey's explanation of SGML (1994):

"SGML became an international standard in 1986. It is not itself an encoding scheme, but a metalanguage within which encoding schemes can be defined. It far surpasses other encoding mechanisms in power and flexibility and provides a way of using the same electronic text for many different purposes. Since it consists of a plain ASCII file, it is completely independent of any particular hardware or software, and can be transmitted across all networks.

"The basic principle of SGML is 'descriptive,' not 'prescriptive' markup. An SGML-encoded text is viewed as a collection of objects within an overall hierarchic structure. It is up to the designer of an SGML document to determine what objects should be encoded or tagged. Typical objects could be title, chapter, page, verse, stanza, act, scene, quotation, name, date, list, etc. They can also be analytical features such as word class tags or other forms of linguistic, literary or historical interpretation. Metadata or descriptive information about the text can also be encoded as SGML objects. The applications program determines what happens to those objects when the text is processed. An object called a title could be italicized if the application is to display or print the text. It could be searched if the application is to retrieve all titles that contain a specific term. It could even be a hypertext link to another document."

• HTML as example of encoding schemas for full texts in digital media : 32

HTML (hypertext markup language) is probably the most widely used encoding schema for digital texts, especially on the world-wide web. It permits the formatting of texts for different sized screens and also the chunking of texts into small documentary units with both internal and external linking via hyperlinks. As noted, it falls into the larger category of schemas referred to as SGML (standard generalized markup language).

• links and documentary units in full texts in HTML : 33

Many word or text processing programs, such as Microsoft Word, permit one to save a text in HTML. Thus, it is very easy to automatically convert a traditional linear text into an HTML text. However, such a simple conversion does not provide any hyperlinks within the text, nor does it divide the text up into meaningful chunks or documentary units. It may be encoded in HTML, but it is not really a hypertext, because there are no hyperlinks. A much more sophisticated analysis program, or human analysis, is required for converting a traditional linear text into a hypertext with internal links and appropriate documentary units.

• HTML versus XML : 34

The University of Washington's UW Computing & Communications (2002) explains why "HTML Is Not Enough":

"HTML is the most successful programming language ever created, so why move on to something else?

• problems with HTML : 35

"Problems with HTML:

- **For Presentation Only:**

"HTML is a presentation language intended to specify how a page will appear when displayed in a browser. HTML tags allow you to identify text blocks as headings, paragraphs, list items, etc., but not by other logical types such as price, dates, or location.

• 36

"Even in terms of presenting information HTML is very limited, in that much of its content is in an aggregate form which cannot be analyzed, searched, manipulated, or edited. For example, consider the presentation of mathematical equations with integrals, matrices, and the like. In HTML this is usually presented as a GIF or PostScript file, and while it looks pretty, you cannot *do* anything with it — you can't locate common sub-expressions, substitute one expression for another, or feed the GIF file into a symbolic mathematical analyzer.

• 37

"Or consider a 3D graphic image: in HTML this is either presented as a static picture, or as a link to a special purpose program that allows only those manipulations explicitly enabled by the programmer.

• syntax in HTML : 38

- **Flexible Syntax:**

"HTML syntax is not strict, making it difficult to develop dynamic page designs controlled by programming languages such as JavaScript. In addition, its loose syntax invites varying interpretation by different browsers.

• tags in HTML : 39

- **No New Tags:**

"You cannot add new tags to HTML. The set of tags available is fixed and cannot be extended.

Chapter 21. Full-Text Display (Section 21.2)

• searches of full texts in HTML : 40

- **Dumb Searches:**

"Because HTML is not 'aware' of what a text block is, other than how it is to be presented, searches of HTML documents usually must be string searches, thus, the term 'Penguin' could refer to a bird, a hockey team, or a publishing firm. Searching for text strings alone creates huge numbers of false matches.

• bandwidth needs of HTML : 41

- **High Bandwidth Needs:**

"Since HTML cannot effectively process, edit, or manipulate information, except through special purpose scripts, interactions with data bases on servers require extensive back-and-forth communication between client and server.

• international aspects of HTML : 42

- **Limited International Capabilities:**

"Lack of full and consistent Unicode support limits the ability of HTML to support different character sets for the world's languages."

• relationship of SGML with HTML, XML : 43

UW Computing & Communications (2002) summarizes the relations among SGML, HTML, & XML as follows:

- "Both HTML and XML are derived from the Standard Generalized Markup Language (SGML).
- "HTML: Loose syntax and structure, some tags. HTML uses a non-strict version of SGML's syntax and structure and a limited set of SGML tags for identifying logical types of text blocks (paragraphs, headings, etc.) for presentation.
- "XML: Strict syntax and structure only. XML uses a strict form of SGML syntax and structure, which can be used to create whole new sets of tags according to the informational and logical needs of a particular situation."

• types of XML : 44

Numerous specialized versions of XML have been created for special purposes and special types of texts. Here is the listing of types from UW Computing & Communications (2002):

- XHTML: eXtensible Hypertext Markup Language
- MathML: Math Markup Language
- VML: Vector Markup Language
- SMIL: Synchronized Multimedia Integration Language
- X3D: 3D Graphics Markup Language
- OFX: Open Financial eXchange
- CDF: Channel Definition Format
- rlMXL: Rick & Larry's Most eXcellent Language

• views of Hockey (Susan) on TEI : 45

According to Hockey (1994), the Text Encoding Initiative (TEI), another in the family of SGML family of encoding schemas, was created to deal with the complexity of texts in humanities scholarship:

Chapter 21. Full-Text Display (Section 21.2)

"Humanities texts are complex in nature. They can include a critical apparatus, marginal notes, variant spellings, words in other languages and character sets. They also exhibit different logical structures, including, in some cases, multiple parallel referencing schemes. These features must be represented adequately in the text in order for the text to be useful. Many different ways have been devised for encoding these features, but by the mid 1980's it was recognized that there were problems with all of them. It was not possible to extend any of them easily to deal with other kinds of texts. Some represented only one theoretical view of the text. Others concentrated on the typographic appearance of the text, leading to ambiguity when, for example, italic can be used for a title, a foreign word or an emphasized word. All were specific to one or two programs. In addition, there was no accepted mechanism for providing information about the source of a text and the rationale for the encoding. Much time was wasted in converting texts from one encoding scheme to another.

• beginnings of TEI : 46

"In late 1987 a planning meeting, held at Vassar College and attended by international experts in humanities computing, determined that it was time to create a common encoding scheme which would satisfy as many purposes as possible. Previous efforts to create a common encoding scheme had foundered but they had all been before the existence of the Standard Generalized Markup Language (SGML).

• guidelines for TEI : 47

"The TEI Guidelines give recommendations both on what features to encode and how to encode them. They include features which are explicitly marked and those which are the result of analysing the text. Very few of the 400 tags are mandatory. The basic philosophy is 'if you want to encode this feature, do it this way.' The encoding process is incremental so that new markup can be added to a text without altering what is already there. Multiple and possibly conflicting views can be encoded within the same text and a method of documenting the encoding is provided.

• 48

"The Guidelines are built on the assumption that virtually all texts share a common core of features to which can be added tags for specific disciplines or applications. The TEI's modular DTD [document type definition] makes this possible. The user chooses an appropriate base tag set for which at present prose, verse, drama, spoken texts, print dictionaries and terminological data are provided. The common core and documentation tags are automatically included. The user may then select additional tagsets if he or she needs, for example, the critical apparatus, hypertext linking, or names and dates. The construction of the TEI DTD has thus been likened to the preparation of a pizza, where the base and the toppings are chosen.

• headers for TEI : 49

"A TEI conformant text consists of a header followed by the text itself. The header consists of a set of SGML elements which provide documentation about the text and its encoding. It represents the first attempt to provide a method of in-file documentation for electronic texts which can be processed by the same software as the text itself. It provides metadata which is needed by librarians who will catalogue the text, scholars who will use the text, and software programs which will operate on the text.

• 50

"The header has four major sections. The file description contains a bibliographic description of the electronic text and can be used as a chief source by cataloguers. It is the only part of the header that has mandatory elements. These include the title statement which gives the title of the work and those responsible for its intellectual content, the publication statement which provides information about the publication or distribution of the text, and the source description which records details of the source from which the electronic text was derived. The encoding description

Chapter 21. Full-Text Display (Section 21.2)

documents the editorial principles used in the transcription of the text, for example the treatment of hyphenation, quotations and spelling variation, and any sampling methods used. The profile description is most relevant for spoken texts where it documents the participants in the conversation. The revision history provides a change log indicating who made each change to the text and when. For a corpus or composite text, there is one header which includes elements common to the entire corpus and individual headers for each text within the corpus.

• **encoding of full texts with TEI : 51**

"The text itself consists of optional front matter, followed by the body, followed by optional back matter. Instead of trying to define elements for every possible subdivision within all text types, the TEI uses a generic subdivision element <div> which carries an attribute indicating the type of subdivision, for example <div type=stanza>. <Div>s can be numbered as <div0>, <div1> etc. if this is convenient. Within a prose text a <div> contains any one or more paragraphs tagged.

• **52**

"In verse, <div>s contain lines tagged <l> which are optionally grouped into line groups tagged <lg>. Depending on the nature of the text, paragraphs or lines are found within <div>s in drama. The core tags such as quotations, lists, names, abbreviations, notes, bibliographic citations may appear anywhere."

• **TEI in digital libraries : 53**

Hockey (1994) also comments on the relevance of TEI for digital libraries, including many of the full-text IR databases now being designed and implemented:

"The TEI's application of SGML satisfies many requirements of the digital library. Its scope already covers the major text types and, because of the modular DTDs, it is easily extended to new text types. It can handle multiple views and interpretations of a text and, through the header, it provides mechanisms for documenting the text. Furthermore, the use of SGML is not restricted to [language] text. It can be used to describe images and other non-[language]-textual material and thus provides the link between a digital image of a [language] text and its transcription. The TEI has extended the cross-referencing systems within SGML to enable them to point to complete texts or sections of text stored elsewhere as images or transcriptions." (Note: in this book, we use "text" for all forms of messages, so we have inserted "[language]" in this paragraph to clarify the type of text that Hockey refers to.)

• **TEI versus HTML : 54**

Hockey (1994) also comments on the relationships between HTML and TEI:

"It is important to understand the relationship between the TEI and the Hypertext Markup Language (HTML). HTML is a somewhat limited SGML application, which concentrates on markup for the presentation of information. It is less suitable for encoding text which is to be analysed in some way, for example by a retrieval program, but it can be used to display the results of an analysis of a more richly marked up text such as one encoded in the TEI scheme. However HTML has introduced many more people to the concept of structured text, and has contributed significantly to the spread of SGML."

• **software for SGML : 55**

Even in 1994, there was a growing body of software programs designed to handle SGML-encoded texts. Hockey (1994) describes some of them:

"Many publishers are now adopting SGML for their electronic publications and much more SGML-based software is available now than a few years ago. Tools such as Author/Editor and Omnimark can be used to aid the production of SGML-encoded text. Products like PAT, Dynatext and Explorer allow the user to search and browse structured text and some, like Panorama, a public domain version of Explorer, can be launched from the World Wide Web and work with any arbitrary DTD."

• impact of TEI : 56

Hockey (1994) concludes:

"Using a powerful SGML-encoding scheme like the TEI provides an opportunity to rethink the way we work. At any level, creating an electronic text implies some interpretation of the source material. SGML allows more levels of interpretation to be embedded in a text than other markup schemes. It thus provides many more possibilities for using that text. However those who insert the markup become responsible for some of the intellectual content of the text. Decisions need to be made as markup is inserted, and it is the markup which determines how words are indexed and thus how they can be retrieved. At present it is not clear whose role this is. In current projects, it is variously being handled by scholars, student assistants, librarians, publishers, and software developers, some of whom may be more familiar with the source material than others. What is important is that documentation such as that provided in the TEI header is supplied so that users of the text know what they have got."

21.3. Browsing Full Texts Online

• 57

Obviously, once a full text has been retrieved, it must be used if its potential is to be realized. Some users will print texts out on paper and peruse them as they have for centuries. But researchers are now focusing on methods and algorithms to make the human scanning or browsing of texts online more comfortable.

• size of documentary units in full texts in digital media : 58

A crucial aspect of full digital texts is their size — the size of the documentary unit that has been indexed and retrieved, as discussed in some detail in chapter 6. Small documentary units, such as a paragraph or a single image (and its description), can be easily scanned, especially if words related to a search requests are highlighted. It is longer texts, sometimes consisting of thousands or hundreds of thousands of words or images, that are problematic.

• analysis of full texts for passage retrieval : 59

Thus, researchers are working on procedures to perform a new round of IR within texts, developing methods for summarizing and displaying the potential relevance of portions of longer texts with respect to an initial or revised search query.

• views of Hearst (Marti) on analysis of full texts : 60

Marti Hearst (1995) introduced "TextTiles" and "TileBars," which use a term distribution and co-occurrence algorithm to identify segments (TextTiles) of longer texts that deal with separate subtopics. TileBars are then used to display the distribution and frequency of search terms in the TextTiles, with black bars indicating high frequency, white bars indicating no occurrence, and varying shades of gray indicating intermediate frequencies. The length of the TileBar indicates the relative size of its TextTile.

• 61

TileBars can be used to compare the treatment of a search topic among multiple documents.

• views of Harper (David et al.) on analysis of full texts : 62

In contrast, David Harper et al. (2004) have focused on finding the most relevant portions of single large texts. Their "ProfileSkim" algorithm divides a long text into "text windows," each containing the same number of words. Then using a language modeling algorithm (see section 8.3) based on term frequency and distribution, they calculate a predicted retrieval score for each text window. These retrieval scores are displayed in a histogram-type bar graph in which each text segment is represented by a vertical bar. The height of the bar indicates the predicted relevance of its text segment, to which the user may go by clicking on the bar. In their 1995 paper, Harper et al. compare the effectiveness of their ProfileSkim algorithm with the traditional display of full texts, in which search terms are highlighted and users simply skim the text on their own. Users had more success in identifying important passages in a long text (as identified separately in advance by human indexing) using the ProfileSkim approach.

• 63

This is a new area of research, so we can expect more work in this area to unfold in the coming years. Fundamentally, this is IR at the micro level (within documents), as opposed to IR at the macro level (across collections or even the entire world-wide web), which was described in chapter 8.

21.4. Our Examples.
21.4.1. A Book.

• 64

Our printed book is indeed a full-text database, but the design of printed books is based on hundreds of years of expert experimentation and experience. We don't propose to second-guess the current patterns of printed book design, except for the designation of documentary units. We have already decided to follow the recommendation of the NISO *Guidelines for indexes and related information retrieval devices* (Anderson 1997a) and use the paragraph as the documentary unit for indexing, rather than the traditional page. This is covered in chapter 6 on documentary units.

• 65

Our book can also be published electronically in a hypertext format, although users should also have the option to see images of the printed text (e.g., in .pdf files). Text should be encoded using an appropriate XML or TEI schema.

• 66

Since the documentary unit for the book is the paragraph, each paragraph will be treated as a separate hypertext page, with sequential links to previous and following paragraphs, as well as hyperlinks to related documentary units. A header will display chapter and section titles plus index headings for the paragraph being displayed.

• 67

These titles and headings serve as brief topical summaries of the paragraph, which can help the user decide whether to actually read the paragraph. Such brief summaries help to implement the important principle of "eliminability" — making is possible for a user to eliminate an irrelevant message before wasting too much time with it.

• 68

Here is a preliminary typescript design of a single paragraph display. Remember that such preliminary designs are conveyed here in simple typescript in order to emphasize that screen designs can be portrayed simply, with pen or pencil on paper, or typescript. These designs should be passed on to professional graphic and type designers to select appropriate typefaces and for graphic enhancement. Underlines indicates hyperlinks to related displays:

Chapter 21. Full-Text Display (Section 21.4.2)

```
===============================================================================
                         INFORMATION RETRIEVAL DESIGN
     [Change display] [index] [contents] [search] [previous] [next] [return]

Chapter: 12. Syntax

Section: 12.2.2.3. Ad hoc string syntax (NEPHIS).

Index String: use of NEPHIS for book indexes.

Text:
     NEPHIS or other types of string indexing syntax can be used in a variety of
     types of index. NEPHIS has been found to be a useful tool for back-of-the-
     book indexes, especially for authors who want to index their own books and
     for other novice indexers. Such beginning indexers typically have little or
     no experience in formulating appropriate headings for indexes. Frequently,
     they ignore the need for syntax, using too many single term headings, with no
     context. This results in too many locators under single headings, such as:

     United States 33, 44-45, 50, 53, 60-67, 70, 72,
         75-79, 80, 83, 86, 90-100, 121-123, 144-147, 149,
         155-158, 160-171, 175, 188, 201, 222-223.
===============================================================================
```

• options for display of full texts : 69

Across the top of the display are the following options:

• [Change display] — This would change the display to a visual image of the printed text, with no titles or index headings at the head of each paragraph.

• [index] — This would return the user to the displayed alphabetical subject index.

• [contents] — This would return the user to the table of contents.

• [search] — This would take the user to the electronic full-text search interface. It would be nice to make available search and browse techniques such as TileBars and ProfileSkim, as described in section 21.3.

• [previous] — This would take the user to the immediately preceding paragraph or element within the book.

• [next] — This would take the user to the next paragraph or element within the book.

• [return] — This would return the user to whatever display was shown previously, e.g., the displayed alphabetical index, the table of contents, a paragraph linked to the current paragraph, or an electronic search screen.

21.4.2. An Indexing and Abstracting Service.

• 70

Our A&I service design provides for digital full-text access for high-use documents via the electronic version of the service; for other documents, only surrogates are provided. The print version of the A&I service is a reference IR database, with only surrogates provided, which include locators for the full texts elsewhere.

Chapter 21. Full-Text Display (Section 21.4.2)

• access to full texts : 71

For full texts, some access is provided via links to outside sources (publisher databases, digital libraries, websites, etc.) while some texts are included in the A&I service database itself. The choice depends on various licensing and copyright issues that are outside the scope of this book. However, we have control over formatting only for those texts included within our IR database. But even here, some licensing or copyright agreements may not permit us to convert texts into the type of hypertext presentation we advocate. For those texts for which we have permission to reformat, text will be encoded using an appropriate XML or TEI schema.

• display of full texts in electronic indexing and abstracting services : 72

The display of full-text documents in our electronic A&I service will be similar to their display in our electronic book. Users may retrieve full documents or special parts, such as charts, tables, or key illustrations, via displayed indexes, both alphabetical or classified. They may also retrieve individual paragraphs, or screens of text, via electronic full-text searches.

• 73

Once a user calls up a particular document or paragraph, chart, illustration or diagram, they will have the option of choosing either of the two display formats described previously: (1) original text format, in which the text is displayed without interruption more or less as in print documents, or (2) hypertext display, in which each documentary unit is prefaced with classification caption(s) and index headings. Of course, some documents begin life as electronic texts, so option (1) may not always be available.

• 74

If the original text was printed on paper, then the original text format display should be a visual recreation of the original text, complete with illustrations in their original positions.

• 75

The hypertext display should look something like this (using section 1.3 of this book as source text). Hyperlinks to related text segments are indicated by underlines:

```
=======================================================================
            BLISTER — Bibliography of Library & Information Science &
                        Technology: Evaluation & Research
   [Change display] [index] [contents] [search] [source] [previous] [next] [return]

   Classification Caption: information retrieval databases. terminology.
                           definitions.

   Index String: databases. models: hypertext databases.

   Source: Anderson, James D.; Pérez-Carballo, José (2005). Information retrieval
           design. Scarecrow Press. Section 1.3.

   Text:
      hypertext database. With the advent of the world-wide web, hypertext data-
      bases have become more and more common. According to FOLDOC (1997, "hyper-
      text"), hypertext refers to a "collection of documents (or 'nodes') contain-
      ing cross-references or 'links' which, with the aid of an interactive browser
      program, allow the reader to move easily from one document to another." In a
      hypertext IR database, some of these documents may be summary records or sur-
      rogates, which can lead the user to documents containing the full text of
      messages.
=======================================================================
```

Chapter 21. Full-Text Display (Section 21.4.3)

Across the top of the display are the following options:

- [Change display] — This would change the display to a visual image of the printed text, with no classification caption or index headings at the head of each display.
- [index] — This would return the user to the displayed alphabetical subject index.
- [contents] — This would return the user to the table of contents of the A&I service, which consists of a classification for library and information science, appropriate for topical browsing.
- [search] — This would take the user to the electronic full-text search interface. It would be nice to make available search and browse techniques for analysis and passage retrieval within full texts such as TileBars and ProfileSkim, as described in section 21.3.
- [Source] — takes the user to a full citation for the source of the article.
- [previous] — This would take the user to the immediately preceding paragraph or element within a document or preceding document within a classified array of documents.
- [next] — This would take the user to the next paragraph or element within a document or the next document within a classified array of documents.
- [return] — This would return the user to whatever display was shown previously, e.g., a displayed alphabetical index, the classified table of contents, a paragraph, element or document linked to the current display, or an electronic search screen.

21.4.3. A Full-Text Encyclopedia/Digital Library.

• 76

When a user selects an electronic encyclopedia article or a paragraph, diagram, table, map or illustration within an article, they will have the same options for display as described for our electronic book and A&I service: a seamless linear text display or a hypertext display.

• 77

The seamless linear text display will be similar to what an encyclopedia article looks like in print. The user can scan or read the text using the usual screen navigation tools.

• 78

The hypertext display will provide direct access to data from all the fields described in the record structure for the electronic encyclopedia (chapter 20). The text will be encoded using an appropriate XML or TEI schema. Here is an example. Hyperlinks are indicated by underlines. In the actual display, such links would be indicated by highlighting and underlines:

Chapter 21. Full-Text Display (Section 21.4.3)

• 79

```
================================================================================
              WELIS: WORLD ENCYCLOPEDIA OF LIBRARY AND INFORMATION SCIENCE
      [Change display] [index] [contents] [search] [previous] [next] [return]
      [Author] [Outline] [Source] [Topic] [Summary] [Comments] [Citations] [Links]

Article: Anderson, James D. Representation and Organization of Knowledge.

Topic: knowledge; messages; documents. representation; organization;
           cognitive psychology; cognitive science.

Heading:    Introduction

Paragraph #1: Knowledge resides in the human mind. Humans have learned how to
      represent knowledge in messages recorded in documents, through which we en-
      deavor to convey parts and aspects of our knowledge to others — to inform
      them by providing potential information. In the context of library and in-
      formation science, the organization of knowledge (often called the organiza-
      tion of information) is the organization of documented messages in which
      knowledge or information is represented. The organization of knowledge
      within the mind, or brain, is a primary focus of cognitive psychology and
      cognitive science.
================================================================================
```

• 80

The options across the top of the screen perform the following functions:

• [Change display] — This would change the display to a visual image of a continuous printed linear text, with no captions, topic descriptors, or headings at the top of each display.

• [index] — This would return the user to the displayed alphabetical subject index.

• [contents] — This would return the user to the table of contents, which consists of a classification for library and information science, appropriate for topical browsing.

• [search] — This would take the user to the electronic full-text search interface.

• [previous] — This would take the user to the immediately preceding paragraph or element within an article or the preceding article within the classified array of articles.

• [next] — This would take the user to the next paragraph or element within within an article or the next article within the classified array of articles.

• [return] — This would return the user to whatever display was shown previously, e.g., an alphabetical displayed index, the classified table of contents, a paragraph, element or article linked to the current display, or an electronic search screen.

• 81

The options on the second line at the top of the screen take the user to particular indexes or sections of the encyclopedia database:

• [Author] takes the user to an author entry consisting of biographical information, a listing of articles within the encyclopedia, and references to other publications.

• [Outline] displays an outline of the full article, with hyperlinks to each section.

• [Source] takes the user to a full citation for the source of the article.

• [Topic] displays an index string for the article as a whole, rather than the particular paragraph in the immediate display.

• [Summary] displays the summary or abstract of the full article.

Chapter 21. Full-Text Display (Section 21.4.3)

- [Comments] displays user comments about the article.
- [Citations] displays list of references and/or suggestions for further reading at the end of the article.
- [Links] displays titles of related articles. These serve as general cross references. Specific links are placed within the text of paragraphs to lead users to discussions related to a displayed paragraph.

Chapter 22. Implementation and Evaluation

• 1

Congratulations! If you have been making decisions as you have read the previous chapters about the many options available for the design of IR databases, your design should now be complete, or nearly complete.

• 2

Now it is time for implementation, and once your design is implemented, at lease as a prototype, it is time for on-going evaluation and testing. Revisions and changes can be made on the basis of evaluation results, so that your design can always be responsive to the changing needs and preferences of your users.

• implementation. testing, and evaluation of IR databases: outside scope of book : 3

This book has focused on design issues and options. Just as the essential preliminary user needs assessment and market analysis that precedes design was outside the scope of this book, so too are implementation, testing, and evaluation.

• software for IR databases : 4

Implementation will involve searching for and selecting appropriate software for your design. This is not an easy task. Most commercially available software for databases are designed for concrete entity and event databases, not IR databases. Most commercial database software is based on the relational model, which has rarely been successful for IR databases (Green 1996). As noted briefly in section 1.3, most IR databases use the flat-file model for their databases, with separate records for each documentary unit

• software for indexing and abstracting services : 5

Most large-scale indexing and abstracting services have commissioned software tailored to their particular IR database designs. This is generally very expensive, and is appropriate only for well-funded large-scale operations. Companies that do offer IR database production and management software include Access Innovations (and its Data Harmony Division, www.dataharmony.com), Cuadra Associates (www.cuadra.com), and Inmagic (www.inmagic.com).

• software for IR databases in libraries; software for OPACs : 6

Most libraries use OPAC software, which is designed around the international standard MARC format.

• software for digital libraries : 7

Digital libraries are still relatively new, and most software is still in the developmental stage, created especially for digital library initiatives. As digital libraries mature, software packages for digital libraries should become more readily available.

• software for personal IR databases : 8

The Institute for Scientific Information sells several software packages designed for individual students and scholars and their personal IR databases (http://www.isinet.com/products/infomanage/ accessed 9-6-2004). These include:

- Endnote: "EndNote offers a breadth of bibliographic formatting options to suit most academic disciplines, from the sciences to the humanities. EndNote's availability on both Macintosh and Windows as well as the cross-platform compatibility, make it an ideal choice for mixed-platform environments" — ISI.

Chapter 22. Implementation and Evaluation

- Reference Manager: "Reference Manager is a feature-rich writing tool for researchers that offering a spell checker, keyword synonyms to manage imported terms, and wizards to help users create bibliographic styles easily. Designed for Windows, Reference Manager offers unparalleled functionality and flexibility. Reference Manager lets the user perform key operations across multiple databases. The Network edition provides multi-user read and write access, making it the perfect tool for workgroups." — ISI.

- ProCite: "ProCite is the indispensable tool for users with distinctive bibliographic data management needs. ProCite has advanced searching and sorting functions to make data easily accessible to the user. ProCite can generate a bibliography, organized by subject headings, and can even produce an index. These unique features make it the popular choice for those who build and maintain special collections. (ProCite for Macintosh does not include the ability to search bibliographic resources on the Internet.)" — ISI.

• testing and evaluation of IR database designs : 9

Once an IR database has been implemented, at least as a prototype, using some appropriate software, it is time for testing and evaluation. Ideally, initial testing and evaluation will take place prior to formal publication, or launching of a new IR database.

• IR database producers versus IR database vendors : 10

Testing and evaluation is complicated if IR database production is separated from distribution, as is often the case. Many large-scale IR database producers focus only on the creation of records for documentary units. They may also maintain an indexing thesaurus. These records, and also the thesaurus, may be provided to any number of different vendors, and it is generally the vendors who provide the search interface.

• omission of IR database features by IR database vendors : 11

It is not uncommon for vendors not to bother to implement important features provided by IR database producers. For example, the *MLA international bibliography* has used a fully faceted classification since 1981, but no vendor has made this faceted classification available to end users for browsing purposes. A database vendor may make a thesaurus available, but as a separate database that may or may not be integrated into the search or browse interface for the IR database itself.

• 12

Ideally, the testing and evaluation of an IR database design must include all features, most especially its search interface.

• readings on testing and evaluation of IR databases : 13

We conclude with some recommended readings on the testing and evaluation of IR databases:

First some classics:

- Lancaster, F. Wilfrid (1969). MEDLARS: Report on the evaluation of its operating efficiency. *American documentation*. 20(2): 119-142; 1969 April. Lancaster refined a technique of failure analysis for this evaluation, seeking to investigate reasons why relevant documents were not retrieved.

- Lancaster, F. Wilfrid (1979). *Information retrieval systems: characteristics, testing, and evaluation*. 2nd ed. New York: Wiley; 1979. xiv, 222 p. (Information science series) ISBN 0-471-04673-6. This important book has many chapters focusing on testing and evaluation: 8. Criteria by which information services may be evaluated; 9. Evaluating the effectiveness of information services; 14. Improving the performance of an information service on the basis of evaluation results; 15. the evaluation of machine-readable data bases and information services derived from them; 16. Cost-effectiveness and cost-benefit evaluation; 17. Evaluation of a national information

Chapter 22. Implementation and Evaluation

system; 19. A brief history of evaluation; Appendix 1. Interview guide used in evaluation of AGRIS (International Information System for the Agricultural Sciences and Technology).

- Lancaster's 1979 classic was later "revised, retitled, and expanded" by Lancaster and Amy J. Warner in 1993 (*Information retrieval today*. Arlington, VA: Information Resources Press, c1993. xviii, 341 p. ISBN 0-87815-064-1), but this new edition has only two chapters that focus on evaluation: 9. Evaluative criteria and evaluation procedures; 10. Factors affecting performance in information retrieval.

• measurement for testing and evaluation of IR databases : 14

All testing and evaluation involves measurement. Two important books of the 1990s addressed the many technicalities of careful and accurate measurement of the attributes and performance of IR databases and their users. They are:

- Boyce, Bert R.; Meadow, Charles T.; Kraft, Donald H. (1994). *Measurement in information science*. San Diego: Academic Press, c1994. xvii, 283 p. (Library and information science). ISBN 0-12-121450-8.

- Tague-Sutcliffe, Jean (1995). *Measuring information: an information services perspective*. San Diego: Academic Press, c1995. xii, 206 p. (Library and information science). ISBN 0-12-682660-0.

• evaluation of library performance : 15

A must less technical approach, aimed at librarians, was provided by the American Library Association in 1996. While focusing on all library services, chief among these is the library's IR database — the library catalog or OPAC:

- Zweizig, Douglas; Johnson, Debra Wilcox; Robbins, Jane; Besant, Michelle (1996). *The tell it! manual: the complete program for evaluating library performance*. Chicago: American Library Association, 1996. vii, 270 p. ISBN 0-8389-0679-6. See especially the following chapters: 12. Evaluation methods, by Johnson; 13. Choosing an evaluation method, by Johnson; 14. Questionnaires, by Keith Curry Lance & Johnson; 15. Interviewing, by Robbins; 16. Focus groups, by Johnson; 17. Gathering numbers for evaluation, by Zweizig; 18. Observation, by Zweizig & Johnson; 19. Attitude measurement, by Ronald Powell; 20. Making sense of narrative responses, by Besant.

• failure analysis in testing and evaluation of IR databases : 16

In 1982, following the pioneering footsteps of F. W. Lancaster's evaluation of MEDLARS (which later became MEDLINE), "the National Library of Medicine awarded Drexel's College of Information Studies a contract to evaluate NLM's coverage and indexing of the literatures of the Medical Behavioral Sciences (MBS). ... The bases for the comparisons were test retrievals and 'failure analysis'" (McCain, White & Griffith 1987a). The Drexel researchers published several papers describing their methods and results:

- Griffith, Belver C.; White, Howard D; Drott, M. Carl; Saye, Jerry. D. (1986). Tests of methods for evaluating bibliographic databases: an analysis of the National Library of Medicine's handling of literatures in the medical behavioral sciences. *Journal of the American Society for Information Science*. 37(4): 261-270; July 1986.

- McCain, Katherine W.; White, Howard D; Griffith, Belver C. (1987a). Comparing retrieval performance in online data bases. *Information processing & management*. 23(6): 539-553; 1987.

- McCain, Katherine W.; White, Howard D; Griffith, Belver C. (1987b). Test retrieval as a measure of system performance: MEDLINE and the medical behavioral sciences. In Hurd, Julie M.; Davis, Charles H., eds. *ASIS '86. Proceedings of the 49th ASIS Annual Meeting*. Volume 23;

Chapter 22. Implementation and Evaluation

28 Sept.-2 Oct. 1986; Chicago, IL. Medford, NJ: Learned Information, for the American Society for Information Science, 1987: 199-203.

- White, Howard D; Griffith, Belver C. (1987). Quality of indexing of online data bases. *Information processing & management.* 23(3): 211-224; 1987.

• beta testing of IR databases : 17

When an IR database is completely integrated (that is, database records and thesaurus are not shipped off to separate vendors to be searched using the vendor's interface), the IR database producer may use beta testing of a new IR database. Beta testing involves placing the IR database with real users to try it out and test its performance. Here is a short article that reviews the issues of beta testing:

- Sweetland, James H. (1988). Beta tests and end-user surveys: are they valid? *Database.* 11(1): 27-32; Feb. 1988.

• qualitative studies of IR databases : 18

Traditionally, testing and evaluation of IR database performance have been based on quantitative studies, using such measures as recall and precision (see chapter 9). However, such quantitative approaches are not appropriate when users are provided the opportunity to browse displayed indexes and make relevance or utility decisions as they explore options. Julian Warner has written a critique of the traditional preoccupation of IR research and IR database design with recall and precision, suggestion that in the new environment, exploratory capability and the criterion of enhanced choice is more appropriate:

- Warner, Julian (1999). "In the catalogue ye go for men": evaluation criteria for information retrieval systems. *Information research.* 4(4). Available at: http://informationr.net/ir/4-4/paper62.html. Accessed 9-29-2003.

• 19

Often qualitative methods focus on users, user needs, user behavior, and user satisfaction, so that they these methods can be as appropriate for the initial user needs assessment that precedes IR database design, as they are for on-going assessment and evaluation of operational IR databases:

- Kyrillidou, Martha; Heath, Fred M., eds. (2001). Measuring service quality. *Library trends.* 49(4): 541-799; Spring 2001. This special issue focuses on methods and issues related to assessing the quality of information services, broadly defined. Two constituent articles of special interest are:

- Cullen, Rowena (2001). Perspectives on user satisfaction surveys. *Library trends.* 49(4): 662-686; Spring 2001.

- Hernon, Peter; Nitecki, Danuta A. (2001). Service quality: a concept not fully explored. *Library trends.* 49(4): 687-708; Spring 2001.

- Kochtanek, Thomas R.; Hein, Karen K. (1999). Delphi study of digital libraries. *Information processing & management.* 35(3): 245-254; May 1999. The Delphi technique, named for the Greek oracle, is designed to help experts reach a consensus on issues presented to them. Experts could be frequent users of an IR database.

- Morrison, Heather G. (1999). Online catalogue research and the verbal protocol method. *Library hi tech.* 17(2): 197-206; 1999. The verbal protocol method — asking users to think out loud as they pursue tasks, is widely used not only for the evaluation of OPACs, but also for all types of electronic IR databases.

Chapter 22. Implementation and Evaluation

- Kerslake, Evelyn; Goulding, Anne (1996). Focus groups: their use in LIS research data collection. *Education for information*. 14: 225-232; Oct. 1996. Focus groups are another popular technique to gather input from users.

- Eager, Carolyn; Oppenheim, Charles (1996). An observational method for undertaking user needs studies. *Journal of librarianship and information science* (Folkestone, England). 28(1): 15-23; March 1996. This "observational technique involves the researcher being with the subject continuously throughout the day and observing their actions [sic]."

- Sandstrom, Pamela Effrein (1994). An optimal foraging approach to information seeking and use. *Library quarterly.* 64(4): 414-449; Oct. 1994. "Optimal foraging theory, derived from evolutionary ecology, [is useful] for its potential to clarify and operationalize studies of scholarly communication." Foraging is a type of browsing, which is very important in modern IR databases. The last section is entitled: "Modeling the behavior of scholarly information users."

- Fidel, Raya (1993). Qualitative methods in information retrieval research. *Library & information science research.* 15(3): 219-247; Sum. 1993. Raya Fidel is one of the leading researchers on IR database performance and human information seeking behavior.

- Gothberg, Helen M. (1990). The library survey: a research methodology rediscovered. *College & research libraries.* 51(6): 553-559; Nov. 1990.

- Cherry, Joan M. (1990). Methods of studying database users: the role of surveys, laboratory studies, and field studies. *Canadian journal of information science.* 15(2): 17-29; July 1990.

- Glazier, Jack D.; Powell, Ronald R., eds. (1992). *Qualitative research in information management.* Englewood, CO: Libraries Unlimited; 1992. xiv, 238 p. ISBN 0-87287-806-6. This book opens with "Qualitative research methodologies for library and information science: an introduction," by Glazier. Other chapters include "The case study method," by Raya Fidel; "From the mind's eye of the user: the sense-making qualitative-quantitative methodology, by Brenda Dervin; "Focused group interviews," by Karen Markey Drabenstott; "Structured participant observation," by Robert Grover and Glazier; and "Qualitative research: an annotated bibliography," by Gemma DeVinney.

Glossary

Terms with their own definitions are printed in boldface in other definitions.

abstract entity. Abstract entities are abstractions — constructs abstracted from (drawn from, based on) experience or thought — that can't be seen or touched but whose existence is made known indirectly through various recognized symptoms or indicators. Examples include the American Medical Association, Rutgers University, communism, Islam, and the theory of relativity. In the case of organizations and corporations, many are incorporated (embodied, from Latin "in" plus "corpus" = "body") through law. *See also* **concrete entity**; **entity**; and chapter 2.

ad hoc string syntax. Ad hoc ("to this") string syntax provides a means for coding natural language statements so that a computer program can convert them into meaningful index **headings**. The statements can be already existing, such as **document** titles, or they can be created as part of the **indexing** process. The coding tells the computer how to break up the statement into individual **terms**, how to arrange the terms within headings, and which terms to place in lead position as access points in a **displayed index**. **NEPHIS** (Nested Phrase Indexing System) is the ad hoc string syntax used for the index of this book. *See also* section 12.2.2.3.

ad hoc syntax. Ad hoc ("to this") syntax refers to syntax that is developed "on the spot" for a one-time indexing project, as opposed to an ongoing indexing operation, such as a regularly updated **IR database** or indexing and abstracting service. The most common example of ad hoc syntax is that used in most back-of-the-book **indexes**. Indexers who create the detailed indexes to individual books rarely use a pre-established system of **syntax**, but rather put **terms** together as they see fit for the particular situation. Because such a book index is a one-time operation, there is no need to record practice for the sake of long-term consistency, although good indexers attempt to maintain consistency throughout a single index. *See also* section 12.2.7.

analysis base. *See* **indexable matter**.

automatic indexing. Automatic indexing refers to **indexing** by machine, or the analysis of **text** by means of computer algorithms. The focus is on automatic methods used behind the scenes with little or no input from individual searchers, with the exception of **relevance feedback**. Thus automatic indexing does not include searching options and techniques used by human searches, such as methods for creating effective search statements, adding weights to terms, specifying proximity requirements, using truncation, wild cards, or combining terms with boolean or role operators. *See also* section 8.3.

best match syntax. Best match syntax refers to a growing variety of electronic term-matching methods that apply techniques for predicting potential **relevance** of **documentary units** in response to a search statement and then ranking documentary units according to predicted "relevance" scores. Because the most common approaches are based on some method of assigning weights to **terms** (search terms, index terms or both), this type of **syntax** can be called "weighted term syntax." Particular models of weighted term syntax include the **vector space model**, the **probabilistic model**, and the **language model**. *See also* sections 8.3.5 and 12.3.2.

bibliographic coupling. Bibliographic coupling is a special form of **clustering** based on reference citations. The underlying idea is that two or more **documents** are related ("bibliographically coupled") if they share the same reference citations. The more reference citations they share (the higher the threshold), the more closely related they may be. *See also* **co-citation**; and section 8.3.12.1.

Glossary

bibliography. In this book, we have subsumed the term "bibliography" under the broader, newer term **"IR database**," but "bibliography" and "bibliographies" are fine old **terms** that mean writing (graphy) about books (biblio), thus they have come to mean lists and descriptions of books. There is no reason to limit their meaning to "books," because the "biblio" part of the word comes from the Greek for papyrus leaves! So by extension, bibliographies can deal with **messages, texts,** and **documents** in any **format** and **medium**, just as IR databases do.

boolean syntax. *See* **exact match syntax**.

bound term. A bound term is a **compound term** consisting of two or more words, sometimes representing two or more concepts, which almost always occur together and have come to be considered a single concept. "Information science," for example, could be factored into "science" and "information," but the bound term "information science" is the name of a discipline and to decompose it would be misleading. Proper names of multiple parts are also bound terms, e.g., "United States." "Birth control" is a bound term whose meaning is different than its component parts, because the bound term means control or prevention of conception, as opposed to the control of birth. *See also* **complex term**; **term**.

catalog, cataloging. A catalog is an **index** for a particular collection of **messages** (plus **texts** and **documentary units**) or of objects (such as a mail order catalog of clothing or a museum's exhibition catalog). A union catalog is an index for several collections. Cataloging is the process of creating a catalog, so it is a type of **indexing**.

cataloging. *See* **catalog, cataloging**.

chain syntax. Chain syntax or chain indexing is a **syntax** technique to create alphanumeric **indexes** to **classification** headings that have been arranged in a non-alphabetical relational classified order. The terms of a classification **heading** or caption are arranged as a chain of **terms** in the order opposite their use in the classification. Each of these terms may become a lead term in the alphanumeric index, following by subsequent terms for context. *See also* section 12.2.4.1.

citation index. Reference citations have always been a useful basis for indicating (**indexing**!) possibly useful relationships. Almost every writer of a term paper, to say nothing of more serious researchers, has pursued reference citations in good **documents** as a way to find other documents of interest. In effect, a string **cluster** is created, with each link through a reference citation leading to an older document that was cited in the newer document. This kind of citation indexing can only lead backwards in time, because it is impossible to cite a document that has not yet been created! Creating indexes that could trace reference citations forward in time was extremely laborious before the advent of the computer. Such citation indexing was limited largely to the legal literature until the Institute for Scientific Information (1961, 1969, 1976) introduced the *Science citation index* in 1961, followed by the *Social science citation index* in 1969 and the *Arts and humanities citation index* in 1976. These **indexes** have now become standard tools, available in both print and electronic forms. They permit the user to begin with a given document and to trace its citation in subsequent documents forward in time. To the extent that a reference citation indicates a link between **messages** related with respect to topic, purpose, meaning or significance, these links can be quite useful for IR searching. *See also* **bibliographic coupling; co-citation**; and section 8.3.12.

class. A grouping of items sharing some similarity. *See also* **classification**.

classification. Classification literally means to place items in **classes**, resulting in groupings of items sharing some similarity. By extension, it can refer to the creation and/or naming of these classes. By further extension, it often includes the arrangement of classes in a logical, relational, non-alphanumeric order. At the fundamental level, **indexing** and classification are the same process, because in both operations, **messages** must be analyzed, and based on this analysis, grouped into categories or classes. Finally, these groupings must be named and arranged to provide access. At the more superficial level, but reflecting its most common usage, classification refers to the logical, relational (non-alphanumeric) arrangement of classes, in contrast to alphanumeric indexes in which classes are simply arranged in alphanumeric order on the basis of their names.

classing. The act creating classes and assigning items to classes or placing items into classes. *See also* **classification**.

clustering. "Clustering" means to create or identify groupings or clusters of items. At one level, "**classing**," "**classification**," and clustering all mean the same thing — the assembling of items into groups or categories. However, the term "clustering" is used more often when the classing, or gathering together, is done through automatic, or algorithmic, means. The term "classing" or "classification" usually implies human judgment.

co-citation. Like **bibliographic coupling**, co-citation is a form of **clustering** based on reference citations. In co-citation clustering, however, clusters are not based on reference citations shared by **documents** (as in bibliographic coupling) but on two or more documents being cited together in a subsequent document. If new papers, hot off the press, frequently cite both documents A and B, then, the reasoning goes, documents A and B must be related, and the more often documents are co-cited (cited together in later documents), then the closer the relationship is. Because new documents keep coming out, with different sets of reference citations, the co-citation clusters keep changing over time, showing new patterns of emerging relationships among documents, authors, and the topics they address. This constant change, incorporating new citation patterns, is the basis of the claim (or hope) of its proponents that these co-citation clusters can identify hot topics and emerging research fronts. *See also* section 8.3.12.2.

co-extensive headings. *See* **statement/heading specificity**.

complex term. Sometimes "complex term" is used for a single phrase denoting more than two distinct concepts. The Library of Congress introduced the complex term "telephone assistance programs for the poor" in 1990. This single **term** could be broken up into separate terms for "telephones," "assistance programs" and "poor people," so it could qualify as an example of a complex term. *See also* **bound term**; **compound term**.

compound term. "Compound term" can refer to a term consisting of more than one word, but more often it refers to a **term** consisting of more than concept, such as "juvenile delinquency," which includes the concepts of both "young person" and "delinquency." *See also* **bound term**; **complex term**.

concrete entity. Concrete entities are those one can see and touch (at least in theory), like persons, tables, chairs. Imaginary concrete entities such as unicorns, Paul Bunyan, angels and faeries (if they are imaginary), can play the same types of roles in **messages** as do concrete real entities, so for **facet analysis**, they can be considered a type of concrete entity. *See also* **abstract entity**; **entity**; and chapter 2.

concrete entity and event database. **Databases** can also be characterized by the nature of the objects or phenomena that they are designed to describe. Concrete entity and event databases organize **data** about real **concrete entities** and events. Examples include airline databases that contain data about airplanes and all their parts, their maintenance, their crews, particular flights, passengers, fares, supplies, including which passengers get special meals, etc.; or bank databases that contain data about all customers, all their accounts, their balances and every banking transaction. The focus of these databases is on concrete entities and concrete events. In contrast, **IR database**s are designed to describe **messages**.

Glossary

These messages, of course, may be about concrete entities and events, but just as often, they can be about **abstract entities** or ephemeral phenomena, such as theories, feelings, emotions, and aesthetics. *See also* section 1.6.

data. *See* **datum, data**

database. "Database" is a relatively new word for a collection of **data** that is organized for retrieval. It is sometimes restricted to organized collections of data in electronic media, but in this book, the term "database" is used for any collection of data organized for retrieval, regardless of **medium**, so that printed **indexes, catalogs**, encyclopedias, and similar reference works constitute examples of databases as well as electronic retrieval tools on CD-ROM or available online or via the world-wide web. (There is a brief note on the origin of this term in section 1.1 and a recap on **IR databases** versus other types of databases in section 1.6.)

Databases (along with the systems for access that accompany those in electronic form) can be categorized in many ways: by mission or purpose (such as MIS: management information systems), by subject areas (such as GIS — geographical information systems), by models of organization (such as **relational, hypertext, object-oriented, flat-file**), or by phenomena represented by data (such as real, **concrete entities** (things, objects!) and events versus **messages** about entities and events, including **abstract entities**, imaginary entities and fictitious events). This book focuses on databases designed for the purpose of facilitating discovery and retrieval of messages of all types, so our databases are called "information retrieval databases" or, for short, **IR databases**. Their purpose is information retrieval. The primary data in such databases describe messages rather than concrete entities and events. *See also* sections 1.5 and 1.6.

datum, data. A "datum" (singular of data) may be considered to be a single fact or item of evidence. To be informative, a datum needs one or more additional data of different sorts to provide context. Thus it can be said that a **message** (potential **information**) needs at least two data. A set of numerical data, such as "70, 90, 28, 64," is meaningless unless some explanation is provided. Do these data refer to temperatures? sport scores? or what? Similarly, a simple datum regarding color, such as "red," carries much more meaning when it is combined with at least one more datum, such as "chair." Data are often presented in tables, along with explanations, e.g., average temperatures by month and place or the scores of yesterday's football games. Because **IR databases** focus on messages, they rarely deal with raw data except in the context of messages, where data are interpreted. *See also* **knowledge**.

descriptive cataloging, descriptive indexing. "Descriptive cataloging" is an old and honorable term that refers to the description and **indexing** of **texts** and **documents** with respect to features other than the content, purpose, or meaning of the text's **message**. Such features include the authors and other creators of texts (editors, composers, illustrators, translators, artists, etc.); the names or titles of texts (including subtitles, parallel titles, alternate titles, running titles etc.); the publishers or manufacturers and distributors of documents; the size and **medium** of documents; and the symbol set and code used to encode the text. Codes and symbols used to encode texts include natural languages and their writing systems (French, German, Chinese), but also codes and symbols for music, dance, chemistry, mathematics, etc., and, at another level, codes for the representation of messages in digital media. Names and index **terms** are established for the most important of these features. Descriptive cataloging (along with **subject cataloging**) is part of the process for making a **catalog**. "Descriptive indexing" is a rarely used term for the same process outside of the context of catalogs for particular collections of documents.

descriptive indexing. *See* **descriptive cataloging**.

Glossary

descriptor. The term "descriptor" is usually reserved for a **term** that is part of a controlled indexing language. Such indexing languages are often listed in a **thesaurus**. For each concept included in the indexing language, one **descriptor** will be chosen to represent the concept, and all other terms that can be used for the same concept are linked to the descriptor by means of cross references. Thus, if a thesaurus uses the descriptor "lawyer," then it might not use the terms "attorney," "barrister," "solicitor," or "counselor-at-law." Each of these alternative terms would be linked to the preferred descriptor "lawyer" and would be given the status of un-used synonymous or **equivalent terms**. (Equivalent terms are terms that are not truly synonymous, but are close enough so that they can be considered equivalent in the context of an **IR database**. Anyone who knows the English legal system knows that "barrister" and "solicitor" are not exactly the same as U.S. "lawyers," but in many databases, the distinction would not be important enough to make, so that "barrister" and "solicitor" could be considered equivalent to "lawyer.") *See also* **vocabulary control/vocabulary management**.

digital library. Digital libraries are **full-text databases** that replicate, in digital **media**, many of the functions of traditional libraries. They tend to contain a purposefully selected collection of **texts** plus various means of access to these texts. *ODLIS: Online Dictionary of Library and Information Science* (Reitz 2000) defines "digital library" simply as: "A library in which a significant proportion of the resources are available in digital (machine-readable) **format**, as opposed to print or microform. The process of digitization began with **indexes** and abstracting services, then moved to periodicals and reference books."

direct file. A direct file is generally the original file of **documentary unit records** or **surrogates**. From it, an **inverted file** is created by extracting search **terms** and rearranging them for quick access and processing by computer algorithm. *See also* **non-displayed index**.

displayed index. Displayed indexes are **indexes** that are displayed for direct examination, browsing, or scanning by users, as opposed to **non-displayed indexes** that are meant for computer manipulation and are not displayed for human examination. *See also* chapter 11.

document. A document is a combination of **text** and **medium**. Texts cannot exist without embodiment in some medium, whether ephemeral, like airwaves, or longer lasting, like paper, film, or electronic media for digital data. Usually we use "document" to refer only to texts recorded in the longer-lasting media, and it is these documents that are susceptible to **indexing** and later retrieval.

documentary domain. Documentary domain is the territory (domain) from which **documents** are gathered for an **IR database**. Two IR databases can have identical **subject scopes** and identical **documentary scopes**, yet provide very different coverage because of different documentary domains. An IR database that obtains documents only from the holdings of one library, for example, will have very different coverage compared to an IR database that combs the entire world for documents that fall within its subject and documentary scopes.

documentary scope. Documentary scope defines and describes the kinds of **messages**, **texts**, and **documents** a user can retrieve via an **IR database** in terms of non-topical features, such as authorship or kinds of authors; **media**; codes and symbols systems used to encode messages as texts, including the various human languages used for creating language texts; the forms, **formats**, and genres of texts; the complexity or technical level of messages, including the kinds of audiences for whom they are intended (children, professionals, general public, etc.); points of view, biases, and methodological approaches characterizing the treatment of topics in messages; time and place of creation, manufacture or publication, etc. *See also* chapter 3.

Glossary

documentary unit. A documentary unit is the portion of a **document** that can be directly retrieved by an **IR database**. Documentary units may be complete documents, such as complete books, or complete periodical articles. Or they may be parts of complete documents — chapters in books, or paragraphs or charts or diagrams or illustrations in periodical articles. This same variety in the size of documentary units applies to all **media**. An IR database for videotapes, for example, might retrieve only complete videotapes (so that the documentary unit is the complete tape), or it might be able to retrieve individual frames or short sequences of frames, in which cases, either the individual frames, or the short sequences of frames, constitute the documentary units. In all cases, the documentary unit is the unit that is analyzed for **indexing** (either by machine algorithm or by human inspection). Consequently, the documentary-unit is also called the "unit-of-analysis." "Bibliographic unit" has also been used for this concept, indicating the unit described and retrievable via a **bibliography**. Small documentary units have also been called "information units," but one should hope that all documentary units will be informative! *See also* **indexable matter**; and chapter 6.

domain. *See* **documentary domain**; **subject domain**.

end-user thesaurus. Traditionally, **thesauri** were designed to guide indexers, who were compelled to use preferred term from **indexing thesauri** for every concept. There are no preferred terms in an end-user thesaurus. Instead, for every concept included, all variant, synonymous, and **equivalent terms** are displayed, along with narrower, broader, and other related **terms**. The purpose is to help searchers find all as many relevant terms as possible for their searches.

entity. Entities, or things, are one of the fundamental **facets** in **facet analysis** for **indexing** and **classification**. Ranganathan referred to the entity facet as the "personality" facet, because he focused on the defining characteristics of entities (their personalities!). Entities include **concrete entities** (living beings and inanimate objects, naturally occurring or human-made, whether real or imaginary) and **abstract entities** (institutions, theories, ideologies, etc.).

entry. In **displayed indexes**, an entry represents and points to a **documentary unit**. An entry consists of a **heading** (of one or more terms) and a single **locator**, such as "United States 23" or "United States. history. civil war. bibliography 44." The locator leads to the documentary unit. In this example the locators 23 and 44 might refer to particular paragraphs or pages or to entries in a list of document citations or to **documents** on shelves or in a filing cabinet. *See also* **entry array**.

entry array. When two or more **entries** have identical **headings** or subheadings, these duplicate headings are usually merged for display, resulting in entry arrays that might look something like this:

```
United States
    Armed Forces
        Afro-Americans. Bibliography   25
                        History   24, 30, 339
        California. History. 20th century   54
        China. History. 20th century   332
            Military life. History   442
        Gays   74-80, 445-450
            Government policy   76
            History. 20th century   78-80
            Legal status, laws, etc. 76-78
```

In this example, there are three separate entries for "United States. Armed Forces. Afro-Americans. History." They have been merged to save space and make the display of the index more convenient for the user. Each separate locator indicates a separate entry in an **index**.

Glossary

equivalent term. Equivalent terms are synonymous terms but also **terms** that are not truly synonymous, but are close enough so that they can be considered equivalent in the context of an **IR database**. Anyone who knows the English legal system knows that "barrister" and "solicitor" are not exactly the same as U.S. lawyers, but in many databases, the distinction would not be important enough to make, so that "barrister" and "solicitor" could be considered equivalent to "lawyer."

exact match syntax. Exact match syntax for electronic matching of **terms** in **non-displayed indexes** requires that terms associated with **documentary units** match exactly the requirements of the search statement. Most often exact match syntax is implemented using boolean operators; it is often called "boolean syntax." Note however that the requirements of the boolean "or" operator permit terms linked with "or" to be either present or absent. Only documentary units whose terms match search statements exactly (within the parameters provided by search syntax options such as truncation, proximity ranges, and stemming) are retrieved. *See also* **best match syntax;** and section 12.3.1.

exhaustivity. Exhaustivity of **indexing** refers to the detail with which the topics and features of **messages, texts,** and **documentary units** are described. How many different **descriptors** or **terms** are used to describe the content or features of a typical documentary unit? This number of terms or descriptors is a measure of exhaustivity. *See also* chapter 9.

facet. Facets are fundamental categories, aspects, or "faces" of phenomena not unlike the journalist's "who, what, where, when, why." Facets represent fundamental characteristics by which any message can be analyzed and described. Facets also represent the important aspects of a subject area that form the basis for creating and arranging a relational classification. Thus a classification of literature might be arranged by the facets of language, nationality, genre, period, writer, theme, etc. The term comes from the French diminutive for "face," "facette" (Webster's 1966). Examples of generic facets are:

- entities or things (persons, artifacts, natural objects, animals and plants, institutions, and other **abstract entities**, etc.)
- attributes or constituent materials
- actions (operations, processes, and events)
- places
- times

Specialized **IR databases** will make use of much more specialized facets. *See also* chapter 2.

facet analysis. The analysis of topics with respect to their basic aspects or **facets**. *See also* chapter 2.

faceted syntax. Faceted syntax is used when there is a need or desire to have the individual **terms** or **descriptors** in an **index** heading arranged in some meaningful order. Terms are assigned to facet categories and these categories are used to determine the order of terms in the **heading**. *See also* section 12.2.2.2.

flat-file database. A flat-file database is an **IR database** based on the flat-file data model. In contrast to the rather sophisticated and highly structured **relational** and **object-oriented** models, a simple flat-file data model calls for nothing more than "a single file containing many **records**, each of which contains the same set of fields" (FOLDOC 2002, "database"). This simple model, sometimes called a "flat file" design, is quite common for IR databases.

format. Texts come in many shapes and styles, influenced by the **medium** on or in which a **message** is encoded, by the meaning and purpose of the message, and by the intended recipients of the message. Shape and style contribute to something we usually call format. It covers a wide spectrum of attributes,

Glossary

such as literary genre (poetry, narrative, drama, essay, speech, fiction, etc.), type of presentation (chart, diagram, picture, cartoon, list, etc.), and type of publication (such as book versus pamphlet versus broadside or poster on paper media, slide versus motion picture in film media). D. W. Langridge (1992, p. 28) suggests six types of attributes related to "the method of selection, arrangement or display" of message content under the heading of format: 1. order, how material is arranged, e.g., alphanumerically, chronologically, or in some classified order according to mutual relations of message content or features; 2. literary forms or genres (poetry, drama, essay, narrative fiction, short story); 3. reductions (abstracts, excerpts, quotations, summaries); 4. collections (encyclopedias, compendia, handbooks, readers); 5. keys to other documents (**indexes, bibliographies, catalogs**); and 6. rules (**standards**, codes, recipes). The distinction between "format" and "medium" is sometimes fuzzy. For example, the meaning of "book" usually includes its medium (paper) as well as its shape (leaves bound together along one edge). When the content of a book is moved to electronic media, is it still a book? Probably the meaning of "book" will continue to shift as the media on or in which book-like messages are conveyed change over time. After all, our word "book" came from the Anglo-Saxon word for beech tree, because ancient runes were once written on beech bark! The connection in German is quite close: "Buche" for "beech tree" and "Buch" for "book."

free-text term. Often shortened to "free text," "free-text term" usually refers to the use of uncontrolled words or **terms** from natural language **text** for **indexing** or searching. When one searches the actual text of a **document**, one is searching the free-text terms that are found in the document. The difference between "free-text terms" and just "terms" is that sometimes terms may be standardized, at least a little, with respect to format, and they may also have links with the most common synonyms or **equivalent terms**, even if they are not controlled to the extent of **descriptors**. In this paragraph, every term or phrase is a free-text term. Some of the smaller words (such as "of," "the," "to," etc.) may be listed on a **stop list** of unsearchable terms — terms that cannot be searched for by themselves, but they are still free-text terms! "Keyword" is often used to indicate the more important free-text terms.

full-text database. Full-text databases are **IR databases** that contain the full text of the **documents** that they describe and organize for retrieval. Such **texts** may be based on a variety of representation codes, such as linguistic, pictorial, musical, mathematical, etc. We have long had full-text databases in print **media**. Examples include handbooks and encyclopedias. In addition, monographs with their own back-of-the-book indexes also qualify as full-text databases, because the text of the monograph is presented together with an **index**, and this index describes and reorganizes the content and other features of the text for retrieval. But usually, "full-text database" refers to electronic databases.

generic posting. Generic posting is the use of a broader more generic **term** in addition to a specific term to represent a topic or feature of a **message, text** or **documentary unit**. Some experts make a distinction between "generic posting" and "**up-posting**," limiting "generic posting" to the use of a broader, more generic term in place of a specific term (e.g., using "furniture" in place of "sofas") while using "up-posting" for the use of both a specific term and a broader, more generic term (using both "sofas" and "furniture").

heading. In **displayed indexes** (indexes that are designed for visual inspection by humans as opposed to **non-displayed indexes** that are searched by computer algorithm), index **terms** are combined into **headings** consisting of multiple terms. It is possible to have index headings with only single terms, but headings of two or more terms are more meaningful, because the lead term is modified or amplified or described by the subsequent term or terms. The subsequent term or terms create a context for the first, or lead, term. Compare, for example, the meaning of the simple heading "United States" versus the more detailed meaning of "United States — history — civil war — bibliography." In the second heading,

Glossary

"United States" has been modified or defined by aspect or approach (history), event or period (civil war), and format (bibliography). An index heading is an essential part of an index entry. When displayed **indexes** are displayed in classified rather than alphanumeric order, the headings are often called "captions."

hierarchical specificity. This type of **specificity** has nothing to do with the **specificity** relationship between the meaning of a **term** and the **message, text,** or **documentary unit** to which it refers. Instead it relates to the relative narrowness or breadth of the meaning of a term in a **hierarchy**. Weinberg and Cunningham (1984, 1985) used this definition in comparisons with **operational specificity**. Thus this hierarchical term-term relationship is entirely different from the term-document relationship that forms the basis of the semantic term-document relational definition of "specificity" as used in this book. *See also* section 10.1.

hierarchy. From the Greek for "hierarch" or "high priest," "hierarchy" is now used to indicate an array of **terms** or **descriptors** or categories arranged from broader to narrower. There is a strong theoretical proposition that broader-narrower relationships exist only within **facets** (Kwasnik 1999).

HTML (HyperText Markup Language). *See* **text encoding schemas**.

human indexing. Human indexing is indexing done by humans based on analysis using the human intellect. *See also* section 8.2.

hypermedia Hypermedia is really **hypertext**. The medium is electronic and digital. It is the format that is hypertextual.

hypertext. Hypertext is **text** displayed in an interactive **format** so that a user (a reader or viewer or listener) has the capability of skipping around from place to place rather freely. The various parts of the text are linked via hyperlinks. Hypertext can be contrasted with traditional static linear text. *See also* section 21.1.

hypertext database. With the advent of the world-wide web, hypertext databases have become more and more common. According to FOLDOC (2002, "hypertext"), "hypertext" refers to a "collection of **documents** (or 'nodes') containing cross-references or 'links' which, with the aid of an interactive browser program, allow the reader to move easily from one document to another." In a hypertext **IR database**, some of these documents may be summary **records** or **surrogates**, which can lead the user to documents containing the full **text** of **messages**. Also, in this context, "documents" may be **documentary units** of any size, e.g., paragraphs or individual images.

index, indexing. An index is any device that is (or can be) used to indicate or point to something of interest. Indexing is the creation of such indexes. Indexes are used in many fields in addition to library and information science, such as the consumer price index in economics, where the index points to the rise and fall of prices. In information retrieval, an index is used to indicate the content and features of **messages,** their **texts** and **documentary units,** and their location and/or the location of particular content or features within these messages, texts, and documentary units. There are many types and varieties of indexes, corresponding to types of **IR databases** listed in section 1.5. Indexes are produced in many different ways, both by human analysis and computer algorithmic processing.

indexable matter. Indexable matter is the actual portion of a **documentary unit** on which **indexing** or **classification** is based — on which index **terms** or **headings** are based or from which terms are extracted. Not all indexes need to be based on the entire **text** of a **message**. Sometimes a message can be adequately summarized by a part of its text. Thus, if an index does not need to be very detailed, a good title might be sufficient to represent the message of a periodical article for purposes of indexing or clas-

Glossary

sification. In that case, the title could be the indexable matter for the documentary unit — the periodical article. Abstracts of scholarly articles are a common example of indexable matter. Many indexing and abstracting services base their indexing and classification only on the abstracts of the messages that they cover. For important messages, the entire text of the message may need to be consulted, thereby making the entire text the indexable matter. Sometimes, whole categories of messages may be excluded from indexable matter (and also from **documentary domain**). An index for a scholarly journal, for example, may index only substantive research articles and exclude from indexable matter all advertisements, letters to the editor (unless they comment on articles that are indexed), announcements, calls for papers, etc. ("Indexable matter" is also called "analysis base," because it constitutes the base, or basis, of analysis — the text on which analysis is based.) *See also* chapter 7.

indexer thesaurus. Traditionally, **thesauri** were designed to guide indexers, who were compelled to use the preferred term in a thesaurus for every concept. Each preferred term is generally accompanied with synonymous, **equivalent**, variant, narrower, broader, and other related **terms**. Sometimes source and scope notes are included. Although designed for indexers, indexing thesauri can be very helpful for searchers as well. *See also* **end-user thesauri**.

information. This is a slippery concept that is best avoided, except in terms like "information science" (the established name of a discipline) and "information retrieval" (the name of a primary focus in information science). The problem with "information" is that it has come to have too many meanings, and it is therefore often vague and unclear. On the one hand, it is used to refer to the process of informing or becoming informed. But more frequently, it is used to stand for **data, messages, texts,** and **documents**, whether or not these are actually informative for a person confronting them. Does it really make sense to call ancient Greek manuscripts "information" if one can't even read them?

IR database (information retrieval database). Also called "bibliographic databases," "document databases," "textual databases," "textbases." The basic definition for the term "IR database" as used in this book is any **database** in any **medium** used for discovering and retrieving **messages, texts,** and **documents**. Thus, it includes the whole gamut of IR databases presented to users via online connections, the world-wide web, CD-ROMs, or in print on paper: indexing and abstracting services (regardless of medium), library **catalogs** (including OPACs, online public access catalogs, and older card catalogs), **bibliographies**, and **indexes**, including back-of-the-book indexes (which can now be presented electronically with electronic books!).

Thus IR databases have as their primary purpose the organization of **data** about messages, texts, and documents to facilitate their retrieval. For the most part, IR databases are not directly concerned with **concrete entities** or events, except as they are represented as topics of messages or features of texts. In contrast to typical **concrete entity and event databases**, the numbers and variety of concrete entities and events, and other topics, that can be represented in texts is enormous and their mutual relationships multitudinous, so that usually there is no attempt to structure their relationships in advance. Hence, IR databases are often called "unstructured," or their data is called "unstructured information." This is why IR databases in electronic media most often use the **flat-file model**.

Despite this general focus on the content and features of messages and texts, many IR databases must also deal with concrete entities and events related to the creation and transmission of messages and texts. They must describe the concrete documents in which messages and texts reside and the persons and organizations that create, manufacture, publish and send these documents.

In contrast to concrete entity and event databases however, IR databases are just as likely to focus on abstract, fictitious or imaginary entities, attributes and events, as compared to real concrete entities and

Glossary

events. Examples of abstract, fictitious or imaginary phenomena include hypotheses, theories, opinions, beliefs, aesthetics, feelings, emotions, and mythical or fictional figures, characters and events.

IR system (information retrieval system or information storage and retrieval system). IR systems are the systems that make it possible to search **IR databases**. They provide the **search interfaces** that permit users to compose searches and match them against database indexes (**non-displayed indexes**) or to browse indexes that are displayed for visual inspection (**displayed indexes**). Often the search system is so integrated into the database itself that it is inseparable. This is especially true for print-on-paper databases, such as printed **indexes, catalogs, bibliographies**, handbooks and encyclopedias. In electronic retrieval, however, the information retrieval system may be completely separate, so that the same IR database can be vended or made available by different vendors or agencies, each of which provides an entirely different information retrieval system, with entirely different search interfaces, different search engines, different search commands, and different display options.

inverse document frequency. Inverse document frequency (IDR) is a measure of how infrequently a **term** occurs in **documents** in a collection or **IR database**, hence the term "inverse" document frequency. Sometimes term frequency (TF) within documents does not help much in distinguishing one **text** from another within a single collection or IR database. Take librarianship, for example. The word "library" will probably occur in most if not all texts in a collection or IR database on librarianship, so the mere fact that it occurs frequently in a text doesn't tell us very much. But comparing frequency counts in single texts with the overall occurrence for the same words in an entire collection or IR database often helps to pinpoint the more important terms. We can identify words that are unusually frequent in particular texts — words that occur frequently in some texts but do not occur frequently across the entire collection. This relative frequency can be more useful in finding useful documents than simple word frequency within documents. The fewer the documents that have a term (or the lower its frequency in most texts), the higher the IDF score. The IDF score can be combined with term frequency (TF) within particular documents to help identify useful documents. *See also* section 8.3.5.

inverted file. An inverted file or inverted index is "a sequence of (key, pointer) pairs where each pointer points to a **record** in a **database** which contains the key value in some particular field. The **index** is sorted on the key values to allow rapid searching for a particular key value .... The index is 'inverted' in the sense that the key value is used to find the record rather than the other way round. For databases in which the records may be searched based on more than one field, multiple indices may be created that are sorted on those keys" (FOLDOC 2002). The "key" in this FOLDOC definition may be any **descriptor**, **term**, or **keyword**, including names of authors or other features, such as languages, **formats, media**, etc. In contrast a **direct file** is generally the original file of **documentary unit surrogates** (records). Search terms (keys) are extracted from the records in such a direct file and rearranged for quick access and processing by computer algorithm. *See also* **non-displayed index**.

keyword indexing. Keyword indexing is based on words (keywords) in natural language **text**. It is commonly the basis for electronic searching of **non-displayed indexes** or full texts, but it is also the basis for some popular **natural language syntax** for **displayed indexes**. KWIC (KeyWord In Context) syntax creates a **heading** for every keyword in a text segment (title or other statement), with the rest of the text segment used for context preceding and following the keyword in the original word order. In KWIC, the keyword (and sorting word) is in the middle of the heading. KWOC (KeyWord Out of Context) pulls the key word out of its context to place it in its traditional place at the left of the heading. KWAC (KeyWord Alongside Context) attempts to restore some context by keeping the original word order, but placing words that appear preceding the key word at the end of the heading. *See also* sections 8.3.2 and 12.2.5. Examples of KWIC, KWAC and KWOC headings are in sections following 12.2.5.

Glossary

knowledge. "Knowledge" refers to what someone knows. It resides in the mind and the brain, but it can be reflected in **messages**. "Wisdom" refers to the wise use of knowledge. It is not technically correct to say that knowledge resides in messages. According to the definitions for "**text**" and "**document**," messages are embodied by organized sets of symbols (texts) recorded on **media** (documents). But these messages and texts can refer to what persons know, think, believe, feel, and understand, so it is entirely proper to say that messages, texts, and documents record, reflect, and convey the knowledge of a person, a group, or an entire culture.

KWAC index. *See* **keyword indexing**.

KWIC index. *See* **keyword indexing**.

KWOC index. *See* **keyword indexing**.

language model syntax. Throughout the history of **automatic indexing** based on term weighting and **relevance** prediction, two major theoretical models have emerged: the **vector-space model** and the **probabilistic model**. Recently, a "language model" for IR has been proposed, as a modification or simplification of the probabilistic model. The differences are subtle. Instead of attempting to predict the probability of **document** relevance for an IR query statement, the language model is used to predict probable query search **terms**. Retrieval is effected when predicted (highly probably) search terms match the actual search terms of users. Like all basic models, language model probabilities are based, for the most part, on term frequencies within documents and the **inverse document frequency** of terms across collections or **IR databases** (Ponte & Croft 1998).

latent semantic indexing. Latent semantic indexing (LSI) is one of the most sophisticated modern attempts at high quality **automatic indexing**. It is based on co-occurrence **clustering** of **terms** and the identification of **documents** associated with these term clusters. By relying on co-occurrence data, LSI is also able to deal with the problem of the variety of terms that can be used to express similar concepts. For example, both "lawyers" and "attorneys" are likely to belong to the same cluster with related terms such as "courts," "trials," "judges," "sentencing," etc. *See also* section 8.3.11.1.

literary warrant. Literary warrant simply means that the vocabulary of indexed or cataloged **documents** should be accepted as terminology for index **headings**, **descriptors**, or preferred **terms** in **thesauri**, because it is warranted (authorized) through actual usage in documents. Literary warrant is complemented by **user warrant**.

locator. The locator is the part of an index **entry** that leads the user to the **documentary unit** to which the index entry refers. It indicates the location of the documentary unit or the location of a representation (**surrogate**) of the documentary unit (such as a citation, abstract, description, or thumb-nail image). The locator can be as brief as a number, representing a page or paragraph in a back-of-the-book **index**, or it can be long enough to include a full citation that can be used to locate a documentary unit, perhaps in a library or on the internet. *See also* chapter 15.

manual indexing. **Indexing** has never been done by the hands! Humans use their intellect, their minds, to index. *See* **human indexing**!

medium. Media (the plural of medium) are the physical substances on which or in which a **text** is recorded and conveyed. Ephemeral media include the airwaves over which sound (including speech) is sent and received. Information retrieval generally deals with longer lasting media, such as stone, clay, metal, paper, film, and the newer media for the recording of electronic digital **data**: disks, tapes and chips made from various forms of plastic, silicon and metal. An important responsibility of our profession is to make sure that the media on which **messages** are recorded can actually be preserved for as long

Glossary

as the messages have value. This is a big challenge, especially for untested newer magnetic and optical media for digital data. One hopes that these modern media, including silicon (ceramic!) chips, will be as long-lasting as their ancient relatives, the clay tablets of the Middle East and elsewhere. And even more important thus far is that the technology required to read various media not be discarded before the texts on older media are transferred to media that can be read.

message. **IR databases** are used to find and retrieve **messages**. A message is the content of a meaningful communication. In order to be communicated — to be sent and to be received, messages must be encoded into **texts**, using symbols or representations that can convey meaning to recipients of the message. And the text of a message must be recorded on a **medium** to create a **document**. A message is potential **information**. If a message is actually received by someone who pays some level of attention to it, that person can be said to have been informed by the message, and the message itself can qualify as information.

metadata. Metadata is **data** about data, or more specifically within our context, data about **messages, texts**, and **documents**. The "meta" of "metadata" comes from the Greek for "along with" or "over," so literally, "metadata" is "along with" data or "over" data. Some experts have suggested that the term "metadata" should be reserved for data about messages, texts and documents that are embedded within the documents themselves. (Other data about messages, texts, and documents could be called bibliographic **records**, or something similar.) Certainly the inclusion of metadata within the document itself is the expectation for metadata that describes a digital document. But any kind of document — digital, print on paper, or of any other medium — can certainly contain its "bibliographic record" within itself, as has long been the practice with CIP (Cataloging in Publication) in printed books. This distinction, between records separate from documents or included in documents, does not seem to be very useful. Thus, metadata may not be very different in meaning or purpose from **surrogates** or records.

natural language syntax. Natural language syntax is **syntax** for **displayed indexes** that is applied to statements or segments of **text** that already exist (i.e., in natural language). Most commonly, it is applied to titles of **documents**. The most common natural language syntaxes are KWIC, KWAC, and KWOC, which are described in the entry for **keyword indexing**. **Permuted syntax** can also be used on natural language **terms**, as well as assigned terms. **Ad hoc string syntax**, such as **NEPHIS**, can also be applied to natural language text or titles. (Many **non-displayed indexes** consist of natural language terms, but the term "natural language syntax" usually refers to syntax used to create displayed indexes.) *See also* section 12.2.5.

NEPHIS. "NEPHIS" stands for "Nested Phrase Indexing System," developed by Timothy Craven (1986). Natural language statements are coded with special symbols to identify phrases that should be lead terms (main **headings**) in an **index** and to arrange remaining terms into meaningful subheadings. *See also* section 12.2.2.3.

non-displayed index. A non-displayed index is one that is not displayed for direct human use. Instead it is designed to be searched by machine, mechanically in the early days and electronically in more recent decades. Only in the past century have we begun creating **indexes** that are used for machine matching rather than for visual inspection by the human eye. The earliest such indexes predated the computer, but they relied on early examples of the same kind of matching techniques (**exact match syntax**) that became nearly universal with the advent of computer-based **IR systems**. An example of a pre-computer non-displayed index are the cards used in the optical coincidence, or **peek-a-boo, retrieval system** that is described in section 5.1.3. Now non-displayed indexes are almost always used by computer programs. Such **indexes** may not even exist until a search is performed. They may be created "ad

Glossary

hoc" or "on the fly" for each search, or **inverted files** of **terms** may be created in advance of searches in order to speed up the machine matching process. Inverted files are created by taking all, or selected, terms from **message**, **text**, or **document** descriptions or from full text, and sorting them in ways that speed up machine processing. *See also* chapter 11.

object-oriented database. A more recent data model for **databases** is called "object-oriented," as in "object-oriented databases," related to object-oriented programming (FOLDOC 2002, "object-oriented database"). In these databases, algorithms for processing **data** are integrated with the data, so that data related to each object of importance have their own associated object-oriented programs.

ontology. In philosophy, ontology refers to the study of existence, or the creation of "a systematic account of existence." From this, the field of artificial intelligence (AI) took the term "ontology" to refer to "an explicit formal specification of how to represent the objects, concepts and other **entities** that are assumed to exist in some area of interest and the relationships that hold among them" (FOLDOC 2002). From the AI field, "ontology" has become a new "in" word referring to **thesauri** and **classifications**: "the hierarchical structuring of **knowledge** about things by subcategorising them according to their essential (or at least relevant and/or cognitive) qualities. ... This is an extension of the previous senses of 'ontology' (above) ..." (FOLDOC 2002). Ontologies are generally created for machine manipulation, whereas thesauri are generally designed for human use. *See also* section 13.3.5.

operational specificity. Elaine Svenonius (1971) redefined **specificity** in terms of the number of **postings** associated with a **term** or **descriptor** and called it "operational specificity." This has also been the definition used in most subsequent information science research on specificity. The fewer the postings, the higher the level of operational specificity. Terms linked to few **documentary units** are considered to be highly specific. Terms linked with many documentary units are considered to lack specificity. Karen Sparck Jones (1972) called this "statistical specificity." *See also* section 10.1.

optical coincidence IR system. *See* **peek-a-boo IR system**.

paradigmatic relationship. Also called "semantic relationship." This is a relationships that always exists based on the definitions of **terms** and permanent relationships among concepts, such as the taxonomic relationships among "dogs," "canines," "mammals," "vertebrates," and "animals." Contrast to **syntagmatic relationship**. *See also* section 12.2.3.1.

peek-a-boo IR system. "Peek-a-boo" is the nick name and the more common name for the "optical coincidence" **IR system**, because light peeking through pin-holes indicates the presence of a hit (one or more **documents** matching search criteria). This was one of the most prominent pre-computer systems for **exact match syntax** (boolean) searching. Cards approximately one foot square were used to represent index **terms** or **descriptors** for topics or features, including names of authors. After a document was indexed, the cards for each term assigned to the document were pulled from an alphabetical file and the document was recorded on the card by drilling a small hole to represent the document number. On each card was a grid with 100 positions along the horizontal and vertical axes, so that 10,000 unique positions were available to represent 10,000 documents. Each document was given a two part number, corresponding to the horizontal and vertical axes, so that document number 59-23 would get a hole drilled exactly 59 spaces to the right of the left margin and 23 spaces down from the top. A highly calibrated drill press was used to make these holes. *See* figure 5.1 for photos of a "peek-a-boo" optical coincidence IR system, with equipment manufactured by the Jonker Corporation, circa 1967. *See also* section 5.1.3.

permuted syntax. Permuted syntax was developed to provide direct access to every two-word pair in an original indexing statement (a document title or a statement prepared by an indexer) or a set of in-

Glossary

dex **terms**, regardless of whether or not these two words appear next to each other in the original statement or set of index terms. Direct access is provided to every keyword (every word not on a **stop list**), and each access word is linked to every other non-stop-list word that occurs in the same index statement or set of terms. Compare permuted syntax with the common syntaxes of **keyword indexing**: KWIC, KWOC, and KWAC. *See also* section 12.2.6.

   postcoordinate, precoordinate syntax. The terms "postcoordinate syntax" and "precoordinate syntax" are used to indicate when **terms** are put together to represent **documentary units**, either before (pre) or after (post) a search begins. All index **headings** that are constructed for **displayed indexes**, which users may browse during the searching process, must of necessity be created before the search, so they are called "precoordinate headings" based on precoordinate syntax. Postcoordinate syntax is used almost exclusively for machine matching, where searchers create search statements, putting terms together at the time of the search, then make use of computer algorithms to find matching **records** or **texts**. *See also* section 12.1

   postings. The term "postings" refers to the assignment or "posting" of a **term** to a **record** for a **documentary unit**. It is used for term-document associations regardless of whether a term was assigned by a human or by machine algorithm. The number of postings is valuable **information** for searchers because it indicates how many **documents** in an **IR database** will be retrieved by a particular term.

   postings specificity. *See* **operational specificity**.

   precision. Precision and **Recall** are traditional measures of retrieval effectiveness. While true recall is difficult, if not impossible, to determine, precision is easy to calculate — at least it would be easy if making **relevance** judgments were easy. It is based only on retrieved **documents**. It's the ratio between the number of relevant documents retrieved over all the documents retrieved — both the relevant documents and the junk:

```
                number of relevant documents retrieved
   precision = ----------------------------------------
                number of all documents retrieved
```
See also section 9.1.2.

   precoordinate syntax. *See* **postcoordinate, precoordinate syntax**.

   probabilistic model syntax. Throughout the history of **automatic indexing** based on **term** weighting and **relevance** prediction, two major theoretical models have emerged: the **vector-space model** and the **probabilistic model**. Probabilistic syntax is based on the probabilistic model, in which statistical **data** for term frequency and distribution is used to predict the probability of relevance. *See also* sections 8.3 and 12.3.2.

   pseudo relevance feedback. Some researchers are experimenting with **relevance feedback** systems that don't require user input or evaluation. The initial search is simply modified on the basis of the most highly-ranked **documents** in the initial retrieval set. This technique is called "pseudo relevance feedback."

   recall. Recall refers to the extent to which an **IR retrieval system**, including the **indexing** provided, is able to retrieve everything useful within its reach in response to a search. Its formal definition is the ratio of the number of relevant **documents** retrieved over all the relevant documents in an **IR database** or collection:

Glossary

$$\text{recall} = \frac{\text{number of relevant documents retrieved}}{\text{number of relevant documents in database or collection}}$$

The denominator of this formula, the total number of relevant documents in an IR database or collection, is impossible to determine. If it were possible, then all relevant documents would be retrieved! Consequently, researchers attempt to estimate the total number of relevant documents, with varying levels of success. *See also* **precision;** and section 9.1.1.

record. A record (or database record) contains the description of a **message**, the **text** in which it is encoded, and the **documentary unit** that contains the text. In some contexts, such a record is now called "**metadata**." All the **information** or **data** in a IR database about a particular message, text and documentary unit goes into its record. Examples of such data include: a citation to the text and its documentary unit, including creator, title, publisher or manufacturer, **format** and **medium**; an abstract or some other description of the message content and features of the message, text, and documentary unit, sometimes including a small picture (thumbnail) of an image **document** or a short segment of sound; and all the content and feature **terms, descriptors** or **headings** associated with the documentary unit. The database record is usually structured or formatted according to some regular pattern. For example, many library catalogs use the MARC (Machine-Readable Cataloging) **record format**, developed initially by the Library of Congress and now a world-wide **standard**. Many IR databases create their own record format. In some database models, especially **relational databases**, the record is not a single unit, but is a node that contains links to all the data related to a particular message, text and documentary unit. For example, the name of a publisher may be recorded in a table of publishers and the name of an author may be in a table of authors. The particular publishers or authors linked to a particular message, text and documentary unit are called into a record or **surrogate display** when that display is requested. *See also* chapter 20.

record format. The record format defines the way that **data** is tagged or labeled and stored in electronic computer-readable **media**. Such electronic **records** are not generally displayed directly to end users, unless specifically requested. Rather they are used to generate the various displays that are especially designed for the end user (such as those described in chapter 16 on **surrogate displays**). The general principle to follow in setting up a record format is that every element of data that will be important for the implementation of any database display or search option should be separately identified. Each of these elements will have a separate field (or subfield) in the record, and each of these fields will have a name or caption, which is abbreviated or represented by some type of tag, label or notation. *See also* chapter 20.

reference database. Reference databases are **IR databases** that point to (refer to!), but do not include, the full text of the **documents** that they describe. Documents are represented by **surrogates**, such as citations, abstracts, excerpts, notes, and pictures.

relational database. One of the most common database models is called "relational," resulting in relational databases. According to *FOLDOC: The Free On-line Dictionary of Computing* (2002), a relational database is one in which "the **data** and relations between them are organized in tables." The name reflects a special way for organizing data and for indicating relations among data or categories of data. The name can be misleading, however, because all **databases**, regardless of data model, describe and display relationships to some degree, in one way or another. *See also* **concrete entity and event database**.

Glossary

relevance. Judgments of relevance are used in information retrieval as an indication of the usefulness of retrieved **documentary units** in response to a request or a search. The common measures of retrieval effectiveness, **recall** and **precision**, are both based on a determination of relevance (*see also* section 9.1). Sometimes researchers try to make distinctions between "relevance," "utility," "pertinence," and similar concepts, or to distinguish types of relevance, such as "topical relevance" as opposed to "user relevance (the idea being that a **document** might be on the topic, and therefore topically relevant, but the user can't use it or doesn't want it — perhaps he or she can't read the language or already has the document or the writing is too complex, etc.).

relevance feedback. Relevance feedback refers to methods for adjusting a search statement based on preliminary **relevance** judgments by the user. The usual approach is for a preliminary search to proceed using **terms** (and modifications such as term weights, truncation, proximity limits, etc.) provided by the user. The results of this initial search are presented to the user, along with an evaluative questionnaire in which the user can indicate preliminary relevance judgments concerning the value of the retrieved **documents**. These judgments are then used by the system to modify the initial search statement (e.g., adding weights to the more successful terms, decreasing weights for the less successful terms or eliminating them altogether), and a second search is performed. This interaction can continue as long as the user wishes. *See also* **pseudo relevance feedback**; and section 8.3.13.

rotated term syntax. This is the simplest of all **string syntax** patterns. All **terms** or **descriptors** assigned to a **documentary unit** are arranged in alphanumeric order within the string, and then each term is rotated out to the lead position, one at a time, for access purposes. *See also* section 12.2.2.1.

search interface. The most important aspect for all **IR databases** is the way in which their content and access options are presented to the user. Database presentation has earned the relatively new name "search interface." We use it in the broadest sense, not only for electronic interfaces for electronic searches, but also for browsing in both electronic and print **media**. All IR databases, regardless of medium, must present their content and their access options to users, so all have search interfaces. *See also* chapter 19.

SGML (Standard General Markup Language). *See* **text encoding schemas**.

specificity. Specificity has been a rather slippery term with respect to its meaning and applications in library and information science. In this book, "specificity" refers to the degree or closeness of fit or correspondence between the meaning of an index **term** or **descriptor** and the topic or feature to which it refers in a **message, text**, and **documentary unit**. This is the "semantic term-document relational definition." *See also* chapter 10, especially section 10.1. where several definitions of specificity are discussed. And *see also* these alternative definitions: **operational specificity, hierarchical specificity**, and **statement/heading specificity**.

standards. Standards are codes of practice on which participants in an operational domain agree in order to promote interoperability, efficiency, and improved service. Since the beginning of librarianship, millennia ago, improvements in practice have come about mainly through the development of new and better standards or codes of practice. Scientific research, as a means to study and understand phenomena and thereby improve practice, is a relatively recent innovation that came into librarianship, for the most part, with the advent and popularity of information science, mostly after World War II. Whereas scientific research is based on empirical testing of hypotheses, standards and codes of practice are based on expert opinion. *See also* section 1.4.

Glossary

statement/heading specificity. This refers to the closeness or accuracy with which a search statement or a complete index **heading** describes the overall content of a **message**, **text** and **documentary unit**. Highly specific search statements or index **headings** are often referred to as "co-extensive" with the scope of the message, text, and documentary unit. Specificity in the sense used in this book refers only to individual index **terms** or **descriptors**, not to strings of terms or multi-term headings or to search statements consisting of multiple terms. However, the specificity of individual terms will contribute to the overall specificity of multi-term headings and to multi-term search statements. The specificity of index headings and search statements can also be increased by adding additional terms. Thus "dogs — New Jersey" can be a more specific heading than "dogs" by itself, or "New Jersey" by itself. And a search for "dogs" and "fleas" can be a more specific search statement than "dogs" by itself or "fleas" by itself, even though the term specificity of "dogs," "New Jersey," or "fleas" has not changed. *See also* section 10.7. The methods for combining terms in index headings and search statements are governed by rules and patterns of **syntax**, not by term specificity. Syntax is the topic of chapter 12.

statistical specificity. *See* **operational specificity**.

stemming. "Stemming" refers to procedures for automatically removing certain common suffixes, or word endings, (and sometimes prefixes, like "re" or "re-" as in "re-indexing") in order to increase the frequency count for important words, and also in order to find word occurrences when the word form in the **text** does not match the word form in the search statement. There are often sets of related words that are derived from a common root and appear in a variety of forms, depending on particular functions in a sentence or variations in meaning. Thus we have "index," "indexes," "indexer," "indexing," "indexable." We also have variants, such as "indices" as another form for the word "indexes." *See also* section 8.3.6. for discussion of stemming algorithms.

stop list. A stop list is a list of insignificant words, designed to eliminate **indexing** of and retrieval by words like "an" and "the." Eliminating stop words can reduce the size of the **index** significantly, and speed up processing. Francis, Kučera and Mackie (1982) suggest that the ten most frequently used words in English can account for twenty to thirty percent of the words in a text. *See also* section 8.3.3.

string indexing *See* **string syntax**.

string syntax. String syntax is the modern version of **subject heading syntax**, inspired by the desire to take advantage of computer technology for the creation of **headings**. Because instructions for the combination of **terms** into headings are programmed for the computer, string syntax tends to be much more regular than the idiosyncratic variety exhibited by subject heading syntax. The name "string syntax" or "string indexing" comes from the custom of displaying headings as strings of terms — terms strung together in various configurations. The variety of string syntax approaches is mostly related to how terms are arranged in these strings. *See also* section 12.2.2.

subject cataloging, subject indexing. Whereas **descriptive cataloging** and **descriptive indexing** focus on the surface features of **texts** and **documents**, subject cataloging and subject indexing focus on analysis, description and **indexing** of the content, purpose or meaning of **messages**, in other words, the topics or subjects of messages and **texts**. The description of certain non-topical features of messages, texts and documents is frequently included in subject cataloging and indexing as well. Examples include special audiences (books for children), special **formats** (poetry, fiction, dictionaries, periodicals, statistics), special aspects or approaches (history, case studies), special **media** (film, video recordings, audio recordings, world-wide web), etc. The goal is to identify and provide access to all important topics and features. The challenge, of course, is figuring out what is, or will be, important for future users!

Glossary

subject domain. The subject domain of an **IR database** sets the **subject scope** into the context of the work or life situation (the domain) in which users will be operating and seeking messages. Typical domains include the various scholarly disciplines, the professions, industries, business, occupations and trades, but also every other sphere of human life and activity, such as sports and recreation, hobbies, religion, entertainment, travel, relationships, child rearing, and home management. Subject domains also include cultural domains, often characterized by such human attributes as economic level, living environment, religious and ethnic heritage, gender, sexual orientation, and age. Subject domain analysis will differentiate between interests and needs in the same subject area for users operating in different subject domains, such as persons seeking novels for entertainment versus literary scholars; week-end soccer players versus sociologists of sport or students of sports medicine; urban high-income African American gay men seeking health information versus low-income, rural, white migrant worker pregnant women. In medicine, for example, researchers, health care practitioners, patients, the general adult public, and children all occupy different subject domains. *See also* chapter 2.

subject heading syntax. Subject headings are the most widely-used type of **pre-coordinate syntax** headings in **indexes** and **catalogs**. They were developed in the 19th century to provide predictable, uniform and direct alphabetical access to topics in library catalogs, indexes, and **bibliographies**. Subject heading syntax consists of main **headings** modified by subheadings or subdivisions representing related topics, places, times, or **formats** and forms of treatment. There are no over-arching syntactic rules. Instead, every heading and every subheading tends to have its own rules. In the United States, the two most widely used subject heading systems are *Sears list of subject headings* (Sears 1997), for smaller libraries, and *Library of Congress subject headings* (Library of Congress 2003) for larger libraries. Specialized lists of subject headings have been developed for many subject areas, such as *MeSH: Medical subject headings* (National Library of Medicine 1999a). *See also* section 12.2.1.

subject indexing. *See* **subject cataloging**.

subject scope. The subject scope of an **IR database** describes the kinds of questions or desires that an IR database can respond to. Generally this can be done by specifying anywhere from ten to thirty categories of topics that the IR database addresses. When IR databases are presented to users electronically, an ideal number of key subject scope categories is between ten and fifteen, because this is the number of topics that can be clearly displayed on an opening electronic **search interface**, where an overall view of the IR database should be presented to potential users. The analysis and definition of a subject scope can often begin with generic categories or **facets** of topics that pertain to all subject fields. These are categories like:

- **entities** or things (persons, artifacts, natural objects, animals and plants, institutions, and other **abstract entities**, etc.)
- attributes or constituent materials
- actions (operations, processes, and events)
- places
- times

Specialized IR databases will have much more specific or narrower categories or facets.

surrogate/surrogation. A surrogate is a representative. A message/text/document surrogate stands in the place of the original full **text** containing the **message** of interest. A message/text/document surrogate represents only certain key aspects of a message, text, and **documentary unit**. Its nature and content will depend on the nature and content of the full documentary unit and the needs of users. Typical components are citations, index **terms**, **headings**, or **descriptors**, abstracts, and thumb-nail illustrations. *See also* **record;** and chapter 14.

surrogate display. **Surrogates** are almost always displayed in stages in both print and electronic **IR databases**. The purpose is to provide to users only what is useful at a particular stage of a search. Surrogate display deals with what portions of surrogates to display and how best to order the elements of a surrogate display in various situations. *See also* chapter 16.

syndetic structure. Syndetic structure consists of cross-reference links between **descriptors** or **headings** in an indexing system. "Syndetic" comes from the Greek words "syn" for "together" and "dein" for "to bind or tie." Thus, the syndetic structure ties or binds the individual descriptors or headings into a complete and connected access system. Syndetic structure results from **vocabulary control and management**, whereby cross references are created linking synonymous, **equivalent**, broader, narrower, or other related descriptors or headings. *See also* chapter 13.

syntactic cross-references. In some types of index heading **syntax**, such as **subject headings**, a **heading** is entered only under a main heading so that there is no direct access through the subheadings in **displayed indexes**. A syntactic cross reference provides indirect access under such subheadings. For example, the subject heading "United States — History — Civil War, 1861-1865 — Bibliography" is not also entered under "civil war," "bibliography," or "history." Therefore, cross references are needed from these terms to the established heading:

```
History
        ======================================================
        | See also names of countries, regions, cities,      |
        | other places and topics followed by the            |
        | subdivision "-- history," e.g., United States --   |
        | History; Piano -- History.                         |
        ======================================================


Civil war
        ======================================================
        | See also names of countries followed by the        |
        | subdivisions "History -- Civil war," e.g.,         |
        | Spain -- History -- Civil war; United States       |
        | -- History -- Civil war                            |
        ======================================================
```

See also section 12.2.8.

syntagmatic relationships. Syntagmatic relationships are non-permanent relationships that exist in life situations and in **messages** and **texts** that describe them, such as a relationship between "dogs" and "breeding" or between "cats" and "care" or "feeding" in the "United States" or "Brazil." These are the kinds of relationships that index **headings** should express through the use of **syntax**. Contrast with permanent **paradigmatic relationships**.

syntax. "Syntax" is a linguistic term meaning (1) "orderly or systematic arrangement," or more precisely, (2) "the arrangement of words as elements in a sentence to show their relationship; sentence structure" (Webster's 1966, p. 1480). It comes from the Greek for putting or arranging together. The first meaning is labeled "obsolete," but it is closer to the meaning intended here in borrowing "syntax" from linguistics and applying it to index **headings** and search statements. "Syntax" is used in this book to mean rules or patterns for the combination of **terms** to form meaningful index **headings** or effective search statements. Index headings consist of terms arranged in a certain order, and they may display a certain structure as well, so the application of the idea of "syntax" seems appropriate. In modern search statements for electronic **IR databases**, the order or particular arrangement of terms is often immaterial, but by extension, the idea of "syntax" is used to refer to the rules or patterns for the combination (as opposed to the arrangement) of terms (for example the use of boolean operators OR, AND, or NOT between terms), and also for the application of techniques for indicating term weights, proximity limits, and truncation, and for **stemming** and similar refinements to influence the results of a search. Here the analogy corresponds to the grammatical use of inflections (word endings or changes in form) to indicate the role of words in a sentence with respect to number (singular or plural), case (subject, object, possessive), gender (male or female) or tense (past, present, future). In short, indexing or searching syntax is used to refer to the rules or patterns for creating index headings or search statements! *See also* chapter 12.

taxonomy. The term "taxonomy" comes from the Greek for arrangement or division ("taxis") and law ("nomos"). Thus it refers to rules of division and arrangement. Such rules can be much more uniform and strict within a facet, so the traditional use of this term for **classification** within a single facet is still appropriate. Thus, the rules for zoological taxonomic classification are often rather narrowly focused on physical characteristics (e.g., back-bones or not, resulting in vertebrates versus invertebrates) and ancestry/evolution.

TEI (Text Encoding Initiative). *See* **text encoding schemas**.

term. A term is a word or a phrase representing a single concept or multiple concepts that are tightly bound together in the context of a particular **IR database**. An "index term" is such a word or phrase associated with a **documentary unit** for the purposes of retrieval. Some concepts need more than one word to express them, for example, "information science" or "venetian blind." Some terms could be divided into two separate terms, but they are used so commonly together in a consistent order that they are considered a single **bound term** or **compound term**. Terms subjected to **vocabulary control and management** are often called **descriptors**. Terms are combined to form index **headings** or search statements.

text. **Messages** are encoded in texts. Texts are meaningful collections of symbols assembled to convey a message. The word "text" is related to the word "textile," and just as textiles consist of organized fibers or threads, a text consists of an organized set of symbols. Spoken language (speech) texts consist of meaningful sequences of sounds (phonemes). Writing is the representation of speech, and it uses visual symbols to represent the sounds of speech (phonemes). Examples of writing symbols include Chinese characters (which represent not only sounds but also meanings), Japanese kana syllabaries (in which each symbol represents a syllable — a combination of a vowel and a consonant), and Roman, Cyrillic, Greek and other alphabets (in which each symbol represents one or more phonemes, with separate symbols for vowels and consonants). In addition to language texts, there are many other kinds of texts that convey messages — musical texts, image texts (such as those embodied in still or moving pictures), three-dimensional texts (such as those created through architecture, sculpture, and industrial design), dance and other performance texts, and mathematical and chemical texts. Music has a well developed symbol system that is used to represent sound, including pitch and length, in visual **media** such as print on paper. We call these texts "scores." Dance choreography can also be represented symbolically, and scientific disciplines like mathematics and chemistry have well developed sets of symbols and codes for representing mathematical and chemical concepts. The symbol systems of art, as in painting and sculpture, are less formal, but most people would agree that paintings and sculpture do convey messages, even if it is not always easy to discern them or to agree on what they are. In painting, the field of iconography is devoted to the study and identification of artistic messages.

Glossary

text encoding schema. Many schemas have been developed for encoding **texts** of various **formats** for electronic digital presentation, analysis and retrieval. These include SGML (Standard General Markup Language), HTML (HyperText Markup Language), XML (eXtensible Markup Language), and TEI (Text Encoding Initiative). *See also* section 21.2.

textual database, textbase. *See* **IR database**.

thesaurus The term "thesaurus" is based on the Greek word for "treasure." The term was adopted by Peter Mark Roget (1779-1869), the compiler of the first modern classified "treasury" of words designed to bring together **terms** with similar meanings as an aid for writers. It is somewhat ironic that the main objective of Roget's thesaurus (and its modern successors) is almost exactly the opposite that of the modern information retrieval thesaurus. While Roget's thesaurus helps writers identify the best term for their particular purpose (an objective that both types of thesauri share!), its main purpose is often seen as encouraging and facilitating variety in expression, something prized in many contexts. The information retrieval thesaurus aims to control or compensate for such variety — to bring together the many terms that might be used to describe essentially the same, or closely related topic, to facilitate searching. The typical thesaurus consists of **records** for terms representing concepts, with links for synonymous, **equivalent**, narrower, broader, and other related terms. *See also* **end-user thesaurus**; **indexing thesaurus**; and chapter 13.

unit of analysis. *See* **documentary unit**.

up-posting. Up-posting is using both a specific **term** and a broader, more generic term to represent a topic or feature in a **message**, **text** or **documentary unit** (e.g., using both "sofas" and "furniture" for a message about sofas). *See also* **generic posting**; **specificity**; and section 10.1.

user warrant. User warrant means that the vocabulary of users or potential users should be accepted as terminology for index **headings**, **descriptors**, or preferred **terms** in **thesauri**, because it is warranted (authorized) through actual usage by users. User warrant is complemented by **literary warrant**.

vector space model syntax. Throughout the history of **automatic indexing** based on **term** weighting and **relevance** prediction, two major theoretical models have emerged: the vector-space model and the **probabilistic model**. Vector space syntax is based on the former, in which statistical data for term frequency and distribution is used to create vectors (like arrows) in multi-dimensional space, the length of the vector representing the importance of the term. Similar vectors are created for search statements, and the combined vectors for **documentary units** that most closely match the combined vectors for a search statement indicate the most promising documentary units, which are retrieved in rank order, based on the degree of vector similarity. *See also* sections 8.3 and 12.3.2.

vocabulary control/vocabulary management. Vocabulary control and management are the efforts to deal with the enormous variability of human language and the unpredictability of how a particular concept might be named in a particular **IR database**. Solutions currently in use, or suggested, to assist searchers with vocabulary problems include:

1. **Syndetic structure** (cross references) for **equivalent**, narrower, broader, and other related **terms** integrated into browsable alphanumeric **displayed indexes**.

2. **Indexing thesauri** designed to guide the assignment of terms by indexers. Such thesauri can guide searchers as well.

3. **End-user thesauri**, designed for searchers rather than indexers. Instead of aiming to control the terminology used by indexers, the purpose of an end-user or searching thesaurus is to help searchers find useful terminology for searches, often for searches across multiple IR databases.

Glossary

4. Co-occurrence term **clustering**. Here computer programs are used to compile lists of terms that occur together most frequently in various contexts. The most frequently co-occurring terms are likely to include terms closely related to the term with which a searcher begins, from which the searcher can select likely terms to improve a search.

5. **Ontologies**. Ontologies for IR attempt (or claim) to raise the level of more traditional **thesauri** to the realms of virtual reality (ontology is the study of being or existence and came into IR from artificial intelligence!). Ontologies are generally created for machine manipulation, whereas thesauri are generally designed for human use.

See also chapter 13.

    weighted term syntax. *See* **best match syntax**.

    XML (eXtensible Markup Language). *See* **text encoding schemas**.

Bibliography

This bibliography consists of citations for every publication cited in the main text of the book. Each citation includes references to the section or sections where the work is cited. Thus, this bibliography can serve as in index to discussions related to particular authors, organizations and their publications. A chapter number without a dot plus section number refers either to a short chapter without sections (e.g., chapter 22), or to the first part of a chapter before the first numbered section. "Pt. 2" refers to the introduction to Part II of the book, between chapters 1 and 2.

Citations follow the U.S.A. national standard ANSI Z39.29-1977 *American National Standard for bibliographic references* (American National Standards Institute 1977). A revision of this standard was approved in 2003. The only significant change for our purposes was moving the placement of dates for periodical articles from the end of the citation, after volume and issue numbering and pagination, to prior to the volume and issue numbering (National Information Standards Organization 2004?). We did not adopt this small change.

ABC-Clio (1999a). America: history and life. Santa Barbara, CA: ABC-Clio. Annual. ISSN 0002-7065. : 12.2.2.1; 17.2.

ABC-Clio (1999b). Historical Abstracts. Santa Barbara, CA: ABC-Clio. Annual. ISSN 0018-2435. : 12.2.2.1.

Aitchison, Jean; Gilchrist, Alan (1987). Thesaurus Construction: A Practical Manual. 2nd ed. London: Aslib, c1987. 173 p. ISBN 0851421970. : 13.3.3.1.4.

Aitchison, Jean; Gilchrist, Alan; Bawden, David (1997). Thesaurus construction and use: a practical manual. 3rd ed. London: Aslib, c1997. xvi, 212 p. ISBN 0851423906. : 13.3.2.

Allen, Bryce L. (1996). Information tasks: toward a user-centered approach to information systems. San Diego: Academic Press; c1996. xiii, 308 p. (Library and information science series). ISBN 0-12-051040-5. : 1.2; pt. 2.

Allen, Bryce L. (1997). Visualization and cognitive abilities. In: Cochrane, Pauline Atherton; Johnson, Eric H.; Roe, Sandra, eds. Visualizing subject access for 21st century information resources. Champaign, IL: Graduate School of Library and Information Science, University of Illinois at Urbana-Champaign; 1998: 63-79. 176 p. (Clinic on library applications of data processing; 1997. ISSN 0069-4789). ISBN 0-87845-103-X. : 19.3.

American Library Association (1980), Filing Committee. ALA filing rules. Chicago: American Library Association; 1980. ix, 50 p. : 1.4; 17.1.

American Library Association (1992), Association for Library Collections and Technical Services, Cataloging and Classification Section, Subject Analysis Committee, Subcommittee on the Display of Subject Headings in Subject Indexes in Online Public Access Catalogs. Headings for tomorrow: public access display of subject headings. Chicago: American Library Association; 1992. xix, 51 p. : 1.4; 17.2.

American Medical Association (2001). JAMA author instructions: preparing structured abstracts. http://jama.ama-assn.org/info/auinst_abs.html. : 14.

American National Standards Institute. *See also* National Information Standards Organization.

American National Standards Institute (1977). ANSI Z39.29-1977 American National Standard for bibliographic references. New York: American National Standards Institute; c1977. 92 p. Revision approved in 2003; see National Information Standards Institute (2004?) : 0.5; 14.2; bibliography.

American Psychological Association (1994). Publication manual of the American Psychological Association. 4th ed. Washington, DC: American Psychological Association; c1994. xxxii, 368 p. ISBN 1557982430. : 14.2.

Anderson, James D. (1979). Contextual indexing and faceted classification for databases in the humanities. In: Information choices and policies: proceedings of the 42nd annual meeting of the American Society for Information Science, volume

Bibliography

16; 1979 October 14-18; Minneapolis, MN. White Plains, NY: Knowledge Industry Publications; 1979: 194-201. xiv, 396 p. ISBN 0-914236-47-4. ISSN 0044-7870. : 2.1; 12.2.2.2; 12.2.4; 17.3.2; 20.2.

Anderson, James D. (1980). Prototype designs for subject access to the Modern Language Association's bibliographic database. In: Raben, Joseph; Marks, Gregory, eds. Data bases in the humanities and social sciences: proceedings of the IFIP Working Conference; 1979 August 23-24; Dartmouth College, Hanover, NH. Amsterdam; New York: North-Holland; 1980: 291-295. xii, 329 p. ISBN 0-444-85499-1. : 2.1; 12.2.2.2; 12.2.4; 17.3.2.

Anderson, James D. (1982). Catalog file display: principles and the new filing rules. Cataloging & classification quarterly. 1(4): 3-23; 1982. : 17.1.

Anderson, James D. (1985). Indexing systems: extensions of the mind's organizing power. Information and behavior. 1:287-323; 1985. : 8.2.1.

Anderson, James D. (1988). Indexing and classification: file organization and display for information retrieval. In: Weinberg, Bella Hass, ed. Indexing: the state of our knowledge and the state of our ignorance: proceedings of the 20th annual meeting of the American Society of Indexers; 1988 May 13; New York, NY. Medford, NJ: Learned Information; 1989: 69-83. x, 134 p. ISBN 0-938734-32-6. : 12.2.4; 17.3.

Anderson, James D. (1990). Ad hoc, user-determined classified displays based on faceted indexing. In: Humphrey, Susanne M.; Kwasnik, Barbara H. Advances in classification research. Medford, NJ: Learned Information, for the American Society for Information Science; 1991: 1-7. Reprinted from Humphrey & Kwasnik. Proceedings of the 1st ASIS SIG/CR Classification Research Workshop. Washington, DC: American Society for Information Science, Special Interest Group/Classification Research; 1990. : 17.3.

Anderson, James D. (1994). Standards for indexing: revising the American National Standard Guidelines Z39.4. Journal of the American Society for Information Science. 45(8): 628-636; 1994 September. : 1.4.

Anderson, James D. (1997a). Guidelines for indexes and related information retrieval devices. Bethesda, MD: NISO Press; 1997. vii, 53 p. (NISO Technical Report; 2). ISSN: 1081-8006. ISBN 1-880124-36-X. : 0.2; 1.3 ("entry"); 1.4; 10.1; 11.1; 12; 12.2.1; 12.2.7; 12.3; 12.4.1; 13.3.2.1; 14.2; 17.1; 18; 18.1.1; 19.1; 20.4.

Anderson, James D. (1997b, 2003). Organization of knowledge. In: Feather, John; Sturges, Paul, eds. International encylcopedia of information and library science. London; New York: Routledge; 1997: 336-353. xxxi, 492 p. ISBN 0-415-09860-2; 2nd ed. London: Taylor & Francis, 2003: 471-490. xxxii, 688 p. ISBN 0-415-25901-0. : 0.2.

Anderson, James D.; Rowley, Frederick A. (1992). Building end-user thesauri from full text. In: Kwasnik, Barbara H.; Fidel, Raya, eds. Advances in Classification Research. Volume 2. Medford, NJ: Learned Information for the American Society for Information Science, 1992: 1-10. Reprinted from Proceedings of the 2nd ASIS SIG/CR Classification Research Workshop. Washington, DC: American Society for Information Science, Special Interest Group/Classification Research, 1991. : 13.3.

Anglo-American cataloguing rules (2002). Prepared under the direction of the Joint Steering Committee for Revision of AACR, a committee of the American Library Association, the Australian Committee on Cataloguing, the British Library, the Canadian Committee on Cataloguing, Chartered Institute of Library and Information Professionals, the Library of Congress. 2nd ed., 2002 revision. Ottawa: Canadian Library Association; Chicago: Library Association; 2002. Looseleaf with multiple pagings. ISBN 0-88802-300-6 (text with binder).: 1.4; 3.1; 9; 14.2.

Art and architecture thesaurus (1990). New York: Oxford University Press: Published on behalf of the J. Paul Getty Trust; 1990. 3 v. ISBN 0195064038. : 13.3.3.1.5.

Art & architecture thesaurus (1994). Toni Petersen, director. 2nd ed. Published on behalf of the Getty Art History Information Program. New York: Oxford University Press; 1994. 5 v. : 1.4.

Artandi, Susan (1976). Machine indexing: linguistic and semiotic implications. Journal of the American Society for Information Science. 27(4): 235-239; 1976 July-August. : 8.2.1.

Association for Library Collections and Technical Services (1992). Headings for tomorrow: public access display of subject headings. Prepared by the Subcommittee on the Display of Subject Headings in Subject Indexes in Online Public Access Catalogs, Subject Analysis Committee, Cataloging and Classification Section, Association for Library Collections and Technical Services. Chicago: American Library Association; 1992. xix, 51 p. ISBN 0-8389-3414-5. : 12.2.1.

Bibliography

Association for Library Collections and Technical Services. Subcommittee on Subject Relationships/Reference Structures (1999). Final report to the ALCTS/CCS Subject Analysis Committee. June 1997. Revised May 1999. http://www.ala.org/alcts/organization/ccs/sac/rpt97rev.html. : 13.3.1; 13.3.3.1.5.

Atherton, Pauline. *See also* Cochrane, Pauline Atherton *(later name)*

Atherton, Pauline (1978). Books are for use. : final report of the Subject Access Project to the Council on Library Resources. Syracuse, NY: Syracuse University, School of Information Studies; 1978. 172 leaves. (Syracuse University. School of Information Studies. Research studies; 4). : 7.1.5.

Austin, Derek (1984). PRECIS: a manual of concept analysis and subject indexing. 2nd ed. With assistance from Mary Dykstra. London: British Library, Bibliographic Services Division; 1984. xi, 397 p. ISBN 0-7123-1008-8. : 8.2.2; 12.2.2.2; 20.4.

Baker, Nicholson (1994). Discards: annals of scholarship. New Yorker. 70(7): 64-86; 4 April 1994. : 5.1.1.

Balnaves, John (1976). Specificity. In: Rayward, W. Boyd, ed. The variety of librarianship: essays in honour of John Wallace Metcalfe. Sydney: Library Association of Australia; 1976: 47-56. 242 p. ISBN 0 909915 42 3. : 10.1.

Barry, Carol L. (1994). User-defined relevance criteria: an exploratory study. Journal of the American Society for Information Science. 45(3): 149-159; 1994 April. 3. : 3.

Bates, Marcia J. (1976). Rigorous systematic bibliography. RQ. 16(1): 7-26; 1976 Fall. : 0.2; 3.12; 4; 8.5.

Bates, Marcia J. (1986). Subject access in online catalogs: a design model. Journal of the American Society for Information Science. 37(6): 357-376; 1986 Nov. : 13.2; 13.3.

Bates, Marcia J. (1989). Rethinking subject cataloging in the online environment. Library resources and technical services. 33(4): 400-412; 1989 Oct. : 13.2; 13.3.

Bates, Marcia J. (1990). Design for a subject search interface and online thesaurus for a very large records management database. In: Henderson, Diane, ed. Information in the year 2000: from research to applications: proceedings of the 53rd annual meeting of the American Society for Information Science, volume 27; 1990 November 4-8; Toronto, Canada. Medford, NJ: Learned Information; 1990: 20-28. p. ISBN , ISSN 0044-7870. : 13.2; 13.3.

Bates, Marcia J. (1998). Indexing and access for digital libraries and the internet: human, database, and domain factors. Journal of the American Society for Information Science. 49(13): 1185-1205; 1998 November. : 0.2; 8.5.

Bates, Marcia J. (2002). The cascade of interactions in the digital library interface. Information processing & management. 38(3): 381-400; 2002 May. : pt. 2.

Beall, Julianne (1995). Summary. In: Holley, Robert P.; McGarry, Dorothy; Duncan, Donna; Svenonius, Elaine, eds. Subject indexing: principles and practices in the 90's: proceedings of the IFLA Satellite Meeting sponsored by the IFLA Section on Classification and Indexing and the Instituto da Biblioteca Nacional e do Livro, Lisbon, Portugal; 1993 August 17-18; Lisbon, Portugal. München; New Providence, NJ: K. G. Saur; 1995: 292-300. x, 302 p. (International Federation of Library Associations and Institutions. Universal Bibliographic Control and International MARC Programme. UBCIM publications; new series v. 15). ISBN 3-598-11251-3. : 12.2.1.2.

Bean, Carol A.; Green, Rebecca (2001). Relationships in the organization of knowledge. Dordrecht, Netherlands; Boston: Kluwer Academic Publishers; c2001. ix, 232 p. (Information science and knowledge management; v. 2). ISBN 0-7923-6813-4. : 17.3.

Bederson, Benjamin B. (2000). Fisheye menus. In: UIST '00: proceedings of the 13th annual ACM symposium on user interface software and technology; 2000 Nov. 5-8; San Diego, CA. Sponsored by ACM SIGGRAPH and ACM SIGCHI, in cooperation with ACM SIGSOFT. New York: Association for Computing Machinery, 2000: 217-225. ix, 248 p. (CHI letters; 2(2)). ISBN 1-58113-212-3. : 17.2; 19.4.

Beghtol, Clare (1986). Bibliographic classification theory and text linguistics: aboutness analysis, intertextuality and the cognitive act of classifying documents. Journal of documentation. 42(2): 84-113; 1986 June. : 8.2.1.; 17.3.

Belkin, Nicholas J.; Croft, W. Bruce (1992). Information filtering and information retrieval: two sides of the same coin? Communications of the ACM. 35(12): 29-38; 1992 December. : 8.3.13.

Bibliography

Belkin, Nicholas J.; Oddy, R. N.; Brooks, H. M. (1982a) Ask for information retrieval: part I. background and theory. Journal of documentation. 38(2): 61-71; 1982. : 13.2.

Belkin, Nicholas J.; Oddy, R. N.; Brooks, H. M. (1982b) Ask for information retrieval: part II. results of a design study. Journal of documentation. 38(3): 145-164; 1982. : 13.2.

Berman, Sanford (1993). Prejudices and antipathies: a tract on the LC subject heads concerning people. With a foreword by Eric Moon. 1993 ed. Jefferson, NC: McFarland & Co.; 1993. xvii, 211 p. ISBN 0899508286. : 12.2.1.

Bertrand, Annick; Cellier, Jean-Marie (1995). Psychological approach to indexing: effects of the operator's expertise upon indexing behaviour. Journal of information science. 21(6): 459-472 ; 1995. : 8.2.

Bertrand, Annick; Cellier, Jean-Marie; Giroux, Luc (1996). Expertise and strategies for the identification of the main ideas in document indexing. Applied cognitive psychology. 10(5): 419-433; 1996 Oct. : 8.2.

Bertrand-Gastaldy, Suzanne; Lanteigne, Diane; Giroux, Luc; David, Claire (1995). Convergent theories: using a multidisciplinary approach to explain indexing results. In: Forging new partnerships in information: proceedings of the 58th annual meeting of the American Society for Information Science, volume 32; 1995 October 9-12; Chicago, IL. Medford, NJ: Information Today; 1995: 56-60. xii, 258 p. ISBN 1-57387-017-X. ISSN 0044-7870. : 8.2.

Blair, David C.; Kimbrough, Steven O. (2002). Exemplary documents: a foundation for information retrieval design. Information processing & management. 38(3): 363-379; 2002 May. : 8.5.

Blair, David C.; Maron, M. E. (1985). An evaluation of retrieval effectiveness for a full-text document-retrieval system. Communications of the ACM, 28(3), 289-299. : 13.2.

Bliss, Henry Evelyn (1997). Bliss bibliographic classification. 2nd ed. Edited by J. Mills and Vanda Broughton, with the assistance of Valerie Lang and Colin Neilson. London; Boston: Butterworths; London; New York: Bowker-Saur; 1977- [continuing]. : 1.4; 17.3.

Booth, A. D. (Andrew Donald) (1969). On the geometry of libraries. Journal of documentation. 25(1): 28-42; 1969 March. : 8.3.7.

Borko, Harold; Bernier, Charles L. (1975). Abstracting concepts and methods. New York: Academic Press; 1975. x, 250 p. (Library and information science). ISBN 0-12-118650-4. : 14; 14.3.

Bose, H. (1990). Universal decimal classification: theory and practice. 2nd rev. and enl. ed. New Delhi: Sterling Publishers; New York: distributed by Apt Books; viii, 192 p. ISBN 8120707168. : 12.2.4; 17.3.

Bowker, Geoffrey C. (1998). The kindness of strangers: kinds and politics in classification systems [example of International classification of diseases]. Library trends. 47(2): 255-292; 1998 Fall. : 17.3.

Bowker, Geoffrey C.; Star, Susan Leigh (1998). How classifications work: problems and challenges in an electronic age [special issue]. Library trends. 47(2): 185-337; 1998 Fall. : 17.3.

Bowker, Geoffrey C.; Star, Susan Leigh (1999). Sorting things out: classification and its consequences. Cambridge, MA: MIT Press, c1999. xii, 377 p. (Inside technology). : 17.3.

Boyce, Bert R.; Meadow, Charles T.; Kraft, Donald H. (1994). Measurement in information science. San Diego: Academic Press, c1994. xvii, 283 p. (Library and information science). ISBN 0-12-121450-8. : 22.

Bredbeck, Gregory W. (2000). Queer theory. In Haggerty, George E., ed. Gay histories and cultures: an encyclopedia. New York: Garland; 2000: 728-729. xlvii, 986 p. (The encyclopedia of lesbian and gay histories and cultures; v. 2). ISBN 0-8153-1880-4. : 8.2.1.

British Standards Institution (1961). Universal decimal classification. Prepared by the B.S.I. under the auspices of the International Federation for Documentation (F.I.D.) and with the concurrence of the Lake Placid Club Education Foundation, New York. B.S. 1000A (F.I.D. No. 289) Abridged English ed. 025.45, 3rd ed., rev. London: British Standards Institution; 1961. 254 p. : 1.4; 12.2.4.; 17.3.

British Standards Institution (1963). Guide to the Universal decimal classification (UDC). B.S. 1000 C: 1963, (F.I.D. No. 345). London: British Standards Institution; c1963. 128 p. : 1.4; 12.2.4; 17.3.

Bibliography

British Standards Institution (1984). British standard recommendations for examining documents, determining their subjects and selecting indexing terms. London: British Standards Institution, c1984. 6 p. (BS 6529: 1984). : 8.2.2.

Brooks, Terrence A. (1998). Orthography as a fundamental impediment to online information retrieval. Journal of the American Society for Information Science. 49(8): 731-741; 1998 June. : 8.3.1.

Broughton, Vanda (2001). Faceted classification as a basis for knowledge organization in a digital environment: the Bliss bibliographic classification as a model for vocabulary management and the creation of multi-dimensional knowledge structures. The new review of hypermedia and multimedia. 7: 67-102; 2001. : 12.2.2.2.1.

Buckland, Michael; Chen, Aitao; Chen, Hui-Min; Kim, Youngin; Lam, Byron; Larson, Ray; Norgard, Barbara; Purat, Jacek (1999). Mapping entry vocabulary to unfamiliar metadata vocabularies. D-lib magazine. 5(1) 1999 January, http://www.dlib.org/dlib/january99/buckland/01buckland.html. : 13.3.

Callan, James P.; Croft, W. Bruce; Broglio, John (1995). TREC and TIPSTER experiments with inquiry. Information processing & management. 31(3): 327-332, 343; 1995 May-June. Reprinted in: Sparck Jones, Karen; Willett, Peter, eds. Readings in information retrieval. San Francisco: Morgan Kaufman Publishers; c1997: 436-439. xv, 589 p. ISBN 1-55860-454-5. : 8.3.8.

Calvert, Drusilla (1996). Deconstructing indexing standards. The indexer. 20(2): 76-78; 1996 October. : 1.4.

Cavnar, William B. (1994). Using an n-gram-based document representation with a vector processing retrieval model. In: Harman, Donna, ed. TREC-3: Proceedings of the Third Text REtrieval Conference; 1994 November 2-4; Gaithersburg, MD. Co-sponsored by the National Institute of Standards and Technology (NIST) and the Advanced Research Projects Agency (ARPA). Gaithersburg, MD: U.S. Depart. of Commerce, Technology Administration, National Institute of Standards and Technology; Washington, D.C.: For sale by the Supt. of Docs., U.S. G.P.O., 1994: 269 ff. (NIST Special Publication; 500-226). http://potomac.ncsl.nist.gov/TREC/t3_proceedings.html; http://trec.nist.gov/. : 8.3.1.

Chan, Lois Mai (1994). Cataloging and classification, an introduction. 2nd ed. New York: McGraw-Hill; c1994. xxii, 519 p. : 8.2.

Chan, Lois Mai (1995). Library of Congress Subject Headings: principles and applications. 3rd ed. Englewood, CO: Libraries Unlimited; c1995. xiv, 541 p. ISBN 1563081954. : 12.2.1.

Chan, Lois Mai (1999). A guide to the Library of Congress Classification. 5th ed. Englewood, CO: Libraries Unlimited; 1999. : 17.3.

Chan, Lois Mai (2002). Exploiting LCSH, LCC, and DDC to retrieve networked resources: issues and challenges. Final version, 4/2/02. http://lcweb.loc.gov/catdir/bibcontrol/chan_paper.html. Accessed 2-20-2003. : 12.2.2.2.1.

Chang, Shan-Ju L. (1993). Toward a multi-dimensional framework for understanding browsing. New Brunswick, NJ: Rutgers University, School of Communication, Information and Library Studies; 1993. 120 p. Unpublished Ph.D. dissertation.

Chang, Shan-Ju; Rice, Ronald E. (1993). Browsing: a multidimensional framework. In: Williams, Martha E., ed. Annual review of information science and technology. Medford, NJ: Learned Information for the American Society for Information Science; 1993: 28: 231-276. : 11.2 .

Chen, Hsinchun; Dhar, V. (1987). Reducing indeterminism in consultation: a cognitive model of user/librarian interaction. In: Proceedings of the 6th National Conference on Artificial Intelligence (AAAI-87); 1987 July 13-17; Seattle, WA: 285-289. : 13.2.

Chen, Hsinchun; Ng, Tobun D.; Martinez, Joanne; Schatz, Bruce R. (1997). A concept space approach to addressing the vocabulary problem in scientific information retrieval: an experiment on the worm community system. Journal of the American Society for Information Science. 48(1): 17-31; 1997 Jan. : 13.2; 13.3.4.

Cherry, Joan M. (1990). Methods of studying database users: the role of surveys, laboratory studies, and field studies. Canadian journal of information science. 15(2): 17-29; July 1990. : 22.

The Chicago manual of style (1993). 14th ed. Chicago: University of Chicago Press; c1993. ix, 921 p. ISBN 0226103897. : 1.4; 8.2; 14.2.

Bibliography

Chowdhury, G. G. (Gobinda G.) (1999). Introduction to modern information retrieval. London: Library Association; 1999. xix, 452 p. : 0.2 .

Chu, Clara M.; O'Brien, Ann (1993). Subject analysis: the critical first stage in indexing. Journal of information science. 19: 439-454; 1993. : 8.2.

CNET Networks (2001). "URL." In: CNET glossary, c1995-2001. http://cnet.com/Resources/Info/Glossary/Terms/url.html (accessed, 8-27-2004). : 15.

Coates, Eric (1988). The role of classification in information retrieval: action and thought in the contribution of Brian Vickery. Journal of documentation. 44: 216-225; 1988 Sept. : 17.3.

Cochrane, Pauline Atherton: *See also* Atherton, Pauline *(earlier name).*

Cochrane, Pauline A. (1986). Improving LCSH for use in online catalogs: exercises for self-help with a selection of background readings. Littleton, CO: Libraries Unlimited; 1986. xiii, 348 p. ISBN 0872874842. : 12.2.1.

Cochrane, Pauline Atherton (1996). [Review of] Subject indexing: principles and practices in the 90's: proceedings of the IFLA Satellite Meeting held in Lisbon, Portugal, 17-18 August 1993, and sponsored by the IFLA Section on Classification and Indexing and the Instituto da Biblioteca Nacional e do Livro, Lisbon, Portugal. Ed. Robert P. Holley and others. UBCIM publications; new series, vol. 15). München, New Providence, R.I. [i.e. NJ]: K. G. Saur, 1995. 302p. (ISBN 3-598-11251-3). Library resources & technical services. 40(3): 185-188; 1996 April. : 12.2.1.2.

Collantes, Lourdes Y. (1995). Degree of agreement in naming objects and concepts for information retrieval. Journal of the American Society for Information Science. 46(2): 116-132; 1995 March. : 8.2; 13.2.

Comaromi, John P. (1981). Book numbers: a historical study and practical guide to their use. Littleton, CO: Libraries Unlimited; 1981. 145 p. ISBN 0-87287-251-3. : 15.

Conway, Martha O'Hara, ed. The future of subdivisions in the Library of Congress Subject Headings system: Report from the Subject Subdivisions Conference; Arlie, VA; 1991 May 9-12. Sponsored by the Library of Congress. Washington, DC: Library of Congress, Cataloging Distribution Service; 1992. iii, 147 p. ISBN 0-8444-0756-9. : 12.2.1; 17.2.

Cooper, William S. (1978). Indexing documents by gedanken experimentation. Journal of the American Society for Information Science. 29(3): 107-119; 1978 May. : 8.1; 8.2.2.2.

Craven, Timothy C. (1986). String indexing. Orlando: Academic Press; 1986. xi, 246 p. ISBN 0121954609. : 1.3 ("entry"); 12.2; 12.2.2.3.

Croft, Bruce (1989). Automatic indexing. In: Weinberg, Bella Hass, ed. Indexing: the state of our knowledge and the state of our ignorance: proceedings of the 20th annual meeting of the American Society of Indexers; 1988 May 13; New York, NY. Medford, NJ: Learned Information; 1989: 86-100. x, 134 p. ISBN 0-938734-32-6. : 8.3.

Cullen, Rowena (2001). Perspectives on user satisfaction surveys. Library trends. 49(4): 662-686; Spring 2001. : 22.

Cutter, Charles Ammi (1876, 1904). Rules for a printed dictionary catalog. Washington, DC: U. S. Government Printing Office; 1876. 89 p. (U.S. Bureau of Education. Special report on public libraries; part II). 4th ed., "rewritten," 174 p. published in 1904 with new title: Rules for a dictionary catalog. : 10.1; 12.2.4; 13.3.3.1.5.

Dahlberg, Ingetraut (1978). A referent-oriented, analytical concept theory for INTERCONCEPT. International classification. 5(3): 143-151; 1978. : 2; 17.3.

Dahlberg, Ingetraut (1981). Conceptual definitions for INTERCONCEPT. International classification. 8(1): 16-22; 1981. : 2; 17.3.

David, Claire; Giroux, Luc; Bertrand-Gastaldy, Suzanne; Lanteigne, Diane; Bertrand, Annick (1995). Indexing as problem solving: a cognitive approach to consistency. In: Forging new partnerships in information: proceedings of the 58th annual meeting of the American Society for Information Science, volume 32; 1995 October 9-12; Chicago, IL. Medford, NJ: Information Today; 1995: 49-55. xii, 258 p. ISBN 1-57387-017-X. ISSN 0044-7870. : 8.2.

Deerwester, Scott C.; Dumais, Susan T.; Furnas, George W.; Landauer, Thomas K.; Harshman, Richard (1990). Indexing by latent semantic analysis. Journal of the American Society for Information Science. 41(6): 391-407; 1990 September. : 8.3.11.1.

Bibliography

Dewey, Melvil (1996, 2003). Dewey decimal classification and relative index. 21st ed. Albany, NY: Forest Press Division of OCLC Online Computer Library Center; 1996. ISBN 0-910608-50-4; 22nd ed. 2003. : 1.4; 12.2.4; 13.3.3.1.3.

Diakoff, Harry (2000). Natural language processing for question answering in a restricted subject domain in the real world. Rutgers Distributed Laboratory for Digital Libraries: Research speakers series, Fall 2000. 2000 Nov. 10. : 13.3.4.

Diener, Richard A. V. (1984). A longitudinal study of the informational dynamics of journal article titles: a treatise in the science of information. New Brunswick: Graduate Program in Library and Information Studies; 1884. xvii, 83 leaves. Thesis (Ph.D.). : 13.3.3.1.5.

Dodd, David G. (1996). Grass-roots cataloging and classification: food for thought from world wide web subject-oriented hierarchical lists. Library resources & technical services. 40(3): 275-286;1996 July. : 12.2.4.

Doszkocs, Tamas E. (1978). An associative interactive dictionary (AID) for online bibliographic searching. In: The information age in perspective: proceedings of the 41st annual meeting of the American Society for Information Science, volume 15; 1978 November 13-17; New York, NY. White Plains, NY: Knowledge Industry Publications; 1978: 105-109. ISBN 0-914236-22-9. ISSN 0044-7870. : 8.3.10.

Drabenstott, Karen Markey. *See also* Markey, Karen *(earlier name)*.

Drabenstott, Karen Markey; Dede, Bonnie A. Roeber; Leavitt, Melanie (1999). The changes of meaning in subdivided subject headings. Cataloging & classification quarterly. 28(3): 19-43; 1999. : 12.2.1.

Drabenstott, Karen Markey; Simcox, Schelle; Fenton, Eileen G. (1999). End-user understanding of subject headings in library catalogs. Library resources & technical services. 43(3): 140-160; 1999 July. : 12.2.1.

Drabenstott, Karen Markey; Vizine-Goetz, Diane (1994). Using subject headings for online retrieval: theory, practice, and potential. Published under the auspices of OCLC Online Computer Library Center, Inc. San Diego: Academic Press; c1994. xviii, 365 p. (Library and information science). ISBN 0-12-221570-2. : 12.2.1; 12.4.1 ;17.2.

Dublin core metadata element set: reference description (1997). 1997 Jan. 15. http://purl.org/metadata/dublin_core_elements. : 3.4.

Dublin Core Metadata Initiative (2002). Dublin Core Metadata Initiative (DCMI) home page. http://dublincore.org/. Accessed 4-16-2002. : 20.5.

Dubois, C. P. R. (1984). The use of thesauri in online retrieval. Journal of information science. 8(2): 63-66; 1984 March. : 13.3.

Dykstra, Mary (1985). PRECIS: a primer. London: British Library, Bibliographic Services Division; 1985. xiii, 262 p. ISBN 0712310223. : 12.2.2.2; 20.4.

Dykstra, Mary (1992). Proposal #2: [the expanded use of free-floating subdivisions in the Library of Congress Subject Headings system]: arguments against. In: Conway, Martha O'Hara, ed. The future of subdivisions in the Library of Congress Subject Headings system: Report from the Subject Subdivisions Conference; Arlie, VA; 1991 May 9-12. Sponsored by the Library of Congress. Washington, DC: Library of Congress, Cataloging Distribution Service; 1992: 39-42. iii, 147 p. ISBN 0-8444-0756-9. : 12.2.1.

Eager, Carolyn; Oppenheim, Charles (1996). An observational method for undertaking user needs studies. Journal of librarianship and information science (Folkestone, England). 28(1): 15-23; March 1996. : 22.

Educational Resources Information Center. Thesaurus of ERIC descriptors. Phoenix, AZ: Oryx Press. [periodically updated]. : 1.4.

El-Hoshy, Lynn M. (1992). Introduction to subdivision practice in the Library of Congress Subject Headings system. In: Conway, Martha O'Hara, ed. The future of subdivisions in the Library of Congress Subject Headings system: Report from the Subject Subdivisions Conference; Arlie, VA; 1991 May 9-12. Sponsored by the Library of Congress. Washington, DC: Library of Congress, Cataloging Distribution Service; 1992: 117-129. iii, 147 p. ISBN 0-8444-0756-9. : 9.2; 12.2.1.

European Communities (1995). Thesaurus Eurovoc. Luxembourg: Office for Official Publications of the European Communities; 1995. 3 v. ISBN 92-77-86348-X. : 13.3.2.1.

Bibliography

Fairthorne, Robert A. (1971). Temporal structure in bibliographical classification. In: Chan, Lois Mai; Richmond, Phyllis A.; Svenonius Elaine, eds. Theory of subject analysis: a sourcebook. Littleton, CO: Libraries Unlimited; c1985: 359-366. xv, 415 p. ISBN 0-87287-489-3. (Reprinted from: Wojceichowski, Jerzy A., ed. Ottawa conference on the conceptual basis of the classification of knowledge, Ottawa, 1971. Pullach/München: Verlag Dokumentation, 1974: 404-412.). : 8.2.

Fallows, James (1996). Navigating the galaxies: New programs are trying to make sense of the uncodified information on the internet. Atlantic monthly. 273(4): 104-107; April 1966. : 5.1.2.

Farradane, Jason (1979). The nature of information. Journal of information science. 1(1): 13-17; 1979 April. : 8.2.1.

Farradane, Jason (1980a). Knowledge, information, and information science. Journal of information science. 2(2): 75-80; 1980 Sept. : 8.2.1.

Farradane, Jason (1980b). Relational indexing. Part I. Journal of information science. 1(5): 267-276; 1980 Jan.; Part II. Journal of information science. 1(6): 313-324; 1980 March. : 12.2.3; 13.3.3.1.5.

Farrow, John F. (1991). A cognitive process model of document indexing. Journal of documentation. 47(2): 149-166; 1991 June. : 8.2.

Feifer, Richard G.; Tazbaz, Denise (1997). Interface design principles for interactive media. Telematics and informatics. 14(1): 51-64; 1997. : 21.1.

Fidel, Raya (1991). Searchers' selection of search keys: I. The selection routine; II. Controlled vocabulary or free-text searching; III. Searching styles. Journal of the American Society for Information Science. 42(7): 490-527; 1995 August. : 8.1; 13.3.

Fidel, Raya (1993). Qualitative methods in information retrieval research. Library & information science research. 15(3): 219-247; Sum. 1993. : 22.

Fidel, Raya; Hahn, Trudi Bellardo; Rasmussen, Edie M.; Smith, Philip J., eds. (1994). Challenges in indexing electronic text and images. Medford, NJ: Learned Information for the American Society for Information Science; 1994. ix, 306 p. (ASIS monograph series). ISBN 0-938734-76-8. : 8; 8.1.

Fillmore, C. J. (1971). Types of lexical information. In: Steinberg, Danny D.; Leon A. Jakobovitz. Semantics: an interdisciplinary reader in philosophy, linguistics and psychology. Cambridge, Eng.: Cambridge University Press; 1971: 370-392. x, 603 p. ISBN 0521078229. : 12.2.3.1.

FOLDOC (2002): The Free On-line Dictionary of Computing. http://wombat.doc.ic.ac.uk/foldoc/index.html or http://foldoc.doc.ic.ac.uk/ Copyright Denis Howe. Accessed 8-8-2002. : 1.3; 6.1; 13.3.5; 21.2.

Foskett, A. C. (Antony Charles) (1982). The subject approach to information. 4th ed. London: Bingley; Hamden, CT: Linnet Books; 1982. xvii, 574 p. ISBN: 0851573134. [Frohmann cites Foskett (1982) for a quote from Foskett. Similar statements occur in this book, but the statement quoted by Frohmann could not be found.] A 5th ed. was published in 1996: London: Library Association Pub., c1996. xv, 456 p. ISBN 1856040488.). : 8.2.1.

Foskett, A. C. (Antony Charles) (1984). Better dead than read: further studies in critical classification [Augmented title: presented at a colloquium held by the Graduate School of Library and Information Science, UCLA, June 1982]. Library resources and technical services. 28: 346-359; 1984 Oct. : 17.3.

Francis, W. Nelson (Winthrop Nelson); Kučera, Henry; Mackie, Andrew W. (1982). Frequency analysis of English usage. : lexicon and grammar. Boston: Houghton Mifflin, c1982. 561 p. ISBN 0395322502. : 8.3.3.

Frohmann, Bernd (1990). Rules of indexing: a critique of mentalism in information retrieval theory. Journal of documentation. 46(2): 81-101; 1990 June. : 8.2.1; 8.2.2; 8.2.2.2; 8.5.1.

Fugmann, Robert (1993). Subject analysis and indexing: theoretical foundation and practical advice. Frankfurt/Main: Indeks Verlag; 1993. xvi, 250 p. (Textbooks for knowledge organization; vol. 1. ISSN 099-8152). ISBN 3-88672-500-6. : 6.1; 8.2.

Furnas, George W.; Landauer, Thomas K.; Gomez, Louis M.; Dumais, Susan T. (1983). Statistical semantics: analysis of the potential performance of keyword information access systems. Bell System technical journal. (62): 1753-1806 (Special issue on human factors in computer systems). Reprinted in: Thomas, John C.; Schneider, Michael L., eds. (1984). Human

Bibliography

factors in computer systems. Norwood, NJ: Ablex Pub. Corp.; c1984: 187-242. xvi, 276 p. (Human/computer interaction). ISBN 0893911461. : 13.3.3.1.2.

Furnas, George W.; Landauer, Thomas K.; Gomez, Louis M.; Dumais, Susan T. (1987). The Vocabulary Problem in Human-System Communication. Communications of the ACM. 30(11): 964-971; 1987 November. : 13.2; 13.3.3.

Furrie, Betty (1998). Understanding MARC bibliographic: machine-readable cataloging. In conjunction with the Data Base Development Department, The Follett Software Co. 5th ed., revised and edited by the Network Development and MARC Standards Office, Library of Congress; 1998. http://www.loc.gov/marc/umb/. Accessed 1-7-2004. : 20.1.

Gibaldi, Joseph (1999). MLA handbook for writers of research papers. 5th ed. New York: Modern Language Association of America; 1999. xvii, 332 p. ISBN 0873529758. : 14.2.

Gilchrist, Alan; Strachan, David, ed. (1990). The UDC: essays for a new decade. London: Aslib, the Association for Information Management, c1990. vi, 97 p. ISBN 0-85142-265-9. : 12.2.4; 17.3.

Glazier, Jack D.; Powell, Ronald R., eds. (1992). Qualitative research in information management. Englewood, CO: Libraries Unlimited; 1992. xiv, 238 p. ISBN 0-87287-806-6. : 22.

Goetz, Diane Vizine: *See* Vizine-Goetz, Diane.

Gomez, Louis M.; Lochbaum, Carol C. (1984). People can retrieve more objects with enriched key-word vocabularies. But is there a human performance cost? In: Interact '84: first IFIP conference on human-computer interaction; 1984 Sept. 4-7; Imperial College of Science and Technology, London. IFIP Task Group on Human-Computer Interaction in association with Association of Computing Machinery (SIGCHI) ... [et al.] [S.l.]: IFIP, c1984. 2 v. : 13.3.3.1.2.

Gomez, Louis M.; Lochbaum, Carol C.; Landauer, Thomas K. (1990). All the right words: finding what you want as a function of the richness of indexing vocabulary. Journal of the American Society for Information Science. 41(8): 547-559. : 13.2.

Gordon, Michael D.; Dumais, Susan (1998). Using latent semantic indexing for literature based discovery. Journal of the American Society for Information Science. 49(8): 674-685; 1998 June. : 8.3.11.1.

Gothberg, Helen M. (1990). The library survey: a research methodology rediscovered. College & research libraries. 51(6): 553-559; Nov. 1990. : 22.

Green, Brian; Bide, Mark (1997). Unique identifiers: a brief introduction. London: Book Industry Communication/EDItEUR; 1997. 9 p. ISBN 1-873671-18-0. http://www.bic.uk/uniquid.html. : 15.

Green, Rebecca (1995a). The expression of conceptual syntagmatic relationships: a comparative survey. Journal of documentation. 51(4): 315-338; 1995 Dec. : 12.2.3.1.

Green, Rebecca (1995b). Syntagmatic relationships in index languages: a reassessment. Library quarterly. 65(4): 365-385; 1995 Oct. : 12.2.3.1.

Green, Rebecca (1995c). Topical relevance relationships: I. why topic matching fails. Journal of the American Society for Information Science. 46(9): 646-653; 1995 Oct. : 12.2.3.1.

Green, Rebecca (1996). The design of a relational database for large-scale bibliographic retrieval. Information, technology and libraries. 15(4): 207-221; 1196 Dec. : 22.

Green, Rebecca (1997). The role of relational structures in indexing for the humanities. Knowledge organization. 24(2): 72-83. : 3; 12.2.3.1.

Green, Rebecca; Bean, Carol A. (1995). Topical relevance relationships: II. an exploratory study and preliminary typology. Journal of the American Society for Information Science. 46(9): 654-662; 1995 Oct. : 12.2.3.1.

Greenberg, Jane. Reference structures: stagnation, progress, and future challenges. Information technology and libraries. 16(3): 108-119; 1997 Sept. : 13.3.1.

Greene, Stephan; Marchionini, Gary; Plaisant, Catherine; Shneiderman, Ben (2000). Previews and overviews in digital libraries: designing surrogates to support visual information seeking. Journal of the American Society for Information Science. 51(4): 380-393; 2000 March 1. : 14; 14.1; 14.2.

Bibliography

Griffith, Belver C.; White, Howard D; Drott, M. Carl; Saye, Jerry. D. (1986). Tests of methods for evaluating bibliographic databases: an analysis of the National Library of Medicine's handling of literatures in the medical behavioral sciences. Journal of the American Society for Information Science. 37(4): 261-270; July 1986. : 22.

Gutwin, Carl; Paynter, Gordon; Witten, Ian H.; Nevill-Manning, Craig G.; Frank, Eibe (1998). Improving browsing in digital libraries with keyphrase indexes. Technical report 98-1, Computer Science Department, University of Saskatchewan, 1998. http://www.cs.usask.ca/faculty/gutwin/1998/keyphind-techreport/html/keyphind-9.html (see also a later version, Gutwin et al. 1999). : 8.3.8.

Gutwin, Carl; Paynter, Gordon; Witten, Ian; Nevill-Manning, Craig; Frank, Eibe (1999). Improving browsing in digital libraries with keyphrase indexes. Decision support systems. 27: 81-104; 1999. : 8.3.8.

Harman, Donna (1991). How effective is suffixing? Journal of the American Society for Information Science. 42(1): 7-15; 1991 January. : 8.3.6.

Harman, Donna (1994). Automatic indexing. In: Fidel, Raya; Hahn, Trudi Bellardo; Rasmussen, Edie M.; Smith, Philip J., eds. Challenges in indexing electronic text and images. Medford, NJ: Learned Information for the American Society for Information Science; 1994: 247-264. ix, 306 p. (ASIS monograph series). ISBN 0-938734-76-8. : 6.4; 8.3; 8.3.1; 8.3.3; 8.3.6.

Harper, David J.; Koychev, Ivan; Sun, Yixing; Pirie, Iain (2004). Within-document retrieval: a user-centered evaluation of relevance profiling. Information retrieval. 7(3): 265-290; 2004 Sept. : 21.3.

Harrison, Lauren Deborah. The impact of thesauri on information retrieval. Ph.D. dissertation. New Brunswick: Rutgers University. School of Communication, Information, and Library Studies; 1998. x, 102 leaves. : 13.3.

Hart, Geoff (2000). Ten technical communication myths. Technical communication. 47(3): 291 ff.; 2000 August, 8 p. Accessed via Academic Search Premier, 4-8- 2002. : 21.1.

Hartley, James (2000). Are structured abstracts more or less accurate than traditional ones? A study in the psychological literature. Journal of information science. 26(4): 273-277; 2000. : 14.

Hartley, James; Davies, Lindsey; Burnhill, Peter (1981). Alphabetization in indexes: experimental studies. The indexer. 12(3): 149-153; 1981 Apr. : 1.4.

Hartley, James; Sydes, Matthew (1996). Which layout do you prefer? An analysis of readers' preferences for different typographic layouts of structured abstracts. Journal of information science. 22(1): 27-37; 1996. : 14.

Head, Alison J. (1997). A question of interface design: how do online service GUIs measure up? Online. 21(3): 20-29; 1997 May-June. : 19.3.

Head, Alison J. (1999). Design wise: a guide for evaluating the interface design of information resources. Medford, NJ: Information Today; c1999; xxiii; 196 p. ISBN 0-910965-31-5. : 19.3.

Hearst, Marti (1995). TileBars: visualization of term distribution information in full text information access, Proceedings of the ACM SIGCHI Conference on Human Factors in Computing Systems (CHI); 1995 May; Denver, CO. pp. 59-66. : 21.3.

Hearst, Marti (1999a). The use of categories and clusters for organizing retrieval results. In: Strzalkowski, Tomek, ed. Natural language information retrieval. Dordrecht, NL; Boston: Kluwer Academic Publishers, c1999: 333-374. xxv, 384 p. (Text, speech, and language technology; v. 7.). ISBN: 0-7923-5685-3. : 8.3.11; 19.3.

Hearst, Marti A. (1999b). User interfaces and visualization. In: Baeza-Yates, Ricardo; Ribeiro-Neto, Berthier. Modern information retrieval. New York: ACM Press; Harlow, England: Addison-Wesley; 1999: 257-323. xx, 513 p. ISBN 0-201-39829-X. : 19.3.

Hearst, Marti; Elliot, Ame; English, Jennifer; Sinha, Rashmi; Swearingen, Kirsten; Yee, Ka-Ping (2002). Finding the flow in web site search: Designing a search system and interface may best be served (and executed) by scrutinizing usability studies. Communications of the ACM. 45(9): 42-49; 2002 Sept. : 17.3.

Heidorn, P. Bryan; Sandore, Beth, eds. (1997). Digital image access & retrieval: papers presented at the 33rd Clinic on Library Applications of Data Processing; 1996 March 24-26. Urbana-Champaign, IL: Graduate School of Library and Information Science; 1997. 191 p. ISBN 0-87845-100-5. : 8.2.2.1.

Bibliography

Hernon, Peter; Nitecki, Danuta A. (2001). Service quality: a concept not fully explored. Library trends. 49(4): 687-708; Spring 2001. : 22.

Hilts, Philip J. (1995). Brain's memory system comes into focus. New York times. Section C: 1, 3; 1995 May 30. (Behind the veil of thought: Fifth article of an occasional series about advances in brain research. "The first article in this series, about evidence for a new theory of consciousness, appeared on March 21. The second article, about the way the brain processes emotion, appeared on March 28. The third one, about the brain's "working memory," appeared on May 2, and the fourth, about music and the brain, appeared on May 16.". : 8.2.

Hjerppe, Roland (1996). Go with the flow, or abide by the side, or watch the wave? Challenges of change for knowledge organization. In: Green, Rebecca. Knowledge organization and change: proceedings of the fourth international ISKO conference; 1996 July 15-18; Washington, DC. Frankfurt/Main: Indeks Verlag; 1996: 10-25. 431 p. (Advances in knowledge organization, v. 5). ISBN 3-88672-024-1. : 13.3.5.

Hjørland, Birger (1997). Information seeking and subject representation: an activity-theoretical approach to information science. Westport, CT: Greenwood Press; 1997. 213 p. (New directions in information management; no. 34). ISBN 0-313-29893-9. : pt. 2; 8; 8.2; 8.2.2.

Hockey, Susan (1994). Describing electronic texts: the text encoding initiative and SGML. 1994. http://www.loc.gov/catdir/semdigdocs/hockey.html. Retrieved 8 August 2002. : 21.2.

Hodge, Gail M.; Milstead, Jessica L. (1998). Computer support to indexing. Philadelphia, PA: National Federationof Abstracting and Information Services; 1998. 118 p. : 8.4.

Hogan, Steve; Hudson, Lee (1998). Constructionism vs. essentialism. In: Hogan, Steve; Hudson, Lee. Completely queer: the gay and lesbian encyclopedia. New York: Henry Holt; 1998: 149-152. xiii, 704 p. ISBN 0-8050-3629-6. : 8.2.1.

Holley, Robert P.; McGarry, Dorothy; Duncan, Donna; Svenonius, Elaine, eds. (1995). Subject indexing: principles and practices in the 90's: proceedings of the IFLA Satellite Meeting sponsored by the IFLA Section on Classification and Indexing and the Instituto da Biblioteca Nacional e do Livro, Lisbon, Portugal; 1993 August 17-18; Lisbon, Portugal. München; New Providence, NJ: K. G. Saur; 1995. x, 302 p. (International Federation of Library Associations and Institutions. Universal Bibliographic Control and International MARC Programme. UBCIM publications; new series v. 15). ISBN 3-598-11251-3. : 12.2.1.

Hsu, Richard C.; Mitchell, William E. (1997). After 400 years, print is still superior. Communications of the ACM. 40(10): 27-28; October 1997. : 5.1.2.

Huffman, Stephen (1995). Acquaintance: language-independent document categorization by n-grams. In: Harman, Donna, ed. TREC-4: Proceedings of the Fourth Text REtrieval Conference; 1995 November 1-3; Gaithersburg, MD. Co-sponsored by the National Institute of Standards and Technology (NIST) and the Defense Advanced Research Projects Agency (DARPA). Gaithersburg, MD: U.S. Depart. of Commerce, Technology Administration, National Institute of Standards and Technology; Washington, D.C.: For sale by the Supt. of Docs., U.S. G.P.O., 1994: 269 ff. (NIST Special Publication; 500-236). http://potomac.ncsl.nist.gov/TREC/t4_proceedings.html; http://trec.nist.gov/. : 8.3.1.

Hull, David A. (1996). Stemming algorithms: a case study for detailed evaluation. Journal of the American Society for Information Science. 47(1): 70-84; 1996 January. : 8.3.6.

Humphrey, Susanne M. (1994). Knowledge-based systems for indexing. In: Fidel, Raya; Hahn, Trudi Bellardo; Rasmussen, Edie M.; Smith, Philip J., eds. Challenges in indexing electronic text and images. Medford, NJ: Learned Information for the American Society for Information Science; 1994: 161-175. ix, 306 p. (ASIS monograph series). ISBN 0-938734-76-8. : 8.4.

Hutchins, W. J. (W. John) (1975). Languages of indexing and classification: a linguistic study of structures and functions. Stevenage, Herts. U.K.: Peter Peregrinus; 1975. viii, 148 p. (Librarianship and information studies; v. 3). ISBN 0-901223-68-9. : 6.1.

Iivonen, Mirja (1994a). Consistency in the selection of search concepts and search terms. Information processing & management. 31(2): 173-190; 1995 March-April. : 8.2; 13.2.

Iivonen, Mirja (1994b). Effect of extending the scope of search concepts on the intersearcher and intrasearcher consistency. In: Albrechtsen, Hanne; Oernager, Susanne, eds. Knowledge organization and quality management. Proceedings of 3rd

Bibliography

International Conference, International Society for Knowledge Organization; 20-24 June 1994; Copenhagen, Denmark. Frankfurt/Main: Index Verlag, 1994: 423-430. : 8.2; 13.2.

Iivonen, Mirja; Kivimäki, Katja (1998). Common entities and missing properties: similarities and differences in the indexing of concepts. Knowledge organization. 25(3): 90-102. : 2.

Information science abstracts (1971). Philadelphia: Documentation Abstracts, inc. ISSN: 0020-0239. : 8.3.7.

Institute for Scientific Information (1961-   ). Science citation index. Philadelphia: ISI. 0036-827X. : 7.1.6; 8.3.12; 12.2.5.

Institute for Scientific Information (1969-   ). Social sciences citation index. Philadelphia: ISI. ISSN 0091-3707. : 7.1.6; 8.3.12; 12.2.5.

Institute for Scientific Information (1976-   ). Arts & humanities citation index. Philadelphia: ISI. ISSN 0162-8445. : 7.1.6; 8.3.12; 12.2.5.

International DOI Foundation (2001). DOI: The Digital Object Identifier System. 2001 April 17. http://www.doi.org. : 15.

International Organization for Standardization (1985). Documentation — methods for examining documents, determining their subjects, and selecting indexing terms. Geneva: ISO; 1985. iii, 5 p. (ISO 5963-1985 (E)). : 8.2.2.

International Organization for Standardization (1986). ISO 2788: Guidelines for the establishment and development of monolingual thesauri. 2nd ed. Geneva: ISO, 1986. : 13.3.3.1.4.

Iwazume, Michiaki; Takeda, Hideaki; and Nishida, Toyoaki (1996). Ontology-based information capturing from the internet. In: Green, Rebecca. Knowledge organization and change: proceedings of the fourth international ISKO conference; 1996 July 15-18; Washington, DC. Frankfurt/Main: Indeks Verlag; 1996: 261-272. 431 p. (Advances in knowledge organization, v. 5). ISBN 3-88672-024-1. : 13.3.5.

Jacsó, Péter (2001). Content evaluation of textual CD-ROM and web databases. Englewood, CO: Libraries Unlimited; 2001.xix, 275 (Database searching series). ISBN 1-56308-737-5. : 19.

Jiménez, Luis A., ed. (1994). Rafael Catalá: del círculo cuadrado a la cienciapoesía: hacia una nueva poética latinoamericana. New Brunswick, NJ: The Ometeca Institute; Kent, WA: Ventura One Publishers; 1994. xv, 232 p. : 6.1.

Jiménez, Luis A. (1995). El arte autobiográfico en Cuba en el siglo XIX. New Brunswick, NJ: The Ometeca Institute; 1995. 188 p. : 6.1.

Jones, Karen Sparck: *See* Sparck Jones, Karen.

Jones, Susan; Hancock-Beaulieu, Micheline (1994). Support strategies for interactive thesaurus navigation. In: Albrechtsen, Hanne; Oernager, Susan, eds. Knowledge organization and quality management: proceedings of the Third International ISKO Conference; 1994 June 20-24; Copenhagen. Organized by the Royal School of Librarianship, Copenhagen, Denmark in cooperation with the International Society for Knowledge Organization. Frankfurt am Main: Indeks Verlag; 1994: 366-373. 457 p. (Advances in knowledge organization; v. 4). ISBN: 3-88672-023-3. : 13.3.

Jorgensen, Corinne (1995). Image attributes: an investigation (indexing systems, retrieval systems, computerized). Syracuse, NY: Syracuse University; 1995. 323 p. Ph.D. dissertation. Citation from Dissertation abstracts international. 57(4)A: 1364). The results of this research are summarized in Jorgensen, Corinne (1998). : 8.2.2.1.

Jorgensen, Corinne (1998). Attributes of images in describing tasks. Information processing & management. 34(2/3): 161-197; 1998 March. : 8.2.2.1.

Jorgensen, Corinne; Liddy, Elizabeth D. (1994). An analysis of information seeking behaviors in index use, or opening Pandora's Box. In: Williams, Martha E., ed. Proceedings of the 15th National Online Meeting; 1994 May 10-12; New York. Medford, NJ: Learned Information; 1994: 233-241. : 19.1.

Jorgensen, Corinne; Liddy, Elizabeth D. (1996). Information access or information anxiety? — an exploratory evaluation of book index features. The Indexer. 20(2): 64-68; 1996 Oct. : 19.1.

Katz, Bill. Cuneiform to computers: a history of reference sources. Lanham, MD: Scarecrow Press; 1998. xvi, 417 p. (History of the book series; no. 4). ISBN: 0-8108-3290-9. : 1.1.

Bibliography

Keister, Lucinda H. (1994). User types and queries: impact on image access systems. In: Fidel, Raya; Hahn, Trudi Bellardo; Rasmussen, Edie M.; Smith, Philip J., eds. (1994). Challenges in indexing electronic text and images. Medford, NJ: Learned Information for the American Society for Information Science; 1994: 7-22. ix, 306 p. (ASIS monograph series). ISBN 0-938734-76-8. : 8.2.2.1.

Kemp, B.; Buckner, K. (1999). A taxonomy of design guidance for hypermedia design. Interacting with computers. 12: 143-160; 1999. : 19.3.

Kerr, R. A. (1995). [Review of] Jiménez, Luis A., ed. Rafael Catalá: del círculo cuadrado a la cienciapoesía. Kent, Washington: The Omoteca [i.e. Ometeca] Institute, 1994. Hispania. 78(3): 511-512; September 1995. : 6.1.

Kerslake, Evelyn; Goulding, Anne (1996). Focus groups: their use in LIS research data collection. Education for information. 14: 225-232; Oct. 1996. : 22.

Kessler, M. M. (Maxwell Mirton) (1963). Bibliographic coupling between scientific papers. American Documentation. 14 (1): 10-25; 1963 January. : 8.3.12.1.

Knowledge organization: official quarterly journal of the International Society for Knowledge Organization. Formerly International Classification. Includes frequent bibliographies of recent literature. : 17.3.

Kochen, Manfred (1974). Principles of information retrieval. Los Angeles: Melville Pub. Co.; 1974. xix, 203 p. (Information sciences series). ISBN 0471496979. : 1.3.

Kochtanek, Thomas R.; Hein, Karen K. (1999). Delphi study of digital libraries. Information processing & management. 35(3): 245-254; May 1999. : 22.

Korfhage, Robert R. (1997). Information storage and retrieval. New York: Wiley Computer Publishing; c1997. xiii, 349 p. ISBN 0-471-14338-3. : 1.3; 8.3.

Kristensen, Jaan; Jarvelin, Kalervo. The effectiveness of a searching thesaurus in free-text searching in a full-text database. International Classification, 17(2): 77-84; 1990. : 13.3.

Krooks, David A.; Lancaster, F. W. (1993). The evolution of guidelines for thesaurus construction. Libri. 43(4): 326-342; 1993 Oct.-Dec. : 13.3.2.

Krovetz, Robert (1993). Viewing morphology as an inference process. In: Korfhage, Robert; Rasmussen, Edie; Willett, Peter, eds. Proceedings of the 16th annual International ACM-SIGIR Conference on Research and Development in Information Retrieval; 1993 June 27-July 1; Pittsburgh, PA. New York, Association for Computing Machinery; c1993: 191-202. xi, 361. ISBN 0-89791-605-0. (Also available as UMass technical report TR-93-35). : 8.3.6.

Krovetz, Robert (1999). Personal correspondence to José Pérez-Carballo. : 8.3.6.

Kowalski, Gerald (1997). Information retrieval systems: theory and implementation. Boston: Kluwer Academic Publishers, c1997. xiii, 282 p. (The Kluwer international series on information retrieval; 1). ISBN: 0-7923-9926-9. : 8.3.

Kurth, Martin; Peters, Thomas A. (1995). Browsing in information systems: an extensive annotated bibliography of the literature. Ann Arbor, MI: Pierian Press, 1995. x, 275 p. (Library hi tech bibliography; v. 10). ISBN 0-87650-341-5 (vol. 10). : 11.2.

Kwasnik, Barbara H. (1989). The influence of context on classificatory behavior. 1989. xiv, 250 leaves. Thesis (Ph. D.)—Rutgers University; 1989. : 17.3.

Kwasnik, Barbara H. (1999). The role of classification in knowledge representation and discovery. Library trends. 48(1): 22-47; 1999 Summer. : 10.1; 17.3.

Kyrillidou, Martha; Heath, Fred M., eds. (2001). Measuring service quality. Library trends. 49(4): 541-799; Spring 2001. : 22.

Lancaster, F. W. (Frederick Wilfrid) (1968). Information retrieval systems: characteristics, testing, and evaluation. New York: Wiley; 1968. xiv, 222 p. (Information sciences series). ISBN 0471512400. A 2nd ed. was published in 1978. : 10.1 .

Lancaster, F. W. (Frederick Wilfrid) (1969). MEDLARS: Report on the evaluation of its operating efficiency. American documentation. 20(2): 119-142; 1969 April. : 22.

Bibliography

Lancaster, F. W. (Frederick Wilfrid) (1979). Information retrieval systems: characteristics, testing, and evaluation. 2nd ed. New York: Wiley; 1979. xiv, 222 p. (Information science series) ISBN 0-471-04673-6. : 22.

Lancaster, F. W. (Frederick Wilfrid) (1986). Vocabulary control for information retrieval. 2nd ed. Arlington, VA: Information Resources Press; 1986. xvii, 270 p. ISBN 0878150536. : 13.3.2.

Lancaster, F. W. (Frederick Wilfrid) (1991, 1998). Indexing and abstracting in theory and practice. Champaign, IL: University of Illinois, Graduate School of Library and Information Science; 1991. xiv, 328 p. ISBN 0-87845-083-1. A 2nd ed. was published in 1998, xiii, 426 p. ISBN 0-87845-102-1. : 8.2; 8.4; 12.3; 14.3.

Lancaster, F. W. (Frederick Wilfrid) ; Warner, Amy J. (1993). Information retrieval today. Arlington, VA: Information Resources Press, c1993. xviii, 341 p. ISBN 0-87815-064-1. : 22.

Landauer, Thomas K. (1985). Experience with an adaptive indexing scheme. In: Borman, Lorraine; Curtis, Bill, eds. Human factors in computing systems: CHI '85 conference proceedings; 1985 April 14-18; San Francisco. Sponsored by the Association for Computing Machinery's Special Interest Group on Computer and Human Interaction (ACM/SIGCHI), in cooperation with the Human Factors Society ... [et al.] New York: Association for Computing Machinery; c1985: 131-135. vii, 231 p. (Special issue of the SIGCHI bulletin). ISBN 0897911490. : 13.3.1; 13.3.3.1.2.

Langridge, D. W. (Derek Wilton) (1992). Classification: its kinds, elements, systems and applications. London; New York: Bowker-Saur; in association with Wagga Wagga, New South Wales: Centre for Information Studies, Charles Sturt University; c1992. 84 p. (Topics in library and information studies). ISBN 0-86291-622-4. : 1.3 ("format") ; 5.4; 17.3.

Layne, Sara Shatford: *See* Shatford Layne, Sara.

Lehnus, Donald J. (1980). Book numbers: history, principles, and application. Chicago: American Library Association; 1980. iv, 153 p. ISBN 0-8389-0316-9. : 15.

Leonard, Lawrence E. (1977). Inter-indexer consistency studies, 1954-1975: a review of the literature and summary of study results. Champaign, IL: University of Illinois, Graduate School of Library Science, 1977. 51 p. (University of Illinois. Graduate School of Library Science. Occasional papers; no. 131. ISSN 0073-5310). : 8.2.

Library and information science abstracts (1969). London: Library Association; 1969 March-April. ISSN 0024-2179. : 8.3.7.

Library literature (1967-1969). Bronx, NY: H.W. Wilson Co. ISSN: 0024-2373. : 8.3.7.

Library of Congress (1980). Library of Congress filing rules. Prepared by John C. Rather and Susan C . Biebel. Library of Congress. Processing Services. Washington, DC: Library of Congress, Cataloging Distribution Service; 1980. 111 p. : 1.4; 12.2.1; 17.1.

Library of Congress (1996). Subject cataloging manual: subject headings. 5th ed. Prepared by The Cataloging Policy and Support Office, Library of Congress. Washington: Cataloging Distribution Service, Library of Congress; 1996. ISBN 0-8444-0906-5. [periodically updated]. : 1.4; 10.1; 12.2.1.

Library of Congress (1999). Free-floating subdivisions: an alphabetical index, prepared by the Cataloging Policy and Support Office, Library of Congress. 11th ed. Washington, DC: Cataloging Distribution Service, Library of Congress. [periodically updated]. : 1.4; 12.2.1.

Library of Congress (2003). Library of Congress subject headings. Washington: Library of Congress, Cataloging Distribution Service. ISSN 1048-9711 [updated annually]. See also website http://lcweb.loc.gov/cds/lcsh.html. : 1.4; 12.2.1; 13.3.1.

Library of Congress (2003a). MARC standards. Washington, DC: Network Development and MARC Standards Office. http://www.loc.gov/marc/. Accessed 1-7-2004. : 20.1.

Library of Congress (2004). Library of Congress classification. Subject Cataloging Division, Processing Services, Library of Congress. Washington: LC. [many volumes, periodically updated]. See also website www.loc.gov/cds/classif.html. (accessed 8-28-2004). : 1.4; 12.2.4.

Liddy, Elizabeth D.; Jorgensen, Corinne (1993). Modeling information seeking behaviors in index use. In: Bonzi, Susan, ed. Proceedings of the 56th annual meeting of the American Society for Information Science; 1993 October 24-28; Columbus, OH. Medford, NJ: Learned Information; 1993: 185-190. ISSN 0044-7870. : 19.1.

Bibliography

Lincoln, Bruce (1989). Discourse and the construction of society: comparative studies of myth, ritual, and classification. New York: Oxford University Press; 1989. ix, 238 p. : 17.3.

Lunin, Lois F. (1994). Analyzing art objects for an image database. In: Fidel, Raya; Hahn, Trudi Bellardo; Rasmussen, Edie M.; Smith, Philip J., eds. (1994). Challenges in indexing electronic text and images. Medford, NJ: Learned Information for the American Society for Information Science; 1994: 57-74. ix, 306 p. (ASIS monograph series). ISBN 0-938734-76-8. : 8.2.2.1.

Lunin, Lois F.; Fidel, Raya, eds. (1994). Perspectives on indexing. Journal of the American Society for Information Science. 45(6): 569-636; 1994 September. : 8.

Maltby, Arthur; Gill, Lindy (1979). The case for Bliss: modern classification practice and principles in the context of the Bibliographic Classification. London: Clive Bingley; 1979. 142 p. : 17.3.2.1.

Marchionini, Gary (1995). Information seeking in electronic environments. New York: Cambridge University Press; c1995. xi, p. (Cambridge series on human-computer interaction; 9). ISBN 0-521-44372-5. : 11.2.

Marchionini, Gary ; Komlodi, Anita (1998). Design of interfaces for information seeking. Annual review of information science and technology. 34: 89-130; 1998. : 19.3.

Markey, Karen. *See also* Drabenstott, Karen Markey *(later name)*.

Markey, Karen (1984). Interindexer consistency tests: a literature review and report of a test of consistency in indexing visual materials. Library and information science research. 6(2): 155-177; 1984 April-June. : 8.2.

Mayfield, James; McNamee, Paul (1998). Indexing using both n-grams and words. In: Voorhees, E. M.; Harman, Donna, eds. TREC-7: Proceedings of the Seventh Text REtrieval Conference; 1998 November 9-11; Gaithersburg, MD. Co-sponsored by the National Institute of Standards and Technology (NIST) and the Defense Advanced Research Projects Agency (DARPA). Gaithersburg, MD: U.S. Depart. of Commerce, Technology Administration, National Institute of Standards and Technology; Washington, D.C.: For sale by the Supt. of Docs., U.S. G.P.O., 1998: 419-424. (NIST Special Publication; 500-242). http://potomac.ncsl.nist.gov/TREC/t7_proceedings.html; http://trec.nist.gov/. : 8.3.1.

McCain, Katherine W.; White, Howard D; Griffith, Belver C. (1987a). Comparing retrieval performance in online data bases. Information processing & management. 23(6): 539-553; 1987. : 22.

McCain, Katherine W.; White, Howard D; Griffith, Belver C. (1987b). Test retrieval as a measure of system performance: MEDLINE and the medical behavioral sciences. In Hurd, Julie M.; Davis, Charles H., eds. ASIS '86. Proceedings of the 49th ASIS Annual Meeting. Volume 23; 28 Sept.-2 Oct. 1986; Chicago, IL. Medford, NJ: Learned Information, for the American Society for Information Science, 1987: 199-203. : 22.

McIlwaine, Ia (1997). The Universal decimal classification: some factors concerning its origins, development, and influence. Journal of the American Society for Information Science. 48: 331-339; 1997 Apr. : 17.3.

McKiernan, Gerry (1997-1999). The big picture (sm): visual browsing in web and non-web databases. In: Cochrane, Pauline Atherton; Johnson, Eric H.; Roe, Sandra, eds. Visualizing subject access for 21st century information resources. Champaign, IL: Graduate School of Library and Information Science, University of Illinois at Urbana-Champaign; 1998: 158. 176 p. (Clinic on library applications of data processing; 1997. ISSN 0069-4789). ISBN 0-87845-103-X. Only the abstract is printed here, with a URL to the 1997 version of The big picture (SM). The updated version may be found at: http://www.public.iastate.edu/~CYBERSTACKS/BigPic.htm. Last visited 03-26-2002; "last modified June 18, 1999.". : 19.3.

Metadata, Dublin core and USMARC (1997). 1997 March 10. 14 p. (LC-MARBI discussion paper; 99). gopher://marvel.loc.gov:70/00/.listarch/usmarc/dp99.doc. : 3.4.

Metcalfe, John Wallace (1976). Information retrieval, British & American, 1876-1976. Metuchen, N.J.: Scarecrow Press; 1976. v, 243 p. ISBN: 0-8108-0875-7. : 1.1.

Miksa, Francis L. (1984). The development of classification at the Library of Congress. University of Ill. at Urbana-Champaign. Graduate School of Lib. & Information Science; 1984. 78 p. : 17.3.

Miksa, Francis L. (1989). The DDC, the universe of knowledge, and the post-modern library. Albany, NY: Forest Press, a Division of OCLC Online Computer Library Center; 1998. vii, 99 p. ISBN 0-910608-64-4. : 2; 2.3; 17.3.

Bibliography

Mills, J.; Broughton, Vanda; Lang, Valerie (1977). Bliss bibliographic classification: introduction and auxiliary schedules. 2nd ed. London: Butterworths; 1987, c1977. xiv, 209 p. : 17.3.2.1.

Milstead, Jessica L. (1984). Subject access systems: alternatives in design. Orlando, FL: Academic Press; 1984. x, 212 p. (Library and information science). ISBN 0-12-498120-8. : 0.2.

Milstead, Jessica L. (1990). Thesaurus software packages. In: Henderson, Diane, ed. Information in the year 2000: from research to applications: proceedings of the 53rd annual meeting of the American Society for Information Science, volume 27; 1990 November 4-8; Toronto, Canada. Medford, NJ: Learned Information; 1990: 3-15. xiv, 393 p. ISBN 0-938734-48-2, ISSN 0044-7870. : 13.3.2.

Milstead, Jessica L. (1992). Methodologies for subject analysis in bibliographic databases. Information processing & management. 28(3): 407-431; 1992. : 8.4.

Milstead, Jessica L. (1994). ASIS thesaurus of information science and librarianship. Medford, NJ: Learned Information, for the American Society for Information Science; 1994. x, 139 p. (ASIS monograph series). ISBN 0-938734-80-6; 2nd ed. published in 1998, Medford, NJ: Information Today for ASIS, 192 p. ISBN 1-57387-050-1; available online at http://www.asis.org/Publications/Thesaurus/tnhome.htm, accessed 8-11-04. : 13.3.2; 13.3.2.1.

Milstead, Jessica L. (1997). Thesauri in a full-text world. In: Cochrane, Pauline Atherton; Johnson, Eric H.; Roe, Sandra, eds. Visualizing subject access for 21st century information resources. Champaign, IL: Graduate School of Library and Information Science, University of Illinois at Urbana-Champaign; 1998: 28-38. 176 p. (Clinic on library applications of data processing; 1997. ISSN 0069-4789). ISBN 0-87845-103-X. An updated online version is available at http://www.jelem.com/full.htm. : 13.3.2.

Milstead, Jessica L. (1999). NISO/APA/ASI/ALCTS workshop on electronic thesauri: planning for a standard. Bethesda, MD: National Information Standards Organization. 1999. http://www.niso.org/thes99rprt.html. : 13.3; 20.6.

Modern Language Association of America. *See also* Gibaldi, Joseph (1999). MLA handbook.

Modern Language Association of America (1997). MLA bibliography worksheet for national literatures. New York: MLA; [1997]. 1 sheet. : 2.1; 8.2.2; 12.2.2.2; 12.2.4; 20.2.

Modern Language Association of America (1999). MLA international bibliography of books and articles on the modern languages and literatures. New York: MLA. annual. ISSN 0024-8215. : 3.7; 12.2.2.2; 12.2.4; 17.2.

Molholt, Pat (1990). Standardizing and codifying related term links for improved information retrieval. In: Fugmann, Robert, ed. Tools for knowledge organisation and the human interface. Proceedings of the 1st International ISKO Conference; 1990 August 14-17; Darmstadt. Frankfurt/Main: Indeks-Verlag; 1990-1991: Part I, 267-275. 2 v. (Advances in knowledge organization, v. 1-2). ISBN 3-88672-020-9 (v. 1), 3-88672-021-7 (v. 2). : 13.3.3.1.5.

Morrison, Heather G. (1999). Online catalogue research and the verbal protocol method. Library hi tech. 17(2): 197-206; 1999. : 22.

Mulvany, Nancy C. (1994). Indexing books. Chicago: University of Chicago Press; c1994. xiii, 320 p. ISBN 0-226-55014-1. : 8.2.

Narayanan, N. Hari; Hegarty, Mary (1998). On designing comprehensible interactive hypermedia manuals. International journal of human-computer studies. 48: 267-301; 1998. : 21.1.

National Information Standards Organization. *See also* American National Standards Institute.

National Information Standards Organization (1984). ANSI/NISO Z39.4 Basic criteria for indexes. Bethesda, MD: NISO; 1984. 24 p. : 1.4.

National Information Standards Organization (1993). ANSI/NISO Z39.19-1993 Guidelines for the construction, format, and management of monolingual thesauri. Bethesda, MD: NISO Press; c1994. xii, 69 p. ISBN 1-880124-04-1. : 1.3; 13.3.2; 13.3.3.1.4.; 13.3.3.1.5.

National Information Standards Organization (1996a). ANSI/NISO Z39.75 Alphabetical arrangement of letters and the sorting of numerals and other symbols. Draft for balloting. Bethesda, MD: NISO Press; 1996. 20 p. : 1.4.

Bibliography

National Information Standards Organization (1996b). Z39.56-1996 Serial item & contribution identifier (SICI). Bethesda, MD: NISO Press; 1996. 36 p. ISBN 1880124289. Examples taken from http://sunsite.berkeley.edu/SICI. : 15.

National Information Standards Organization (1997a). 1996 annual report. Bethesda, MD: NISO; 1997. 28 p. : 1.4; 7.

National Information Standards Organization (1997b). ANSI/NISO Z39.14-1997 Guidelines for abstracts: an American national standard. Approved November 27, 1996 by the American National Standards Institute. Bethesda, MD: NISO Press, c1997. viii, 14 p. (National information standards series. ISSN 1041-5653). ISBN: 1-88012-431-9. : 7.4.2; 14.2; 14.5.2.

National Information Standards Organization (1997c). NISO Press 1997 catalog. Oxon Hill, MD: NISO Press Fulfillment; 1997. 36 p. : 1.4.

National Information Standards Organization (1999). First workshop on linkage from citations to electronic journal literature: a one-day invitational workshop sponsored by NISO, NFAIS, DLF, and the Society of Scholarly Publishers. Funded by the Digital Library Federation and NISO. Washington, DC; 11 Feb. 1999. http://www.niso.org/linkge.html. : 15.

National Information Standards Organization (2000). Z39.84-2000 Syntax for the digital object identifier. http://www.doi.org/handbook_2000/appendix_1.html#A1-NIS. : 15.

National Information Standards Organization (2002). Z39.50 resource page. http://www.niso.org/standards/resources/Z3950_Resources.html#info. Accessed 5-28-2002. : 20.6.

National Information Standards Organization (2004?). Z39.29-200x Bibliographic references. Bethesda, MD: NISO Press; 2004? "This standard has been approved by the voting members and is being readied for publication." — www.niso.org, 4-14-2004. : 0.5; 14.2; 14.5.2; 15.1.2; bibliography.

National Library of Medicine (1999). Medical Subject Headings. Annotated alphabetic list. Bethesda, MD: Medical Subject Headings Section, Library Operations, National Library of Medicine; Springfield, VA: National Technical Information Serivce, distributor. Periodically updated. ISSN 0147-5711. See also NLM Cataloging Webpage: http://www.nlm.nih.gov/tsd/cataloging/mainpge.html. : 1.4; 12.2.1; 12.2.1.1.

Nielsen, Jakob (1999). User interface directions for the web. Communications of the ACM. 42(1): 65-72; 1999 Jan. : 19.3.

NISO: See National Information Standards Organization.

O'Connor, Brian C. (1985). Access to moving image documents: background concepts and proposals for surrogates for film and video works. Journal of documentation. 41: 209-220; 1985 December. : 14.2.

O'Connor, Brian C. (1996). Explorations in indexing and abstracting: pointing, virtue, and power. Englewood, CO: Libraries Unlimited; 1996. xiii, 182 p. (Library and information science text series). ISBN 1-56308-184-9. : 8.2; 14.3.

Olson, Hope Alene (1998). Mapping beyond Dewey's boundaries: constructing classificatory space for marginalized knowledge domains [examining Dewey decimal classification for bias]. Library trends. 47(2): 233-254; 1998 Fall. : 17.3.

Olson, Hope A.; Boll, John J. (2001). Subject analysis in online catalogs. 2nd ed. Englewood, CO: Libraries Unlimited; 2001. xv, 333 p. ISBN 1-56308-800-2. : 20.1.

Oxford English dictionary (1989). 2nd ed. Prepared by J. A. Simpson and E. S. C. Weiner. Oxford, England: Clarendon Press; 1989. 20 v. ISBN 0-19-861218-8. : 1.1; 13.3.5.

Paice, Chris D. (1996). Method for evaluation of stemming algorithms based on error counting. Journal of the American Society for Information Science. 47(8): 632-649; 1996 August. : 8.3.6.

Pao, Miranda Lee (1978). Automatic text analysis based on transition phenomena of word occurrences. Journal of the American Society for Information Science. 29(3): 121-124; 1978 May. : 8.3.7.

Paskin, Norman (1997). Information identifiers. Learned publishing. 10(2): 135-156; 1997 April. http://www.elsevier.com/inca/homepage/about/infoident/. : 15.

Pérez-Carballo, José; Strzalkowski, Tomek (2000). Natural language information retrieval: progress report. Information processing & management. 36(1): 155-178; 2000. : 8.3.8.

Bibliography

Pérez-López, Kathleen Golitko (1995). Management of scientific image databases using wavelets (indexing). Fairfax, VA: George Mason University; 1995. 201 p. Ph.D. dissertation. Citation from Dissertation abstracts international. 56(5)B: 2727). : 8.2.2.1.

Peters, Ronnie (1992). Designing for the computer screen. In: Smith, Linda C.; Dalrymple, Prudence W. Designing information: new roles for librarians. Champaign, IL: Graduate School of Library and Information Science, University of Illinois at Urbana-Champaign; c1993: 147-163. 222 p. (Clinic on library applications of data processing; 1992. ISSN 0069-4789). ISBN 0-87845-088-2. : 19.3.

Poli, Roberto (1996). Ontology for knowledge organization. In: Green, Rebecca. Knowledge organization and change: proceedings of the fourth international ISKO conference; 1996 July 15-18; Washington, DC. Frankfurt/Main: Indeks Verlag; 1996: 313-319. 431 p. (Advances in knowledge organization, v. 5). ISBN 3-88672-024-1. : 13.3.5.

Pollitt, A. Steven (1998). The key role of classification and indexing in view-based searching. International cataloguing and bibliographic control, 27(2), 37-40. : 13.3.

Pollitt, A. Steven; Ellis, Geoffrey P. (1994). Improving search quality using thesauri for query specification and the presentation of search results. In: Albrechtsen, Hanne; Oernager, Susan, eds. Knowledge organization and quality management: proceedings of the Third International ISKO Conference; 1994 June 20-24; Copenhagen. Organized by the Royal School of Librarianship, Copenhagen, Denmark in cooperation with the International Society for Knowledge Organization. Frankfurt am Main: Indeks Verlag; 1994: 382-389. 457 p. (Advances in knowledge organization; v. 4). ISBN: 3-88672-023-3. : 13.3.

Pollitt, A. Steven; Smith, Martin P.; Braekevelt, Patrick A. J. (1997). View-based searching systems — a new paradigm for information retrieval based on faceted classification and indexing using mutually constraining knowledge-based views. Huddersfield, UK: Centre for Database Access Research, School of Computing and Mathematics, University of Huddersfield; 1997? http://www.hud.ac.uk/schools/cedar/bcshci.htm. No longer available; see Pollitt (1998). : 13.3.

Ponte, Jay M.; Croft, W. Bruce (1998). A language modeling approach to information retrieval. In: Proceedings of the 21st annual international ACM SIGIR conference on research and development in information retrieval; 1998; Melbourne, Australia. New York: ACM Press: 175-181. ISBN 1-58113-015-5. : 8.3.

Ranganathan, S. R. (Shiyali Ramamrita, rao sahib) (1965). The Colon classification. New Brunswick, NJ: Graduate School of Library Service, Rutgers, the State University; 1965. 289 p. (Artandi, Susan, ed. Rutgers series on systems for the intellectual organization of information; v. 4). : 2.3; 8.2.2; 17.3.

Raskin, Jef (2000). The humane interface: new directions for designing interactive systems. Reading, MA: Addison-Wesley; 2000. xix, 233 p. ISBN 0-201-37937-6. : 19.3.

Rasmussen, Edie M. (1994). Indexing and retrieval from full-text. Introduction. In: Fidel, Raya; Hahn, Trudi Bellardo; Rasmussen, Edie M.; Smith, Philip J., eds. Challenges in indexing electronic text and images. Medford, NJ: Learned Information for the American Society for Information Science; 1994: 241-245. ix, 306 p. (ASIS monograph series). ISBN 0-938734-76-8. : 8.1.

Reitz, Joan M. (2000). ODLIS: Online Dictionary of Library and Information Science. Danbury, CT: Western Connecticut State University, c2000. http://www.wcsu.ctstateu.edu/library/odlis.html. : 1.3 ("digital library").

Rice, Ronald E.; McCreadie, Maureen; Chang, Shan-Ju L. (2001). Accessing and browsing information and communication. Cambridge, MA: MIT Press; c2001. xiii, 357 p. ISBN 0-262-18214-9. : 11.2.

Richmond, Phyllis A. (1981). Introduction to PRECIS for North American usage. Littleton, CO: Libraries Unlimited; 1981. 321 p. ISBN 0872872408. : 12.2.2.2.; 20.4.

Richmond, Phyllis A. (1988). Precedent-setting contributions to modern classification [American view of Vickery's accomplishments]. Journal of documentation. 44: 242-249; 1988 Sept. : 17.3.

Salton, Gerard (1975a). Dynamic information and library processing. Englewood Cliffs, NJ: Prentice-Hall; c1975. 523 p. ISBN 0-13221325-7. : 8.3.11.

Salton, Gerard (1975b). A theory of indexing. Philadelphia: Society for Industrial and Applied Mathematics. v, 56 p. (Regional conference series in applied mathematics ; 18). : 8.3.

Bibliography

Salton, Gerard (1989). Automatic text processing: the transformation, analysis, and retrieval of information by computer. Reading, MA: Addison-Wesley; 1989. xiii, 530 p. (Addison-Wesley series in computer science). ISBN 0201122278. : 8.3.

Salton, Gerard; Buckley, Christopher (1988). Term weighting approaches in automatic text retrieval. Information processing & management. 24(5)513-523; 1988. Reprinted in: Sparck Jones, Karen; Willett, Peter, eds. Readings in information retrieval. San Francisco: Morgan Kaufman Publishers; c1997: 323-328. xv, 589 p. ISBN 1-55860-454-5. : 8.3.5.

Salton, Gerard; Buckley, Christopher (1990). Improving retrieval performance by relevance feedback. Journal of the American Society for Information Science. 41(4): 288-297; 1990 June. : 8.3.13.

Salton, Gerard; McGill, Michael J. (1983a). Introduction to modern information retrieval. New York: McGraw-Hill, c1983. xv, 448 p. (McGraw-Hill computer science series) ISBN 0070544840. : 8.3; 8.3.11.

Salton, Gerard; McGill, Michael J. (1983b). The SMART and SIRE experimental retrieval systems. Reprinted in: Sparck Jones, Karen; Willett, Peter, eds. Readings in information retrieval. San Francisco: Morgan Kaufman Publishers; 1997: 118-155. 576 p. ISBN 1-55860-454-5. : 8.3.11.

Sandstrom, Pamela Effrein (1994). An optimal foraging approach to information seeking and use. Library quarterly. 64(4): 414-449; Oct. 1994. : 22.

Saracevic, Tefko (1970). On the concept of relevance in information science. Ph.D. dissertation. Cleveland OH: Case Western Reserve University; 1970. xi, 342 leaves. : 9.1.1.

Saracevic, Tefko (1976). Relevance: a review of the literature and a framework for thinking on the notion in information science. Advances in librarianship. 6: 79-138; 1976. (A slightly different version appeared in the Journal of the American Society for Information Science. 26(6): 321-343; 1975 November.). : 9.1.1.

Saracevic, Tefko (1991). Individual differences in organizing, searching and retrieving information. In: Systems understanding people: proceedings of the 54th annual meeting of the American Society for Information Science, volume 28; 1991 October 27-31; Washington, DC. Medford, NJ: Learned Information; 1991: 82-86. xiii, 393 p. ISBN 0-938734-56-3, ISSN 0044-7870. : 8.1; 8.2; 13.2.

Saracevic, Tefko; Kantor, Paul; Chamis, Alice Y.; Trivison, Donna (1988a). A study of information seeking and retrieving. I. Background and methodology. Journal of the American Society for Information Science. 39(3): 161-176; 1988 May. : 8.2.

Saracevic, Tefko; Kantor, Paul (1988b). A study of information seeking and retrieving. II. Users, questions, and effectiveness. Journal of the American Society for Information Science. 39(3): 177-196; 1988 May. : 8.1; 8.2; 13.2.

Saracevic, Tefko; Kantor, Paul (1988c). A study of information seeking and retrieving. III. Searchers, searches, and overlap. Journal of the American Society for Information Science. 39(3): 197-216; 1988 May. : 8.1; 8.2; 13.2.

Satija, Mohinder Partap (1988). Classification: some fundamentals, some myths, some realities. Knowledge organization. 25(1/2): 32-35. : 17.3.

Satija, Mohinder Partap (1992). Ranganathan and classification: a chronology 1924-1992. International classification. 19(1): 3-6; 1992. : 2; 17.3.

Schatz, Bruce R.; Johnson, Eric H.; Cochrane, Pauline A.; Chen, Hsinchun (1996). Interactive term suggestion for users of digital libraries: using subject thesauri and co-occurrence lists for information retrieval. In: Fox, Edward A., Marchionini, Gary, eds. Proceedings of the 1st ACM International Conference on Digital Libraries; 1996 March 20-23; Bethesda, MD. New York: Association for Computing Machinery; c1966: 126-133. viii, 187 p. ISBN 0-89791-830-4. : 13.3.

Schulze, Anna Noakes (2001). User-centered design for information professionals. Journal of education for library and information science. 42(2): 116-122; 2001 Spring. : 19; 19.3.

Schutze, Hinrich; Pedersen, Jan O. (1997). A co-occurrence-based thesaurus and two applications to information retrieval. Information processing & management. 33(3): 307-18; 1997 May. : 13.3.4.

Sears, Minnie Earl (1997). Sears list of subject headings. Ed. by Joseph Miller. 16th ed. New York: H. W. Wilson Co.; 1997. lii, 786 p. ISBD 0-8242-0920-6. : 12.2.1.

Bibliography

Shapiro, Celia D.; Yan, Puck-Fai (1996). Generous tools: thesauri in digital libraries. In: Williams, Martha E., ed. Proceedings of the 17th National Online Meeting; 1996 May 14-16; New York. Sponsored by Information Today, Inc. Medford, NJ: Information Today; 1996: 323-332. xi, 418 p. ISBN 1-573-87026-9. : 13.3.

Shatford Layne, Sara (1994). Some issues in the indexing of images. Journal of the American Society for Information Science. 45(6): 583-588; 1994 September. : 8.2.2.1.

Shneiderman, Ben (1998). Designing the user interface: strategies for effective human-computer interaction. 3rd ed. Reading, MA: Addison Wesley Longman; 1998. xiv, 639 p. ISBN 0-201-69497-2. : 19.3.

Small, Henry G. (1973). Co-citation in the scientific literature: a new measure of the relationship between two documents. Journal of the American Society for Information Science. 24(4): 265-269; 1973 July-August. : 8.3.12.2.

Smith, Howard; Poulter, Kevin (1999). Share the ontology in XML-based tradiing architectures. Communications of the ACM. 42(3): 110-111; 1999 March. : glossary (ontologies).

Smith, Martin P.; Pollitt, A. Steven (1996). Ranking and relevance feedback extensions to a view-based searching system. In: Raitt, David I.; Jeapes, Ben, eds. Online information 95: the 19th International Online Information Meeting; 1995 December 5-7; London. Oxford, UK: Learned Information Europe; 1996: 231-240. ISBN 0-904933-94-6. : 13.3.

Soergel, Dagobert (1974). Indexing languages and thesauri: construction and maintenance. Los Angeles: Melville Pub. Co.; 1974. xliii, 632 p. (A Wiley-Becker & Hayes series book). ISBN 0471810479. : 13.3.2.

Soergel, Dagobert (1985). Organizing information: principles of data base and retrieval systems. Orlando: Academic Press; 1985. xiv, 450 p. (Library and information science series). : 8.2; 8.2.2; 13.3.3.1.3.

Soergel, Dagobert (1999). The rise of ontologies or the reinvention of classification. Journal of the American Society for Information Science. 50(12): 1119-1190; 1999 Oct. : 13.3.5.

Sowa, John (1983). Conceptual structures. Reading MA: Addison-Wesley; 1983. Cited in Vickery (1997). : 13.3.5 .

Sowa, John (1995). Top-level ontological categories. International journal of human-computer studies. 43(5/6): 669-685; 1995. Cited in Poli (1996). : 13.3.5.

Sparck Jones, Karen (1972). A statistical interpretation of term specificity and its application in retrieval. Journal of Documentation. 28(1): 11-21; 1972 March. Reprinted in: Willett, Peter, ed. Document retrieval systems. London: Taylor Graham and the Institute of Information Scientists; c1988: 132-142. 292 p. (The foundations of information science; v. 3). ISBN 0-947568-21-2. : 10.1.

Sparck Jones, Karen (1981a). The Cranfield tests. In: Sparck Jones, Karen, ed. for Cyril Cleverdon. Information retrieval experiment. London; Boston: Butterworths; 1981: 256-284. viii, 352 p. ISBN 0-408-10648-4. : 8.1.

Sparck Jones, Karen, ed. (1981b). Information retrieval experiment. Ed. by Karen Sparck Jones for Cyril Cleverdon. London; Boston: Butterworths; 1981. viii, 352 p. ISBN 0-408-10648-4. : 8.1.

Sparck Jones, Karen (1981c). Retrieval system tests 1958-1979. In: Sparck Jones, Karen, ed. for Cyril Cleverdon. Information retrieval experiment. London; Boston: Butterworths; 1981: 213-255. viii, 352 p. ISBN 0-408-10648-4. : 8.1.

Sparck Jones, Karen (1999). What is the role of NLP in text retrieval? In: Strzalkowski, Tomek, ed. Natural language information retrieval. Dordrecht, NL; Boston: Kluwer Academic Publishers, c1999: 1-24. xxv, 384 p. (Text, speech, and language technology; v. 7.). ISBN: 0-7923-5685-3. : 8.3.8.

Sparck Jones, Karen; Walker, S.; Robertson, S.E. (2000). A probabilistic model of information retrieval: development and comparative experiments. Information processing & management. 36(6): 779-840; 2000 Nov. : 8.3.

Sparck Jones, Karen; Willett, Peter, eds. (1997). Readings in information retrieval. San Francisco: Morgan Kaufman Publishers; 1997. 576 p. ISBN 1-55860-454-5. : 8.3.

Spink, Amanda (1995). Term relevance feedback and mediated database searching: implications for information retrieval practice and systems design. Information processing & management. 31(2): 161-171; 1995 March-April. : 8.3.13.

Stiles, H. Edmund (1861). The association factor in information retrieval. Journal of the Association of Computing Machinery. 8(2): 271-279; 1961 April. : 8.3.11.

Bibliography

Stone, Alva T., ed. (2000). The LCSH century: one hundred years with the Library of Congress subject headings system. Cataloging and classification quarterly. 29(1-2): 1-234; 2000. : 12.2.1.

Strzalkowski, Tomek; Lin, Fang; Pérez-Carballo, Jose (1997). Natural language information retrieval: TREC-6 Report. In: Voorhees, E. M.; Harman, Donna, eds. Information technology: the Sixth Text REtrieval Conference (TREC-6); 1997 Nov. 19-21; Gaithersburg, MD. Co-sponsored by the National Institute of Standards and Technology (NIST) and the Defense Advanced Research Projects Agency (DARPA). Gaithersburg, MD: U.S. Depart. of Commerce, Technology Administration, National Institute of Standards and Technology; Washington, D.C.: For sale by the Supt. of Docs., U.S. G.P.O., 1998: 209-228. xxiv, 788, 252, 8 p. (NIST special publication ; no. 500-240). http://trec.nist.gov/. : 8.3.8.

Strzalkowski, Tomek; Lin, Fang; Wang, Jin; Pérez-Carballo, José (1999). Evaluating natural language processing techniques in information retreival. In: Strzalkowski, Tomek, ed. Natural language information retrieval. Dordrecht, NL; Boston: Kluwer Academic Publishers, c1999: 113-145. xxv, 384 p. (Text, speech, and language technology; v. 7.). ISBN: 0-7923-5685-3. : 8.3.8.

Strzalkowski, Tomek, Pérez-Carballo, Jose and Marinescu, Mihnea (1996). Natural language information retrieval in digital libraries. In: Fox, Edward A., Marchionini, Gary, eds. Proceedings of the 1st ACM International Conference on Digital Libraries; 1996 March 20-23; Bethesda, MD. New York: Association for Computing Machinery; c1966: 117-125. viii, 187 p. ISBN 0-89791-830-4. : 8.3.8.

Sun, Qinglan; Shaw, Debora; Davis, Charles H. (1999). A model for estimating the occurrence of same-frequency words and the boundary between high- and low-frequency words in texts. Journal of the American Society for Information Science. 50(3): 280-286; 1999 March. : 8.3.7.

Svenonius, Elaine (1971). The effect of indexing specificity on retrieval performance. A dissertation submitted to the faculty of the Graduate Library School in candidacy for the degree of doctor of philosophy. Chicago, IL: University of Chicago; 1971. vii, 418 p. Svenonius (1976) puts forth a similar discussion of the meaning and significance of specificity. : 10.1.

Svenonius, Elaine (1976). Metcalfe and the principles of specific entry. In: Rayward, W. Boyd, ed. The variety of librarianship: essays in honour of John Wallace Metcalfe. Sydney: Library Association of Australia; 1976: 171-189. 242 p. ISBN 0 909915 42 3. : 10.1.

Svenonius, Elaine (1992). Ranganathan and classification science. Libri. 42: 176-183; 1992 July/Sept. : 17.3.

Svenonius, Elaine (1994). Access to nonbook materials: the limits of subject indexing for visual and aural languages. Journal of the American Society for Information Science. 45(6): 600-606; 1994 September. : 8.2.2.1.

Svenonius, Elaine (1995). Precoordination or not? In: Holley, Robert P.; McGarry, Dorothy; Duncan, Donna; Svenonius, Elaine, eds. Subject indexing: principles and practices in the 90's: proceedings of the IFLA Satellite Meeting sponsored by the IFLA Section on Classification and Indexing and the Instituto da Biblioteca Nacional e do Livro, Lisbon, Portugal; 1993 August 17-18; Lisbon, Portugal. München; New Providence: K. G. Saur; 1995: 231-255. x, 302 p. (International Federation of Library Associations and Institutions. Universal Bibliographic Control and International MARC Programme. UBCIM publications; new series v. 15). ISBN 3-598-11251-3. : 12.1.

Sweetland, James H. (1988). Beta tests and end-user surveys: are they valid? Database. 11(1): 27-32; Feb. 1988. : 22.

Swift, D. F.; Winn, V. A.; Bramer, D. A. (1977a). Multi-modality in indexing and searching. Journal of informatics. 1(3): 91-95; 1977 December. : 8.2.2.

Swift, D. F.; Winn, V. A.; Bramer, D. A. (1977b). A multi-modal approach to indexing and classification. International classification. 4(2): 90-94; 1977 November. : 8.2.2.

Swift, D. F.; Winn, V. A.; Bramer, D. A. (1978). "Aboutness" as a strategy for retrieval in the social sciences. Aslib proceedings. 30(5): 182-187; 1978 May. : 8.2.2.

Tague-Sutcliffe, Jean (1995). Measuring information: an information services perspective. San Diego: Academic Press, c1995. xii, 206 p. (Library and information science). ISBN 0-12-682660-0. : 22.

Taube, Mortimer (1953). Evaluation of information systems for report utilization. In: Taube, Mortimer; et al. Studies in coordinate indexing. By Mortimer Taube and associates. Washington, DC: Documentation Incorporated; 1953-1965: 1:96-110. 6 v. : 12.1.

Bibliography

Tavris, Carol (1998). The paradox of gender. Scientific American. 279(4): 126-128; 1998 October. : 8.2.1.

Taylor, Arlene G. (1999). The organization of information. Englewood, CO: Libraries Unlimited; 1999. xx, 280 p. (Library and information science test series). ISBN 1-56308-493-7. : 1.1; 8.2; 20.6.

Taylor, Mike (1999). Zthes: a Z39.50 profile for thesaurus navigation. Version 0.3b. 26th July 1999. http://lcweb.loc.gov/z3950/agency/profiles/zthes-03.html. : 13.3.

Thomas, Alan R. (1995). Blissful beliefs: Henry Evelyn Bliss counsels on classification. Cataloging and classification quarterly. 19(3/4): 17-22; 1995. : 17.3.

Thomas, David H. (2001). The effect of interface design on item selection in an online catalog. Library resources and technical services. 45(1): 20-46. : 16.

Tonta, Yasar Ahmet. LCSH and PRECIS in library and information science: a comparative study. Champaign, Ill.: Graduate School of Library and Information Science, University of Illinois at Urbana-Champaign; c1992. 68 p. (Occasional papers; no. 194). : 20.4.

TREC (1992-2001). Text Retrieval Conferences. Voorhees, E. M.; Harman, Donna K., eds. Proceedings of the Text REtrieval Conferences 1-8; 1992-2001; Gaithersburg, MD. Co-sponsored by the National Institute of Standards and Technology (NIST), the Defense Advanced Research Projects Agency (DARPA), and the Advanced Research and Development Activity (ARDA). Gaithersburg, MD: U.S. Depart. of Commerce, Technology Administration, National Institute of Standards and Technology; Washington, D.C.: For sale by the Supt. of Docs., U.S. G.P.O., 1992-2002. http://trec.nist.gov/pubs.html. Accessed 2-3-2003. : 8.1; 8.3.1; 8.3.5.

Unesco (1977). Unesco thesaurus: a structured list of descriptors for indexing and retrieving literature in the fields of education, science, social science, culture, and communication. Compiled by Jean Aitchison. Paris: Unesco; 1977. 2 v. ISBN 9231014692. : 13.3.2.1.

Unesco (1995). Unesco thesaurus: a structured list of descriptors for indexing and retrieving literature in the fields of education, science, social and human science, culture, communication and information. 2nd ed. Paris: Unesco; 1995. 3 v. ISBN 92-3-003100-3. : 13.3.2.1.

Universal decimal classification: *See* British Standards Institution (1961).

Uschold, M.; Gruninger, M. (1996). Ontologies: principles, methods and applications. Knowledge engineering review. 11(2): 93-136; 1996. Cited in Vickery (1997). : 13.3.5.

UW Computing & Communications (2002). An introduction to XML. http://www.washington.edu/computing/training/540/. Last modified: June 10, 2002. Retrieved 8 August 2002. : 21.2.

Vickery, B. C. (Brian Campbell) (1966). Faceted classification schemes. New Brunswick, NJ: Graduate School of Library Service, Rutgers the State University; 1966. 108 p. (Artandi, Susan, ed. Rutgers series on systems for the intellectual organization of information; v. 5). : 2; 8.2.2; 12.2.4; 17.3.

Vickery, Brian Campbell (1991). Eric de Grolier's "big book" on classification [published in 1956, its opinions are still valid]. International classification. 18(3): 170; 1991. : 17.3.

Vickery, B. C. (Brian Campbell) (1997). Ontologies. Journal of information science. 23(4): 277-286; 1997. : 13.3.5.

Wang, Yih-Chen; Vandendorpe, James; Evens, Martha (1985). Relational thesauri in information retrieval. Journal of the American Society for Information Science. 36(1): 15-27; 1985 January. : 13.3.3.1.5.

Warner, Julian (1999). "In the catalogue ye go for men": evaluation criteria for information retrieval systems. Information research. 4(4). Available at: http://informationr.net/ir/4-4/paper62.html. Accessed 9-29-2003. : 22.

Webster's (1966). Webster's new world dictionary of the American language. College ed. Cleveland: World Publishing Co.; c1966. xxxvi, 1724 p. : 1.3 ("syntax"); 2; 12.2.3; 13.3.5; 14.2.

Weibel, Stuart; Jul, Erik; Shafer, Keith (2001). PURLs: persistent uniform resource locators. 2001. http://purl.oclc.org/OCLC/PURL/SUMMARY. An updated version of "PURLs to improve access to Internet." OCLC newsletter. p. 19; 1995 Nov-Dec. : 15.

Bibliography

Weinberg, Bella Hass (1987). Why indexing fails the researcher. In: Information: the transformation of society: proceedings of the 50th annual meeting of the American Society for Information Science, volume 24; 1987 October 4-8; Boston, MA. Medford, NJ: Learned Information; c1987: 241-244. xii, 287 p. ISBN 0-938734-19-9. ISSN 0044-7870. (reprinted in Weinberg 1988b). : 3; 8.2.2.

Weinberg, Bella Hass, ed. (1988a). Indexing: the state of our knowledge and the state of our ignorance: proceedings of the 20th annual meeting of the American Society of Indexers; 1988 May 13; New York, NY. Medford, NJ: Learned Information; 1989. x, 134 p. ISBN 0-938734-32-6. : 8.

Weinberg, Bella Hass (1988b). Why indexing fails the researcher. The indexer. 16: 3-6; 1988. First published in Weinberg (1987). : 8.2.2.

Weinberg, Bella Hass (1998). Can you recommend a good book on indexing?: collected reviews on the organization of information. Medford, NJ: Information Today; 1998. xii, 161 p. ISBN 1-57387-041-2. : 8.

Weinberg, Bella Hass; Cunningham, Julie A. (1984). Term specificity and online postings: inverse relationship? In: Challenges to an information society: proceedings of the 47th annual meeting of the American Society for Information Science, volume 21; 1984 October 21-25; Philadelphia, PA. White Plains, NY: Knowledge Industry Publications; 1984: 144-147. vii, 255 p. ISBN 0-86729-115-X. ISSN 0044-7870. : 10.1.

Weinberg, Bella Hass; Cunningham, Julie A. (1985). The relationship between term specificity in MeSH and online postings in MEDLINE. Bulletin of the Medical Library Association. 73: 365-372; 1985 Oct. : 10.1.

Wellisch, Hans H. (1978). Early multilingual and multiscript indexes in herbals. The indexer. 11(2): 81-102; 1978 Oct. : 1.1.

Wellisch, Hans H. (1980). Indexing and abstracting: an international bibliography. Santa Barbara, CA: ABC-Clio; c1980. xxi, 308 p. ISBN 0-87436-300-4. : 1.1.

Wellisch, Hans H. (1981). How to make an index, 16th century style: Conrad Gessner on indexes and catalogs. International classification. 8(1): 10-15; 1981. : 1.1.

Wellisch, Hans H. (1984). Indexing and abstracting, 1977-1981: an international bibliography. Santa Barbara, CA: ABC-Clio Information Services; 1984. xix, 276 p. ISBN 0-87436-398-5. : 1.1.

Wellisch, Hans H. (1986). The oldest printed indexes. The indexer. 15(2): 73-82; 1986 Oct. : 1.1.

Wellisch, Hans H. (1991). Indexing from A to Z. Bronx, NY: H.W. Wilson, 1991. xxvi, 461 p. ISBN 0-8242-0807-2. : 8.2.

Wellisch, Hans H. (1996). Indexing from A to Z. 2nd ed., rev. and enl. New York: H.W. Wilson; 1995, c1996. xxix, 569 p. ISBN 0-8242-0882-X. : 8.2.

Wellisch, Hans H. (1998). Indexing after the millennium 3: the indexer as helmsman. The indexer. 21:(2): 89; 1998 Oct. : 8.5.1.

Wellisch, Hans H. (1999). Guidelines for the alphabetical arrangement of letters and sorting of numerals and other symbols. Bethesda, MD: NISO Press; c1999. vi, 20 p. (NISO technical report; 3). : 1.4; 17.1; 17.4.1; 17.4.2.

Wellisch, Hans H. (2000). Glossary of terminology in abstracting, classification, indexing, and thesaurus construction. 2nd ed. Medford, NJ: Information Today, in association with the American Society of Indexers; c2000. vii, 77 p. ISBN 1-573-87094-3. : 1.3.

whatis.com Inc. (1998). http://www.whatis.com/. : 3.4.

White, Howard D; Griffith, Belver C. (1987). Quality of indexing of online data bases. Information processing & management. 23(3): 211-224; 1987. : 22.

Wiegand, Wayne A. (1988). The "Amherst method": the origins of the Dewey decimal classification scheme. Libraries and culture. 33(2): 175-194; 1998 Spring. : 17.3.

Wiener, Norbert (1950). The human use of human beings: cybernetics and society. London: Eyre and Spottiswoode; 1950. 241 p.; 2nd ed. rev. Garden City, NY: Doubleday; 1954. 199 p. : 8.5.1.

Bibliography

Will, Leonard (2000). Software for building and editing thesauri. Willpower Information: Information Management Consultants. 2000. http://www.willpower.demon.co.uk/thessoft.htm. : 13.3.2.

Willett, Peter (1988). Recent trends in hierarchic document clustering: a critical review. Information processing & management. 24(5): 577-597; 1988. : 8.3.11.

Willetts, Margaret (1975). An investigation of the nature of the relation between terms in thesauri. Journal of documentation. 31(3): 158-184; 1975 Sept. : 13.3.3.1.5.

Wilson, Mary Dabney (1998). Specificity, syndetic structure, and subject access to works about individual corporate bodies. Library resources & technical services. 42(4): 272-281; 1998 Oct. : 10.1.

Wilson, Patrick (1968). Two kinds of power: an essay on bibliographical control. Berkeley: University of California Press; 1968. 155 p. (University of California publications. Librarianship; 5). : 1.3 ("message"); 4; 8.2; 8.2.2.

Wilson, Patrick (1978). Some fundamental concepts of information retrieval. Drexel library quarterly. 14(2): 10-24; 1978 April. : 8.2.2; 8.5.1.

Wilson, Patrick (1979). The end of specificity. Library resources & technical services. 23(2): 116-122; 1979 Spring. : 10.1.

Witten, Ian H.; Nevill-Manning, Craig G.; McNab, Rodger; Cunningham, Sally Jo (1998). A public library based on full-text retrieval. Communications of the ACM. 41(4): 71-75; 1998 April. : 8.3.8.

Zweizig, Douglas; Johnson, Debra Wilcox; Robbins, Jane; Besant, Michelle (1996). The tell it! manual: the complete program for evaluating library performance. Chicago: American Library Association, 1996. vii, 270 p. ISBN 0-8389-0679-6. : 22.

Index

This index was created using NEPHIS syntax, as described in sections 12.2.2.3 and 12.4.1. Locators refer to chapters (chap.), sections (sec.) or to paragraphs. All locators include a chapter number. Section locators include the full section number (which is included in the headings at the top of each page). Paragraph locators consist of a chapter number, a full stop (dot), and a paragraph number; "pt2" refers to Part II, which falls between chapters 1 and 2. Paragraph numbers can be found on each page of text in the right margin at the head of each paragraph.

The **glossary**, in which definitions and cross references are arranged in alphabetical order, is not included in this index, nor is the **bibliography**, also arranged in alphabetical order by primary author.

A.L.A. filing rules
   as standards for alphanumeric arrangement : 1.85
abbreviations
   in alphanumeric arrangement : 17.19
abstract entities
   concepts : 2.23
   in IR databases : 1.28
   independent existence : 2.22
   universities as example : 2.18
   versus attributes and processes in subject scope analysis : 2.20
   versus concrete entities in subject scope analysis : 2.17
abstracting
   and abstracts.
      readings : sec. 14.3
abstracts
   alternatives to : 14.7
   as basis for indexing : 1.132
   as indexable matter : sec. 7.1.2
   role in information retrieval : 6.28
   types : 14.6
   versus documentary units : 6.27
Abstracts in anthropology
   table of contents : 19.9
accuracy
   of indexing. impact of indexable matter : sec. 7.3
acknowledgments
   to executive director of NISO : 0.14, 15
   to members of NISO Committee YY : 0.14, 15
   to Milstead (Jessica L.) : 0.14
   to scholars and practitioners : 0.15
   to students : 0.12, 0.16
   to Wellisch (Hans H.) : 0.14, 15
acronyms
   for facets. PMEST : 2.77, 78
   in alphanumeric arrangement : 17.19
actions
   and entities.
      combination in *Library of Congress subject headings* : 12.23
      in subject scope analysis : 2.28; examples : 2.46
   names : 2.31

activity theory
   treatment of knowledge organization : 8.58
ad hoc string syntax : sec. 12.2.2.3
   compared to faceted syntax : 12.170
   compared to natural language syntax : 12.171
   definitions : 12.169
   examples of index headings : 12.317, 318
   examples of index statements : 12.316
   for book indexes : 12.313
   NEPHIS : 12.172
ad hoc syntax : sec. 12.2.7
   and systematic syntax. combinations : sec. 12.2.7.1; examples in Psychological abstracts : 12.262
   characteristics : 12.253
   cross references : 12.257; placement : 12.258
   definitions : 12.251
   elements : 12.254
   examples : 12.252
   guidelines : 12.255
   prepositions : 12.255
advisory groups
   selection of useful documents : 8.250
agents
   versus objects in subject scope analysis : 2.30
ALA filing rules
   as standards for alphanumeric arrangement : 1.85
Allen (Bryce L.)
   views on visualization and cognitive abilities : 19.55
alphabetical ... *see:* alphanumeric ...
alphabetico-classed arrangement. *see:* alphanumeric-relational arrangement
alphanumeric arrangement
   abbreviations : 17.19
   acronyms : 17.19
   ampersand : 17.25
   controversies : 17.12
   examples : 17.26
   in hypertext displays : sec. 17.2
   initialisms : 17.20
   lack of consensus among standards : 1.91
   lack of research : 1.87, 88
   non-alphanumeric criteria : 17.21
   numbers : 17.18
   of book indexes : 17.120

alphanumeric arrangement (continued)
   of displayed indexes : 1.144
   punctuation : 17.16
   roman numerals : 17.12
   spaces : 17.15
   standards : 1.82, 17.14
      A.L.A. filing rules : 1.85
      Library of Congress filing rules : 1.83
      NISO : 1.86
   subject headings : 17.22
alphanumeric browsing
   using *Library of Congress subject headings* : 12.70
alphanumeric displays : sec. 17.1
   advantages : 17.6
   in hypertext.
      examples : 17.35
      goals : 17.32
   problematic nature : 17.9
   versus relational classified displays : 12.193, 17.8, 48
alphanumeric indexes
   browsable. display. design features : 19.74; examples : 19.75
   display in printed books : 17.122
   for classified arrangements : 12.219
   in print media.
      preference for : 19.15
   staged display in hypertext : 17.29, 38
   syndetic structure : sec. 13.3.1
alphanumeric-relational arrangement
   of displayed indexes : 1.146
Altavista web search engine
   indexing of image texts : 8.127
America: history and life
   record formats : sec. 20.3
   rotated term syntax : 12.126
American Library Association
   special interest groups : 17.79
   views on display of *Library of Congress subject headings* : 12.82
American Society for Information Science
   endorsement of standards for indexes : 1.99
   opposition to standards for indexes : 1.100
   opposition to terminology for non-displayed indexes : 1.102

Index

American Society for Information Science and Technology
Classification Research SIG : 17.78
special interest groups : 17.77
American Society of Indexers
objections to standards for indexes : 1.97
ampersand
in alphanumeric arrangement : 17.25
analysis
and indexing of documents. methods : chap. 8
computer algorithmic. of texts for indexing : 1.149
guidelines in cataloging and classification at Rutgers University : 8.93
human intellectual. of texts for indexing : 1.148
methods.
  examples : sec. 8.6
methods for book indexes : sec. 8.6.1
methods for digital libraries : sec. 8.6.3
methods for full-text encyclopedias : sec. 8.6.3
methods for indexing and abstracting services : sec. 8.6.2
methods in human indexing.
  British standards : 8.92
  international standards : 8.92
of messages.
  methods : sec. 1.5.6
rules in human indexing : 8.91
standards in human indexing : 8.92
units of. documentary units : 6.6
analytico-synthetic classification syntax : 12.200
Anderson (James D.)
views on human indexing : 8.73
anomalous states of knowledge.
views of Belkin (Nicholas J.) : 13.13
anthropology
indexing and abstracting services : 19.9
apostrophes
treatment in automatic indexing : 8.138
arrangement
> *related terms to consider:* **alphanumeric arrangement; relational classified displays**

alphanumeric. lack of consensus among standards : 1.91; lack of research : 1.87, 88; of displayed indexes : 1.144; standards : 1.82 (*A.L.A. filing rules* : 1.85; *Library of Congress filing rules* : 1.83; NISO : 1.86)
alphanumeric-relational. of displayed indexes : 1.146
classified. *see:* relational classified
of book indexes : sec. 17.4.1
of displayed indexes : 1.142, chap. 17
  examples of policies : sec. 17.4
  options : 17.3
of displayed indexes for digital libraries : sec. 17.4.3
of displayed indexes for electronic books : 17.124
of displayed indexes for electronic encyclopedias : sec. 17.4.3
of displayed indexes for indexing and abstracting services : sec. 17.4.2
of entries : sec. 1.5.5
of facets.
  views of Ranganathan (Shiyali Ramamrita) : 2.78
of facets by other facets : 17.94

arrangement *(continued)*
of facets for databases : 17.84; for document collections : 17.85; for ethnicities : 17.83; for Germanic languages : 17.91; for groups : 17.82; for Indo-European languages : 17.89; for institutions : 17.82; for language families : 17.87; for languages : 17.86; for persons : 17.82; for places : 17.92
of indexes versus classifications : 12.205
of retrieved documentary units.
  methods : 12.288
of subdivisions in *Library of Congress subject headings* : 12.53
of subheadings : 1.84
of terms in end-user thesauri : 13.168
of topics within facets : 17.81
relational classified. of displayed indexes : 1.145; of index headings within facets : 12.208
Artandi (Susan)
views on human indexing : 8.75
artistic works
versus critical works.
  subject scope analysis : 2.69
ASIS thesaurus : 13.111
display : 13.112
facets : 13.113
Association of Library Collections and Technical Services. Subject Analysis Committee
views on term relationships : 13.185
Associative Interactive Dictionary
as example of automatic vocabulary management : 8.200
associative relationships
> *related term to consider:* **related terms**

in thesauri : 13.180
versus hierarchical relationships in thesauri : 13.189, 195
assumptions
of this book : sec. 1.2
attributes
and components of IR databases : pt2.6, pt2.7
and processes versus abstract entities in subject scope analysis : 2.20
in subject scope analysis : 2.25; examples : 2.45
audience
as non-topical feature : sec. 3.6
as searchable feature : sec. 3.6
in documentary scope for indexing and abstracting services : 3.56
audio media
types : 3.20
author processes
role in subject scope versus documentary scope : 2.58
author searches
surrogates.
  display in electronic media : 16.4
  display in print media : 16.37
authority
assessments.
  role of human indexers : 8.253
authority records
MARC formats : 20.7
authors/authorship
and authorship as non-topical feature : sec. 3.1

authors/authorship *(continued)*
and creators.
  types as searchable features : 3.13
corporate bodies : 3.14
exhaustive indexing : 9.3
identification.
  standards : 14.11
in documentary scope for indexing and abstracting services : 3.63
indexes to : 1.114, 115
of IR databases : sec. 1.5.14
automatic clustering
thresholds : 8.217
techniques : 8.218
automatic indexing : 1.149, sec. 8.3
addition of terms to thesauri : 8.197
clustering : sec. 8.3.11
combined with human indexing : 1.150
compared to human indexing : 8.162, 169
  incompatibility : 8.168
cultural factors : 8.38
definition of words : 8.131, 143
documentary units : 6.33
effectiveness : 8.24
exhaustivity for important documents : 9.32; in book indexes : 9.27
feedback : 8.228
for displayed indexes in indexing and abstracting services in print media : 12.329
frequency of words : sec. 8.3.4
human indexing as model : 8.76
identification of phrases : 8.181, 185
  cost versus benefits : 8.180
importance of phrases : 8.178
index terms.
  specificity in book indexes : 10.51
language model : 8.129
of image texts.
  views of Pérez-López (Kathleen Golitko) : 8.111
of language texts versus image texts : 8.5, 126; versus other non-language texts : 8.5; versus sound texts : 8.126
of words : sec. 8.3.1
phrases : sec. 8.3.8
positive vocabulary control : 8.191
probabilistic model : 8.128
recommended resources : 8.130
relevance feedback : sec. 8.3.13
role in high-precision IR : 9.20; in high-recall IR : 9.19
role in information retrieval : sec. 8.5
role of human searching behavior : 8.234
see-also references for equivalent terms : 13.259
stemming : sec. 8.3.6
surrogates. display : 16.22
theoretical models : 8.128
treatment of apostrophes : 8.138; of full stops : 8.136; of hyphens : 8.134; of lower-case letters : 8.144; of numbers : 8.139; of parentheses : 8.137; of punctuation : 8.133; of single characters : 8.142; of slashes : 8.135; of underscores : 8.136; upper-case letters : 8.144
vector-space model : 8.128

Index

automatic indexing *(continued)*
  versus human indexing : 8.2
    allocation : 8.241
    cost-benefit analysis : 8.25
    cultural factors : 8.37
    evidence from use : 8.22
    research : sec. 8.1
    results : 8.3
    user preferences : 8.23
  versus human searching : 8.125
  vocabulary management : sec. 8.3.9, 8.194
automatic term weighting : 12.312
automatic stemming
  user options : 12.324
automatic vocabulary management : sec. 8.3.10
  examples. Associative Interactive Dictionary : 8.200
  impact : 8.208

back-of-the-book indexes. *see:* **book indexes**
Baker (Nicholson)
  views on card catalogs : 5.9
Balnaves (John)
  views on specificity : 10.16
Bates (Marcia J.)
  views on documentary domain : 4.2
  views on IR database design : 0.8
  views on role of human indexing : 8.245
  views on variability of vocabulary : 13.16, 22
Beghtol (Clare)
  views on human indexing : 8.72
Belkin (Nicholas J.)
  views on anomalous states of knowledge : 13.13
best match syntax : sec. 12.3.2, 12.280
  definitions : 12.297
  examples : 12.301
  language model : 12.298
  probabilistic model : 12.297
  ranking : 12.300
  vector space model : 12.297
beta testing
  of IR databases : 22.17
biases
  as non-topical features : 3.40
  as searchable features : 3.40
  in documentary scope : 3.47
Bible verses
  indexes to : 1.117
bibliographic citations
  standard for style : 0.15
bibliographic coupling : sec. 8.3.12.1
  and co-citation as basis for indexing : 8.108
  compared to co-citation : 8.226
  definition : 8.225
bibliographic records
  versus metadata : 20.30
bibliography
  definition : 1.183
Bliss bibliographic classification
  citation order of facets : 17.110
  facets applied to *Library of Congress subject headings* : 12.158
book indexes
  ad hoc string syntax : 12.313
  alphanumeric arrangement : 17.120
  alternative levels of exhaustivity : 9.28
  analysis methods : sec. 8.6.1

book indexes *(continued)*
  application of thesauri : 13.246
  arrangement : sec. 17.4.1
  display in electronic media : 12.319
  documentary domain : sec. 4.3.1
  documentary scope : sec. 3.14.1
  documentary units : sec. 6.5.1, 6.11, 12.314
    locators for, in index entries : 19.85
    in electronic media : 6.37
  double posting for equivalent or synonymous terms : 13.241
  equivalent-term cross references : 13.240; for narrower terms : 13.243; for synonymous terms : 13.240
  exhaustivity of indexing : sec. 9.3.1; for automatic indexing : 9.27; for human indexing : 9.26
  fields in record formats : 20.44
  in electronic media. interface designs : 19.87; record formats : 20.48
  in print media. interface designs : 19.83; vocabulary management : 13.238
  indexable matter : sec. 7.4.1, 7.18
  interface designs : sec. 19.4.1
  locators : 12.314, sec. 15.1.1, 15.7
  media : sec. 5.5.1
  multimedia : 5.33
  permuted index headings versus cross references : 18.16
  record formats : sec. 20.7.1
  run-in layout versus indented layout : 18.18
  see-also references : 13.245
  size : sec. 18.1.1
    estimation : 18.8
    estimation. accuracy : 18.10
    estimation. problems : 18.11
    estimation as guideline for indexing : 18.12
    reduction : 18.15
  specificity of index terms : sec. 10.8.1; of index terms assigned by automatic indexing : 10.51; of index terms assigned by human indexing : 10.50
  subject scope analysis : sec. 2.5.1, 2.88
  surrogates : sec. 14.5.1
    display : sec. 16.1.1
  syntax : sec. 12.4.1
  use of NEPHIS : 12.177
  users : 2.89
    vocabulary : 2.90
  vocabulary management : sec. 13.4.1
    integration : 13.239
Book Item and Component Identifier (BICI) : 15.27
book numbers
  in call numbers : 15.38
  views of Comaromi (John P.) : 15.39
  views of Lehnus (Donald J.) : 15.39
books
  as media for IR databases : sec. 5.1.2
    advantages : 5.10
  displayed indexes and non-displayed indexes : sec. 11.4.1
  in electronic media.
    arrangement of displayed indexes : 17.124
    as hypertext : 6.37, 38
    full-text searching. syntax : 12.320
    full texts. display : sec. 21.4.1.
    indexable matter : 7.23

books *(continued)*
    indexes. browsing : 15.49; locators : 15.47; postings : 15.50
    intermediate surrogates : 16.30
    surrogates. display : 16.28
    topic sentences as intermediate surrogates : 16.31
  indexes for : 2.87
  IR databases for : 1.162
  MARC formats for. examples : 20.5
  printed.
    indexes. size : 18.1
    relational classified displays : 17.123
    surrogates. display : 16.24
    unified surrogates : 16.27
  versus monographs : 3.36
boolean searches
  on optical coincidence (peek-a-boo) retrieval systems : 5.20
boolean syntax. *see:* **exact match syntax**
Booth (A. D.)
  article. Zipfian distributions of words : 8.163
bound terms
  definition : 1.58
  impact on size of thesauri : 13.174
  in end-user thesauri : sec. 13.3.3.1.4
  information science as example : 1.159
  views of standards for thesauri : 13.170
braille media
  for IR databases : 1.178
British standards
  on methods for analysis in human indexing : 8.92
broader terms
  BT as notation for : 13.61
broader-term cross references : 13.61
  in *Library of Congress subject headings* : 12.43
browsability
  among variables in IR research : 8.13
browsable alphanumeric indexes
  display. design features : 19.74; examples : 19.75
browsable displays. *see:* **display**
browsable facets
  display. design features : 19.72; examples : 19.73
browsable indexes
  for end-user thesauri : 13.213
browsing
  alphabetical. using *Library of Congress subject headings* : 12.70
  and navigation : 11.11
  definition : 11.30
  literature reviews : 11.27
  of full texts in digital media : sec. 21.3
  of indexes for electronic books : 15.49
  research in IR : sec. 11.2
  role in IR : 11.25
  role of classification captions : 17.64; of phrases : 8.186
  versus searching using Medical subject headings : 12.101
  views of Chang (Shan-Ju) and Rice, (Ronald E.) : 11.30; of Marchionini (Gary) : 11.31
BT
  as notation for broader terms : 13.61
business
  ontologies : 13.234

Index

call numbers
  book numbers in : 15.38
  classification notation : 15.40
  in libraries : 15.37
    examples : 15.41
    local nature : 15.43
  work marks in : 15.38
card catalogs
  views of Baker (Nicholson) : 5.9
card files
  as medium for IR databases : sec. 5.1.1, 5.7
    disadvantages : 5.8
cataloging
  and classification. guidelines for analysis at Rutgers University : 8.93
  and indexing by document creators : 20.29
  definition : 1.52
  history : 1.1
  principles. role.
    views of Cutter (Charles Ammi) : 13.196
  standards : 1.80
catalogs
  definition : 1.52
  library.
    absence of cross references : 12.49
categories
  expression in subject scope analysis : 2.50
  generic. role in subject scope analysis : 2.12
  in ontologies.
    views of Poli (Roberto) : 13.228; of Sowa (John) : 13.227
  in ontologies versus thesauri : 13.230
  in thesauri.
    definition : 13.164
    not mutually exclusive : 13.166
    size : 13.160
  number in subject scope analysis : 2.8
  of entities in end-user thesauri : 13.161
  of operations and processes in end-user thesauri : 13.163
  postings for, versus postings for descriptors : 17.98
  specialized. role in human indexing : 8.100; in subject scope analysis : sec. 2.1; in subject scope for folklore, language, linguistics : 2.55; in subject scope for literature : 2.53, 54
categorization
  initial. of terms for thesauri : 13.159
  of long arrays of index headings using facets : 12.164
  of subdivisions in *Library of Congress subject headings* : 12.58
  of terms for end-user thesauri : sec. 13.3.3.1.3
CD-ROMs
  as media for IR databases : sec. 5.3.2
censorship
  versus guidance in indexing : sec. 8.5.1
  versus measures of use : 8.248
chain indexes
  creation from classified arrangements : 12.220
  examples : 12.221
chain syntax. : sec. 12.2.4.1
  definition : 12.218
Chan (Lois Mai)
  views on faceted syntax for *Library of Congress subject headings* : 12.157; on human indexing : 8.39

Chang (Shan-Ju)
  and Rice, (Ronald E.). views on browsing : 11.30
channels
  for document transmission. world-wide web : 3.21
  for IR database transmission. world-wide web : sec. 5.3.3
chaos
  and creativity versus stability in IR database design : 1.107
checktags
  use in subject analysis and indexing : 8.239
chemical symbols
  role in index terms : 1.128
Chicago manual of style
  views on human indexing : 8.42
Chinese language
  definition of words : 8.132
choreographers
  indexes to : 1.116
Chowdhury (Gobinda G.)
  views on information retrieval : 0.9
chronological subdivisions
  in *Library of Congress subject headings* : 12.34, 57
citation indexes : sec. 8.3.12
  to newer documents : 8.224
citation links
  to older documents : 8.223
citation order
  of facets : 17.109
    role facets versus type facets : 17.111
  of facets for relational classified displays in print media : 17.74; for shelf arrangement : 17.74; in Bliss *bibliographic classification* : 17.110
citations
  and systematic syntax. combination : 12.263
  reference. as basis for indexing : 1.136
civilization
  role of information retrieval : 1.2
clarity
  of index headings : 12.147
  of rotated term syntax : 12.129
classification
> *related terms to consider:* **faceted classification; enumerative classification; relational classified displays**

  alphanumeric indexes for : 12.219
  and cataloging. guidelines for analysis at Rutgers University : 8.93
  arrangement. versus alphanumeric indexes : 12.205
  arrangement of headings within facets : 12.208
  captions. definitions : 1.62; role in browsing : 17.64; versus index headings : 12.196
  chain indexes for : 12.220
  definition : 1.55, 17.4, 49
  display : 17.53; in hypertext : 12.195, 17.59; postings : 17.69; role of notation : 17.68; on the world-wide web : 12.194; versus alphanumeric display : 12.193
  faceted : 17.61
  faceted. for *MLA international bibliography* : 19.38
  facets for. determination : 17.75
  facets of literature : 17.76
  hierarchical arrangement : 12.209
  MARC format for : 20.7

classification *(continued)*
  notation : 12.212, 17.64, 115; types : 17.116; and captions : 17.63; in call numbers : 15.40; in *Unesco thesaurus* (1977) : 13.89
  of library and information science. retroactive notation : 17.117
  of literature : 17.54
  research : 17.55
  role in searching : 12.194
  role of facets : 17.72
  standards : 1.80
  syntax : sec. 12.2.4, 17.52
  traditional : 17.61; advantages : 17.62
  versus indexing : 17.50
Classification Research SIG
  of American Society for Information Science and Technology : 17.78
classing
  definition : 8.209
clique clusters : 8.215
clump clusters : 8.216
clustering
  automatic. techniques : 8.218; thresholds : 8.217
  by document similarity : 8.212
  definition : 8.209
  dynamic : 8.218
  in automatic indexing : sec. 8.3.11
  of terms for end-user thesauri : sec. 13.3.4; for vocabulary management : 13.220; research : 13.219
  scatter-gather techniques : 8.218
  static : 8.218, 219
  use in searches in indexing and abstracting services in electronic media : 12.328
clusters
  clique : 8.215
  clump : 8.216
  criteria for : 8.210
  role in searching : 8.211
  star : 8.214
  string : 8.213
  types : 8.213
co-author
  Pérez-Carballo (José) : 0.10
co-citation : sec. 8.3.12.2
  and bibliographic coupling as basis for indexing : 8.108
  compared to bibliographic coupling : 8.226
  definition : 8.227
  for identification of research fronts : 8.227
co-occurrence
  frequency. for ranking of related terms : 8.202
  of terms. identification of related terms : 8.201
co-occurrence lists
  and thesauri : 13.27
codes
  and symbols. nature for texts : 5.30; varieties for texts : 5.31; for IR databases : sec. 5.4, 5.32
  for composition of texts : 3.24
  for representation of machine-readable texts : 3.28; of word-processing texts : 3.29
coextensive index headings, subject headings
  in string syntax : 12.127, 128; principles : 12.120
  using faceted syntax for *Library of Congress subject headings* : 12.160
coextensive subject headings principle
  for subject heading systems : 12.115

Index

cognition
  versus culture in human indexing : 8.87
  versus social construction in human indexing : sec. 8.2.1
cognitive abilities
  and visualization. views of Allen (Bryce L.) : 19.55
  impact on visualization : 19.54
cognitive processes
  in human indexing : 8.28, 31
collections
  frequency of words : sec. 8.3.5
  of documents. IR databases for : 1.186; documentary scope descriptions : 3.4, 6
  of documents and anthologies. documentary units : 6.8
  of documents as impetus for design : pt2.4
collocation
  adequacy in natural language syntax : 12.232
  in faceted syntax : 12.155
  in KWIC indexes : 12.236
  in rotated term syntax : 12.149
  of index headings : 12.148
  of minor concepts by generic terms : 10.40
Comaromi (John P.)
  views on book numbers : 15.39
Common Information System (CIS) : 15.28
complex phenomena
  in subject scope analysis. insurance as example : 2.39
complex terms
  definition : 1.59
composers
  indexes to : 1.116
Compositeur, Auteur, Editeur (CAE) : 15.29
compound terms. *see:* **bound terms**
comprehensive searches
  in indexing and abstracting services in electronic media : 12.322; in print media : 12.329
computer-aided indexing
  for indexing and abstracting services : 8.240
computer algorithmic analysis
  of texts for indexing. *see:* automatic indexing
computer-output microfilm
  as medium for IR databases : 5.22
computer programs
  for construction of thesauri : 13.85
computer representation
  internal. not addressed in this book : 1.141
computer screens
  size : 19.64
computer software
  IR databases for : 1.171
concepts
  as abstract entities : 2.23
conceptual levels
  in ontologies : 13.233
concrete entities
  in IR databases : 1.27
  versus abstract entities in subject scope analysis : 2.17
concrete entities and events
  databases for. exclusion from scope of this book : 1.198
  databases for versus IR databases : 1.196, 197, 202
  indexing. compared to indexing of messages : 1.23

concrete entity and event databases
  definitions : 1.20
  versus IR databases : 8.55
concrete events
  in IR databases : 1.27
consistency principle
  in subject heading systems : 12.109
  in human indexing : 8.64
constituent materials
  in subject scope analysis : 2.26
content
  of IR databases.
    separation from search interfaces : 19.37
continuing and integrating resources
  as non-topical features : sec. 3.5; as searchable features : sec. 3.5
controlled vocabularies
  mapping of search terms : 13.28
  multiple. interaction : 13.29
  versus un-controlled vocabularies for indexing : 10.42
controversial documents
  discovery : 8.255
controversies
  in information retrieval : 1.93
Cooper (William S.)
  rules for human indexing. views of Frohmann (Bernd) : 8.114
  views on human indexing : 8.115; on variables in IR research : 8.19
corporate bodies
  as authors : 3.14
  types as searchable features : 3.15
cost-benefit analysis
  of electronic media versus paper : 5.15
  of human indexing versus automatic indexing : 8.25
  of identification of phrases in automatic indexing : 8.180
coverage
  of documentary domain : sec. 4.2
  of IR databases.
    impact of documentary domain : 4.1
Craven (Timothy)
  related term to consider: **NEPHIS (Nested Phrase Indexing System)** [created by Timothy Craven]
  views on purpose of precoordinate syntax : 12.14
creativity
  and chaos versus stability in IR database design : 1.107
criteria
  for allocation of human indexing : 8.247
  for assignment of index terms : 2.65
  for clusters : 8.210
  for index entries : 1.74
  for indexing languages : 12.12
  for precoordinate indexing languages : 12.15
  of evaluation for natural language syntax : 12.230
critical works
  versus artistic works. subject scope analysis : 2.69
cross references
  absence from library catalogs : 12.49
  explanatory : 12.260

cross references *(continued)*
  from equivalent-terms : 13.44; in *Library of Congress subject headings* : 12.40; UF as instruction for creation : 13.54; in OPACs; form : 13.55
  general. in *Library of Congress subject headings* : 12.45
  in ad hoc syntax : 12.257
  in hypertext : 13.207
  in library catalogs : 13.68; OPACs : 13.49
  in thesauri : 13.51
  omission. impact : 13.74; from OPACs : 13.73
  placement. examples : 12.264; in ad hoc syntax : 12.258
  postings data : 13.50
  syntactic : sec. 12.2.8
    definitions : 12.268
    examples : 12.266
    necessity : 12.265
  to broader terms : 13.61; in *Library of Congress subject headings* : 12.43
  to narrower terms : 13.46, 56; in *Library of Congress subject headings* : 12.41; versus specificity : 10.19
  to related terms : 13.46, 64; in *Library of Congress subject headings* : 12.44
  types : 13.43
  user suggested : 12.342
  versus permuted index headings in book indexes : 18.16
cultural domains : 2.4
cultural factors
  in automatic indexing : 8.38
  in human indexing versus automatic indexing : 8.37
culture
  versus cognition in human indexing : 8.87
customization
  of interfaces : 19.61
  views of Head (Alison J.) : 19.62
Cutter (Charles Ammi)
  development of cutter numbers : 15.42
  views on role of principles in cataloging : 13.196; on specificity : 10.4
cutter numbers
  development by Cutter (Charles Ammi) : 15.42

data
  definition : 1.43
  versus information : 1.5; knowledge : 1.5
  views of Korfhage (Robert R.) : 1.41
data mining
  role of surrogates : 14.16
database management systems : 1.198
database records
  definition : 1.76
databases
  compared to libraries to : 1.4
  definition : 1.14, 194
  facets.
    arrangement : 17.84
  for concrete entities and events. exclusion from scope of this book : 1.198; versus IR databases : 1.196, 197, 202
  hybrid. IR databases : 1.201
  models. flat file databases : 1.18; hypertext databases : 1.19; object-oriented databases : 1.17; relational databases : 1.16
  origin as term : 1.3

Index

databases *(continued)*
two basic types : sec. 1.6.1
types : sec. 1.6, 1.15
dates (time)
in rotated term syntax : 12.124
in subject scope analysis : 2.38; examples : 2.49
datum, data
definition : 1.39
decision making
with numerical values in human indexing : 8.124
decision theory
role in rules for human indexing : 8.116
decision trees
for *Library of Congress subject headings* : 12.65
decoration
in search interfaces : 19.65
descriptive cataloging
definition : 1.53
rules for institutions versus societies : 2.19
descriptive indexing
definition : 1.53
descriptors
definition : 1.60
descriptor postings versus category postings : 17.98
design
impetus : pt2.2; role of collections of documents : pt2.4
of displayed indexes : sec. 11.3
of indexes. technical report : 0.5
of IR databases : 1.6
of non-displayed indexes : sec. 11.3
of record formats. principles : 20.3
precursors to : pt2.3
design decisions : pt2
sequence : pt2.9
design features
for display of browsable alphanumeric indexes : 19.74; of browsable facets : 19.72; of electronic search results : 19.78; of vocabulary information for electronic searches : 19.78
for electronic searches : 19.76
for opening screens for IR databases : 19.70
for surrogate displays : 19.80
design options
for IR databases. impact of media : 5.2
interaction : pt2.8
design specifications
for IR databases : 1.206
Dewey decimal classification
display in hypertext : sec. 17.3.1, 17.67, 70
syntax : 12.197
Diener (Richard)
views on term relationships : 13.183
diesel engines
facets for. by Ranganathan (Shiyali Ramamrita) : 2.79
indexing. rules. of Ranganathan : 8.99
digital communication format
MARC format : 20.12
digital libraries
as examples of IR databases : 1.193
definition : 1.31
displayed indexes. arrangement : sec. 17.4.3
displayed indexes versus non-displayed indexes : sec. 11.4.3

digital libraries *(continued)*
documentary domain : sec. 4.3.3
documentary scope : sec. 3.14.3
documentary units : sec. 6.5.3
exhaustivity of indexing : sec. 9.3.3
full texts. display : sec. 21.4.3
hypertext links : 12.341
indexable matter : sec. 7.4.3
indexes. size : sec. 18.1.3
interface design : sec. 19.4.3
locators : sec. 15.1.3
media : sec. 5.5.3
methods of analysis : sec. 8.6.3
natural language syntax : 12.228
record formats : sec. 20.7.3
search options : 12.340
software for : 22.7
specificity of index terms : sec. 10.8.3
subject scope analysis : sec. 2.5.3
surrogates : sec. 14.5.3
display : sec. 16.1.3
syntax : sec. 12.4.3
TEI : 21.53
vocabulary management : sec. 13.4.3
digital media
full texts. browsing : sec. 21.3; display : 21.4
encoding schemas : sec. 21.2 (HTML as example : 21.32); size of documentary units : 21.58
Digital Object Identifier (DOI) : 15.22
components : 15.23
examples : 15.25
resolution : 15.24
digital resources
locators : 15.16
discovery
of controversial documents : 8.255
display
formatted. of surrogates : 16.18, 21
media. of IR databases : chap. 5
of alphanumeric indexes in printed books : 17.122
of *ASIS thesaurus* : 13.112
of book indexes in electronic media : 12.319
of browsable alphanumeric indexes. design features : 19.74; examples : 19.75
of browsable facets. design features : 19.72; examples : 19.73
of classification : 17.53; postings data: 17.69; role of notation : 17.68; in hypertext : 12.195, 17.59
of *Dewey decimal classification* in hypertext : sec. 17.3.1, 17.67, 70
of electronic search results. design features : 19.78; examples : 19.79
of end-user thesauri : sec. 13.3.3.1.8
of faceted classification : sec. 17.3.2, 17.97; in print media : sec. 17.3.2.1
of faceted index headings : 12.136; for indexing and abstracting services : 12.337
of full surrogates : 16.6
of full texts : chap. 21; examples : sec. 21.4; options : 21.69; in digital libraries : sec. 21.4.3; in digital media : 21.4; in electronic books : sec. 21.4.1; in electronic encyclopedias : sec. 21.4.3; in electronic indexing and abstracting services : 21.72; in indexing and abstracting services : sec. 21.4.2
of index headings in hypertext media : 17.42

display *(continued)*
of indexes. standards : 19.16
of *Library of Congress subject headings* : 12.58, 61; views of American Library Association : 12.82; of Drabenstott and Vizine-Goetz : 12.65
of MARC records : 16.19
of multiple hierarchical levels in *Unesco thesaurus* (1995) : 13.102
of original formats of full texts : 21.17
of relational syntax : 12.189
of results for electronic searches : 17.130
of string indexing in hypertext : 17.40
of subject headings in hypertext : 17.35, 39; in online public access catalogs : 1.90
of surrogates : chap. 16; examples : sec. 16.1; format options : 16.11; general options : 16.8; order of fields : 16.15, 20; research : 16.5
of surrogates based on automatic indexing : 16.22
of surrogates for author searches in electronic media : 16.4; in print media : 16.37
of surrogates for indexing and abstracting services : sec. 16.1.2;
of surrogates for subject searches in electronic media : 16.4; in print media : 16.36
of surrogates in book indexes : sec. 16.1.1; in digital libraries : sec. 16.1.3; in electronic books : 16.28; in electronic encyclopedias : sec. 16.1.3; in electronic media : 16.39; in libraries : 16.16; in print media : 16.35; in printed books : 16.24; in tables of contents : 16.25, 38
of term relationships in thesauri : 13.191
of thesauri for searching : 13.30
work of Pollitt (A. Steven, et al.) : 13.31
of vocabulary information for electronic searches. design features : 19.78; examples : 19.79
staged. of alphanumeric indexes in hypertext : 17.29, 38; of faceted index headings in hypertext : 17.44; of index headings in hypertext : 17.43; of surrogates in electronic media : 16.3; of surrogates in print media : 16.2
versus content of surrogates : 14.4
displayed indexes : 1.139
advantages : 11.18
alphanumeric arrangement : 1.144
alphanumeric. syndetic structure : sec. 13.3.1
alphanumeric-relational arrangement : 1.146
and non-displayed indexes. differences : 12.10; examples : sec. 11.4; for books : sec. 11.4.1; in indexing and abstracting services : sec. 11.4.2
arrangement : chap. 17, 1.142; examples of policies : sec. 17.4; options : 17.3; for digital libraries : sec. 17.4.3; for electronic books : 17.124; for electronic encyclopedias : sec. 17.4.3; for indexing and abstracting services : sec. 17.4.2
based on automatic indexing in indexing and abstracting services in print media : 12.329
challenges : 11.20
characteristics : 11.17
design : sec. 11.3
disadvantages : 11.19

Index

displayed indexes *(continued)*
   faceted relational classified. dynamic postings : 13.33, 17.99
   for indexing and abstracting services in electronic media : 17.129; in print media : 17.128
   history : 11.6
   in electronic media : sec. 11.1; presentation of see-also references : 13.251
   in print media. type size : 18.17
   index headings. merging : 18.4
   postings. for electronic books : 17.127
   psychological advantages : 17.2
   purpose : 17.1; in indexing and abstracting services : 12.338
   relational classified arrangement : 1.145
   scope notes : 12.261
   size : chap. 18, sec. 18.1
   versus non-displayed indexes : chap. 11, 11.2; calculation of exhaustivity : 9.22; syntax : 11.9; in digital libraries : sec. 11.4.3; in encyclopedias : sec. 11.4.3
   vocabulary management : 8.195
distributions
   of words in texts : sec. 8.3.7
   Zipf's law : 8.160
document creators
   cataloging and indexing by : 20.29
document descriptions
   fields for. in record formats : 20.18
document numbers
   indexes to : 1.121
document retrieval
   versus information retrieval : 6.1
document similarity
   as basis for clustering : 8.212
document titles
   as basis for index headings : 12.226
   in documentary scope for indexing and abstracting services : 3.64
document transmission
   channels. world-wide web : 3.21
document weights
   calculation for relevance prediction : 8.152
documentary domain
   coverage : sec. 4.2
   descriptions. role : 4.10
   examples : sec. 4.3
   for book indexes : sec. 4.3.1
   for digital libraries : sec. 4.3.3
   for full-text encyclopedias : sec. 4.3.3
   for indexing and abstracting services : sec. 4.3.2
   for IR databases : chap. 4
   impact on coverage of IR databases : 4.1
   monitoring : sec. 4.2
   views of Bates (Marcia J.) : 4.2; of Wilson (Patrick) : 4.3
documentary features
   role in human indexing : 8.30
documentary scope : chap. 3
   and subject scope. relation to rules for human indexing : 8.96
   based on specific documents : sec. 3.11
   biases : 3.47
   descriptions. for IR databases for collections of documents : 3.4, 6; for IR databases for single documents : 3.5; importance for IR database producers : 3.3; importance for users : 3.2

documentary scope *(continued)*
   examples : sec. 3.14
   for book indexes : sec. 3.14.1
   for digital libraries : sec. 3.14.3
   for full-text encyclopedias : sec. 3.14.3
   for indexing and abstracting services : sec. 3.14.2; audience : 3.56; authorship : 3.63; document titles : 3.64; formats : 3.54; language : 3.57; levels of treatment : 3.56; media : 3.53; methodological approaches : 3.65; periodicity : 3.55; place of publication : 3.58; points of view : 3.65; qualitative criteria : 3.61; searchable features : 3.62; specific documents : 3.60; time of publication : 3.59
   objective qualitative criteria : 3.46
   points of view : 3.47
   qualitative criteria : sec. 3.12
   versus subject scope : 2.57, 62, 3.1; methodological approaches : 2.63; role of author processes : 2.58
documentary units : chap. 6
   and links in full texts in HTML : 21.33
   as units of analysis : 6.6
   definition : 1.56
   examples : sec. 6.1, sec. 6.5
   features. facets : 12.159
   for automatic indexing : 6.33
   for book indexes : sec. 6.5.1, 6.11, 12.314; in electronic media : 6.37
   for collections of documents and anthologies : 6.8
   for digital libraries : sec. 6.5.3
   for full-text encyclopedias : sec. 6.5.3
   for full-text searching : 6.42
   for high-use documents in indexing and abstracting services : 6.41
   for hypertext : 6.20; on world-wide web : 6.21
   for indexing and abstracting services : sec. 6.5.2, 6.7, 40
   for mixed-text documents : 7.4
   for music : 6.10
   for video recordings and motion pictures : 6.9
   in book indexes. locators in index entries : 19.85
   in library catalogs : 6.24
   multiple : sec. 6.4; in full-text IR databases : 6.32
   pages versus paragraphs : 6.12, 12.315
   paragraphs : 6.17; advantages : 6.13; NISO recommendation : 6.15; for electronic texts : 6.14
   relationship to exhaustivity : 9.24
   role in IR databases : 6.34
   size : 6.3; among variables in IR research : impact on indexable matter : 7.6; relationship to exhaustivity : 9.5; 8.10; in full texts in digital media : 21.58
   small. IR databases for : 1.184
   smaller. advantages : 6.25
   smaller. in full-text IR databases : 6.30; in reference IR databases : 6.29
   text sections : 6.16
   types and sizes : sec. 1.5.12
   versus abstracts : 6.27
   versus surrogates : sec. 6.3; in reference IR databases : 6.26
documentation
   role in information retrieval : 6.2

documents
   analysis and indexing. methods : chap. 8
   collections. as impetus for design : pt2.4; IR databases for : 1.186; documentary scope descriptions : 3.4, 6
   collections and anthologies. documentary units : 6.8
   complete. IR databases for : 1.185; versus parts of documents : 6.5
   definition : 1.51
   high-use. documentary units in indexing and abstracting services : 6.41; full texts as indexable matter : 7.26; indexable matter : 7.25
   important. allocation of human indexing : 8.242; exhaustivity of automatic indexing : 9.32; exhaustivity of human indexing : 9.31
   indexes to documents as topics : 1.117
   inequality : 8.256
   mixed-text. documentary units : 7.4; indexable matter : 7.4
   proximity to IR databases : sec. 1.5.11
   routine. exhaustivity : 9.30
   selection for IR databases. principles : 4.5
   types : sec. 1.5.9
   useful. selection by advisory groups and indexing staff : 8.250; use of human indexing for identification : 8.244
domain. *see:* **documentary domain; subject domain**
domain analysis
   as basis for rules for human indexing : 8.105
   functions : 2.1
   role in information understanding : 8.60
double posting
   for equivalent and synonymous terms in book indexes : 13.241
Drabenstott (Karen Markey); Vizine-Goetz (Diane)
   views on display of *Library of Congress subject headings* : 12.65
Dublin Core
   as metadata. role in surrogates : 14.17
   core elements : 20.31; formats versus media : 3.30; qualifiers for : sec. 20.5.1
   metadata records. examples : sec. 20.5.2; by Joseph (Michael) : 20.35
   purpose : 20.28
   record formats for internal metadata : sec. 20.5
   websites : 20.27; metadata : 20.27
dynamic clustering : 8.218

economic aspects
   of indexable matter : 7.5
editors
   indexes to : 1.115
electronic books
   arrangement of displayed indexes : 17.124
   full texts. display : sec. 21.4.1.
   hypertext indexes : 17.125
   indexes. browsing : 15.49; locators : 15.47; postings : 15.50, 17.127; vocabulary management : 13.250
   intermediate surrogates : 16.30
   non-displayed indexes : 13.252
   postings in displayed indexes : 17.127
   surrogates. display : 16.28
   topic sentences as intermediate surrogates : 16.31

Index

electronic encyclopedias
  arrangement of displayed indexes : sec. 17.4.3
  full texts. display : sec. 21.4.3.
  hypertext links : 12.341
  indexes. size : sec. 18.1.3
  interface designs : sec. 19.4.3
  locators : sec. 15.1.3
  record formats : sec. 20.7.3
  search options : 12.340
  surrogates : sec. 14.5.3; display : sec. 16.1.3
  syntax : sec. 12.4.3
  vocabulary management : sec. 13.4.3
electronic indexing and abstracting services
  full texts. display : 21.72
electronic interfaces. *see:* **search interfaces**
electronic IR databases
  search interfaces : sec. 19.2; problems and opportunities : 19.35
electronic media
  as standard for IR databases : 5.16
  book indexes. interface designs : 19.87; record formats : 20.48
  books. as hypertext : 6.37, 38; full-text searching. syntax : 12.320; indexable matter : 7.23
  display of book indexes : 12.319; of surrogates for author searches : 16.4; of surrogates for subject searches : 16.4
  displayed indexes : sec. 11.1; presentation of see-also references : 13.251; for indexing and abstracting services : 17.129
  documentary units for book indexes : 6.37
  indexing and abstracting services. comprehensive searches : 12.322; interface designs : 19.94; locators : 15.54; postings : 15.55; targeted searches : 12.327; use of clustering in searches : 12.328; use of proximity requirements in searches : 12.326; use of truncation in searches : 12.325; vocabulary management for non-displayed indexes : 13.262
  IR databases : sec. 5.3, 1.176; interfaces : sec. 19.4
  non-displayed index searching : 5.25
  reading versus searching : 5.13
  surrogates. display : 16.39; staged display : 16.3
  types for IR databases : 5.26
  unit of manipulation : 5.24
  versus paper. cost : 5.15; for IR databases : 5.14
electronic search results
  display. design features : 19.78; examples : 19.79
electronic searches
  bypassing vocabulary management : 8.198
  design features : 19.76
  display of results : 17.130
  display of vocabulary information. design features : 19.78; examples : 19.79
  examples : 19.77
  vocabulary management : 8.196
electronic texts
  paragraphs as documentary units : 6.14
eliminability principle
  in string syntax : 12.128
EMTREE thesaurus
  facets : 13.32

encoding schemas (for digital texts)
  related terms to consider: **HTML; SGML; TEI; XML**
  for full texts in digital media : sec. 21.2; HTML as example : 21.32
encyclopedias
  displayed indexes versus non-displayed indexes : sec. 11.4.3
  electronic. *see:* **electronic encyclopedias**
  exhaustivity of indexing : sec. 9.3.3
  full-text. as examples of IR databases : 1.193; documentary domain : sec. 4.3.3; documentary scope : sec. 3.14.3; documentary units : sec. 6.5.3; indexable matter : sec. 7.4.3; media : sec. 5.5.3; methods of analysis : sec. 8.6.3; subject scope analysis : sec. 2.5.3;
  specificity of index terms : sec. 10.8.3
end-user thesauri : sec. 13.3.3
  bound terms : sec. 13.3.3.1.4
  browsable indexes : 13.213
  categories of entities : 13.161; of operations and processes : 13.163
  clustering of terms : sec. 13.3.4
  compilation : sec. 13.3.3.1; procedures : 13.129
  display : sec. 13.3.3.1.8
  equivalent terms : sec. 13.3.3.1.6; versus variant terms : 13.205
  examples : 13.124
  experimental research : 13.23
  facets : 13.155; primary facets : 13.156
  gathering terms : 13.123, 202; choice : 13.204
  lead-in terms : 13.122
  phrases from full text : 13.146; identification : 13.143
  relational classified displays : 13.214
  search options : 13.212
  searching : 13.215
  stop list terms : 13.152
  term records : 13.157
  terms. categorization : sec. 13.3.3.1.3; from texts. selection : 13.141; indexers as source : 13.148; search statements as source : 13.131; selection : sec. 13.3.3.1.2; sorting : 13.154, 168; sources : sec. 13.3.3.1.1; users as source. views of Landauer (Thomas K.) : 13.132
  used for terms versus equivalent terms : 13.210
  variant forms : sec. 13.3.3.1.6
  versus indexing thesauri : 13.120; differences : 13.121
entities
  related term to consider: **abstract entities**
  and actions. combination in *Library of Congress subject headings* : 12.23
  categories in end-user thesauri : 13.161
  in subject scope analysis : 2.16; examples: 2.44
  messages and texts as entities : 2.21
  parts of. in subject scope analysis : 2.24
entries. *see:* **index entries**
entry arrays. *see:* **index entry arrays**
enumerative classification
  use in indexing and abstracting services in print media : 19.14
  versus faceted classification : 17.72
equivalence relationships
  in thesauri : 13.178

equivalent-term cross references : 13.44
  for equivalent terms in book indexes : 13.240
  for narrower terms in book indexes : 13.243
  for synonymous terms in book indexes : 13.240
  in *Library of Congress subject headings* : 12.40
  in OPACs. form : 13.55
  terminology : 13.244
  UF as instruction for creation : 13.54
equivalent terms
  and synonymous terms. vocabulary management : 8.192
  cross references in book indexes : 13.240
  definition : 1.60
  double posting in book indexes : 13.241
  in end-user thesauri : sec. 13.3.3.1.6
  see-also references in automatic indexing : 13.259
  versus used for terms in end-user thesauri : 13.210; variant terms in end-user thesauri : 13.205
essentialism
  versus social constructionism in gender studies : 8.83
Eurovoc thesaurus : 13.104
  microthesauri : 13.108
  term records : 13.105
evaluation
  and testing of IR database designs : 22.9;
  and testing of IR databases : chap. 22; failure analysis : 22.16; measurement : 22.14; outside scope of book : 22.3; readings : 22.13
  criteria for natural language syntax : 12.230
  of importance. expert judgment versus use : 8.249
  of KWIC index syntax : 12.235
  of library performance : 22.15
events
  in subject scope analysis : 2.36; examples : 2.47
exact match syntax : sec. 12.3.1; 12.280
  absence of ranking : 12.287
  definition : 12.281
  disadvantages : 12.291
  examples : 12.285
  history : 12.282
  impact : 12.286
  narrowing of searches : 12.289
  syntactic operators : 12.284; meaning : 12.292
examples
  actions in subject scope analysis : 2.46
  ad hoc string syntax. index headings : 12.317, 318; index statements for : 12.316
  ad hoc syntax : 12.252; and systematic syntax in *Psychological abstracts* : 12.262
  alphanumeric arrangement : 17.26
  alphanumeric displays in hypertext : 17.35
  arrangement of displayed indexes. policies : sec. 17.4
  attributes in subject scope analysis : 2.45
  automatic vocabulary management. Associative Interactive Dictionary : 8.200
  best match syntax : 12.301
  call numbers in libraries : 15.41
  chain indexes : 12.221
  cross references. placement : 12.264
  Digital Object Identifier (DOI) : 15.25

Index

examples *(continued)*
display of browsable alphanumeric indexes : 19.75; of browsable facets : 19.73; of electronic search results : 19.79; of full texts : sec. 21.4; of surrogates : sec. 16.1; of vocabulary information for electronic searches : 19.79
displayed indexes and non-displayed indexes : sec. 11.4
displayed indexes. arrangement. policies : sec. 17.4
documentary domain : sec. 4.3
documentary units : sec. 6.1, sec. 6.5
end-user thesauri : 13.124
entities in subject scope analysis : 2.44
events in subject scope analysis : 2.47
exact match syntax : 12.285
exhaustivity of indexing : sec. 9.3
expert systems for subject analysis and indexing. MedIndEx : 8.238
faceted index headings from Modern Language Association : 12.140
faceted syntax : 12.131; for *Library of Congress subject headings* : 12.161; in indexing and abstracting services : 12.334
high exhaustivity : 9.8
indexable matter : sec. 7.1
IR database design : 1.190
IR databases. digital libraries : 1.193; full-text encyclopedias : 1.193; indexing and abstracting services : 1.192; monographs : 1.191
KWAC indexes : 12.241
KWIC indexes : 12.234; in indexing and abstracting services in print media : 12.330
KWOC indexes : 12.239
locators : sec. 15.1
low exhaustivity : 9.7
MARC formats for books : 20.5; for name authorities : 20.8
media for IR databases : sec. 5.5
metadata records using Dublin Core : sec. 20.5.2
NEPHIS coding : 12.174
NEPHIS index headings : 12.175
notation in *Universal decimal classification* : 12.216
opening screens for IR databases : 19.71; for electronic searches : 19.77
permuted syntax : 12.248
places in subject scope analysis : 2.48
policies for arrangement of displayed indexes : sec. 17.4
Publisher Item Identifier (PII) : 15.18
record formats : sec. 20.7
rotated term syntax : 12.123
search interfaces : 19.53
Serial Item & Contribution Identifier (SICI) : 15.20
specificity : sec. 10.3, sec. 10.8
subject scope analysis : sec. 2.5
surrogate displays : 19.81
surrogates : sec. 14.5
syntactic cross references : 12.266
syntax : sec. 12.4; impact on precision : 12.4
text encoding schemas : 21.19
time in subject scope analysis : 2.49
vocabulary management : sec. 13.4
exhaustivity : chap. 9
alternative levels for book indexes : 9.28

exhaustivity *(continued)*
among variables in IR research : 8.12
calculation : sec. 9.2; terms versus headings : 9.21; in displayed indexes versus non-displayed indexes : 9.22
definition : 9.1
examples : sec. 9.3
for book indexes : sec. 9.3.1
for digital libraries : sec. 9.3.3
for indexing for encyclopedias : sec. 9.3.3
for indexing and abstracting services : sec. 9.3.2
for routine documents : 9.30
high exhaustivity. advantages : 9.6; examples : 9.8
impact on indexable matter : 7.6; on recall and precision : sec. 9.1.3, 9.9
interactions with specificity and vocabulary management : 10.44
low exhaustivity. advantages : 9.6; examples : 9.7
of automatic indexing for important documents : 9.32; in book indexes : 9.27
of human indexing for important documents : 9.31; in book indexes : 9.26
range : 9.4
relationship to documentary units : 9.24 to size of documentary units : 9.5
versus specificity : sec. 10.2
experimental research
on end-user thesauri : 13.23
expert judgment
application to world-wide web and internet : 8.257
in indexing : 8.252
versus use in evaluation of importance : 8.249
versus user preferences in IR database design : 8.251
expert systems
for subject analysis and indexing. examples. MedIndEx : 8.238
expert users
versus novice users : 1.10
experts
importance of non-topical features for : 3.8
versus novices.
interfaces. views of Raskin (Jef) : 19.59
exploration searches : 13.11
extraction
of index terms : 1.152; and assignment of index terms. combination : 1.154

facet analysis
avoiding meaningless categories : 2.51
by reference librarians : 2.42
role of Ranganathan (Shiyali Ramamrita) : sec. 2.3, 2.13
facet arrangement. *see:* facet order
facet indicators
in faceted syntax : 12.134
in *Universal decimal classification* : 12.215
facet order
in faceted classification. flexibility : 17.73
in Modern Language Association classification : 12.211
faceted classification
construction : sec. 17.3.2
display : sec. 17.3.2, 17.97; in print media : sec. 17.3.2.1

faceted classification *(continued)*
dynamic postings : 13.33, 17.99
facet order.
flexibility : 17.73
of *MLA international bibliography* : 19.38
syntax : 12.202
versus enumerative classification : 17.72
versus traditional classification for hypertext displays : 17.61
faceted index headings
display : 12.136
examples from Modern Language Association : 12.140
for indexing and abstracting services. display : 12.337; format : 12.336; generation : 12.335
staged display in hypertext : 17.44
faceted syntax : sec. 12.2.2.2
collocation : 12.155
compared to ad hoc string syntax : 12.170; to rotated term syntax : 12.132, 145
definition : 12.130
examples : 12.131
facet indicators : 12.134
for *Library of Congress subject headings* : sec. 12.2.2.2.1; coextensive index headings : 12.160; examples : 12.161; testing : 12.168; views of Chan (Lois Mai) : 12.157
in indexing and abstracting services : 12.332; examples : 12.334; indexing worksheet : 12.333
in specialized domains : 12.139
PRECIS : 12.133
role definers : 12.135, 144
role indicators : 12.134
facets
acronyms for. PMEST : 2.77, 78
and hierarchical relationships : 10.21
antecedents : 2.14
arrangement. views of Ranganathan (Shiyali Ramamrita) : 2.78; by other facets : 17.94; classified. within facet : 12.208; of topics : 17.81
browsable display. design features : 19.72; examples : 19.73
categorization of multiple index headings : 12.164
citation order : 17.109; role facets versus type facets : 17.111; for relational classified displays in print media : 17.74; for shelf arrangement : 17.74; in *Bliss bibliographic classification* : 17.110
definition : 2.77
for classification. determination : 17.75
for classification of literature : 17.76
for databases. arrangement : 17.84
for document collections. arrangement : 17.85
for end-user thesauri : 13.155
for ethnicities. arrangement : 17.83
for features of documentary units : 12.159
for Germanic languages. arrangement : 17.91
for groups. arrangement : 17.82
for Indo-European languages. arrangement : 17.89
for institutions. arrangement : 17.82
for language families. arrangement : 17.87
for languages. arrangement : 17.86
for library and information science : 17.80; special interest groups as sources : 17.77

Index

facets (continued)
 for literature. fields in record formats : 20.19
 for persons. arrangement : 17.82
 for places. arrangement : 17.92
 fundamental : 2.15
 in *ASIS thesaurus* : 13.113
 in *EMTREE thesaurus* : 13.32
 in subject scope analysis : 2.83
 of *Bliss bibliographic classification* applied to *Library of Congress subject headings* : 12.158
 of Ranganathan (Shiyali Ramamrita) for diesel engines : 2.79
 primary. for end-user thesauri : 13.156
 role in classification : 17.72
 tests for membership : 2.82
 versus topical groupings in subject scope analysis : 2.80, 84
 versus topics. number : 2.86
failure analysis
 in testing and evaluation of IR databases : 22.16
Fairthorne (Robert)
 views on human indexing : 8.46
Farradane (Jason)
 views on human indexing : 8.70; views on relational indexing : 12.185; views on term relationships : 13.182
features
 indexes to : 1.114, 118
 non-topical. identification in human indexing : 8.108; in subject scope analysis : 2.56; versus topics : sec. 3.13 (clear distinctions : 3.49)
 of documentary units. facets : 12.159
 role as topics : 2.60
 versus topics : 2.59; distinguishing : 2.61, 66; role of methodological approaches : 2.64; on opening screens : 2.75
feedback
 in automatic indexing : 8.228
 in searching : 8.228
fiction
 indexes to : 1.120
 IR databases for : 1.164
fictitious entities
 in IR databases : 1.28
field research
 on use of thesauri : 13.24
field tags
 for term records : 13.158
fields
 in MARC formats : 20.6
 in record formats for book indexes : 20.44; for facets of literature : 20.19
 order in display of surrogates : 16.15, 20
film media
 IR databases for : 1.165
filtering
 relevance feedback : 8.233
first lines
 as basis for indexing : 1.137
fish-eye menu displays : 17.34
flat file databases
 as models for databases : 1.18
folklore
 specialized categories in subject scope : 2.55
foreword
 by Jessica Milstead : sec. 0.1

form subdivisions
 in *Library of Congress subject headings* : 12.26, 90
 versus topical subdivisions. confusion in *Library of Congress subject headings* : 12.90
formats
 as non-topical features : sec. 3.4
 as searchable features : sec. 3.4
 definition : 1.50
 for faceted index headings for indexing and abstracting services : 12.336
 for KWIC indexes : 12.238
 for language texts : 3.26
 for music : 3.25
 for surrogates : 14.5
 in documentary scope for indexing and abstracting services : 3.54
 presentation. media formats : 3.31
 presentation. physical formats : 3.31
 terminology : 3.27
 versus media in Dublin Core metadata : 3.30
Foskett (A. C.)
 views on human indexing : 8.69
frame-based structures
 in indexing : 12.192
free-text terms
 definition : 1.61
frequency
 inverse document. of words : 8.151
 of co-occurrence. ranking of related terms : 8.202
 of words. in automatic indexing : sec. 8.3.4; in collections : sec. 8.3.5; impact of stemming : 8.155; use in ranking of texts : 8.150
frequent users
 versus new users : 1.10
Frohmann (Bernd)
 views on human indexing : 8.67, 78; on rules for human indexing : 8.103; on rules for human indexing of Cooper (William S.) : 8.114; on social context of human indexing : 8.88
Fugmann (Robert)
 views on human indexing : 8.43
full stops (dots, periods)
 treatment in automatic indexing : 8.136
full-text databases. *see:* **full-text IR databases**
full-text encyclopedias
 as examples of IR databases : 1.193
 documentary domain : sec. 4.3.3
 documentary scope : sec. 3.14.3
 documentary units : sec. 6.5.3
 indexable matter : sec. 7.4.3
 media : sec. 5.5.3
 methods of analysis : sec. 8.6.3
 subject scope analysis : sec. 2.5.3
full-text IR databases : 1.179
 definition : 1.30
 multiple documentary units : 6.32
 smaller documentary units : 6.30
 thesauri : 13.82
full-text searching
 documentary units : 6.42
 of books in electronic media. syntax : 12.320
full-text sources
 variability of vocabulary : 13.19

full texts
 access : 21.71
 analysis. views of Harper (David et al.) : 21.62; views of Hearst (Marti) : 21.60; for passage retrieval : 21.59
 as basis for indexing : 1.130
 as indexable matter : sec. 7.1.8; for high-use documents : 7.26
 display : chap. 21; examples : sec. 21.4; options : 21.69
 encoding with TEI : 21.51
 in digital libraries. display : sec. 21.4.3
 in digital media. browsing : sec. 21.3; display : 21.4; encoding schemas : sec. 21.2 (HTML as example : 21.32); size of documentary units : 21.58
 in electronic books. display : sec. 21.4.1.
 in electronic encyclopedias. display : sec. 21.4.3.
 in electronic indexing and abstracting services. display : 21.72
 in indexing and abstracting services. display : sec. 21.4.2
 links and documentary units in HTML : 21.33
 original formats. display : 21.17
 searches in HTML : 21.40
Furnas (George W. et al.)
 views on variability of vocabulary : 13.14

gedanken experimentation
 role in rules for human indexing : 8.116
gender
 role in human indexing : 8.85
 social construction : 8.86
gender studies
 essentialism versus social constructionism : 8.83
generic categories
 role in subject scope analysis : 2.12
generic posting
 and up-posting versus specificity : 10.19
generic terms
 collocation of minor concepts : 10.40
genres
 as non-topical features : sec. 3.4
 as searchable features : sec. 3.4
 for language texts : 3.26
 indexes to : 1.120
 of music : 3.25
 terminology : 3.27
 versus styles in music : 3.25
geographic subdivisions
 in *Library of Congress subject headings* : 12.30, 59
geographical information systems : 1.168
Germanic languages
 facets. arrangement : 17.91
Green (Rebecca)
 views on syntagmatic relationships in indexing : sec. 12.2.3.1.
Greene (Stephan et al.)
 views on purpose of surrogates : 14.8
guidance
 versus censorship in indexing : sec. 8.5.1
guidelines
 for ad hoc syntax : 12.255
 for analysis in cataloging and classification at Rutgers University : 8.93

Index

guidelines *(continued)*
  for indexing. subjective nature : 8.94
    views of Hjørland (Birger) : 8.95
  for search interfaces : 19.69
  for surrogates : sec. 14.2

hardware
  for IR databases : 1.205
Harper (David et al.)
  views on analysis of full texts : 21.62
Head (Alison J.)
  views on customization of interfaces : 19.62
headings. *see:* **index headings; subject headings**
Hearst (Marti A.)
  views on search interfaces and visualization : 19.50; on analysis of full texts : 21.60
hierarchical arrangement
  in classification : 12.209
hierarchical displays
  in thesauri. term relationships : 13.190
  in *Unesco thesaurus* (1977) : 13.92
hierarchical levels
  multiple. display in *Unesco thesaurus* (1995) : 13.102
hierarchical relationships
  and facets : 10.21
  in thesauri : 13.179
  versus associative relationships in thesauri : 13.189, 195
  versus roles : 10.31
hierarchical specificity : 10.24
Historical abstracts
  record format : sec. 20.3
  table of contents : 19.10
history
  indexing and abstracting services : 19.10
  of cataloging : 1.1
  of displayed indexes : 11.6
  of exact match syntax : 12.282
  of indexing : 1.1
  of IR databases : 1.1
  of librarianship : 1.1
  of non-displayed indexes : 11.7
  of syntax in *Library of Congress subject headings* : 12.21
Hjerppe (Roland)
  views on ontologies versus knowledge organization systems : 13.226
Hjørland (Birger)
  views on guidelines for indexing : 8.95; on human indexing : 8.57; on nature of subjects : 8.61
Hockey (Susan)
  views on SGML : 21.31; on TEI : 21.45
homographs
  in thesauri : sec. 13.3.3.1.7
homonymy principle.
  for subject heading systems : 12.106
HTML
  and XML. relationship with SGML : 21.43
  as example of encoding schemas for full texts in digital media : 21.32
  bandwidth needs : 21.41
  definition : 21.24
  international aspects : 21.42
  international standards body : 21.27
  links : 21.25; and documentary units in full texts : 21.33

HTML *(continued)*
  problems : 21.35
  searches of full texts : 21.40
  syntax : 21.38
  tags : 21.24, 26, 39
  versus TEI : 21.54; XML : 21.34
human analysis
  methods for human indexing : 8.27
human-computer interaction : sec. 19.3, 19.2
human indexers
  contributions. identification : 8.254
  role in assessments of authority : 8.253
human indexing : sec. 8.2, 1.148
  allocation. criteria : 8.247; to important documents : 8.242
  analysis steps : 8.32
  and automatic indexing. combination : 1.150
  application of views of Wittgenstein (Ludwig) : 8.78
  as model for automatic indexing : 8.76
  cognition versus social construction : sec. 8.2.1
  cognitive processes : 8.28, 31
  compared to automatic indexing : 8.162, 169; incompatibility : 8.168
  compared to keywords based on Zipfian distributions : 8.167
  consistency : 8.64
  culture versus cognition : 8.87
  exhaustivity for important documents : 9.31; in book indexes : 9.26
  identification of non-topical features : 8.108
  index terms. specificity in book indexes : 10.50
  methods for analysis. British standards : 8.92; international standards : 8.92
  methods of human analysis : 8.27
  numerical values for decision making : 8.124
  of image texts. recommended resources : 8.112; rules : sec. 8.2.2.1
  positive attributes : 8.77
  probabilistic rules : sec. 8.2.2.2
  request-oriented. qualitative judgments : 8.102
  role. views of Bates (Marcia J.) : 8.245
  role in high-precision IR : 9.20
  role of documentary features : 8.30; of gender : 8.85; of specialized categories : 8.100
  rules : sec. 8.2.2, 8.91; domain analysis as basis : 8.105; limitations : 8.101; relation to subject scope and documentary scope : 8.96; role of decision theory : 8.116; role of gedanken experimentation : 8.116; role of utility theory : 8.116; views of Frohmann (Bernd) : 8.103
  rules of Cooper (William S.). views of Frohmann (Bernd) : 8.114
  social context. views of Frohmann (Bernd) : 8.88
  specialized rules : 8.97
  standards for analysis : 8.92
  use for identification of useful documents : 8.244
  variability : 8.63
  versus automatic indexing : 8.2, 8.258; allocation : 8.241; cost-benefit analysis : 8.25; cultural factors : 8.37; evidence from use : 8.22; research : sec. 8.1; results : 8.3; user preferences : 8.23

human indexing *(continued)*
  views of Anderson (James D.) : 8.73; of Artandi (Susan) : 8.75; of Beghtol (Clare) : 8.72; of Chan (Lois Mai) : 8.39; of Chicago manual of style : 8.42; of Cooper (William S.) : 8.115; of Fairthorne (Robert) : 8.46; of Farradane (Jason) : 8.70; of Foskett (A. C.) : 8.69; of Frohmann (Bernd) : 8.67, 78; of Fugmann (Robert) : 8.43; of Hjørland (Birger) : 8.57; of Lancaster (F. W.) : 8.45; of Mulvany (Nancy) : 8.33; of O'Connor (Brian) : 8.47; of Soergel (Dagobert) : 8.44; of Taylor (Arlene) : 8.56; of Wellisch (Hans) : 8.48; of Wilson (Patrick) : 8.51
human intellectual analysis
  of texts for indexing : 1.148
human searching
  versus automatic indexing : 8.125
human searching behavior
  role in automatic indexing : 8.234
hybrid databases
  IR databases : 1.201
hypertext
  alphanumeric displays. examples : 17.35; goals : 17.32
  automatic conversion of linear text : 21.15
  books in electronic media : 6.37, 38
  constrained : 21.13
  conversion of linear text : 21.9
  cross references : 13.207
    display. of classification : 12.195, 17.59; of *Dewey decimal classification* : sec. 17.3.1, 17.67, 70; of string indexing : 17.40; of subject headings : 17.35, 39
  documentary units : 6.20; on world-wide web : 6.21
  guidelines : 21.8
  interactivity : 21.6
  relational classified displays. research : 17.56
  staged display of alphanumeric indexes : 17.29, 38; of faceted index headings : 17.44; of index headings : 17.43
  versus linear text : sec. 21.1
hypertext databases
  as models for databases : 1.19
hypertext displays
  advantages : 17.31
  alphanumeric arrangement : sec. 17.2
  scrolling : 17.32
  traditional classification versus faceted classification : 17.61
  visual limitations : 17.30
hypertext indexes
  for electronic books : 17.125
hypertext links
  in digital libraries : 12.341
  in electronic encyclopedias : 12.341
hypertext locators
  indicators of postings : 15.12
hypertext media
  display of index headings : 17.42
hyphens
  treatment in automatic indexing : 8.134

icons
  versus words : 19.56
  views of Raskin (Jef) : 19.58

Index

identification
  of phrases in automatic indexing : 8.185; cost versus benefits : 8.180
  of word roots in stemming : 8.156
illustrators
  indexes to : 1.115
image texts
  and sound texts. terminology : 8.113
  automatic indexing. views of Pérez-López (Kathleen Golitko) : 8.111
  human indexing. recommended resources : 8.112; rules : sec. 8.2.2.1
  indexing. views of Jorgensen (Corinne) : 8.110; by Altavista web search engine : 8.127
  versus language texts. automatic indexing : 8.5, 126; as indexable matter for world-wide websites : 7.15
imaginary entities
  in IR databases : 1.28
importance
  evaluation. expert judgment versus use : 8.249
important documents
  exhaustivity of automatic indexing : 9.32; exhaustivity of human indexing : 9.31
inconsistency
  in searching : 8.66
indented layout
  versus run-in layout for book indexes : 18.18
index entries
  arrangement : sec. 1.5.5
  criteria : 1.74
  definition : 1.68
  locators for documentary units in book indexes : 19.85
  numbers of. determination : 1.71
index entry arrays
  definition : 1.69
  presentation : 1.70
index headings
  related term to consider: **subject headings**
  based on document titles : 12.226; on natural language text : 12.225
  clarity : 12.147
  coextensive. in string syntax : 12.127, 128; using faceted syntax for *Library of Congress subject headings* : 12.160
  collocation : 12.148
  compared to search statements. syntax : 12.1, 6
  definition : 1.62
  display in hypertext media : 17.42
  examples based on ad hoc string syntax : 12.317, 318
  faceted. display : 12.136; examples from Modern Language Association : 12.140; staged displa. in hypertext : 17.44; for indexing and abstracting services (display : 12.337; format : 12.336; generation : 12.335)
  in displayed indexes. merging : 18.4
  locators. number of : 1.73
  multiple. categorization using facets : 12.164
  nonsensical. in permuted indexes : 12.250
  permuted. versus cross references in book indexes : 18.16
  precoordinate. : 12.8
  predictability : 12.156
  purpose : 12.7
  staged display in hypertext : 17.43
  syntax : chap. 12; definition : 1.63

index headings *(continued)*
  versus classification captions : 12.196; search statements : 11.1
  within facets. classified arrangements : 12.208
index statements
  examples for ad hoc string syntax : 12.316
index terms
  assigned by automatic indexing. specificity in book indexes : 10.51
  assigned by human indexing. specificity in book indexes : 10.50
  assignment : 1.153; criteria : 2.65
  combination. methods : sec. 1.5.8, 1.156; necessity : 1.155
  definition : 1.58
  extraction : 1.152
  extraction and assignment. combination : 1.154
  postcoordinate combination : 1.158
  precoordinate combination : 1.157
  precoordinate combination and postcoordinate combination : 1.159
  role of chemical symbols : 1.128; of common words : 1.124; of mathematical symbols : 1.127; of musical symbols : 1.129; of numbers : 1.125; of proper nouns : 1.124; of symbols : 1.126; of words : 1.123
  selection. methods : sec. 1.5.7
  specificity in book indexes : sec. 10.8.1; in digital libraries : sec. 10.8.3; in encyclopedias : sec. 10.8.3; in indexing and abstracting services : sec. 10.8.2
  specificity versus scope : 10.3
  types of : sec. 1.5.2
indexable matter : chap. 7
  abstracts : sec. 7.1.2
  complete texts versus partial texts : 7.2
  definition : 1.57, 7.1
  economic aspects : 7.5
  elimination of types of messages : sec. 7.1.9
  examples : sec. 7.1, sec. 7.4
  extent. among variables in IR research : 8.11
  for book indexes : sec. 7.4.1, 7.18
  for books in electronic media : 7.23
  for digital libraries : sec. 7.4.3
  for full-text encyclopedias : sec. 7.4.3
  for high-use documents : 7.25
  for indexing and abstracting services : sec. 7.4.2
  for maps : 7.28
  for mixed-text documents : 7.4
  for non-language-based texts : 7.3
  for world-wide websites. language-based texts versus image texts : 7.15
  full texts : sec. 7.1.8
  full texts for high-use documents : 7.26
  impact of exhaustivity of indexing : 7.6
  impact of size of documentary units : 7.6
  impact on accuracy of indexing : sec. 7.3
  initial paragraphs : sec. 7.1.4
  internal indexes : sec. 7.1.5
  lead paragraphs : 7.29
  opening screens of world-wide websites : sec. 7.1.7
  preliminary matter : sec. 7.1.3
  reference citations : sec. 7.1.6
  role for world-wide web search engines : 7.14
  tables of contents : sec. 7.1.5
  titles : sec. 7.1.1; adequacy : 12.231
  variations : 7.7
  varieties : sec. 1.5.3

indexable matter *(continued)*
  versus subject scope : sec. 7.2
indexers
  and searchers. variability of vocabulary : 13.17
  as source of terms for end-user thesauri : 13.148
indexes
  attributes : 1.111
  back-of-the-book. *see:* **book indexes**
  definition : 1.34
  design. technical report : 0.5
  display. standards : 19.16
  for digital libraries. size : sec. 18.1.3
  for electronic books. browsing : 15.49; locators : 15.47; postings : 15.50; vocabulary management : 13.250
  for electronic encyclopedias. size : sec. 18.1.3
  for indexing and abstracting services. size : sec. 18.1.2
  for printed books. size : 18.1
  internal. as indexable matter : sec. 7.1.5
  kinds of objects represented : sec. 1.5.1
  presentation : sec. 1.5.4
  repetition of recurring elements : 19.29
  searching. methods : sec. 1.5.4
  size. determination : 18.2; estimation : 18.3; impact of syntax : 12.184; relationship to document size : 18.14
  standards. endorsement by American Society for Information Science : 1.99; impossibility : 1.106; lack of consensus : 1.105; objections of American Society of Indexers : 1.97; opposition : 1.96; opposition from American Society for Information Science : 1.100; role of NISO Committee YY : 0.4, 1.95
  stop lists for reducing size : 8.146
  syntax as essential attribute : 12.5
  to .... *see:* **indexes to ...** (separate main heading)
  types : 1.110
  versus classifications. arrangement : 12.205
  versus IR databases : 1.204
  versus vocabulary lists in non-displayed indexes : 11.13
indexes to
  authors : 1.114, 115
  Bible verses : 1.117
  choreographers : 1.116
  composers : 1.116
  document numbers : 1.121
  documents : 1.117
  editors : 1.115
  features : 1.114, 118
  fiction : 1.120
  genres : 1.120
  illustrators : 1.115
  institutions : 1.117
  international standard numbers : 1.121
  laws : 1.117
  lexicographers : 1.116
  novels : 1.120
  painters : 1.116
  places : 1.117
  poems : 1.120
  publishers : 1.115
  quotations : 1.117
  science fiction : 1.120
  sculptors : 1.116
  short stories : 1.120

Index

indexes to *(continued)*
  subjects : 1.117
  titles : 1.119
  topics : 1.114
  translators : 1.115
indexing
  accuracy. impact of indexable matter : sec. 7.3
  and analysis of messages, texts, documents. methods : chap. 8
  and cataloging by document creators : 20.29
  and subject analysis. expert systems. examples. MedIndEx : 8.238; use of checktags : 8.239
  and subject analysis in indexing and abstracting services : sec. 8.4
  based on abstracts : 1.132; on bibliographic coupling and co-citation: 8.108; on first lines : 1.137; on full text : 1.130; on introductory matter : 1.135; on lead paragraphs : 1.133; on reference citations : 1.136; on tables of contents : 1.134; on titles : 1.131
  censorship versus guidance : sec. 8.5.1
  computer algorithmic analysis of texts : 1.149
  controlled vocabularies versus un-controlled vocabularies : 10.42
  exhaustive. of authors : 9.3
  exhaustivity : chap. 9; calculation : sec. 9.2; definition : 9.1; examples : sec. 9.3; for book indexes : sec. 9.3.1; for digital libraries : sec. 9.3.3; for encyclopedias : sec. 9.3.3; for indexing and abstracting services : sec. 9.3.2; impact on indexable matter : 7.6; impact on recall and precision : sec. 9.1.3; versus specificity : sec. 10.2
  expert judgment : 8.252
  frame-based structures : 12.192
  guidelines. subjective nature : 8.94; views of Hjørland (Birger) : 8.95
  high-threshold of importance. role in high-precision IR : 9.18
  history : 1.1
  human intellectual analysis of texts : 1.148
  multiple approaches in IR databases : 8.4
  of concrete entities and events. compared to indexing of messages : 1.23
  of image texts. views of Jorgensen (Corinne) : 8.110
  of image texts by Altavista web search engine : 8.127
  of messages : 1.24; compared to indexing of concrete entities and events : 1.23
  of proper nouns : 8.179
  role of machines versus humans : 8.258
  role of syntax : 12.2
  rules for *MLA international bibliography* : 8.98
  specificity of vocabulary : chap. 10
  standards : 1.81
  syntagmatic relationships. views of Green (Rebecca) : sec. 12.2.3.1.
  versus classification : 17.50
  vocabulary. size. impact of specificity : sec. 10.6
indexing and abstracting services
  arrangement of displayed indexes : sec. 17.4.2
  as examples of IR databases : 1.192
  computer-aided indexing and subject analysis : 8.240
  contents of surrogates : 14.22

indexing and abstracting services *(continued)*
  displayed indexes and non-displayed indexes : sec. 11.4.2
  displayed indexes. purpose : 12.338; in electronic media : 17.129; in print media : 17.128;
  documentary domain : sec. 4.3.2
  documentary scope : sec. 3.14.2; audience : 3.56; authorship : 3.63; document titles : 3.64; formats : 3.54; language : 3.57; levels of treatment : 3.56; media : 3.53; methodological approaches : 3.65; periodicity : 3.55; place of publication : 3.58; points of view : 3.65; qualitative criteria : 3.61; searchable features : 3.62; specific documents : 3.60; time of publication : 3.59
  documentary units : sec. 6.5.2, 6.7, 40; for high-use documents : 6.41
  exhaustivity of indexing : sec. 9.3.2
  external locators : 15.56
  faceted index headings. ; display : 12.337; format : 12.336; generation : 12.335
  faceted syntax : 12.332
  faceted syntax. examples : 12.334; indexing worksheet : 12.333
  for anthropology : 19.9
  for history : 19.10
  for information science : 19.12
  for sociology : 19.11
  full texts. display : sec. 21.4.2
  in electronic media. comprehensive searches : 12.322; full texts. display : 21.72; interface designs : 19.94; locators : 15.54; postings : 15.55; targeted searches : 12.327; use of clustering in searches : 12.328; use of proximity requirements in searches : 12.326; use of truncation in searches : 12.325; vocabulary management for non-displayed indexes : 13.262
  in print media. comprehensive searches : 12.329; displayed indexes based on automatic indexing : 12.329; interface designs : 19.92; internal locators : 15.53; KWIC indexes. examples : 12.330; search interfaces : 19.6; use of enumerative classification : 19.14; vocabulary management : 13.258
  indexable matter : sec. 7.4.2
  indexes. size : sec. 18.1.2
  interface designs : sec. 19.4.2
  internal locators : 15.5
  locators : sec. 15.1.2
  media : sec. 5.5.2
  methods of analysis : sec. 8.6.2
  opening screens. subject scope : 2.95
  record formats : sec. 20.7.2. 20.15
  selective searches : 12.331
  software : 22.5
  specificity of index terms : sec. 10.8.2
  subject analysis and indexing : sec. 8.4
  subject scope analysis : sec. 2.5.2
  subject scope. presentation : 2.94
  surrogates : sec. 14.5.2; display : sec. 16.1.2; role of keywords : 14.23
  syntax : sec. 12.4.2
  tables of contents : 19.7
  terminology : 6.39
  vocabulary management : sec. 13.4.2

indexing languages
  criteria : 12.12
  precoordinate. criteria : 12.15
indexing odds-payoff chart : 8.119
indexing processes
  recommended resources : 8.6
indexing rules
  social construction. application of views of Wittgenstein (Ludwig) : 8.80
indexing staff
  and advisory groups. selection of useful documents : 8.250
indexing systems
  postcoordinate. on paper media : 5.18
indexing theory
  compared to queer theory : 8.81
indexing thesauri : sec. 13.3.2
  examples : sec. 13.3.2
  versus end-user thesauri : 13.120; differences : 13.121
indexing worksheets
  for faceted syntax in indexing and abstracting services : 12.333
Indo-European languages
  facets. arrangement : 17.89
inequality
  of documents : 8.256
information
  definition : 1.38, 44
  versus data : 1.5
  views of Korfhage (Robert R.) : 1.41
  visualization : 19.51
information architects
  role : 1.207
information content
  of IR databases. overviews : 19.52
information needs and desires
  categories : 13.3
information professionals
  responsibility in absence of standards : 1.109
information retrieval. *see:* **IR (information retrieval)**
information science
  as example of bound term : 1.159
  indexing and abstracting services : 19.12
  paradigms : 8.59
Information science abstracts
  table of contents : 19.12
information seeking
  research : 13.13
information seeking situations
  continua : 13.12
information understanding
  role of domain analysis : 8.60
initialisms
  in alphanumeric arrangement : 17.20
institutions
  indexes to : 1.117
  versus societies in descriptive cataloging : 2.19
insurance
  as example of complex phenomena in subject scope analysis : 2.39
integrating and continuing resources
  as non-topical features : sec. 3.5; as searchable features : sec. 3.5
interaction
  among design options : pt2.8
  in hypertext : 21.6

603

Index

interface designs
> *related term to consider:* **search interfaces**

for book indexes : sec. 19.4.1; in electronic media : 19.87; in print media : 19.83
for digital libraries : sec. 19.4.3
for electronic encyclopedias : sec. 19.4.3
for indexing and abstracting services : sec. 19.4.2; in electronic media : 19.94; in print media : 19.92
guidance. literature about : 19.48; taxonomy of : 19.46

internal locators
for indexing and abstracting services : 15.5

internal metadata
record formats using Dublin Core : sec. 20.5

international aspects
of HTML : 21.42

International Standard AudioVisual Number (ISAN) : 15.32

International Standard Bibliographic Description (ISBD) : 16.17

International Standard Music Number (ISMN) : 15.30

international standard numbers
indexes to : 1.121

International Standard Recording Code (ISRC) : 15.31

International Standard Work Code (ISWC) : 15.33

international standards
on methods for analysis in human indexing : 8.92

international standards body
for HTML : 21.27

internet
and world-wide web. application of expert judgment : 8.257

internet resources
IR databases for : 1.172

interoperability
for metadata schemas : 20.38; standards : 20.40
vocabulary data. standards : 20.41

introductory matter
as basis for indexing : 1.135

inverse document frequency
of words : 8.151

inverted files
as non-displayed indexes : 11.8, 12.271
definition : 12.272

IR (information retrieval)
components of problems : 1.7
controversies : 1.93
documentary units as limiting factor : 6.23
high-precision. role of automatic indexing : 9.20; role of high-threshold indexing : 9.18; role of human indexing : 9.20
high-recall. role of automatic indexing : 9.19
natural laws : sec. 6.2
political aspects : 8.107
purposes for diverse users : 8.104
role in support of civilization : 1.2
role of abstracts : 6.28
role of automatic indexing : sec. 8.5
role of browsing : 11.25; research : sec. 11.2
role of documentation : 6.2
role of relational classified displays : 17.57
standards : 1.94
versus document retrieval : 6.1
views of Chowdhury (Gobinda G.) : 0.9

IR (information retrieval) *(continued)*
wants versus needs : 8.106

IR database design
chaos and creativity versus stability : 1.107
examples : 1.190
expert judgment versus user preferences : 8.251
fundamental issues : 0.3
implementation : chap. 22; outside scope of book : 22.3
standards : sec. 1.4
terminology : 1.11
testing and evaluation : 22.9
views of Bates (Marcia J.) : 0.8; views of Milstead (Jessica L.) : 0.7

IR database designers
role : 1.207

IR database features
omission by IR database vendors : 22.11

IR database producers
importance of documentary scope descriptions for : 3.3
versus IR database vendors : 22.10

IR database vendors
omission of IR database features : 22.11
versus IR database producers : 22.10

IR databases : sec. 1.6.2
abstract entities : 1.28
alternative names for : 1.29
as hybrid databases : 1.201
as messages, texts, and documents : 5.1
attributes : 1.111, pt2.6; list : pt2.7
authorship : sec. 1.5.14
beta testing : 22.17
braille media : 1.178
card files as favored medium : 5.7
CD-ROMs as media : sec. 5.3.2
channels of transmission. world-wide web : sec. 5.3.3
codes and symbols : sec. 5.4, 5.32
components : 1.204, pt2.6
concrete entities : 1.27
concrete events : 1.27
content. separation from search interfaces : 19.37
coverage. impact of documentary domain : 4.1
defining characteristics : 4.4
definitions : 0.1, 1.22
design : 1.6
design options. impact of media : 5.2
design specifications : 1.206
documentary domain : chap. 4
documentary units : 6.34
examples. digital libraries : 1.193; full-text encyclopedias : 1.193; indexing and abstracting services : 1.192; monographs : 1.191
fictitious entities : 1.28
for .... *see:* **IR databases for** ... *(separate main heading)*
full-text. smaller documentary units : 6.30
hardware : 1.205
history : 1.1
imaginary entities : 1.28
in libraries. software : 22.6
indexing. multiple approaches : 8.4
key entities. messages : 1.200

IR databases *(continued)*
media : sec. 1.5.10; examples : sec. 5.5; for display : chap. 5; options : 5.4; books : sec. 5.1.2 (advantages : 5.10); card files : sec. 5.1.1 (disadvantages : 5.8); computer-output microfilm : 5.22; electronic media : sec. 5.3, 1.176 (as current standard : 5.16; interfaces : sec. 19.4; types : 5.26); microforms : 1.175, sec. 5.2; paper : 1.174, sec. 5.1 (versus electronic media : 5.14);
mental images : 11.21
online access : sec. 5.3.1
opening screens. design features : 19.70; examples : 19.71
paper. as favored medium : 5.5; paper formats : 5.6
periodicity : sec. 1.5.13
personal. software : 22.8
presentation : 1.141
primary sources versus secondary sources : sec. 4.1
proximity of documents : sec. 1.5.11
qualitative studies : 22.18
reference. documentary units versus surrogates : 6.26; smaller documentary units : 6.29
secondary sources : 4.7
selection of documents. principles : 4.5
software : 1.205, 22.4
sound media : 1.177
special types. paper as medium : 5.17
subject domains : 2.10
testing and evaluation : chap. 22; measurement : 22.14; outside scope of book : 22.3; readings : 22.13
text options : 5.3
types : sec. 1.5, 1.195
unit of manipulation : 5.23
versus concrete entity and event databases : 1.196, 197, 202, 8.55
versus indexes : 1.204

IR databases for
books : 1.162
collections of documents : 1.186; documentary scope descriptions : 3.4, 6
complete documents : 1.185
computer software : 1.171
fiction : 1.164
film media : 1.165
internet resources : 1.172
machine-readable texts : 1.170
maps : 1.168
monographs : 1.162
motion pictures : 1.165
music : 1.169
periodicals : 1.161
photographic media : 1.165
pictures : 1.167
poetry : 1.163
single documents. documentary scope descriptions : 3.5
slides : 1.165
small documentary units : 1.184
sound recordings : 1.169
videotapes : 1.166

IR protocols
Z39.50 standard : 20.42

IR research
conflation of variables : 8.18, 20
role of users : 8.8

Index

IR research (continued)
  TREC. role of users : 8.21
  variables : 8.9; views of Cooper (William S.) : 8.19; browsability : 8.13; exhaustivity : 8.12; extent of indexable matter : 8.11; size of documentary units : 8.10; specificity : 8.12a; surrogation : 8.17; syntax : 8.14; vocabulary management : 8.16
IR systems
  definition : 1.33
ISO standards
  for SGML : 21.22

Jorgensen (Corinne)
  views on indexing of image texts : 8.110
Joseph (Michael)
  metadata records using Dublin Core : 20.35
judges
  of relevance : 1.78

key entities
  for IR databases. messages : 1.200
keyword indexes : sec. 8.3.2
  natural language syntax : 12.233
keyword searches
  using *Library of Congress subject headings* : 12.75
keywords
  based on Zipfian distributions. compared to human indexing : 8.167
  definition : 1.61
  effectiveness : 8.166
  identification based on transition points in Zipfian distributions : 8.161, 165
  role in surrogates in indexing and abstracting services : 14.23
knowledge
  anomalous states. views of Belkin (Nicholas J.) : 13.13
  definition : 1.40, 45
  versus data : 1.5
  views of Korfhage (Robert R.) : 1.41
knowledge discovery
  role of surrogates : 14.16
knowledge organization
  treatment by activity theory : 8.58
knowledge organization systems
  versus ontologies. views of Hjerppe (Roland) : 13.226
known items
  searches with known vocabulary : 13.4; with unknown vocabulary : 13.5
Korfhage (Robert R.)
  views on data, information, knowledge, wisdom : 1.41
Kuhr (Pat)
  and Michel (Dee). compilation of term relationships : 13.186
KWAC indexes : sec. 12.2.5.3
  definition : 12.241
  example : 12.241
  phrases : 12.242
  word pairs : 12.242
KWIC indexes : sec. 12.2.5.1
  collocation : 12.236
  definitions : 12.234
  display. in *Unesco thesaurus* (1977) : 13.91

KWIC indexes (continued)
  examples : 12.234; in indexing and abstracting services in print media : 12.330
  format : 12.238
  syntax. evaluation : 12.235
KWOC indexes : sec. 12.2.5.2
  definition : 12.239
  example : 12.239
  phrases : 12.240
  word pairs : 12.240

Lancaster (F. W.)
  views on human indexing : 8.45
Landauer (Thomas K.)
  views on users as source of terms for end-user thesauri : 13.132
language
  as non-topical feature, as searchable feature : sec. 3.8
  human. richness : 13.2
  in documentary scope for indexing and abstracting services : 3.57
  specialized categories in subject scope : 2.55
language-based texts
  versus image texts as indexable matter for world-wide websites : 7.15
language families
  facet. arrangement : 17.87
language model
  for automatic indexing : 8.129
  for best match syntax : 12.298
language texts
  formats : 3.26
  genres : 3.26
  versus image texts. automatic indexing : 8.5, 126
  versus non-language texts. automatic indexing : 8.5
  versus sound texts. automatic indexing : 8.126
languages
  facets. arrangement : 17.86
latent semantic indexing : sec. 8.3.11.1
  vocabulary management : 8.222
laws
  indexes to : 1.117
  of information retrieval : sec. 6.2
lead-in terms
  in end-user thesauri : 13.122
lead paragraphs
  as basis for indexing : 1.133
  as indexable matter : 7.29
Lehnus (Donald J.)
  views on book numbers : 15.39
levels
  of treatment as non-topical feature : sec. 3.6; as searchable feature : sec. 3.6; in documentary scope for indexing and abstracting services : 3.56
lexicographers
  indexes to : 1.116
librarianship
  history : 1.1
libraries
  call numbers : 15.37 (examples : 15.41; local nature : 15.43)
  compared to databases : 1.4
  IR databases. software : 22.6
  locators : 15.36
  surrogates. display : 16.16

library and information science
  classification. retroactive notation : 17.117
  facets : 17.80; special interest groups as sources : 17.77
library catalogs : 1.181
  related term to consider: **OPACs**
  cross references : 13.68; absence : 12.49
  documentary units : 6.24
Library of Congress
  views on specificity : 10.5
Library of Congress classification
  syntax : 12.201
Library of Congress filing rules
  as standard for alphanumeric arrangement : 1.83
Library of Congress subject headings : sec. 12.2.1, 12.18
  alphabetical browsing : 12.70
  application of facets of *Bliss bibliographic classification* : 12.158
  arrangement of subdivisions : 12.53
  broader term cross references : 12.43
  categorization of subdivisions : 12.58
  chronological subdivisions : 12.34, 57
  combination of entities and actions : 12.23
  compared to vocabulary of users : 13.15
  comprehensibility : 12.84
  confusion between form subdivisions versus topical subdivisions : 12.90
  decision trees : 12.65
  display : 12.58, 61; views of American Library Association : 12.82; views of Drabenstott and Vizine-Goetz : 12.65
  equivalent term cross references : 12.40
  exact-match searches : 12.66
  faceted syntax : sec. 12.2.2.2.1; coextensive index headings : 12.160; examples : 12.161; testing : 12.168; views of Chan (Lois Mai) : 12.157
  form subdivisions : 12.26, 90
  general cross references : 12.45
  geographic subdivisions : 12.30, 59
  keyword searches : 12.75
  main headings : 12.22
  modernization : 12.51
  narrower term cross references : 12.41
  national authority file : 12.55
  professional and research literature : 12.96
  recommendations for improvement : 12.52
  related term cross references : 12.44
  search decision trees : 12.81
  specificity : 10.18
  subdivision by place versus topic : 12.37
  subdivision practice : 12.25
  subdivisions : 12.60; conference on future : 12.52
  syndetic structure : 12.38
  syntax : 12.20; history : 12.21
  topical subdivisions : 12.36
  types of subject headings : 12.19
library performance
  evaluation : 22.15
linear text
  conversion to hypertext : 21.9; automatic : 21.15
  versus hypertext : sec. 21.1
linguistics
  specialized categories in subject scope : 2.55

Index

links
  in HTML : 21.25; and documentary units in full texts : 21.33
  in postcoordinate syntax : 12.275
literary study
  methodological approaches : 3.39
literary warrant principle.
  for subject heading systems : 12.111
literature
  facets. fields in record formats : 20.19; for classification : 17.76
  record formats : 20.17
  specialized categories in subject scope : 2.53, 54
locators : chap. 15
  as indicators of postings : 15.11
  chapter and paragraph numbers : 15.44
  definition : 1.68, 75, 15.1
  examples : sec. 15.1
  external : 15.2; for indexing and abstracting services : 15.56
  for book indexes : sec. 15.1.1, 12.314
  for digital libraries : sec. 15.1.3
  for digital resources : 15.16
  for electronic encyclopedias : sec. 15.1.3
  for indexes in electronic books : 15.47
  for indexing and abstracting services : sec. 15.1.2; in electronic media : 15.54
  for nonbook media : 15.13
  for webpages : 15.14
  hypertext. indicators of postings : 15.12
  in book indexes : 15.7
  in index entries in books : 19.85
  in libraries : 15.36
  in rotated term syntax : 12.125
  internal : 15.4; for indexing and abstracting services : 15.5; in print media : 15.53
  invisible : 15.6
  numbers of. under headings : 1.73
  paragraph numbers : 15.45
  ranges. indication : 15.9
  sequences of : 1.72
  visible : 15.6
lower-case letters
  treatment in automatic indexing : 8.144

machine-readable texts
  codes for representation : 3.28
  IR databases for : 1.170
machine searching
  surrogates : sec. 14.4
machine translation
  ontologies : 13.233
machines
  versus humans in indexing : 8.258
main headings
  in *Library of Congress subject headings* : 12.22
management information systems : 1.198
maps
  indexable matter : 7.28
  IR databases for : 1.168
MARC formats : sec. 20.1
  as digital communications format : 20.12
  fields : 20.6
  for authority records : 20.7
  for books. examples : 20.5
  for classification data : 20.7
  for name authorities. examples : 20.8

MARC formats *(continued)*
  versus record formats for indexing and abstracting services : 20.15
  websites : 20.14
MARC records
  display : 16.19
Marchionini (Gary)
  views on browsing : 11.31
mark-up languages. *see:* **encoding schemas (for digital texts)**
mathematical symbols
  role in index terms : 1.127
measurement
  for testing & evaluation of IR databases : 22.14
measures
  of use versus censorship : 8.248
media
  as non-topical feature : sec. 3.3
  as searchable feature : sec. 3.3
  audio. types : 3.20
  CD-ROMs for IR databases : sec. 5.3.2
  definition : 1.49
  electronic. as standard for IR databases : 5.16; types for IR databases : 5.26; unit of manipulation : 5.24; versus paper. cost : 5.15
  for book indexes : sec. 5.5.1
  for digital libraries : sec. 5.5.3
  for display of IR databases : chap. 5
  for full-text encyclopedias : sec. 5.5.3
  for indexing and abstracting services : sec. 5.5.2
  for IR databases : sec. 1.5.10; examples : sec. 5.5; books : sec. 5.1.2 (advantages : 5.10); card files : sec. 5.1.1 (disadvantages : 5.8); computer-output microfilm : 5.22; microforms : 1.175, sec. 5.2; paper : 1.174, sec. 5.1 (versus electronic media : 5.14)
  for reading. advantages of paper : 5.12
  impact on design options for IR databases : 5.2
  in documentary scope for indexing and abstracting services : 3.53
  nonbook. locators : 15.13
  paper. postcoordinate indexing systems : 5.18; for special types of IR databases : 5.17
  terminology : 3.27
  versus formats in Dublin Core metadata : 3.30
  visual. types : 3.19
media formats
  versus presentation formats : 3.31
media options
  for IR databases : 5.4
Medical subject headings : sec. 12.2.1.1
  browsing versus searching : 12.101
MedIndEx
  as examples of expert systems for subject analysis and indexing : 8.238
mental images
  of IR databases : 11.21
menu displays
  fish-eye. : 17.34
messages
  analysis. methods : sec. 1.5.6
  analysis and indexing. methods : chap. 8
  as key entities for IR databases : 1.200
  characteristics : 1.8
  definition : 1.35
  from nature : 3.16
  indexing : 1.24; compared to indexing of concrete entities and events : 1.23

messages *(continued)*
  types. elimination as indexable matter : sec. 7.1.9
  varieties : 1.5
  versus works : 1.36
  without human authors : 3.16
metadata
  definition : 20.4
  Dublin Core. formats versus media : 3.30; role in surrogates : 14.17
  for Dublin Core website : 20.27
  internal. record formats using Dublin Core : sec. 20.5
  versus bibliographic records : 20.30
metadata records
  using Dublin Core. example : sec. 20.5.2; by Joseph (Michael) : 20.35
metadata schemas : sec. 20.5.2
  examples : 20.43
  interoperability : 20.38; standards : 20.40
  isolation versus consensus : 20.37
  number : 20.36
methodological approaches
  as non-topical feature : sec. 3.7
  as searchable feature : sec. 3.7
  as topic versus feature : 2.64
  in documentary scope for indexing and abstracting services : 3.65
  in literary study : 3.39
  in subject scope vs documentary scope : 2.63
methods
  for analysis. of messages : sec. 1.5.6; of documents, messages, texts : chap. 8; examples : sec. 8.6; for book indexes : sec. 8.6.1; for digital libraries : sec. 8.6.3; for full-text encyclopedias : sec. 8.6.3; for indexing and abstracting services : sec. 8.6.2
  for analysis in human indexing : 8.27; British standards : 8.92; international standards : 8.92
  for arrangement of retrieved documentary units : 12.288
  for combination of index terms : sec. 1.5.8, 1.156
  for searching of indexes : sec. 1.5.4
  for selection of index terms : sec. 1.5.7
Michel (Dee)
  and Kuhr (Pat). compilation of term relationships : 13.186
microfilm
  computer-output. as media for IR databases : 5.22
microforms
  as media for IR databases : 1.175, sec. 5.2
microthesauri
  in *Eurovoc thesaurus* : 13.108
  in *Unesco thesaurus* (1995) : 13.99
Milstead (Jessica L.)
  acknowledgments : 0.14
  foreword : sec. 0.1
  views on IR database design : 0.7
minor terms
  vocabulary management : 8.193
MLA International Bibliography : 2.54
  faceted classification : 19.38; facet arrangement : 12.211; syntax : 12.203
  faceted index headings. examples : 12.140
  opening screen. subject scope : 2.74
  record formats : sec. 20.2
  rules for indexing : 8.98

Index

models
  for databases. flat file databases : 1.18; hypertext databases : 1.19; object-oriented databases : 1.17; relational databases : 1.16
Modern Language Association of America. *see: MLA international bibliography*
monitoring
  of documentary domain : sec. 4.2
monographic databases : 1.187
monographic series : 3.35
monographs
  as examples of IR databases : 1.191
  IR databases for : 1.162
  revised frequently. versus serials : 3.34
  versus books : 3.36
  versus serials as non-topical features : sec. 3.5
  versus serials as searchable features : sec. 3.5
motion pictures
  and video recordings. documentary units : 6.9
  IR databases for : 1.165
multi-word phrases
  in permuted syntax : 12.247
multiformats
  versus multimedia : 3.32
multimedia
  for book indexes : 5.33
  versus multiformats : 3.32
Mulvany (Nancy)
  views on human indexing : 8.33
music
  documentary units : 6.10
  formats : 3.25
  genres : 3.25
  IR databases for : 1.169
  styles versus genres : 3.25
musical symbols
  role in index terms : 1.129

name authorities
  MARC formats. examples : 20.8
names
  for actions : 2.31
narrower-term cross references : 13.46, 56
  in *Library of Congress subject headings* : 12.41
narrower terms
  equivalent-term cross references for. in book indexes : 13.243
  NT as notation for : 13.56
  versus related terms in syndetic structure : 13.57
  versus related terms in thesauri : 13.57
narrowing
  of searches with exact match syntax : 12.289
national authority file
  for *Library of Congress subject headings* : 12.55
National Information Standards Organization (NISO). *see:* **NISO**
natural language syntax : sec. 12.2.5
  adequacy of collocation : 12.232
  compared to ad hoc string syntax : 12.171
  criteria for evaluation : 12.230
  effectiveness : 12.227, 229
  in digital libraries : 12.228
  in keyword indexes : 12.233
  versus permuted syntax : 12.246
  word pairs : 12.243

natural language text
  as source for index headings : 12.225
nature
  messages from : 3.16
navigation
  browsing : 11.11
needs
  versus wants in information retrieval : 8.106
needs assessment
  not in scope of this book : 1.9
negative vocabulary control : 8.149
NEPHIS (Nested Phrase Indexing System)
  as example of ad hoc string syntax : 12.172
  coding examples : 12.174
  index headings. examples : 12.175
  notation : 12.173
  syntax algorithm. explanation : 12.176
  use for book indexes : 12.177
Nested Phrase Indexing System. *see:* **NEPHIS (Nested Phrase Indexing System)**
new users
  versus frequent users : 1.10
Nielsen (Jakob)
  views on scrolling : 19.66
NISO (National Information Standards Organization)
  executive director. acknowledgment : 0.14, 15
  standards for alphanumeric arrangement : 1.86
NISO Committee YY
  members. acknowledgment : 0.14, 15
  new standard for indexes : 0.4, 1.95
non-book media
  locators for : 15.13
non-displayed indexes : 1.140
  advantages : 11.14
  characteristics : 11.12, 12.270
  definition : 12.279
  design : sec. 11.3
  disadvantages : 11.16
  for electronic books : 13.252
  history : 11.7
  inverted files : 11.8, 12.271
  role of search interfaces : 1.104
  searches. presentation of suggestions for vocabulary management : 13.253
  syntax. alternative options : 12.296; major types : 12.280
  terminology for : 1.103; opposition from American Society for Information Science : 1.102
  versus displayed indexes : chap. 11, 11.2; differences : 12.10; examples : sec. 11.4; for books : sec. 11.4.1; in digital libraries : sec. 11.4.3; in encyclopedias : sec. 11.4.3; in indexing and abstracting services : sec. 11.4.2; calculation of exhaustivity : 9.22; syntax : 11.9
  versus vocabulary lists : 12.276
  vocabulary lists versus indexes : 11.13
  vocabulary management for indexing and abstracting services in electronic media : 13.262
non-displayed searching
  in electronic media : 5.25
non-language texts
  versus language texts. automatic indexing : 8.5
non-topical features
  as searchable features : 3.11
  audience : sec. 3.6
  authors and authorship : sec. 3.1

non-topical features *(continued)*
  biases : 3.40
  combined with topics in searches : 3.7
  continuing and integrating resources : sec. 3.5
  examples : 3.10
  formats : sec. 3.4
  genres : sec. 3.4
  identification in human indexing : 8.108
  importance for experts : 3.8
  in subject scope analysis : 2.56
  language : sec. 3.8
  levels of treatment : sec. 3.6
  media : sec. 3.3
  methodological approaches : sec. 3.7
  monographs versus serials : sec. 3.5
  periodicity : sec. 3.5
  place of publication : sec. 3.9
  point of view : sec. 3.7
  role in relevance judgments : 3.9
  terminology : 3.66
  time of publication : sec. 3.10
  titles : sec. 3.2
  versus topics : sec. 3.13; clear distinctions : 3.49
notation
  and captions for classification : 17.63
  BT for broader terms : 13.61
  for classification : 17.64, 115; types : 17.116; in call numbers : 15.40; in *Unesco thesaurus* (1977) : 13.89
  for relational syntax : 12.187
  for thesauri. translation into natural human language : 13.59
  in NEPHIS : 12.173
  in *Unesco thesaurus* (1977) : 13.90
  in *Universal decimal classification*. examples : 12.216; compared to relational syntax : 12.217
  NT for narrower terms : 13.56
  retroactive. for classification of library and information science : 17.117
  role in classification systems : 12.212; in display of classification : 17.68
  RT for related terms : 13.64
  UF for un-used terms : 13.52
novels
  indexes to : 1.120
novices
  versus experts : 1.10; interfaces for. views of Raskin (Jef) : 19.59
NT
  as notation for narrower terms : 13.56
numbering
  of paragraphs : 6.15; methods : 15.8
numbers
  in alphanumeric arrangement : 17.18
  role in index terms : 1.125
  treatment in automatic indexing : 8.139

object-oriented databases
  as models for databases : 1.17
objects
  versus agents in subject scope analysis : 2.30
O'Connor (Brian)
  views on human indexing : 8.47
odds-payoff indexing chart : 8.119
online access
  for IR databases : sec. 5.3.1
online public access catalogs. *see:* **OPACs**

Index

ontologies : sec. 13.3.5
  categories. views of Poli (Roberto) : 13.228; of Sowa (John) : 13.227
  compilation : 13.235
  conceptual levels : 13.233
  definition : 13.221
  for business : 13.234
  for machine translation : 13.233
  versus knowledge organization systems. views of Hjerppe (Roland) : 13.226
  versus thesauri : 13.225; categories : 13.230; term relationships : 13.230
  views of Vickery (Brian C.) : 13.232, 236
  weak structures : 13.231
OPACs
  related term to consider: **library catalogs**
  cross references : 13.49; omission : 13.73
  display of subject headings : 1.90
  equivalent-term cross references. form : 13.55
opening screens
  for indexing and abstracting services. subject scope : 2.95
  for IR databases. design features : 19.70; examples : 19.71
  MLA international bibliography. subject scope : 2.74
  of world-wide websites as indexable matter : sec. 7.1.7
  presentation of subject scope : 2.72
  Queer resources directory. subject scope : 2.73
  topics versus features : 2.75
operations
  and processes.
    categories in end-user thesauri : 13.163
  in subject scope analysis : 2.29
  versus processes in subject scope analysis : 2.35
optical coincidence IR systems. *see:* **peek-a-boo IR systems**

pages
  versus paragraphs as documentary units : 6.12, 12.315
painters
  indexes to : 1.116
paper formats
  for IR databases : 5.6
paper media
  advantages. for reading : 5.12
  for IR databases : 1.174, sec. 5.1; as favored medium : 5.5; for special types : 5.17
  postcoordinate indexing systems : 5.18
  versus electronic media. cost : 5.15; for IR databases : 5.14
paradigms
  of information science : 8.59
paragraph numbers
  as locators : 15.45
paragraphs
  as documentary units : 6.17; advantages : 6.13; NISO recommendations : 6.15; for electronic texts : 6.14
  lead (initial). as basis for indexing : 1.133; as indexable matter : sec. 7.1.4, 7.29
  numbering : 6.15; methods : 15.8
  versus pages as documentary units : 6.12, 12.315

parentheses
  treatment in automatic indexing : 8.137
parts of entities
  in subject scope analysis : 2.24
parts of documents
  versus complete documents : 6.5
passage retrieval
  analysis of full texts : 21.59
peek-a-boo IR systems : sec. 5.1.3, 5.19
  boolean searches : 5.20
Pérez-Carballo (José)
  as co-author : 0.10
Pérez-López (Kathleen Golitko)
  views on automatic indexing of image texts : 8.111
periods (full stops, dots). *see:* **full stops (dots, periods)**
periodicals
  IR databases for : 1.161
periodicity
  as non-topical feature, as searchable feature : sec. 3.5
  in documentary scope for indexing and abstracting services : 3.55
  of IR databases : sec. 1.5.13
permuted indexes
  nonsensical index headings : 12.250
permuted syntax : sec. 12.2.6
  definition : 12.245
  example : 12.248
  multi-word phrases : 12.247
  versus natural language syntax : 12.246
Persistent Uniform Resource Locator (PURL) : 15.35
personal IR databases
  software : 22.8
Peters (Ronnie)
  views on search interfaces : 19.63
photographic media
  IR databases for : 1.165
phrases
  from full text for end-user thesauri : 13.146; identification : 13.143
  identification in automatic indexing : 8.181, 185 (cost versus benefits : 8.180); in searching : 8.181
  in automatic indexing : sec. 8.3.8; importance : 8.178
  in KWAC indexes : 12.242
  in KWOC indexes : 12.240
  role in browsing : 8.186
physical formats
  versus presentation formats : 3.31
pictures
  IR databases for : 1.167
place of publication
  as non-topical feature, as searchable features : sec. 3.9
  in documentary scope for indexing and abstracting services : 3.58
placement
  of cross references. examples : 12.264
places
  examples in subject scope analysis : 2.48
  facets for. arrangement : 17.92
  in subject scope analysis : 2.37
  indexes to : 1.117
  versus topics. subdivisions in *Library of Congress subject headings* : 12.37

plural "s" suffixes
  stemming : 8.157
PMEST
  acronyms for facets : 2.77, 78
poems, poetry
  indexes to : 1.120
  IR databases for : 1.163
points of view
  as non-topical feature, as searchable features : sec. 3.7
  in documentary scope : 3.47; for indexing and abstracting services : 3.65
Poli (Roberto)
  views on categories in ontologies : 13.228
political aspects
  of information retrieval : 8.107
Pollitt (A. Steven, et al.)
  work on display of thesauri for searching : 13.31
postcoordinate combination
  and precoordinate combination of index terms : 1.159
  of index terms : 1.158
postcoordinate indexing systems
  on paper media : 5.18
postcoordinate search statements : 12.9
  versus precoordinate index headings : 1.66
postcoordinate syntax : sec. 12.1, sec. 12.3
  definition : 1.65, 12.273
  links : 12.275
  used with precoordinate syntax : 12.274
  versus precoordinate syntax : 12.269
postcoordination
  versus precoordination. views of Svenonius (Elaine) : 12.11
postings data
  dynamic. in faceted relational classified displayed indexes : 13.33, 17.99
  for categories versus descriptors : 17.98
  for indexing and abstracting services in electronic media : 15.55
  in cross references : 13.50
  in display of classification : 17.69
  in displayed indexes for electronic books : 17.127
  in indexes for electronic books : 15.50
  indicators for hypertext locators : 15.12
  locators as indicators : 15.11
  number and specificity : 10.8
PRECIS
  as example of faceted syntax : 12.133
precision
  and recall : sec. 9.1; impact of exhaustivity : 9.9; of exhaustivity : sec. 9.1.3; of specificity : sec. 10.5; inverse relationship : 9.15
  definition : sec. 9.1.2
  high-precision. role of automatic indexing : 9.20; of high-threshold indexing : 9.18; of human indexing : 9.20
  impact of specificity : 10.35; of syntax : 12.3 (examples : 12.4)
precoordinate combination
  and postcoordinate combination of index terms : 1.159
  of index terms : 1.157
precoordinate index headings : 12.8
  versus postcoordinate search statements : 1.66
precoordinate index terms
  role in search statements : 1.67

Index

precoordinate indexing languages
criteria : 12.15
precoordinate syntax : sec. 12.1, sec. 12.2
definition : 1.65
purpose. views of Craven (Timothy) : 12.14
used with postcoordinate syntax : 12.274
versus postcoordinate syntax : 12.269
precoordination
versus postcoordination. views of Svenonius (Elaine) : 12.11
predictability
of index headings : 12.156
preferred terms
in thesauri. choice : 13.204
versus gathering terms in thesauri : 13.203
preliminary matter
as indexable matter : sec. 7.1.3
prepositions
in ad hoc syntax : 12.255
presentation
of indexes : sec. 1.5.4
of IR databases : 1.141
presentation formats
versus media formats : 3.31; physical formats : 3.31
primary sources
versus secondary sources for IR databases : sec. 4.1
principles
for application of subject heading systems : 12.113
for coextensive index headings in string syntax : 12.120
for coextensive subject headings in subject heading systems : 12.115
for consistency in subject heading systems : 12.109
for construction of subject heading systems : 12.103
for design of record formats : 20.3
for homonymy in subject heading systems : 12.106
for literary warrant in subject heading systems : 12.111
for naming in subject heading systems : 12.110
for selection of documents for IR databases : 4.5
for semantics in subject heading systems : 12.107
for specific index headings in string syntax : 12.120
for specific subject headings in subject heading systems : 12.115
for subject heading systems : sec. 12.2.1.2
for subject indexing policy in subject heading systems : 12.114
for synonymy in subject heading systems : 12.105
for syntax in subject heading systems : 12.108
for uniform headings in subject heading systems : 12.104
for user needs in subject heading systems : 12.112
print displays
visual resolution : 17.41
print interfaces. *see:* **search interfaces**
print media
alphanumeric indexes. preference for : 19.15
book indexes. interface designs : 19.83; vocabulary management : 13.238

print media *(continued)*
display of faceted classification : sec. 17.3.2.1; of surrogates for author searches : 16.37; for subject searches : 16.36
displayed indexes. type size : 18.17; for indexing and abstracting services : 17.128
indexing and abstracting services. comprehensive searches : 12.329; displayed indexes : 17.128 (based on automatic indexing : 12.329); interface designs : 19.92; internal locators : 15.53; KWIC indexes. examples : 12.330; search interfaces : 19.6; use of enumerative classification : 19.14; vocabulary management : 13.258
relational classified displays. citation order of facets : 17.74
search interfaces : sec. 19.1, 19.2
surrogates. display : 16.35; staged display : 16.2
print media IR databases
search options : 19.13
printed books
indexes. alphanumeric. display : 17.122; size : 18.1
relational classified displays : 17.123
surrogates. display : 16.24; unified surrogates : 16.27
printed indexes
vocabulary management : 19.17
probabilistic model
for automatic indexing : 8.128
for best match syntax : 12.297
probabilistic rules
for human indexing : sec. 8.2.2.2
processes
and attributes versus abstract entities in subject scope analysis : 2.20
and operations. categories in end-user thesauri : 13.163
in subject scope analysis : 2.34
versus operations in subject scope analysis : 2.35
proper nouns
in indexing : 8.179
role in index terms : 1.124
properties
in subject scope analysis : 2.27
proximity requirements
use in searches in indexing and abstracting services in electronic media : 12.326
pseudo relevance feedback : 8.235
Psychological abstracts
example of ad hoc syntax with systematic syntax : 12.262
publications
related to this book : 0.6
Publisher Item Identifier (PII) : 15.17
examples : 15.18
publishers
indexes to : 1.115
punctuation
in alphanumeric arrangement : 17.16
in automatic indexing : 8.133
purpose
of information retrieval for diverse users : 8.104
of subject scope analysis : 2.85
of this book : 0.1, 11, sec. 1.1, pt2.1

qualifiers
for core elements of Dublin Core : sec. 20.5.1
qualitative criteria
in documentary scope : sec. 3.12; for indexing and abstracting services : 3.61
objective. in documentary scope : 3.46
qualitative judgments
in request-oriented human indexing : 8.102
qualitative studies
of IR databases : 22.18
Queer resources directory
opening screen. subject scope : 2.73
queer theory : 8.82
compared to indexing theory : 8.81
quotations
indexes to : 1.117

Ranganathan (Shiyali Ramamrita)
facet analysis : sec. 2.3, 2.13
facets for diesel engines : 2.79
rules for indexing about diesel engines : 8.99
views on arrangement of facets : 2.78
ranking
absence in exact match syntax : 12.287
in best match syntax : 12.300
of related terms by frequency of co-occurrence : 8.202
of texts. use of word frequency : 8.150
Raskin (Jef)
views on icons : 19.58; on interfaces for experts versus novices : 19.59
reading
media. advantages of paper : 5.12
versus searching on electronic media : 5.13
recall
and precision : sec. 9.1; impact of exhaustivity : sec. 9.1.3, 9.9; of specificity : sec. 10.5; inverse relationship : 9.15
definition : sec. 9.1.1
high-recall. role of automatic indexing : 9.19
impact of specificity : 10.36
impossibility of calculation : 9.11
versus relative recall : 9.12
record formats : chap. 20
design. principles : 20.3
examples : sec. 20.7
fields for book indexes : 20.44; for document descriptions : 20.18; for facets of literature : 20.19
for a class IR database : sec. 20.4
for *America: history and life* : sec. 20.3
for book indexes : sec. 20.7.1
for book indexes in electronic media : 20.48
for digital libraries : sec. 20.7.3
for electronic encyclopedias : sec. 20.7.3
for *Historical abstracts* : sec. 20.3
for indexing and abstracting services : sec. 20.7.2; versus MARC formats : 20.15
for internal metadata using Dublin Core : sec. 20.5
for literature : 20.17
for *MLA international bibliography* : sec. 20.2
for rotated term syntax : 20.21
purpose : 20.2
reference citations
as basis for indexing : 1.136
as indexable matter : sec. 7.1.6

Index

reference IR databases : 1.180
  definition : 1.32
  documentary units versus surrogates : 6.26
  smaller documentary units : 6.29
reference librarians
  facet analysis : 2.42
related-term cross references : 13.46, 64
  in *Library of Congress subject headings* : 12.44
related terms
  related term to consider: **associative relationships**
  identification by term co-occurrence : 8.201
  ranking by frequency of co-occurrence : 8.202
  RT as notation for : 13.64
  versus narrower terms in syndetic structure : 13.57; in thesauri : 13.57
relational classified displays : sec. 17.3, 17.4
  advantages : 17.7
  for printed books : 17.123
  in end-user thesauri : 13.214
  in hypertext. research : 17.56
  in print media. citation order of facets : 17.74
  in *Unesco thesaurus* (1977) : 13.95
  of displayed indexes : 1.145
  on world-wide web : 17.60
  role in information retrieval : 17.57
  versus alphanumeric displays : 17.8, 48
relational databases
  as model for databases : 1.16
relational indexing
  views of Farradane (Jason) : 12.185
relational syntax : sec. 12.2.3
  display : 12.189
  notation : 12.187; compared to *Universal decimal classification* : 12.217
  relational indicators : 12.186
  use : 12.188
relevance
  definition : 1.77, 9.13
  judges of : 1.78
relevance feedback
  in automatic indexing : sec. 8.3.13
  in filtering : 8.233
  in selective dissemination of information : 8.233
  procedures : 8.231
  pseudo : 8.235
  purpose : 8.229
relevance judgments
  role of non-topical features : 3.9
  role of user attributes : 3.10
request-oriented human indexing
  qualitative judgments : 8.102
research
  experimental. on end-user thesauri : 13.23
  field. on use of thesauri : 13.24
  lack of. on alphanumeric arrangement : 1.87, 88
  on automatic indexing versus human indexing : sec. 8.1
  on browsing in IR : sec. 11.2
  on classification : 17.55
  on clustering of terms for vocabulary management : 13.219
  on information seeking : 13.13
  on relational classified displays in hypertext : 17.56
  on solutions for vocabulary problems : 13.21
  on surrogate display : 16.5

research (continued)
  on syndetic structure. proposal : 13.75
  on term relationships in thesauri : 13.187
  on vocabulary problems : sec. 13.2
  versus standards. views of Saracevic (Tefko) : 1.89
research fronts
  identification by co-citation : 8.227
retrieved documentary units
  arrangement. methods : 12.288
retroactive notation
  for classification of library and information science : 17.117
Rice, (Ronald E.)
  and Chang (Shan-Ju). views on browsing : 11.30
role definers
  in faceted syntax : 12.135, 144
role facets
  versus type facets in citation order of facets : 17.111
role indicators
  in faceted syntax : 12.134
roles
  use in subject scope analysis : 2.67
  versus hierarchical relationships : 10.31
roman numerals
  in alphanumeric arrangement : 17.12
rotated term syntax : sec. 12.2.2.1
  clarity : 12.129
  collocation : 12.149
  compared to faceted syntax : 12.132, 145
  dates (time). treatment : 12.124
  definitions : 12.122
  examples : 12.123
  in *America history & life* : 12.126
  locators : 12.125
  record formats : 20.21
RT
  as notation for related terms : 13.64
rules
  for analysis in human indexing : 8.91
  for human indexing : sec. 8.2.2; domain analysis as basis : 8.105; limitations : 8.101; relation to subject scope and documentary scope : 8.96; of Cooper (William S.). views of Frohmann (Bernd) : 8.114; role of decision theory : 8.116; of gedanken experimentation : 8.116; of utility theory : 8.116; views of Frohmann (Bernd) : 8.103 of image texts : sec. 8.2.2.1; specialized : 8.97
  for indexing about diesel engines by Ranganathan : 8.99; for *MLA international bibliography* : 8.98
run-in layout
  versus indented layout for book indexes : 18.18
Rutgers University
  guidelines for analysis in cataloging and classification : 8.93

Saracevic (Tefko)
  views on research versus standards : 1.89
scatter-gather clustering : 8.218
science fiction
  indexes to : 1.120
scientific research
  related term to consider: **research**
  versus standards : 1.79

scope
  of this book : 0.2, 1.203; exclusion of databases for concrete entities and events : 1.198
  versus specificity of index terms : 10.3
scope notes
  in displayed indexes : 12.261
screens
  opening. *see:* **opening screens**
scrolling
  in hypertext displays : 17.32
  views of Nielsen (Jakob) : 19.66
sculptors
  indexes to : 1.116
search decision trees
  for *Library of Congress subject headings* : 12.81
search engines
  world-wide web. role of indexable matter : 7.14
search interfaces : chap. 19
  and visualization. views of Hearst (Marti A.) : 19.50
  customization : 19.61; views of Head (Alison J.) : 19.62
  decoration : 19.65
  electronic interfaces. versus print interfaces. comparison : 19.39
  examples : 19.53
  for electronic IR databases : sec. 19.2; problems and opportunities : 19.35
  for experts versus novices. views of Raskin (Jef) : 19.59
  for indexing and abstracting services in print media : 19.6
  for IR databases in electronic media : sec. 19.4
  for print media : sec. 19.1, 19.2
  guidelines : 19.69
  impact : 19.3
  importance : 19.1
  integration of thesauri : 13.26
  role in non-displayed indexes : 1.104
  separation from content of IR databases : 19.37
  views of Peters (Ronnie) : 19.63; of Shneiderman (Ben) : 19.67
search options
  for digital libraries : 12.340
  for electronic encyclopedias : 12.340
  in end-user thesauri : 13.212
  in print media IR databases : 19.13
search statements
  as source of terms for end-user thesauri : 13.131
  multiple terms. suggestions for vocabulary management : 13.263
  postcoordinate : 12.9
  purpose : 12.7
  role of precoordinate index terms : 1.67
  syntax : chap. 12; definition : 1.63
  versus index headings : 11.1; syntax : 12.1, 6
search terms
  mapping to controlled vocabulary : 13.28
searchable features
  audience : sec. 3.6
  biases : 3.40
  continuing and integrating resources as - : sec. 3.5
  formats : sec. 3.4
  genres : sec. 3.4

Index

searchable features *(continued)*
  in documentary scope for indexing and abstracting services : 3.62
  language : sec. 3.8
  levels of treatment : sec. 3.6
  media : sec. 3.3
  methodological approaches : sec. 3.7
  monographs versus serials : sec. 3.5
  non-topical features : 3.11
  periodicity : sec. 3.5
  place of publication : sec. 3.9
  point of view : sec. 3.7
  time of publication : sec. 3.10
  titles : sec. 3.2
  types of authors and creators : 3.13
  types of corporate bodies : 3.15
searchers
  and indexers. variability of vocabulary : 13.17
searches
  boolean. peek-a-boo (optical coincidence) IR systems : 5.20
  broad-scoped. versus narrow-scoped searches : 10.34
  comprehensive. in indexing and abstracting services in electronic media : 12.322; in print media : 12.329
  exact-match. *Library of Congress subject headings* : 12.66
  for known items with known vocabulary : 13.4; with unknown vocabulary : 13.5
  for unknown items with known vocabulary : 13.8; with unknown vocabulary : 13.9; and vague concepts : 13.10
  in non-displayed indexes. presentation of suggestions for vocabulary management : 13.253
  narrow-scoped. versus broad-scoped searches : 10.34
  narrowing with exact match syntax : 12.289
  non-topical features combined with topics : 3.7
  of exploration : 13.11
  of full texts in HTML : 21.40
  selective. in indexing and abstracting services : 12.331
  targeted. in indexing and abstracting services in electronic media : 12.327
  use of clustering in indexing and abstracting services in electronic media : 12.328
  use of proximity requirements in indexing and abstracting services in electronic media : 12.326
  use of truncation of indexing and abstracting services in electronic media : 12.325
searching
  by means of classification systems : 12.194; clusters : 8.211
  display of thesauri : 13.30; work of Pollitt (A. Steven, et al.) : 13.31
  feedback : 8.228
  full-text. documentary units : 6.42; of books in electronic media (syntax : 12.320)
  identification of phrases : 8.181
  inconsistency : 8.66
  non-displayed. in electronic media : 5.25
  of indexes. methods : sec. 1.5.4
  versus browsing using *Medical subject headings* : 12.101
  versus reading on electronic media : 5.13
  with end-user thesauri : 13.215
Sear's list of subject headings : 12.97

secondary sources
  for IR databases : 4.7; versus primary sources : sec. 4.1
see-also references : 13.45
  related terms to consider: **narrower-term cross references; broader-term cross references; related-term cross references**
  for equivalent terms in automatic indexing : 13.259
  from unused headings : 19.33
  general : 13.67
  in book indexes : 13.245
  omission : 13.47
  placement : 19.20, 31
  presentation in displayed indexes in electronic media : 13.251
  problems : 19.18
  terminology : 19.19, 25
see references. *see:* **equivalent-term cross references**
selection
  of documents for IR databases. principles : 4.5
  of index terms. methods : sec. 1.5.7
  of useful documents by advisory groups and indexing staff : 8.250
selective dissemination of information
  relevance feedback : 8.233
selective searches
  in indexing and abstracting services : 12.331
semantics principle.
  for subject heading systems : 12.107
serial databases : 1.188
Serial Item & Contribution Identifier (SICI) : 15.19
  examples : 15.20
serials
  versus monographs as non-topical feature : sec. 3.5; as searchable feature : sec. 3.5
  versus revised monographs : 3.34
series
  monographic - : 3.35
SGML
  definition : 21.21
  ISO standard : 21.22
  relationship with HTML and XML : 21.43
  software : 21.55
  views of Hockey (Susan) : 21.31
shelf arrangement
  citation order of facets : 17.74
Shneiderman (Ben)
  views on search interfaces : 19.67
short stories
  indexes to : 1.120
signals
  definitions : 1.42
single characters
  treatment in automatic indexing : 8.142
single documents
  IR databases for. documentary scope descriptions : 3.5
size
  of book indexes : sec. 18.1.1; estimation : 18.8 (accuracy : 18.10; problems : 18.11; as guideline for indexing : 18.12); reduction : 18.15
  of computer screens : 19.64
  of displayed indexes : chap. 18, sec. 18.1

size *(continued)*
  of documentary units : 6.3; impact on indexable matter : 7.6; relationship to exhaustivity : 9.5; among variables in IR research : 8.10; in full texts in digital media : 21.58
  of indexes. determination : 18.2; estimation : 18.3; impact of syntax : 12.184; relationship to document size : 18.14; for digital libraries : sec. 18.1.3; for electronic encyclopedias : sec. 18.1.3; for indexing and abstracting services : sec. 18.1.2; for printed books : 18.1
  of surrogates : 14.5
  of thesauri. impact of bound terms : 13.174;
  of vocabulary for indexing. impact of specificity : sec. 10.6
slashes
  treatment in automatic indexing : 8.135
slides (photographic)
  IR databases for : 1.165
social construction
  of gender : 8.86
  of indexing rules. application of views of Wittgenstein (Ludwig) : 8.80
  versus cognition in human indexing : sec. 8.2.1
social constructionism
  versus essentialism in gender studies : 8.83
social context
  of human indexing. views of Frohmann (Bernd) : 8.88
societies
  versus institutions in descriptive cataloging : 2.19
Sociological abstracts
  table of contents : 19.11
sociology
  indexing and abstracting services : 19.11
Soergel (Dagobert)
  views on construction of thesauri : 13.83; on human indexing : 8.44; on Ontologies : 13.223
software
  for digital libraries : 22.7
  for indexing and abstracting services : 22.5
  for IR databases : 1.205, 22.4; in libraries : 22.6
  for personal IR databases : 22.8
sorting. *see:* **arrangement**
sound media
  for IR databases : 1.177
sound recordings
  IR databases for : 1.169
sound texts
  and image texts. terminology : 8.113
  versus language texts. automatic indexing : 8.126
Sowa (John)
  views on categories in ontologies : 13.227
spaces
  in alphanumeric arrangement : 17.15
Sparck Jones (Karen)
  views on specificity : 10.22
special interest groups
  as sources of facets for library and information science : 17.77
  of American Library Association : 17.79
  of American Society for Information Science and Technology : 17.77

Index

specialized categories
role in human indexing : 8.100
specialized domains
faceted syntax : 12.139
specialized rules
for human indexing : 8.97
specific documents
in documentary scope for indexing and abstracting services : 3.60
specific index heading principle
in string syntax : 12.120
specific subject heading principle
for subject heading systems : 12.115
specificity
among variables in IR research : 8.12a
and number of postings : 10.8
as closeness of relationship between index term and topic : 10.1
definitions : sec. 10.1, 10.6, 16
examples : sec. 10.3, sec. 10.8
hierarchical : 10.24
impact. on recall : 10.36; of free uncontrolled vocabulary : 10.41; of vocabulary control : 10.39; on precision : 10.35; on precision and recall : sec. 10.5; on size of vocabulary for indexing : sec. 10.6;
in *Library of Congress subject headings* : 10.18
interactions with exhaustivity and vocabulary management : 10.44
of index terms in book indexes : sec. 10.8.1 (assigned by automatic indexing: 10.51; assigned by human indexing : 10.50); in digital libraries : sec. 10.8.3; in encyclopedias : sec. 10.8.3; in indexing and abstracting services : sec. 10.8.2
of vocabulary for indexing : chap. 10
operational : 10.8, 9; versus semantic specificity : 10.11
practical : sec. 10.4
semantic. versus operational specificity : 10.11
statement/heading : sec. 10.7
versus broader-narrower cross references : 10.19; exhaustivity of indexing : sec. 10.2; scope of index terms : 10.3; syntax : sec. 10.7; up-posting and generic posting : 10.19; vocabulary of users : 10.33
views of Balnaves (John) : 10.16; of Cutter (Charles Ammi) : 10.4; of Library of Congress : 10.5; of Sparck Jones (Karen) : 10.22; of Svenonius (Elaine) : 10.7; of Weinberg (Bella Hass) : 10.24; of Wilson (Patrick) : 10.18
stability
versus chaos and creativity in IR database design : 1.107
standards
absence of. resulting responsibility of information professionals : 1.109
for alphanumeric arrangement : 1.82, 17.14; lack of consensus : 1.91; *A.L.A. filing rules* : 1.85; *Library of Congress filing rules* : 1.83; NISO : 1.86
for analysis in human indexing : 8.92
for cataloging : 1.80
for classification : 1.80
for display of indexes : 19.16
for identification of authors : 14.11

standards (continued)
for indexes. endorsement by American Society for Information Science : 1.99; impossibility : 1.106; lack of consensus : 1.105; objections of American Society of Indexers : 1.97; opposition : 1.96 (from American Society for Information Science : 1.100); role of NISO Committee YY : 0.4, 1.95
for indexing : 1.81
for information retrieval : 1.94
for interoperability of metadata schemas : 20.40; of vocabulary data : 20.41
for IR database design : sec. 1.4
for surrogates : sec. 14.2, 14.10
for thesauri. views on bound terms : 13.170
impossibility. in periods of instability : 1.108
versus research. views of Saracevic (Tefko) : 1.89; scientific research : 1.79
star clusters : 8.214
static clustering : 8.218, 219
stemming
automatic. user options : 12.324
for automatic indexing : sec. 8.3.6
identification of word roots : 8.156
impact : 8.159; on frequency of words : 8.155
of multiple suffixes : 8.158
of plural "s" suffixes : 8.157
stop list terms
in end-user thesauri : 13.152
stop lists
as negative vocabulary control : sec. 8.3.3
choice of words : 8.147
for reducing size of indexes : 8.146
number of words : 8.148
user-defined. : 12.323
string clusters : 8.213
string indexing
display in hypertext : 17.40
string indexing syntax : sec. 12.2.2
coextensive index headings : 12.127, 128; principles : 12.120
compared to subject heading syntax : 12.127
definition : 12.118
eliminability principle : 12.128
objectives : 12.183
specific index headings. principles : 12.120
structured data : 1.25
style
for bibliographic citations : 0.17
styles
versus genres in music : 3.25
subdivision
by place versus topic. in *Library of Congress subject headings* : 12.37
practices. in *Library of Congress subject headings* : 12.25
subdivisions, subheadings
arrangement : 1.84; in *Library of Congress subject headings* : 12.53
categorization. in *Library of Congress subject headings* : 12.58
in *Library of Congress subject headings* : 12.60; conference on future : 12.52
subheadings. *see:* subdivisions, subheadings
subject analysis and indexing.
expert systems. examples. MedIndEx : 8.238; use of checktags : 8.239
in indexing and abstracting services : sec. 8.4

subject cataloging
definition : 1.54
subject domain : chap. 2
of IR databases : 2.10
versus subject scope : 2.3
subject domain analysis
functions : 2.5
necessary detail : 2.2
value : 2.6
subject domain description
goals : 2.9
subject heading syntax : sec. 12.2.1
compared to string syntax : 12.127
subject heading systems
principles : sec. 12.2.1.2; principles for: application : 12.113; coextensive subject headings : 12.115; consistency : 12.109; construction : 12.103; homonymy : 12.106; literary warrant : 12.111; naming : 12.110; semantics : 12.107; specific subject headings : 12.115; subject indexing policy : 12.114; synonymy : 12.105; syntax : 12.108; uniform headings : 12.104; user needs : 12.112
subject headings

> *related terms to consider:* **Library of Congress subject headings; Medical subject headings; Sear's list of subject headings**

alphanumeric arrangement : 17.22
development in 19th century : 12.16
display in hypertext : 17.35, 39; in OPACs : 1.90
future : 12.116
in the United States : 12.17
types in *Library of Congress subject headings* : 12.19
versus terms in syndetic structure : 13.42
subject indexing
definition : 1.54
subject indexing policy principle.
for subject heading systems : 12.114
subject scope : chap. 2
and documentary scope. relation to rules for human indexing : 8.96
presentation : sec. 2.2; on opening screens : 2.72; for indexing and abstracting services : 2.94, 95; for *MLA international bibliography* : 2.74; for *Queer resources directory* : 2.73
specialized categories for folklore : 2.55; for language : 2.55; for linguistics : 2.55; for literature : 2.53, 54
versus documentary scope : 2.57, 62, 3.1; role of author processes : 2.58; methodological approaches : 2.63
versus indexable matter : sec. 7.2; subject domain : 2.3
subject scope analysis
abstract entities versus attributes and processes : 2.20
actions : 2.28
agents versus objects : 2.30
and subject domain analysis. functions : 2.5; necessary detail : 2.2; value : 2.6
attributes : 2.25
avoiding meaningless categories : 2.51
complex phenomena. insurance as example : 2.39
concrete entities versus abstract entities : 2.17

612

Index

subject scope analysis *(continued)*
  constituent materials : 2.26
  entities : 2.16
  events : 2.36
  examples : sec. 2.5; of actions : 2.46; of attributes : 2.45; of entities : 2.44; of events : 2.47; of places : 2.48; of time : 2.49
  expression of categories : 2.50
  facets : 2.83
  for artistic works versus critical works : 2.69; book indexes : sec. 2.5.1, 2.88; digital libraries : sec. 2.5.3; for full-text encyclopedias : sec. 2.5.3; for indexing and abstracting services : sec. 2.5.2; for this book : 2.91
  functions : 2.1
  generic categories. role : 2.12
  goals : 2.4, 2.43
  non-topical features : 2.56
  number of categories : 2.8
  operations : 2.29
  parts of entities : 2.24
  places : 2.37
  processes : 2.34
  processes versus operations : 2.35
  properties : 2.27
  purpose : 2.85
  specialized categories : sec. 2.1
  time : 2.38
  topical groupings versus facets : 2.80, 84; deficiency of topical groupings : 2.81
  use of roles : 2.67
subject scope description
  goals : 2.8
subjects
  indexes to : 1.117
  nature. views of Hjørland (Birger) : 8.61
suffixes
  multiple. stemming : 8.158
  plural "s." stemming : 8.157
surrogate displays
  design features : 19.80
  examples : 19.81
surrogates, surrogation : chap. 14
  among variables in IR research : 8.17
  based on automatic indexing. display : 16.22
  content : 14.3, 5; in indexing and abstracting services : 14.22
  definition : 14.1
  display : chap. 16; examples : sec. 16.1; options : 16.8; format options : 16.11; order of fields : 16.15, 20; research : 16.5
  display versus content : 14.4
  examples : sec. 14.5
  for author searches. display in electronic media : 16.4; in print media : 16.37
  for machine searching : sec. 14.4
  for subject searches. display in electronic media : 16.4; in print media : 16.36
  format : 14.5
  formatted display : 16.18, 21
  full. display : 16.6
  guidelines : sec. 14.2
  in book indexes : sec. 14.5.1; display : sec. 16.1.1
  in digital libraries : sec. 14.5.3; display : sec. 16.1.3
  in electronic books. display : 16.28
  in electronic encyclopedias : sec. 14.5.3; display : sec. 16.1.3

surrogates, surrogation *(continued)*
  in electronic media. display : 16.39
  in indexing and abstracting services : sec. 14.5.2; display : sec. 16.1.2; role of keywords : 14.23
  in libraries. display : 16.16
  in print media. display : 16.35
  in printed books. display : 16.24
  in tables of contents. display : 16.25, 38
  intermediate. for electronic books : 16.30; topic sentences : 16.31
  purpose : sec. 14.1; views of Green et al : 14.8
  role in data mining, knowledge discovery : 14.16
  role of Dublin core metadata : 14.17
  size : 14.5
  staged display in electronic media : 16.3; in print media : 16.2
  standards : sec. 14.2, 14.10
  unified : 16.7; for printed books : 16.27
  versus documentary units : sec. 6.3; in reference IR databases : 6.26
Svenonius (Elaine)
  views on precoordination versus postcoordination : 12.11; on specificity : 10.7
symbols
  and codes. nature. for texts : 5.30; varieties. for texts : 5.31; for IR databases : sec. 5.4, 5.32
  role in index terms : 1.126
syndetic structure
  as vocabulary management : 12.50
  definition : 12.38, 13.40
  in alphabetical displayed indexes : sec. 13.3.1
  in *Library of Congress subject headings* : 12.38
  in thesauri : 13.51
  narrower terms versus related terms : 13.57
  purpose : 13.41, 13.48
  research. proposal : 13.75
  subject headings versus terms : 13.42
  types : 13.43
synonymous terms
  and equivalent terms. vocabulary management : 8.192
  double posting in book indexes : 13.241
  equivalent-term cross references in book indexes : 13.240
synonymy principle.
  for subject heading systems : 12.105
syntactic cross references : sec. 12.2.8
  definition : 12.268
  examples : 12.266
  necessity : 12.265
syntactic operators
  in exact match syntax : 12.284; meaning : 12.292
syntagmatic relationships : 12.191
  definition : 12.190
  views of Green (Rebecca) : sec. 12.2.3.1.
syntax

> *related terms to consider:* **ad hoc string syntax; ad hoc syntax; analytico-synthetic classification syntax; best match syntax; chain syntax; exact match syntax; faceted syntax; natural language syntax; permuted syntax; postcoordinate syntax; precoordinate syntax; relational syntax; rotated term syntax; string indexing syntax; subject heading syntax; systematic syntax**

syntax *(continued)*
  absence in vocabulary lists : 12.278
  among variables in IR research : 8.14
  as essential attribute of indexes : 12.5
  definition : 12.1
  examples : sec. 12.4
  for book indexes : sec. 12.4.1
  for digital libraries : sec. 12.4.3
  for displayed indexes versus non-displayed indexes : 11.9
  for electronic encyclopedias : sec. 12.4.3
  for full-text searching of books in electronic media : 12.320
  for index headings : chap. 12; definition : 1.63
  for indexing and abstracting services : sec. 12.4.2
  for non-displayed indexes. alternative options : 12.296; major types : 12.280
  for search statements : chap. 12; definition : 1.63
  for string indexing : sec. 12.2.2
  impact on precision : 12.3; examples : 12.4
  impact on size of indexes : 12.184
  in classification : 17.52
    in *Dewey decimal classification* : 12.197
  in faceted classifications : 12.202
  in HTML : 21.38
  in index headings compared to search statements : 12.1, 6
  in *Library of Congress classification* : 12.201
  in *Library of Congress subject headings* : 12.20; history : 12.21
  in Modern Language Association classification : 12.203
  in *Universal decimal classification* : 12.215
  postcoordinate : sec. 12.1
  precoordinate : sec. 12.1, sec. 12.2
  role in indexing : 12.2
  versus specificity : sec. 10.7
syntax principle
  for subject heading systems : 12.108
systematic syntax
  and ad hoc syntax. combinations : sec. 12.2.7.1; example in *Psychological abstracts* : 12.262
  and citations. combinations : 12.263

tables of contents
  as basis for indexing : 1.134
  as indexable matter : sec. 7.1.5
  for *Abstracts in anthropology* : 19.9
  for *Historical abstracts* : 19.10
  for indexing and abstracting services : 19.7
  for *Information science abstracts* : 19.12
  for *Sociological abstracts* : 19.11
  surrogates. display : 16.25, 38
tags
  in HTML : 21.24, 26, 39
  in record formats : 20.3
taxonomy
  definition : 19.47
Taylor (Arlene)
  views on human indexing : 8.56
technical report
  on design of indexes : 0.5
TEI (text encoding initiative)
  beginnings : 21.46
  definition : 21.29
  encoding of full texts : 21.51

Index

TEI (text encoding initiative) *(continued)*
  guidelines : 21.47
  headers : 21.49
  impact : 21.56
  in digital libraries : 21.53
  versus HTML : 21.54
  views of Hockey (Susan) : 21.45
term records
  conceptually similar. merger : 13.167
  field tags : 13.158
  for end-user thesauri : 13.157
  for thesauri. card format : 13.84
  in *Eurovoc thesaurus* : 13.105
  in *Unesco thesaurus* (1977) : 13.88; (1995) : 13.103
term relationships
  related terms to consider: **equivalence relationships; hierarchical relationships; associative relationships**
  compilation by Michel (Dee) and Kuhr (Pat) : 13.186
  in thesauri : sec. 13.3.3.1.5, 13.176; attitudes of users : 13.188, 194; display : 13.191; hierarchical display : 13.190; more detailed relationships : 13.181; during compilation : 13.192; examples : 13.177; research : 13.187; versus ontologies : 13.230
  views of Association of Library Collections and Technical Services. Subject Analysis Committee : 13.185; of Diener (Richard) : 13.183; of Farradane (Jason) : 13.182; of Wang, Vandendorpe, and Evens : 13.184
term weighting
  automatic methods : 12.312
terminology
  for formats : 3.27
  for genres : 3.27
  for image texts and sound texts : 8.113
  for indexing and abstracting services : 6.39
  for media : 3.27
  for non-displayed indexes : 1.103; opposition from American Society for Information Science : 1.102
  for non-topical features : 3.66
  in equivalent-term cross references : 13.244
  of IR database design : 1.11
terms
  addition to thesauri in automatic indexing : 8.197
  co-occurrence. identification of related terms : 8.201
  definition : 1.58
testing
  and evaluation of IR database designs : 22.9; of IR databases : chap. 22; failure analysis : 22.16; measurement : 22.14; outside scope of book : 22.3; readings : 22.13
  of faceted syntax for *Library of Congress subject headings* : 12.168
text encoding initiative. *see:* TEI (text encoding initiative)
text encoding schemas
  definition : 21.20
  examples : 21.19
  purpose : 21.18
texts
  related term to consider: **full texts**
  analysis and indexing. methods : chap. 8
  and messages as entities : 2.21

texts *(continued)*
  codes and symbols. nature : 5.30; varieties : 5.31
  composition. codes : 3.24
  computer algorithmic analysis for indexing : 1.149
  definition : 1.47
  distributions of words : sec. 8.3.7; Zipf's law : 8.160
  electronic. paragraphs as documentary units : 6.14
  human intellectual analysis for indexing : 1.148
  language. formats : 3.26; genres : 3.26
  language-based. versus image texts as indexable matter for world-wide websites : 7.15
  machine-readable. codes for representation : 3.28
  non-language-based. indexable matter : 7.3
  ranking. use of word frequency : 8.150
  sections as documentary units : 6.16
  types : 1.48
  varieties : 3.23
  versus exemplars : 1.37
  word-processing. codes for representation : 3.29
thematic roles : 12.191
theoretical models
  for automatic indexing : 8.128
thesauri
  related terms to consider: **EMTREE thesaurus; Unesco thesaurus; Eurovoc thesaurus; ASIS thesaurus;** end-user thesauri; indexing thesauri
  addition of terms in automatic indexing : 8.197
  and co-occurrence lists. combining : 13.27
  application to book indexes : 13.246
  associative relationships : 13.180
  categories. definitions : 13.164; size : 13.160; not mutually exclusive : 13.166
  construction. books on : 13.81; computer programs : 13.85; views of Soergel (Dagobert) : 13.83
  cross references : 13.51
  display for searching : 13.30; work of Pollitt (A. Steven, et al.) : 13.31
  end-user. experimental research : 13.23
  equivalence relationships : 13.178
  for full-text IR databases : 13.82
  gathering terms. versus preferred terms : 13.203
  hierarchical displays. term relationships : 13.190
  hierarchical relationships : 13.179; versus associative relationships : 13.189, 195
  homographs : sec. 13.3.3.1.7
  integration with search interfaces : 13.26
  more detailed term relationships : 13.181
  narrower terms versus related terms : 13.57
  notation. translation into natural human language : 13.59
  preferred terms. selection : 13.204
  size. impact of bound terms on - : 13.174
  source of term "thesaurus" : 13.80
  standards. views on bound terms : 13.170
  syndetic structure : 13.51
  term records. card format : 13.84

thesauri *(continued)*
  term relationships : sec. 13.3.3.1.5, 13.176; attitudes of users : 13.188, 194; display : 13.191; during compilation : 13.192; examples : 13.177; research : 13.187
  terms. initial categorization of - : 13.159
  use. field research : 13.24
  versus ontologies : 13.225; categories : 13.230; term relationships : 13.230
thresholds
  in automatic clustering : 8.217
time. *see:* dates (time)
time of publication
  as non-topical feature, as searchable feature : sec. 3.10
  in documentary scope for indexing and abstracting services : 3.59
title indexes : 1.131
titles
  adequacy as indexable matter : 12.231
  as basis for indexing : 1.131, 12.226
  as indexable matter : sec. 7.1.1
  as non-topical feature, as searchable feature : sec. 3.2
  indexes to : 1.119
topical groupings
  deficiency in subject scope analysis : 2.81
  versus facets in subject scope analysis : 2.80, 84
topical subdivisions
  and form subdivisions. confusion in *Library of Congress subject headings* : 12.90
  in *Library of Congress subject headings* : 12.36
topics
  arrangement within facets : 17.81
  combined with non-topical features in searches : 3.7
  indexes to : 1.114
  role of features : 2.60
  versus facets. number : 2.86
  versus non-topical features : 2.59, sec. 3.13; clear distinction 2.61, 66, 3.49; on opening screens : 2.75; role : 2.64
  versus places. subdivision in *Library of Congress subject headings* : 12.37
translators
  indexes to : 1.115
transmission
  channels for IR databases. world-wide web : sec. 5.3.3
treatment level
  as non-topical feature, as searchable feature : sec. 3.6
  in documentary scope for indexing and abstracting services : 3.56
TREC
  IR research. role of users : 8.21
truncation
  use in searches of indexing and abstracting services in electronic media : 12.325
type size
  for displayed indexes in print media : 18.17

UF
  as instruction for creation of equivalent-term cross references : 13.54
  as notation for un-used terms : 13.52

Index

underscores
 treatment in automatic indexing : 8.136
***Unesco thesaurus* (1977)** : 13.87
 classification notation : 13.89
 hierarchical displays : 13.92
 KWIC display : 13.91
 notation : 13.90
 relational displays : 13.95
 term records : 13.88
***Unesco thesaurus* (1995)** : 13.98
 display of multiple hierarchical levels : 13.102
 microthesauri : 13.99
 term records : 13.103
Uniform Resource Names (URN) : 15.34
United States
 in subject headings : 12.17
units of analysis
 documentary units : 6.6
Universal decimal classification
 compared to relational syntax. notational symbols : 12.217
 facet indicators : 12.215
 notation. examples : 12.216
 syntax : 12.215
universities
 as example of abstract entities : 2.18
unstructured data : 1.26
up-posting
 and generic posting. versus specificity : 10.19
upper-case letters
 treatment in automatic indexing : 8.144
URLs
 instability : 15.15
use
 measures of. versus censorship : 8.248
 versus expert judgment in evaluation of importance : 8.249
use references. *see:* **equivalent-term cross references**
used for terms
 versus equivalent terms in end-user thesauri : 13.210
useful documents
 identification. through of human indexing : 8.244
 selection. by advisory groups and indexing staff : 8.250
user attributes
 role in relevance judgments : 3.10
user-defined stop lists : 12.323
user needs
 necessity for understanding : 2.7
user needs principle.
 for subject heading systems : 12.112
user needs assessment : pt2.5
user options
 for automatic stemming : 12.324
user preferences
 for automatic indexing versus human indexing : 8.23
 versus expert judgment in IR database design : 8.251
user studies
 not in scope of this book : 1.9
user-suggested cross-references : 12.342
users
 as source of terms for end-user thesauri. views of Landauer (Thomas K.) : 13.132
 attitudes toward term relationships in thesauri : 13.188, 194

users
 characteristics : 1.8
 diverse. purposes of information retrieval : 8.104
 of book indexes : 2.89; vocabulary : 2.90
 role in IR research : 8.8; TREC : 8.21
 vocabulary. compared to *Library of Congress subject headings* : 13.15
utility theory
 role in rules for human indexing : 8.116

variability
 in human indexing : 8.63
 of vocabulary. views of Furnas (George W. et al.) : 13.14
variables
 in IR research : 8.9; conflation : 8.18, 20; browsability : 8.13; exhaustivity : 8.12; extent of indexable matter : 8.11; size of documentary units : 8.10; specificity : 8.12a; surrogation : 8.17; syntax : 8.14; vocabulary management : 8.16; views of Cooper (William S.) : 8.19
variant forms
 in end-user thesauri : sec. 13.3.3.1.6
variant terms
 versus equivalent terms in end-user thesauri : 13.205
vector-space model
 for automatic indexing : 8.128
 for best match syntax : 12.297
Vickery (Brian C.)
 views on ontologies : 13.232, 236
video recordings
 and motion pictures. documentary units : 6.9
videotapes
 IR databases for : 1.166
visual media
 types : 3.19
visual resolution
 of print displays : 17.41
visualization
 and search interfaces. views of Hearst (Marti A.) : 19.50
 impact of cognitive abilities : 19.54; views of Allen (Bryce L.) : 19.55
 of information : 19.51
vocabulary
 controlled. mapping of search terms : 13.28
 for indexing. size. impact of specificity : sec. 10.6
 free uncontrolled. impact on specificity : 10.41
 of users. compared to *Library of Congress subject headings* : 13.15; versus specificity : 10.33
 of users of book indexes : 2.90
 specificity for indexing : chap. 10
 variability. among searchers and indexers : 13.17; in full-text sources : 13.19; views of Bates (Marcia) : 13.16, 22; views of Furnas (George W. et al.) : 13.14
vocabulary control
 related term to consider: **vocabulary management**
 impact on specificity : 10.39
 negative (stop lists) : sec. 8.3.3, 8.149
 positive. in automatic indexing : 8.191

vocabulary data
 standards for interoperability : 20.41
vocabulary information
 display for electronic searches. design features : 19.78; examples : 19.79
vocabulary lists
 absence of syntax : 12.278
 versus non-displayed indexes : 11.13, 12.276
vocabulary management : chap. 13
 among variables in IR research : 8.16
 automatic : sec. 8.3.10; examples. Associative Interactive Dictionary : 8.200; impact : 8.208
 by means of syndetic structure : 12.50
 bypassing. in electronic searching : 8.198
 clustering of terms : 13.220; research : 13.219
 examples : sec. 13.4
 for book indexes : sec. 13.4.1; in print media : 13.238; integration : 13.239
 for digital libraries : sec. 13.4.3
 for displayed indexes : 8.195
 for electronic encyclopedias : sec. 13.4.3
 for electronic searching : 8.196
 for indexes in electronic books : 13.250
 for indexing and abstracting services : sec. 13.4.2; in print media : 13.258
 for non-displayed indexes for indexing and abstracting services in electronic media : 13.262
 for printed indexes : 19.17
 in automatic indexing : sec. 8.3.9, 8.194
 in latent semantic indexing : 8.222
 interactions with specificity and exhaustivity : 10.44
 of equivalent terms and synonymous terms : 8.192
 of minor terms : 8.193
 suggestions. optional status : 13.264; presentation for searches in non-displayed indexes : 13.253; for multiple terms in search statements : 13.263
vocabulary problems : sec. 13.1
 research : sec. 13.2
 solutions : sec. 13.3; research : 13.21

Wang, Vandendorpe, and Evens
 views on term relationships : 13.184
wants
 versus needs in information retrieval : 8.106
webpages
 locators : 15.14
websites
 for Dublin Core : 20.27
 for MARC formats : 20.14
 indexable matter. language-based texts versus image texts : 7.15
 opening screens as indexable matter : sec. 7.1.7
weighted term syntax. *see:* **best match syntax**
Weinberg (Bella Hass)
 views on specificity : 10.24
Wellisch (Hans H.)
 acknowledgments : 0.14, 15
 views on human indexing : 8.48
Wilson (Patrick)
 views on documentary domain : 4.3; on human indexing : 8.51; on specificity : 10.18
wisdom
 definition : 1.40, 46
 views of Korfhage (Robert R.) : 1.41

Index

Wittgenstein (Ludwig)
   application of views to human indexing : 8.78;
      to social construction of indexing rules :
      8.80

word pairs
   in KWAC indexes : 12.242
   in KWOC indexes : 12.240
   in natural language syntax : 12.243

word-processing texts
   codes for representation : 3.29

word roots
   identification in stemming : 8.156

words
   automatic indexing : sec. 8.3.1
   choice for stop lists : 8.147
   common. role in index terms : 1.124
   definition. in automatic indexing : 8.131, 143;
      in Chinese language : 8.132
   distribution in texts : sec. 8.3.7; Zipf's law :
      8.160; impact of stemming : 8.155; use for
      ranking of texts : 8.150
   frequency. in automatic indexing : sec. 8.3.4;
      in collections : sec. 8.3.5
   inverse document frequency : 8.151
   number. in stop lists : 8.148
   role in index terms : 1.123
   versus icons : 19.56
   Zipfian distribution. transition points : 8.164;
      in article by Booth (A. D.) : 8.163

work marks
   in call numbers : 15.38

works
   versus messages : 1.36

world-wide web
   and internet. application of expert judgment :
      8.257
   as channel for transmission of documents :
      3.21; of IR databases : sec. 5.3.3
   documentary units for hypertext : 6.21
   relational classified displays : 12.194, 17.60

world-wide web search engines
   role of indexable matter : 7.14

world-wide websites. *see:* websites

XML
   and HTML.
     relationship with SGML : 21.43
   definitions : 21.28
   types : 21.44
   versus HTML : 21.34

Z39.50 standard
   for information retrieval protocols : 20.42

Zipfian distributions
   keywords compared to human indexing : 8.167
   of words.
     transition points : 8.164
   of words in article by Booth (A. D.) : 8.163
   transition points.
     identification of keywords : 8.161, 165

Zipf's law
   on distributions of words in texts : 8.160

About the Authors

JAMES D. ANDERSON (B.A., Harvard College, M.S.L.S., D.L.S., Columbia University) is professor emeritus of library and information science in the School of Communication, Information, and Library Studies at Rutgers the State University of New Jersey. He was associate dean of this school from 1983 through 1997. His library career included service at Sheldon Jackson College, Sitka, Alaska, and the Multnomah County Public Library (Portland, Oregon). He taught at Columbia, St. John's, and the City University of New York before coming to Rutgers in 1977, where he specialized in the design of information retrieval databases. Major projects included the international bibliography and database of the Modern Language Association of America and the bilingual (French and English) *Bibliography of the History of Art*, sponsored by the J. Paul Getty Trust and the French Centre National de la Recherche Scientifique in Paris. At Rutgers he also chaired the President's Select Committee for Lesbian and Gay Concerns, and fought for equal benefits for lesbian and gay employees, without success. He left Rutgers in 2003 to protest the new president's proclamation that less than half benefits for lesbian and gay employees was a "reasoned response." For the Presbyterian Church (U.S.A.) he edited and published the journal *More Light Update* on lesbian, gay, bisexual, and transgender issues from 1980 to 2003. See the Bibliography for his relevant publications.

JOSE PEREZ-CARBALLO (B.A. Universidad Nacional Autónoma de México, Ph.D., New York University) is associate professor of computer information systems at California State University, Los Angeles. He specializes in IR systems for academia and industry. He has participated in several collaborations in TREC (Text Retrieval Conferences) focusing on the interactive and natural language processing tracks. After five years at Rutgers University, where he taught and pursued research in human information behavior and web resource design in the School of Communication, Information, and Library Studies, he joined a company in Cupertino, California as an knowledge architect. He worked there on the design and implementation of domain specific knowledge representation systems for facilitating user interaction with large IR databases and in the application of natural language processing to enhance the performance of IR systems. His publications related to this book are listed in the Bibliography.